T0217701

# Lecture Notes of the Institute for Computer Sciences, Social-Informatics and Telecommunications Engineering    43

Kandeepan Sithamparanathan
Mario Marchese   Marina Ruggieri
Igor Bisio (Eds.)

# Personal
# Satellite Services

Second International ICST Confernce, PSATS 2010
Rome, Italy, February 4-5, 2010
Revised Selected Papers

 Springer

Volume Editors

Kandeepan Sithamparanathan
Create-Net, Cognitive Information Networks Group,
Future Network Infrastructure and Service Platforms,
Povo, 38123, Trento, Italy
E-mail: kandeepan@ieee.org

Mario Marchese
Igor Bisio
Universita of Genova, Department of Communications,
Computer and System Sciences
16145 Genova, Italy
E-mail: {mario.marchese; igor}@unige.it

Marina Ruggieri
University of Roma Tor Vergata, CTIF Italy
00133 Rome, Italy
E-mail: ruggieri@uniroma2.it

Library of Congress Control Number: 2010928054

CR Subject Classification (1998): C.2, K.6.5, E.3, D.4.6, J.1, H.4

ISSN    1867-8211

ISBN    978-3-642-13617-7 Springer Berlin Heidelberg New York

springer.com

© ICST Institute for Computer Sciences, Social Informatics and Telecommunications Engineering 2010

Typesetting: Camera-ready by author, data conversion by Scientific Publishing Services, Chennai, India
Printed on acid-free paper       SPIN:      06/3180      5 4 3 2 1 0

# Proceedings

The Second International ICST Conference on Personal Satellite Services 2010 (PSATS 2010) was held at the Starhotels Michael Angelo Hotel, Rome in Italy during February 4–5, 2010, jointly organized by CREATE-NET (Italy), University of Genoa (Italy) and Eutelsat (France).

The PSATS 2010 scientific conference was a two-day event emphasizing many aspects of satellite communications ranging from satellite communications, networks, navigation to quantum satellite communications presenting several high-quality technical and scientific papers. The first day of PSATS 2010 had four regular tracks of technical paper presentations, and the second day included four special sessions on the recent advancements in satellite communications. All the presentations were followed up by fruitful question-and-answer sessions and debates leading to immense knowledge sharing in the respective fields.

The conference included a keynote speech, four regular technical tracks and four special sessions consisting of 33 high-quality scientific papers. The four technical tracks included (1) Satellite Communications: Coding and Modulations; (2) Satellite Communications: Multimedia Integration; (3) Satellite Network: Quality of Service and Architectures; and (4) Satellite Networks: Applications and Services. The four technical tracks were complemented by four special sessions on: (1) Delay-Tolerant Networks; (2) Quantum Satellite Communications; (3) Access Quality Processing and Applications of Satellite Imagery; and (4) Satellite Emergency Communications.

The keynote speech titled "ICT Evolution and the Opportunities for Satellite Communications", was given by Giovanni E. Corazza, who is the Head of the Department of Electronics Computer Science and Systems (DEIS) at the University of Bologna, Italy. Professor Giovanni was the recipient of the IEEE 2009 Satellite Communications Distinguished Service Award and is the founder of the Integral Satcom Initative (ISI) the European technology platform on satellite communications. His speech emphasized the DNA of ICT evolution and identifying the opportunities for satellite communications. The keynote speech was well received and discussed among the participants.

The conference had close to 50 participants both from the industrial and the academic sectors from various parts of the world such as Japan, France, Greece, Spain, UK and Italy. The logistical organization of the conference is highly commendable and a special acknowledgment is due to Barbara Torok from ICST for running the event smoothly. The conference provided tea and coffee breaks as well as lunch at the hotel for all the participants throughout the conference. A Gala Dinner event was also organized on the first day of the conference. The quality of the venue, services provided by the hotel staff and especially the quality of food and drinks were all highly spoken about during the conference by the participants and the Organizing Committee as well.

Last but not least, I would like to thank the Organizing Committee members, Special Session Chairs, the Technical Program Committee members, and all the authors and reviewers who contributed immensely towards the success of this event. Also, on behalf of the Organizing Committee and the Steering Committee of PSATS, I would like to thank the ICST for sponsoring this event, and CREATE-NET, University of Genoa, and Eutelsat for their extended support in making this event a successful one.

We very much look forward to another successful conference in 2011 in Malaga with PSATS 2011, and in the forthcoming years.

Marina Ruggieri
Mario Marchese
Kandeepan Sithamparanathan

# Organization

## General Chair

| | |
|---|---|
| Marina Ruggieri | University of Rome, "Tor Vergata", Italy |
| Mario Marchese | University of Genoa, Italy |
| Kandeepan Sithamparanathan | Create-Net, Italy |

## Steering Committee Chair

Imrich Chlamtac      President, Create-Net, Italy

## General Vice-Chairs

| | |
|---|---|
| Alessandro Vanelli-Coralli | University of Bologna, Italy |
| Haitham Cruickshank | University of Surrey, UK |

## Technical Program Committee Chairs

| | |
|---|---|
| Claudio Sacchi | University of Trento, Italy |
| Giovanni Giambene | University of Sienna, Italy |
| Mauro De Sanctis | University of Rome, Tor Vergata", Italy |

## Industrial Chair

Agnelli Stefano      ESOA/Eutelsat, France

## Advisory Committee

| | |
|---|---|
| Giovanni E. Corazza | University of Bologna, Italy |
| Abbas Jamalipur | University of Sydney, Australia |
| Sam Reisenfeld | Macquarie University, Australia |
| Sandro Scalise | German Aerospace Centre, Germany |
| Takaya Yamazato | Nagoya University, Japan |
| Tarik Taleb | Tohuku University, Japan |

## Publications Chair

Igor Bisio      University of Genoa, Italy

## Local Chair

Tommaso Rossi                    University of Rome, "Tor Vergata", Italy

## Conference Coordinators

Barbara Torok                    ICST, Belgium

## Website Chair

Lorenzo Mucchi                   University of Florence, Italy

## Special Session on Delay-Tolerant Networks

Haitham Cruickshank              University of Surrey, UK
Carlo Caini                      University of Bologna, Italy

## Special Session on Quantum Satellite Communications

Paolo Villoresi                  University of Padua, Italy
Rupert Ursin                     Austrian Academy of Science, Austria

## Special Session on Access Quality Processing and Applications of Satellite Imagery

Giuseppe Conti                   Fondazione Graphitech, Italy
Mattia Crespi                    University of Rome "La Sapienza", Italy

## Special Session on Satellite-Based Emergency Services

Mauro De Sanctis                 University of Rome, "Tor Vergata", Italy
Simone Morosi                    University of Florence, Italy

## Technical Program Committee

Alban Duverdier                  Centre National d'Etudes Spatiales - CNES, France
Fatih Alagoz                     Bogazici University, Turkey
Franco Davoli                    University of Genoa, Italy
Thierry Gayraud                  Laboratory for Analysis and Architecture of
                                 Systems: LAAS-CNRS, France
Gianluca Reali                   University of Perugia, Italy
Maurizio Mongelli                University of Genoa, Italy
Francesco Potorti                Institute of Information Science and Technologies:
                                 ISTI -CNR, Italy
Sandro Scalise                   German Aerospace Centre: DLR, Germany

# Table of Contents

## Track 4 - Satellite Networks: Applications and Services

## Special Session 1 - Delay Tolerant Network

## Special Session 2 - Quantum Satellite Communications

## Special Session 3 - Access Quality Processing and Applications of Satellite Imagery

## Special Session 4 - Satellite Based Emergency Services

# Track 1
# Satellite Communications: Coding and Modulation

# Overview of PHY-Layer Design Challenges and Viable Solutions in W-Band Broadband Satellite Communications

Claudio Sacchi[1] and Tommaso Rossi[2]

[1] University of Trento
Department of Information Engineering and Computer Science (DISI)
Via Sommarive 14, I-38050, Povo (Trento), Italy
sacchi@disi.unitn.it
[2] University of Rome,"Tor Vergata"
Department of Electronics
Via del Politecnico 1, Rome, Italy
tommaso.rossi@uniroma2.it

**Abstract.** The exploitation of Extremely High Frequency (EHF) bands for broadband satellite communications really represents a challenging frontier for aerospace R&D. In few time, ALPHASAT mission (through the Technology Demonstration Payload 5) should test Q/V band (40-50GHz) digital satellite transmission. Moreover, a lot of effort is spent to study the feasibility of broadband links in W-band (70-110GHz). This paper is devoted at showing the most relevant challenges to be faced in the effective PHY-layer design of W-band satellite connections. Some practical solutions will be analyzed together with a look to future solutions in phase of testing. From the proposed analysis, it is clear that effects of nonlinear distortions and phase noise should be adequately counteracted by considering spectrally-efficient solutions. In such a perspective, it seems that efficient coded modulations employed together with appropriate pulse shaping can be regarded as effective PHY-layer solutions for future high-frequency and high-data rate connections.

**Keywords:** Satellite communications, EHF communications, gigabit connectivity, Modulation, Pulse shaping, Channel coding.

## 1 Introduction

The future exploitation of higher frequency bands for broadband aerospace communications will provide new opportunities, but also generate critical challenges to be adequately considered. It is known by literature [1] that the rush towards higher and higher frequencies will characterize future R&D on satellite communications. The objective is to reach "gigabit connectivity" by aerospace links in order to make such a radio segment a potential "backbone on the air" for global wireless connectivity [2]. Such objective is not realistically achievable by exploiting currently saturated bandwidth (Ku and Ka bands).

K. Sithamparanathan et al. (Eds.): PSATS 2010, LNICST 43, pp. 3–18, 2010.
© Institute for Computer Sciences, Social-Informatics and Telecommunications Engineering 2010

Some proposals for the exploitation of Q/V-bands (31-60 GHz) and W-band (75-110 GHz) in satellite communications are being recently issued [3]. W-band seems to provide a very favorable "attenuation window" related to Oxygen absorption [4]. In addition, W-band is still scarcely used for data transmission (only analog radar applications are supported in those frequencies [3]) and, therefore, interference level is very low. For these reasons, despite the increasing attenuation due to rain, water vapor and clouds, W-band is regarded as a good candidate for supporting future broadband services in the millimeter wave domain.

The exploitation of Q/V band is in advanced phase. In fact, the satellite mission ALPHASAT, whose launch is forecast in 2011, will embark a Q/V band payload in order to perform two experiments [5]: a propagation experiment targeted at evaluating 2nd order statistics of atmospheric attenuation and a communication experiment devoted at testing Propagation Impairment Mitigation Technique (PIMT) and Adaptive Coding and Modulation (AMC). On the other hand, the experimentation of W-band for data transmission is currently in a very early stage. In recent years, Italian Space Agency (ASI) issued two "startup experiments" proposed by Ruggieri et. al.: DAVID-DCE (Digital Audio-Video Interactive Distribution – Data Collection Experiment) [3] [6] and WAVE (W-band Analysis and evaluation) [7] [8].

Preliminary on-going experimentations evidenced the actual possibility of exploiting W-band for broadband connections at very high data rates. Nevertheless, some areas of uncertainty and risk can hinder the efficient exploitation of these large and almost interference-free bandwidth portions. These are related to: a) non-idealities of communication payloads (phase-noise, linear and nonlinear distortions, timing uncertainties etc.) [9] and b) lack of knowledge of signal propagation modalities in W-band. PHY-layer design should carefully take into account all these problems in order to provide the desired quality of service. The analysis of requirements of an efficient W-band satellite PHY-layer should start from the known issues that can be listed as follows [9]:

1) heavy pathloss due to high carrier frequency;

2) presence of nonlinear distortions due to the necessity of using High Power Amplifiers (HPAs) and Travelling Wave Tube Amplifiers (TWTAs) at the maximum level of power efficiency (W-band power resources are quite scarce and should be intensively exploited);

3) presence of time and frequency uncertainties (symbol unbalance, phase noise) that become more and more relevant as the data rate increases;

4) finite system passband and nonideal bandpass characterization of the satellite system (presence of linear distortion);

5) spectrum management issues, related to the presence of other transmitters exploiting adjacent bandwidth portions (in practical satellite applications, bandwidth resources are always limited and spectrum is always shared by a variety of users).

In this paper, all these critical issues about broadband W-band PHY-layer design will be considered, together with an overview of some feasible solutions in terms of modulation format, channel coding and advanced pulse shaping. The introduction to W-band PHY-layer design will be presented in Section 2. Coded modulation solutions based on Manchester-coded BPSK and trellis-coded QAM will be analyzed in the presence of nonlinear distortions and phase-noise (Section 3). Innovative strategies of PHY-layer design based on UWB pulse-shaping techniques (namely: Prolate Spheroidal Wave Functions (PSWF)) will be considered in the perspective of gaining robustness against channel distortion without sacrificing spectral efficiency (Section 4). A look to advanced solutions considering together turbo-coded modulation techniques and adaptive pulse shaping will be mentioned (Section 5). Paper conclusions will be drawn in Section 6.

## 2 PHY-Layer Design for W-Band Satellite Communications: Critical Aspects

### 2.1 Radio Interface Design Issues

W-band satellite communications is a novel and very interesting field of research that shall be deeply investigated in order to design the proper radio interface.

W-band satellite communication shows some interesting characteristics that can be very attractive, both for commercial and dual-use applications, such as good interference protection, through the use of very narrow spot beams.

Antennas operating in this band have a higher directivity than antennas (of the same size) operating at lower frequencies, so the interference between adjacent satellite position is reduced; moreover this high directivity makes it possible the use of high-gain spot beam satellite antennas, increasing down-link power flux density and saving satellite power (one of the most important resource of the platform); moreover high frequency reuse can be realized, exploiting the bandwidth resource in a very efficient way.

Another important improvement provided by EHF is the reduction of all RF hardware equipment. This makes the use of W-band particularly attractive with respect to realization of portable terminals and smaller satellite payloads, for example in the context of space exploration, where mass and size are one of the most important mission driver. On the other hand, W-band telecommunications technologies are currently under development; some equipment has been already used for satellite Earth observation applications (i.e.: cloud profiling) and terrestrial radar applications and need to be slightly changed to be used for TLC applications but other critical components shall be completely developed. In this frame, one of the most critical issues is the power generation: therefore, very low HPA back-off level shall be used.

The most relevant sources of signal degradation in a W-band geostationary satellite link are amplifiers, oscillators and frequency Doppler. HPA are hardware components explicitly required in order to guarantee suitable transmission power, taking into account the very high pathloss typical of EHF GEO satellite transmissions. HPAs exhibit two relevant distortions that can severely affect the received signal: nonlinear distortion due to the saturating characteristic of the amplifier and linear bandpass distortion due to non-ideal bandpass characterization of RF amplifier circuitry. The nonlinear saturation of AM/AM characteristic may involve a noticeable alteration of the envelope of the RF modulated signal [10]. On the other hand, nonlinear AM/PM characteristic introduces a phase drift that fluctuates in dependence of the signal amplitude excursions [10].

Linear bandpass distortion consists of a frequency-selective alteration of the RF modulated signal amplitude, due to the "bell-shaped" bandpass characteristics of HPAs, together with a phase distortion mainly due to the frequency-selective group delay of front-end filters [11]. The degradation of the transmitted signal due to linear and nonlinear distortions causes Inter-Symbol-Interference and relevant phase jitters at the receiver side. Moreover, spectral re-growth involved by nonlinear effects [11] will cause adjacent channel interference and violation of spectral mask requirements, as shown in [12].

With a commonly-accepted degree of approximation (see e.g. [9]), we can say that nonlinear distortion of the satellite modem chain is imposed by HPAs, linear amplitude distortion is mostly imposed by amplifiers (HPAs and LNAs, Low Noise Amplifier) and, finally, the linear group delay distortion is mainly imposed by front-end filters.

EHF satellite links are affected also by relevant frequency uncertainties. High-frequency oscillators present both in the up-conversion and in the down-conversion stages are not ideal and they can exhibit high levels of phase noise. Consequently, we have a frequency instability that may impact on the performance of the carrier recovery loop in terms of longer acquisition time, frequency mistracking, and may yield to a residual phase jitter able to significantly lower final BER performance.

## 2.2 Atmospheric Attenuation and Rain Fading

As previously introduced, one of the main drawbacks of W-band satellite links is the large atmospheric fade experienced when rainfall occurs along the path, in addition to the gaseous atmospheric absorption by oxygen and water vapor; this attenuation shall be carefully taken into account in W-band link testing simulation, in particular rain fading time-series shall be synthesized.

In literature there are different methodologies used for rain attenuation time-series synthesis for EHF satellite links [13]; the most important are: spectral model, synthetic storm techniques, two-sample model, second-order Markov chain and N-states Markov chain models. These models are used for link operating in Ka and Q/V bands, being obtained from empirical measurements performed during scientific satellite missions [14]. Most of these models cannot be effectively used for W band rain attenuation time-series synthesis because they need data from empirical measurements as input; as a matter of fact, no attenuation record database is available for W band satellite link. In this framework, the N-state Markov chain model could be considered as one of the best choices in order to achieve some results. This model does not require empirical measurements; the only inputs are the link characteristics (including rain attenuation cumulative distribution function), the geographical meteorological data of the ground station and the fade slope characteristics. The N-states Markov chain model [15] is divided into two sub-models. The first one is referred to as macroscopic model and provides a time series consisting of two possible states: "rain" and "no rain". The second part of the model is the so-called microscopic model. Its task is to fill the boxes of "rain" states obtained from the macroscopic model. The microscopic model provides the short-term dynamic behavior of rain attenuation (using the information provided by the fade slope distribution). In order to generate complete long-term time-series the two time-series obtained from the previous parts have to be combined. The transition probabilities of the N-states Markov chain model are based on ITU-R Recommendation [16]. An example of W-band synthesized rain attenuation series (related to 1 day observation) has been shown in [29].

## 3   PHY-Layer Solutions Based on Coded Modulations

### 3.1   Manchester-Coded Split-Phase BPSK Modulation

The choice of using a Split-Phase Manchester-Coded BPSK modulation was considered both in DAVID-DCE experiment and in WAVE mission. The reason of such a choice is to have the availability of a tone carrier in the spectrum in order to make easier carrier recovery in the presence of relevant frequency uncertainties (i.e. high Doppler shift and phase noise). Moreover SP-BPSK with Manchester coding presents a constant envelope that is good to counteract nonlinear distortions due to HPA. The mathematical expression for the transmitted signal is given as follows:

$$s_k(t) = \sqrt{2P} \sum_{k=0}^{+\infty} \exp\left(j\omega_c t + b_k \phi_m\right) \quad \frac{kT_b}{2} \le t < \frac{(k+1)T_b}{2} \tag{1}$$

where $\omega_c$ is the RF radian frequency, $b_k \in \{-1,1\}$ is the binary Manchester symbol level of half-bit time duration, $\phi_m = 60°$ is the modulation index, and $P$ is the carrier power. Fig. 1 shows the amplitude spectrum of the transmitted signal. The pattern of the signal spectrum points out the presence of a residual carrier in the hole spacing two sidelobes [17].

The presence of the residual carrier is very useful in terms of the carrier recovery. A simple second-order Phase-Locked-Loop (PLL) circuit [18] can be employed for carrier recovery; provided that the bit-rate is much larger than the Doppler shift (otherwise the loop filter cannot isolate the carrier row [19]). Results shown in [9] about carrier recovery in the presence of high Doppler and high phase noise for a simulated W-band data link at 100 Mb/s of channel data rate fully confirms the claim that carrier recovery really becomes simple, robust and effective.

SP-BPSK modulation with Manchester coding may present some advantages that have been previously mentioned. However, its employment in broadband W-band satellite applications is not really convenient. In fact, this modulation is spectrally inefficient (spectral efficiency less than 0.5 bit/sec/Hz) and power demanding (3dB of power waste due to the presence of the residual carrier in the spectrum). Moreover, being baseband Manchester-coded binary signal continuously transient, the demodulation and synchronization process can suffer a lot from symbol duration unbalance [9]. The total performance degradation encountered at the demodulator side is about 4.25 dB with respect to the ideal case [9] that is surely relevant.

The channel bit-error-rate achieved by simulations is reported in Fig. 2 (see the complete simulation settings in [9]). Considering the channel data rate of 100 Mb/s, the $E_b/N_0$ value of 15dB corresponds to the "clear-sky" working point of the satellite link budget fixed at a $C/N_0$ equal to 95 dBHz [9]. At this working point, a BER value of $8 \cdot 10^{-4}$ is measured in the absence of symbol unbalance that is acceptable in the perspective of the use of a Reed-Solomon channel coding RS(255,223) upon the recommendation of the Consultative Committee for Space Data System (CCSDS) [20]. However, in the presence of a 52% of symbol unbalance (ideal value: 50%), the BER increases up to $3 \cdot 10^{-3}$ that is above the waterfall zone of the error curve of the RS(255,223) coding and quite close to the error-floor zone.

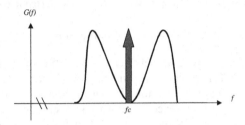

**Fig. 1.** Amplitude spectrum of the Manchester-coded Split-Phase BPSK signal

To sum up, SP-BPSK solution with Manchester coding can be considered a valuable arrangement to be pretty sure to succeed to transmit "something in the sky" without caring too much about the bandwidth and power expense. It may be proposed as a "backup" solution for preliminary testing operations.

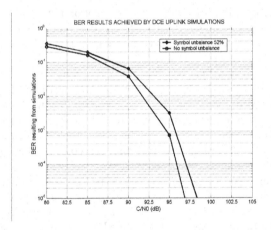

**Fig. 2.** BER performances achieved by SP-BPSK Manchester-coded modulation: simulation results of DAVID-DCE data collection uplink (channel data-rate 100 Mb/s)

### 3.2  Trellis-Coded Modulation (TCM)

The use of TCM for gigabit/sec connections over LEO satellite networks working in W-band has been explored by Sacchi and Grigorova in [21]. The basic idea underlying Trellis-Coded-Modulation consists of transmitting $m$ bits/waveform in each signaling interval of duration $T$, using a modulator with a set of $M$ waveforms. In general $M = 2^{m+1}$. The redundancy in the number of available waveforms is exploited through a proper choice, made on the basis of the past transmitted signals through the memory of the channel encoder: i.e.: a convolutional encoder represented by its trellis diagram [22]. The decoding process is performed by means of a Viterbi-based soft maximum-likelihood decoding algorithm acting on the unquantized demodulator outputs. TCM transmitters can gain efficiency with respect to the corresponding waveform uncoded modulation (from 3 to 6dB as stated by Ungerboeck in [22]), without sacrificing data or requiring more bandwidth. In our specific application context, we considered the use of M-QAM modulation with TCM. A mixed phase-amplitude modulation instead of a phase-shift-keying modulation might not seem best-suited solution for an uplink satellite application. In fact, according to [11], a power back-off has been introduced depending on the AM/AM and AM/PM amplifier saturating characteristics. But, as contrast, constant-envelope PSK modulations are very vulnerable to the effects of phase distortions (involved by amplifiers and filters), phase noise, and exhibit relevant performance degradation in the presence of additive Gaussian noise with respect to M-ary QAM modulations. In [18], the SNR degradation involved by the use of an M-PSK instead of the corresponding M-QAM has been measured in 1.65dB for an 8-QAM, 4.20dB for a 16-QAM and 9.95dB for a 64-QAM. This performance gain inherent to the use of M-QAM instead of M-PSK is only partially eroded by the backoff and, in such a way, the coding gain can be fully exploited. The waveforms used for carrying the modulated TCM symbols are the usual rectangular Non-Return-to-Zero (NRZ). Therefore, the absence of linear filtering and, consequently, the availability of infinite bandwidth have been supposed. The TWTA memoryless non-linear model proposed by Saleh in [10] and parameterized in terms of Clip Level (CL) has been considered by authors of [21].

The following state-of-the-art TCM modulation schemes have been experimented, fixing a data bit-rate of 1Gb/s:

- 8-state systematic encoder at rate 2/3 jointly with 8-QAM modulation. Given a 1Gb/s of pure data rate, we shall obtain a symbol rate of 500Mbaud/sec and an occupied RF bandwidth (referred to the sinc main lobe) of about 500MHz (theoretical spectral efficiency $\eta$=2b/s/Hz);

- 8-state systematic encoder at rate 3/4, jointly with a 16-QAM modulation. Given a 1Gb/s of pure data rate, we shall obtain a symbol rate of 333Mbaud/sec and an occupied RF bandwidth (referred to the sinc main lobe) of about 333MHz (theoretical spectral efficiency $\eta$=3b/s/Hz);

- 8-state systematic encoder at rate 5/6, jointly with a 64-QAM modulation. Given a 1Gb/s of pure data rate, we shall obtain a symbol rate of 200Mbaud/sec and an occupied RF bandwidth (referred to the sinc main lobe) of about 200MHz (spectral efficiency $\eta$=5b/s/Hz).

In order to appreciate the effects of phase-noise on TCM performances, the state-of-the art carrier recovery loop of [23] has been adopted by authors of [21] in their simulations. The loop of [23] is based on the improvement of the well-know Rustako and Greenstein's carrier recovery circuit presented in [24].

Simulation results about TCM modulation for W-band satellite connections are shown in Fig.3. A saturating nonlinear distortion (CL=5dB) has been considered, with a power back-off equal to 3dB. BER results are shown vs. phase-noise standard deviation for all the above-mentioned TCM configurations. In such a way, we have a comparative overview of different TCM configurations, each one requiring a different amount of bandwidth. It is worth noting that all TCM configurations fall inside the "low-quality" band when the phase noise standard deviation is higher than 12°. Phase-noise standard deviation of the order of 10° is quite common to be encountered in W-band connection with non-ideal high-frequency oscillators. The problem is related to the coherent detection using a carrier recovery loop. It is known by literature [25] that a generic carrier recovery loop, in the presence of phase noise, converges to the expected frequency with a residual phase jitter $\varphi_{jitt}$ that is expressed as follows:

$$\varphi_{jitt} = \sqrt{2 \int_{B_L}^{R_s/2} S_\phi(f) df} \tag{2}$$

where $B_L$ is the carrier loop bandwidth [18], $R_s$ is the symbol rate, and $S_\phi(f)$ is the one-sided PSD, converted from dBc/Hz to rad$^2$/Hz. It is clear that the sharp reduction in the PSD obtained at the lowest frequency offset values is of paramount importance to reduce the residual phase jitter.

Some interesting measurements about residual phase jitter concerning the application of Trellis-Coded-Modulation (TCM) have been reported in Table 1. In the first column of the table values are shown of $L(f_m)$ (measured in dBcarrier/Hz) accounting the phase-noise level at the output of an oscillator, in the second column the corresponding values of the phase-noise standard deviation are listed. Note that, as expected, the residual jitter increases as the modulated signal bandwidth increases. Values reported in Tab.1 clearly motivate results shown in Fig.3.

## 4   PHY-Layer Solutions Based on Adaptive and Spectrally Efficient Pulse Shaping

In Section 3.2, the ideal hypothesis of unlimited bandwidth availability has been assumed and, consequently, the use of rectangular pulse as digital waveform has been considered by authors. Such a solution is advantageous in terms of resilience against nonlinear distortions. In fact, phase modulations (PSK) using such kind of waveforms are characterized by constant envelope and, for this reason, they are irrespective of envelope clipping. But, as contrast, rectangular pulses are unlimited in bandwidth with high-power sidelobes. The resulting modulated signal would span its bandwidth on a very large frequency range with relevant power level measured outside the main spectral lobe. Considering that satellite channels are closely located, adjacent channel interference (ACI) would become a major issue that might severely limit the spectral efficiency and, definitely, the achievable capacity. Another drawback of rectangular pulses is related to their sensitivity to linear bandpass filtering. In order to avoid waveform corruption and subsequent ISI (Inter Symbol Interference), a very large system passband is required, say, e.g.: 5-10 times the baud-rate [26][27].

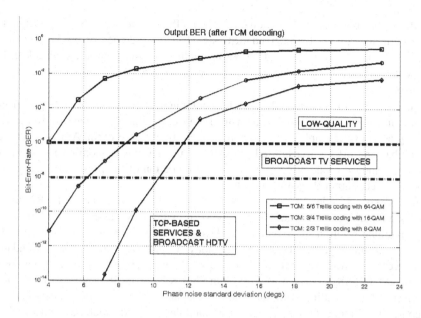

**Fig. 3.** Data BER provided at the output of the different TCM decoders, versus phase-noise standard deviation, for $CL$=5dB and $C/N_0$=106.75dBHz

**Table 1.** Residual phase jitter (deg.) in a 1Gb/s W-band LEO connection using TCM

| $L(f_m)$ | $\varphi_{jtt}(8-QAM)$ | $\psi_\phi(16-QAM)$ | $\psi_\phi(64-QAM)$ |
|---|---|---|---|
| -70dBc/Hz | 19.85 | 16.21° | 12.81 |
| -75dBc/Hz | 11.16 | 9.11° | 7.21 |
| -80dBc/Hz | 6.27 | 5.12° | 4.05 |
| -85dBc/Hz | 3.52 | 2.88° | 2.27 |

For the above reasons, the use of band-limited pulse shaping may be envisaged for broadband satellite applications. A well-known band-limited pulse is the raised cosine (RSC) [26]. RSC is commonly employed in satellite communications in combination with QAM (Quadrature Amplitude Modulation) (or QPSK, Quadrature Phase-Shift Keying) modulation, implementing the so-called RSC-filtered QAM (or QPSK) [26]. RSC is intrinsically ISI-free (it fulfills Nyquist's conditions) and can be generated by means of digital FIR (Finite Impulse Response) filters. Moreover, it is much less sensitive to filtering than rectangular pulse. The main disadvantages of RSC are: a) unlimited pulse duration in time that may involve inter-pulse interference (IPI), in particular when the transmission rate is very high and b) very relevant envelope fluctuations of the RF (Radio Frequency) modulated signal resulting in high values of the Peak-to-Average-Power-Ratio (PAPR). As RF power amplifiers usually employed in W-band satellite connections (like Traveling Wave Tube Amplifiers – TWTA) efficiently work in nonlinear saturation zone, the transmitted signal can be severely affected by waveform corruption and ISI. As noted in [27], no ISI-free point can be observed in the eye-pattern diagram of the received RSC signal in the presence of nonlinear distortions. Therefore, the use of raised cosine in satellite communications, advisable from the spectral efficiency viewpoint, requires appropriate countermeasures against nonlinear distortions.

The usual solution considered in satellite communications is to sacrifice power efficiency in order to avoid nonlinear distortion effects. This is realized by fixing the working point of the amplifier at the border of the linear zone of the AM/AM characteristic, backing off the transmitted power [11]. In such a way, nonlinear distortions would be removed at the price of a substantial reduction of the power efficiency due to the involved Output Back-Off (OBO).

The necessity of sidelobe power reduction and constant envelope of the RF signal makes Gaussian Minimum Shift Keying (GMSK) modulation a feasible and theoretically favorable solution to W-band PHY-layer design. GMSK is a modulation technique widely employed in terrestrial telephony, in particular in the GSM standard. More recently, GMSK also found some interesting applications in satellite communications [28]. GMSK is derived by Minimum Shift Keying (MSK) signal that is a form of Offset-QPSK signaling with sinusoidal pulse shaping [26]. MSK is characterized by constant envelope (being a frequency modulation) and sidelobes considerably lower than QPSK, but at the expense of a significantly larger main lobe [26]. For GMSK, unmodulated data (rectangular-shaped pulses) are processed by a LPF filter, having Gaussian-shaped frequency response, before the data are frequency-modulated onto the carrier [26]. This filter greatly reduces the spectral sidelobes with respect to MSK signals. The introduction of the Gaussian filter involves a decrease of efficiency due to the increase of ISI. Literature points out that a good compromise for relatively low sidelobes and tolerable ISI is given by a bandwidth of the Gaussian LPF that equals 0.3 times the bit-rate [26]. GMSK may represent a good PHY-later solution for satellite communications thanks to some unquestionable advantages in terms of ACI reduction and resilience against nonlinear distortions. The main problem of GMSK is related to the reduced spectral efficiency with respect to QPSK and RSC-filtered QAM/QPSK. In fact, the main lobe of GMSK is about 1.5 times larger than the main lobe of usual (not filtered) QPSK and 2 times larger (and even more) than that of RSC-filtered QPSK [26]. This fact should be adequately taken into account when dealing with finite and non-ideal bandpass characteristics of satellite systems.

A very innovative solution in the satellite communications panorama has been proposed in [29] Prolate Spheroidal Wave Functions (PSWF) were firstly studied by D. Slepian and H. Pollack (Bell Labs) in 1961 [30]. The fundamental concept standing at the basis of PSWF is to concentrate the energy of the pulse in limited regions, both in time and frequency domains. PSWFs are characterized by some interesting properties, i.e.:

- Pulse waveforms of different orders are mutually orthogonal;
- Pulse width and pulse bandwidth can be simultaneously controlled to match with arbitrary spectral masks (adaptive pulse shaping);
- Pulse width and bandwidth are the same for all orders;

- by definition, PSWFs exhibit an optimized tradeoff between concentration of the energy in a finite time window and in a finite bandwidth: this means that the resulting modulated signal is characterized by "almost finite" pulse duration and, at the same time, "almost limited" bandwidth.

PSWF found interesting applications in UWB applications thanks to spectral compactness and full shaping programmability (they can be employed in cognitive radio systems).For our aims, it is very interesting to note that PSWFs of order 1 and order 2 are characterized by surprising envelope compactness, as shown in Fig.4. This observation suggested us to use order 1 and order 2 PSWFs as in-phase and in-quadrature component of a 4-level modulation that should present "almost constant" envelope. To this aim, the 4-ary Pulse Shape Modulation (PSM) scheme proposed in [31] is employed (4-ary mapping is reported in Tab.2). In Tab.3, the value of Peak to Average Power Ratio (PAPR) is shown for 4-ary PSM and RSC-filtered QAM with different roll-off.

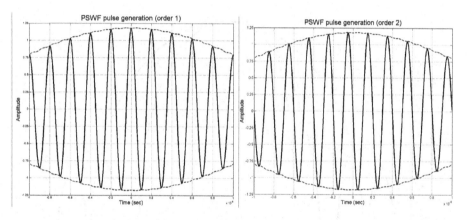

**Fig. 4.** PSWF pulse shaping: order 1 PSWF (left side), order 2 PSWF (right side)

**Table 2.** 4-level PSM mapping

| SYMBOL | 1ST ORDER PSWF (PULSE 1) | 2ND ORDER PSWF (PULSE 2) |
|--------|--------------------------|--------------------------|
| 00 | -pulse 1 | -pulse 2 |
| 01 | -pulse1 | pulse 2 |
| 11 | pulse 1 | pulse 2 |
| 10 | pulse 1 | -pulse 2 |

Numerical values reported in Tab.3 evidenced the potential advantages taken by PSWF in terms of envelope compactness. The PAPR value yielded by the 4-level PSM signal is very close to the ideality, whereas RSC-filtered QAM, as already noted by literature, exhibits high PAPRs. Fig.5 shows the power spectra of different pulse-shaped modulations used in the framework of W-band satellite connections at 1Gb/s of channel data rates. It is clear that the sidelobe power of conventional QAM using rectangular pulses is not acceptable in terms of adjacent channel interference. RSC-filtered QAM is bandlimited and, therefore, it is optimal from the viewpoint of sidelobe power reduction. However, the use of RSC-filtered QAM in satellite communications is viable only by backing off transmitted power. Sidelobe power of 4-ary PSM modulation is comparable with that one of GMSK. The main advantage taken by 4-ary PSM with respect to GMSK is related to the reduced width of the main spectral lobe.

**Table 3.** Peak-to-Average-Power-Ratio (PAPR) for different pulse shaping

| PULSE SHAPING | PAPR VALUE |
|---|---|
| RSC-filtered QAM (roll-off 0.5) | 3.22 dB |
| RSC-filtered QAM (roll-off 0.35) | 3.80 dB |
| 4-ary PSM | 1.04 dB |
| GMSK, QAM | 0dB |

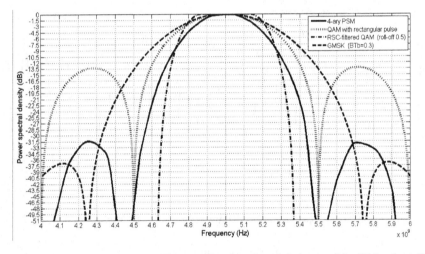

**Fig. 5.** Power spectral density of different pulse-shaped modulation used for W-band satellite links working in the framework of gigabit connectivity

Other results have been shown in Fig.6, where curves BER vs. per-bit signal-to-noise ratio have been shown for different pulse-shaped modulated signals employed to transmit data at a channel data-rate of 1Gb/s over a geostationary forward W-band satellite link. In this figure, the presence of nonlinear amplifier and linear passband distortions has been taken into account, without considering the presence of phase-noise at this stage. One can note that 4-ary PSM and GMSK outperform RSC-filtered QAM, this last one transmitted with a power back-off. This improvement is motivated by the fact that 4-ary PSM and GMSK can be transmitted at the saturation point of the non-linear amplifier, without any power back-off. In this comparison, 4-ary PSM is the winner because BER performances are rather close to those ones of GMSK, but the spectral efficiency of 4-ary PSM is better than GMSK one (see Fig.4).

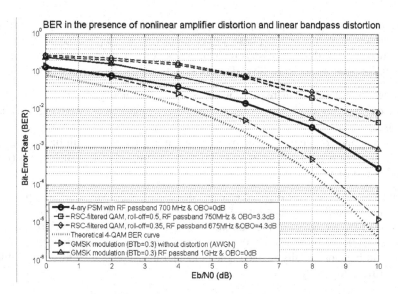

**Fig. 6.** BER results of different pulse-shaped modulations in the presence of nonlinear amplifier distortion and linear passband distortion

Some simulation results achieved in the presence of phase noise are also available, but not reported here for sake of brevity. Using a state-of-the-art carrier recovery loop already considered for pulse-shaped UWB transmission [33], the effect of phase noise is again relevant and the amount of phase noise at the input of the demodulator should be adequately reduced (maximum acceptable phase-noise standard deviation = 10°).

## 5  Possible Novel Trends in PHY-Layer Design for W-Band Gigabit Connections

In the previous sections, some open issues about W-band satellite PHY-layer design have been highlighted. The biggest issue to be considered seems related to residual phase jitters involved by phase noise that can affect coherent demodulation. As shown in Fig.3 showing results achieved by TCM, a nasty error floor can be noted for phase noise standard deviation larger than 12°. Similar results have been mentioned (but not shown) in Section 4 dealing with pulse-shaped modulations. Phase noise can be reduced at the source, by using low noise oscillators. Hardware technologies for W-band low noise oscillator consider the use of GaAs MBE material [34] or the so-called Gunn oscillators [35], based on the Gunn diode characterized by a dynamic negative resistance. The cost of this kind of hardware, however decreasing with time, is often not very affordable.

A possible alternative solution should rely in the adoption of differential modulation. It is known that differential modulation is insensitive with respect to phase jitters, as it evaluates the difference between two received samples in order to decide the transmitted symbol. In this framework, it is worth mentioning the work of Howard and Schlegel [36], where a novel approach for turbo-coded differential modulation is shown. The robustness of the proposed coded-modulation scheme is appreciated also in the presence of noticeable phase jitters thanks to a simple channel estimation scheme that can avoid the necessity of channel state information knowledge.

A novel perspective for PHY-layer design can rely on these three hypothetic pillars:

- Coded-modulation to increase robustness without reducing spectral efficiency;
- Differential modulation in order to counteract phase jitters deriving by phase-noise;
- Efficient and adaptive pulse shaping design in order to cope with future spectrum management regulatory issues and to reduce the impact of link distortions (linear and nonlinear).

It should be noted that the proposed analysis doesn't consider any kind of atmospheric effect, which is still to be appreciated. A credible model of W-band channel attenuation, derived by an intensive measurement campaign, will be a key priority issue in the future satellite missions working at these frequencies. Considerations made in this paper might be substantially revised when channel measurements will be available to the scientific community.

# 6 Conclusion

In this paper an overview of the most challenging aspects related to the PHY-layer design in W-band broadband satellite communications is presented, together with some feasible solutions presented in literature. The most relevant issues that should be considered by PHY-layer designers are related to the presence of frequency uncertainties and phase noise at the input of the coherent demodulators. Another aspect to be carefully considered concerns with the presence of nonlinear distortions in the link due to high-power amplifiers. The introduction of power back-off in order to avoid distortion effects should be carefully analyzed, considering the link budget constraints that in W-band satellite connections are often very tight. The use of spectrally efficient coded modulations should be envisaged, together with the design of adaptive and programmable pulse shaping able at reducing sidelobe power. Possible steps-ahead with respect to state-of-the-art might be related to the use of turbo-coded differential modulations jointly with adaptive pulse shaping. This novelty in terms of PHY-layer design should be effectively tested only when a precise assessment of the W-band satellite channel in terms of reliable statistics will be available. In our opinion, this last one is the most relevant uncertainties that still hinder the effective exploitation of W-band for broadband commercial services.

## Acknowledgements

This work has been partially supported by the Italian Ministry of University and Scientific Research, under the framework of SALICE (Satellite-Assisted Localization and Communication systems for Emergency services) research project (COFIN 2007RFTYY7_002).

# References

1. Farserotu, J., Prasad, R.: A Survey of Future Broadband Multimedia Satellite Systems, Issues and Trends. IEEE Comm. Mag., 128–133 (2000)
2. Ibnkahla, M., Rahaman, Q.M., Sulyman, A.Y., Al-Asady, H.A., Yuan, J., Safwat, A.: High-Speed Satellite Mobile Communications: Technologies and Challenges. Proceedings of the IEEE 92(2), 312–339 (2004)
3. De Fina, S., Ruggieri, M., Bosisio, A.V.: Exploitation of the W-band for High-Capacity Satellite Communications. IEEE Trans. on AES 39(1), 82–93 (2003)
4. Pinhasi, Y., Yahalom, A., Harpaz, O., Vilner, G.: Study of Ultra-wideband Transmission in Extremely High Frequency (EHF) Band. IEEE Trans. on Antennas and Propagat. 52(11), 2833–2842 (2004)
5. Gallinaro, G., Speziale, V., Vernucci, A.: The Alphasat Q/V-band Experimental Mission (TDP#5): Objectives and Opportunities (2006),
   http://www.satexpo.it/documenti/200628gio_isi_ga2.pdf
6. Ruggieri, M., De Fina, S., Pratesi, M., Salome', A., Saggese, E., Bonifazi, C.: The W-band Data Collection Experiment of the DAVID Mission. IEEE Transactions on AES 38(4), 1377–1387 (2002)
7. Jebril, A., Lucente, M., Ruggieri, M., Rossi, T.: WAVE – A new mission in W band. In: Proc. of 2005 IEEE Aerospace Conf., Big Sky (MT), March 5-12 (2005)
8. Lucente, M., Rossi, T., Jebril, A., Ruggieri, M., Iera, A., Molinaro, A., Pulitanò, S., Sacchi, C., Zuliani, L.: Experimental Missions in W-Band: a Small LEO Satellite Approach. IEEE Systems Journal 2(1), 90–102 (2008)
9. Sacchi, C., Gera, G., Regazzoni, C.: W-band Physical Layer Design Issues in the Context of the DAVID-DCE Experiment. Int. Jour. of Satellite Communications and Networking 22(2), 193–215 (2004)
10. Saleh, A.A.M.: Frequency-independent and frequency-dependent nonlinear models of TWT amplifiers. IEEE Trans. Commun. COM 29(11), 1715–1720 (1981)
11. Tirrò, S. (ed.): Satellite Communication Systems Design. Plenum Press, New York (1993)
12. Fikart, J.L., Kocay, B.: Cost Effective Operating Power Specification of Ka-Band MMICS for Multimedia Satellite Interactive Terminals. In: Proc. of 1999 IEEE MTT-S Symposium on Technologies for Wireless Applications, pp. 247–252 (1999)
13. Polonio, R., Riva, C.: ITALSAT propagation experiment at 18.7, 39.6 and 49.5 GHz at Spino D'Adda: three years of CPA statistics. IEEE Trans. on Antennas and Propagat. 46(5), 631–635 (1998)
14. Lemorton, J., Castanet, L., La coste, F., Riva, C., Matriccciani, E., Fiebig, U.C., Van De Kamp, M., Martellucci, A.: Development and validation of time-series synthesizers of rain attenuation for Ka-band and Q/V-band satellite communication systems. Int. Jour. of Satellite Comm. and Networking 25(5), 575–601 (2007)
15. Castanet, L., Deloues, T., Lemorton, J.: Methodology to simulate long-term propagation time-series from the identification of attenuation periods filled with synthesized events. In: Int. Workshop on Satellite Communications from Fade Mitigation to Service Provision, Noordwijk, NL (2003)
16. ITU-R Recommendation P.1623: Prediction method of fade dynamics on Earth-space path, Geneva (CH) (2005)
17. Pahvalan, K., Levesque, A.: Wireless Information Networks. Wiley, New York (1995)
18. Proakis, J.G.: Digital Communications (new ed.). McGraw-Hill, New York (2000)
19. Kantak, A.V.: A Method for obtaining Signal Components and Their Power Content of Residual Carrier Signal. IEEE Trans on EMC 33(3), 269–270 (1991)

20. Recommendation on Telemetry Channel Coding, issued by: Consultative Committee for Space Data System (CCSDS), Oxfordshire, UK (2001)
21. Sacchi, C., Grigorova, A.: Use of Trellis-Coded Modulation for Gigabit/sec Transmissions over W-Band Satellite Links. In: Proc. of 2006 IEEE Aerospace Conf., Big Sky, MT (2006), vailable on CD-ROM
22. Ungerboeck, G.: Trellis-coded Modulation with Redundant Signal Sets – Part II: State of the Art. IEEE Comm. Mag. 25, 12–21 (1987)
23. Sacchi, C., Musso, M., Gera, G., Regazzoni, C., De Natale, F.G.B., Jebril, A., Ruggieri, M.: An Efficient Carrier Recovery Scheme for High-Bit-Rate W-Band Satellite Communication Systems. In: Proc. of 2005 IEEE Aerospace Conference, Big Sky, Montana, USA (2005) (available on CD-ROM)
24. Rustako, A.J., Greenstein, L.J., Roman, R.R., Saleh, A.M.: Using Times-Four Carrier Recovery in M-QAM Digital Radio Receivers. IEEE Journal on Selec. Areas in Communications SAC 5(3), 524–533 (1987)
25. Jeruchim, M.C., et al.: Simulation of Communication Systems. Kluwer, Dordrecht (2000)
26. Couch II, L.W.: Digital and Analog Communication Systems, 7th edn. Pearson – Prentice Hall, Upper Saddle River, NJ (2007)
27. Martin, W.L., Nguyen, T.M.: CCSDS-SFCG Efficient Modulation Methods Study: A comparison of Modulation Schemes, Phase 2: Spectrum Shaping, CCSDS Tech. Rep. (1994)
28. Rice, M., Oliphant, T., Haddadin, O., McIntire, W.: Estimation Technique for GMSK using Linear Detectors in Satellite Communications. IEEE Trans. on AES 43(4), 1484–1495 (2007)
29. Sacchi, C., Rossi, T., Menapace, M., Granelli, F.: Utilization of UWB Transmission Techniques for Broadband Satellite Connections operating in W-band. In: Proc. of 1st IEEE EHF-AEROCOMM Workshop Conf. (in conjunction with IEEE Globecom 2008), New Orleans, LA (2008)
30. Slepian, D., Pollak, H.O.: Prolate Spheroidal Wave Functions, Fourier Analysis and Uncertainty. I. Bell System Tech. J. 40, 43–64 (1961)
31. Usuda, K., Zhang, H., Nakagawa, M.: M-ary pulse shape modulation for PSWF-based UWB systems in multipath fading environment. In: Proc. IEEE Globecom 2004 Conf., Dallas (TX), pp. 3498–3504 (2004)
32. Howard, S.L., Schlegel, C.: Differential Turbo-Coded Modulation With APP Channel Estimation. IEEE Trans on Comm. 54(8), 1397–1406 (2006)
33. Cabric, D., Chen, M.S.W., Sobel, D.A., Wang, S., Jang, J., Brodersen, R.: Novel Radio Architectures for UWB, 60GHz and Cognitive Wireless Systems. EURASIP Jour. on Wireless Comm. and Networking 2006 Article ID 17957, 1–18 (2006)
34. Eisele, H.: GaAs W-band impatt diodes for very low-noise oscillators. Electronics Letters 26(2), 109–110 (1990)
35. Carlstrom, J.E., Plambeck, R.L., Thornton, D.D.: A continuously tunable 65-115-GHz Gunn oscillator. IEEE Trans. on Microwave Theory and Techniques MT-33, 610–619 (1985)
36. Howard, S.L., Schlegel, C.: Differential Turbo-Coded Modulation with APP Channel Estimation. IEEE Trans. on Comm. 54(8), 1397–1405 (2006)

# FM Discriminator for AIS Satellite Detection

Maria Angeles Jurado Gallardo[1,2] and Ghislain Ruy[1]

[1] LuxSpace, Chateau de Betzdorf, Building B, L-6815 Betzdorf, Luxembourg
[2] University of Luxembourg, 6 rue Coudenhove-Kalergi, L-1359 Luxembourg
marian.jurado@uni.lu, ruy@luxspace.lu

**Abstract.** The Automatic Identification System (AIS) is a tracking system used on ships for several decades to improve traffic monitoring and safety at sea in a short range. The modulation technique used is Gaussian Minimum Shift Keying (GMSK).

Recently, the idea of receiving AIS signals from space arose. This presents mainly two challenges. The first one is that received signals present a large Doppler range due to the satellite speed. The second one is the simultaneous reception of signals from ships because of the broad satellite coverage.

In this paper, a novel non-coherent GMSK demodulator is proposed to handle the large Doppler shift problem based on several FM discriminators in parallel. A frame collision detection algorithm is presented but the collision problem is not addressed.

In addition, computer simulated and real signals are used to study the receiver performance on an AWGN channel.

**Keywords:** AIS, GMSK, FM discriminator, Doppler.

## 1 Introduction

AIS stands for Automatic Identification System and is a telecommunication system defined for navigation safety purposes. It is required by the International Convention for the Safety of Life at Sea (SOLAS) convention and defined by the International Telecommunication Union (ITU) in Rec. ITU-R 1371-1 [1].

Ships exchange information such as position, speed, course and identification number every few seconds. The main objective is to avoid collisions among ships and also to localize certain vessels, for example, in search and rescue operations or ship carrying out illegal trade. In order to accommodate all vessel transmissions, a time multiplexing scheme is used.

This is of interest in areas close to the shore or between ships at open sea. However, the coverage range of AIS is not very large. It depends on the height of the antenna but nominally is around 20 nautical miles (nm) or 37 km. The position of vessels out of this range from the shore is unknown and it can only be received by ships nearby.

K. Sithamparanathan et al. (Eds.): PSATS 2010, LNICST 43, pp. 19–34, 2010.

The solution is to develop a space based system to receive AIS signals sent from these extensive maritime zones. This idea consists of implementing a constellation of Low Earth Orbit (LEO) satellites that detect and decode AIS messages and send them to the earth stations for database storing and further processing. Considering AIS signals with 12.5 W power transmission and an satellite altitude no longer than 1000 km for LEO orbits, reception of AIS signals from a spaceborne platform is feasible.

The main drawback of satellite detection is the Doppler range expected at reception. If a satellite speed of 7 km/s is considered, the Doppler range is approximately ±3.8 kHz. This maximum shift corresponds to approximately 40 % of the bit rate. Usually, frequency estimation methods handle shifts of 15 % of the bit rate like, for example, in [2]. In the effort to design a robust and efficient spaceborne AIS receiver that handles this Doppler range, we present a novel algorithm based on an FM discriminator.

Another important issue is that the coverage for an AIS sensor in space would be a much larger area on the ground than the system was originally designed for. As a consequence, collisions among signals from ships separated by a large distance will occur. More information about this is provided in the next section.

The structure of this paper is organized as follows. Section 2 presents the scenario for AIS satellite detection. The relevant technical aspects of AIS are introduced in Section 3 followed by the description of the signal model in Section 4. A novel algorithm for demodulating Gaussian Minimum Shift Keying (GMSK) signals with high Doppler range is derived in Section 5. Results for simulated and real AIS signals are contained in Section 6, as well as the Bit Error Rate (BER) performance of the system. Sections 7 and 8 finish with conclusions and possible future developments.

## 2  Scenario

This research work is part of a larger AIS project. The aim of this project is to improve the global maritime surveillance through the implementation of AIS message satellite detection using a constellation of LEO satellites. AIS signals are received and decoded. The resulting information is relayed via satellite feeder links to appropriately located ground stations, as shown in Fig. 1.

An initial demonstration system will consist of a single LEO satellite. For later operational systems, it is envisioned that a relatively small constellation of LEO satellites would be used; consequently satellite coverage of a given ship location will not be continuous.

As the satellite antenna beam covers a large geographical area, transmissions by multiple AIS ship transmitters are received simultaneously. With many ships in the Field Of View (FOV), interference problems will occur and AIS messages from some of the ships may not be detected. An example of this is described in [3] and is presented hereunder. Fig. 2 depicts the coverage area in North Sea for several AIS cells (small circles) and for an airplane at 12 km altitude (large circle). The observation area corresponding to the aircraft altitude is around 440 nm of

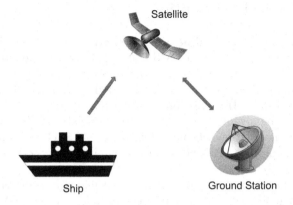

Fig. 1. Satellite Detection of AIS

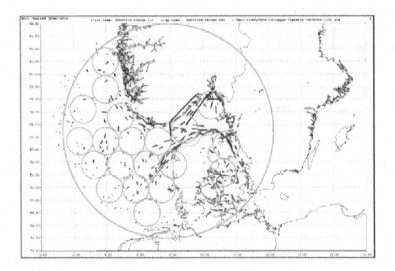

Fig. 2. Ship Distribution in North Sea [3]

diameter. In this range, multiple AIS cells become visible. As a consequence, simultaneous arrival of frames can produce collisions. For a LEO satellite, the coverage area is 2880 nm of diameter, including Europe and a wide sea area. Thus, the number of cells visible for the satellite is larger, increasing the probability of signal collision.

According to the study presented in [4], a satellite constellation with continuous coverage could handle up to 1300 ships with a ship information update rate of once per hour with a ship detection probability of better than 99 %. This shows that spaceborne AIS message reception is possible but not by a standard AIS receiver.

# 3   AIS Technical Description

In this section, a brief technical description of AIS is presented. Further information about the characteristics of AIS transmission can be found in [1].

The AIS system operates in the Very High Frequency (VHF) maritime mobile band. Two parallel channels have been allocated: *AIS 1* at 161.975 MHz and *AIS 2* at 162.025 MHz. Transmissions can use one of the two defined settings: *high* with 25 kHz bandwidth (most frequently utilized) and *low* with 12.5 kHz bandwidth. The modulation scheme specified for AIS is GMSK with maximum Bandwidth-Time product (BT) equals 0.4 for high setting mode and with data rate 9600 bps [1].

AIS works autonomously, automatically, continuously and operates primarily in broadcast mode using Time Division Multiple Access (TDMA) schemes. The access schemes to accommodate all users are Self Organized TDMA (SOTDMA), Random Access TDMA (RATDMA) and Fixed Access TDMA (FATDMA). Each channel AIS is divided into frames of one minute duration. Frames are synchronized with the Coordinated Universal Time (UTC) time standard and each one contains 2250 Time Slots (TS), thereby providing 4500 TS per minute considering both channels. The duration of a TS is: $60/2250 = 26.7$ ms or: $9600 \times 60/2250 = 256$ bits.

There are 22 AIS message types defined with different purposes. Their occupancy ranges from one to five TS depending of the type. The type relevant for us is the *position report* kind, used by ships to provide identification and navigational data. Its structure is shown in Fig. 3.

| Ramp Up | Training Seq. | Start Flag | Data | FCS | End Flag | Buffer |
|---------|---------------|------------|------|-----|----------|--------|

**Fig. 3.** Structure of the AIS Position Report Message

The transmission starts with an 8-bit ramp up followed by a 24-bit training sequence, consisting of alternating zeros and ones. Then a start flag, which is a standard High-level Data Link Control (HDLC) to identify the beginning of the frame. This is followed by the data, which has 168 bits length for position report messages type, and a Frame Check Sequence (FCS), that uses the Cyclic Redundancy Check (CRC) 16-bit polynomial to calculate the checksum. The end flag marks the end of the frame and is identical to the start flag. Finally, there is a 24-bit buffer to compensate bit stuffing, distance delays, repeater delay and jitter synchronization.

Each parameter field is defined with the most significant bit first. The total length is 256 bits, which corresponds to the length of one TS. The message duration is an important parameter because frequency and/or phase recovery algorithms for coherent demodulation usually require longer bit sequences, as in [5] for example, where around 1000 bits are required for the estimation.

Messages are Non-Return to Zero Inverted (NRZI) encoded before being output on the VHF data link.

## 4 Signal Model

The model of the transmitted AIS signal is presented in this section.

GMSK is a kind of Minimum Shift Keying (MSK) modulation with a Gaussian pulse shaping filter of an appropriate bandwidth defined by BT. The BT value is the product of B, the premodulation Gaussian filter bandwidth, and T the bit period, which is the inverse of the bit rate. Like MSK, the modulation index of GMSK is 0.5.

The advantage of using the Gaussian filter is that the generated signal has low side lobes, narrower main lobe than in MSK and smoother phase transitions. Another important property of MSK signals is that they have constant envelope making the modulation scheme more immune to noise and amplitude variations.

According to [6], two methods can be used to generate a modulated GMSK signal: a Gaussian filter followed by an FM modulator or a Gaussian filter and Quadrature Phase Shift Keying (QPSK) modulation.

The time domain impulse response of the Gaussian Low Pass Filter (GLPF) is given by [7]:

$$h(t) = \sqrt{\frac{2\pi}{\ln 2}} \mathrm{B} \exp\left(-\frac{2\pi^2}{\ln 2} \mathrm{B}^2 t^2\right) . \tag{1}$$

The impulse response has to be truncated and scaled depending on the BT value to ensure that the response of the filter to a single bit produces a phase change of $\pm\pi/2$. For BT = 0.4, the filter length is three symbol periods. The impulse response has to be also time shifted in order to have a causal signal.

When a rectangular pulse centred in the origin with unit amplitude and T duration passes through this filter, the response is:

$$g(t) = \frac{1}{2\mathrm{T}} \left[ Q\left(2\pi\mathrm{B}\frac{t - \mathrm{T}/2}{\sqrt{\ln 2}}\right) - Q\left(2\pi\mathrm{B}\frac{t + \mathrm{T}/2}{\sqrt{\ln 2}}\right) \right] , \tag{2}$$

where $Q(t)$ is the $Q$-function:

$$Q(t) = \int_t \frac{1}{\sqrt{2}} \exp\left(-x^2/2\right) dx . \tag{3}$$

Therefore, the signal obtained after the Gaussian filter is:

$$x(t) = \sum_i s_i g(t - iT) , \tag{4}$$

being $s_i$ the symbols to transmit.

The drawback of using GMSK is that since GMSK has a narrower main lobe than MSK, pulses spread over a longer time causing Intersymbol Interference (ISI). The presence of ISI makes the demodulation at the receiver more complex.

Either if the FM modulator or the quadrature modulator is used, the GMSK modulated signal is given by:

$$z(t) = A\cos(2\pi f_c t + \theta(t) + \theta_0) \,, \tag{5}$$

with A constant amplitude, $f_c$ carrier or modulation frequency and $\theta_0$ the initial phase at $t = 0$. $\theta(t)$ is related to the message information by:

$$\theta(t) = 2\pi k_f \int_{-\infty}^{t} x(\tau)d\tau \,, \tag{6}$$

where $k_f$ is the frequency deviation in volts per hertz.

## 5    GMSK Demodulator

Three different techniques can be used for GMSK demodulation ([8]): coherent detection, differential detection and FM discriminator. The last two are non-coherent detection and are usually utilized to demodulate FM. The coherent detection method is similar to the one used for MSK demodulation. In this paper, we chose to utilize a non-coherent scheme. The reason behind is that coherent demodulation requires accurate frequency, phase and clock recovery and, as mentioned above, the maximum Doppler shift is out of the range of the frequency recovery algorithms studied.

The differential detection and the FM discriminator are compared in [9] drawing the conclusion that the BER performance of the FM discriminator is better. This is due to the fact that the differential detection utilizes the phase and the amplitude of the signal and the FM discriminator uses only the phase. As a result, the FM discriminator is not affected by the amplitude noise. This problem, could be overcome with a limiter but in any case, the results of our tests conclude also that the FM discriminator has better BER performance and thus it is the best option. The block diagram of the discriminator is based on [10] and described in the following.

### 5.1    Description

The spaceborne AIS receiver developed consists of several branches in parallel with an FM discriminator in each branch. Every discriminator is centred at a different frequency to cope with the large Doppler range of the received signals. This idea comes from the bank of filters used in radar to treat different frequencies.

The block diagram of each FM discriminator is shown in Fig. 4. It is composed of the following elements: an I & Q demodulator, a phase derivator and a GLPF. Basically, the discriminator maps the frequency of the I & Q components to a voltage using a differential estimation algorithm.

Considering an AWGN channel with noise $n(t')$, $r(t')$ is defined by:

$$r(t') = A\cos(2\pi(f_c + f_d)t' + \theta(t') + \theta_0) + n(t') \,, \tag{7}$$

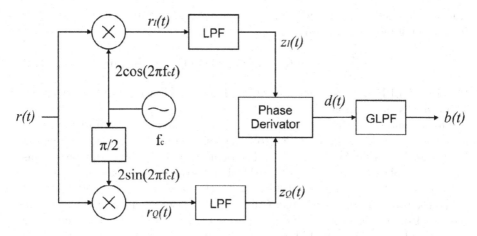

**Fig. 4.** FM Discriminator Block Diagram

being $f_d$ the Doppler frequency shift and $t' = t + \varepsilon$. $\varepsilon$ is the time needed by the signal to travel from the ship to the satellite. It needs to be estimated. From now on, and for the sake of simplicity, we consider $\theta_0 = 0$. We assume also, and only for the following mathematical description, that $\varepsilon = 0$ ($t' = t$). The estimation of $\varepsilon$ is explained afterwards.

The input passband signal $r(t)$, centred at an Intermediate Frequency (IF) is filtered by a reception filter with a wide enough bandwidth to consider the Doppler range. The filtered signal is input to the bank of branches and in each one is multiplied by a Local Oscillator (LO) centred at a different frequency, generating the I and Q signals in baseband. For the branch in the middle, the LO frequency is $f_c$. The following mathematical development is for the middle branch. The same procedure can be applied for the other branches. Noise is not considered for simplicity.

$$\begin{aligned}
r_I(t) &= r(t)2\cos(2\pi f_c t) = 2A\cos(2\pi(f_c + f_d)t + \theta(t))\cos(2\pi f_c t) \\
&= A\left[\cos(2\pi f_d t + \theta(t)) + \cos(2\pi(2f_c + f_d)t + \theta(t))\right] \\
r_Q(t) &= r(t)2\sin(2\pi f_c t) = 2A\cos(2\pi f_c t + \theta(t))\sin(2\pi f_c t) \\
&= A\left[\sin(2\pi f_d t + \theta(t)) + \sin(2\pi(2f_c + f_d)t + \theta(t))\right] .
\end{aligned}$$ (8)

After that, the I and Q signals pass through a LPF to eliminate the $2f_c$ component generated by the mixer:

$$\begin{aligned}
z_I(t) &= A\cos(2\pi f_d t + \theta(t)) \\
z_Q(t) &= A\sin(2\pi f_d t + \theta(t)) .
\end{aligned}$$ (9)

First, the phase derivator obtains the phase of the baseband signal by computing the arctangent of $z_I(t)$ and $z_Q(t)$.

$$y(t) = \arctan(\frac{z_Q(t)}{z_I(t)}) = \arctan\left(\frac{A\sin(2\pi f_d t + \theta(t))}{A\cos(2\pi f_d t + \theta(t))}\right) = 2\pi f_d t + \theta(t) .$$ (10)

And as a second step, it performs the derivation of the arctangent respect to time. Taking into account Eq. 6:

$$d(t) = \frac{dy(t)}{dt} = 2\pi f_d + Cx(t) \text{ , where C is a constant .} \tag{11}$$

Finally, a GLPF eliminates the out of band noise facilitating the hard decision. The result is the demodulated signal $b(t)$.

The advantage of this demodulator is that is simple, not need of carrier or initial phase recovery, leading also to a very simple implementation in a Field Programmable Gate Array (FPGA). The demodulated signal at the output has constant amplitude independently of the signal level at the input.

Nevertheless, there are also disadvantages: the noise is amplified when no signal is received and there is a Direct Current (DC) offset when the received signal presents Doppler, as shown in Eq. 11. This is the reason why the discriminators are in parallel, as mentioned above.

However, an advantage can be gained from the DC offset because its value is proportional to the Doppler shift. Hence, Doppler is calculated and compensated, the signal is centred around zero and the symbol decision is correctly taken. To estimate the DC shift, a mean filter is used taking advantage from the fact that the training sequence consists of alternating zeros and ones. Consequently, the frame DC is obtained by calculating the mean value of this segment.

Now we consider the case that $\varepsilon \neq 0$. AIS signals are UTC synchronized but the exact moment of reception at the satellite is not known. For detecting the presence of a frame and also recovering the synchronization, the following technique is used.

At the same time that the signal is being demodulated, a correlation is performed to compare the demodulated signal at the output of the FM discriminator with the waveform of the training sequence and the start flag (32 bits in total) which are called preamble in the following. In this manner, when the preamble is contained in the demodulated signal, the correlation function has a peak marking the beginning of the frame and, hence, the beginning and end of a symbol. That is how $\varepsilon$ is estimated. The peak can be a maximum or a minimum depending on the initial state of the NRZI encoding (1 or -1). The advantage of this technique is that is amplitude independent because, as mentioned above, the demodulated signals have the same output amplitude.

The correlation has to be performed in every branch of the demodulator. The reason is that when the training sequence is being demodulated, the frequency has not been compensated yet and the demodulated signal has a DC component, as it is shown in Section 6. Therefore, there are as many correlators as FM discriminators. Fig. 5 depicts the parallel structure that detects the peak correlation to estimate $\varepsilon$. If a frame is detected, the Doppler shift is estimated from the middle demodulated signal. $\lfloor \; \rfloor$ represents the rounding to the nearest integer smaller than the element.

Once the demodulation is done and the synchronization is recovered, the detection starts, working with the middle branch of the demodulator. The other branches are only utilized for detection of the correlation peaks. By using an

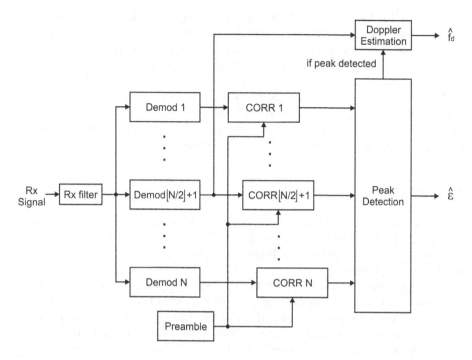

**Fig. 5.** Demodulator Block Diagram

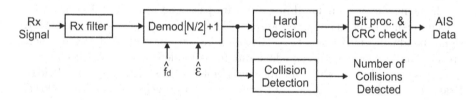

**Fig. 6.** Signal Detection and Further Processing

Integrate & Dump filter, the receiver integrates the signal over one symbol to take the decision. The process continues until the end of the frame (identified by the end flag). The CRC is checked and if the message is correct, further processing is done to obtain human read information. This is shown in Fig. 6.

Complexity is not added due to the parallel structure because the intention of the AIS project, is to implement the design in an FPGA, which allows the implementation of parallel configurations. Consequently, the receiver can perform in real time.

## 5.2 Collision Detection

A fairly high collision rate is expected over dense traffic zones. Therefore, every attempt must be made to retrieve the maximum information from the signals.

Based on the fact that GMSK signals have constant amplitude, if the received signal presents a change in the amplitude, it is likely that a collision between two or more frames has occurred. Therefore, the amplitude of the received signal is obtained by using the I and Q components defined in Eq. 9. Hence: $(z_I(t)^2 + z_Q(t)^2) = A^2$.

Then, to detect the amplitude variation, the variance of the amplitude is calculated, providing a method to detect the presence of collisions. This is a first attempt to estimate the collision rate. However, the focus of this research is on the large Doppler range rather than in the collision problem.

# 6    Results

In this section, the performance of the proposed demodulator is evaluated, firstly with computer simulated signals and then with real AIS signals recorded through an aircraft. Finally, the receiver BER performance is displayed and compared with theoretical results.

A compromise has to be found for the number of branches in the demodulator. The more branches, the smaller the frequency interval between LO frequencies and hence, the narrower the bandwidth of the LPFs from Fig. 3. As a consequence, there is less noise passing through the filter, making the detection easier. The drawback is that the complexity of the demodulator increases: several FM discriminators and correlation calculations running in parallel. For this case, five branches have been chosen.

The signals used (simulated and real) are passband centred at 12 kHz as IF. This frequency is high enough because, as BT = 0.4 and T = 1/9600, the GMSK signal bandwidth is B = 3840 Hz. The sampling rate is 96 ksps, therefore, there are 10 samples per symbol. The demodulator is implemented in ANSI C.

From the five branches, the middle one (number 3) has a LO centred at 12 kHz. Branches 1 and 2 have higher LO frequencies and branches 4 and 5 have lower LO frequencies.

## 6.1    Computer Simulated AIS Signals

Synthesized signals have been created to determine the performance of the demodulator. To simplify, an AWGN channel has been considered, though in reality some interference may disturb the communication.

The test consists of three AIS frames with different amplitudes and Doppler frequency shifts. They are synchronized in consecutive TS. The beginning of each TS is marked in the figures corresponding to this validation with synthesized signals. In the following, the amplitude and correlation values displayed in the figures are normalized to one.

Fig. 7 displays the demodulated baseband signals. The training sequences of the frames have a DC shift (indicated with a circle) because the mean value of the training sequence has still not been calculated. After the frequency compensation, the signal is centred around the axis, which is required for the bit

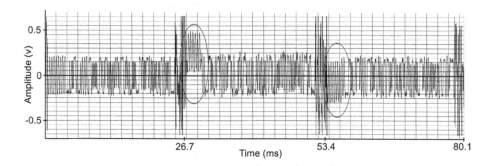

**Fig. 7.** Doppler Correction

decision. Since the first frame has a very small Doppler shift, 14 Hz, the demodulated signal is centred around the axis. The second one has a positive Doppler, 3547 Hz, being the training sequence above the zero axis. The training sequence of the last frame is below the axis because its Doppler is -1018 Hz.

In Fig. 7, one of the advantages of the receiver is appreciated: the demodulated signals have all the same amplitude. However, a disadvantage is also visible: the white Gaussian noise between the frames is amplified.

For detection, the synchronization needs to be recovered to identify the symbol start and end. To this aim, the correlation over the preamble is performed, as mentioned previously, for the different branches. Fig. 8 presents the parallel correlations for the three signals.

The correlation peak involved in the synchronization for the first frame corresponds to branch 3 because the first signal has a very small Doppler shift. The second one, has the peak at branch 1 (for large positive Doppler shift) and the third frame has two peaks: in branch 3 and 4, being the peak in branch 4 the minimum and the one involved in the synchronization recovery.

Fig. 9 illustrates the synchronization process. The upper part of the figure depicts the training sequence, start flag and the beginning of the first AIS frame from Fig. 7. The lower part corresponds to the correlation function. As can be seen, the correlation peak, a minimum in this case, corresponds to the end of the preamble, thus being possible to determine the bit beginning.

## 6.2  Real AIS Signals

For the test with real messages, the signals recorded from an aircraft have been used. The purpose of the flight was to record AIS signals sent from ships in similar conditions as with satellite reception. The altitude of the aircraft is 4500 m. As the speed of the airplane is much slower than the satellite speed, the expected Doppler range for these signals is small, around ±200 Hz and the frequency compensation is not needed. For LEO satellites, the expected Doppler range is ±3.8 kHz. For this reason, the presented AIS receiver is needed. The demodulated signals are depicted in Fig. 10.

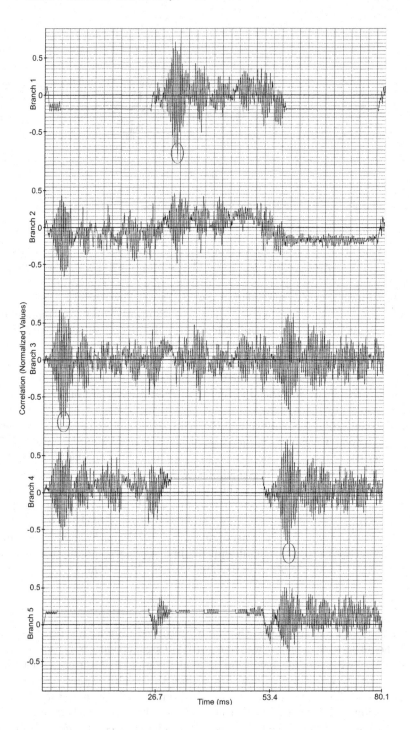

**Fig. 8.** Correlation Functions for Synchronization

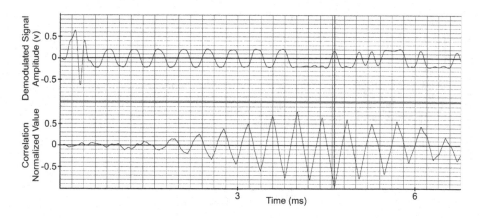

**Fig. 9.** Synchronization Through Correlation Function

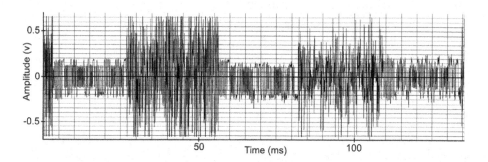

**Fig. 10.** Demodulated Real AIS Signals

The correlation peaks corresponding to branch 3 are displayed in Fig. 11. As mentioned above, peaks can be maximum or minimum. For the first two frames the peak is a maximum and for the last one is a minimum.

### 6.3 Receiver BER Performance

Finally, the BER performance of the GMSK receiver is shown in Fig. 12.

The line with round points is our receiver BER performance. It is compared to the theoretical BER curve achieved by a non-coherent MSK receiver (line with square points). For GMSK, the theoretical curve is slightly shifted to the right due to ISI. As can be seen, the curve of the receiver is, in average, 4 dB from the theoretical curve achieved by a non-coherent GMSK receiver with $BT = 0.4$.

In the received real signals, it has been observed that some signals have a very low Signal-to-Noise Ratio (S/N). For that reason, further improvements have to be done to make the BER performance closer to theory.

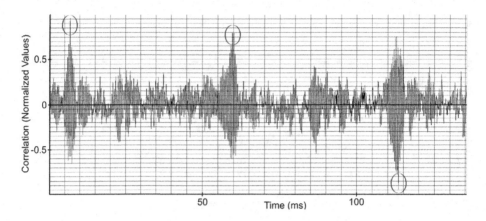

**Fig. 11.** Correlation Result of Real AIS Signals

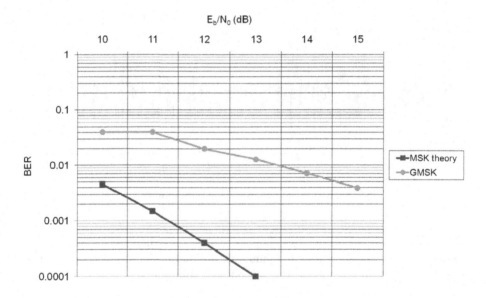

**Fig. 12.** Demodulator BER Performance

## 7   Conclusions

In this paper the structure of a spaceborne AIS receiver has been presented and analysed. The purpose of this demodulator is to receive the AIS messages sent by ships, in order to identify the position of all ships over the world, improving the maritime surveillance.

Space based reception introduces a large Doppler frequency shift of the received signals, which is in the range of $\pm 3.8\,\mathrm{kHz}$ due to the satellite speed. To cope with this issue, the receiver is implemented with several branches in parallel centred at a different demodulation frequency. The number of branches of the proposed receiver is five. Each branch is based on an FM discriminator that performs the derivation of the arctangent to obtain the signal, which is contained in the phase of received signal.

The main advantages of this robust scheme is that, as it is non-coherent, there is no need to recover the frequency of the arriving signals with a small margin of error ($\pm 1$ Hz). Our algorithm performs a rough frequency compensation by the calculation of the signal DC offset. This approximation is good enough ($\pm 100$ Hz error) to centre the demodulated signal around the axis for hard detection, leading to an easier implementation.

In addition to the FM discriminator, the receiver includes a bit synchronization algorithm by obtaining the correlation of the demodulated signals with a known waveform, the preamble.

In presence of AWGN channel, the BER performance of the GMSK demodulator showed a 4 dB loss respect to the theoretical curve. The disadvantage is that a coherent demodulation scheme has always theoretically 3 dB better BER performance. For that reason, a coherent demodulator could be considered for further developments.

The receiver has also been tested with real AIS signals recorded from an airplane. Real messages can be demodulated properly and the information is recovered. However, some of the recorded frames have a very low S/N, not being possible to demodulate them with the receiver presented here.

The collision in a TS among signals from different ships is a quite likely event. Some preliminary tests performed with the receiver show that if two frames collide only the frame with higher amplitude can be obtained if the Signal-to-Interference ratio is large enough (10 dB). As a consequence, the receiver presented here can detect if a collision has occurred or not in a TS, but is not able to demodulate the two (or more) signals colliding.

## 8    Future Work

As a first implementation, the demodulator consists of five branches. Fewer amount of branches is not advisable because of the large Doppler range. A possibility is then to try seven branches, which complicates the demodulator structure. However, at the same time allows to reduce the bandwidth of the filters in the branches, increasing the S/N and improving the BER performance, placing it closer to the theoretical values.

Another detection schemes may be used instead of Integrate and Dump, such as Decision Feedback Equaliser (DFE), to cope with the ISI inherent to GMSK modulation. Moreover, possible designs for coherent demodulation schemes can be studied to increase the receiver performance respect to BER.

Finally, a scheme to deal with signal collisions will be analysed since, so far, these are only detected.

**Acknowledgements.** This research has been carried out in cooperation with LuxSpace and the University of Luxembourg. It is supported by AFR (Aides à la Formation-Recherche) from the Government of Luxembourg. Special thanks to Prof. Dr. Ulrich Sorger.

# References

1. ITU: Recommendation ITU-R M.1371-2, Technical characteristics for a universal shipborne automatic identification system using time division multiple access in the VHF maritime mobile band, last version (2006)
2. Morelli, M., Mengali, U.: Joint Frequency And Timing Recovery For MSK-Type Modulation. IEEE Transactions on Communications (June 1999)
3. Narheim, B.T.: NCUBE-1 and 2 AIS Detection Probability, Norwegian Defence Research Establishment (2007)
4. Høye, G.K., Eriksen, T., Meland, B.J., Narheim, B.T.: Space-based AIS for Global Maritime Traffic Monitoring. Norwegian Defence Research Establishment (2007)
5. Bianchi, P., Loubaton, P., Sirven, F.: Blind Joint Estimation of the Technical Parameters of Continuous Phase Modulated Signals, France (2003)
6. Hull University: Appendix D: Digital Modulation and GMSK, http://www.emc.york.ac.uk/reports/linkpcp/appD.pdf
7. Haykin, S.: Communication Systems, 4th edn., pp. 396–400. John Wiley & Sons, New York (2001)
8. Mehrotra, A.: GSM System Engineering, The Artech House Mobile Communication Series, pp. 216–217 (1996) ISBN: 0-89006-860-7
9. Schiphorst, R., Hoeksema, F., Slump, K.: Bluetooth demodulation algorithms and their performance, Netherlands
10. Turletti, T.: GMSK in a nutshell. Massachusetts Institute of technology (1996)

# Simulation of a Feasible Galileo System Operating in L1 and E5 Bands

Spyridon K. Chronopoulos, Christos Koliopanos, Antigoni Pappa,
and Constantinos T. Angelis

Department of Informatics and Telecommunications
Technological Educational Institute of Epirus, Arta, Greece
schrono@cc.uoi.gr, hkoliopanos@teleinfom.teiep.gr,
antigoni.pappa@gmail.com, kangelis@teiep.gr

**Abstract.** Galileo is the program that has been launched by the European Union for the purpose of building a Global Navigation Satellite System (GNSS) for serving civilians and to exist under civil control. Our project combines many previous researched scenarios for Galileo system to a final one, which has been simulated and adjusted to meet the most demanding standards (of proposed GNSS services). The final simulated scenario is consisted of 30 (27+3 spare) satellites allocated in 3 orbital planes.

**Keywords:** Galileo, GPS, GNSS, BPSK, BOC, EIRP, RAAN, Satellite coverage, Satellite access time, BER.

## 1 Introduction

GPS was built by the US as a revolutionary precise positioning system in order to play a key role in various military operations. But almost twenty years ago a change of scene took place considering the need for additional GPS civil services. Due to its primary goal and institutional status, GPS cannot guarantee such kind of services which would keep up the pace with the actual increasing rate of satellite demanding applications.

Galileo will fill the actual gap of high quality satellite services absence, in terms of performance, better signal tracking and therefore position accuracy. In comparison to GPS it will not be controlled by any government. GNSS Supervisory Authority and the Concessionaire will be responsible for the whole project.

The Galileo system will be consisted of 27 satellites in MEO (Medium Earth Orbit) with 3 additional spare satellites intended for broadcasting navigational signals. This constellation will provide 4 kinds of navigation services such as Open Service, Safety-of-Life Service, Commercial Service and Public Regulated Service [1]. Consequently, development of scientific fields such as GNSS-R altimeter for characterizing mesoscale ocean feature, sea-ice altimetry and soil moisture monitoring will be major breakthroughs of GNSS reflectometry [2].

In this paper, taking into consideration previous mentioned needs for better performance we study various proposed scenarios for Open Service (L1 and E5 frequency bands). This is the first stage of our work followed by the second stage where

K. Sithamparanathan et al. (Eds.): PSATS 2010, LNICST 43, pp. 35–43, 2010.
© Institute for Computer Sciences, Social-Informatics and Telecommunications Engineering 2010

we investigate the feasibility of combining all proposed systems to a final and even better one. In this way, we conclude in constructing a scenario consisted of a constellation of 30 satellites (27 + 3 spares). Final stage is devoted in the simulation procedures and results.

## 2  Technical Specifications of the Proposed Galileo System

Binary offset carrier (BOC) modulation will be used for the purpose of sharing the same centre frequency among various GNSSs. It has advantages compared to BPSK modulation from the aspect of frequency correlation function. In this function the main lobe of BOC signal is narrower and in turn provides higher positioning accuracy [3], [4].

The Galileo Open Service signal (L1) will be consisted from BOC signals. Symbolic expression of BOC($f_S$, $f_C$) is transformed to BOC(1,1) for a given subcarrier frequency of $f_S$ = 1.023 MHz and chipping rate of $f_C$ = 1.023 MHz. Signal characteristics for the simulated Galileo system including Data rates and Chip rates are summarized in Table 1 [5], [6].

**Table 1.** Signal characteristics of the simulated Galileo system

| Standard | Galileo E1 | E5a |
|---|---|---|
| Frequency (MHz) | 1575.42 | 1176.45 |
| Bandwidth (MHz) | 4.092 | 25.575 |
| Modulation | BOC(1,1) | BPSK |
| Data rate (bps) | 250 | 50 |
| Chip rate (Mcps) | 1.023 | 10.23 |

For the purpose of simulating Galileo system under real conditions, we included in our scenario signal propagation characteristics. These characteristics consisted of free space path loss, Ionospheric and Tropospheric path delay, Ionospheric and Tropospheric amplitude scintillation, Ionospheric and Tropospheric phase scintillation, Ionospheric refraction, Ionospheric Doppler shift, foliage attenuation, worst case scenario for attenuation by water vapor and oxygen, worst case scenario for rainfall, clouds and fog attenuation. Total signal attenuation was equal to 189.3 dB, satellite and user gain antenna equal to 14 dB and 0 dB respectively [7], [8].

EIRP of each satellite was equal to 12.3 dBW and all receivers' sensitivity equal to -144 dBm [5].

Orbital parameters of all satellites were based on our modifications of GIOVE-A satellite. Apogee and perigee altitude was equal to 23616 km. Inclination and argument of perigee was equal to 56 deg and 317 deg respectively. Right ascension of the ascending node (RAAN) and true anomaly had various values according to 3 satellite planes defined by Walker tool in Satellite toolkit [9], [10].

Table 2 shows all orbital characteristics of 30 satellites constituting the proposed Galileo system.

**Table 2.** Orbital parameters of simulated Galileo system (apogee and perigee altitude equals to 23616 km and mean motion equals to 1.6713 revs/day for all satellites)

| Proposed Satellite name | Inclination (deg) | Argument of perigee (deg) | RAAN (deg) | True Anomaly (deg) |
| --- | --- | --- | --- | --- |
| GioveA101 spare | 56 | 317 | 186 | 0 |
| GioveA102 | 56 | 317 | 186 | 36 |
| GioveA103 | 56 | 317 | 186 | 72 |
| GioveA104 | 56 | 317 | 186 | 108 |
| GioveA105 | 56 | 317 | 186 | 144 |
| GioveA106 | 56 | 317 | 186 | 180 |
| GioveA107 | 56 | 317 | 186 | 216 |
| GioveA108 | 56 | 317 | 186 | 252 |
| GioveA109 | 56 | 317 | 186 | 288 |
| GioveA110 | 56 | 317 | 186 | 324 |
| GioveA201 spare | 56 | 317 | 306 | 12 |
| GioveA202 | 56 | 317 | 306 | 48 |
| GioveA203 | 56 | 317 | 306 | 84 |
| GioveA204 | 56 | 317 | 306 | 120 |
| GioveA205 | 56 | 317 | 306 | 156 |
| GioveA206 | 56 | 317 | 306 | 192 |
| GioveA207 | 56 | 317 | 306 | 228 |
| GioveA208 | 56 | 317 | 306 | 264 |
| GioveA209 | 56 | 317 | 306 | 300 |
| GioveA210 | 56 | 317 | 306 | 336 |
| GioveA301 spare | 56 | 317 | 66 | 24 |
| GioveA302 | 56 | 317 | 66 | 60 |
| GioveA303 | 56 | 317 | 66 | 96 |
| GioveA304 | 56 | 317 | 66 | 132 |
| GioveA305 | 56 | 317 | 66 | 168 |
| GioveA306 | 56 | 317 | 66 | 204 |
| GioveA307 | 56 | 317 | 66 | 240 |
| GioveA308 | 56 | 317 | 66 | 276 |
| GioveA309 | 56 | 317 | 66 | 312 |
| GioveA310 | 56 | 317 | 66 | 348 |

## 3 Results and Discussion

In order to demonstrate the efficiency of the proposed Galileo system, we inserted a vehicle in our simulation. Vehicle was set to move on an ideal straight line ranging from Thessaloniki (Greece) to Berlin (Germany). Average speed of 80 km/h was assumed. Hardware characteristics of portable Galileo system which were located on the vehicle and onboard satellites are described in the previous section. For the purpose of confirming good theory of operation, coverage (FOM satisfaction) and access time graphs are presented. Coverage is the existence of a clear line of sight from one object to another. Also, Access tool allows determining the times one object can access another object. It models transmission according to the constraints set by the user [10].

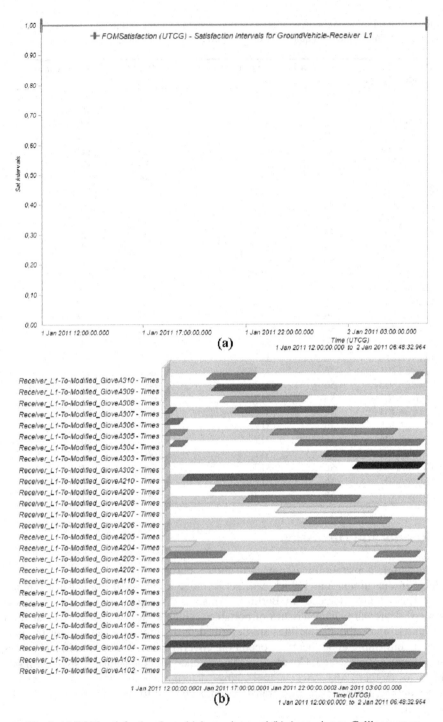

**Fig. 1.** (a) FOM satisfaction for vehicle receiver and (b) Accessing to Galileo system

FOM satisfaction diagram (Fig. 1a) for vehicle receiver (bands L1+E5a) shows real time coverage from Galileo system. In turn, this is essential for accomplishing real time accessing. The previous principle is shown in Fig. 2b by presenting each satellite access time in relation to vehicle receiver. Time gaps were expected due to medium earth orbits of Galileo system. Nevertheless, they do not affect the final outcome of accomplishing real time data transfer, because multi-locking procedure of several Galileo satellites at the same time gives excellent results.

In Fig. 2a is presented the simulation scenario of Galileo system and moving vehicle in 2 dimensions. Fig. 3 shows real time accessing in 3D representation (denoted with lines ranging from each satellite to vehicle).

Using link budget analysis, we investigated BER performance for all Galileo satellite links of the moving vehicle. BER was found in most occasions not to supersede the value of $10^{-3}$ [11]. The previous result is linked with worst case scenario noise, included in simulation computations.

Also, diagrams are shown (Fig 4) which are related with accessing Galileo system (27 satellites) from its spare satellites. These diagrams explain the reason of choosing the certain spare satellites orbital parameters (Table 2). Graphical results which are derived from Fig.3 (a) (b) and (c) are summarized in Table 3.

**Table 3.** Observations in accessing Galileo system from each spare satellite

| Real time accessing specifications | Accessing from GioveA101 spare | Accessing from GioveA201 spare | Accessing from GioveA301 spare |
|---|---|---|---|
| Absence of satellite accessing | GioveA106 | GioveA206 | GioveA306 |
| Time accessing under conditions (with gaps) | GioveA203 | GioveA303 | GioveA104 |
|  | GioveA204 | GioveA304 | GioveA105 |
|  | GioveA307 | GioveA108 | GioveA208 |
|  | GioveA308 | GioveA109 | GioveA209 |
| Real time access | All others | All others | All others |

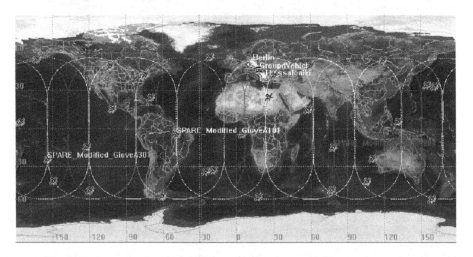

**Fig. 2.** 2D representation of Galileo system (only spare satellites orbits are shown)

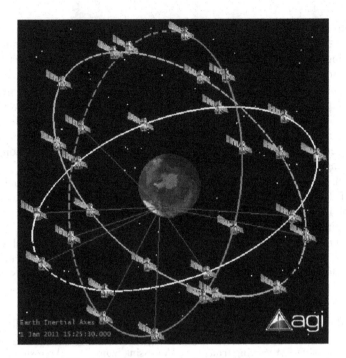

**Fig. 3.** 3D representation of simulated system

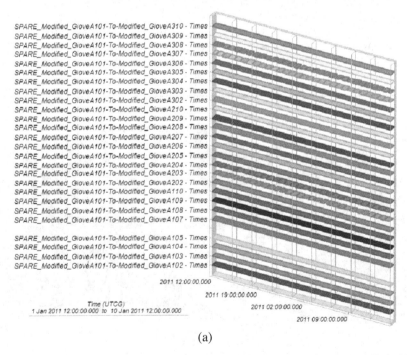

(a)

**Fig. 4.** Time accessing for spare satellites (a) GioveA101, (b) GioveA201 and (c) GioveA301

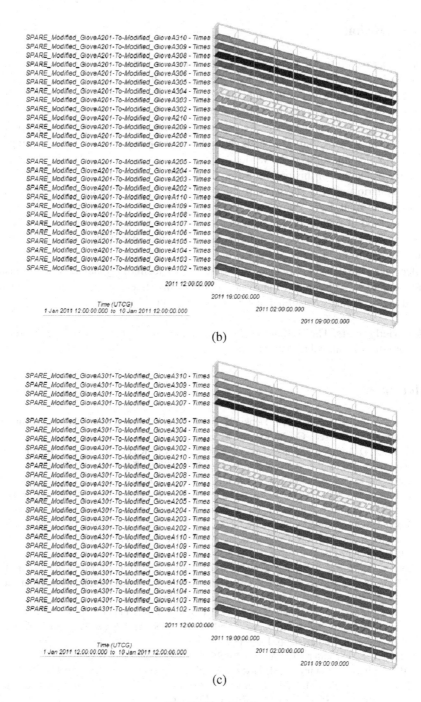

(b)

(c)

**Fig. 4.** (*Continued*)

# 4 Conclusion

In this paper we presented a study that has been based on the modification of an existing satellite called GIOVE-A. The main purpose was to find all orbit parameters of a satellite constellation that could constitute Galileo system. Consequently simulation of this system was conducted in order to determine good theory of operation even under worst case scenario noise. Results confirmed the feasibility of the proposed system working in L1 and E5a bands through the existence of real time accessing to various mobile units all over the world.

Another outcome of this project would be to investigate and if possible to develop a new scenario unifying services provided by GPS, GLONASS and Galileo for the benefit of the final user. A next step to our research will be also to investigate (based on our method of finding orbit elements for Galileo system) the feasibility of GPS III system under real conditions in order to verify its interoperability even under worst jamming conditions. Finally, a simulation will be conducted for unifying services of Galileo and GPS III systems using the outcome of technology based on previously manufactured or researched hardware components like synthetically generated, phased-array antennas for global navigation systems [12].

**Acknowledgments.** The Authors would like to thank AGI, Inc. for the license to use STK for educational and research purposes.

# References

1. Moudrak, A., Konovaltsev, A., Denks, H., Hammesfahr, J.: GNSS Development: Bringing New Benefits to Users. GeoInformatics Magazine 10(1), 54–59 (2007)
2. Buck, C., D'Addio, S.: Status and Perspectives of GNSS-R at ESA. In: IEEE International Geoscience and Remote Sensing Symposium, IGARSS 2007, pp. 5076–5079 (2007)
3. Grein, N., Olynik, M., Clayton, M.: Galileo BOC(1,1) Prototype Receiver Development. In: ION GNSS 2004, pp. 2604–2610. The Institute of Navigation, Inc., Manassas (2004)
4. Yoo, S.H., Yoo, S., Ahn, S., Yoon, S., Kim, S.Y.: Two-Stage Search Scheme for High-Ordered BOC Modulation in Future GNSS. In: The third International Technical Conference on Circuits/Systems, Computers and Communications (ITC-CSCC), pp. 1333–1336. IEICE, Japan (2008)
5. Detratti, M., Lopez, E., Perez, E., Palacio, R.: Dual-Band RF Front-End Solution for Hybrid Galileo/GPS Mass Market Receivers. In: 5th IEEE Consumer Communications and Networking Conference, pp. 603–607. IEEE, New York (2008)
6. Sand, S., Mensing, C., Ancha, S., Bell, G.: Communications and GNSS based Navigation: A Comparison of Current and Future Trends. In: 16th IST Mobile and Wireless Communications Summit, Budapest, pp. 1–5 (2007)
7. Schuller, E., Schuller, T.: Active GNSS Networks and the Benefits of Combined GPS+Galileo Positioning. Inside GNSS Magazine, 46–55 (November/December 2007)
8. Hein, G.W., Irsigler, M., Avila-Rodriguez, J.A.: GNSS System of Systems: Envisioning a Future. Inside GNSS Magazine, 64–73 (May/June 2007)

9. European Space Agency, `http://www.esa.int/esaCP/index.html`
10. Analytical Graphics, Inc., `http://www.agi.com`
11. Nandra, A., Govil, J., Govil, J.: Optimization of Satellite Link Design. In: Proceedings of the 2008 Spring simulation multiconference, pp. 225–230. The Society for Modeling and Simulation International, San Diego (2008)
12. Solovied, A., Graas, F.V., Miller, M., Gunawardena, S.: Synthetic Aperture GPS Signal Processing - Concept and Feasibility Demonstration, Inside GNSS Magazine, 37–46b, Gibbons Media & Research LLC. (May/June 2009)

# Compensations of Nonlinear Effects of TWTA for Signal Super-Positioning Satellite Communication Systems

Kenta Kubo[1], Shigeo Naoi[2], Yozo Takeda[2], Ryusuke Miyamoto[1], Takao Hara[1], and Minoru Okada[1]

[1] Graduate School of Information Science, Nara Institute of Science and Technology
8916-5 Takayamacho, Ikoma, Nara, 630-0101 Japan
Tel.: +81-743-72-5348; Fax: +81-743-72-5349
{kenta-k,miya,takao-ha,mokada}@is.naist.jp
[2] SKY perfect JSAT Corporation
1-14-14 Akasaka, Minato, Tokyo, 107-0052 Japan
Tel.: +81-3-5571-7800
{naoi-shigeo,y-takeda}@sptvjsat.com

**Abstract.** The Carrier Super-Positioning Satellite System is a promising telecommunication system because the frequency efficiency is double that of existing satellite systems. In this technique, we can use the same frequency band for inbound and outbound signals which are currently used in separated bands. Interference canceller used in the carrier super-positioning system is degraded a lot by the nonlinear distortion of satellite TWTA. This paper proposes and verifies a method of compensation of nonlinearity for the interference canceller. It becomes clear that, by intentionally giving the same nonlinearity as that of the satellite to the generated replica, significant part of the interference caused by the nonlinearity can be removed.

**Keywords:** satellite communication, interference canceller, nonlinear distortion, frequency reuse technology, TWTA.

## 1   Introduction

As the traffic demand for high-speed images increases, along with severe compentition in the market environment, the effective utilization of frequency resources of satellite communications is more important than ever. Frequency reuses by carrier super-positioning is one of the efficiency method [1]. This is not only for effective use of the band but also for the demand on the expansion of applications by reducing the channel cost.

Many activities, including our own, for the studies of interference canceller used in this system have been reported for the last few years [2]-[12]. All these reports show that the interference canceller performs well in the linear systems. In this study including our previous one however, it has been verified that it is not true in the nonlinear system[10]. The interference is remainded un-cancelled

K. Sithamparanathan et al. (Eds.): PSATS 2010, LNICST 43, pp. 44–59, 2010.

if the signal is distorted and degrades the BER performance of wanted signals. The distortion is due to AM/AM and AM/PM conversion of the satellite TWTA.

In general, as for the compensation of nonlinear effects, many studies have been reported. Some of them propose a pre-compensation that reshapes the signals at the transmitted side[13]. However, they are all about regular signal transmission for non-superposed carriers or about amplifier devices; very few are about interference cancellers for carrier super-positioning.

In order to minimize the effects of such nonlinear distortion, this paper proposes a method to compensate the nonlinearity of the satellite in the canceller unit put in the receiver. As described in the many reference papers, it is common for the interference canceller for frequency superposing to generate replica of outbound signal and subtract it from received signal[6]-[9]. Both inbound signal and outbound signal are contained in the received signal. The outbound signal returned from the satellite is the unwanted signal which has to be cancelled in this case since the station does not want to receive outbound signal but want to receive inbound signal. Here it can be notified that the received signal sent back from the satellite transponder is distorted if the signal is fed to the nonlinear region of satellite TWTA while the replica generated in the canceller is free from the distortion. The canceller has been suffered from the performance degradation due to this difference between received signal and the replica.

Our proposal is to compensate the nonlinearity for the canceller by simply giving distortion to the replica too. Then difference should be erased if the replica is distorted in the same way as the received signal is done by the TWTA.

This paper first explains the effects of TWTA onto the interference canceller, then shows the improvement of the performance of the canceller by our proposed method.

## 2    Interference Canceller

Fig.1 shows two typical network configurations for carrier super-positioning network. Fig.1(a) is for point-to-point paired carrier network. Both outbound (OB) and inbound (IB) carriers are superposed in the same frequency band. The level of both OB and IB carriers are the same in this case since size of antennas are the same for both stations. In this network, interference canceller is required to put at both stations.

On the other hand, Fig.1(b) shows the point-to-multipoint network called VSAT (Very Small Aperture Terminal) system. This network is composed of one large Hub station and many remote stations, and a wider band OB carrier is sent from Hub station to remote stations and plural narrower band IB carriers are from remotes to Hub. Since different diameter of antenna are used for Hub and remote stations in the VSAT system, the carrier level (power density) of OB is generally much higher than those of IB carriers. The difference is generally as well as 10dB and more. The interference canceller is then required only in the Hub station but not required in remotes since remote stations can demodulate high level OB carrier (wanted signal) as it is.

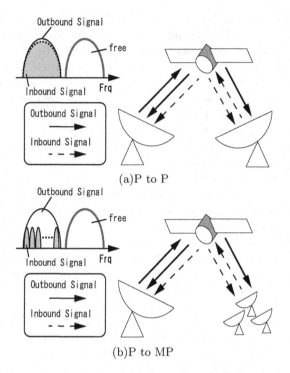

Fig. 1. Carrier Super-Positioning System

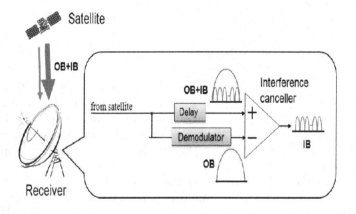

Fig. 2. Replica generation by demodulation

Interference canceller is realized by generating replica of unwanted signal and subtracting it from received signals. Two methods have been proposed by us. One is to demodulate unwanted signal from received signals and generating replica [5]. The other method is to shift transmitting signal with the amount of delay of one round trip time [11][12]. The former (method 1) is simple and useful for VSAT system but the accuracy of replica is affected by the bit error at the demodulation of unwanted signal. The latter (method 2) is not affected by such bit error but is required to measure the satellite one round trip delay accurately and continuously. The concept of interference canceller of method 1 is shown in Fig.2. In Fig.2, upper part is the path for received signal (OB+IB) and the lower part is for the path to demodulate unwanted signal and to generate replica (unwanted OB). Then, wanted signals (IB) are extracted at the output of the canceller.

## 3   Nonlinear Effects

### 3.1   Theoretical Description

In the satellite communications, the transponder TWTA is generally operated in the region of near saturation in order to use power effectively. Then, the signals amplified there suffer from the effects of inter-modulation and distorted due to the AM/AM and AM/PM conversion. Fig.3 shows the typical AM/AM and AM/PM conversion characteristics of the TWTA used in the conventional communications satellite. The amplitude and phase of the signal provided to the nonlinear amplifier are converted to new amplitude and phase respectively

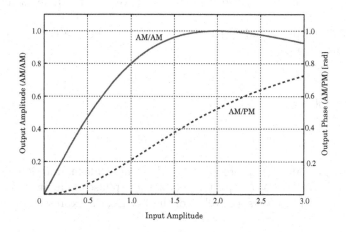

**Fig. 3.** Nonlinear characteristics of TWTA

**Table 1.** Parameters of TWTA characteristics

| $\alpha_x$ | 1.0 |
|---|---|
| $\beta_x$ | 0.25 |
| $\alpha_\phi$ | $\pi/12$ |
| $\beta_\phi$ | 0.25 |

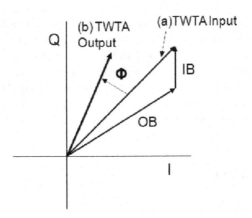

**Fig. 4.** Signal vectors of TWTA Input and Output

according to the conversion characteristics shown in Fig.3. Fig.4 shows vector diagram of input and output signal through the TWTA. Composite signal(a) of OB and IB is fed to TWTA and converted to the TWTA output signal(b). Here, if the power of OB is much larger than that of IB, the conversion which the composite signal is received by the nonlinearity is the same as that OB is received.

The TWTA output signal $u(t)$ against to the input signal $s(t)$ can be expressed by the equation(1) [14]

$$u(t) = s(t)G[s(t)] \tag{1}$$

where the amplifier gain $G[s(t)]$ is

$$G[s(t)] = \frac{1}{|s(t)|} g(|s(t)|) \exp(jf(|s(t)|)) \tag{2}$$

The function $g(r)$ and $f(r)$ represent AM/AM (amplitude modulation/amplitude modulation) and AM/PM (amplitude modulation/phase modulation) conversion characteristics of TWTA respectively. For the TWTA, the expressions for $g(r)$ and $f(r)$ are

$$g(r) = \frac{\alpha_x r}{1 + \beta_x r^2} \tag{3}$$

$$f(r) = \frac{\alpha_\phi r^2}{1 + \beta_\phi r^2} \tag{4}$$

where $\alpha_x$ is the small-signal gain, and $g_{max} = \frac{1}{\sqrt{\beta_x}}$ is the amplifier input saturation voltage. $\alpha_\phi$ and $\beta_\phi$ is the parameters which decide AM/PM conversion characteristics. The AM/AM and AM/PM characteristics of TWTA and the parameters used in above equations are shown in Fig.3 and Table 1 respectively.

Here, let's consider that the power of IB is smaller enough, then the received signal fed to the input of the canceller is expressed by $u(t)$ shown in equation(1). On the other hand the replica which is provided to another input of the canceller is just expressed by $s(t)$. The difference between these two signals $R(t)$ is the remained signal which behaves as interference in this system.

$$R(t) = u(t) - s(t) \qquad (5)$$

where $R(t)$ can be considered as the remained signal caused by the nonlinear effects. And we can define the suppression of the interference canceller $\delta$ in the nonlinear system by the ratio of the power of unwanted signal at the canceller input and the power of remained interference signal as

$$\delta = \frac{\overline{u(t)^2}}{\overline{R(t)^2}} \qquad (6)$$

By the way, as easily expected in equation(5),$R(t)$ is zero since $u(t) = s(t)$ in the linear system if other factors such as quantizing error, carrier and timing synchronization errors etc.,in the canceller are ideally zero. As shown in equation (5) and (6), interference power is generated due to the nonlinear distortion of unwanted signal in the satellite transpoder. Our intention is, as mentioned above, to compensate the distortion by giving the same distortion to the replica. The principle of our proposal is simple. Namely, $R(t)$ becomes zero if we substitute $u(t)$ for $s(t)$ in equation (5).

Here the issue is how to estimate the nonlinear characteristics of satellite TWTA in the canceller unit. It is possible to know the TWTA nonlinearity itself by getting the data of transponder from the network operator. However even though it is possible, we still have to know the operation point of the satellite TWTA since the uplink power to the satellite frequently deviates due to the rain attenuation or to the other reasons. An approach to estimating nonlinearity is explained later.

### 3.2    Evaluation of Nonlinear Effects

A. **Perfomance Degradation.** The nonlinear verification test of interference canceller has been conducted by both computer simulation using reference model and laboratory test using FPGA based hardware prototype. The network simulated here is the VSAT system in which the level difference between OB and IB is 13 dB (refer to Fig.1(b)). One of the important performance parameters for the canceller is the purity of extracted inbound signal (wanted signal). The purity can be evaluated by the suppression of unwanted signal. The transmission path model used in the simulation is shown in Fig.5. The parameters used for the simulation is shown in Table 2. Simulated results of suppression performances are shown in Fig.6 and Fig.7.

Fig.6 shows both spectrum of received signals (which includes both 5MHz outbound and 1MHz inbound carriers) and extracted inbound signal in the linear

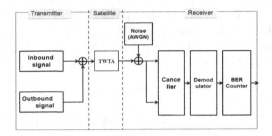

**Fig. 5.** Transmission Path Model of Computer Simulation

**Table 2.** Simulation parameters

| Moduration Level | QPSK(OB)DQOSK(IB) |
|---|---|
| Symbol Rate | 5Msymbol/s 1Msymbol/s |
| Power Density Difference (D/U) | 13[dB] |
| The number of IB | 4 |
| Channel Model | AWGN |
| HPA Model | TWTA |
| Input Back-off | 0-10[dB] |

system. Fig.7 is those in the nonlinear system operated at 0dB IBO (Input Back Off). As shown in these figures, the inbound signal (wanted signal ) is well extracted in case the system is linear but is not in the case the system is nonlinear. That is, signal to interference ratio (D/U ratio) in the nonlinear system is only 10 dB or lower.

Fig.8 shows hardware test results of both received signal spectrum and the extracted IB signal. Though similar test have been conducted but the results of hardware test is worse than those of computer simulation. The D/U ratio of extracted signal is only 6-7 dB in this case. The hardware test has been conducted by using method 2 [11].

*B.* **Compensation of Nonlinear Effects.** As mentioned before, our proposal is to give the replica the same nonlinear characteristics and compensate the satellite nonlinearity as shown in Fig.9. Fig.9 shows the basic block diagram in which the compensation is put at the output of outbound signal demodulator. The upper side of this block diagram is the path where the received signals (OB+IB) are provided to the canceller as they are. These signals are distorted if the satellite transponder is operated in the nonlinear region. And the lower path is to generate replica of OB (unwanted signal). The output of the demodulator is fed to the circuit where the same nonlinearity shown in Fig.3 is numerically given to the demodulated replica. Here, the nonlinearity can be simply realized by baseband processing of I and Q vector of PSK signal.

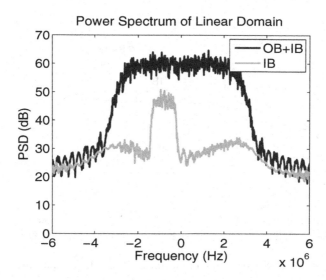

**Fig. 6.** Power spectrum of received signals(OB+IB) and extracted IB signal (Linear case)

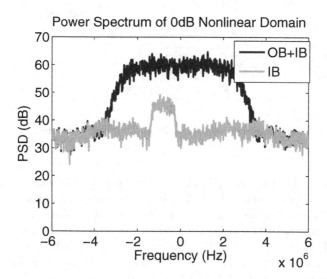

**Fig. 7.** Power spectrum of received signals(OB+IB) and extracted IB signal (Nonlinear IBO=0dB)

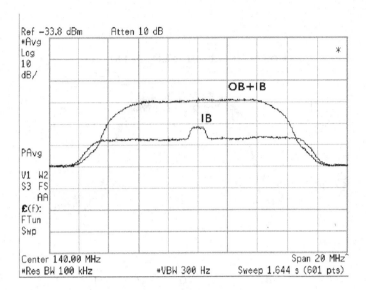

**Fig. 8.** Measured spectrum of output of FPGA based canceller

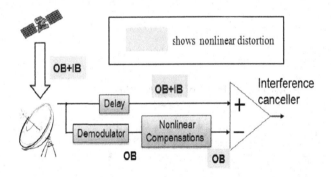

**Fig. 9.** Interference cancellar introduced nonlinear compensations

Firstly, the effects of the compensation on the purity of inbound signal after cancellation has been evaluated. Fig.10 shows the spectrum form of canceller input (IB+OB) and canceller output (IB). The operating point of the satellite TWTA is saturation (IBO=0dB). The ratio of the power density of OB to IB signal is 13 dB in this case. And the canceller output is for both cases of with and without compensator. As shown in this figure, it is clear that the purity of extracted IB is improved about 10 dB by adopting compensation.

Then lets show the BER performance of IB signal after cancellation. Fig.11 and Fig.12 show them for the case input back off (IBO) is 2 dB and 10 dB respectively. Fig.11 is the case which is the nonlinear system. In case IBO=2 dB, the improvement by the compensation is obvious though the improvement

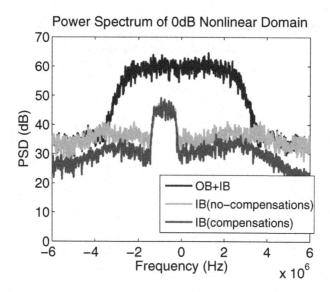

**Fig. 10.** Power spectrum of IBO=0[dB]

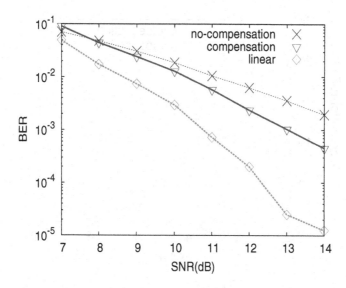

**Fig. 11.** BER performance of inbound signal(IBO=2[dB])

for the latter case is small. The system of the latter case (IBO=10dB) is close to linear and the degradation itself is very small whatever the compensation exists or not. Fig.13 shows the improvement of BER performance by the compensation for various input back off (IBO). In this simulation, it was assumed that the input back off for both satellite TWTA and the nonlinearity intentionally given

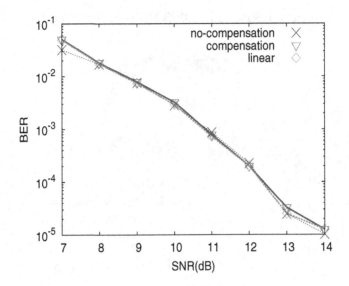

**Fig. 12.** BER performance of inbound signal(IBO=10[dB])

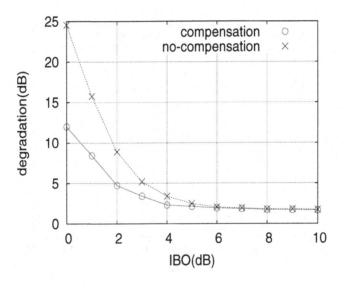

**Fig. 13.** BER degradation at $10^{-4}$

to the canceller for compensation are the same. It can be said that the significant improvement is obtained by the proposed compensation.

*C.* **Automatic Tracking of TWTA Back Off.** In the previous section, it becomes clear that the nonlinear compensation works as far as the operating point (back off) of both satellite TWTA and the nonlinearity given to the replica

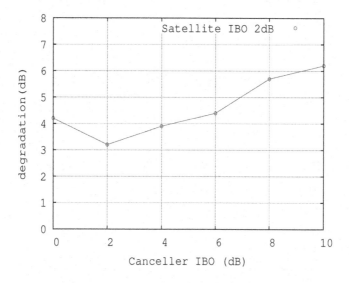

**Fig. 14.** BER degradation of IB signal at $10^{-3}$

in the canceller is the same. For this, it is necessary for the canceller to know the operating point of the satellite.

Here we propose a method to track the back off of satellite TWTA automatically. Before introducing the proposed method, it is illustrative to review the performance of the compensator when the back off of the canceller has mismatch with that of the satellite TWTA.

Fig.14 shows the BER degradation of IB (wanted) signal as a function of the difference between back off of satellite TWTA and that of nonlinearity given to the replica. The degradation is minimum when the values of both back off are identical.

On the other hand, Fig. 15 shows the remained signal level of unwanted signal, that is interference power, at the output of the canceller for three different cases of back off of replica nonlinearity (0, 3, 6 dB) while keeping the satellite TWTA is the same (3 dB). This test was conducted by feeding OB signal only to the canceller. As shown in this figure, the power of remained unwanted signal proportionally increases as the difference between back off of the two nonlinearities is larger. This property can be expressed as shown in Fig.16. By utilizing this property, it is possible to estimate the satellite back off at the canceller unit in the earth station.

We prepare three paths in the canceller unit as shown in Fig.17. These three can be easily realized by signal processing without significant increase of hardware cost. One nonlinear element is provided to each path with three different back off such like $y$ dB for upper path, $x$ dB for middle path and $\frac{x+y}{2}$ dB for lower path. Here, the output level of nonlinear element of each path is normalized to be constant for any input back off. By this approach, we should get three

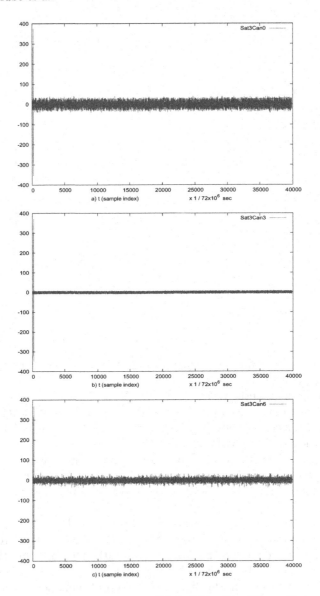

**Fig. 15.** Remained Unwanted Signal Level for Three Cases
a) Satellite IBO 3dB Canceller IBO 0dB
b) Satellite IBO 3dB Canceller IBO 3dB
c) Satellite IBO 3dB Canceller IBO 6dB

different levels of remained unwanted signals at the output of each path in Fig.17. Actually, wanted signal (IB) is extracted at the output of canceller. Therefore it is necessary to extract unwanted signal only from those wanted and unwanted power at the output. In order to do this, correlation technique by multiplying

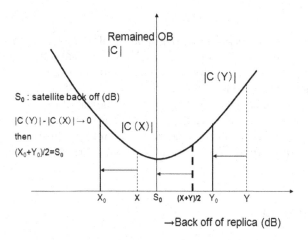

**Fig. 16.** Automatic Back Off Tracking

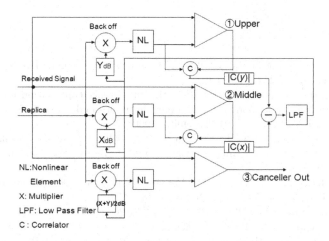

**Fig. 17.** Proposed Configuration of Satellite TWTA Back Off Tracking

replica signal to the canceller output is adopted here. By this operation, we can get the absolute value of correlation for three each path which has back off of $y$ dB, $x$ dB and $\frac{x+y}{2}$ dB.

Here let them be $|C(y)|, |C(x)|$ and $|C(\frac{y+x}{2})|$ respectively. Then, these are expressed as shown in Fig 16. By designing the automatic control which works so as to make the error $e = |C(y)| - |C(x)|$ becomes zero, then the back off $\frac{x+y}{2}$ dB at this moment should approach to the value of satellite TWTA back off $s_0$. The lower path in Fig. 17 is finally just the canceller output which nonlinearity is the same as the satellite. Thus the tracking loop of satellite TWTA back off can be realized by this method.

# 4  Conclusion

In order to minimize the performance degradation of frequency super-positioning interference canceller due to the nonlinearity of the satellite transponder, a method to compensate it by intentionally implementing same nonlinearity in the canceller is proposed. The study results show that it decreases the significant amount of degradation specifically in case the satellite is operated in the deep nonlinear region. Considering the case that the operationg point of satellite TWTA may change, we proposed a method of adaptive adjustment of both operating points of satellite nonlinearity and the nonlinearity given to the canceller for compensation.

# Acknowledgment

The authors would like to thank SKY Perfect JSAT Corporation in Japan for their supports of this reserch.

# References

1. Ishida, N.: Common-band satellite communication system. IEICE Transactions J82-B (8), 1531–1537 (1999)
2. Toshinaga, H., Kobayashi, K., Kazuma, H.: Interference cancellation for multimedia satellite communication systems employing superposed transmission, Technical Report of IEICE, SAT2000-86 (December 2000)
3. Dankberg, M.D., Miler, M.J., Mulligan, M.G.: Selfinterference Cancellation For Two-Party Relayed Communication, January 21.3. The ViaSat Inc.,United States Patent (1997) Patent No.5596439
4. Hara, T., Ichikawa, M., Okada, M., Yamamoto, H.: Canceller Design for Carrier Super-Positioning for Frequency Reuse Satellite Communications. IEICE Transactions of Communications J88-B (7), 1300–1309 (2005)
5. Osato, M., Kobashi, H., Hara, T., Okada, M., Yamamoto, H.: Simplified canceller for multi-level modulation super-positing for frequency reuse satellite communications. In: ICT 2006 (May 2006)
6. Kobashi, H., Osato, M., Hara, T., Okada, M., Yamamoto, H.: Signal cancellation for satellite frequency reuse by super-positioning multi-level modulation. In: IEEE-ISCC 2006 (June 2006)
7. Ichikawa, M., Hara, T., Okada, M., Yamamoto, H., Andou, K.: Fast and accurate canceller super-positioning for vsat frequency reuse. In: IEEE-WCNC 2005, new Orleans (March 2005)
8. Osato, M., Kobashi, H., Omaki, R.Y., Hara, T., Okada, M.: Development of signal canceller in the carrier super-positioning satellite networks. In: International Conference on Wireless and Mobile Communications 2007(ICWM 2007), guadeloupe (March 2007)
9. Kuroda, S., Tanaka, S., Miyamoto, R., Hara, T., Okada, M.: A configuration of carrier super-positioning satellite system using extended matched filter, IEICE Technical Report, SAT2008-57, pp.23-28 (December 2008)

10. Uratani, T., Miyamoto, R., Hara, T., Okada, M.: Performance of an interference canceller for P-MP satellite networks with nonlinear TWTA. In: ISCCSP 2008, Malta (March 2008)

11. Hara, T., Kuroda, S., Tanaka, S., Miyamoto, R., Okada, M.: Frequency Reuse of Satellite Communications and its Strategic Applications. In: Pacific Telecommunications Council (PTC 2009), Honolulu, Hawaii, USA (January 2009)

12. Kuroda, S., Tanaka, S., Naoi, S., Takeda, Y., Miyamoto, R., Hara, T., Okada, M.: Development of an Interference Canceller in Satellite Communications using a Muti-level Modulation with Superposed Transmission. IEICE Trans. Commun. E92-B (11), 3354–3364 (2009)

13. Kojima, M., Suzuki, Y., Hasimoto, A., Sujikai, H., Tanaka, S., Kimura, T., Shogen, K.: Non-linear Compensation Technique Based on Signal Point Error Estimation on Satellite Transmission System. IEICE Technical Report SAT2008-66, pp.37–42 (Febuary 2009)

14. Santella, G., Mazzenga, F.: A model for performance evaluation in schemes in presence of non-linear distortions. In: Proc.of IEEE VTC 1995, pp. 830–834 (1995)

# Track 2
# Satellite Communications:
# Multimedia Integration

# Comparative Analysis of Image Compression Algorithms for Deep Space Communications Systems

Igor Bisio, Fabio Lavagetto, and Mario Marchese

Department of Communications, Computer and System Science
University of Genoa
{igor.bisio,fabio.lavagetto,mario.marchese}@unige.it

**Abstract.** In deep communications systems bandwidth availability, storage and computational capacity play a crucial role and represent precious, as well as limited, communications resources. Starting from this consideration, high efficient image compression coding algorithms may represent a key solution to optimize the resources employment. In this paper two possible approaches have been considered: JPEG2000 and CCSDS Image Compression, which is specifically designed for satellite and deep space communications. In more details, two coders have been compared in terms of performance: *JasPer*, which is an implementation of the JPEG2000 standards, and the BPE, which is based on the CCSDS recommendations. The proposed comparison takes into account both the quality of the compressed images, by evaluating the Peak Signal to Noise Ratio, and the time needed to compress the images: the Compression Time. The latter parameters, which concerns the computational complexity of the compression algorithm, is very interesting for deep space systems because of their limited computational and energy resources.

**Keywords:** Deep Space Communications Systems, Image Compression, JPEG2000, CCSDS Compression, PSNR, Compression Time.

## 1 Introduction

In deep communications system bandwidth availability, storage and computational capacity play a crucial role and represent precious, as well as limited, communications resources. Starting from this consideration, high efficient image compression coding algorithms may represent a key solution to optimize the resources employment.

JPEG2000 is a wavelet-based image compression standard and coding system. It was created by the Joint Photographic Experts Group committee in the year 2000 with the intention of superseding their original discrete cosine transform-based JPEG standard. On the other hand, The Consultative Committee for Space Data Systems (CCSDS) data compression working group has adopted a recommendation for image data compression that proposes an algorithm based on a two dimensional discrete wavelet transform of the image, followed by progressive bit-plane coding of the transformed data. The algorithm can provide both lossless and lossy compression, and allows a user to directly control the compressed data volume or the fidelity with which the wavelet-transformed data can be reconstructed. CCSDS approach represents a low computational load compression

K. Sithamparanathan et al. (Eds.): PSATS 2010, LNICST 43, pp. 63–73, 2010.
© Institute for Computer Sciences, Social-Informatics and Telecommunications Engineering 2010

and, as a consequence is suitable for both frame-based image data and scan-based sensor data, and has applications for near-earth and deep-space missions.

In this work, both JPEG2000 and CCSDS algorithms have been taken into account and compared in terms of performance. In more detail, two main performance parameters have been considered: Peak Signal to Noise Ratio (PSNR) and Compression Time.

The former (PSNR) is a measure used to evaluate the quality of a compressed image with respect the original. This quality index is defined as the ratio of the maximum power of a signal and the power of noise that can invalidate the fidelity of his compressed version. PSNR is usually expressed in terms of the logarithmic scale of decibels. It is worth noting that in this context the noise concept comes from the amount of information that is lost during the compression with respect the original image. PSNR is often used as an indicator of perceptual quality: higher PSNR often results for compressed image more pleasing to the human eye.

The latter parameter, the Compression Time, is the time needed by an algorithm to compress an image starting from the original one.

In general the simplicity, fastness, and small storage necessities of an algorithm make it easy to be realized in hardware and suitable for space borne application. With respect to JPEG2000, CCSDS approach is aimed at reducing the computational load of the compression algorithm by maintaining the overall quality of the compressed images.

Nevertheless, the proposed comparison shows that the performance are strictly dependent on the practical implementation of the algorithm and, in particular, it is shown that among the employed coders the JPEG2000 one have lower Compression Time with respect to CCSDS based coder.

The remainder of this paper is structured as follows. Section 2 shortly focuses on the considered Image Compression Approaches (JPEG2000 and CCSDS) and their possible implementation (*JasPer* and BPE coders). Section 3 illustrates the considered terms of the proposed performance comparison (PSNR and Compression Time). Performance comparison of the described approaches is presented in Section 4, whereas final remarks and conclusions are drawn in Section 5.

## 2  Image Compression Approaches: JPEG2000 and CCSDS

### 2.1  JPEG2000

JPEG2000 [1] is the well known new image compression standard for web and distribution on PDAs, phones, PCs, televisions, etc. It represents the evolution of the famous JPEG format and, even if equipped with highly innovative features, JPEG2000 is not intended, at least in the short term, to replace JPEG, but rather is expected a transition during which the new standard will integrate and expand the features offered by JPEG.

In summary, the salient features of JPEG 2000 are:

   □   It is a unique coding system that can deal effectively with images from different sources, with different needs compression.

☐  Allows both lossy compression (lossy), is that no loss compression (lossless).

☐  It produces images with better visual quality, especially at low bit-rate compared to those achievable with JPEG, thanks to the properties of the wavelet transform.

☐  Allows you to change and, possibly, to decode any image regions, working directly on data in compressed form.

☐  It can create scalable compressed images in terms of resolution both in the level of detail, leaving the implementer the freedom to choose how much information and what parts of the image can be used for decompression.

☐  Introduces the concept of *Region of Interest* (ROI) of an image.

Indeed, one of the novelties introduced in JPEG2000 is the opportunity to emphasize the importance of certain regions of the image, favoring the encoding of coefficients belonging to these areas. The use of ROI is particularly suitable for the encoding of images in which some parts are more important than their surroundings.

Moreover JPEG2000 can achieve high compression rates by maintaining acceptable image quality and there is the possibility of including, in a file that contains an image coded with JPEG2000, information on intellectual property and copyrights.

### 2.1.1  JPEG2000 Considered Implementation: JasPer

There are several distributions that allow to create JPEG2000 encoding, certainly the most important are the implementation *Kakadu* (downloadable from the web site http://www.kakadusoftware.com/) and the *JasPer* Project (download http://www.ece.uvic.ca/~mdadams/jasper/), which is interesting for its peculiarity of being open source and can therefore exploit all the functionality of JPEG2000. *Kakadu* needs instead of purchasing.

*JasPer* [2] is a software-based implementation of the codec specified in the JPEG2000 standard. The development of this software had two motivations: firstly, the implementers wanted to develop a JPEG2000 implementation using the standard as only reference. Secondly, by conducting interoperability testing with other JPEG2000 implementations, implementers might find ambiguities in the text of the standards, allowing them to be corrected.

In more detail, the design of the *JasPer* software was driven by several key concerns: fast execution speed, efficient memory usage, robustness, portability, modularity, maintainability, and extensibility. Since fixed-point operations are typically faster than their floating-point counterparts on most platforms, and some platforms lack hardware support for floating-point operations altogether, *JasPer* implementers elected to use only fixed-point operations in their software to match the objectives of high portability and fast execution speed.

The *JasPer* software is written in the C programming language. This language was chosen mainly due to the availability of C development environments for most of computing platforms.

The *JasPer* software consists of about 20,000 lines of code in total. This code is spread across several libraries. There are two executable programs, the first is the encoder, and the second is the decoder. The *JasPer* software can, moreover, handle image data in a number of popular formats (e.g., PGM/PPM, Windows BMP, and Sun Raster file).

## 2.2 CCSDS

The Consultative Committee for Space Data Systems (CCSDS) data compression working group has adopted a recommendation for image data compression. The algorithm adopted in the recommendation consists of a two-dimensional discrete wavelet transform of the image, followed by progressive bit-plane coding of the transformed data [4]. The algorithm can provide both lossless and lossy compression, and allows a user to directly control the compressed data volume or the fidelity with which the wavelet-transformed data can be reconstructed. The algorithm is suitable for both frame-based image data and scan-based sensor data, and has applications for near-Earth and deep-space missions. The standard is moreover accompanied by free software sources as briefly described in the sub-section below.

### 2.2.1 CCSDS Considered Implementation: BPE

Concerning the implementations of the CCSDS standard, there are only two: one developed by the University of Nebraska, "BPE" (http://hyperspectral.unl.edu) and one by the Universitat Autonoma de Barcelona, the "B Software" (http://www.gici.uab.cat/TER/). In this paper the first distribution, built in C + +, has been employed. Actually the TER, written in JAVA, has been used, but as a converter of raw images to pgm.

## 3  Terms of Comparison: PSNR and Compression Time

### 3.1  Peak Signal to Noise Ratio

Peak Signal-to-Noise Ratio (PSNR) is a measure used to evaluate the quality of a compressed image from the original [5]. This quality index is defined as the ratio of the maximum power of a signal and the power of noise that can invalidate the fidelity of its compressed representation. Because many signals have a very wide dynamic range, PSNR is usually expressed in terms of the logarithmic scale of decibels as will be done in the presented comparison.

It is worth noting that the noise is not related to the typical channel noise (e.g., thermal noise) or with the attenuation due to the distance between source and destination, or by other disturbs (e.g., electrical storm burst). The noise considered concerns, in the framework of this paper, the amount of information that is lost during the operation of lossy compression with respect to the original image.

PSNR is often used as an indicator of perceptual quality in the sense that a higher PSNR often results in a compressed image more pleasing to the human eye. Nevertheless, this measure must be analyzed with caution because it happens that compressed images with values of PSNR lower than others are more similar to the original one.

Independently of that consideration, it is possible to consider PSNR a fully reliable indicator in all cases in which it is used to compare results obtained from the same coder (or similar coders) [6].

From the analytical viewpoint, it is possible to define the PSNR from another well known estimator: the Mean Square Error (MSE) as reported in [6, 7]. It expresses the difference between the MSE of observed data and the values of estimated figures. Denoting by $I$ the original image and the compressed image with $K$, both of dimension $m \times n$, the following quantity is defined as MSE between the two images:

$$MSE = \sum_{0}^{m-1} \sum_{0}^{n-1} \left\| I(i,j) - K(i,j) \right\|^2 \qquad (1)$$

It represents the standard norm between correspondent pixels of the original image and compressed one. If the MSE is equal to 0 would mean that there is no difference between the two images.

Starting from equation (1), it is possible to compute the PSNR as follows:

$$PSNR = 20\log_{10}\left( \frac{MAX\{I\}}{\sqrt{MSE}} \right) \qquad (2)$$

Typically, 0.25 dB are considered a significant improvement of the image compression method, valuable from the viewpoint of human perception.

### 3.2  Compression Time

Another important aspect that has been taken into consideration in the evaluation of the compression algorithms is the compression time because, nevertheless the careful studies in the literature, some expected results may fails when the implementation aspects are taken into account. In more details, methods such as the CCSDS, studied to have low computational loads, may be unready to be employed due to their row implementation that need to be further developed.

In this paper, the standard JPEG2000 is assumed as reference from the performance viewpoint. It is however worth noting that JPEG2000 is valid for several environments and it is very complex and, for this reason, expensive from the computational viewpoint.

Therefore, as also described in previous section, it was born an image compression algorithm developed by the CCSDS studied to create a standard that focuses exclusively on the transmission of image through satellite and deep space transmission devices where the problem of energy consumption and, as a consequence, of computation load (and therefore of the compression time) becomes critical.

As will be shown later, however, the envisaged increased compression speed of the CCSDS approach, at the moment, does not exist, and indeed the JPEG2000 algorithm in many cases is faster.

## 4  Performance Comparison

### 4.1  Reference Scenario

Most of the tests were carried out using an image test taken directly from the site of CCSDS (http://cwe.ccsds.org/sls/docs/sls-dc/). That image (b3.raw) has a resolution of 1024 * 1024 pixels, and is encoded with 8 bits/pixel.

Below are reported several figures that analyze the performance of two approaches: JPEG2000 (*JasPer* coder) and CCSDS (BPE coder). The two considered approaches are absolutely identical in the processing of the original data in the Discrete Wavelength Transform domain but they differ in the coding of the transformed data. Firstly, coded images with the algorithm CCSDS will be examined. They have been processed with DWT 9/7 floating point and with four different rates (bit per pixel): 0.25 bpp, 0.5 bpp, 1 bpp and 2 bpp. Also different sizes of code blocks (8, 16, 32, 64) entering in to the coder itself have been tested. Analogously, the JPEG2000 algorithm, with the same processor, same rate and same size of code blocks has been evaluated.

As regards the calculation of PSNR, it should be noted that the *JasPer* open source package available is an executable that takes as input two images, in pgm format, and allows calculating various statistics, such as MSE and PSNR.

Differently, it is more complicated to determine the PSNR in the case of CCSDS algorithm, since that is not available a library that helps to calculate the statistics of the image. In this case, an ad-hoc algorithm to calculate precisely the PSNR has been developed. This program was written in Matlab, takes two input raw images and computes the MSE, thus giving the value of PSNR. Obviously the employed images are those before and after encoding CCSDS.

Concerning the compression time, the comparison has been performed in the following way: the *time* command has been exploited. In practice, the time spent in the execution of the compression from the first to the last line of code has been computed. Obviously that computation is influenced the type of hardware configuration and the processes running on your computer when launching the executable. For this reason the tests performed were made from the same machine on the same day, and with the same hardware configuration. Moreover, for each test, there have been seven measures. The result suggested in the graphs is the result of an arithmetic average on these measures.

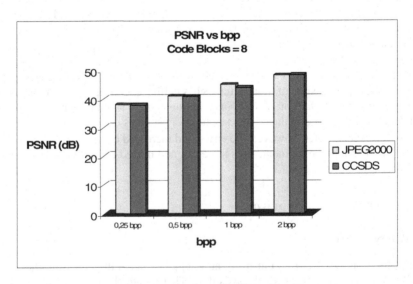

**Fig. 1.** PSNR vs. bpp (Code Blocks = 8)

## 4.2 PSNR Comparison

In the following figures, the PSNR obtained by employing the described image compression algorithms has been reported in the several situations, in terms of bpp and Code Blocks, mentioned above.

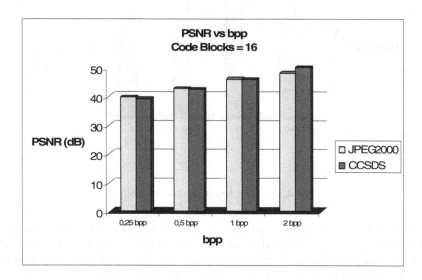

**Fig. 2.** PSNR vs. bpp (Code Blocks = 16)

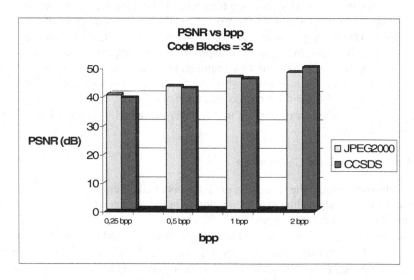

**Fig. 3.** PSNR vs. bpp (Code Blocks = 32)

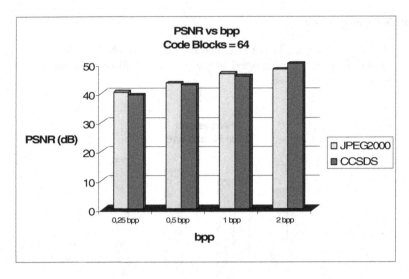

**Fig. 4.** PSNR vs. bpp (Code Blocks = 64)

The analysis shows that the variation of the size of code blocks does not affect particularly the value of PSNR significantly. It remains fairly constant, except for cases where the code blocks have size equal to 8 (please note that size 8 means equal to 8 * 8, then a total of 64 blocks input to the coder) that is lower that about 2 dB.

Concerning the rate, as expected, increasing the compression, and thus reducing the rate, the quality decreases more significantly. It also indicates how the choice of encoding blocks of size 8 is always the worst from the performance point of view.

The JPEG2000 has a gain of at least 1 dB compared to the CCSDS in all scenarios, except for case in which the image is compressed with 2 bpp. In such cases, in fact, the CCSDS performs better, and this improvement increases with the size of the blocks. In the case of "high quality", where the test image has been encoded at 2 bpp with Code Blocks = 64, the difference is estimated at 2.34 dB.

In general, from the test performed in this paper the superior quality of JPEG2000 has been observed.

### 4.3  Compression Time Comparison

In the following figures, the Compression Time obtained by employing the described image compression algorithms has been reported in the several situations also considered previously, in terms of bpp and Code Blocks.

These graphs are very interesting. The Figures, from 4 to 8, show that the compression time of JPEG200 decreases significantly with the increasing of the size of the blocks. As a consequence, in addition to increasing the quality, it also increases the efficiency. Differently, for the algorithm CCSDS, the block size does not have any impact on the compression time.

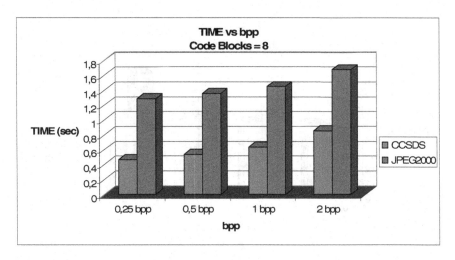

**Fig. 5.** Time vs. bpp (Code Blocks = 8)

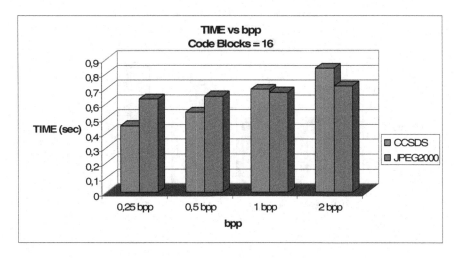

**Fig. 6.** Time vs. bpp (Code Blocks = 16)

Except for the case of Figure 5, in which the CCSDS behaves much better than the JPEG2000 (the compression time equal to half of the reference standard), it is possible to observe the compression times are similar. Moreover, it is possible to observe a different trend compared to what was expected when the block size is equal to 32 and 64: in such cases, the JPEG2000 algorithm is more efficient than the CCSDS.

This result was originally unexpected at the time of the analysis, since the CCSDS was designed, by its express declaration, with the intent to be more efficient than JPEG2000.

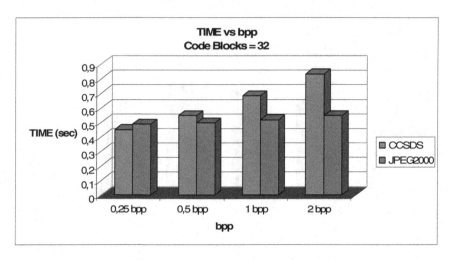

**Fig. 7.** Time vs. bpp (Code Blocks = 32)

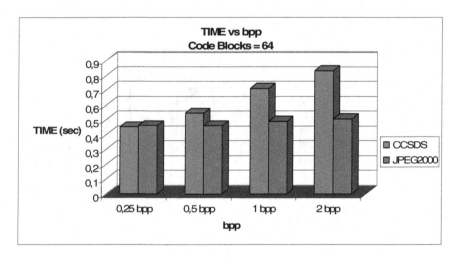

**Fig. 8.** Time vs. bpp (Code Blocks = 64)

The key point is the considered implementation: the problem that affect the CCSDS' compression time does not concern the algorithm, but its implementation. In fact, the *JasPer* software has been optimized over time while the CCSDS coder is still under development.

## 5   Conclusions

This work focused on the comparison between two possible image compression approaches. The first algorithm, briefly described and evaluated, is based on the

JPEG2000 standard. The second algorithm is based on the CCSDS recommendation for image compression for satellite and deep space communication systems.

Nevertheless the nature of the latter algorithm, though to be simple and to have a limited computational complexity, the current implementation of it, the BPE coder considered in this paper, has good PSNR performance but does not guarantee a really reduced image compression time. On the other hand, the JPEG2000 coders, in particular the JasPer, being optimized guarantees good PSNR performance and also better compression time with respects the CCSDS coder.

In practice, from the results reported in this work, the CCSDS image compression coders need to be further enhanced before their practical employment in satellite and deep space transmission systems.

# References

1. Taubman, D.S., Marcellin, M.W.: JPEG 2000: Image Compression Fundamentals, Standards and Practice. Kluwer International Series in Engineering and Computer Science (2000)
2. Adams, M.D., Kossentini, F.: JasPer: A Software-Based JPEG-2000 Codec Implementation. In: Proc. IEEE International Conference on Image Processing, Vancouver, BC, Canada, October 2000, vol. 2, pp. 53–56 (2000)
3. International Standard ISO/IEC 15444-1, JPEG2000 Core Coding System (December 2000)
4. Yeh, P., Armbruster, P., Kiely, A., Masschelein, B., Moury, G., Schaefer, C., Thiebaut, C.: The New CCSDS Image Compression Recommendation. In: Proc. IEEE Aerospace Conference, Big Sky, Montana, March 5-12 (2005)
5. Web site,
   http://en.wikipedia.org/wiki/Peak_signal-to-noise_ratio
6. Huynh-Thu, Q., Ghanbari, M.: Scope of validity of PSNR in image/video quality assessment. IEEE Electronics Letters 44(13), 800–801
7. Thomos, N., Boulgouris, N.V., Strintzis, M.G.: Optimized Transmission of JPEG2000 Streams Over Wireless Channels. IEEE Transactions on Image Processing 15(1), 54–67

# Ka-Band Satellite Consumer Triple-Play and Professional Video Services

Guillaume Benoit, Hector Fenech, Stefano Pezzana, and Alessia Tomatis

Eutelsat, 70 rue Balard, 75015 Paris, France +33 1 53 98 47 47
{gbenoit,hfenech,spezzana,atomatis}@eutelsat.fr

**Abstract.** This article presents Eutelsat European Ka-band implementation of the broadband ToowayTM service and its evolution through a dedicated Ka-band exclusive satellite (KA-SAT). It also explains Eutelsat's choice in selecting the Ka-band for interactive services, broadcast video and IPTV services, demonstrating the optimal consumer service synergy between existing Ku-band and new Ka-band services.

KA-SAT satellite is not focusing only on consumer triple-play services. Indeed, Eutelsat strategy consists in offering also professional video and data services in Ka-band (video distribution, video contribution, e-cinema, file transport) sharing the same transparent satellite bandwidth and the same ground segment infrastructure.

For those professional video applications the last content processing (SVC) and satellite transport (DVB-S2 ACM) techniques are under deployment and this paper will present simulation results and link budgets estimations for a large number of future commercial applications.

## 1 Introduction

Eutelsat operates 25 satellites in the geostationary arc from 15°W to 70.5°E offering a variety of services from corporate networks to broadcasting. The HOT BIRD™ constellation at 13°E constitutes the prime position for DTH (Direct to Home) and cable broadcasting, utilizing the full Ku-band spectrum from 10.70 GHz to 12.75 GHz. There are 102 transponders delivering about 1400 TV channels. The HOT BIRD™ service area reaches some 120 million satellite and cable households.

Video services contribute to approximately three quarters of Eutelsat revenue. With DTH and cable broadcasting, the main objective is to cover as many households as possible through a single service area. However, the requirements of broadband access move away from broadcast to unicast as the data accessed on the Internet by a given user is generally intended for that given user at that given instant.

The KA-SAT system calls for specific system concepts which are different from those of DTH systems. The main objective is to ensure that the cost for the system capacity permits a competitive consumer interactive service.

K. Sithamparanathan et al. (Eds.): PSATS 2010, LNICST 43, pp. 74–85, 2010.

## 2  The KA-SAT Satellite

KA-SAT will be the first European multi-beam satellite to operate exclusively in Ka-band and dedicated to providing broadband and broadcast services in Extended Europe. It will be launched 3rd quarter 2010 and positioned to be compatible with the 13 degrees East location in geostationary orbit, where the Eutelsat's HOT BIRD broadcast satellites are operated.

The satellite is being manufactured by EADS-Astrium based on their Spacebus 3000 platform. KA-SAT will operate simultaneously 82 spotbeams, which makes it the largest multi-beam Ka-band satellite ever ordered worldwide and also offering the largest service area. The satellite will feature a high level of frequency re-use. The spacecraft is equipped with four multi-feeds deployable antennas with enhanced pointing accuracy and a high efficiency repeater. The cells cover Europe and parts of the Middle East and North Africa as shown in Figure 1. Efficient frequency reuse enables the system to achieve a total capacity that is in excess of 70 Gbps. The introduction of KA-SAT will triple the total capacity commercialized by Eutelsat.

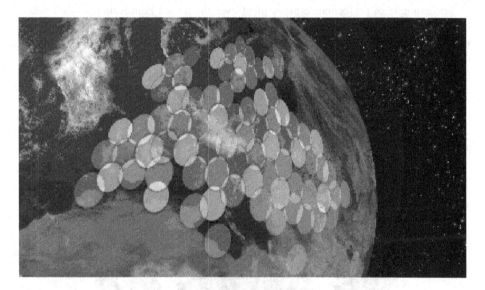

**Fig. 1.** KA-SAT illustrative coverage

The KA-SAT satellite will form the cornerstone of a major new infrastructure in Europe and the Mediterranean Basin that will also comprise eight gateways, interconnected by fibre and connected to the Internet backbone. Each gateway will manage broadband connections between the Internet and the users via a group of spotbeams on the satellite. The overall network will be managed by Eutelsat's Skylogic subsidiary from its Turin teleport in Italy.

KA-SAT supports a variety of broadband services ranging from consumer services (including triple- play solutions), professional services (e.g. SNG, occasional use, and platform contributions) and TV broadcast services. In addition KA-SAT will be an opportunity to open up a new resource optimised for the development of local and regional television channels targeting specific geographical audiences.

KA-SAT's innovative design will enable the provision of up to 900 Mbit/s of capacity for each spotbeam, which will be shared on the forward and return paths. This exceptionally high throughput heralds the arrival of future video applications requiring very high bit rates, notably HD digital cinema and 3D television.

## 3  KA-SAT Performance Assessment

The design of the KA-SAT system has been also based on a detailed link budget assessment in order to optimise all the system parameters. The present section provides an assessment of KA-SAT performance on the Forward Link.

An approach based on the Adaptive Coding Modulation (ACM) has been of valuable importance for the optimisation of the system performance to the different propagation condition inside the KA-SAT service area. The Modulation/Code (MOD/COD) thresholds are based on DVB-S2 standard [1].

The example of performance assessment over the Italian Peninsula affords a good example for the wide diversity that prevails in terms of geographical, atmospheric and climatic conditions. All performances shown are given for illustrative purposes only and are not contractual binding.

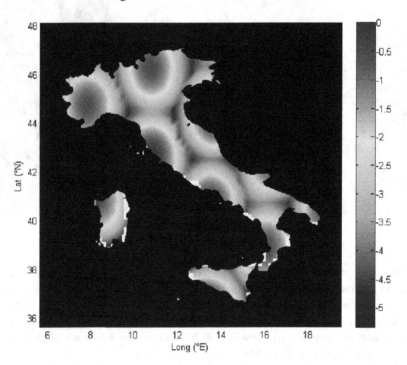

**Fig. 2.** KA-SAT Forward Overall Performance (clear sky condition) over Italian Peninsula

In this context, the overall performance is expressed as the normalised carrier-to-noise+interference ratio calculated at each point of the coverage, and expressed as C/(N+I). Figure 2 shows the KA-SAT overall performance over the Italian Peninsula in clear sky conditions on the Forward Link.

Figure 3 below shows a possible MOD/COD assignment based on this performance in clear sky conditions. The MOD/COD thresholds are based on the DVB-S2 standard [1]. By assigning a specific MOD/COD value to each individual terminal, it is possible to take advantage of the KA-SAT's multi-spot coverage and adapt efficiently to the diverse geographical and atmospheric conditions that prevail.

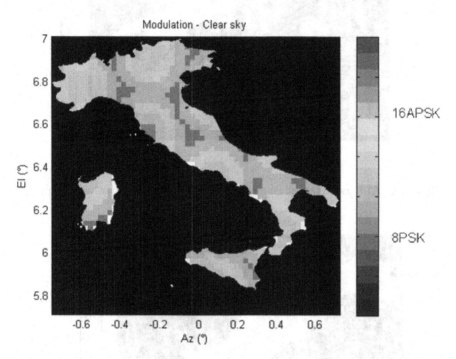

**Fig. 3.** Possible MODCOD Assignment (clear sky condition) over Italian Peninsula on the Forward Link

Figure 4 below shows the KA-SAT's overall performance (normalised C/(N+I)) over the Italian Peninsula with rain-fade conditions on the user downlink of the Forward Link assuming a downlink availability of 99.9%.

Figure 5 below shows a MOD/COD assignment based on this performance in rain conditions, using the ACM capabilities of the DVB-S2 standard [1]. By assigning an adaptive MOD/COD value to each individual terminal, it is possible to adapt efficiently to the diverse weather conditions of the Italian Peninsula. From this Figure, one can obtain the minimum rate that can be guaranteed 99.9% of the time to each location.

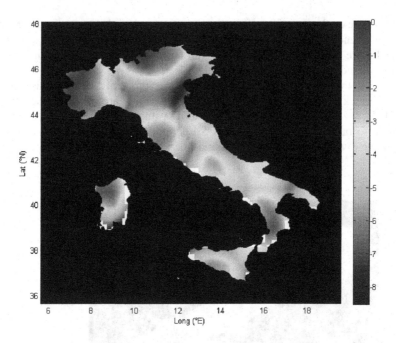

**Fig. 4.** KA-SAT Forward Overall Performance (rain fade condition) over Italian Peninsula

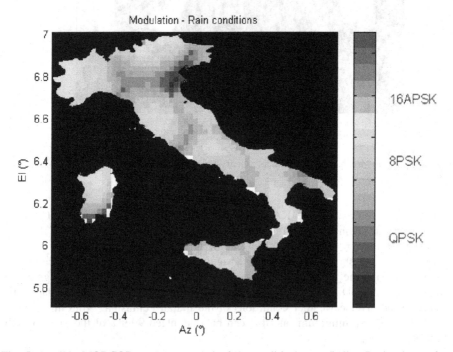

**Fig. 5.** Possible MODCOD Assignment (rain fade condition) over Italian Peninsula on the Forward Link

A similar performance analysis can be conducted for the Return Link. The performance assessment over the full KA-SAT coverage has demonstrated a traffic capacity in excess of 70 Gbps and the ability of providing services comparable to ADSL2+.

# 4 The Tooway™ Service

Consumer broadband expectations (triple play) are in continuous evolution for high bandwidth consuming applications such as Web TV, VoIP, music, P2P, online gaming, database and video. These applications must be accessible at higher speeds and lower prices. KA-SAT will form the cornerstone of a major new satellite infrastructure that will significantly expand capacity for consumer broadband services across Europe and the Mediterranean Basin (triple play), while providing new opportunities for professional services like:

- Broadband internet access for SOHO market,
- Close user group of terminals,
- Regional video services,
- Service restoration.

## 4.1 Consumer TriplePlay Services

**Broadband Internet Access**
Households located within KA-SAT's coverage who do not have access to ADSL will be able to benefit from Tooway™ for full satellite-based broadband connectivity. The potential ADSL un-served market for pure satellite broadband services in 2010 is estimated to be 6 million homes in Western Europe and 8 million homes in Eastern Europe.

Capitalizing on the Ka-band capacity that is already available via Eutelsat's existing resource, on HOT BIRD™ 6 and the Ku-band capacity on EUROBIRD™ 3, Eutelsat has already introduced Tooway™ for consumer broadband access using the SurfbeamTM system developed by ViaSat:

- HOT BIRD™ 6 was the first European commercial satellite with a Ka-band payload and was a real opportunity for Eutelsat to deploy a full Ka-band system in Europe as done already by WildBlue in USA, awaiting KA-SAT.
- EUROBIRD™ 3 was the first Eutelsat satellite specifically designed for broadband applications in Ku-band and offers strong coverage over Eastern parts of Europe where HOT BIRD™ 6 is not able to provide Ka band Tooway™ services.

The current ToowayTM service definition over HOT BIRD™ 6 and EUROBIRD™ 3 is allowing download up to 3.6Mbps and upload up to 384Kbps. The service differentiation is done on volume consumption per month through a Fair Access Policy (FAP). To promote a fair access use of service and avoid abuse, when consumption is above volume thresholds, the service remains available but at a lower speed.

KA-SAT with the new SurfbeamTM generation system from ViaSat will allow much higher throughput and volume for each subscriber at a price comparable to ADSL and cable modem connections.

**VoIP Services**

Voice over IP is also an expectation of any broadband subscriber interested in good call quality at low cost, taking advantage of competition between all the VoIP operators. VoIP through Tooway™ is already available and marketed by several service distributors. The new generation of Surfbeam™ manufactured by ViaSat will provide the same VoIP capabilities with QoS.

**TV Services**

As KA-SAT will be collocated at Eutelsat's HOT BIRD™ TV premium neighborhood, the IPTV services delivered via Tooway™ will complement and enrich the DTH TV offer using new combined Ku/Ka-band receive terminals. Indeed as Tooway™ is delivering ADSL-like services via satellite, Tooway™ subscribers will expect to be able to access IPTV services with VoD and PVR features. IPTV offers will benefit from the new techniques including DVB-S2 VCM/ACM mode and H.264 SVC coding in order to guarantee higher bit rates and quality standards.

-      **DVB-S2 VCM/ACM**

In the DVB-S2 standard, the VCM (Variable Code and Modulation) mode is defined to avoid feedback from each terminal for waveform efficiency configuration. In such a case, a specific link budget is performed for each terminal and a static efficiency is defined for each of them according to the availability needed. In this case, the adaptive linked to the evolution of the weather is lost, but there are no longer constraints for the worst link budget applied for the entire spot. The ACM (Adaptive Code and Modulation) needs a terminal feedback on the return channel and allows each terminal to receive the best efficiency related to its fading conditions.

-      **H.264 SVC**

The SVC (Scalable Video Coding) is a feature developed for H.264 (MPEG-4 Part 10) source coding, which allows transmitting the same video sequence coded with:

- spatial scalability
- temporal scalability
- SNR/Fidelity/Quality scalability

SVC is being developed to be basically applied to mobile ecosystems (DVB-SH) and ADSL video services but it will have important legacy applications for IP video services over Ka band satellite systems.

As an example, the same video sequence can be coded in SD and HD format:

-      SD 720x576i @50 Hz
-      HD 1920x1080p @ 60 Hz

Combined with SVC the HD format could be received by a terminal in clear sky conditions as the SD format could be received by another terminal affected by fading conditions (e.g. rain). In case of stringent fading conditions an SD program with lower bit rate will be available in order to maintain TV service.

Applied to satellite, the SVC feature with DVB-S2 VCM/ACM capability will allow to not multicast the full 3 programs detailed in the figure below but only one program with 3 layers protected with different efficiencies. The bit rates and the efficiencies of interest are under study.

| Definition | MPEG4 encoding bit rate *under study* | DVB-S2 Efficiency *under study* | Example of quality |
|:---:|:---:|:---:|:---:|
| SD | 1Mbps | QPSK 2/3 1.33 |  |
| SD | 2.5Mbps | QPSK 5/6 1.66 |  |
| HD | 8Mbps | 8PSK 2/3 1.99 |  |

**Fig. 6.** Image source from Institut Nachrichtentechnik Heinrich-Hertz-Institut

Eutelsat is participating in an ESA project (SVConS) with other companies (NOMOR, Fraunhofer HHI and IIS) which are assessing the performances of SVC over satellite links.

A complete range of simulations is running and preliminary results will be available beginning of 2010.

## 4.2 Video Services

Three main video services will be covered with KA-SAT.

### DTT Primary Distribution
All the countries which are implementing a DTT network on their territory are facing the same problem: it would not be possible to cover 100% of the population with the transmission from DTT terrestrial headends.

On the top of that, it will be impossible to feed all the terrestrial headends by fiber and/or microwave links.

KA-SAT will be the natural solution to:

- feed the terrestrial headends not connected by fiber.
- complement the DTT offer with DTH reception for households not receiving DTT.

Thanks to the spot beam coverage of KA-SAT, this solution will be complete the existing national distribution with regional distribution. Regional DTT channels can be inserted in the national MUXes only in the spots covering the region of interest.

This will avoid the distribution of all the regional channels in the DTT MUXes optimizing the bandwidth utilization and saving CAPEX (headends equipment optimization).

The DTT primary distribution in Ka-band will achieve with a dish size of 120 cm an acceptable operational availability.

Figure 7 is depicting a hybrid solution which will consist in the transport of the DTT multiplexes via satellite for the feeding of headends and complementary DTH reception.

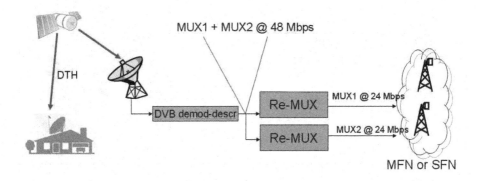

**Fig. 7.** Primary DTT distribution

**Professional Video Contribution**

In order to complement the offer of SNG services a professional contribution system is under development in order to allow the implementation of video contributions on KA-SAT.

This system will allow the uplink of a video contribution (SD or HD, 4:2:2 profile) under a spot of KA-SAT and the potential distribution of this signal on some or all the 82 spots via the fibre ring.

This terminal will feature a professional indoor unit with enhanced throughput performances, a most powerful ODU and bigger size Ka-band dish (with an option for auto-deploy systems).

| Diameter | SSPA | Bitrate | Application |
|----------|------|---------|-------------|
| 60cm | 4W | 5 Mbps | 1 SDTV channel |
| 120cm | 4W | 10 Mbps | 1 HDTV channel |
| 120 cm | 10W | 15 Mbps | 2 HDTV channels |

## DTH Broadcast Services

The pan-european coverage of KA-SAT can be used for DTH broadcasting. It will complement and enrich the offer from the HotBird™ fleet at 13°East.

This offer currently provides more than 1400 TV channels over all Europe, Middle East and North Africa; with KA-SAT this offer can be extended with regional channels and new actors in the Digital TV scenarios.

KA-SAT broadcast services will benefit of a full redundant fiber ring relaying the 10 Ka-band gateways and allowing multiple insertion points for local video contributions.

**Fig. 8.** KA-SAT Gateway system

This architecture will allow distributed video platforms (optimized CAPEX and OPEX) as well as local video insertion for regional content (via fiber and/or KA-SAT contribution).

The use of DVB-S2 will optimize the bandwidth utilization with typical DTH reception diameters (70 cm).

Figure 9 is depicting a typical architecture of a DTH video platform on KA-SAT. The platform will be located in the central KA-SAT hub and will distribute the DTH contents along the fibre inter-POP ring for the uplink from the different gateways.

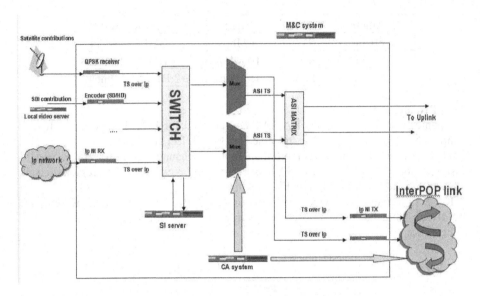

**Fig. 9.** KA-SAT DTH service platform

Figure 10 is depicting a typical Tooway ™ residential installation under KA-SAT. The service will include triple-play services (including IPTV and push-VoD services) and DTH broadcast services.

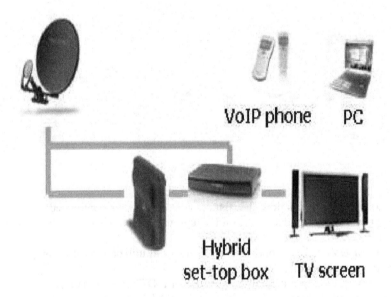

**Fig. 10.** Residential Tooway™ installation

# 5 Conclusions

Through the high power and broad coverage of its HOT BIRD™ broadcast satellites, Eutelsat has built the world's leading video neighborhood, assembling over 1400 channels.

In 2010 with the launch of KA-SAT, Eutelsat will triple the total capacity commercialized by its in-orbit resource and drive broadband to new frontiers.

By uniting these leading-edge Ku and Ka-band technologies at one satellite neighborhood, Eutelsat is developing a unique infrastructure in Europe able to:

- deliver a full range of digital services to consumers (DTH and interactive services such as triple play),
- take advantage of a new band (Ka) enabling Ku band capacity to be preserved for TV broadcasting,
- satisfy a real and common solution to the digital divide over the full Europe area,
- extend the market of professional applications via satellite with lower OPEX and CAPEX saving, enabling new opportunities by taking advantage of the spot beam coverage of KA-SAT.

Thanks to KA-SAT and the new generation Surfbeam™ system from ViaSat, the Tooway™ service will increase the throughput in services and applications without sacrificing service availability.

# Reference

[1] ETSI EN 302 307 V1.1.1, Digital Video Broadcasting (DVB); Second generation framing structure, channel coding and modulation systems for Broadcasting, Interactive Services, News Gathering and other broadband satellite applications (June 2006)

# On the Consideration of an UMTS/S-UMTS Based GEO-MSS System Architecture Design

Jianjun Wu, Yuxin Cheng, Jiancheng Du, Jian Guo, and Zhenxing Gao

State Key Laboratory of Advanced Optical Communication Systems and Networks,
EECS, Peking University, Beijing 100871, P.R. China
{just,chengyx,dujc,guoj,gaozx}@pku.edu.cn

**Abstract.** To address the special requirements of China's future public satellite mobile network (PSMN), three system architecture schemes are proposed in this paper basing on different satellite payload processing modeling. Finally, one of them, i.e., the so-called passive part on-board switching based architecture, is selected as a proposal for further design and development of China's PSMN system, which essentially compatible to the 3GPP/UMTS R4 reference model.

**Keywords:** MSS, GEO, UMTS, network architecture.

## 1 Introduction

In order to extend and complement the current PLMN service coverage, to promote the emergency communications ability during disaster rescues, and to protect the rare space resource, that is, 115.5°E & 125.5°E S-band orbits, which China is holding with highest priority till now, the idea of establishing China's own public satellite mobile network (PSMN) has been proposed repeatly since the 3rd quarter of 2008. Several earlier fundings have been launched respectively by those related national divisions, among which the Ministry of Science and Technology of China (MSTC), is the most progressive one to start the relevant research and development activities.

So far, there are several mobile satellite systems which are already in sucessful commercial operation or right now under construction all over the world. The typical mobile satellite service (MSS) systems include: the 2G compatible systems, e.g., Iridium[1], Globalstar[2], Thuraya[3], ACeS; the 3G compatible system, i.e., the Inmarsat BGAN[4]; and so-called next generation system, i.e., MSV[5], Terrestar[6]. Undoubtedly, these MSS systems will be provided as a beneficial basis of the design and construction of China's future PSMN.

Among the above mentioned satellite systems, though some are successful deploied systems, and some are even designed in advanced technologies as adopted in the terrestrial counterpart systems, none could definitely address the prerequistes imposed by the Ministry of Science and Technolgy of China (MSTC). According to MSTC, the future PSMN should: first, base on 3G or 3G beyond techinology; and second, support a limited number of shorter-latency voice service real-time links, if not the whole. In this situation, a research group was organized by MSTC to setup the

K. Sithamparanathan et al. (Eds.): PSATS 2010, LNICST 43, pp. 86–95, 2010.

early stage work, in which we as a member mainly focus on the system network architecture design.

This paper is organized as following, section 2 lists the PSMN system main design features, network domains partition, and satellite payload configurations; section 3, 4 and 5 discribe three architecture schemes based on different satellite processing models; section 6 evaluates those three schemes, and makes a final decision; and finally, section 7 gives out a short summary.

## 2  System Description

### 2.1  Main System Features

In general, the PSMN system we are designing is nevertheless a typical satellite communications system, as illustrated in Fig.1.

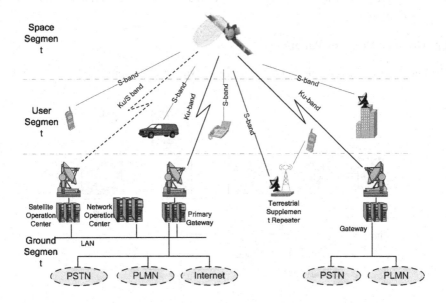

**Fig. 1.** The PSMN system organization diagram

There are several main design features of PSMN which should be listed before the system network architecture is described. These relevant features range from satellite orbit selection to communications technology evaluation, as well as radio interface decision.

- **GEO orbits:** mainly due to the requirement of the satellite network file approved by ITU in 2004, the GEO orbits will be chosen for the PSMN of China, which will reduce the system complexity to some extent, but result in  longest transmiting latency[7];

- **3G Technology**: it is one of the prerequistes imposed by the MSTC to design a 3G compatible mobile satellite telecommunications system, which can provide higher data rate sevices, not only the low rate voice sevice;
- **WCDMA Air-interface**: since applying CDMA2000 will suffer the patent problems, meanwhile TD-SCDMA is difficult to be employed within the satellite based system, the WCDMA becomes an appropriate choice of the system air-interface;
- **3GPP R4 Reference Model**: among the 3GPP/UMTS releases, namely, Release 99, 4, 5, 6, 7, 8, 9 and 10, the R4 release[8] includes a mature and stable network architecture version, which is divided into RAN and CN fields, CS and PS domains, and most importantly, has a bearer independent CN;
- **CN indepentent to PLMN**: the lowest integration level of satellite communications system and terrestrail tele-communications systems has to be chosen in China, for the licenses of the 3G telecommunications service were issued respectively to different operators, i.e., China Mobile, China Unicom and China Telecom.

## 2.2 Network Domains Partition

The Fig.2 shows the basic domains in UMTS network architecture.

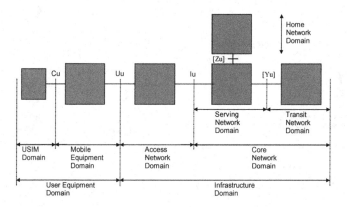

**Fig. 2.** The basic domains in UMTS network

where Cu is the reference point between USIM and ME; Iu is the reference point between Access and Serving Network domains; Uu is the reference point between User Equipment and Infrastructure domains, an UMTS radio interface; [Yu] is the reference point between Serving and Transit Network domains, and [Zu] is the reference point between Serving and Home Network domains.

To simplify the architecture design and description, a more general network partition model of the PSMN is illustrated in Fig.3, as following.

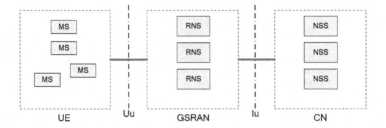

**Fig. 3.** Network domains partition model of the PSMN

where UE represents the user equipment domain, in which the MS is the mobile station; GSRAN represents the GEO satellite radio access network domain, in which RNS is the radio network sub-system; CN is the core network domain, in which NSS is the network switch sub-system.

### 2.3 Satellite Payload Configurations

As a MSS system, the satellite payload configuration becomes the key factor of the system network architecture design. In general, there are 5 possible payload configuration types, including,

- Transparent bent-pipe configuration
- Passive part on-board switching configuration
- Active part on-board switching configuration
- Passive full on-board switching configuration
- Active full on-board switching configuration

Anyway, those full on-board switching configurations couldn't be implemented under current technical level in China. To be practical, one of the other three configurations will be the optimal choice. More details on these three configurations and related system architecture designs will be presented and discussed in the following sections.

## 3   Transparent Bent-Pipe Based Scheme

The transparent bent-pipe model is the simplest model for satellite processing. It is divided into 2 functional entities, i.e., ULPU (User Link Processing Unit) and FLPU (Feeder Link Processing Unit), which respectively interface with the User Link and Feeder Link, as illustrated in Fig.4. The processings here within the ULPU and FLPU, may be as simple as only playing the role of an amplifier of RF signals.

Based on above satellite payload modeling, the related system architecture can be simply organized, as showed in Fig.5. As we can see, this is compatible with the 3GPP/UMTS R4 architecture[9], meanwhile taking into account the impact of the space segment, namely, the satellite.

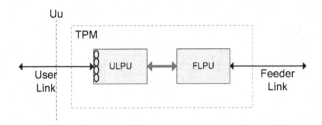

**Fig. 4.** Transparent bent-pipe model block diagram

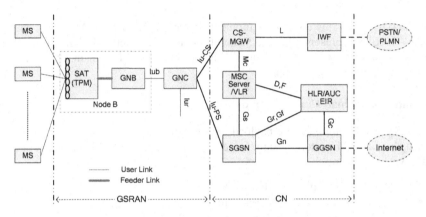

**Fig. 5.** Transparent bent-pipe based architecture scheme

As traditional UMTS/S-UMTS architecture, the network architecture of PSMN is also divided into two part, the Radio Access Network (RAN) and the Core Network (CN).

However, the RAN here is named as GSRAN (GEO Satellite Radio Access Network), since it is extended via the introduction of satellites in the high altitude space. The GSRAN consists of the following entities, such as, multi-spotbeam satellite, GNB (Gateway-station Node B), GNC (Gateway-station Network Controller). The GNB integrating with the transparent satellite together forms a terrestrial Node B entity. Thus, the GSRAN in total plays a role of UTRAN of the terrestrial celluar systems.

Likely, the CN in PSMN consists of those traditional functional entities, i.e., HLR (Home Location Register), VLR (Visitor Location Register), AUC (Authentication Center), EIR (Equipment Identity Register), MSC Server (Mobile-services Switching Center Server), CS-MGW (Circuit Switched-Media Gateway Function), IWF (Interworking Function), SGSN (Serving GPRS Support Node), GGSN (Gateway GPRS Support Node), etc. These entities act actuall the same as those in the terrestrial systems based on 3GPP/UMTS R4.

The communications procedure in this system will be the same as that in the 3GPP/UMTS system. However, since no on-board processing and switching, it can operates in double-hop communications mode.

## 4  Passive Part On-Board Switching Based Scheme

The passive part-switch on-board processing model is a hybrid model, mainly a transparent bent-pipe together with an capacity-limited on-board passive switch processing part. The passive switching here means that the on-board processor only executes switching function, while the routing control instructions come from other entities, e.g., those entitis in the ground segment. Obviously, the on-board switching is the only way to realize single hop voice communications links.

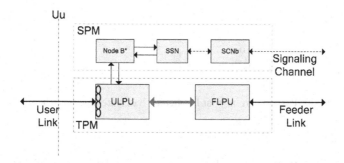

**Fig. 6.** Passive part-switch model block diagram

The passive part-switch model is illustrated in Fig.6, where the TPM means transparent processing module, and the SPM means switch processing module. The passive part-switch model comprises componets as following,

- **ULPU:**    User Link Processing Unit
- **FLPU:**    Feeder Link Processing Unit
- **Node B\*:** Part-functional Node B on board;
- **SSN:**    Satellite Switching Network on board;
- **SCNb:**    Satellite Control Node-b, a control signaling interface node;

The network architecture above generally looks like the transparent bent-pipe case, except the introduing of a satellite control signaling branch. This branch consists of several new added functional entities in the PSMN system network architecture, as demonstrated in Fig.7,

**1) GSRAN domain:**

- **SCN** (Satellite Control Node): a node to control satellite payload, especially the on-board switching network;
- **SRC** (Satellite Route Controller): an entity to manage satellite switching resource and to decide the routing strategy;

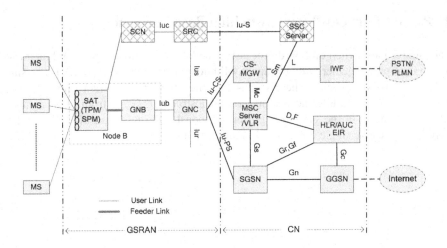

**Fig. 7.** Passive part on-board switching based architecture scheme

**2) CN domain:**

- **SSC Server** (Satellite Switching Coordination Server): an device to coordinate the necessary operations among the SRC and the MSC servers, e.g., charging.

There are also some new defined interfaces and related protocols in the PSMN system network architecture, including,

- **Iuc:** interface between SCN and SRC, with an also new defined interface protocol SCNAP (Satellite Control Node Application Part);
- **Ius:** interface between SRC and GNCs, with an also new defined interface protocol SRCAP (Satellite Routing Control Application Part );
- **Iu-S:** interface between SRC and SSC Server, with an also new defined interface protocol SSCAP (Satellite Switching Coordination  Application Part);
- **Sm:** interface between SSC Server and MSC Servers, while using common CN interface protocol, such as MAP, BICC, etc.;

As to the communications procedure in this system, it will be much the same as that in the 3GPP/UMTS system, except that the voice traffic will be bypassed via the satelliter on-board processor after the calling setup, only if the SRC can find out enough on-board resource and issue an on-board switching instruction. By this way, single hop voice connectivity is realized.

## 5   Active Part On-Board Switching Based Scheme

Much like the passive part-switch model, the active part-switch model is also a hybrid model, except an on-board active switching processor instead of the passive one. The acttive switching means that the on-board processor not only executes switching function, but also fulfils single-hop routing, which is assumed to be the role of the ground segment of the system at the passive model.

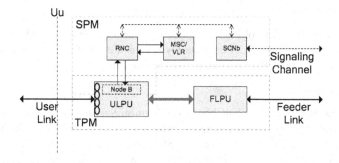

**Fig. 8.** Active part-switch model block diagram

The active part-switch model is illustrated in Fig.8. The TPM and SPM hold the same function as in the passive model. The active part-switch mode comprises the following components,

- **ULPU:**   User Link Processing Unit
- **FLPU:**   Feeder Link Processing Unit
- **Node B:**  Full-functional Node B on board;
- **RNC:**    Radio Network Controller on board;
- **MSC/VLR:** Mobile-services Switching Center/ Visitor Location Register on board;
- **SCNb:**   Satellite Control Node-b, a control signaling interface node;

It should be noticed that in the active part-switch model, the Node-B entity on the satellite is embeded into the ULPU module as a portion of it.

The network architecture based on this on-board processor model is essentially the same as the passive one, while the later has a simpler satellite control signaling branch. The system network architecture is demonstrated in Fig.9,

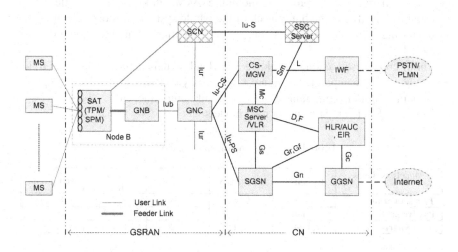

**Fig. 9.** Active part on-board switching based architecture scheme

**1) GSRAN domain:**

- **SCN** (Satellite Control Node): a node to control satellite payload. In contrast to the passive case, the SCN here mainly acts as the interfaces bridge between satellite and ground infrastructure parts, such as, Iur, Nc, E, & G;

**2) CN domain:**

- **SSC Server** (Satellite Switching Coordination Server): an device to coordinate the necessary operations among the On-board processor and the MSC servers, e.g., charging. On the other hand, SSC Server is also the interface converging point of the ground CN domain, which maintains the connectivities with the relevant CN functional entities on the satellite via the SCN.

There are less new defined interfaces and related protocols in this kind of PSMN system network, including,

- **Iu-S:** interface between SCN and SSC Server, with an also new defined interface protocol SSCAP (Satellite Switching Coordination Application Part);
- **Sm:** interface between SSC Server and MSC Servers, while using common CN interface protocol, such as MAP, BICC, etc.;

The communications procedure in this network architecture will be generally the same as that in the 3GPP/UMTS system, since the satellite can be treated as a small copy of the ground infrastructure. Meanwhile, the single hop voice links can be setup faster than in the passive scheme by this way.

## 6  Comparison and Discussion

Though the above 3 system architecture schemes are proposed for the China's PSMN, only one of them can be employed in the future. As we all know, the satellite processing capability is always the bottle-neck of the whole system, thus one scheme will be chosen basing on the comparison among 3 above mentioned satellite on-board processor models.

A brief comparison among the above 3 payload models is presented in the following Table 1. The comparing items are satellite payload resource usage, complexity, power comsump-tion, communications delay, link setup time, etc.

Table 1. A brief comparison among 3 models

**Table 1.** A brief comparison among 3 models

| Models vs. Items | Resource | Complxity | Power | Comm. delay | Setup time |
|---|---|---|---|---|---|
| **Trans. bent-pipe** | Low | Low | Low | Large | Large |
| **Passive part-switch** | Medium | Medium | Medium | Small | Large |
| **Active part-switch** | High | High | High | Small | Small |

As mentioned before, GEO system has a large transmission delay, i.e., about 0.27s for a loop, thus it will spend about 0.54s for the double hop mode. However, commercial real-time voice service generally requires less latency than 0.4s. To satisfy this requirement, single hop system is undoubtedly neccesary, which results in the inevitable satellite on-board switching[9].

Having considered these comparison results, together with the system design prerequistes in mind, we decide to apply the passive part-switch proceesing model based system network architecture as the basis of our further system design.

## 7  Summary

As a preparation of China's future PSMN plan, three system network architecture schemes are proposed in this paper for China's future GEO satellite mobile telecommunications system, which all are compatible to the 3GPP/UMTS R4 reference model. One of them, i.e., the passive part on-board switching based scheme, is selected finally basing on the comparison of their satellite on-board processing models, which in general addresses better the special design require-ments of the Ministry of Science and Technology of China.

However, the results presented here are schematic, and also simple to some extent. Further research efforts may focus largely on the detailed designs of the proposed entities, interfaces, protocols, and control procedures.

## References

1. Iridium Satellite LLC web page, http://www.iridium.com/
2. Globalstar INC web page, http://www.globalstar.com/
3. Thuraya Telecommunications Company web site, http://www.thuraya.com/
4. Inmarsat PLC web site, http://www.inmarsat.com/
5. Mobile Satellite Ventures web site, http://www.msvlp.com/
6. Terrestar Corporation web site, http://www.terrestar.com/
7. Lloyd's Satellite Constellations Overview,
   http://personal.ee.surrey.ac.uk/Personal/L.Wood/
   constellations/references.html
8. 3rd GPP Technical Specification Group Services and Systems Aspects: Network architecture, Release 4, 3GPP TS 23.002 V4.8.0 (2003-2006)
9. Satellite component of UMTS/IMT-2000: General aspects and principles, ETSI TR 101 865 v1.2.1. (2002-2009) (technical report)

# Track 3
# Satellite Networks: Quality of Service and Architectures

# End-to-End QoS Evaluation of IP-Diffserv Network over LEO Satellite Constellation

Lukman Audah, Zhili Sun, and Haitham Cruickshank

Centre for Communication System Research (CCSR)
University of Surrey, Guildford, UK
{l.audah,z.sun,h.cruickshank}@surrey.ac.uk

**Abstract.** In this paper, we present an end-to-end QoS simulation studies on internetworking of remote LAN and long range communications over LEO-Iridium satellites constellation taking SuperJARING network in Malaysia as an example. A macro level network simulation scenario based on actual network topology in Malaysia is implemented as Diffserv network model using the Network Simulator-2 (NS-2). Web traffic (HTTP) is used as the internet traffic models in the simulation analysis. All simulations are carried out in error-free and link-loss environment. In error-free simulations, the accumulative network traffic loads are varied from 20%, 50% and 80% while in link-loss environment simulations only 20% traffic load is used with bit error rate (BER) varied from $1 \times 10^{-5}$, $1 \times 10^{-4}$ and $2 \times 10^{-4}$. The results show clearly that QoS can be achieved with IP Diffserv over satellites constellation like Iridium.

**Keywords:** End-to-end QoS, IP over satellites, Differentiated Services (Diffserv).

## 1 Introduction

The current Internet architecture operates mostly based on connectionless Internet Protocol (IP) system that provides best effort services. This means the IP routers treat all packet streams equally without given any preferential treatment to the higher priority traffic streams. Furthermore, the IP routers route packets based on shortest path first (SPF) algorithm without regard to the overall link utilization. Consequently, the all shortest paths links become congested and over-utilized capacity while the other paths with slightly longer distance become under-utilized in link capacity. These whole things eventually cause poor Quality of Service (QoS) to the entire packet transmission services.

The IETF has proposed Differentiate Services (Diffserv) as a better solution to provide QoS guarantees in IP networks. Compared to its predecessor like the Integrated Services (Intserv) which provides services based on per-microflow state, Diffserv outsmarts Intserv in providing better end-to-end QoS and preferential treatment. Diffserv discriminates different traffic flows which have same commonality to finite aggregate of classes and provides a more scalable solution for QoS in IP networks by simplifying the complexity functions such as traffic classification and traffic conditioning within the edge routers [1][2].

K. Sithamparanathan et al. (Eds.): PSATS 2010, LNICST 43, pp. 99–113, 2010.

However, Diffserv alone is not the complete solution without adopting Traffic Engineering (TE) to overcome the link congestion and inefficiency of network resource distribution. Traffic Engineering might enhance the end-to-end QoS performance and resource utilization in any IP packet network system. It is important to achieve the end-to-end QoS target because the Internet user's perception of service quality is based on end-to-end network performance.

Previous related studies on end-to-end Internet QoS of IP-Diffserv [3][4][5][6][7] only analyzed a micro scale of wired/wireless terrestrial network topology. None of them have analyzed the global scale of Internet data transmissions over both terrestrial and satellite and also adopting actual network topology in the simulation scenario. We believe that it is important to analyze end-to-end QoS based on the actual network topology of both terrestrial and satellite networks because this reflects the current and future Internet data transmission. Furthermore, simulation measurement and evaluation of end-to-end QoS parameters using common Internet traffic (HTTP, FTP, VoIP) for multiple client-server communications might give better foresight on the future network design with QoS guarantees for many users.

We aim to evaluate the network performance and build a base-work for future generation Internet over satellite to study the outcome of IP-Diffserv and TE in the end-to-end QoS performance. This paper presents the end-to-end QoS simulation studies from a macro level perspective which involves both terrestrial and inter-satellites communications. The end-to-end QoS parameters include packet delivery ratio, packet dropped distribution, average end-to-end packet delay and average session throughput using Hyper Text Transfer Protocol (HTTP) application on long range communications over LEO-Iridium satellites constellation between a remote local area network (LAN) and Diffserv network. A macro level network scenario that imitates the actual geographical topology in Malaysia is proposed as an example in implementing the IP-Diffserv and TE model. In addition, the simulation analysis also emulates the common speed of Internet services in Malaysia which is 1Mb/s. Simulations are done in error-free and link-loss environments. In error-free simulations, the accumulative background traffic loads are varied from 20%, 50% and 80% of the Diffserv core-link capacity while in link-loss environment simulations only 20% background traffic load is used with bit-error-rate (BER) varied from $1 \times 10^{-5}$, $1 \times 10^{-4}$ and $2 \times 10^{-4}$. All simulations and analysis of the above mentioned network model are done using the Network Simulator-2 (NS-2- version 2.33).

## 2   Simulation Framework and Configuration

This section describes in detail the parameters used for the IP-Diffserv and the network system of both terrestrial and LEO-Iridium satellites simulation configuration. In addition, measurement methodologies for QoS parameters like packet delivery ratio (PDR), total packets dropped distribution, average end-to-end packet delay and average session throughput are also explained in this section.

### 2.1   Satellite Networking Simulation in NS-2

Simulation of satellite networks that follows the exact technical parameters often requires a detailed modeling of radio frequency characteristics (interference, fading), protocol interactions (e.g. interaction of residual burst errors on link with error checking codes), and second-order orbital effects (precession, gravitational anomalies, etc.). However, in order to study the fundamental characteristics of satellite networks from a networking perspective, some features might be omitted. As an example, simulation analysis of TCP performance over satellite has little effect with detailed propagation channel model which could be characterized to first order by the overall packet loss probability [8][9]. In this paper, LEO-Iridium satellites constellation are used in order to create a framework to study the QoS effects of transport, routing and handover protocol in end-to-end data transmissions. The following are the parameters description and Table- 1 shows all LEO-Iridium satellites constellation parameters that can be simulated in NS-2 [8].

**Basic constellation definition:** Define the satellite altitude, number of satellites, number of planes, and number of satellites per plane.

**Orbits:** Define the orbit inclination ranging from 0 to 180 degrees. Inclination above 90 degrees corresponds to retrograde orbits. However, orbit eccentricity and nodal precession are not modeled in NS-2. In addition, inter-satellites spacing within a given plane and relative phasing between planes are set to be fixed.

**Inter-satellite (ISL) links:** Define the polar orbiting constellations, intraplane and interplane satellite links. Intraplane ISL correspond to the communications between satellites in the same plane which are never deactivated or handed off. In addition, Interplane ISL referring to the communications between satellites of neighboring co-rotating planes. Both ISL will be deactivated near the poles when exceeding ISL threshold because the satellite antenna unable to track these links in the Polar Regions.

**Table 1.** LEO-Iridium satellites parameters [8][9]

| Parameter | Value |
|---|---|
| Altitude | 780Km |
| Planes | 6 |
| Satellites per plane | 11 |
| Inclination (degree) | 86.4 |
| Interplane separation (degree) | 31.6 |
| Seam separation (degree) | 22 |
| Elevation mask (degree) | 8.2 |
| Intraplane phasing | YES |
| Interplane phasing | YES |
| ISL per satellite | 4 |
| ISL bandwidth | 25 Mb/s |
| Uplink/downlink bandwidth | 1.5 Mb/s |
| Cross-seam ISL | NO |
| ISL latitude threshold (degree) | 60 |

**Ground to Satellite (GSL) links:** Define the communications between satellites and terrestrial links network. GSL are periodically handed off when the elevation angle drop below the elevation mask. In this paper, there are two GSL which locations are set in London, UK ($51.53^0$, $-0.08^0$) and Kuala Lumpur, Malaysia ($3.13^0$, $101.70^0$).

**Elevation Mask:** Define the elevation angle of GSL link can be operated. When a GSL terminal that correspond to a satellite drops below the elevation mask, it will search for a new satellite above the elevation mask. Each GSL terminal will check for handoff opportunities when the timeout interval specified by the user is exceeded. Both GSL in this paper initiate handoff asynchronously.

## 2.2 Simulation Scenario

The proposed simulation scenario as shown in Figure 1 consists of two main components which are the terrestrial and satellite networks. The terrestrial network on the right side is designed such that it imitates the macro level of actual geographical topology in Malaysia. The way of imitation is by assigning an edge router to represent each of the 11 Cities/Counties which connects to other 6 interconnected routers (red color) that form the Diffserv core links. Each of the 11 edge router (green color) is further connected to client (orange color) and server (blue color) nodes. So, there are 11 pairs of client and server nodes, 11 Diffserv edge routers and 6 core routers which in total are 39 nodes in the terrestrial network. The Diffserv parameters and policies are assigned to those 11 edge routers and 6 core routers which control the packet streams transmission within the Diffserv network domain. The assignment of client-server pair location is done randomly with the fact that all links must be utilized by the traffic flows. The path taken by the traffic flows from each pair of client/server node is determined by the Link State Routing Protocol.

In addition, there are another 66 LEO-Iridium satellites constellation and 2 ground to satellite links (GSL) located at London and Kuala Lumpur. The satellites form a bridge from a server node located in a remote LAN in UK to a client node in Malaysia. It should be noted that a single client node generates HTTP connections from a *"cloud"* of web clients while a single server node accepts and serves HTTP connection destined for a *"cloud"* of web servers. The link bandwidth for Core Links, C1 to C7, follow the Optical Carrier (OC-192) specification which is approximately 10Gb/s while the Edge Links, E1 to E11, follow the OC -24 specification which is approximately 1.25Gb/s [10]. A reduction of a hundred folds in the link bandwidth is done in order to speed up the simulation time and to accommodate the limited capacity of computer hard disk space.

The Core Links propagation delays approximation varies according to actual distance in Malaysia geography. The propagation delay for link C1=20ms, C2=25ms, C3=25ms, C4=30ms, C5=30ms, C6=25ms and C7=25ms. The Edge Link propagation delay is fixed to 5ms while the client/server Link is 1ms. Based on Figure 1, each pair of client and its designated server node is labeled with the same name (e.g. HTTP1, HTTP2 and etc). The paths that packet streams take across the network system are determined by the Link State (LS) routing protocol. The LS governs all the Layer 3 network routing process for terrestrial network while routing process in LEO satellites network is govern by a centralize routing genie. The routing genie determines the global satellites topology, computes new data routes for all nodes and built a forwarding table on each node [8]. In addition, it computes the shortest path data route based on the current propagation delay of a link as the cost metric.

Moreover, all simulations in NS-2 involve one type of Internet application traffic which is the Hyper Text Transfer Protocol (HTTP). A client-server pair generates thousands of different HTTP request-response sessions based on 20%, 50% and 80% of traffic loads. Calculation of the traffic load is divided in two categories which are based on the terrestrial Diffserv core links capacity and the satellite links bandwidth. As an example for 20% of traffic load simulation, all 10 server nodes in terrestrial network generate an average aggregate background traffic that approximate to the 20% of the Diffserv core links capacity which is 20Mb/s while the other server node (HTTP5) located in remote LAN in UK generates an average data rate that approximate to the 20% of uplink/downlink of GSL bandwidth which is 300Kb/s. These traffic loads parameters are determined by the inter-arrival time of each new request-response session. The traffic load also corresponds to the amount of packet streams been injected to the network system. In this paper, we want to demonstrate the effect of the background traffic generated by client/server pairs (except HTTP5) to the QoS of Internet data transmission over LEO-Iridium satellites constellation.

In addition, each HTTP session involves an average of 10Kbytes of HTTP response file transfer size. The average inter-arrival time between each generated HTTP session is modeled by Exponential distribution while the average HTTP response file transfer size is modeled by Pareto distribution. A HTTP session represents a complete request-response pair that follows both Exponential and Pareto distribution between a server-client pair. NS-2 has both distribution functions built in it and could be generated using Random Number Generator (RNG). In order to set the Pareto file transfer size distribution, the average value of 10Kbytes and Pareto shape parameter of 1.5 are passed to the Pareto type of Random Variable function. It produced a series of file size distribution with an average of 10Kbytes. It should be noted that the 10Kbytes parameter is taken based on the majority of Internet file transfer size as measured in the previous studies [11][12]. On the other hand, an average of HTTP session inter-arrival time parameter is passed to the Exponential type of Random Variable.

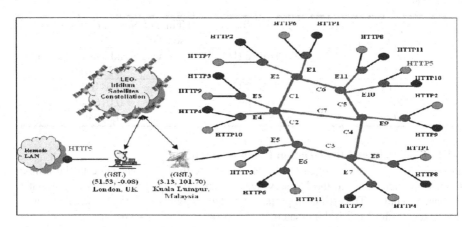

**Fig. 1.** Simulation scenario in Network Simulator 2 (NS-2)

As mentioned previously, the two types of traffic loads are generated according to the inter-arrival time of new HTTP sessions which varies from 20%, 50% and 80%. Therefore, there are two HTTP session inter-arrival variables used in all simulations which one is according to Diffserv core links capacity (background traffic) and the other one according to uplink/downlink GSL bandwidth (traffic from HTTP5). As an example for 20% of traffic load simulation, the average inter-arrival time, $i$, measured in second is calculated using the following formula:

$$i(s) = \frac{(N) \times (Fs) \times 8}{Bw} \qquad (1)$$

The $N$ parameter is the number of nodes involve in generating the traffic flows while the $Fs$ parameter is the average HTTP Response file size (10400 bytes) sent by the server nodes. An average of one TCP segment size is 1040 bytes of which the 1000 bytes is the Data and 40 bytes is the TCP header. An average of a file transfer is assumed to contain 10 Kbytes of Data which in total including header is approximately $1.04 \times 10^4 \times 8$bits . The $Bw$ parameter is the link bandwidth measured in b/s. In this paper, we define $Bw$ in two different values which one of them (100 Mb/s) is used to calculate the inter-arrival time of the background traffic generated by 10 pairs of client/server nodes (except HTTP5) and the other one (1.5 Mb/s) is for the main traffic flows across LEO-Iridium satellites constellation. Table 2 lists the average inter-arrival time of HTTP session parameters for every pair of client/server (HTTP1-HTTP11) according to 20%, 50% and 80% of traffic loads.

Moreover, all link-loss environment simulations in this paper used one-way random link loss error model. Link loss error model is configured on all Diffserv Edge Links with bit error rate (BER) $1 \times 10^{-5}$, $1 \times 10^{-4}$ and $2 \times 10^{-4}$. The loss module is placed right after link's queue element and before the link's delay element. This means a packet will be marked as 'error' and dropped as soon as it enters the Diffserv edge link. The error model follows uniform distribution with minimum and maximum value of 0 and 1 respectively.

**Table 2.** Average inter-arrival time of HTTP sessions according to 20%, 50% and 80% of traffic loads

| Traffic Load | Average Inter-arrival Time of New HTTP Session (second) | |
|---|---|---|
| | Main Traffic (HTTP5) | Background Traffic (except HTTP5) |
| 20% | 0.27733 | 0.04160 |
| 50% | 0.11093 | 0.01664 |
| 80% | 0.06933 | 0.01040 |

### 2.2.1 Flow Path and Propagation Delay Estimation

Table 3 shows the paths taken by the HTTP5 flow from a server node in the remote LAN to a client node in the Diffserv network (based on Figure 1), and its estimated propagation delay. The estimated propagation delay might vary based on the path variation taken in the LEO-Iridium satellites network. It was obtained without taking into account the queuing delay at each link. The value of 157.162ms is calculated based on the paths taken by HTTP5 flows in the early data transmission as stated in the NS-2 satellite output trace file. Based on the output trace file, the propagation paths in LEO-Iridium satellites network stated in term of (latitude, longitude) locations are $GSL_{(UK)}$ $(51.53°, -0.08°)$, node(2) $(65.21°,7.83°)$, node(1) $(32.67°,2.31°)$, node(12) $(48.97°,$ $35.75°)$, node(23) $(32.66°, 65.51°)$, node(34) $(48.97°, 98.94°)$, node(33) $(16.33°,95.86°)$ and $GSL_{(KL)}$ $(3.13°, 101.70°)$. The one way link propagation delay $(t_{sat\text{-}prop})$ in LEO-Iridium satellites network is calculated using some trigonometry formulas as discussed in [13], without taking into account the queuing delay at each satellite links. The value is equal to the summation of propagation delay from earth terminal in UK to the current nearest satellite above it $(t_{uplink})$, propagation delay within satellites network $(t_{inter\text{-}sat})$ and propagation delay from satellite to earth terminal in KL, $(t_{downlink})$. Following are the formulas used to calculate the estimated $t_{sat\text{-}prop}$ [13]:

$$t_{sat-prop} = t_{uplink} + t_{inter-sat} + t_{downlink} \tag{2}$$

$$t_{uplink} = \frac{d_{ts}}{c} \tag{3}$$

$$d_{ts} = \sqrt{(x_{sat} - x_{term(UK)})^2 + (y_{sat} - y_{term(UK)})^2 + (z_{sat} - z_{term(UK)})^2} \tag{4}$$

$$t_{inter-sat} = \frac{d_{is}}{c} \tag{5}$$

$$d_{is} = \sqrt{(x_{sat(i+1)} - x_{sat(i)})^2 + (y_{sat(i+1)} - y_{sat(i)})^2 + (z_{sat(i+1)} - z_{sat(i)})^2} \tag{6}$$

$$t_{downlink} = \frac{d_{st}}{c} \tag{7}$$

$$d_{st} = \sqrt{(x_{term(KL)} - x_{sat})^2 + (y_{term(KL)} - y_{sat})^2 + (z_{term(KL)} - z_{sat})^2} \tag{8}$$

Where:

$d_{ts}$ = Distance from earth terminal in UK to satellite

$d_{is}$ = Distance between satellite$_{(i)}$ and satellite$_{(i+1)}$

$d_{st}$ = Distance from satellite to earth terminal in KL

$x_{sat}$ = $(R+h)\cos\theta_{sat}\cos\phi_{sat}$ , $y_{sat} = (R+h)\cos\theta_{sat}\sin\phi_{sat}$ , $z_{sat} = (R+h)\sin\theta_{sat}$

$x_{term()}$ = $R\cos\theta_{term()}\cos\phi_{term()}$ , $y_{term()} = R\cos\theta_{term()}\sin\phi_{term()}$ , $z_{term()} = R\sin\theta_{term()}$

$\theta$ = latitude, $\phi$ = longitude

$R$ = 6378.137 Km (earth radius), $c = 299792$ Km/s (light speed), $h = 780$ Km

**Table 3.** Flow paths from server node to client node and its estimated propagation delay

| HTTP Flow | Paths Taken | Estimated Propagation Delay |
|---|---|---|
| HTTP5 | $GSL_{(UK)}\rightarrow$ LEO Satellites$\rightarrow GSL_{(KL)}\rightarrow$ E5$\rightarrow$ C2$\rightarrow$ C1$\rightarrow$ C6$\rightarrow$ E10 | $\approx 157.162$ms |

In order to calculate the link propagation delay from $GSL_{(UK)}$ to the nearest satellite (node(2)) above it, both coordinate locations of $GSL_{(UK)}$ and node(2) are inserted in equation (4) and then equation (3) which yield $t_{uplink}$ = 6.173ms. The inter-satellite links propagation delays are calculated using equation (6) and equation (5) for every pair of satellite ($sat_{i+1}$ and $sat_i$), using node(2), node(1), node(12), node(23), node(34) and node(33) coordinates which then yield $t_{inter-sat}$ = 13.448ms + 12.253ms + 11.358ms + 12.253ms + 13.458ms = 62.770ms. In addition, the downlink propagation delay is calculated using equation (8) and equation (7) with $GSL_{(KL)}$ and node(33) coordinates which then yield $t_{downlink}$ = 6.219ms. Therefore, the total propagation delay in LEO-Iridium satellites network is $t_{sat-prop}$ = 6.173ms+ 62.770ms + 6.219ms = 75.162ms. Meanwhile, the propagation delay across E5, C2, C1, C6 and E10 nodes within Diffserv network domain from $GSL_{(KL)}$ to the designated HTTP5 client node is 82ms, as previously described in section 2.2. Finally, the end-to-end link propagation delay for HTTP5 is $t_{tot-prop} = t_{sat-prop} + t_{terrestrial-prop}$ = 75.162ms + 82ms = 157.162ms.

### 2.2.2  Link Loss

All link-loss environment simulations in this paper used one-way random link loss error model. Link loss error model is configured on all Diffserv edge links with bit error rate (BER) $1x10^{-5}$, $1x10^{-4}$ and $2x10^{-4}$. The loss module is placed right after link's queue element and before the link's delay element. This means a packet will be marked as 'error' and dropped as soon as it enters the edge link. The error model follows uniform distribution with minimum and maximum value of 0 and 1 respectively.

## 3  Result and Discussion

The following are the results and discussions based on HTTP simulations in NS-2. The results are divided into error-free (traffic loads of 20%, 50% and 80%) and with link-loss condition (BER = $1x10^{-5}$, $1x10^{-4}$ and $2x10^{-4}$) for traffic flows over LEO-Iridium satellites network. All QoS parameters results obtained from the NS-2 simulations are calculated as averages for all HTTP sessions generated by HTTP5 client/server pair. Simulation time is set to 300 second because there are more than 2GB of the output trace file produced for each traffic load category.

### 3.1  Packet Delivery Ratio (PDR)

Figure 2 shows the Packet Delivery Ratio (PDR) for HTTP5 Request and Response packets transmission over LEO-Iridium satellites network. The PDR is calculated as the ratio between the Received Request/Response packets and Sent Request/Response packets type. It measures the percentage of successful end-to-end data transmission. Although all packets are guaranteed to be delivered from source to destination by the TCP, not all packets received are the original packets sent by the source. Some of the packets are lost and need to be retransmitted. Therefore, the PDR shows the ratio between total sent packets including retransmission packets and total received packets.

The PDR is inversely proportional to the increment of traffic load, the lower the traffic load the higher would be the PDR. The PDR is higher in lower traffic load because the links still could sustain the traffic burst. Fewer packets are lost in lower traffic load.

However, the PDR is lower in higher traffic load because the links become saturated with traffic burst which eventually cause many packets being dropped. Moreover, compared to the two types of PDR in HTTP5 flows, most of the Response PDR is a lower than the Request PDR. This mainly because the average total size of response packets (10Kbytes) is much higher than the response packets (550bytes) and many of them will be dropped either by Diffserv elements or due to the narrowband in satellite links. Based on Figure 2, the PDR values are much above 96% in all traffic load variation. This is due to the flow control by TCP in order to provide a reliable data transmission.

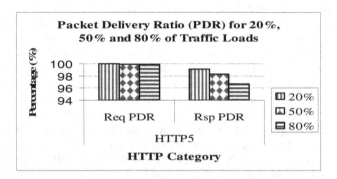

**Fig. 2.** Packet Delivery Ratio (PDR) for 20%, 50% and 80% of traffic loads

Figure 3 shows the PDR of HTTP5 flows for 20% traffic load with BER from $1x10^{-5}$, $1x10^{-4}$ and $2x10^{-4}$. The PDR of HTTP5 flows are inversely proportional to the increment of BER. The higher the BER, the lower would be the number of successful transmitted packets. Based on the graph, the PDR could be considered higher which is above 80% in the worst case of BER equal to $2x10^{-4}$. The main reason is because the HTTP5 flows operate in low bandwidth of 20% traffic load in which the links could still sustained the traffic burst. Furthermore, the results shows that link-loss in Diffserv network domain did not give significant effect on short HTTP sessions when operate in lower traffic load.

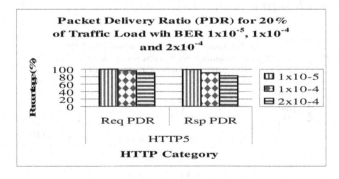

**Fig. 3.** Packet Delivery Ratio (PDR) for 20% of traffic load with Bit Error Rate (BER)

## 3.2 Total Packets Dropped Distribution

Figure 4 shows the distribution of total dropped HTTP Request, Response, SYN/ACK and FIN/ACK type of packets during 300 second of simulation time. It should be noted that the SYN/ACK and FIN/ACK are small packets of 40 bytes size which sent by the HTTP client and server upon connection establishment or connection tear down. The SYN/ACK means SYN or ACK packet type sent by the client. In addition, the FIN/ACK means FIN or ACK packet type sent by the server. The total packets dropped include the packets dropped due to buffer overflow and also Diffserv RED buffer early packets dropped. As traffic loads increase from 20% to 80%, the numbers of packets dropped are drastically increased. This is because greedy flows are se-verely punished by the Diffserv RED buffers. The increment of traffic loads will cause the current average buffer size to grow larger as many packets need to queue before being transmitted. Diffserv marks the packet flows that have accumulative sending rate more than the 1 Mb/s and dropped those packets probabilistically when the current average RED buffer size exceeds the minimum threshold. All packets are then dropped when the buffer size exceeds the maximum threshold. Based on the graph, the HTTP Response packets are dropped much more than the SYN/ACK and FIN/ACK packets. This is because the HTTP Response packets are larger (average size of 10 Kbytes) than the SYN/ACK and FIN/ACK packets (40 bytes each). Larger packets will quickly fill the queue buffer which will then trigger the Diffserv RED monitoring element that estimates the current queue size. Besides that, the total pack-ets dropped not only due to the Diffserv RED buffers but also due to the narrowband links in the satellites network.

Figure 5 shows the total packets dropped distribution in link-loss simulation envi-ronment for 20% of traffic load with BER $1x10^{-5}$, $1x10^{-4}$ and $2x10^{-4}$. The number of packets dropped increase proportionally with the increment of BER. Compared to Figure 4, flows in lower traffic load did not much penalized by Diffserv and the pack-ets dropped mainly due to the link-loss error model implemented on the Diffserv net-work boundary.

Based on Figure 4, the total HTTP packets dropped in 20%, 50% and 80% of traf-fic load are 102 packets, 545 packets and 1877 packets respectively. Meanwhile, the total HTTP packets dropped for $1x10^{-5}$, $1x10^{-4}$ and $2x10^{-4}$ of BER are 104 packets, 1284 packets and 2734 packets respectively. From these values, we could see that the

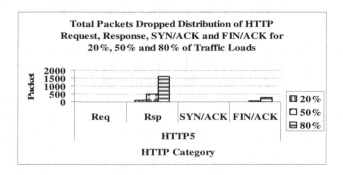

**Fig. 4.** Total packets dropped distribution for 20%, 50% and 80% of traffic loads

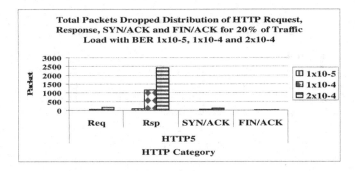

**Fig. 5.** Total packets dropped distribution for 20% of traffic load with Bit Error Rate (BER)

increment of BER in lower traffic load (20%) has cause larger number of packets to be dropped compared to the number of packet dropped in higher traffic load.

### 3.3 Average End-to-End Packet Delay

Unlike in the previous sections that describe QoS parameter based on per packet basis, this section and the following section discuss the QoS parameters based on average number of completed HTTP sessions,. The average end-to-end packet delay involves three main factors which are the propagation delay, queuing delay, and delay due to other traffic condition (e.g. link-loss with bit-error-rate). Table 3 already states the one-way propagation delay over LEO-Iridium satellites network from server node to its correspondence client node without taking into account the queuing delay. The propagation delay in satellites network may vary due to the handover process and various paths taken by the packets streams. For all error-free simulations (20%, 50% and 80% of traffic loads) in this paper, the additional factor due to other traffic condition could be neglected and the end-to-end delay only involves propagation delay and queuing delay. We estimate the average end-to-end delay ($D_{avg}$) using the following equation based on summation of session duration ($t_s$) per total received of HTTP request/response packets ($P_{s\text{-}tot}$) and then divided the value with the total number of completed HTTP sessions ($S_{tot}$) generated by HTTP5 client/server pair for the whole simulation time.

$$D_{avg} = \left[ \frac{\sum \frac{t_s}{P_{s\text{-}tot}}}{S_{tot}} \right] \qquad (9)$$

Based on Figure 6, as the traffic loads increase from 20% to 80%, the links become busy with traffic burst and the service time at each queue buffer become lower than the incoming traffic flows which eventually cause buffer to overflow. This has caused many packets need to be retransmitted to complete a session transfer. The session duration becomes higher in order to complete a HTTP request-response and as the result the average end-to-end delay becomes higher too in every HTTP session. In addition, many packets are dropped in higher traffic load due to Diffserv RED buffer

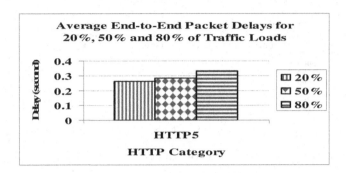

**Fig. 6.** Average end-to-end packet delays for 20%, 50% and 80% of traffic loads

early drop action which also cause many packets need to be retransmitted to complete a HTTP session. This Diffserv policy had severely punished greedy flows and eventually causes the increment of average end-to-end delay.

Figure 6 shows the average end-to-end packet delays ($D_{avg}$) for 20%, 50% and 80% of traffic loads are 0.2626 second, 0.2837 second and 0.3324 second respectively. Based on previous mentioned assumption that the delay due to other network condition (e.g. link-loss with bit-error-rate) could be neglected in all error-free simulations, we then estimate the average end-to-end queuing delay using the following formula:

$$D_q = D_{avg} - t_{tot-prop} \qquad (10)$$

Therefore, the average end-to-end queuing delays for 20%, 50% and 80% of traffic loads are 105.438ms, 126.538ms and 175.238ms respectively.

Figure 7 shows the average end-to-end packet delays for HTTP5 flows in 20% of traffic load with BER of $1\times10^{-5}$, $1\times10^{-4}$ and $2\times10^{-4}$. Based on the graph, the average end-to-end packet delay is proportionally increased with the increment of BER. The higher the BER, the longer time needed to send a packet from server node to client node or from client node to server node. This is mainly because many packets are dropped in higher BER and need to be retransmitted. Based on Figure 5, the average end-to-end delays ($D_{avg(BER)}$) with BER $1\times10^{-5}$, $1\times10^{-4}$ and $2\times10^{-4}$ are 0.2690 second, 0.3594 second and 0.5184 respectively.

The integration of random error-model to create some network scenario variations in all link-loss simulations has caused additional packet delay apart from the propagation delay ($t_{tot-prop}$) and queuing delay ($D_q$). Based on the delay parameters obtained previously, we then estimate the additional average end-to-end delay ($D_{add}$) due to the BER variation using the following formula:

$$D_{add} = D_{avg(BER)} - D_{q(20\%)} - t_{tot-prop} \qquad (11)$$

Therefore, the additional average end-to-end delays due to the network condition variation with BER of $1\times10^{-5}$, $1\times10^{-4}$ and $2\times10^{-4}$ are 6.4 ms, 96.8 ms and 255.8 ms respectively.

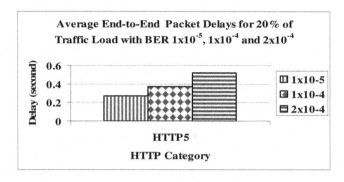

**Fig. 7.** Average end-to-end packet delays for 20% of traffic load with Bit Error Rate (BER)

## 3.4 Average HTTP Session Throughput

The instantaneous session throughput is measured in bit/s based on the amount of successfully received bit in each HTTP session divided by the session duration time. The instantaneous throughput is estimated by summing all the amount of successfully received HTTP Request and Response bits ($B_{tot}$) and then divided by the session duration time ($t_s$). The average session throughput ($T_{s\text{-}avg}$) is then estimated using equation (12) by summing all instantaneous session throughputs and divided by total number of completed HTTP session ($S_{tot}$). This section could be regarded as the conclusion of the previous sections because it shows the final results after taking into account the effect of all the QoS parameters mentioned previously.

Figure 8 shows the average HTTP5 session throughputs for 20%, 50% and 80% traffic loads. Indeed the variation of average session throughput is very much depending on the end-to-end delay and consequently the session duration. The longer the paths taken from source to destination, the longer would be the time needed to transmit a packet due to propagation delay and queuing delay at each node, and as the result the longer time needed to complete a HTTP session. In addition, the low PDR and high drop rate also contribute to the lower throughput in higher traffic load. The average session throughputs for 20%, 50% and 80% of traffic loads are 40.157 Kb/s, 37.75 Kb/s and 32.601 Kb/s respectively.

$$T_{s\text{-}avg} = \left[ \frac{\sum \frac{B_{s-tot}}{t_s}}{S_{tot}} \right] \tag{12}$$

Figure 9 shows the average session throughput for HTTP5 flows for 20% of traffic load in link-loss environment simulations. Based on the graph, the average session throughput is inversely proportional to the increment of BER. Based on the graph, the average session throughputs with BER of $1\times10^{-5}$, $1\times10^{-4}$ and $2\times10^{-4}$ are 39.099 Kb/s, 28.167 Kb/s and 21.188 Kb/s respectively. From those values, we found that the decrements of average session throughput are much higher in link-loss environment compared to the decrement of those values in higher traffic load. This mainly due to the high packets loss and high average session duration as the BER increased from $1\times10^{-5}$ to $2\times10^{-4}$.

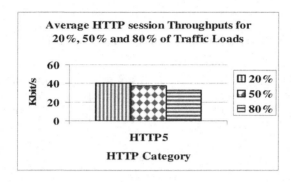

**Fig. 8.** Average HTTP session throughputs for 20%, 50% and 80% of traffic loads

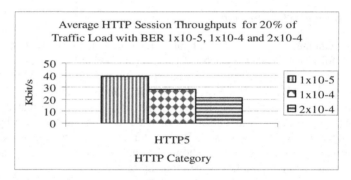

**Fig. 9.** Average HTTP session throughputs for 20% of traffic load with Bit Error Rate (BER)

## 4  Conclusion and Future Research

In this paper, we studied end-to-end QoS of IP-Diffserv over satellites network model in NS-2. The QoS simulation parameters are considered including packet delivery ratio (PDR), total packets dropped distribution, end-to-end packet delay and average session throughput. Network traffic involves many short session of web transmissions in both terrestrial and over LEO-Iridium satellites. In addition, the simulations involve error-free (20%, 50% and 80% of traffic loads) and link-loss (only 20% of traffic load with BER $1x10^{-5}$, $1x10^{-4}$ and $2x10^{-4}$) simulation environment. The results show that the end-to-end service quality is inversely proportional to the increment of both back-ground traffic load and BER. The higher the background traffic load and BER, the lower would be the service quality. Diffserv is just the mechanism to reduce those effects and preserve the end-to-end internet service quality and network performance.

As for the future research, some improvements can be done on both satellite and the Diffserv network system in order to provide better end-to-end QoS for satellite-terrestrial communications. As for the Diffserv network system, we suggest that it should be combined with traffic engineering mechanism like multi protocol label switching (MPLS) for fast switching and optimum packet routing. This will greatly reduce the buffering process delay at all Diffserv routers. However, this can be further improved by adding the adaptive admission control at the Diffserv ingress/egress routers for service differentiation and traffic flow management. The adaptive admission control mechanism will be based on periodic rate measurement information at every Diffserv routers which will then passed to the ingress/egress routers for further actions. Based on that information, the system must be able to provide alternative routing paths and efficient resource reservation for the traffic flows in case of network environment variation (e.g. link-loss, traffic load and etc). Meanwhile, the satellites network must be enhanced in the software part with on-board traffic flows processing and efficient buffer management.

# References

1. Nichols, K., Blake, S., Baker, F., Black, D.: Definition of the Differentiated Services Field (DS Field) in the IPv4 and IPv6 Headers. IETF Network Working Group, RFC 2474 (1998)
2. Blake, S., Black, D., Carlson, M., Davies, E., Wang, Z., Weiss, W.D.: An Architecture for Differentiated Services. IETF Network Working Group, RFC 2475 (1998)
3. Zhang, G., Mouftah, H.T.: End-to-End QoS guarantees over Diffserv Networks. In: 6th IEEE Symposium on Computer and Communications (2001)
4. Yang, J., Ye, J., Papavassiliou, S.: Enhancing End-to-End QoS Granularity in Diffserv Networks via Service Vector and Explicit Endpoint Admission Control. Journal of IEEE Communications Proceedings 151, 77–81 (2004)
5. Yang, J., Ye, J., Papavassiliou, S., Ansari, N.: Decoupling End-to-End QoS Provisioning at Routers in the Diffserv Network Model. In: IEEE Global Telecommunications Conference, GLOBECOM (2004)
6. Zhou, L., Pung, H.K., Ngoh, L.H.: A Cross-Domain Framework for Coordinated End-to-End QoS Adaptation. In: 33rd IEEE Conference on Local Computer Networks, LCN (2008)
7. Myounghwan, L., Copeland, J.A.: An Adaptive End-to-End Delay Assurance Algorithm with Diffserv Architecture in IEEE 902.11e/IEEE 802.16 Hybrid Mesh/Relay Networks. In: Proceeding of 18th International Conference on Computer Communications and Networks, ICCCN (2009)
8. Fall, K., Varadhan, K.: The NS Manual. University California, Berkeley (2008)
9. Pattan, B.: Satellite-Based Cellular Communication. McGraw-Hill, New York (1997)
10. Optical Carrier, http://en.wikipedia.org/wiki/Optical_carrier
11. Crovella, M.E., Bestavros, A.: Self-Similarity in World Wide Web traffic: Evidence and possible cause. IEEE/ACM Transaction on Networking 5, 835–846 (1996)
12. Sikdar, B., Kalyanaraman, S., Vastola, K.S.: An Integrated Model for the Latency and Steady-State Throughput of TCP Connections. Performance Evaluation 46, 139–154 (2001)
13. Makki, S., Pissinou, N., Daroux, P.: A New Routing Algorithm for Low Earth Orbit Satellite Networks. In: 10th International Conference on Computer Communications and Networks Proceedings (2001)

# A Cross-Layer Approach to Dynamic Bandwidth Allocation in Satellite Networks

Andrea Fiaschetti[*], Antonio Pietrabissa, and Laura Pimpinella

Department of Computer and Systems Science – University of Rome "La Sapienza"
Via Ariosto 25, 00185 Rome, Italy
Ph.: +39-347-0138146; Fax: +39-06-77274033
{fiaschetti,pietrabissa,pimpinella}@dis.uniroma1.it

**Abstract.** This work presents an innovative cross-layer approach to dynamic bandwidth allocation (BoD) in Satellite DVB-RCS networks. The algorithm is based on the assumption that, by managing the traffic at IP level through interaction with MAC level, a meaningful reduction in packet loss can be achieved, thus resulting in better resource exploitation. The proposed mechanism has been embedded in a consolidated control scheme for dynamic bandwidth allocation ([23], [1]). The interaction consists in the computation of the exact amount of MAC cells to send to the air interface during the next frame; based on this computation, the proper number of IP packets are segmented, transmitted to the MAC layer and queued in the MAC buffers. In this way, a twofold result is obtained: 1) no duplication of the scheduling function, scheduling can be performed at IP layer only, and 2) avoidance of overflows of MAC buffers. Simulations results, obtained by Opnet®, confirm the effectiveness of the proposed approach.

**Keywords:** Cross-layer, Bandwidth on demand, DVB-RCS Satellite Network.

## 1 Introduction

Traditional design paradigm in communication network, and all the more so in satellite networks, is based on the separation of different layers and the optimization of distinct parts, in order to reduce the complexity and the effort of the initial design; the interaction and interoperability among different layers and various equipments from diverse manufacturers will be obtained through the use of standardized interfaces. However in a complex system (such as a satellite network), there exists strict interdependence among layers, so the above mentioned design paradigm with tight modularity and layer independence may lead to sub-optimal or non-optimal performances and this means a non-efficient resources exploitation. The need of information exchange is evident if we consider, for example, the transport layer protocols, that require to take into account the problem of propagation delays, link impairments and bandwidth asymmetry; moreover if we consider that error correction schemes are implemented both at physical, link and (in some cases) transport layers, inefficiencies and redundancies given by a classic approach are immediate. In order to overcome these obstacles, it is necessary to explore a

---

[*] Corresponding author.

K. Sithamparanathan et al. (Eds.): PSATS 2010, LNICST 43, pp. 114–129, 2010.
© Institute for Computer Sciences, Social-Informatics and Telecommunications Engineering 2010

new design paradigm that propose innovative protocol architectures that violate the reference layered architecture, for example, by allowing direct communication between protocols at non-adjacent layers or sharing state variables between layers to obtain performance gains. This "violation" is known as "cross-layer design".

The cross layer approach described in this work continues a previous work ([23]) on Bandwidth on Demand procedure. The satellite control structure that computes the satellite terminal bandwidth request described in [23] hasn't got any control on packet flows from IP level to MAC level. We extend the work in [23] by introducing a disabling signal from MAC layer to IP layer, the so called "back-pressure signal", that prevent the transmission of packets to the MAC layer, if MAC buffer queues reach a defined threshold (congestion state). In this way, MAC layer functionality is kept as simple as possible: during the congestion, packet dropping (if needed) is performed at the IP layer; at the end of the congestion state, the IP level scheduler select the IP packets with the most stringent delay requirements.

The work is structured as follows: in Section 2, the problem of cross-layer as reported in literature is introduced, Sections 3 and 4 describe the system architecture and the BoD control scheme presented in [23], whereas section 5 describes the cross-layer mechanism and theoretical approach to compute the threshold level. The paper ends with a description of the system implementation and a discussion on simulation results.

## 2   Layers Interactions in Satellite Networks

According to recent studies carried out in [19], since satellite network scenario is moving towards a full IP integration, cross-layer is particularly significant to overcome some architectural problems. They are, for example, TCP erroneous inference of congestion state (the absence of an ACK is also due to wireless channel degradation); resources wasting while allocating bandwidth to users with very bad channel conditions; the necessity of intra and inter satellite handover and consequent rerouting that could bring to connection dropping; packet losses due to buffer overflows in real time streaming during congestion situations or particular bad wireless conditions.

In spite of this, it is worthwhile mentioning some recent works in literature to describe the progress reached in cross-layer design (in general) and in satellite networks (in particular). Most of them are related to scheduling techniques and design. For example in [3], the scheduling at the data link layer divides the traffic in two categories and applies a weighted policy mechanism to respect the QoS constraints, while at the physical layer users adapt their modulation and coding according to traffic conditions with the help of a perfect estimation of wireless channel conditions obtained by prediction-based algorithm.

In [20], QoS guarantees for CDMA networks are provided by means of cross-layer optimization across the physical and network layer. At the physical layer, the QoS requirements are specified in terms of a target signal-to-interference ratio (SIR) requirement, and optimal target powers are dynamically adjusted according to the current number of users in the system. At the network layer, both the blocking probabilities as well as call connection delay constraints are considered.

A packet scheduling algorithm in satellite digital multimedia broadcasting system is developed in [8], namely "combined delay and rate differentiation" (CDRC); this algorithm takes into account QoS parameters to prioritise different contents among different services in a dynamic environment. Moreover, in [9] the application and transport layers exchange information about QoS requirements together with MAC layer that adapts its packet scheduling decision in order to achieve QoS targets, while respecting the power constraints given by the lower layers.

In [10], an innovative allocation algorithm is presented, based on cross-layer interaction between TCP and MAC layers; it aims at synchronizing the requests of resources with the TCP transmission window trend, thus reducing delays and increasing air interface utilization; this is also the case of [11], where a new technique called "ACK compaction" is discussed to overcome the physical delay problems that leads to a sub-optimal behaviour of TCP protocol.

In [12] two different methodologies are presented: a reservation-based medium access control scheme, which uses cross-layer interaction with the physical layer to measure channel condition and predict performances through a Markov chain formulation (dynamic cross-layer), and a Neyman-Pearson MAC design optimization (static cross-layer). These two techniques, coupled to physical measures, aim at predicting optimal decision for traffic management.

The innovation proposed in this paper consists in the introduction of a cross-layer mechanism between MAC layer and IP layer, aiming at reducing expensive packet losses in the air interface; this interaction is obtained by means of a control signal that enable-disable the packet flow from IP to MAC level, according to congestion conditions.

## 3  System Architecture and Control Scheme

The Scenario considered in this work (see Fig. 1) consists of a DVB-RCS (ETSI 2003) geostationary satellite network with on board switching capabilities, Satellite Terminals (STs) provide Local Area Network with the access to the network, Gateways (GW) connect the satellite network to the core network (i.e. to the Internet) and a Network Control Centre located on earth that manages the satellite network resources. The NCC is in charge to prevent collisions between packets transmitted by different STs through a dynamic bandwidth assignment procedure. Each ST computes the bandwidth request and sends it to the NCC; after a period of latency, the NCC communicates the bandwidth assigned to the STs. Due to the latency of the satellite network, the traffic is being divided into two main classes: high-priority service class and low-priority service class.

The high-priority service classes require a static bandwidth assignment, due to the excessive latency of the BoD request assignment cycle. In the case of low priority classes it is possible to assign the bandwidth in a dynamic way.

The corresponding network model is depicted in Fig. 2. In DVB-RCS satellite networks, each ST has a periodic opportunity to send bandwidth requests; thus, the network model is a discrete-time system with sampling time $T_C$ equal to the time period between two consecutive bandwidth requests (*control time*).

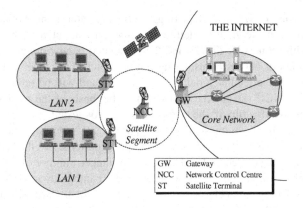

**Fig. 1.** Satellite reference scenario

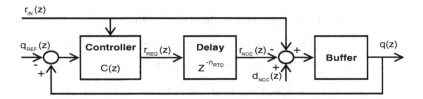

**Fig. 2.** Control scheme of the Satellite Network Model

The system model consists of 4 elements:

- **Source Traffic.** It is the traffic received by each ST during the *kth* time interval and it is modeled by an input bit rate, $r_{IN}(k)$, which is non-negative and limited by a maximum rate, $r_{MAX}$ :

$$0 \le r_{IN}(k) \le r_{MAX} \tag{1}$$

- **ST MAC Buffer.** It collects the MAC cells waiting for transmission in the uplink and it is modeled by an integrator. Let $q(k)$ denote the queue length in this buffer at time $t = kT_C$: the variation of $q(k)$ is given by the input rate $r_{IN}(k)$ minus the transmission rate assigned by the NCC, $r_{NCC}[k]$. The following equations hold:

$$q'(k) = q(k-1) + T_C \cdot r_{IN}(k) - T_C \cdot r_{NCC}(k-1) \tag{2}$$

$$q(k) = \sigma(q'(k)) \tag{3}$$

where $\sigma(x)$ is a saturation function such that $\sigma(x) = x$ if $x \ge 0$, $\sigma(x) = 0$ otherwise.

- *Satellite Network Delay and NCC.* In geostationary satellite networks, the STs and the NCC communicate via the satellite; the time interval between the transmissions of a bandwidth request by the ST and the associated bandwidth allocation is fixed and equal to about 600ms (considering physical and MAC layer delays). This interval constitutes the feedback delay of the system and will be referred to as *round trip delay*. The NCC assigns the bandwidth on the basis of the requests and of the available link bandwidth: if the network is not congested, the assigned bit rate $r_{NCC}(k)$ is equal to the requested one: $r_{NCC}(k)=r_{REQ}(k - n_{RTD})$, where $n_{RTD}$ is the *round trip delay* expressed in number of sampling periods. For the sake of simplicity, in this paper $n_{RTD}$ is considered equal to an integer number of $T_C$[1]. Conversely, if the network is congested, the NCC assigns less bandwidth according to a predefined fairness policy: $r_{NCC}(k) < r_{REQ}(k - n_{RTD})$. Thus, the transmission delay and the NCC can be modeled as a delay block cascaded to an additive disturbance $d_{NCC}(k)$, defined as follows:

$$d_{NCC}(k) = r_{REQ}(k - n_{RTD}) - r_{NCC}(k) \qquad (4)$$

The use of the additive disturbance models the state of the network as follows:

$$\begin{cases} d_{NCC}(k) = 0 & \text{if the network is not congested} \\ d_{NCC}(k) > 0 & \text{if the network is congested} \end{cases} \qquad (5)$$

To compute the unused assigned bandwidth, has been introduced the wasted rate parameter, defined as follows:

$$r_w(k) = \sigma(-\frac{q'(k)}{T_c}) \qquad (6)$$

Thus, $r_w(k)$ is null if the link utilization is achieved and positive otherwise.

With reference to the developed model, the targets of the BoD protocol can be expressed as follows:

1. The *wasted bit rate* should be null, i.e., $r_W(k) = 0$, which means that bandwidth is not wasted (*Full Link Utilization*).
2. When no congestion is occurring, $q(k)$ should be as small as possible.
3. In case of congestion, $q(k)$ grows regardless of the request policy; the objective, in this case, is that the system should recover the normal behavior when the congestion ends (*congestion recovery*).

- *BoD Controller.* The BoD Controller $C(z)$ is situated in the ST and it computes the rate requested based on the input rate fed the network and on the MAC buffer measurement.

---

[1] Generally, this is not true and $n_{RTD}=n+ \varepsilon$, where $n$ is an integer number and $\varepsilon$ is a real number between 0 and 1; in this case, the generic quantity $x(k - n_{RTD})$ is computed as follows: $x(k - n_{RTD}) = (1-\varepsilon) \cdot x(k-n) + \varepsilon \cdot x(k-n-1)$.

## 4  Dynamic Capacity Assignment

The structure of the BoD scheme was already presented in [21], and is detailed in Fig. 3: the bandwidth requests $r_{REQ}(k)$ is computed as the sum of two parts: rate-based and queue-based:

$$
\begin{aligned}
r_{REQ}(k) &= r_{IN}(k) + r_Q(k) = \\
&= r_{IN}(k) + Z^{-1}\{K(z)[q_{REF}(z) - q(z)]\}
\end{aligned}
\tag{7}
$$

The expression of the queue based part is given by:

$$
r_Q(k) = \frac{1}{T_C}\left( q(k) - q_{REF}(k) - T_C \sum_{i=1}^{n_{RTD}} r_Q(k-i) \right)
\tag{8}
$$

Where $q_{REF}(k)$ is given by:

$$
q_{REF}(k) = T_C \sum_{i=0}^{T_{RTD}} r_{IN}(k-i)
\tag{9}
$$

In [23] and [22], a parameter $\alpha \in [0, 1]$ is introduced to regulate the 'aggressiveness' of the request policy. In particular, the reference queue is computed as follows:

$$
q_{REF}(k) = \alpha T_C \sum_{i=0}^{T_{RTD}} r_{IN}(k-i)
\tag{10}
$$

and, consequently, the request is computed as follows:

$$
r_{REQ}(k) = \left( \frac{1}{T_C} q(k) - \sum_{i=1}^{n_{RTD}} r_{REQ}(k-i) + (1-\alpha)\sum_{i=0}^{n_{RTD}} r_{IN}(k-i) \right)
\tag{11}
$$

By setting $\alpha = 1$, the same request policy of [21] is obtained, guaranteeing the full link utilization; by decreasing the value of $\alpha$, a more aggressive request policy is obtained, which achieves lower queuing delays at the price of some bandwidth waste.

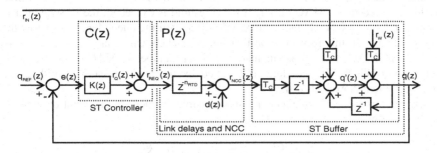

**Fig. 3.** System reference scheme

Finally, in [23], a Multi Model Reference Control approach has been chosen to set dynamically the value of $\alpha$, in order to achieve the full link utilization when the network is congested (and thus the bandwidth is a precious resource which must not be wasted), and favor better performance in terms of queuing delays (by lowering $\alpha$) as the network load decreases.

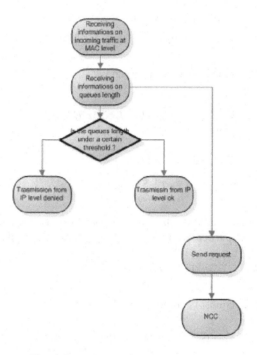

**Fig. 4.** Back Pressure Functional Diagram

The proposed back-pressure algorithm is based on the request computed according to the BoD algorithm of equation (9'''). The objective is to compute the dynamic threshold value $q^*(k)$ which represents the maximum number of MAX cells which should be stored in the MAC buffer. If the threshold is exceeded, the IP scheduler is blocked, and no MAC cell enters the MAC buffer until the queue length is below the threshold again (in this respect, note that the IP packets which are transmitted from the IP to the MAC layer are segmented in a given number of MAC cells; thus, it is likely that, when the IP scheduler is blocked by the back pressure-algorithm, the MAC queue length exceeds $q^*(k)$).

At time $k$, from (1), (2), (3) and (11) it is possible to calculate the worst-case queue length as follows:

$$\hat{q}(k+1) = T_C r_{\max} + T_C \sum_{i=1}^{n_{RTD}} r_{REQ}(k-i) + (1-\alpha)T_C \sum_{i=1}^{n_{RTD}} r_{IN}(k-i) \qquad (12)$$

where $n_{RTD}$ is the number of control time in a round trip delay. This queue length is achieved if the MAC buffer is fed with the maximum allowed rate $r_{MAX}$, during the current round tripe time and represent the maximum amount of packet that could be sent to the air interface.

For comparison purposes, we also developed a 'static' approach, which computes a fixed threshold. This static approach is also more easily implemented, since it does not require measures of the MAC cells entering the MAC buffer. The static threshold is straightforwardly computed from the control system equations via theoretical considerations. Control system theory, which was used to develop the BoD algorithm, provides the Final Value Theorem, which states that the stationary value achieved by the system can be computed as follows:

$$\lim_{t \to \infty} y(t) = \lim_{z \to 1} \left[ (z-1)y(z) \right] \tag{13}$$

where $y(t)$ is the system output and $y(z)$ is its Z-tranform.

In our system, the output is the queue length $q(k)$, the input is the reference queue length $q_{REF}(k)$ given by equation (10); the transfer function between $q_{REF}(k)$ and $q(k)$ is immediate (see [23] for detailed demonstration):

The static threshold is then calculated in the worst-case (i.e., for $\alpha = 1$) as in the following equation:

$$\lim_{z \to 1} \frac{r_{max}}{1-z} \left\{ \frac{q(z)}{r_{IN}(z)} + \frac{q(z)}{q_{ref}(z)} \frac{q_{ref}(z)}{r_{IN}(z)} \right\} = (1 + n_{RTD})T_c r_{max} \tag{14}$$

where $r_{IN}(t)$ is set equal to the maximum rate available for on-demand traffic $r_{MAX}$. Note that equation (14) is also obtained by computing the worst-case dynamic threshold, i.e., by computing eq. (15) with $\alpha = 1$ and by considering that the request was the maximum allowed during the last round trip delay, i.e., $r_{REQ}(k - i) = r_{MAX}$, $i = 1,\ldots,n_{RTD}$:

$$q_{MAX}^{*}(k+1;\alpha = 1) = T_C r_{MAX} + T_C \sum_{i=0}^{n_{RTD}} r_{MAX} = T_C(1 + n_{RTD})r_{MAX} \tag{15}$$

## 5   System Implementation

The simulations of the proposed approach were developed using the OPNET® Modeler 11.5A PL3 (Build 3408) tool by OPNET® Technologies.

The implementation of the thresholds computed via the control theory has been implemented in the Scheduler module at IP level and in the DAMA_Agent module at MAC Level (Fig. 5).

The DAMA Agent is in charge of measuring the queue size at MAC level and of comparing this value to a threshold. Every $T_C=96ms$ time interval the DAMA Agent computes the gap between the threshold and the real value of the MAC queues size and sends it with a proper signaling message to the scheduler. The scheduler receives the message and extracts the value of the threshold. Then, it is in charge of sending to the lower layer the proper amount of bits (to avoid the overflow of the MAC queues). When congestion occurs, the DAMA Agent computes a negative value of the bit to send from the IP level to the MAC level so a disabling signal is generated and the transmission is denied.

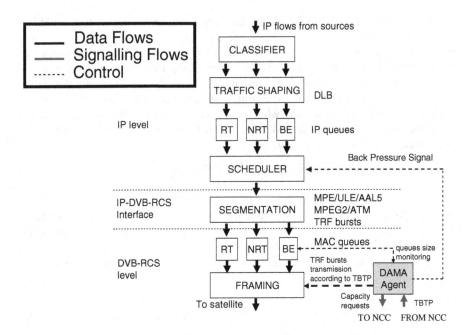

**Fig. 5.** Satellite Terminal system architecture

## 6   Simulation Results

Two simulation sets has been performed:

Simulation Set A )    The system runs under no threshold at MAC level;
Simulation Set B )    The system runs under a back-pressure algorithm;
The simulation parameters are shown in the following tables.

**Table 1.** Simulation Parameters: High Priority Traffic

|  | Voice | Video |
|---|---|---|
| Interarrival Time [s] | Constant (0.02) | Uniform (0.008, 0.01) |
| Packet Size [bits] | Constant (1280) | Normal (1150, 450) |

**Table 2.** Simulation Parameters: Low Priority Traffic

|  | Multimedia Streaming | Data |
|---|---|---|
| Interarrival Time [s] | Uniform (0.0005, 0.00265) | Exponential (0.2) |
| Packet Size [bits] | Poisson (10800) | Pareto (6000, 1.5) |

**Table 3.** Opnet simulation parameters

| Simulation # | 3 |
|---|---|
| Simulation Length [sec] | 450 |
| Terminal Satellite (STs) | 7 |
| Estimated Load [Mbit] | 45 |
| Sampling Time [msec] | 0.069632 |

**Table 4.** Simulation parameters high priority traffic

| | Max Delay |
|---|---|
| High priority Traffic [s] | 0.15 |
| Low priority Traffic [s] | 2 |
| Best Effort Traffic [s] | 5 |

## 6.1 Simulation Set A

The first simulation set shows the results obtained when no threshold is computed. The result shows that the MAC queuing delay reaches the maximum tolerated delays for both high- and low-priority MAC queues, entailing MAC layer cell dropping.

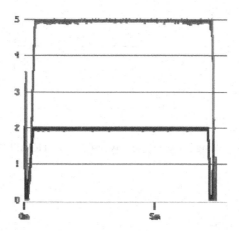

**Fig. 6.** Best Effort (black line) and Low priority (grey line) MAC Queuing delay

## 6.2 Simulation Set B

The second simulation set evaluates the performance in terms of delay for both the static and dynamic threshold approaches. With a static approach the number of packet losses at MAC level is reduced with respect to the original control scheme, because only the exact amount of packet is sent to the lower layer and can be transmitted; however the delay is still considerable and almost constant (the threshold is static!).

By using a dynamic approach the system is able to adapt to traffic condition thus minimizing better the delay of packets waiting in the MAC queues and reducing as well the packet losses.

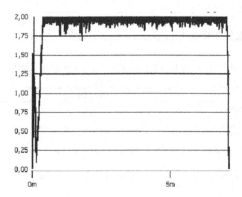

**Fig. 7.** IP queuing delay high priority traffic (STATIC APPROACH)

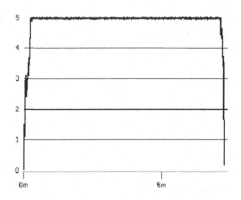

**Fig. 8.** IP queuing delay low priority traffic (STATIC APPROACH)

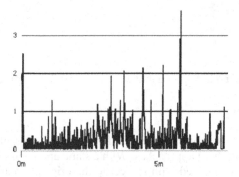

**Fig. 9.** MAC Queuing Delay Best Effort Traffic (STATIC APPROACH)

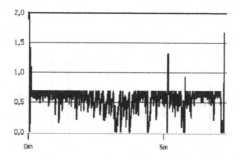

**Fig. 10.** MAC Queuing Delay Non Real Time Traffic (STATIC APPROACH)

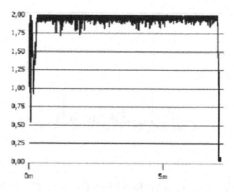

**Fig. 11. IP** Queuing delay Non Real Time (DYNAMIC APPROACH)

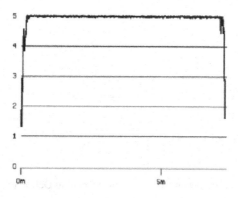

**Fig. 12.** Queuing delay Best Effort (DYNAMIC APPROACH)

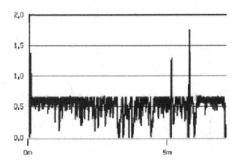

**Fig. 13.** MAC Queuing delay Non Real Time (DYNAMIC APPROACH)

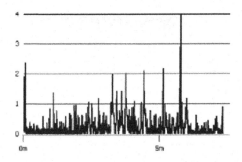

**Fig. 14.** MAC Queuing delay Best Effort (DYNAMIC APPROACH)

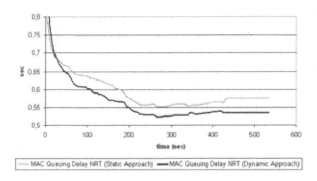

**Fig. 15.** Non Real Time MAC Average Queuing Delay comparisons

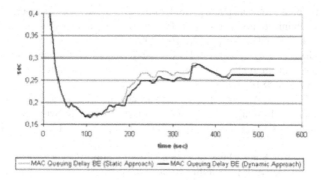

**Fig. 16.** Best Effort MAC Average Queuing delay comparisons

## 7  Conclusions

The proposed approach is built on the problem of cross-layer control between IP and MAC level. By computing a threshold that sets the maximum value that MAC queues can reach, it is possible to stop the traffic flow from IP to MAC level in congestion states. Both a worst-case static and a dynamic threshold were theoretically computed based on the control theoretical BoD scheme proposed in [22].

Summarizing the chosen approach meets the following targets:

- it avoids the duplication of the scheduling and dropping functionalities at the IP and MAC layers;
- It avoids MAC buffer overflows and consequent MAC cells dropping, which would result in partial transmissions of IP packets;
- when a congestion state occurs, packets are accumulated in the IP queues and not in the MAC queues, so that, in case of need, packets are dropped at IP layer; as the congestion ends, the IP scheduler is able to use all its discrimination capability by selecting the IP packets with the most stringent delay requirements.

## References

[1] Pimpinella, L., Fiaschetti, A., Pietrabissa, A.: Dynamic Bandwidth Allocation in Satellite Networks. In: Proceedings of IEEE European Conference on Control (August 2009)

[2] Kota, S.L.: Broadband satellite networks: trends and challenges. In: IEEE Conference on Wireless Communications and Networking, 2005, March 13-17, vol. 3, pp. 1472–1478 (2005)

[3] Sali, A., Widiawan, A., Thilakawardana, S., Tafazolli, R., Evans, B.G.: Cross-Layer Design Approach for Multicast Scheduling over Satellite Networks. In: 2nd International Symposium on Wireless Communication Systems, 2005, September 5-7, pp. 701–705 (2005)

[4] Ibnkahla, M., et al.: speed satellite mobile communications: technologies and challenges. Proceedings of the IEEE 92(2), 312–339 (2004)

[5] Sunheui, R., et al.: Rate adaptation with hybrid ARQ based on cross layer information for satellite communication systems. In: IEEE International Symposium on Consumer Electronics, 2004, September 1-3, pp. 165–168 (2004)

[6] Kota, S., Giambene, G., Candio, N.L.: Cross-layer approach for an air interface of GEO satellite communication networks. International Journal of Satellite Communications and Networking 25(5), 481–499 (2007)

[7] Giambene, G., et al.: Access Schemes and Packet Scheduling Techniques. In: Giambene, G. (ed.) Adaptive Resource Management and Optimization in Satellite Networks: Optimization and Cross-Layer Design, April 2007, ch. 15, pp. 119–175. Springer, Heidelberg (2007)

[8] Du, H., et al.: Combined Delay and Rate Differentiation Packet Scheduling for Multimedia Content Delivery in Satellite Broadcast/Multicast Systems. To be published in Proceedings of IEEE International Conference on Communications, 2007, June 24-28 (2007)

[9] Du, H., et al.: Cross-Layer Packet Scheduling for Multimedia Data Delivery in Broadcast/Multicast Satellite Systems. In: Proceedings of AIAA 25th International Conference on Communications Satellite Systems Conference, 2007, pp. 10–13 (April 2007)

[10] Chini, P., et al.: Dynamic Resource Allocation based on a TCP-MAC Cross-Layer Approach for Interactive Satellite Networks. In: 2nd International Symposium on Wireless Communication Systems, 2005, September 5-7, pp. 657–661 (2005)

[11] Fairhurst, G., et al.: Performance issues in asymmetric TCP service provision using broadband satellite Communications. Proceedings of the IEE 2001 148(2), 95–99 (2001)

[12] Maharshi, A., Lang, T., Swami, A.: Cross-layer designs of multichannel reservation MAC under Rayleigh fading. IEEE Transactions on Signal Processing 2003 51(8), 2054–2067 (2003)

[13] Srivastava, V., Motani, M.: Cross-layer design: a survey and the road ahead. IEEE Communications Magazine 43(12), 112–119 (2005)

[14] Shakkottai, S., Rappaport, T.S., Karlsson, P.C.: Cross-layer design for wireless networks. IEEE Communications Magazine 41(10), 74–80 (2003)

[15] Tse, D.: Forward Link Multiuser Diversity through Proportional Fair Scheduling. Presentation at Bell Labs (August 1999)

[16] Wang, Y., et al.: Protocol Design and Optimization for Delay/Fault-Tolerant Mobile Sensor Networks. In: 27th International Conference on Distributed Computing Systems, p. 7 (2007)

[17] Lang, T., Naware, V., Venkitasubramaniam, P.: Signal processing in random access. IEEE Signal Processing Magazine 21(5), 29–39 (2004)

[18] Wang, Q., Abu-Rgheff, M.A.: Cross-layer signalling for next-generation wireless systems. In: IEEE Conference on Wireless Communications and Networking, March 2003, vol. 2, pp. 1084–1089 (2003)

[19] Giambene, G., Kota, S.: Cross-layer protocol optimization for satellite communications networks: a survey. International Journal of Satellite Communications and Networking 24(5), 323–341 (2006)

[20] Comaniciu, C., Poor, H.V.: Jointly optimal power and admission control for delay sensitive traffic in CDMA networks with LMMSE receivers. IEEE Transaction on Signal Processing 51(8), 2031–2042 (2003)

[21] Delli Priscoli, F., Pietrabissa, A.: Design of a bandwidth-on-demand (BoD) protocol for satellite networks modeled as time-delay systems. Automatica, International Federation of Automatic Control 40(5), 729–741 (2004), doi:10.1016/j.automatica.2003.12.013

[22] Pietrabissa, A., Inzerilli, T., Alphand, O., Berthou, P., Mazzella, M., Fromentin, E., Gayraud, T., Lucas, F.: Validation of a QoS Architecture for DVB/RCS Satellite Networks via a Hardware Demonstration Platform. Computer Networks 49(6), 797–815 (2005), doi:10.1016/j.comnet.2005.01.018

[23] Pietrabissa, A.: A Multi-Model Reference Control Approach for Bandwidth-on-Demand in Satellite Networks. Control Engineering Practice, International Federation of Automatic Control 16(7), 847–860 (2008), doi:10.1016/j.conengprac.2007.10.001

# End-to-End QoS Measurement over a DVB-RCS Satellite Network

M. Ali[1], L. Liang[1], Z. Sun[1], H. Cruickshank[1], P. Thompson[1], L.M. Audah[1],
T. Bouquentar[2], and N. Alagha[2]

[1] CCSR, University of Surrey, Guildford, Surrey, GU2 7XH, UK
{m.ali,l.liang,z.sun,h.cruickshank,p.thompson,l.audah}@surrey.ac.uk
[2] European Space Agency, Netherlands
{tajani.bouqentar,nader.alagha}@esa.int

**Abstract.** Satellites play an important role in the future network due to their wide area coverage and for providing connectivity in remote regions of the world. This paper presents the end-to-end quality of service (QoS) measurements taken employing a European Space Agency (ESA) testbed over DVB-RCS infrastructure, in collaboration with University of Surrey, UK.

The applications chosen for these experiments are file transfer (FTP), web browsing (HTTP) and video streaming. File transfer and web browsing require reliable transport mechanism as a corrupted bit will hinder the intact data delivery. Therefore, these applications use transmission control protocol (TCP) as the transport protocol. TCP involves a three way handshake, which introduces extra delay during data transfer. Video streaming is a real time application. It is time-sensitive and requires lesser reliability compared to FTP and Web services. Hence, it employs user datagram protocol (UDP) at the transport layer, which do not offer any guarantee of reliable data delivery but timely. The parameters that have been used to evaluate quality of service (QoS) are packet delivery time, file download time, round trip delay, packet sizes and packet loss.

The paper presented measurement results and comparative analysis of the QoS of the applications over the DVB-RCS testbed.

**Keywords:** QoS, DVB-RCS, Satellite network.

## 1 Introduction

Satellite systems are integrated with the global information infrastructure as one of the major technologies providing both television broadcast services and Internet access. These systems are supporting the same Internet applications, services, and protocols as the terrestrial networks. Standards for satellite systems are required to be optimized for Internet access. Open standards have proven their merit in improving the telecommunications commercial market. In urban areas, Internet access is available via terrestrial networks, whereas, infrastructure deprived rural areas rely on wireless connectivity for this facility [8]. It takes a

K. Sithamparanathan et al. (Eds.): PSATS 2010, LNICST 43, pp. 130–144, 2010.
© Institute for Computer Sciences, Social-Informatics and Telecommunications Engineering 2010

long time to develop terrestrial networks to these rural areas. So, satellites can offer Internet access to such remote regions.

Satellites are characterized by their long propagation delay; hence, quality of service (QoS) needs to be handled correctly in these networks. In this paper, we are presenting the end-to-end QoS measurements taken in digital video broadcast-return channel via satellite (DVB-RCS) environment. The applications to be tested are file transfer (FTP), web browsing (HTTP) and video streaming and these applications will be used for the underlying services when taking measurements. The different QoS parameters considered are packet delivery time, file download time, round trip delay, packet size and packet loss.

This paper is divided into the following sections: Section 2 is an overview of DVB-RCS standard; Section 3 is a description of the ESA testbed used to perform the experiments; Section 4 describes the different applications used to perform the tests; the performance metrics are briefly reviewed in Section 5; the results have been analyzed in Section 6; and finally, Section 7 concludes the paper.

## 2    DVB-RCS Standard

The DVB Project (digital video broadcasting, DVB) started the development of a system for digital television broadcasting via satellite (DVB-S) [3] in 1992 and finalized the specification in 1993 [9]. Since then, the DVB-S has become the preferred format for satellite broadcasting worldwide. Initially, to support Internet services for DVB-S, the return channel used terrestrial networks. The emergence of digital video broadcast-return channel via satellite (DVB-RCS) [4] transformed the one-way DVB-S system into an interactive system and eliminated cables in the return path for Internet. The second generation of the DVB-S standard (DVB-S2) was finalized in 2006 with a considerable improvement in power and bandwidth efficiency. The DVB-S2 standard also allowed for Adaptive Coding and Modulation for interactive services with a significant gain in the overall system capacity and reduction of link margin.

The DVB-RCS standard was developed in 1997 and finally accepted as a European Telecommunications Standards Institute (ETSI) specification in March 2000. In September 2001, the guideline document was published. Early trial products were tested in 2000-2002, and the systems started getting stable, mature and widely acceptable during 2002. Satellite standardization organizations, operators, and manufacturers have made great progress over the last years to achieve a viable solution for interactive services via satellite [8].

In the forward link, DVB-RCS is based on the DVB-S and DVB-S2 standards. It employs time-division multiplexing at a data rate up to tens of megabits per second. In order to provide Internet access and interactivity, it uses the existing moving pictures expert group-2 (MPEG-2) transport stream to encapsulate IP packets. This encapsulation is performed according to the DVB specification. The return link in DVB-RCS employs a multiple-frequency time-division multiple-access (MF-TDMA) scheme. It allows a group of terminals to communicate using a set of carrier frequencies, each of which is divided into time slots.

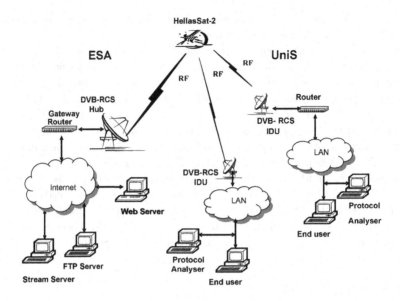

**Fig. 1.** ESA Testbed

The allocation mechanism is based on the statistical multiplexing principle, to utilize the satellite bandwidth optimally. This allocation is managed from the network control centre (NCC) at the gateway. The NCC is responsible for synchronization of the system, via the network clock reference (NCR). It transmits a number of specific system tables in order to update the terminals about issues related to quality of service (QoS), service level agreement (SLA), bandwidth allocation, etc.

## 3    The ESA DVB-RCS Testbed

A DVB-RCS testbed at the European Space Agency (ESA) is used for this end-to-end QoS measurement. As shown in Figure 1, the testbed consists of a gateway and two satellite terminals. The satellite capacity used in these experiments is provided by HellasSat-2 satellite. The available uplink bandwidth is 512 kbps and for downlink, it is 4 Mbps. Various applications and servers are installed on the local area networks (LAN) connected to the gateway and the terminals.

The testbed deploys performance enhancing proxies (PEP) to improve the performance of TCP based traffic. TCP deduces congestion in the network from delay and loss. Due to the long propagation delay in satellites, it takes a long time for TCP to increase its transmission rate and maintain a good throughput. PEPs split a single TCP connection into multiple connections. Splitting the connection allows to maneuver with different parts of the connection according to the condition of the satellite link [5].

# 4   Applications for Experimentation

Different applications that are tested on the testbed are described in the following subsections. The details of these applications are available in their corresponding standards, but an overview is necessary to understand the results. The softwares installed on the clients and servers are also described.

## 4.1   File Transfer

File Transfer Protocol (FTP) is a method of downloading files from and uploading files to another system using TCP over a network. It operates in a client/server paradigm. FTP uses two separate connections to send files. One TCP connection is used to send control messages, such as user identification, password, etc., and the other is used to send data. As FTP sends the control messages separately, so it is referred as an out-of-band protocol. There are a number of commands used in FTP for managing the sessions. The commands, from client to server, and replies, from server to client, are sent across the control connection in 7-bit ASCII format. Thus, these commands are human readable. Each command consists of four uppercase ASCII characters, some with optional arguments. Some of the more common commands are listed below:

- USER username: Used to send the user identification to the server
- PASS password: Used to send the user password to the server
- LIST: List all the files in the current directory in the server
- RETR filename: Used to retrieve (i.e., get) a file from the current directory of the server
- STOR filename: Used to store (i.e., put) a file in the current directory of the server

Each of these commands is followed by a reply from the server. The replies are three-digit numbers, with an optional message following the number. Some typical replies, along with their possible messages, are listed below:

- 331 Username OK, password required
- 230 User logged in, proceed
- 200 Command OK
- 125 Data connection already open; transfer starting
- 150 File status OK; about to open data connection
- 226 Transfer complete
- 221 Goodbye

A client utility (ftp) invokes the file transfer. In addition to the original ftp utility, there are many textual and graphical FTP client programs, including most browsers, which run under different operating systems. We used ftp as the client program for the end-to-end QoS measurements. There are also many FTP server programs. One of the available servers included in Linux is Very Secure FTP daemon (vsftpd) package.

## 4.2   Web Browsing

Web browsing is based on the HyperText Transfer Protocol (HTTP). It also works in a client/server model. The client and server programs exchange HTTP messages to transfer web content. The client program is the browser that opens the Web pages and offers other features like playing audio and video, upload-ing and downloading files, filling forms, etc. Popular Web browsers are Firefox, Netscape, lynx and Internet Explorer. On the server side, the Web server, houses the web content. HTTP uses TCP as the transport protocol. One of the world-wide deployed, Linux based Web server is Apache. In its latest versions, if support for IPv6 is available in the operating system, its IPv6 listening sockets open by default [6].

Like file transfer, HTTP also exchanges request and response messages. The typical methods and their purpose in a request message are as follows:

- GET: Request an object from the server
- POST: Filling form on a web page
- HEAD: Similar to GET used for debugging

The majority of the HTTP request messages use the GET method to retrieve objects from web servers during browsing. In the HTTP response messages, the replies are identified by the status code. Some of the commonly used status codes are listed below:

- 200 OK: Request succeeded and the information is returned in the response
- 301 Moved Permanently: Requested object has been moved permanently
- 400 Bad Request: The request could not be understood by the server
- 404 Not Found: The requested document does not exist on this server

## 4.3   Video Streaming

In this class of applications, clients request on-demand compressed video files that are stored on servers. A client typically begins playout of the video a few seconds after it begins receiving the file from the server. The client will be playing out video from one location in the file while it is receiving later parts of the file from the server. Both TCP and UDP are used in video streaming.

For the purpose of our test, VLC media player [1] is used. It is a lightweight media player that can play numerous video formats. It is supported by Windows, Linux and PocketPC/WinCE handhelds. It can also be used as a streaming server.

## 5   Performance Metrics

The performance of different applications described, is measured, using the ESA DVB-RCS testbed. Wireshark [2], formerly known as Ethereal, a packet analyzer is used to capture packets at the client and server to measure and calculate different performance metrics. The end-to-end QoS parameters measured are described in the following subsections.

## 5.1  Delay

Delay is the transit time between the client and the server observed by the packets. In satellite networks, this time is dominated by the propagation delay. The processing time for the encapsulation of IP packet in MPEG stream also adds to the overall delay. In addition to this, other factors adding to the delay are router queues and number of hops in the path. A simple way to calculate the delay is to synchronize the client and the server and calculate the time difference. One way for synchronization is to use Network Time Protocol (NTP) server [7].

## 5.2  Jitter

Jitter is the variation in delay of consecutive packets. It is due to the variable time elapsed in the queues of the routers in the path. Packet time-stamps are used to measure jitter. The delay experienced in router queue is dependent on the scheduling policy of the router and the congestion in the network. In satellite networks, devices like modem, the modulator in the hub and the IP encapsulator also introduce jitter. Another similar parameter dependent on time-stamps is packet inter-arrival time.

## 5.3  Packet Size

Packet size affects different applications. Larger packets experience more packet loss and delay as compared to smaller packets. Smaller packets are vulnerable to higher jitter in contrast with larger ones.

## 5.4  Packet Loss

Packet loss occurs due to network congestion and buffer overflow at routers. In satellites, it is due to the wireless nature of the transmission link. In satellite networks, it could be due to weather conditions, improper line up, interference, etc. It can be reduced by retransmission or error recovery mechanisms. Some applications cannot tolerate packet loss beyond a certain threshold.

# 6  Results and Analysis

The experiments have been performed for different applications as mentioned earlier. These applications are analyzed in the following subsections.

## 6.1  File Transfer

For analysis of file transfer using file transfer protocol (FTP), two files of different sizes have been chosen to compare the results. One file is 500 kilobytes and the second is 50 megabytes. These files have been uploaded (via put command) from client (Surrey) to server (ESA) and downloaded (via get command) in the reverse direction.

The round trip time (RTT) for the control commands for these operations is tabulated in Table 1. The RTT ranges from 550-700 milliseconds, which is the typical range for a geostationary satellite. The RTT values in the second row of Table 1 are higher as these values include the password typing time from the user. The upload time of the files is 10 times the download time because of the difference in the uplink and downlink data rates offered by the satellite network. The transfer rate in downloading is high than uploading due to the high bandwidth available on the downlink.

The role of performance enhancing proxies (PEP) deployed in the satellite network can be depicted from the histograms shown in Figure 2 and 3. These histograms have been generated from the FTP data being uploaded/downloaded and the acknowledgements being received from the PEP rather than from the recipient. As very few packets are exchanged while downloading the 500 KB file, hence, the density of packets is very low than during upload, resulting in a different shape of histogram. Similarly, less packet exchange can be depicted from the vertical scale of the figures during download of the 50 MB file, as compared with the upload.

The IP packet length of different packets during the upload and download is shown in Figure 4 and Figure 5, respectively. The packets on the right side show the packets depicting the FTP data and the packets on the left side are the TCP acknowledgements. Some packets in between are the last portion of the FTP data and control commands. It can be deduced from these results that

**Table 1.** Round Trip Time for Request and Response pairs (milliseconds)

| FTP Request | FTP Response | Upload (put) | | Download (get) | |
|---|---|---|---|---|---|
| | | 500 KB | 50 MB | 500 KB | 50 MB |
| USER | 331 Password required | 620.621 | 610.481 | 604.685 | 652.596 |
| PASS | 230 Access granted | 748.752 | 701.774 | 724.554 | 944.772 |
| PORT | 200 PORT Successful | 618.772 | 596.778 | 608.898 | 613.617 |
| STOR/ RETR | 150 Opening BINARY mode | 680.763 | 629.675 | 680.800 | 687.860 |
| QUIT | 221 Goodbye | 615.153 | 662.917 | 605.296 | 618.140 |
| Total upload/download time (seconds) | | 18.470 | 2085.830 | 1.640 | 228.040 |
| Transfer rate (kbps) | | 221.600 | 196.400 | 2511.760 | 1796.160 |

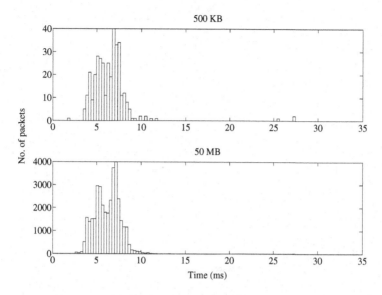

**Fig. 2.** RTT for ACK from PEP in upload of a 500 KB and a 50 MB file

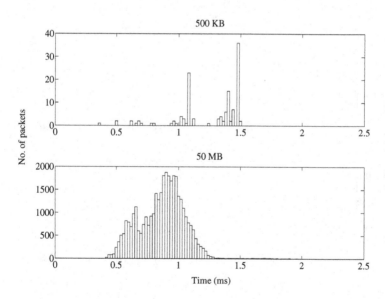

**Fig. 3.** RTT for ACK from PEP in download of a 500 KB and a 50 MB file

during upload, the percentage of TCP ACKs is more than the FTP data. It is understood that this is due to the lower bandwidth available on the uplink resulting in more TCP retransmissions and duplicate ACKs. On the other hand, during download, plenty of bandwidth is available, so more FTP data can be sent

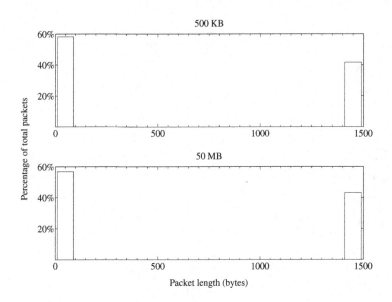

**Fig. 4.** IP packet length during upload of a 500 KB and a 50 MB file

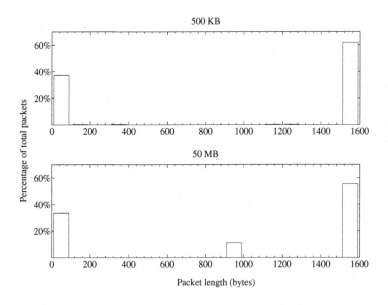

**Fig. 5.** IP packet length during download of a 500 KB and a 50 MB file

and less ACKs are required due to the cumulative acknowledgement phenomenon of TCP. In downloading the 50 MB file, mostly FTP data packets are 1500 bytes and quite a lot of them are 932 bytes, so there is a prominent bar near 1000 byte scale on the histogram in Figure 5.

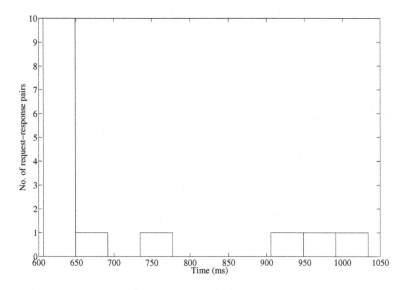

**Fig. 6.** RTT for HTTP request-response pairs

During the upload and download of the 500 KB and 50 MB files, most of the frames have inter-arrival time in the microsecond and millisecond range. Some packets exhibit more inter-arrival time depicting the user password typing time, the time taken by server to open ports for data transfer during execution of PORT command, total file transfer time and user idleness to execute the QUIT command.

## 6.2   Web Browsing

To analyze web browsing which is based on hypertext transfer protocol (HTTP), an Apache server is installed on the server (ESA) and a website is hosted on it. The client (Surrey) browses that website via Firefox. Meanwhile packets are captured with Wireshark on both the client and server.

The round trip time (RTT) for the HTTP request-response pairs is shown in Figure 6. Most of the RTT values are within the stated range for a geostationary satellite, but some are higher due to the delay incurred in transferring the large objects from web server to the browser.

TCP acknowledgements for the GET requests from the client are analyzed to find their RTT. It is observed that the ACKs are coming from the performance enhancing proxy (PEP) rather than the server as inferred from the time scale in Figure 7.

The IP packet length of the packets captured during browsing the website is illustrated in Figure 8. The first bar represents the TCP ACKs, the second is HTTP responses and the third is HTTP requests. The size of the request and response data is same because each request has a single response.

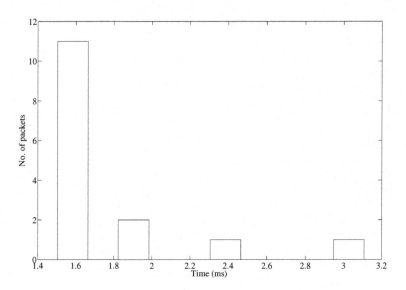

**Fig. 7.** RTT for ACK from PEP for GET requests from client

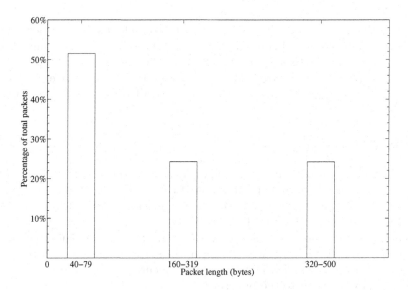

**Fig. 8.** IP packet length during browsing

The inter-arrival time of the frames during browsing is shown in Figure 9. Majority of the frames have inter-arrival times in the range of microsecond and millisecond. Some of the frames show more inter-arrival time due to the time spent in opening the browser and clicking the hyperlinks on the webpage by the user.

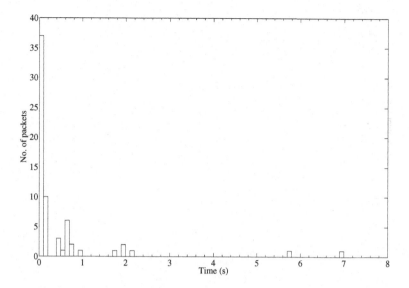

**Fig. 9.** Frame inter-arrival time during browsing

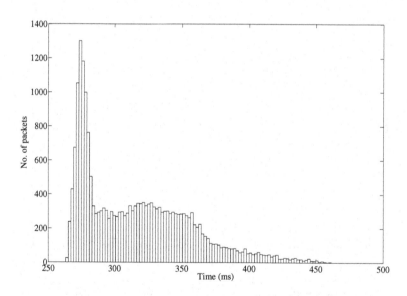

**Fig. 10.** One-way delay for video streaming

## 6.3    Video Streaming

For analysis of video streaming using user datagram protocol (UDP), a video clip has been streamed from the server (ESA) using the media player VLC and the stream is watched at the client (Surrey) with same media player.

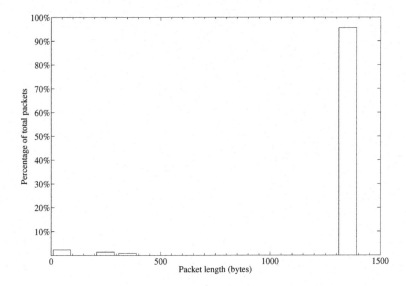

**Fig. 11.** IP packet length of streaming video packets

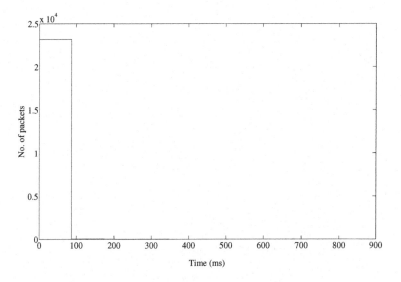

**Fig. 12.** Frame inter-arrival time for video streaming

The propagation delay for geostationary satellite is 250-270 milliseconds. The one-way delay observed between the streaming server and client is shown in Figure 10. The reasons for additional delay are jitter, buffering, playout delay etc.

The IP packet length captured in streaming the video is shown in Figure 11. Most of the streaming packets are 1344 bytes in length, which is shown by a prominent bar in the histogram.

The inter-arrival time of the frames is shown in Figure 12. As for the other two applications, file transfer and web browsing, video streaming also has inter-arrival time in microsecond and millisecond range.

Multimedia applications, like, video streaming, are sensitive to packet loss. The packet loss measured during streaming the video clip from server to client is 1.563% which is within acceptable range.

## 7   Conclusion

This paper presented the evaluation of the end-to-end QoS for different applications over a DVB-RCS satellite network. The results show the role of performance enhancing proxies (PEP) in the satellites for TCP-based applications. PEPs reduce the time of acknowledging the packets transmitted over satellites. The frame inter-arrival time for file transfer and web browsing is quite comparable while it is much less in video streaming than these two applications. It is due to the fast nature of UDP guaranteeing no reliability. More than 90% of packets in UDP based application are of same length due to no acknowlegements while, in TCP based applications, at least 30-60% of the packets are small in size and are used for acknowledgements. These acknowledgements can be further reduced by developing algorithms to reserve more bandwidth for TCP based applications over satellites.

These experiments can be tested on an IPv6 DVB-RCS satellite network testbed for comparison. More accuracy can be achieved by using GPS system for synchronization of client and server, which is more precise than the Network Time Protocol (NTP).

## Acknowledgment

The authors acknowledge the support of the European Space Agency (ESA) and the Framework 6 Network of Excellence, SatNEx II.

## References

1. VLC media player, http://www.videolan.org/vlc
2. Wireshark, http://www.wireshark.org
3. Digital Video Broadcasting(DVB), Framing structure, channel coding and modulation for 11/12 GHz satellite services (1997)
4. Digital Video Broadcasting(DVB); Interaction channel for Satellite Distribution Systems (2005)
5. Feighery, P., Scott, K., Goldsmith, D.: Using Performance Enhancing Proxies with Demand Assigned Multiple Access systems. In: Proc. IEEE Military Communications Conference MILCOM 2008, pp. 1–7, November 16–19 (2008)

6. Hadid, I., Gordon, D.: Apache Talking IPv6. Linux Journal (2003)
7. Mills, D.L.: NTP: Network Time Protocol (NTP) Version 3 Specification, Implementation and Analysis (March 1992)
8. Skinnemoen, H., Leirvik, R., Hetland, J., Fanebust, H., Paxal, V.: Interactive IP-network via Satellite DVB-RCS. IEEE Journal on Selected Areas in Communications 22(3), 508–517 (2004)
9. Sun, Z.: Satellite Networking: Principles and Protocols. John Wiley & Sons, Chichester (2005)

# Track 4
# Satellite Networks: Applications and Services

# Towards an IP/GSE-Only Signalling Framework for DVB Transmission Systems

Nimbe L. Ewald and Gorry Fairhurst

Electronics Research Group, Department of Engineering,
University of Aberdeen, AB24 3UE, UK
{n.l.ewald,g.fairhurst}@abdn.ac.uk

**Abstract.** An Internet Protocol/Generic Stream Encapsulation (IP/GSE) signalling framework is proposed to replace the current MPEG-2 Transport Stream (TS) Table-based signalling system and to enable smoother convergence of Digital Video Broadcasting (DVB) transmission systems and IP networks. GSE suitability is explained and a review of IP-based signalling techniques is presented in order to select the optimal candidate methods for this architecture.

**Keywords:** GSE, DVB, IP signalling, MPEG-2 TS Tables.

## 1 Introduction

IP-based signalling procedures for content metadata currently take place in DVB networks, e.g. acquisition of an Electronic Service Guide (ESG) in a DVB-H system. However, the signalling for network metadata is still being performed through MPEG-2 encoded Tables conveyed by the TS even though the second generation of DVB systems can also support the Generic Stream (GS).

The GS is expected to be used for IP-based services, where IP packets can be encapsulated using the Generic Stream Encapsulation (GSE) protocol [1]&[2] as an adaptation layer that provides efficient IP packet encapsulation and fragmentation.

In current network signalling, two sets of MPEG-2 encoded Tables are necessary for DVB system signalling, the Program Specific Information (PSI) and the System Information (SI) defined by MPEG and DVB, respectively. Tables are segmented in Sections, directly encapsulated in TS packets and sent with high repetition rates (e.g. 25 ms) to allow fast acquisition and updating. Figure 1 shows the protocol stack for current network signalling in a generic second generation DVB system.

In the current TS-based signalling framework, the receiver, initially, filters the Tables with fixed Packet Identifier (PID) field in the TS packet header, such as the Program Access Table (PAT). Next, it extracts the PID of the Network Information Table (NIT) that contains the tuning parameters. It accesses NIT and obtains the PAT PID of the respective TS. Finally, the receiver acquires the PAT and obtains the PIDs of the Program Map Tables (PMTs) where the PIDs of the audio/video Program Elements can be found. Thus, TS signalling strongly depends on PIDs filtering.

If signalling were conveyed by GSE packets instead of TS packets, there would not be a direct equivalent to the PID filters used for TS given that GSE does not contain a

K. Sithamparanathan et al. (Eds.): PSATS 2010, LNICST 43, pp. 147–162, 2010.

PID field. Thus, in an IP/GSE-only signalling framework, the receiver will need to identify which BB frames or GSE packets carry the network signalling information that it requires. In addition, for the realisation of this architecture, it will also be necessary to determine the respective Network Discovery and Selection (ND&S) procedures and a new flexible signalling metadata syntax. To clarify, Service Discovery and Selection (SD&S) methods are used for content metadata (e.g. ESG) discovery whilst ND&S are defined to be used for network metadata (e.g. PAT-like records) in this paper.

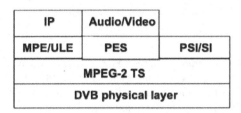

**Fig. 1.** Protocol stack for a generic DVB system

IP-based ND&S techniques will provide network bootstrapping and network selection in a similar manner to PAT. A new syntax with extensibility features, different from the present MPEG-2, will allow the easy modification of the signalling metadata. This network metadata is expected to experiment continuous change with the convergence of DVB and IP networks given that this union will enable DVB transmission networks to become networks functioning as a part of the Internet infrastructure. Even when the IP/GSE signalling framework intends to be DVB generic, the focus is on DVB-S2 in this paper.

This paper is divided as follows: GSE suitability for signalling is briefly examined in section 2, a review of current IP-based signalling procedures is given in section 3, the IP/GSE-only signalling framework is proposed in section 4 while section 5 concludes the paper.

## 2   GSE Protocol

The GSE protocol, defined in [1]&[2], provides flexible fragmentation, opposite to the fixed size of 188B TS packets, and extensibility through its extension headers. Figure 2 shows the GSE header format, the shadowed areas indicate optional fields thus the minimum header length is 4B.

The 1-bit S and E flags along with the FragID are used to indicate fragmentation. If both are set, the PDU encapsulated in the payload is not fragmented. Otherwise, the PDU is a fragment and the Total length and the Fragment ID provide the length of the PDU before fragmentation and the identification to allow re-assembly or loss detection at the receiver buffer. A CRC-32 is added to the last fragment to check the payload integrity.

The GSE length field allows encapsulation of a PDU with a length of up to 4096B, which can, potentially, improve bandwidth efficiency given that the Table Sections should not be larger than 1024B. Therefore, one 1024B-Section could be sent as the payload of a GSE packet with an overhead of 4B (plus higher-layer headers) instead of fragmenting it into 188B-TS packets. In addition, if the Table comprises several Sections, these can be sent in the same payload, as long as the size is lower or equal to 4096B, through the use of the PDU-Concat extension header [3].

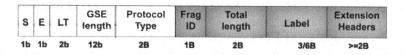

| S | E | LT | GSE length | Protocol Type | Frag ID | Total length | Label | Extension Headers |
|---|---|---|---|---|---|---|---|---|
| 1b | 1b | 2b | 12b | 2B | 1B | 2B | 3/6B | >=2B |

**Fig. 2.** GSE header format [2]

The Protocol Type field denotes the protocol of the PDU in the payload, e.g. IPv4 or IPv6. Potentially, a new Type field can be defined to identify the GSE packets carrying network metadata signalling.

GSE extension headers [3] are envisaged to provide a range of features to GSE. Besides the PDU-Concat extension header, the TS-Concat extension could be used during the transition from the TS to the GS. So concatenated TS packets would comprise the GSE payload. A new extension header could be defined to identify network signalling. Potentially, a security model can be implemented through the use of GSE security extensions (if these are standardised).

## 3  IP-Based Signalling Systems

The current literature was surveyed to determine the status and deployment of GSE-only signalling systems. The only standards-related documentation found in the area of GSE-only signalling was that of the DVB TM-GBS Common Metadata Toolkit (CMT) sub-group. There was also preliminary work on a GS/address resolution in the IETF IPDVB working group [4]. This lack of work on GSE-only signalling is the result of the currently limited availability of chipsets that support a GS interface to the S2 waveform. There are not known operational systems that have use the GS, all current systems use the TS, and may, in the first stage, decide to employ signalling using the TS SI/PSI Tables.

This section provides a survey of current systems employing IP signalling in DVB and non-DVB transmission networks. It seeks to understand the different signalling mechanisms and to identify suitable candidate methods that could be used to derive an IP/GSE signalling framework.

### 3.1  Metadata Signalling over DVB Systems

Different approaches of IP-based signalling procedures for content, applications and services over DVB systems are described below. Particular emphasis is given to the bootstrapping mechanisms.

### 3.1.1  IP Datacast over DVB-Handheld (DVB-H)

DVB-H [5] is a broadcast system for the delivery of digital content and services using IP-based mechanisms for terminals with constrained computational resources and battery. It uses PSI/SI Tables to perform signalling combined with content metadata, as shown in Figure 3. A PSI/SI generator, in the broadcast network, creates DVB-H specific descriptors and MPEG-2 encoded Tables such as NIT, PAT, PMT and the IP/MAC Notification Table (INT). Some of these tables are adapted whilst others are created specifically for the system, e.g. the INT exists only in DVB-H systems to signal the availability and location of IP streams in DVB networks. A DVB-H receiver includes a PSI/SI handler that extracts and interprets the PSI/SI signalling to configure the terminal for the IP service received over DVB-H.

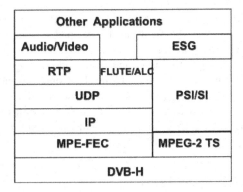

**Fig. 3.** DVB-H system protocol stack

A bootstrap entry point discovery can be performed using any of the following options: a preconfigured address at the receiver, a manually entered ESG bootstrap entry point information (provided out of band) and an entry point determined by terminal provisioning.

Once the network bootstrap stream is identified, the network bootstrap metadata can be received, to identify the IP platform (network service). The INT bootstrap information may be included in a SI/PSI table, e.g. the PAT or NIT tables.

The content is described using the ESG, content discovery follows the network bootstrap. The ESG bootstrap uses descriptors transported by the Asynchronous Layer Coding (ALC) using a File Delivery over Unidirectional Transport (FLUTE) session via UDP for broadcast channels or transported by HTTP over TCP for interactive channels. This specifies all the available ESGs in an IP platform. The appropriate ESG is selected using the ESG bootstrap information. The ESG content metadata describes the different IP-based services available in the handheld terminal's region.

The ESG data model is described by eXtensible Markup Language (XML) Schemas [6] that define ESG bootstrap descriptors and ESG fragments (e.g. Service, Service Bundle, Content fragment). Two compression algorithms, GNU- ZIP (GZIP) [7] and the Binary MPEG format for XML (BiM) [8] are recommended. GZIP is intended to be used for handheld terminals because of its simplicity.

XML fragments form the majority of the ESG information. However, part of the acquisition information contains Session Description Protocol (SDP) [] files that allow the end-device to locate service streams and configure service consumption applications appropriately. Once the ESG is acquired, service discovery is available through the information contained in it.

### 3.1.2  IP Datacast over DVB-Satellite Services to Handheld (DVB-SH)

The announcement of services and ESG delivery in DVB-SH networks for "regionalised ESGs" is described in [10]. The delivery of ESGs for DVB-SH Single Frequency Networks (SFN) is identical to that for DVB-H networks. In Multi Frequency Networks (MFNs), content regionalisation is possible therefore the ESG delivery uses additional descriptors and procedures. However, the mechanism is not changed even if, for example, there are new ESG bootstrap descriptors to indicate the local provider: information is transmitted using FLUTE sessions for broadcast channels and via HTTP for interactive channels.

As in the previous case, the bootstrap, transmission and syntax for DVB-SH refers to the content metadata while network signalling is carried in MPEG-2 PSI/SI Tables providing the information to bind PIDs with well-known IP addresses.

### 3.1.3  Interactive Applications and Services in Hybrid Broadcast/Broadband Environments

The DVB TM-MIS (Middleware for Interactive Services) group developed a specification, Blue Book A.137 [11], on signalling for interactive services or applications in hybrid broadcast / broadband networks. This specification builds on the work of [12]. It defines the application metadata signalling for two syntaxes, MPEG-2 and XML Document Type Definitions (DTDs) encoding, for broadcast and broadband networks (it is assumed that a return channel is in use), respectively. It is intended to define how interactive applications and services are to be announced and deployed. This should apply to any interactive application or service independent of the technology.

In a broadcast network, the receiver identifies the applications associated with a service through the MPEG-2-encoded Application Information Table (AIT) [13] whose location is retrieved from the PMT. The AIT contains application metadata such as its type, identifier, control code, priority and storage information.

In a broadband network, the SD&S procedures for DVB-IPTV described in [12] and in section 3.2.1 are followed to acquire the interactive applications through the XML-encoded AIT transported through HTTP1.1, multicast is not defined. In broadcast networks, Digital Storage Media-Command and Control (DSM-CC) [14] object carousel is used. It is also possible to signal applications using both syntaxes for hybrid broadcast/broadband networks.

### 3.2  Content Metadata Signalling over Non-DVB Systems

Current IP-based SD&S procedures in non-DVB transmission systems are described below.

### 3.2.1 Transport of MPEG-2 TS DVB Services over IP Networks

ETSI TS 102 034 [12], also known as the DVB-IPTV book, defines a framework for delivery of MPEG-2 services over bidirectional IP networks. The syntax and transmission of SI/PSI signalling is the usual MPEG-2 encoded Sections in TS packets, as shown in Figure 4, and transported by UDP/IP, which reduces the efficiency of the system.

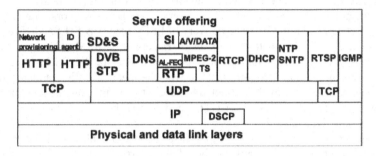

**Fig. 4.** Protocol stack for DVB-IP services [12]

The service discovery is defined in three steps. First, the service discovery entry points are found (bootstraping). Then, for each service discovery entry point, the service provider discovery information is acquired. Finally, for each service provider, the DVB-IP service discovery information is obtained.

Service discovery entry points can be well-known multicast addresses. Also, they can be acquired using multicast Domain Name Server Service (mDNS SRV) records [15]. In addition, SD&S entry point addresses can be obtained using an mDNS SRV record received via the Dynamic Host Configuration Protocol (DHCP) option 15. Alternatively, entry points can be given in the configuration data received on a provisioned network.

The service provider and DVB-IP service discovery information are carried in multicast and unicast modes. DVBSTP [12] is defined for the delivery of the mentioned content metadata records in multicast mode while HTTP is used for unicast.

Several types of record can be provided by the DVB-IP service discovery information (e.g. Broadcast, Content on Demand, Package). One of them, the Broadcast service discovery information presents two types of record, TS Full SI and TS Optional SI. TS Full SI provides information to create a list of available services and to find available live media broadcast services which have embedded SI, then, information on individual services is acquired from the transport stream by the usual PIDs scan. For the TS Optional SI record only PSI information, PAT and PMT, is embedded, i.e. it does not contain SI information.

XML Schemas are defined for all DVP-IP discovery information records and BiM is recommended for compression.

### 3.2.2 The Internet Media Guide (IMG)

The IETF MMUSIC working group defined the Internet Media Guide (IMG) framework and requirements [16]. An IMG provides "an envelope for metadata formats and session descriptions defined elsewhere with the aim of facilitating structuring, versioning, referencing, distributing and maintaining such information" [16]. Thus, the IMG methods and protocols refer to content metadata.

Existing Internet protocols and standards are proposed to be used with the IMG framework. For example, SDP is a candidate method to convey session-level parameters. Because of limitations in SDP flexibility for extensions, SDP would only be used just to carry a small subset of IMG metadata. SDP with negotiation capabilities (SDPng) could also be used, as SDP, to carry session-level parameters. However, extensions and integration with other description formats are allowed because of SDPng XML-based format.

However, there are sets of mechanisms needed to meet the requirements of IMGs. Four specific mechanisms are identified [16], 1) a multicast-unidirectional, capable announcement protocol, 2) the design of a new multicast-unidirectional protocol based on ALC/FLUTE is recommended, 3) use of existing unicast protocols for subscribe and announcement/notification, e.g. the Session Initiation Protocol (SIP), SIP events (IETF RFCs 3261 and 3265, respectively) and HTTP and 4) definition of a metadata envelope.

The metadata model should allow reusing and extending the set of metadata and enable the use of different syntaxes (e.g. SDP, MPEG-7, XML). However, these design decisions were based on the need for Internet content discovery and selection.

### 3.2.3  The Open IPTV Forum (OIPF)

The OIPF [17] defines a set of specifications for an end-to end platform for the deployment of IPTV services in managed and unmanaged (open Internet) networks. In managed networks, a WAN gateway may act as DHCP server and Network Address Translator (NAT) to allow communication among the Application Gateway (AG), the IP Multimedia Subsystem Gateway (IG) and the Open IPTV Terminal Function (OITF) within the residential network. In unmanaged networks, the OITF is allowed to send/receive messages from the Internet.

For managed networks, the WAN gateway assigns IP addresses to the AG, IG and OITF so the configuration information (e.g. DNS server) is obtained directly by them. In case of unmanaged networks, the WAN gateway (acting as a NAT) translates the IP address to be recognizable to the provider's addressing plan. When an OITF powers up, it should automatically discover the IG using the Universal Plug and Play (UPnP) discovery mechanism (described in section 3.2.5).

Three steps are defined to enable SD&S of IPTV services, which are based on those of DVB-IPTV described in section 3.2.1 [12]. In managed networks, the WAN gateway provides the IP address to start the IPTV service provider discovery phase. Once the entry points are found, the terminal retrieves the IPTV service provider information, which can be given as a web page or as a XML record. SIP/SDP over HTTP is used to obtain this information. Once a service provider is selected, its IPTV service information can be obtained as a web page or as a XML record (e.g. DVB-IP records). This signalling is performed over HTTP (unicast) and over DVBSTP (multicast).

In unmanaged networks, the terminal requests the IPTV service provider information using HTTP. In this case, the terminal finds the entry points by either manual, pre-configured or DHCP configuration.

SD&S metadata uses and extends the XML Schemas defined by DVB-IPTV [12]. The OIPF framework allows discovering servers via web-based applications, the extensions allow signalling these from within SD&S records.

### 3.2.4 Universal Plug and Play (UPnP)

The UPnP Forum [18] defines an architecture for pervasive network connectivity of intelligent devices, which supports zeroconf and automatic discovery of devices. Devices are classified as controlled devices or control points. Controlled devices function as servers, responding to requests from a control point. The steps needed for a device to use UPnP networking are: IP addressing, discovery, description, control, eventing and presentation.

Addressing is performed using standard IP methods. If the controlled device or control point does not provide a DHCP server, it must implement a DHCP client and will look for a DHCP server to obtain an IP address. If a DHCP server is not found, they implement Auto-IP, that is, intelligently choose an IP address from a set of link-local IP addresses.

Once a controlled device or control point obtained an IP address, discovery takes place. It is possible to know the appliance's (or services) UPnP type, its universally unique identifier and a URL to its description through discovery messages. Discovery allows a controlled device to advertise its services to control points and, similarly, it allows a control point to find interesting controlled devices. If a controlled device or control point are new in the network, they send multicast discovery messages. In the case of the control point, to a specific IP address on port 1900 or on a manually entered port.

Discovery messages are carried using the Simple Service Discovery Protocol (SSDP), defined by Microsoft and Hewlett-Packard [18]. It uses part of the header field format of HTTP1.1. Since SSDP is only partially based on HTTP1.1, it is carried by UDP instead of TCP.

After a controlled device has been discovered by a control point, description takes place to discover services and capabilities. These are retrieved from a URL (provided during the discovery phase). Each service included in the device contains URLs for service description, control and eventing, respectively. Each device description includes descriptions of all embedded devices and a URL for presentation of the aggregate. The descriptions are in XML syntax, thus specific Schemas have been developed for this purpose. No compression method is recommended for XML. HTTP1.1/TCP provides the transport for the description phase and the control, eventing and presentation stages.

Once the device description and its services are known, a control point may request a certain service to perform an action and, consequently, it may receive responses indicating the result of the action as well as polling for values. This is done by sending/receiving control messages, expressed in XML, to/from the control URL (previously sent in the device description) using the Simple Object Access Protocol (SOAP).

Finally, eventing and presentation take place. The control points listens to updates in variables during eventing whilst they can retrieve a presentation page during presentation by subscribing/retrieving the corresponding URLs (acquired during description phase). XML Schemas are also developed for these message sets.

UPnP requires bi-directional connectivity and it is not suitable for unidirectional network signalling. In addition, UPnP, including SSDP, are proprietary standards as compared to mDNS which is an open standard.

### 3.2.5 ATSC Systems

*3.2.5.1   A/92 ATSC Delivery of IP Multicast Sessions over Data Broadcast.* The procedures for signalling an IP multicast service over an ATSC A/90 Data Broadcast System are described in [19]. An IP multicast session is announced by SDP. The Session Announcement Protocol (SAP), defined in IETF RFC 2974, is used to encapsulate the SDP protocol in UDP datagrams.

An IP multicast receiver uses signalling metadata, i.e. Tables, to bind the IP multicast media and SDP announcement streams to specific MPEG-2 Program Elements. For this purpose, an optional descriptor listing the MAC multicast addresses where a given MPEG-2 Program Element can be found, is defined for the Data Service Table (DST).

The procedure for the acquisition of an IP Multicast service involves the Program and System Information Protocol (PSIP), MPEG and A/90 Tables. The DST contains Tap structures that are used to find Program Elements in lower layers. This Tap structure includes an *associationTag* to allow the identification of the location of the IP multicast Program Element PID. This location is obtained by matching the *associationTag* in DST with the association tag in PMT.

The location of the SDP streams is also indicated in the PMT since the SDP datagrams are encapsulated as DSM-CC addressable sections. The *deviceId* field of these addressable sections represents the SDP IP multicast address, thus the receiver filters these sections based on the value of this field. Optionally, the MAC address descriptor in the DST can be used to discover multicast addresses.

*3.2.5.2   A/153 ATSC-Mobile DTV Standard.* Also called the ATSC mobile/handheld (M/H) system [20], it uses a portion of the capacity of a mobile DTV link to provide mobile/pedestrian/handheld broadcasting services, while the remainder can be used for HD television. The protocol stack for the ATSC-M/H system is shown in Figure 5, where FIC stands for Fast Information Channel and provides bootstrap signalling.

The FIC channel provides a network bootstrap method that is specified outside of the normal frame payload, and hence is independent of the data channel carrying Reed-Solomon (RS) frames. It provides the binding information between the M/H services and the M/H ensembles. The M/H ensemble is a set of consecutive RS frames having the same FEC coding. Information such as the M/H ensemble ID, Tables carried by the ensemble, number of services carried by the ensemble and M/H service ID is carried by the FIC. The key result is that the receiver can access the FIC information very rapidly instead of having to decode every RS frame.

The procedure for acquiring an M/H service consists of two steps: access to the M/H ensemble and then, access to the IP level M/H service through the Service Map Table (SMT) which lists the IP address for each service.

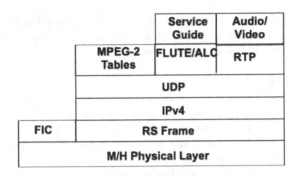

**Fig. 5.** Simplified protocol stack for ATSC-Mobile DTV [20]

The Service Guide for ATSC-M/H services is based on XML Schemas. SDP records are used to deliver the session descriptions using FLUTE transport. The Service Guide Delivery Descriptor (SGDD) is an XML document used by the broadcast system to describe the structure and declare the content of the Service Guide. If the Service Guide is to be available over an interactive channel, the broadcast system should advertise the whole guide (or some portions) over the interactive channel by setting an alternative access URL in the appropriate SGDD(s).

The use of a dedicated signalling channel (FIC) allows the control information to be acquired faster; however once this bootstrap is complete, the method relies on Tables conveyed by UDP over IP/RS frame. This technology is an optimisation of the physical layer to address the requirements for rapid tuning and separation of content and network signalling.

# 4   IP/GSE-Only Signalling Framework

The first step towards network discovery and selection is to filter signalling information at the adaptation layer, that is, to identify the GSE packets conveying signalling information. Next, IP-based network bootstrapping procedures will be performed, and finally, network selection will be carried out. It is also considered to modify the current MPEG-2 syntax of the signalling metadata to one that allows extensibility.

## 4.1   GSE Signalling Identification

The candidate procedures for locating signalling are identified in Table 1. The methods are listed by increasing amounts of information that would need to be parsed by a receiver joining the network. Some of these procedures may be jointly used, e.g. placement of a GSE packet with signalling information at a known position and a dedicated GSE Type field.

For candidate method 1, a specific DVB-S2 ModCod could be chosen. Method 3 is similar to the technique used in the DVB-H systems. Candidate methods 1-4 can eliminate the need for a receiver to process non-signalling BBframes. Candidate methods 1-3 require changes to DVB second generation standards but they also represent a faster acquisition of the signalling.

**Table 1.** Candidate methods for identification of GSE packets conveying network signaling

| No. | Candidate method | Filtering level |
|---|---|---|
| 1 | Assignment of a particular physical frame format | BB frame |
| 2 | Use of fields in the BB header | BB frame |
| 3 | Alignment of signalling transmission to a time-slicing frame | BB frame |
| 4 | Placement of a GSE packet containing signalling at a known position | BB frame |
| 5 | Allocation of a dedicated GSE Type field value | GSE packet |
| 6 | Allocation of a dedicated Label/NPA | GSE packet |
| 7 | Allocation of a dedicated new Tag in the GSE header | GSE packet |
| 8 | Allocation of a dedicated IP address | IP packet |
| 9 | Allocation of a dedicated UDP port | UDP packet |

Candidate methods 4-9 operate on the contents of the BBframe, method 4 exploits the flexible placement of fragments provided in GSE. Methods 5-7 operate at an equivalent level. Given GSE support for multiple label formats and the need to support multiple network services, it seems the most consistent and flexible method at this level would be to use a 2B optional Type extension header to identify network signalling. Well-known Type values will need to be specified for other protocol headers to allow correct processing by the receiver stack.

The location of signalling through the GSE Type field  (method 5) can resemble the current location of signalling in the TS, e.g. a well-known Type value will carry the PAT, which will indicate the Type fields of the PMT. A well-known IP address (method 8) may be also used for the network bootstrap, as in mDNS.

It is suggested therefore to further evaluate the following techniques: assignment of a particular physical frame format for signalling (if efficient and available at the physical layer),  use of fields in the BB header or PL header to indicate signalling content (if available at the physical layer), alignment of signalling transmission to a time-slicing frame (subject to analysis of cost and complexity), placement of a GSE packet containing signalling information at the start of a frame, allocation of a dedicated GSE optional 2B Type field value for all signalling PDU and allocation of a dedicated Label/NPA or IP address for signalling (possibly using multicast SRV records for bootstrap).

## 4.2 ND&S Procedures

In common with IP-based systems providing content discovery and selection, a two-stage approach is recommended for network discovery and selection.

Once the GSE packets carrying signalling metadata are filtered through some of the methods described in section 4.1, a bootstrap will be performed to select the appropriate network signalling information. The appropriate network signalling information can then be used to select the required network service.

A bootstrap method eliminates the need to manually enter a bootstrap entry point (e.g. configuring IP/NPA addresses out of band, or using device configuration). Instead the device only has to be configured with the logical name for the network to which it is attach.

Most procedures that were described in section 3 have been defined for bootstrapping of content metadata. However, some of these mechanisms may also be candidate methods for bootstrapping of the network information.

### 4.2.1  Network Bootstrapping

The format of network bootstrap information can be a Table structure (as current MPEG-2 Tables) that maps logical names to appropriate discovery entry points (as in INT) or a multicast service discovery using DNS SRV records to specify the network service discovery entry points, similar to the procedure recommended for DVB-IPTV [12]. This approach is now common in IP networks, e.g. the service discovery information is provided, by default, on the Internet Assigned Numbers Authority (IANA) registered well-known *dvbservdsc* port 3937 via TCP and UDP and on the IANA registered well-known *dvbservdisc* multicast addresses 224.0.23.14 for IPv4 and FF0X:0:0:0:0:0:0:12D for IPv6.

The bootstrap information may also need to support network topology information as that supplied by NIT. In broadcast links, this information may be sent by as a SRV record over mDNS using a well-known multicast address or as a Table directly over UDP using a well-known multicast address. For bidirectional links, a Table could be sent over SSDP/UDP or a SRV record can be transmitted over mDNS or over DHCP option 15. However, the use of SSDP is not recommended since it is a proprietary standard.

### 4.2.2  Transmission of Network Signalling Metadata

The candidate methods in Table 2, reviewed in section 3, can be considered for transport of content metadata for multicast and unicast delivery.

From all the candidates listed in Table 2, DVBSTP [12] was specifically defined for content metadata delivery in architectures compliant with DVB-IPTV and OIPF [12]&[17]. DVBSTP is used for delivery of SD&S XML records over IP multicast systems. It defines the type of payload carried through its Payload ID field (e.g. Content on Demand, Broadcast discovery information) as well as the type of compression encoding, if any, indicated by the Compression field. Its header would add an overhead of at least 12B per Section. Even though DVBSTP may be able to provide signalling identification though its Payload ID field, a receiver would need to process all GSE packets in order to retrieve the signalling packets since the signalling identifier would be in the header of DVBSTP at the transport layer level.

**Table 2.** Candidate methods for transport of network signalling metadata

| Candidate method | Mode |
| --- | --- |
| DVBSTP/UDP | Multicast |
| ALC/FLUTE/UDP | Multicast |
| SDP/ALC/FLUTE/UDP | Multicast |
| SSDP/HTTP/UDP | Multicast |
| SDP/SAP/UDP | Multicast |
| HTTP/TCP | Unicast |
| SIP/SDP/HTTP/TCP | Unicast |
| SOAP/HTTP/TCP | Unicast |

Since the requirements of the network signalling metadata are different from those of the content metadata, the transport protocols listed above may not be suitable. For example, DVBSTP and TCP add an overhead of at least 12B and 20B, respectively, and provide reliability, which is not needed for network signalling given its high repetition rates. DVBSTP indicates the type of XML-record carried and the type of compression used. These two features are desirable for the transport protocol that will be carrying the signalling metadata. In addition, a field to indicate if payload encryption is used should be also considered. Thus, the development of a new lightweight transport protocol providing the features above mentioned and a small overhead (1 or 2 B) will be analysed.

### 4.3 Syntax of Network Signalling Metadata

It is desirable that the network signalling metadata present a more extensible syntax than that of MPEG-2. SDP, SDPng and XML have been identified as candidate methods for network signalling metadata.

SDP is only a format for session description without flexibility while SDPng could be an optimal syntax given that it allows XML DTDs and Schemas as extensions. However, SDPng work was abandoned so specifications were not defined.

XML DTDs and Schemas are commonly used for content metadata in current DVB systems (section 3). XML is a verbose syntax however compression algorithms have been developed with satisfactory results. In [21], XML Schemas were specifically developed for PSI/SI Sections, BiM and GZIP algorithms were implemented and their compression rates compared. Then, they are sent over DVBSTP via UDP/IP. Two sets of DVB-S and DVB-T signalling streams were captured to validate this analysis. The comparison considered three cases: **1)** Sections are compressed with GZIP, **2)** Sections are converted to XML and compressed with GZIP and **3)** Sections are converted to XML and compressed with BiM. The dictionary-based compression approach of BiM was able to offer significant benefit by exploiting knowledge of the syntax of the XML information.

The key advantages of XML are that it represents information in a human readable format, is easy to extend, and can use comments to document a configuration. BiM provides a good compression rate, although future transports may need to also consider newer methods that are also emerging, which could offer further improvements in performance. An XML approach seems attractive for an IP-only solution.

### 4.4 IP/GSE-Only Signalling Framework

Figure 6 shows the potential protocol stack for the IP/GSE-only signalling architecture. Once a receiver is turned on, it should be able to identify the GS conveying signalling metadata (the bootstrap) and configure an appropriate filter to receive this traffic (preferably without incurring the cost of reading all GS packets in the BBframe), through one of the mechanisms given in section 4.1. This may also require a method to efficiently identify this signalling flow within the multiplex.

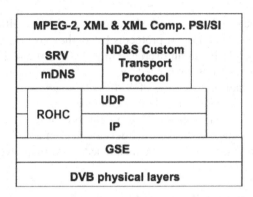

**Fig. 6.** Prospective protocol stack for the IP/GSE-only signalling framework

Once the bootstrap filter is configured, the receiver will extract the bootstrap information, containing the basic signalling information, to allow network discovery and selection (e.g. using mDNS). The SRV records may replace PAT function. That is, PIDs could be substituted by IP addresses and UDP ports from which the (possibly XML-based) NIT-like information and, consequently, the tuning parameters can be obtained. Similarly, IP addresses and UDP ports could replace the PIDs of the MPEG-2 Program Elements and PAT. This data could be directly encapsulated into GSE or IP encapsulated. The end result will be the signalling metadata of the required network. A preferred method will be identified.

Network discovery requires the receiver to filter a specific signalling stream that identifies a network service and defines how to provide address resolution to the specific services being offered (e.g. to bootstrap an ESG). The signalling metadata will use a transport protocol, linked to the chosen procedure to implement network discovery. The prospect of a new lightweight transport protocol for signalling metadata will be analysed further. This protocol should provide means to identify the payload, to indicate the type of compression and if encryption is present.

A signalling format based on XML Schemas seems attractive. This will allow easily extension of this metadata according to the specific system physical layer, e.g. new descriptors for emerging systems. Since, XML is a verbose syntax, compression should be applied through BiM and GZIP. New compression algorithms need to be evaluated, e.g. Efficient XML Interchange (EXI). Also, hybrid systems using both syntaxes, MPEG-2 and XML, should be considered, as in [11] (section 3.1.3).

A separate set of content SRV records, which indicate the IP addresses and ports providing certain services using existing IP-based mechanisms can also be developed (e.g. acquisition of ESG-like information).

RTP with an extension header containing a Network Time Protocol (NTP) timestamp or RTCP carrying NTP and RTP timestamps may be used for synchronisation of the system, as suggested in [21].

Methods to further reduce the signalling capacity requirements will be studied. GSE may use PDU-Concat to improve encapsulation overhead. Signalling information with the same repetition rates may be bundled into one larger signalling block. This may improve compression rates. The use of header compression, e.g. Robust

Header Compression (ROHC), defined in IETF RFC 4815, on UDP and IP headers will be also analysed to identify compression gains.

# 5 Conclusions and Future Work

Since current DVB transmission systems still perform network signalling through MPEG-2 TS packets, this paper presents a proposal for an IP/GSE-only signalling framework to replace it. This architecture would allow DVB systems to converge with IP networks in a smoother manner. Thus, DVB systems will become part of the Internet and will be able to provide traditional IP network services.

GSE suitability for DVB network signalling was explained. Current IP-based procedures for SD&S in DVB and non-DVB networks were examined in order to identify candidate methods for the IP/GSE signalling framework. Importantly, a range of techniques for identification of GSE packets, conveying network signalling, was also proposed.

As future work, each of the methods proposed to identify signalling at the physical and GSE layer will be analysed in depth. GSE security header extensions will be also further studied. MPEG-2 PSI/SI Tables will be captured and translated into XML Schemas. The performance of compression algorithms, such as BiM or EXI, on this XML data will be evaluated. The DVB system efficiency with these XML-based Tables will be analytically calculated considering the use of GSE PDU-Concat extensions and IP/UDP header compression.

**Acknowledgments.** The European Space Agency (ESA) under contract 22471/09/NL/AD has funded this work. The authors would like to thank Ana Yun Garcia and Isaac Moreno Asenjo for their help in preparing this paper.

# References

1. Cantillo, J., Collini-Nocker, B., De Bie, U., Del Rio, O., Fairhurst, G., Jahn, A., Rinaldo, R.: GSE: A Flexible, yet Efficient, Encapsulation for IP over DVB-S2 Continuous Generic Streams. Int. J. Satellite Comms. Net. 26, 231–250 (2008)
2. ETSI TS 102 606: Digital Video Broadcasting (DVB); Generic Stream Encapsulation (GSE) Protocol (2007)
3. Fairhurst, G., Collini-Nocker, B.: Extension Formats for Unidirectional Lightweight Encapsulation (ULE) and the Generic Stream Encapsulation (GSE). IETF RFC 5163 (2008)
4. Fairhurst, G., Montpetit, M.-J.: Address Resolution Mechanisms for IP Datagrams over MPEG-2 Networks. IETF RFC 4947 (2007)
5. ETSI TS 102 469: Digital Video Broadcasting (DVB); IP Datacast over DVB-H: Architecture (2006)
6. World Wide Web Consortium (W3C), Extensible Markup Language (XML) 1.0, 5th edn., http://www.w3.org/TR/REC-xml/REC-xml-20081126.xml
7. Deutsh, P.: GZIP file format specification version 4.3, IETF RFC 1952 (1996)
8. ISO/IEC 23001-1 (MPEG-B): Information Technology – MPEG Systems Technologies – Binary MPEG format for XML

9. Handley, M., Jacobson, V., Perkins, C.: SDP, Session Description Protocol, IETF RFC 4566 (2006)
10. ETSI TS 102 592-2: Digital Video Broadcasting (DVB); IP Datacast: Electronic Service Guide (ESG) Implementation Guidelines; Part 2: IP Datacast over DVB-SH (2009)
11. DVB Document A137: Signalling and carriage of interactive applications and services in hybrid broadcast/broadband environments (2009)
12. ETSI TS 102 034: Digital Video Broadcasting (DVB); Transport of MPEG-2 TS Based DVB Services over IP Based Networks (2007)
13. ETSI TS 101 812: Digital Video Broadcasting (DVB); Multimedia Home Platform (MHP) Specification 1.0.3 (2006)
14. ISO/IEC 13818-6: Information technology – Generic coding of moving pictures and associated audio information – Part 6: Extensions for DSM-CC (1998)
15. Gulbrandsen, A., Vixie, P., Esibov, L.: A DNS RR for specifying the location of services (DNS SRV), RFC 2782 (2000)
16. Nomura, Y., Walsh, R., Luoma, J.-P., Asaeda, H., Schulzrinne, H.: A Framework for the Usage of Internet Media Guides (IMGs), IETF RFC 4435 (2006)
17. Open IPTV Forum, http://www.openiptvforum.org
18. UPnP Forum, http://www.upnp.org
19. ATSC Standard: Delivery of IP Multicast Sessions over ATSC Data Broadcast, A/92 (2002)
20. ATSC Standard: ATSC-Mobile DTV Standard, Part 1-ATSC Mobile Digital Television System (A/153 Part 1: 2009) (2009)
21. Foellscher, H.: Transmission of Media Content on IP-based Digital Broadcast Platforms, Institute for Communications Technology, Technical University of Braunschweig, Dissertation (2007)

# No-Reference H.264/AVC Statistical Multiplexing for DVB-RCS

Hamed Ahmadi Aliabad[1], Sandro Moiron[1,2], Martin Fleury[1,*], and Mohammed Ghanbari[1]

[1] University of Essex,
Colchester, United Kingdom
{hahmada,fleum,ghan}@essex.ac.uk
[2] Instituto de Telecomunicações
Leiria, Portugal
smoiron@co.it.pt

**Abstract.** Replacement of MPEG-2 by the H.264/AVC codec for satellite video services, including aggregated video for the DVB-RCS uplink, presents an opportunity to develop efficient statistical multiplexing. In this paper, a scheme is developed that effectively models the relationship between number of non-zero coefficients and video quality. The result is the ability to equalize video quality, reduce quality fades, and smooth the overall bitrate presented. The number of channels in the multiplex can be increased through the scheme if there is a need to achieve an average of 40 dB PSNR across all inputs.

**Keywords:** DVB-RCS, DTH, H.264/AVC, look-ahead statistical multiplexing.

## 1 Introduction

In the current economic environment, there is a strong incentive to reduce costs for service providers of TV satellite broadcasting, even though revenues remain buoyant for the satellite companies themselves. To a certain extent this applies to content distribution and more especially it applies to Direct-to-Home (DTH) broadcast and its successor Digital Video Broadcasting (DVB)-Return Channel via Satellite (DVB-RCS) [1]. DVB-RCS replaces the terrestrial uplink of DTH with a satellite uplink with several Mbps available, thus further increasing the attraction of the DTH offering for certain markets in terms of massive coverage and low installation costs. One way DVB-RCS costs may be reduced is through efficient statistical multiplexing. In statistical multiplexing, a constant bitrate, the transponder's bandwidth, is allocated according to the coding complexity of the constituent video streams. Efficient statistical multiplexing can improve received video quality at the receiver, and may even increase the number of TV channels carried by a transponder [2]. In business terms it is acknowledged that the revenue that can be potentially generated from combining video streams within a multimedia channel [3] is related to the quality of the video delivered to end users. Statistical multiplexing can reduce deep quality fades [4], thus

---

* Corresponding author.

K. Sithamparanathan et al. (Eds.): PSATS 2010, LNICST 43, pp. 163–178, 2010.

increasing the quality of experience. Though there may be times in which the content of a majority of multiplexed TV channels demands a large bandwidth allocation, the essence of well-managed statistical multiplexing is that the duration of these intervals is short.

The H.264/Advanced Video Codec (AVC) [5] has provided an opportunity for countries that are contemplating digital video broadcasting, as it can be adopted in one step, rather than in the two-step process of earlier adopters that opted for the Moving Pictures Experts Group (MPEG)-2 codec. Other countries such as Portugal and Brazil have introduced H.264/AVC-based services. H.264/AVC can use the same MPEG-2 Transport Stream (TS) [6] as previously employed by the MPEG-2 codec itself. The MPEG-2 TS [7] can assemble up to 6 or 10 or even 20 independent television programs. Programs bitrates can be constant or variable. In the case of variable data rate, these rates can be controlled based on the requirements of the system prior to multiplexing (statistical multiplexing). The H.264/AVC codec significantly improves compression ratios [8] by as much as 50%, especially for SDTV. It is reported [9] that little prior research has been conducted on statistical multiplexing of H.264/AVC streams, even though this codec is now preferred for emerging national applications of HDTV and within wireless systems such as 3GPP's MBMS.

Assuming live or pre-encoded Constant Bitrate (CBR) video as used in the paper, the basic system is based on finding the number of non-Zero coefficients (NNZC) of the input sequences to the multiplex. (The scheme can be modified to work for Variable Bitrate (VBR) video.) These coefficients are those transform coefficients in the encoded bitstream that have not been reduced to zero by the quantization process. The NNZC allows the spatial complexity of the video sequence to be judged and by implication the coding complexity required to achieve a given quality. Notice that coding complexity is a measure of the coding bits required for compression and not the computational complexity. Specifically the NNZC of an individual macroblock was found to be logarithmically proportional to the coding complexity of that macroblock. Notice that because the system is intended for broadcast quality TV, the spatial coefficients dominate the bitstream. At low bit rates, the data given over to motion vectors and headers in the compressed bitstream [3] must be taken into account. As this is a no-reference system, a method is required to estimate the video quality (Peak Signal-to-Noise Ratio (PSNR)) based on knowledge of the NNZC. To do so required an estimate of the video quality from the average quantization parameter (QP), which, in a production system, can be extracted from the encoded bitstream without full decode.

Once the relative coding complexity is determined across the sequences, the video quality is equalized across the input sequences. This operation is performed at each Group-of-Pictures (GOP) boundary, though a refined version could also include scene change detection. (A GOP in broadcast TV normally consists of 12 or 15 pictures or frames (if progressively transmitted) corresponding respectively to about half a second at 12 or 15 frames/s.) The CBR rates are subsequently adjusted on a GOP-by-GOP basis to produce what has been called 'semi-CBR-VBR' streams [10]. Research in [11] also presents a CBR multiplex of streams previously stored at a high quality. In implemented systems, such as that from Scopus [12] for the MPEG-2 codec, VBR video can be smoothed [13] prior to complexity analysis. However, it is important to note that H.264/AVC video bitstreams have been found to be significantly more variable [14] than even MPEG-4 part 2 streams, due to the variety of coding modes available in H.264/AVC.   It is also reported [14] that, after H.264/AVC frame size smoothing, the output remained significantly more variable than *unsmoothed* MPEG-4 part 2 output for the same films. CBR encoding allows planning of storage capacity and in video-on-demand schemes, it allows the bandwidth from a server to be tightly controlled. If the CBR video is not pre-encoded at a high rate (prior to transcoding) then image 'dissolves', fast 'action' and scenes with camera motion (pans, zooms, tilts, ...) all suffer. However, scenes with limited motion such as head-and-shoulder news sequences are not much affected by CBR encoding.

The envisaged system is shown in Fig. 1 in which a bitrate transcoder bank modifies the input after NNZC statistics have been extracted in the compressed domain. For an example of a commercial transcoder bank for a different purpose refer to [15]. In Fig. 1, the statistical multiplexor receives $n$ compressed bitstreams which pass through a bank of bit-rate transcoders to adjust the combined bitrate according to the output channel constraint. The bandwidth share is defined by the statistical bandwidth manager which receives content complexity measures (*parameters*) from each transcoder and returns the appropriate bandwidth share ($\alpha$). Modification of the bitrate in the compressed domain is known as dynamic rate shaping [16]. Frequency domain transcoding [17] has the advantage that latency is reduced by only requiring an entropic decode. In H.264/AVC, the Context Adaptive Variable Length (CAVLC) decode and bit-stream parsing on average take only 13% of the computational complexity of a full decode [18]. The complexity of the Context Adaptive Binary Arithmetic Coding (CABAC) option is estimated [19] to add approximately 12% of the CAVLC timing to the overall time (at a potential reduction in bitrate of up to 16%).

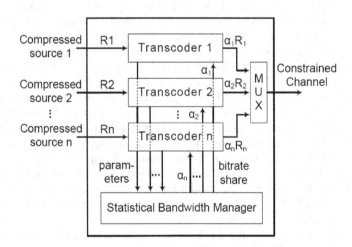

**Fig. 1.** Statistical multiplexor architecture

The advantages of the proposed GOP-based dynamic rate control were found to be: a modest but worthwhile overall gain across the channels in video quality (PSNR); quality equalization across the video stream multiplex components; for the test example a stream quantity gain of about 1.5, i.e. more channels at the target PSNR of 40 dB; and a considerable reduction in bitrate burstiness of the video streams. It is known [20] that quality fluctuations have a significant impact on the subjective quality. The proposed scheme is based on empirically derived equations. Because the system is GOP-based it is probably easily integrated into GOP-based call-admission-control or bandwidth allocation systems for satellite channels [21], replacing H.264/AVC for MPEG-2 streams. In the DVB-RCS system, statistical multiplexing of aggregated user video traffic could additionally take place at the terrestrial hub, if the return channel were to be used for user video applications such as remote learning and telemedicine.

The remainder of this paper is organized as follows. Section 2 discusses related work on statistical multiplexing, covering related issues such as buffer management. Section 3 is an extended analysis of the methodology. This will be of interest to those wishing to construct their own statistical multiplexing system, based on their own likely video payload. Section 4 is an evaluation using a carousel of video sequences in each multiplexed stream. Finally, Section 5 draws some conclusions and makes suggestions for future work.

## 2  Related Work

Statistical multiplexing techniques vary according to their complexity. In [22], a relatively simple form of statistical multiplexing was applied in which the same QP was applied to all video frames within a multiplexed group to achieve a target bit rate. A binary chop search across the range of available QPs was conducted. This procedure in the tests appeared to achieve its objective even though *no direct* account was taken of content complexity. In [11], a more computationally intensive scheme was applied in which statistical multiplexing based on spatial complexity statistics was applied to a set of rate-distortion controlled MPEG-2 video encoders. Their method is further discussed below but first we make a preliminary distinction.

There are two different ways for a statistical multiplexing algorithm to determine the bit rates of the encoders. Firstly, the feedback approach uses information from channel utilization and video coding complexity, which can be a by-product of the encoding procedure. The result of this process is a signal that is applied to the video encoders to determine their bit rates based on previous behavior. Secondly, the look-ahead approach uses the video statistics before encoding to find out each video's complexity and its assigned share of the bandwidth. It gains these statistics by pre-processing the future video frame. Then, with the information gathered from all videos, it calculates the amount of bandwidth for each of the video channels and applies the result to the encoders in order to set their bit rates. These techniques are applicable for the case of raw video as an input source.

Böröczky et al. [11] used the feedback approach in their joint rate control algorithm. They defined GOP boundaries or scene changes in a program as the point at which the MPEG-2 encoders bit rate was changed. This method provides two advantages. Firstly, during a GOP the encoder outputs at a constant bit rate. Therefore, the resulting bit streams are piecewise CBR. Secondly, this method does not need any preprocessing of the input video. The second advantage is important because processing raw video is computationally demanding and causes delay in the system. A limit was set to the bit rate changes during the same scene at GOP boundaries to prevent a noticeable change of quality in that scene. A control method was also developed to avoid buffer overflow and underflow. The method predefines two guard bounds at the top and bottom of the channel buffer. The information on channel buffer occupancy due to these guard-bands and the complexity of each input channels GOPs are jointly fed into the control algorithm to compute the bit rate of the individual encoders.

The process of obtaining statistics from video for determining the content coding complexity in the feedback approach is based on predicting the complexity from the previous frames' statistics. This can degrade the output video quality at scene changes, though some allowance for this problem can be made by using a sliding window GOP prediction method. As an alternative, He and Wu [23] used a lookahead approach in which the frame differences for each input video after encoding are found in order to estimate the variance of the number of DCT transform coefficients. These statistics in turn allow the rates for the input videos to be predicted for a desired constant distortion and a given encoder configuration. Processing is on a frame-by-frame basis but the average rate for any output video is then found for a given lookahead number of frames. For each output video, the predicted rate is normalized by the sum of all the other rates to determine the change to the encoding rate. Once a set of relative rates are found, these are then reduced step-by-step until encoder output buffer constraints are met. To avoid buffer overflow a similar two threshold system to that of [11] is used.

## 3  Methodology

### 3.1  Codec Software Modifications

Though a bitrate transcoder is under active development, for research purposes a decoder and encoder were used in back-to-back fashion, Fig. 2. In fact this is an example of the look-ahead method of statistical multiplexing. Again for research purposes, the H.264/AVC JM reference software was employed. The JM software (version 15.1) is written in the C programming language to ensure the fastest possible software-only processing time. In order to acquire the NNZC for each macroblock (MB) from the JM decoder, the decoder was modified as follows. The decoder obtains the coefficients from its input, arranges them in MB format, and then starts to decode each MB. The easiest method is to dump the NNZC is to obtain them prior to the decoding process of each MB. In the source codes of the decoder program in "image.c" inside "void decode_one_slice", the function "read_one_  macroblock(img, currSlice, currMB);" constructs an MB coefficient matrix and stores it in "img->cof" for a 4×4 transform and in "img->mb_rres" for an 8×8 transform. After this line "decode_  one_macroblock(img, currMB, dec_picture);" is executed which decodes the stored MB coefficient. Between these two lines is the place in which the additional code is added to dump the number coefficients and also to calculate and dump the total number of NNZC of a GOP.

In the experiments, the bitrate is changed during the encoding process. There is a feature in the encoder setting by the name of "ChannelType" which can be set to "time varying channel". By testing this feature it became clear that the CBR encoder changes the bitrate once by multiplying it by a constant factor during encoding. By exploiting this feature code was developed to oblige the encoder to change its bitrate at the start of each GOP.

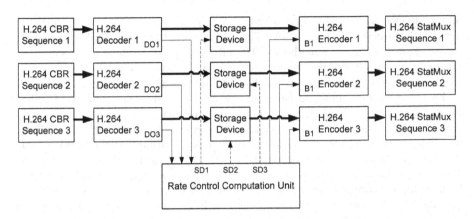

**Fig. 2.** Look-ahead implementation of statistical multiplexor

For the sake of simplicity, Common Intermediate Format (CIF) resolution sequences (352 × 288 pixels/frame) test sequences were employed rather than SDTV. By 2006 there were already a variety of hardware H.264/AVC codecs available [24] though with a reduced selection of features. Blu-ray specifies H.264/AVC High Profile as one of its three formats and H.264/AVC High Profile is selected for the Memory Stick Video format.

### 3.2  Relationship between NNZC and PSNR

The first step toward implementation of a statistical multiplexor was to establish the relationship between PSNR and the NNZC. To estimate this relationship on a GOP basis, several sequences were encoded and decoded at different bitrates. The chosen sequences for this step were the well-known Mobile, Foreman, News, Stefan, Bus and Akiyo. The sequences were chosen based on their temporal and spatial complexity to represent different video characteristics. 'Complexity' in this context refers to the coding complexity involved in compressing the sequence. A more complex sequence requires more bits to compress to achieve a given video quality. Spatial complexity refers to the level of detail within each frame, whereas temporal complexity refers to the level of disparity between successive frames.

These sequences were encoded in CBR mode at 256, 512, 768 kbit/s, and 1, 1.5, 2, 2.5 and 3 Mbit/s. The PSNR of each frame were obtained from output of the encoder, and then the average PSNR of each GOP was calculated. (GOP structure IBBPBBP…, intra-refresh rate 12 frames.) The total NNZCs of a GOP, which was obtained during the decoding process, was paired with the average PSNR value of the corresponding GOP. Figure 3 plots the relationship between PSNR and NNZC per GOP for a selection of these sequences. The rates plotted are across the given bitrate ranges for all of the selected video sequences, except for Akiyo. For Akiyo, the results shown correspond to the range 512 kbit/s to 1 Mbit/s. At bitrates higher than this the QP of the encoder is reduced to its minimum level due to the simplicity of Akiyo sequence contents. Consequently, in later experimental results (though obviously not in Fig. 3) Akiyo was excluded. Other plots in Fig. 3 illustrate the differing coding

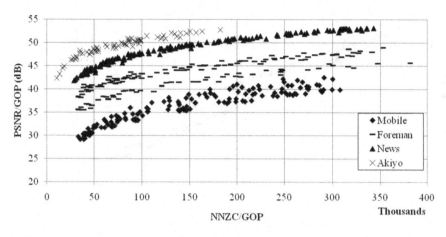

**Fig. 3.** NNZC per GOP versus average PSNR per GOP for selected video sequences

complexity of the sequences, with plots lower on the vertical axis representing more complex sequences. For equal NNZC/GOP, it is reasonable and expected that quality decreases for 'complex' sequences. Equally, when NNZC increases, it is reasonable and expected that also the quality increases.

An estimation equation based on these results was extracted as follows:

$$PSNR = 4.8 \ln (NNZC) + psnr' \text{ (dB)} \tag{1}$$

Where psnr' represents the zero-crossing value of the fitted curve, which depends on the coding complexity of the sequence as a whole.

### 3.3  No-Reference PSNR Estimation

Obviously, psnr' cannot be found without reference to the input raw (YUV) video which is often not feasible. However, the QP is available from the encoded bitstream. The encoder in CBR mode allocates the bit budget for each frame in the sequence based on frame type, GOP size, GOP structure and the bitrate. The encoder assigns an initial QP and then starts the encoding process of the first frame. After the encoding of the first frame the number of bits used for this frame is observed. This number is compared with the bit budget which was allocated for this frame and as a result the QP is adjusted to maintain the allocated bitrate for the GOP. For a certain bitrate, a complex frame needs to be compressed more than a simple frame and consequently it receives a higher QP.

To find this relationship between PSNR and QP, the average PSNR of each GOP is paired with the corresponding QP. Figure 4 shows that relationship for a selection of the input sequences and bitrates previously described. This relationship can be estimated by a linear equation:

$$PSNR = (-0.89) \times QP + 60.93 \text{ (dB)}. \tag{2}$$

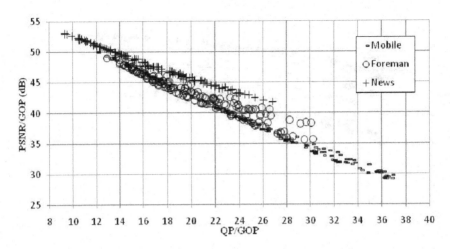

**Fig. 4.** QP per GOP versus average PSNR per GOP for selected video sequences

Equation (2) has a smaller margin of error for lower QP or equivalently higher bitrates. In the scenario envisaged in this paper, the input video streams are encoded at high bitrates to make the process of statistical multiplexing possible. Therefore, this estimate can be used with acceptable accuracy.

At this point, with the estimated average PSNR (ePSNR), the total NNZCs for all GOPs so far (tNNZC) and the average QP (avgQP) of the decoded GOP, using (1) and (2), psnr' can be calculated as:

$$ePSNR = (-0.89) \times avgQP + 60.93 \ (dB) \tag{3}$$

$$psnr' = ePSNR - 4.8 \times \ln(tNNZC) \ (dB) \tag{4}$$

and thus

$$PSNR = 4.8 \times \ln(NNZC) - 0.89 \times avgQP + 60.93 - 4.8 \ln(tNNZC) \ (dB). \tag{5}$$

Equation (5) is the main tool of this scheme as it permits per GOP PSNR to be found.

### 3.4  Relating PSNR to CBR Bitrate

In the encoding procedure of a codec operating in CBR mode, the best achievable way to assign the new bitrate for next encoded GOP is to oblige the encoder to change its bitrate. Therefore, (5) must be related to bitrate. After that, it becomes possible to allocate the bitrate based on the quality (PSNR) of a GOP. This requires that the relationship between NNZC and the number bits used per GOP is known. For this purpose, the total number of bit used per GOP (bits/GOP) is paired with the total NNZC for the corresponding GOP. The relationship is linear with a good accuracy at higher bitrates. Figures 5 and 6 show this relationship for three different GOPs of four different sequences (Mobile, Foreman, News and Stefan), encoded at 256 kbit/s to 3 Mbit/s. The GOP size or width does not disturb the linear relationship between bits/GOP and number of NNZC per GOP. No clear trend is discernible though for Mobile the results for a GOP size of 12 of separated from the other two GOP sizes.

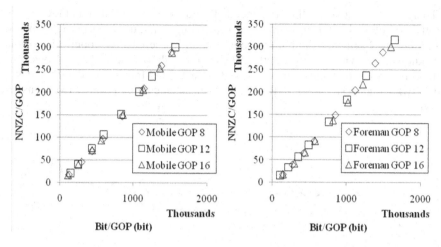

**Fig. 5.** NNZC per GOP versus bits/GOP for Mobile and Foreman at different GOP sizes

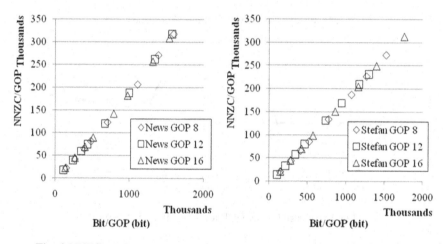

**Fig. 6.** NNZC per GOP versus bits/GOP for News and Stefan at different bitrates

By analyzing these data, the following equation (6) was found to be a reasonable estimation basis for conversion between NNZC and bits per GOP.

$$NNZC = 0.2 \times (bits/GOP) - 65536 \qquad (6)$$

### 3.5  Calibration Tests

In order to test the scheme, combined sequences of a set of the reference video sequences were CBR encoded at 3 Mbit/s. Each of three combined sequences contained 900 frames consisting of FNS (Foreman + News + Stefan), NMF (News + Mobile + Foreman) and WHB (Flower + Highway + Bus). In tests these H.264/AVC encoded combined sequences were the inputs of the statistical multiplexing system.

To apply the first step, all of the encoded sequences are decoded and the avgQP and tNNZC of each GOP was obtained. Processing continues on a per GOP basis. Therefore, the latency of the multiplexing system is one GOP or about 0.5 s. As is well known, live video is frequently delayed for a short time for the purposes of editing. Figures 7, 8 and 9 show the avgQP of each GOP for each of the FNS, NMF and WHB sequences. The ePSNR of each GOP is calculated through (3) by using avgQP.

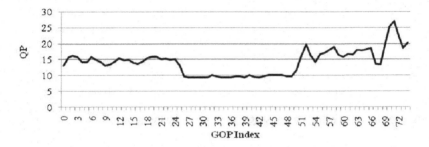

**Fig. 7.** Average QP per GOP for the FNS sequence set

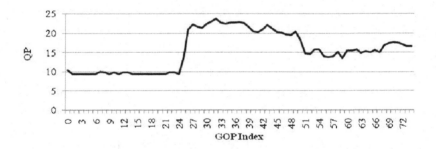

**Fig. 8.** Average QP per GOP for the NMF sequence set

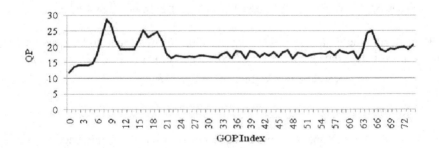

**Fig. 9.** Average QP per GOP for the WHB sequence set

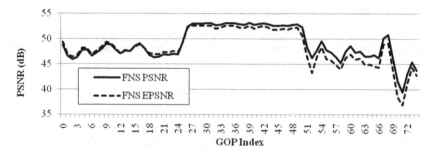

**Fig. 10.** Estimated PSNR (ePSNR) and calculated PSNR for the FNS combined sequence

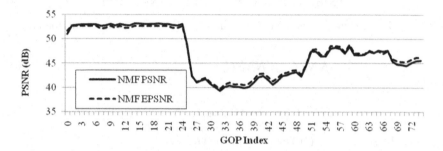

**Fig. 11.** Estimated PSNR (ePSNR) and calculated PSNR for the NMF combined sequence

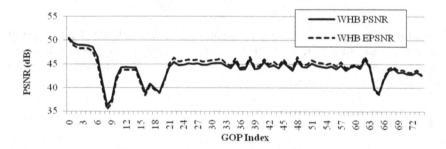

**Fig. 12.** Estimated PSNR (ePSNR) and calculated PSNR for the WHB combined sequence

The result of the above calculation for all of the sequences and the correct PSNR value obtained from the encoder output are presented in Figures 10, 11 and 12. It will be apparent that there is a good match between the estimated PSNR and the calculated PSNR.

The estimated PSNR (ePSNR) is then used to calculate the psnr' or the constant part of eq. (1) for each GOP, by means of eq. (4). The total bitrate of the statistical multiplexing system is taken to be 3 Mbit/s for test purposes. Hence, the first condition for calculation of the bitrate allocation is defined as follows:

$$\text{Bitrate}_1(t) + \text{Bitrate}_2(t) + \text{Bitrate}_3(t) = 3 \text{ Mbit/s} \tag{7}$$

where indices 1, 2 and 3, represent the FNS, NMF and WHB sequences over time t. Making use of (6), (7) can be converted to the following form, NNZC and per GOP (with GOP size = 12 frames and frame rate = 25 fps).

$$NNZC_1 + NNZC_2 + NNZC_3 = 0.2 \times (3 \text{ Mbit/s} \times \frac{12}{25}) - 3 \times 65536 \tag{8}$$

The second condition to satisfy a statistical multiplexing system is to normalize the overall quality, which happens if at each sampling time the quality of all of the streams becomes equal. This fact defines the second condition of this process, which is:

$$PSNR_1(GOP) = PSNR_2(GOP) = PSNR_3(GOP). \tag{9}$$

By substituting (1) into (9) and equating, equations (10) and (11) are easily found.

$$NNZC_2 = NNZC_1 \times e^{\frac{psnr_1 - psnr_2}{4.8}} \tag{10}$$

$$NNZC_3 = NNZC_1 \times e^{\frac{psnr_1 - psnr_3}{4.8}} \tag{11}$$

Subsequently, substituting (10) and (11) into (8) results in:

$$NNZC_1 = \frac{105382}{1 + e^{\frac{psnr_1 - psnr_2}{4.8}} + e^{\frac{psnr_1 - psnr_3}{4.8}}} \tag{12}$$

In the final calculation step, by using (6) again Bitrate$_{1-3}$ are calculated at the start of each GOP. These bitrates are the input of the second stage of this system which consists of the final set of encoders. The final encoders apply these bitrates through the method described in Section 3.1

## 4  Evaluation

The proposed scheme was evaluated through comparison of the system output quality with conventional equal allocation of bitrate multiplexing. Figures 13, 14 and 15 illustrate the average PSNR of each GOP for the three experimental sequences, according to whether the proposed scheme is applied (StatMux) or whether the available 3 Mbit/s bandwidth is allocated at 1 Mbit/s per video sequence. It is immediately clear that in Fig. 14, the constant bitrate allocation results in a deep quality fade. All of the three encoded sequences at 1 Mbit/s, contain at least one GOP with average PSNR below 30 dB. Therefore, the CBR process results are not suitable for broadcasting because of the noticeable quality degradation. On the other hand, the minimum average GOP PSNR for the statistical multiplexing scheme was about 34 dB, which is an acceptable quality.

The average PSNR over all frames was calculated for both statistical multiplexing and constant CBR mode, and demonstrated in Table 1. The overall quality difference is 0.42 (dB) gained by the proposed statistical multiplexing scheme. The standard deviation of the PSNR is also calculated as a measure of variation of the PSNR around its average. The PSNR standard deviation of the statistical multiplexing scheme is lower by a considerable extent. This result illustrates the success of the scheme in equalizing the quality across the three sequences. Because of the quality fade for constant CBR (Fig. 14 and drops below 30 dB) and because of the low over-all quality of the WHB sequence (Table 1), it would be necessary to send just two sequences at a rate of 1.5 Mbit/s each for fixed rate transport. Therefore, for this example, the number of programs that can be sent at 40 dB has been increased by a factor of 1.5.

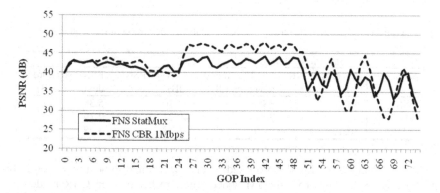

**Fig. 13.** Average PSNR/GOP for constant allocation of bandwidth and the proposed statistical multiplexing scheme on the FNS combined sequence

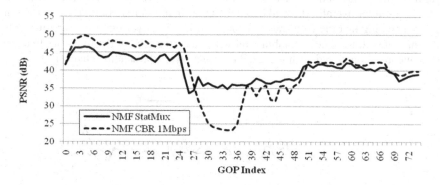

**Fig. 14.** Average PSNR/GOP for constant allocation of bandwidth and the proposed statistical multiplexing scheme on the NMF combined sequence

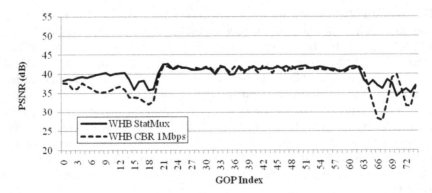

**Fig. 15.** Average PSNR/GOP for constant allocation of bandwidth and the proposed statistical multiplexing scheme on the WHB combined sequence

**Table 1.** Per sequence average PSNR and standard deviation of the sequences

| | Statistical multiplexing | | CBR | |
|---|---|---|---|---|
| Sequence | Average PSNR (dB) | PSNR standard deviation (dB) | Average PSNR (dB) | PSNR standard deviation (dB) |
| **FNS** | 40.57 | 3.00 | 41.70 | 5.38 |
| **NMF** | 40.39 | 3.47 | 40.21 | 7.39 |
| **WHB** | 40.04 | 2.10 | 38.68 | 3.68 |

A further gain from using the proposed scheme was found to be a reduction in bitrate fluctuations arising from the JM codec software behavior in CBR mode. The codec selects I- and B-frame QPs intelligently to avoid too rapid transitions in quality. Unfortunately, if at scene changes the new scene is more complex, then a large fluctuation in bitrate occurs. It was observed that the proposed scheme results in smoother resulting bitrate fluctuations than when requests are made for a uniformly constant bitrate. The total overall bitrate allocation (rather than requested bitrate) is shown in Fig. 16, showing that the fixed rate allocation results in larger bitrate excursions. It is clear that rate adjustment in combination with buffering is required to ensure that the instantaneous allocation does not exceed the capacity of the satellite channel.

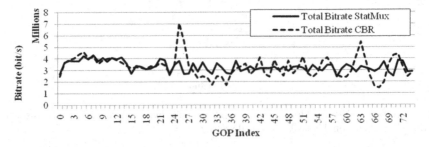

**Fig. 16.** Allocated bitrate/GOP for constant allocation of bandwidth and the proposed statistical multiplexing scheme for the overall multiplex

# 5  Conclusion

The H.264/AVC results in approximately a doubling in compression efficiency relative to MPEG-2. The resulting bitstream is easily accommodated in an MPEG-2 TS. In this paper, we have demonstrated a statistical multiplexing scheme based on spatial complexity modeling equations parameterized by the per-GOP NNZC. For 40 dB PSNR video streams, the scheme significantly reduces PSNR fluctuations. True VBR video may result in too frequent bitrate oscillations and in this paper, a GOP-by-GOP semi-VBR scheme has been investigated. This implies that the latency of the scheme is the time taken to process a GOP, normally about 0.5 s. Aggregated user video inputs may occur in the DVB-RCS system, with the video bitrates close to those described in this paper. Therefore, this is one application of the proposed scheme. Future work should account for the impact of scene changes. The JM software implementation of H.264/AVC operating in CBR mode avoids rapid changes in quality by modifying the output bitrate. The proposed scheme additionally counters the bitrate fluctuations that occur due to the behavior of the codec at scene changes.

# References

1. Neal, J., Green, R., Landovskis, J.: Interactive channel for multimedia satellite networks. IEEE Commun. Mag. 39, 192–198 (2001)
2. Tandberg Television Ltd.: Reflex and data Reflex statistical multiplexing system. White Paper, Slough, UK (2008)
3. Seeling, P., Reisslein, M.: The rate variability-distortion (VD) curve of encoded video and its impact on statistical multiplexing. IEEE Trans. Broadcast 51(4), 473–492 (2005)
4. Kuhn, M., Antkowiak, J.: Statistical multiplex what does it mean for DVB-T? FKT Fachzeitschrift für Fernsehen, Film und elektronische Medien (2000)
5. Wiegand, T., Sullivan, G.J., Bjøntegaard, G., Luthra, A.: Overview of the H.264/AVC video coding standard. IEEE Trans. Circuits Syst. Video Technol. 13(7), 560–576 (2003)
6. Wenger, S.: H.264 over IP. IEEE Trans. Circuits Syst. Video Technol. 13(7), 645–656 (2003)
7. Fischer, W.: Digital video and audio broadcasting technology, 2nd edn. Springer, Berlin (2008)
8. Ghanbari, M., Fleury, M., Khan, E., et al.: Future Performance of Video Codecs, research report for Office of Communications (Ofcom), London (November 2006)
9. Vukadinovic, V., Huschke, J.: Statistical multiplexing gains of H.264/AVC video in E-MBMS. In: 3rd Int. Symp. on Wireless Pervasive Computing, pp. 468–474 (2008)
10. Ghanbari, M., Azari, J.: Effect of bit rate variation of the base layer on the performance of two-layer video codecs. IEEE Trans. Circuits Syst. Video Technol. 4(1), 8–17 (1994)
11. Böröczy, L., Ngai, A.Y., Westermann, E.F.: Statistical multiplexing using MPEG-2 video encoders. IBM J. of Research and Development 43(4), 511–520 (1999)
12. Scopus Video Networking: Advanced encoding mechanism and statistical multiplexing. White Paper, Sunnyvale, CA (2006)
13. Zhang, Z.-L., Kurose, J., Salehi, J.D., Townsley, D.: Smoothing, statistical multiplexing and call admission control for stored video. IEEE J. Sel. Areas Communs 15(6), 1148–1166 (1997)

14. van der Auwera, G., David, P.T., Reisslein, M.: Traffic and quality characterization of single-layer video streams encoded with the H.264/MPEG-4 Advanced Video Coding standard and Scalable Video Coding extension. IEEE Trans. Broadcast 54(3), 698–718 (2008)
15. Kasai, K., Nilsson, M., Jebb, T., Whybray, M., Tominaga, H.: The development of a multimedia transcoding system for mobile access to video conferencing. IEICE Trans. on Communs. 10(2), 2171–2181 (2002)
16. Eleftheriadis, A., Batra, P.: Dynamic rate shaping of compressed digital video. IEEE Trans. Multimedia 8(9), 297–314 (2006)
17. Assunção, P.A., Ghanbari, M.: A frequency-domain video transcoder for dynamic bit-rate reduction of MPEG-2 bit streams. IEEE Trans. Circuits Syst. Video Technol. 8(8), 953–967 (1998)
18. Malvar, H., Hallapuro, A., Karczewicz, M., Kerofsky, L.: Low complexity transform and quantization in H. 264/AVC. IEEE Trans. Circuits Syst. Video Technol. 13(7), 598–603 (2003)
19. Saponara, S., Blanch, C., Denolf, K., Bormans, J.: The JVT advanced video coding standard: Complexity and performance analysis on a tool-by-tool basis. In: Int'l. Packet Video Workshop, Nantes, France (April 2003)
20. Ghinea, G., Thomas, J.P.: QoS impact on user perception and understanding of multimedia video clips. In: ACM Int'l. Conf. on Multimedia, pp. 49–54 (1998)
21. De Rango, F., Tropea, M., Fazio, P., Marano, S.: Call admission control for aggregate MPEG-2 traffic over multimedia geo-satellite networks. IEEE Trans. Broadcast. 54(3), 612–622 (2008)
22. Wang, L., Vincent, A.: Joint rate control for multi-program video coding. IEEE Trans. Consumer Electron. 42(3), 300–305 (1996)
23. He, Z., Wu, D.O.: Linear rate control and optimum statistical multiplexing for H. 264 video broadcast. IEEE Trans. Multimedia 10(7), 1237–1249 (2008)
24. Marpe, D., Wiegand, T., Sullivan, G.J.: The H.264 / MPEG4 Advanced Video Coding standard and its applications. IEEE Commun. Mag. 44(8), 134–144 (2006)

# The Interplanetary Network Node: Architecture and Preliminary Performance Evaluation

Giuseppe Araniti[1], Igor Bisio[2], and Mauro De Sanctis[3]

[1] Department of Computer, Mathematics, Electronic and Transports
University of Reggio Calabria
araniti@unirc.it
[2] Department of Communications, Computer and System Science
University of Genoa
igor.bisio@unige.it
[3] Department of Electronic Engineering
University of Rome Tor Vergata
mauro.de.sanctis@uniroma2.it

**Abstract.** In the framework of the so called InterPlaNetary (IPN) Internet, the paper surveys possible advanced communications and networking solutions applied by a specific IPN node architecture. The proposed solutions have been preliminarily evaluated by using the ns2 simulator by considering possible network status changes due to the nodes' movements, typical in the deep space scenario. In particular, the performance study on one hand highlights the role of the Multicast and, on the other hand, it shows the effects of new possible control approaches such as the dynamic Link Selection in the IPN network. The performance study represents the main paper contribution.

**Keywords:** Interplanetary Networks Architecture, Advanced IPN Node, Multicast, Link Selection.

## 1 Introduction

The IPN Internet, described in [1] and here synthesised, is supposed to be split into different sub-networks that encounter different problems and, as a consequence, different technical challenges. The IPN includes the IPN Backbone Network, IPN External Networks, and PlaNetary (PN) Networks. The IPN Backbone Network provides a common infrastructure for communications among Earth, planets, moons, space probes and spacecrafts through satellites, which operate as network nodes allowing transmissions over deep space channels. The IPN External Network consists of nodes that are spacecrafts flying in deep space between planets, space probes, and orbiting space stations. Nodes of the IPN External Network have both long and short-haul communication capabilities. The former are employed if the nodes are at long distance from the other IPN nodes, the latter are employed at nodes flying in proximity of other ones.

The PN Network is composed of the PN Satellite Network and the PN Surface Network. The former includes links among surface nodes, orbiting satellites and IPN Backbone Nodes, providing a relay service between surface network and backbone

K. Sithamparanathan et al. (Eds.): PSATS 2010, LNICST 43, pp. 179–190, 2010.
© Institute for Computer Sciences, Social-Informatics and Telecommunications Engineering 2010

network and between two or more parts of the surface network. The latter provides the communication links between surface elements, such as rovers and sensor nodes which may have the communication capability towards satellites. It also provides a wireless backbone over the planet employed by surface elements that cannot communicate with satellites directly.

In this paper, the study of a specific IPN network architecture has been proposed. That network, depicted in Fig. 1, is exactly composed as described previously. In more detail, three PN networks have been included in the architecture. Two PN networks are employed over a remote planet (e.g., Mars) and over the Moon. In both cases, the Surface PN network is composed of two landers (MS1 and MS2 over the remote planet and LS1 and LS2 over the Moon), able to transmit information such as images, sensed data (e.g., temperature, humidity etc.), towards the PN Satellite Network. PN satellite networks are structured with four orbiting satellites (MO1, MO2, MO3 and MO4) in the case of the remote planet and two orbiting satellites around the Moon (LO1 and LO2).

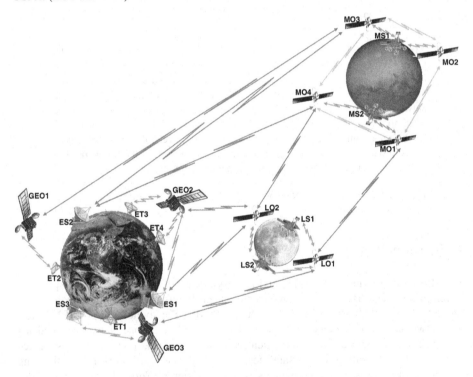

**Fig. 1.** Interplanetary Network Architecture

Over Earth, the PN surface network is composed of six surface nodes. They are typically the destination of the information sent from remote planets and, simultaneously, the source of possible control messages transmitted towards the IPN nodes (e.g., from Mission Control Centres). In detail, Earth Surface nodes are the ones of the well-known DSN - Deep Space Network (ES1, ES2 and ES3) and other possible nodes, such as Space Science Research Centres, distributed over the planet (ET1, ET2

ET3 and ET4). Concerning the PN Satellite Network, three Geostationary satellites (GEO1, GEO2 and GEO3) have been included in the architecture. They are supposed spaced of 120° so allowing the maximum coverage of Earth surface. Each orbiting satellite of the IPN network has been also considered as a node of the Backbone Network. Satellites can exchange information each other, if a link is available among them. No External Networks have been considered in this architecture.

All details concerning the link: available data rate, propagation delays, network movement and the consequent link blackouts, will be reported in the following.

It is worth noting that this architecture, as well as the analysis reported in the following, is a synthesis of the main contributions of the paper [2] by the same authors, here reported for the sake of completeness.

The remainder of this paper is structured as follows. Section 2 reports the simulative IPN network study concerning bandwidth availabilities, delays and link blackouts. Section 3 revises a functional architecture suited to be employed in the IPN scenario and, in particular, analyses the Multicast Transmission [3] and Link Selection [4] necessities with an introductive performance investigation carried out again by *ns-2* simulation. Conclusions are drawn in Section 4.

## 2  IPN Network Architecture Study

The analysis of the proposed architecture (described in Section 1) has been carried out for a sample period of 24 hours and in this analysis only the former cause has occurred. The architecture considered in this paper is an example of a possible realization of IPN Internet with planetary networks on Earth, Moon and Mars and the performance evaluation of link parameters (i.e., availability, delay and path loss) have been used for the simulation of networking solutions (Section 3).

It is worth noting that no cable connections between ground stations have been considered and landers can only communicate with the relative planetary network of orbiters.

Furthermore, the lunar lander LS1 is positioned on the dark side of the Moon, and hence, it could not communicate directly with the Earth without using a Lunar relay orbiter. Lunar orbiters has the further task to relay the communications between Mars and Earth when direct communication is not possible. The average blackout duration for a selected set of IPN links between external nodes is summarized in Table 1.

**Table 1.** Average blackout duration for a selection of IPN links

| Link | Average blackout duration | Link | Average blackout duration |
|------|--------------------------|------|--------------------------|
| LO1-GEO1 | 2286 s | LO1-MO1 | 2157 s |
| LO1-GEO2 | 2496 s | LO1-MO2 | 2258 s |
| LO1-GEO3 | 2170 s | LO1-MO3 | 1209 s |
| LO2-GEO1 | 2453 s | LO1-MO4 | 1209 s |
| LO2-GEO2 | 2410 s | LO2-MO1 | 2157 s |
| LO2-GEO3 | 2156 s | LO2-MO2 | 2258 s |
| ES1-LO1 | 10230 s | LO2-MO3 | 1209 s |
| ES1-LO2 | 8939 s | LO2-MO4 | 1209 s |
| ES1-MO1 | 6797 s | ES1-MO3 | 17198 s |
| ES1-MO2 | 6726 s | ES1-MO4 | 17199 s |

From the values of the average blackout duration, it can be noticed that the DSN Earth station ES1 (Canberra), and hence similarly ES2 (Goldstone) and ES3 (Madrid), shows a long blackout duration of the links to the Lunar or Martian orbiters. However, this is overcome by using alternative links through three GEO satellites.

Another important aspect of the system architecture is the propagation delay. The mean value of the propagation delay is shown in Table 2 for a selection of IPN links. The propagation delay can be as long as 20 minutes in the case of Mars-Earth connection. However, since the shortest path from Mars to Earth (i.e. the MSx-MOy-ESz path) is not always available, in many cases the total end-to-end delay can be much higher.

**Table 2.** Average propagation delay for a selection of IPN links

| Link | Average propagation delay | Link | Average propagation delay |
|------|---------------------------|------|---------------------------|
| LO1-GEO1 | 1.25 s | LO1-MO1 | 1210 s |
| LO1-GEO2 | 1.25 s | LO1-MO2 | 1210 s |
| LO1-GEO3 | 1.25 s | LO1-MO3 | 1210 s |
| LO2-GEO1 | 1.25 s | LO1-MO4 | 1210 s |
| LO2-GEO2 | 1.25 s | LO2-MO1 | 1210 s |
| LO2-GEO3 | 1.25 s | LO2-MO2 | 1210 s |
| ES1-LO1 | 1.3 s | LO2-MO3 | 1210 s |
| ES1-LO2 | 1.3 s | LO2-MO4 | 1210 s |
| ES1-MO1 | 1210 s | ES1-MO3 | 1210 s |
| ES1-MO2 | 1210 s | ES1-MO4 | 1210 s |

The data rate of each link has been computed on the basis of the DVB-S2 standard and with realistic values of transmission power and antenna size [9]. The performance of the DVB-S2 standard in terms of Bit Error Rate (BER) versus Signal to Noise Ratio (SNR) $E_s/N_0$ follows a threshold behavior which is due to the adopted modulation and coding schemes. In fact when the SNR is lower than the required $E_s/N_0$ the BER is very large, while when the SNR is larger than the required $E_s/N_0$ the performance of the system is quasi error free (BER=$10^{-10}$) [10]. Therefore, a constant data rate has been considered. It has been computed in each link for the maximum distance (worst case) by using the lowest modulation index and code rate (i.e. QPSK 1/4) with a packet length of 64800 bits. However, since the DVB-S2 standard foresees adaptive coding and modulation schemes and the propagation losses are highly variable, another possible approach is to consider variable data rates on the basis of the selected modulation and coding scheme for every set of propagation losses.

**Table 3.** Data rate for a selection of IPN links

| link | forward link data rate | reverse link data rate |
|------|------------------------|------------------------|
| LOx-GEOx | 100 kbps | 100 kbps |
| LOx-MOx | 1 kbps | 1 kbps |
| ESx-GEOx | 10000 kbps | 10000 kbps |
| ESx-LOx | 1000 kbps | 100 kbps |
| ESx-MOx | 10 kbps | 1 kbps |

The parameters reported in Table 1, 2 and 3 have been presented in [2] and they represent the input of the simulations performed with *ns2* and described in the following Section.

## 3  The IPN Node Functional Architecture

A possible functional architecture suited to be employed in IPN networks has been proposed starting from its definition originally proposed in [5]. In this Section, moreover, the introductive performance investigation of some features of the proposed node (Multicast Transmission and Link Selection) have been included.

The envisaged IPN Node architecture is reported in Fig. 2. It includes the Bundle Layer and a Higher Convergence Layer that act as bridge between two different portions: a standard stack (e.g., the TCP/IP one) used to connect common network devices to the IPN Node and the space protocol stack suited to be employed in the IPN

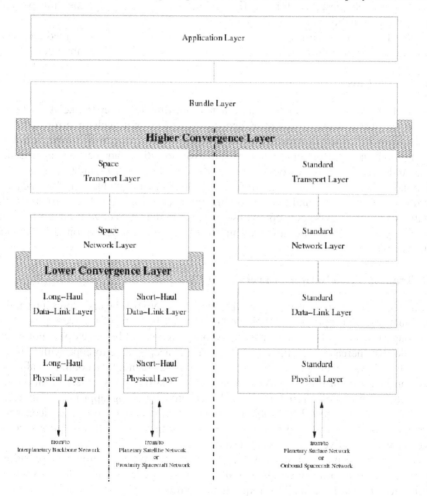

**Fig. 2.** IPN Node Protocol Stack

environment. The Higher Convergence Layer will allow managing traffic flows both sent by standard hosts and DTN-compatible hosts. It acts as adaptation layer and realizes the backward compatibility with common protocol stacks. After the adaptation phase all packets become bundles, the transmission unit of DTNs, and they are sent though specific transport and network layers designed for the space portion of the IPN network. The IPN Node transport and network protocols parameters will be adaptively optimized starting from the employed channel conditions. Data Link and Physical Layers have been again differentiated into two families: Long and Short-haul. In the former case, the lower layers solutions will be specialized for very long distance channels (e.g., between satellites of the IPN backbone). In the latter case, solutions are suited to be used in short distance channels (e.g., between spacecrafts and proximity satellites of the IPN network or between PN satellites and planet surfaces). The Lower Convergence Layer acts as selector between the Long or Short-haul layers in dependence on the position of the IPN network elements. Long and Short-haul protocols, opportunely designed for the IPN environment, allow implementing possible adaptive functionalities of the lower layers.

In the following, each layer of the IPN node has been briefly described and some considerations concerning the related open research issues have been included.

### 3.1 Bundle Layer

To match the IPN environment requirements, the Bundle Layer [6] needs to be extended. In more detail, its current specification does not include error detection mechanisms of bundles. It opens the doors to the employment of application layer coding, both in terms of source coding and error detection and recovery approaches. Other important open issues related to the Bundle Layer will be taken into account: the bundle size optimization and the related problem of fragmentation; the study and the design of common bundle layer routing approaches for the IPN environment; the Quality of Service (QoS) concept, whose meaning in the IPN network differs from the common one, together with new QoS mechanisms suited to be exploited in the considered environment.

### 3.2 Transport and Network Layers

The performance issues of the space transport and network layers represent another important research topic of the IPN node design [1]. In terms of recovery procedures and congestion control schemes, new transport protocol will be developed. For example, Additive Increase / Multiplicative Decrease concepts, able to cope with blackout events by taking advantage of probing packets will be taken into account to realize the transport layer. In turn, in the case of unavailable or strongly asymmetric return links, the transport protocol's reliability will be ensured by using appropriate strategies based on erasure codes. The problem of congestion events occurring at deep space IPN Node will be also solved by considering call admission and flow control schemes together with effective storage routing strategies.

The IPN Node protocol stack will also support the point-multipoint applications. Multicast/broadcast transmissions will allow reaching several IPN nodes, so optimizing the resource utilization. This requires the introduction of Multicast Transmission approaches whose possible enhancements will be object of future and extensive research.

In this sub-section some preliminary simulation results, carried out by means of *ns2* simulator, have been provided. They show the impact of multicast data delivery in deep space exploration missions. In particular, it has been highlighted the advantages that could be obtained utilizing groups oriented applications respect to point-to-point transmissions in the IPN scenario.

It is worth noting that, in the depicted IPN topology, (reported in Fig. 1) two different kind of Multicast Connections could be thought: *(i) Multicast Forward Connections* (MFC), where sources are, for instance, Earth Mission Centers and receivers are the deep space nodes; *Multicast Reverse Connections* (MRC), for communications from remote planets to Earth. As mentioned in the introduction, the *MFC* could be used for Mission Applications to provide control information and to upgrade the software implemented in the IPN nodes. While, *MRC* could be utilized for Scientist and Public Applications to receive planetary images, videos and experimental results acquired by space stations.

In the following simulation campaign, the network architecture of Fig. 1 has been considered. It has been assumed, for each link, the propagation delay and data rate values reported in Section 4. The results highlight how a multicast approach could lead to a most efficient resource management compared with Unicast techniques. For instance, considering a scenario where a terrestrial node (i.e., ES1) sends data to receivers of a multicast group located on two different planets and supposing that four receivers belong to such a multicast group (two scattered on the Moon and the other ones located on Mars) the situation is as follows. Unicast approach foresees four connections between sender and receivers; this means that the same information is sent on the channel four times. Therefore, in this case a Unicast approach increases the accesses to the links needed to forward the same packet. Clearly, such a issue is more manifest when the number of receivers increases. While, a multicast approach always foresees the same number of accesses (i.e., one each planet) regardless of the number of receivers belonging to the same multicast group. These result are depicted in Fig. 3 varying the number of multicast receiver for region/planet. The obtained result demonstrates that a multicast approach in IPN networks gives the following advantages: *(i)* it reduces the links utilization, saving radio resources that could be utilized to supply transmission of further services; *(ii)* it optimizes the memorization units size (buffer size) and reduces the signalization due to acknowledgment procedures and routing.

The next results concern how Unicast and Multicast transmissions affect the buffer size (in terms of maximum number of packets that can be memorized) of IPN nodes. We assumed that the buffer size is equal for each IPN node. Fig. 4 depicts the obtained results for a MFC connection in term of Packet Delivery Ratio (PDR).

How mentioned above Unicast transmissions foresee that the same information is sent on the channel for all the receivers. From Fig. 3 such a issue affects the limits in terms of buffer size more in Unicast approach than in Multicast ones, clearly. On the other hands whether the buffer size is increased then the PDR also increases. From a buffer size equal to 500 packets (i.e. 83,4% of the overall forwarded traffic) there are not loss due to congestion of the buffers, considering multicast transmission.

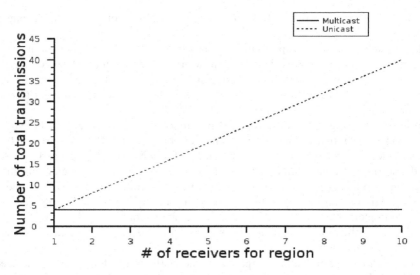

**Fig. 3.** Number of accesses to the links varying the number of receivers per region

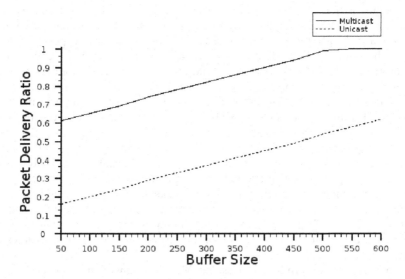

**Fig. 4.** MCF: PDR varying buffer size

In this case, the bottlenecks in the nodes MO1 and LO1 are the main reason of packets loss. Therefore, also in this case a Multicast approach improves the performances in IPN network with respect to Unicast transmission. Moreover, it is worth noting that these results have been obtained by considering unreliable traffic only. This means that a packet is removed from the buffer as soon as it is sent on the radio link. In case of reliable Multicast transmissions the propagation delays on the links have to be taken into account; they clearly can get worse the performance showed in Fig. 3 in both Unicast and Multicast approach, but affecting Unicast Transmissions significantly.

Future activities are aimed to improve the performance of Multicast Transmission in IPN network implementing DTN paradigm. In particular, the research activity will deal with the following issues: *(i)* definition of procedures for notifications and registration/de-registration of multicast groups; *(ii)* definition of multicast routing protocols that utilize models based on both tree or mesh topologies, in order to minimize the path length between source and destinations and to increase the probability that the bundle is delivered to as many destination nodes as possible; *(iii)* definition of transport and bundle layers suitable to provide end-to-end reliable connections, defining efficient transmission and retransmission procedures. In this context, the storing functionalities for the store-and-forward policies have to be design in order to guarantee data persistence in DTN nodes also for relatively large time slots. For dealing with that, DTN aggregates data into bundles and stores them in persistent storage of different IPN nodes so that in case of loss of connectivity, the bundles could be retransmitted from the closest storage points rather than from the source node. A key Bundle Protocol innovation is known as *Custodial Delivery*. The memorization functionality in DTN nodes will be considered as a new network resource that has to be administered and protected. Fundamental open issues in the definition of a new protocol stack are related to these topics. At the moment, the Bundle Protocol specifies the procedures for supporting custodial delivery of bundles destined to unicast applications. However, it does not discuss how *Custodial Delivery* should be provided for bundles destined to multicast groups (multicast bundle). There is a strong motivation for using custodial multicast in IPN to preserve the already-scarce resource of bandwidth during transmission and retransmission procedures [2].

### 3.3  Data Link and Physical Layers

Data Link Layers protocols of the IPN node include functionalities concerning the medium access control (MAC) and error control functions. Also in this case, advanced network control features need to be considered and they are aimed at optimizing the utilization of IPN channels. For both Long and Short-haul physical layers, specific solutions will be studied in terms of bandwidth/power efficient modulations and low complexity channel codes with high coding gain. Waveforms design and the exploitation of Ultra WideBand (UWB) systems needs to be considered with the goal to reduce the complexity of the system and the sensitivity to IPN channels' non-linearity.

Also space physical layer solutions that exploit Extremely High Frequency (EHF) bands can be taken into account. EHF employment, in particular the W-band, represents an answer to the needs of IPN links: the saturation of lower frequency bands, the growth of data-rate request and the reduction of mass and size of equipment. Considering that the main disadvantage of the use of W-band frequencies is the atmospheric attenuation, the benefits of its employment could be fully exploited in deep space channels where the atmosphere is absent. The reduced antenna size due to the use of higher frequencies represents a further advantage of this choice.

### 3.4  Convergence Layers

Convergence Layers, both Higher and Lower, and IPN Network Control approaches concern another group of innovative solutions, envisaged in this work, which needs to be developed. As previously said, the action of the Higher Convergence Layer is to offer a common interface to the transport layers (space and standard). The Lower Convergence Layer will offer a common interface towards data link and physical layers and vice versa and it will offer innovative control functions in terms of selection of the opportune lower layer stack (e.g., vertical handover) by considering the situation in which the IPN Node operates (long- or short-haul network segment).

## 3.5 Network Controls

In order to smooth the effect of the intrinsic heterogeneity of the IPN network, adaptive mechanisms [7], based on the cross-layer principle [1], are needed. It means that appropriate solutions are necessary to harmonize each single layer solution and jointly optimize the capabilities of IPN Node layers. For example, the transport and network protocol parameters need to be dynamically tuned in dependence on the channel status. The same concept holds true for all protocol layers, also with respect to the position of the IPN Node within the IPN topology.

In the set of possible Network Controls, a partially unexplored solution concerns the Link Selection strategies based on the exploitation of the Bundle Layer of the DTN paradigm. In more detail, Link Selection techniques, also called Congestion Aware Routing, have been proposed in [4] where the mathematical framework has been formalised. It has been taken as example in this paper.

In synthesis, the approaches proposed allow selecting a forwarding link, among the available ones, by optimising one or different metrics, simultaneously. In fact, in this paper, the optimization of one metric has been considered: the Bundle Buffer Occupancy (BBO). The Bundle Buffer Occupancy is the ratio between the number of bundles stored in the bundle layer buffer and the maximum size of the buffer itself. The evaluated Link Selection technique is based on its minimization.

The performance analysis has been conducted by taking network topology depicted in Fig. 1 as reference and by considering the bandwidth capacities and propagation delays reported in the analysis of Section 4. All the link blackouts, due to IPN node movements, have been also included in the simulations whose results have been reported in the following. Moreover, each node implements a bundle layer buffer size equal to 400 bundles. Constant Bit Rate (CBR) traffic sources are considered: they are kept active for 50 s each hour of simulation and generate data bundles of 64 Kbytes at rate of 1 bundles/s, yielding 512 Kbit/s. Furthermore, in this case, the traffic sources have been set on the planetary regions, and in particular the traffic sources are the nodes MS1 and MS2 from the remote planet, LS1 and LS2 from the Moon. They send data over Earth to ET1, ET2, ET3 and ET4, respectively, which are set as receivers. The simulation duration was of 7200 s (2 hours out of 24, which is the duration of the analysis proposed in Section 4) for each test carried out by *ns2* simulations.

The proposed results concern a macroscopic analysis of the Link Selection method's performance. It looks into performance provided by the whole network and, in this view, two metrics have been considered: Bundle Loss Rate (BLR) and Data Delivery Time (DDT) coherently with [4]. The first is defined as ratio between the number of received and of transmitted bundles. The second accounts for the time interval required to complete the data delivery to destinations. It is possible to observe, in Fig. 5, the Bundle Loss Rate (BLR %) performance for each Flow where

Flow1 is the data flow between LS1 to ET1, Flow2 is the data flow between LS2 to ET2, Flow3 is the data flow between MS1 to ET3 and Flow4 is the data flow between MS2 to ET4. The BLR measured highlights quite effective results. This means that a Link Selection Control (or Congestion Aware Routing) allows reaching good network performance also in challenging network as the IPN ones. In more detail, Flow1 is privileged with respect to the others. Actually, it is mainly due to the simulated period: in the first 2 hours, out of 24, the link blackouts have penalized Flow4 and, partially, Flow2 and Flow3. Moreover, Flow3 and Flow4 experience very low link capacities over the IPN network due to the very high distance between Mars and Earth.

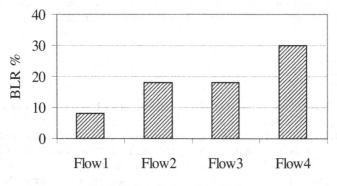

**Fig. 5.** Bundle Loss Rate [%]

On the other hand, as far as Data Delivery Time (DDT) is concerned, it can be observed from Fig. 6 that the Link Selection solution offer satisfactory performance. The shown DDT can appear very high but the enormous propagation delays and the very small available link capacities do not allow better performance. It is obvious in particular in case of transmissions from the remote planet (Mars in Fig. 1): they require almost the overall time that has been simulates (about two hours). Transmission from the Moon requires about 260 [s] in average.

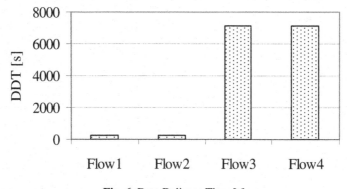

**Fig. 6.** Data Delivery Time [s]

However, from the introductive evaluation proposed, it is worth noting that the proposed control technique have promising performance. This opens the doors to future extensions and investigations that will analyse in-depth the performance of the Link Selection over the considered network architecture.

## 4 Conclusions

The presented work describes possible networking solutions jointly used with novel network control procedures that allow the optimization of the IPN network performance so guaranteeing a reliable and efficient communication process over the IPN Internet. These solutions will be the object of ongoing and future research that will be developed as extension of this work, which represents an introductive overview of them.

## References

1. Akyildiz, I., et al.: The State of the Art in InterPlaNetary Internet. IEEE Communications Magazine, 108–118 (July 2004)
2. Araniti, G., Bisio, I., De Sanctis, M.: Interplanetary Networks: Architectural Analysis, Technical Challenges and Solutions Overview. In: Proc. IEEE International Communications Conference 2010 (ICC 2010), Capetown, South Africa (June 2010) (to appear)
3. Symington, S., Durst, R.C., Scott, K.: Custodial Multicast in Delay Tolerant Networks. In: 4th IEEE Consumer Communications and Networking Conference, CCNC 2007, January 2007, pp. 207–211 (2007)
4. Bisio, I., de Cola, T., Marchese, M.: Congestion Aware Routing Strategies for DTN-based Interplanetary Networks. In: IEEE GLOBECOM 2008, New Orleans, LA, USA (November-December 2008)
5. Araniti, G., Bisio, I., De Sanctis, M.: Towards the Reliable and Efficient Interplanetary Internet: a Survey of Possible Advanced Networking and Communications Solutions. In: proc. SPACOMM 2009, Colmar, France (July 2009)
6. Cerf, V., et al.: Protocol Specification. IETF RFC 4838, experimental (April 2007)
7. Peoples, C., et al.: A Reconfigurable Context-Aware Protocol Stack for Interplanetary Communication. In: Proc. IWSSC 2007, Salzburg, Austria, September 2007, pp. 163–167 (2007)

# WiFi Assisted GPS for Extended Location Services

Saverio Cacopardi[1], Mauro Femminella[1], Gianluca Reali[1], Andrea Sedini[1], Fortunato Palella[2], Maurizio Turina[2], Andrea Vignoli[2], Giuseppe Confessore[2], Emanuela Scacchi[2], and Angela Maria Saraceno[2]

[1] Department of Electronic and Information Engineering - University of Perugia
Via G. Duranti 93, 06125 Perugia, Italy
name.surname@diei.unipg.it
[2] Consorzio Technos Reat Aerospace
02100 Rieti, Italy

**Abstract.** This paper shows a lightweight technique for extending the positioning capabilities of a global navigation satellite system to areas characterized by reduced satellite visibility. This technique includes the presence of a WiFi coverage, used to implement the *virtual satellite* concept. In particular we assume that a customer terminal can receive both Global Positioning System (GPS) signals and WiFi beacons broadcasted by an access point (AP). We show that if such beacons include the geo-referenced position of the relevant AP, the suitable usage of this information allows determining the GPS receiver position even if only three satellites are visible. Experimental results show that the achievable performance are similar to that obtainable by a plain GPS receiver using four visible satellites.

**Keywords:** WiFi, GPS, hybrid positioning, performance analysis.

## 1 Introduction

The growing diffusion of location based services using the GPS has driven a lot of research efforts for defining effective solutions for augmenting the GPS coverage [1]. It is known that a GPS receiver can fix its position by processing signals received by at least *four* satellites. In this paper we show a *lightweight* solution for extending the use of the GPS in areas where only *three* GPS satellites are visible. We propose to integrate the information received by a GPS receiver from *three* satellites with an equivalent information obtainable from an AP compliant with the IEEE 802.11 radio technologies (commonly referred to as WiFi). This information consists of the geo-referenced position of a such an AP, through which a fourth *virtual satellite* is constructed so that the receiver position can be fixed. The shown algorithm makes use of the AP position only, and does not include any other information, such as the distance from GPS receiver to AP, the estimation of which is typically critical due to site-dependent signal path loss and multipath propagation.

K. Sithamparanathan et al. (Eds.): PSATS 2010, LNICST 43, pp. 191–202, 2010.

We stress that we do not propose to integrate the GPS with a WiFi positioning system, as frequently appears in the literature [2]. Our approach is much simpler, and consists of integrating the information received from GPS satellites with a further static information obtainable from an existing WiFi network.

The idea of using less than four satellites for fixing a position on the earth surface is not novel. For example [3] shows a Chinese proposal, based on a satellite system alternative to GPS, working for a limited range of latitudes. [3] includes a derivation of the geometric errors due to the use of a constellation of three satellites. This aspect is indeed the crucial point of using fewer than four satellites. In this regard, the importance of our proposal consists of providing performance similar to that achievable by using four satellites, obtained through a ligthweight and easy to implement solution.

The AP coordinates can be easily integrated in WiFi beacons broadcasted periodically, typically every 100 ms. Beacon frames are made of both mandatory and optional components, referred to as Information Elements (IE). Thus, the AP position may be either included in a new, dedicated IE, published within beacons, or embedded in the AP Service Set Identifier (SSID) IE, which usually reports the network name but could, in principle, include any type of information. In addition, if codified into a dedicated IE, it could be also obtainable with the classic probe request/probe response mechanism to save wireless bandwidth ([15] reports a study about the overhead of embedding information into WiFi beacons). In any case, all these approaches does not require to associate to the AP to obtain the information on AP position.

This approach could also be integrated with the use of inertial systems, which are mainly used in vehicular environments in order to improve performance of navigation systems. In fact, inertial system performance degradates very quickly when GPS satellites are not visible and receiver does not move over a straigh line [14].

A GPS receiver has to determine four unknowns, which are its own coordinates and clock bias. Thus a system of at least four equations including these unknowns is needed. In our approach three equations consist of the pseudo-range equations of the three visible satellites. The fourth equation is a suitably modified pseudo-range equation using the AP as an equivalent *virtual satellite*. This point is quite critical, since the relevant geometric trilateration could lead to numerical problems. Thus, the selection of a suitable position for the virtual satellite is crucial. The position estimaiton algorithm works well only if the fourth satellite forms a good geometry with the other three visible satellites, which is typically represented by the so called geometric dilution of precision (GDOP) [9].

This manuscript shows the experimental performance of our proposal. Experiments have been done by using a GPS station ASHTECH Z-12 equipped with a choke ring antenna (J.PSREGANT-DD-E) and a receiver (Topcon ODYSSEY-E) driven by a rubidium atomic clock. The experimental results show that the position fixing capabilities of a GPS receiver using three satellites and implementing our proposal are similar to those of a plain GPS receiver using four satellites if its distance to the AP is within some specific values.

## 2  The GPS Operation

The GPS navigation data are organized in frames [10], including ephemeris and correction clock parameters, by which a receiver can estimate its distance to the sending satellite, referred to as pseudorange. This estimation is done by the difference between the local reception time and the time when the satellite signal has been trasmitted. Since this estimation happens at different times, and the receiver clock is not synchronized with the satellite clock, it is necessary to use time difference of arrival (TDOA) techniques to fix the receiver position.

In this way, for each visible satellite a GPS receiver constructs a navigation equation including pseudorange, satellite position, unknown clock bias, unknown receiver coordinates, and other minor error contributions not included in this letter for brevity. A Cartesian reference system with the origin of coordinate axes located at the center of the earth allows it to easily formulate a navigation equation. Let $\mathbf{S_i}$ be the coordinate vector of the $ith$ satellite and $\rho_i$ its estimated pseudorange. If we represent the receiver position coordinate vector as $\mathbf{X_{rec}}$ and the receiver clock bias as $\Delta b$, we can write:

$$\| \mathbf{S_i} - \mathbf{X_{rec}} \| - \Delta b = \rho_i \, , i = 1, .., 4 \tag{1}$$

where the operator $\| \cdot \|$ is the euclidean norm on $\mathcal{R}^3$. Bancroft [4] has suggested to model the navigation equation as a hyperbolic equation, and has provided an exact non iterative solution. Through a geometric approach, Abel [5] has investigated the existence and uniqueness of the system solution. Another way to solve the system of pseudorange equations consists of applying the Newton method. Since the number of unknowns is four, three receiver coordinates and clock bias, the minimal number of needed visible satellites is four. The use of more observable data (i.e. more visible satellites) allows improving the estimation accuracy.

## 3  Joint WiFi-GPS Operation

When only three satellites are visible, they are not sufficient to fix the receiver position. Thus, additional information, eventually obtainable from other sources, is needed. We propose to use a geo-referenced WiFi AP which broadcasts its coordinates by including them in broadcasted beacons. If a GPS receiver is equipped by a WiFi network interface, as most of current commercial devices, it can receive and use the information broadcasted by such an AP. In case of different available APs, we assume to use the one closest to the receiver, estimated through the RSSI measures collected by the WiFi card. This way, it is possible to complete the set of equation necessary to solve the receiver position. This additional information could be used in many ways. We propose an algorithm that can reuse the processing algorithms already implemented in GPS receivers. Below we illustrate the processing steps, the relevant approximations and their effect on estimation accuracy.

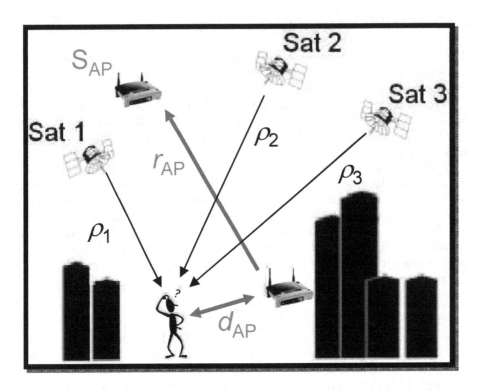

**Fig. 1.** Construction of the WiFi-based virtual satellite

*Step 1*: The first step consists of a preliminary estimation of the receiver clock bias. To this aim, we approximate the receiver position with the AP position, which is $d_{AP} = \| \mathbf{X_{rec}} - \mathbf{X_{AP}} \|$ meters away from the GPS receiver (see Fig. 1).

For each visible satellite it is possible to construct a navigation equation where the only unknown is the receiver clock bias, as follows:

$$\| \mathbf{S_i} - \mathbf{X_{AP}} \| - \Delta b = \rho_i , i = 1,..,3 \tag{2}$$

where $\mathbf{X_{AP}}$ is the coordinate vector of the AP. Thus, three estimates of the receiver clock bias are obtained, and their average is an input to the second step.

*Step 2*: The second step consists of introducing a *virtual satellite*, the coordinates of which are referred to as $\mathbf{S_{AP}}$, and constructing a modified system of equations that allows estimating the receiver position.

This new system of equations is made of three navigation equations, relevant to the visible satellites, and a fourth modified navigation equation, relevant to the virtual satellite.

The determination of the position of the virtual satellite is crucial for obtaining a good estimation of the position of the GPS receiver. In fact, the pseudorange measurements are typically affected by both sistematic errors (bias) and random errors. These errors have clearly an impact on the accuracy of the estimated receiver position, expressend by the GDOP, defined as follows.

From (1) we can write the jacobian $\mathbf{H}$ of $\rho(\mathbf{X_{rec}})$:

$$\mathbf{H} = \begin{pmatrix} \frac{\partial \rho_1}{\partial x}, & \frac{\partial \rho_1}{\partial y}, & \frac{\partial \rho_1}{\partial z}, & \frac{\partial \rho_i}{\partial \delta b} \\ .. & .. & .. & .. \\ \frac{\partial \rho_4}{\partial x}, & \frac{\partial \rho_4}{\partial y}, & \frac{\partial \rho_4}{\partial z}, & \frac{\partial \rho_4}{\partial \delta b} \end{pmatrix} \tag{3}$$

Matrix $\mathbf{H}$ plays a role of measure matrix and if we assume $\hat{\mathbf{X}}$ to be an estimate of the position and $\mathbf{X_{rec}}$ the exact position, the equation of the residue become:

$$\delta\rho \approx \mathbf{H}\,(\,\hat{\mathbf{X}} - \mathbf{X_{rec}}\,) \tag{4}$$

By inverting this relation we can obtain:

$$(\,\hat{\mathbf{X}} - \mathbf{X_{rec}}\,) = (\mathbf{H^T H})^{-1}\,\mathbf{H^T}\,\delta\rho \tag{5}$$

The matrix $\mathbf{Cov} = (\mathbf{H^T H})^{-1}$ is the covariance matrix of position and clock bias. The GDOP is defined as:

$$GDOP = \frac{\sqrt{tr(\mathbf{Cov})}}{\sigma_0} \tag{6}$$

where $\sigma_0$ is the ranging error variance and the operator $tr(\mathbf{A}))$ is the trace of the matrix $\mathbf{A}$.

Similarly, the dilution of precision may also be related to individual geometric and temporal quantities; HDOP, PDOP, VDOP, and TDOP refers to the horizontal, position, vertical, and time dilution of precision, respectively [9].

In order to obtain a relible position estimation, we need to place the virtual satellite in a position producing a good GDOP. Our approach aims to emulate the GPS operation under unobstructed satellite visibility. Thus we have decided to locate the virtual satellite in a position compliant with the GPS satellite constellation. In other words, the virtual satellite is located by the software of the GPS receiver in a position where a GPS satellite would be visible without the obstructing objects close to the GPS receiver. Thus, the GPS receiver needs to be aware of the satellite ephemerides. This is not a challenging problem, since they could be either collected during the satellite visibility periods, since each satellite broadcasts its own ephemeris and clock correction data, or easily downladed through already available ephemeris distribution services, accessible through either the WiFi connection or a cellular network, similarly to what happens for the Assisted GPS [13]. Clearly, among the candidate satellite positions we select the one providing the best GDOP value. Hence, the needed fourth navigation equation can be constructed by approximating again the receiver position with the AP position; thus we can replace the pseudo-range with the geometric distance $r_{AP}$ between the AP and the known (virtual) $\mathbf{S_{AP}}$ position as follows:

$$\| \mathbf{S_{AP}} - \mathbf{X_{rec}} \| = r_{AP} \tag{7}$$

where $r_{AP}$ is the euclidean distance between the AP and the virtual satellite.

The solution of this modified system of equations is an estimation of the GPS receiver position. We have used the iterative Newton method, using as the starting point the preliminary estimation of the receiver clock bias obtained in *step 1* and the known AP position. Below we illustrate the impact of the approximations introduced on the estimation accuracy.

## 4    Results

In order to analyze our positioning algorithm, we have implemented a software tool in C language, used to process the receiver independent exchange format[11] (RINEX).[1] The block diagram of this tool is shown in Fig. 2.

We have processed data obtained by a receiver located at the Topography Lab at the University of Perugia [12]. The accurate world geodetic system 84 (WGS84) coordinates of the receiver have been obtained from the Italy geographic military institute (IGM95) network. Ephemeredis, pseudoranges, and ionospheric parameters are extracted and a channel is associated with each satellite. The position of the GPS receiver is available with a resolution of few cm, and we have assumed this position as the "true" reference receiver position for subsequent processing.

In order to analyze the achievable performance, we have done experiments by randomly selecting four satellites out of the visible ones.

The same set of data has been processed by our hybrid positioning algorithm, which uses three satellites and an AP located at variable distance from the GPS receiver.

For evaluating the location estimation error we have used the great circle distance metric. We have used a spherical model of the earth and assumed that the altitude of the receiver is the same of the known accurate position of the GPS receiver. Since the position estimated is close to the reference position, the great circle arc between these two points can be regarded, with a good approximation, as a straight line. Its length may be taken as a measure of the distance between the estimated position and the accurate position. Experiments have been realized by considering a maximum tolerable GDOP value equal to 3. Above this threshold all relevant satellite positions over the GPS constellation have been discarded. Conversely, all satellite positions obtained from the available ephemerides generating a GDOP value lower than or equal to 3 have been used one by one for locating the virtual satellite and construct the fourth navigation equation. Below we show the results collected during an observation window of one hour, by collecteing GPS observations each second. Our algorithm succeded in finding a solution with the desired GDOP for about 50% of the observations by using three satellites and an AP with a GDOP threshold equal to 3.

---

[1] The RINEX is an internationally accepted data exchange format for GPS receivers. The information is organized in three parts: observation data, navigation data, and meteorological data. Pseudorange values can be obtained by observation data, ephemeredis and ionospheric parameters by navigation data.

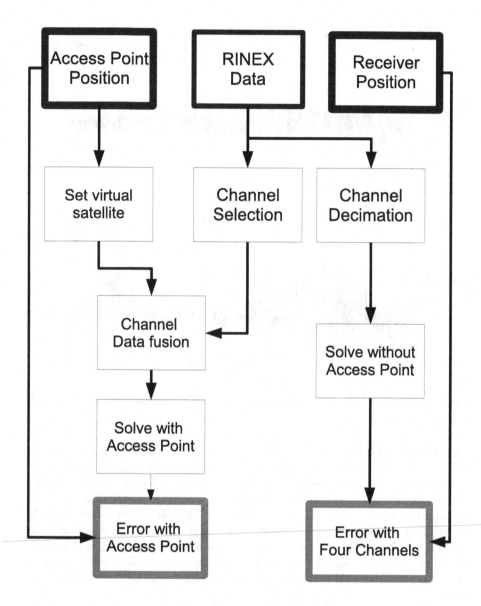

**Fig. 2.** Flow Graph of data processing

Fig. 3 shows a realizaton of the estimation of error magnitude obtained by both a hybrid receiver with three satellites and an AP placed at a distance of 20 m (a), and a plain GPS receiver using four satellites (b). It appears that the need of using the only four visible satellites, modeled by selecting four random satellites out of the set of visible ones, can deteriarate performance of a plain GPS receiver, while by suitably positioning the virtual satellite allows obtaining

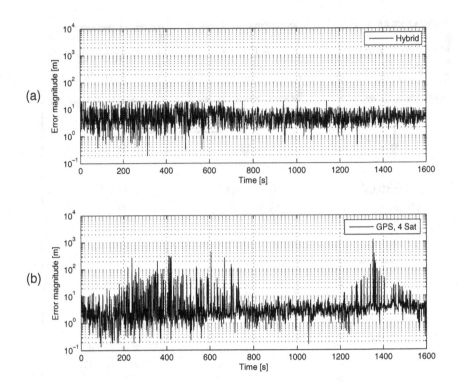

**Fig. 3.** Error magnitude as a function of time; the AP is 20m away from the GPS receiver

a low GDOP value (up to 3 in our experiments), hence a lower error magnitude. However, when the geometry of the four satellites is good (i.e., low GDOP), the plain GPS receiver outperforms the hybrid one. Nevertheless, we can also observe that the errors induced by our approximations are substantially lower than the distance between the GPS receiver and the AP, which is the error that would be made by simply approximating the receiver position by the AP position. To go further, we have made a statistical analysis on the achieved results. It is worth noting that in the hybrid operation the mean error magnitude, shown in Fig. 4, ranges between 0.2 and 0.3 times the distance between the GPS receiver and the AP.

In addition, when the AP is quite close to the GPS receiver, namely for 10, 20, and 30 m, the average error obtained with the proposed solution is even better than the one relevant to the usage of four satellites, whereas the estimation error is comparable for 40 m. In conclusion, it is evident that performance of the hybrid receiver is equivalent to that achievable by a plain GPS receiver working by four satellites and, in some situations, can be compared also with that relevant to the use of more satellites. Thus, the objective of extending positioning service to areas with difficult satellite visibility is achievable.

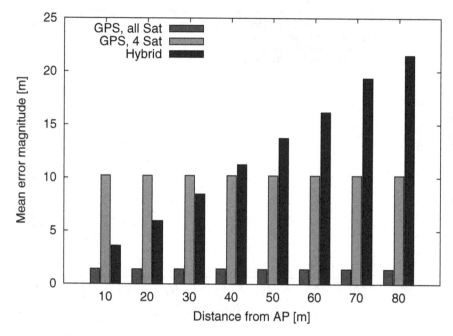

**Fig. 4.** Mean error at various AP distances from the GPS receiver

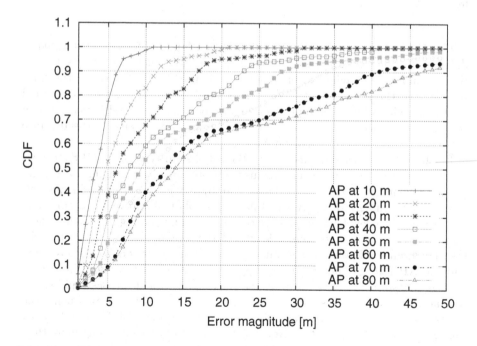

**Fig. 5.** Cumulative Distribution Functions of error at various AP distances from the GPS receiver

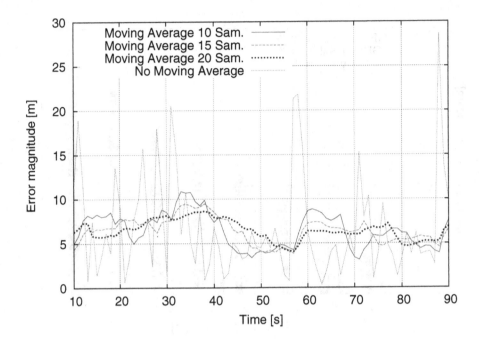

**Fig. 6.** Effect of a moving average filtering on error magnitude; the AP is 20m away from the GPS receiver

Fig. 5 shows the cumulative error distribution function for the AP located at different distances from the GPS receiver. It appears that for all analysed cases, the probability of having an error up to half the distance between the GPS receiver and the AP is about 90%. This is an excellent results when compared with the trivial solution of approximating the position of the GPS receiver with the one of the AP. In addition, this result is not dependent on the distance between the GPS receiver and the AP.

Fig. 6 and Fig. 7 are relevant to the AP located 20 m away of the GPS receiver. Fig. 6 shows the error magnitude versus time, obtained by averaging 10, 15, and 20 subsequent estimates. It is evident that by using a filtering technique (we have used a simple moving average) it is posssible to improve the accuracy of the system, since few bad samples are compensated by good ones. Finally, Fig. 7 shows the maximum error versus length of the moving average filter. Clearly, the maximum reachable error is equal to the distance between the GPS receiver and the AP (20 m) and this may happen for a single sample measure. If we average measures over few samples, the maximum error decreases rapidly. For instance, by using three samples (this implies waiting 3s before producing the solution in our testbed) we have obtained a improvement of 20%, and by six samples it increases up to 33%. Asymptotically (in practice by using more than 100 samples), the maximum error converges towards 8 m, which is very close to the average error (5.94 m). Clearly, if samples are provided by the GPS device

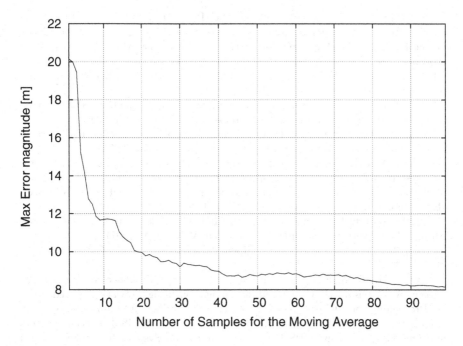

**Fig. 7.** Maximum error vs. length of the moving average filter; the AP is 20m away from the GPS receiver

at higher rate than one per second, the performance can be largely improved with reduced latency.

## 5    Conclusion

We have shown a solution for augmenting GPS potentials by the use of WiFi. If a GPS receiver can receive the coordinates of a geo-referenced AP, it can combine three navigation equations, relevant to three visible satellites, and the AP position information. This hybrid approach can provide performance similar to the one achievable by using four satellites, thus providing a significant extension of the area where the GPS can work. The proposed approach highly outperforms the trivial solution of simply approximating the GPS receiver position with that of the AP. In the future we will include the optimal AP selection in case different AP are available and the extension of our approach to two visible satellites.

## References

1. Project ICT-217033 "WHERE", Delivrable D1.1, Performance assessment of Hybrid data fusion and tracking algorithms (December 2008)
2. Singh, R., Guainazzo, M., Regazzoni, C.: Location Determination using WLAN in Conjunction with GPS Network. In: IEEE VTC 2004-Spring, Milan, Italy, May 17-19 (2004)

3. Forden, G.: The Military Capabilities and Implications of Chinas Indigenous Satellite-Based Navigation System. Science and Global Security 12, 219–250 (2004)
4. Bancroft, S.: An Algebraic solution of the GPS equations. IEEE Transaction on Areospace and Electronic Systems 21(1), 56–59 (1985)
5. Abel, J., Chaffee, J.: Existence and uniquesses of GPS solutions. IEEE Transaction on Areospace and Electronic Systems 27(6), 951–952 (1991)
6. Abel, J., Chaffee, J.: On the exact solution of pseudorange equations. IEEE Transaction on Areospace and Electronic Systems 30(4), 1021–1030 (1994)
7. Makrand, S.: Recursive Method for optimum GPS satellite solution. IEEE Transaction on Areospace and Electronic Systems 27(2), 751–754 (2001)
8. Lee, H.B.: A novel procedure for assessing the accuracy of hyperbolic multilateration system. IEEE Trans. on Areospace and Elect. Systems 11(1), 2–15 (1975)
9. Yarlagadda, R., Ali, I., Hershey, J.: "GPS GDOP metric". IEE Proceedings on Radar, Sonar, and Navigation 147(5), 259–264 (2000)
10. ICD-GPS-200 Interface controll document, ICD-GPS-200, Arinc Research Corporation, 11770 WarnerAve., Suite 210, Fountain Valley, CA (1991)
11. Gurtner, W.: RINEX: the receiver indipendent exchange format. GPS world 5(7), 49–52 (1994)
12. Laboratorio di Topografia, University of Perugia, http://labtopo.ing.unipg.it/
13. Brown, A.K., Olson, P.: Urban/Indoor Navigation using Network Assisted GPS. In: Proceedings of ION 61st Annual Meeting, Cambridge, MA (June 2006)
14. Davidson, P., Hautamki, J., Collin, J.: Using Low-Cost MEMS 3D Accelerometers and One Gyro to Assist GPS Based Car Navigation System. In: Proceedings of 15th Saint Petersburg International Conference on Integrated Navigation Systems (May 2008)
15. Di Sorte, D., Femminella, M., Reali, G.: Beacon-based Service Publishing Framework in Multi-service Wi-Fi Hotspots. EURASIP Journal on Wireless Communications and Networking, 1–18 (2007)

# Hybrid Satellite-Optical Ring Network for Regional Blackspots in Australia's National Broadband Network

Sithamparanathan Kandeepan[1], Chava Vijaya Saradhi[1],
Sam Reisenfeld[2], Eryk Dutkiewicz[2],
Nicolas Chuberre[3], and Pierre Fraise[3]

[1] CREATE-NET Research Centre, Trento, Italy
kandeepan@ieee.org, saradhi.chava@create-net.org
http://www.create-net.org
[2] Macquarie University, Sydney, Australia
{samr,eryk}@science.mq.edu.au
http://www.mq.edu.au/
[3] Thales Alenia Space, Toulouse Cedex, France
{nicolas.chuberre,pierre.fraise}@thalesaleniaspace.com
http://www.thalesgroup.com/

**Abstract.** Satellite communications is the most prominent solution for covering remote areas for broadband Internet access where long and expensive cables are not feasible to be deployed. The Australia's National Broadband Network (NBN) initiation 'delivering superfast broadband to Australian homes and workplaces' currently face the problem of deploying long fibres to cover regional blackspots considering the geographic structure of the continent. Considering this we present some preliminary ideas to have hybrid satellite-optical broadband networks specifically covering the regional blackspots in Australia based on ring network topologies. We present topologies for the hybrid network and also architecture for the electronic (RF)-optical interface which enables to connect the fibre optical network to the satellites. Furthermore, topologies for the regional fibre optical networks in the blackspot regions are also presented in this paper.

**Keywords:** Hybrid satellite optical networks, Australian National broadband network, coverage of regional blackspots, ring topology.

## 1 Introduction

The Internet in the current era has influenced significantly on the global economic and social aspects. It has been predicted that the Future Internet will play a vital role in every business by connecting millions and millions of people around the globe simultaneously [2]. The Internet traffic is substantially growing at a predicted rate of $50\% - 70\%$ a year and by the year 2012 the IP traffic is expected to be 50 terabits per second. One of the possible solution to address

K. Sithamparanathan et al. (Eds.): PSATS 2010, LNICST 43, pp. 203–217, 2010.
© Institute for Computer Sciences, Social-Informatics and Telecommunications Engineering 2010

the Future Internet requirements is the enhancement of the existing fibre optic telecommunications backbone and infrastructure. Fibre optic communications provide very high speed communications at the expense of cost per cable length and maintenance, and is also unfeasible to be deployed depending on the terrain structure such as mountains etc. This restricts the high speed network coverage for the Future Internet using the fibre optical infrastructure for the extended geographic region.

The telecommunications infrastructure convergence is therefore necessary to cater the demand of Future Internet, and to provide seamless connectivity and services to the users. Extending the geographic coverage is one of the key aspects of Future Internet, and it is a well known that satellite communications provide such extended coverage. With the rapid development of the ground based wired telecommunications infrastructure for global connectivity, mainly the optical fibre communication backbone that has an extensively increasing cost factor associated with the coverage region, it is essential to consider hybrid systems such as satellite-optical hybrid system to deliver extended coverage. The fixed-cost versus benefit (profit) trade-off for deploying long haul fibre optical links to cover regional areas to provide broadband services does not attract any investors and service providers, or in other words it does not seem sensible to have a house built and maintained with a hundred rooms to accommodate five people. Therefore, hybrid satellite-optical systems are considered to provide extended broadband coverage which we consider in this paper.

Here we consider a particular case study for the deployment of the hybrid satellite-optical network, namely in Australia. The Australian government's initiative for a National Broadband Network (NBN) [1] to provide broadband Internet services to every home and business in Australia by 2014 has the potential need to address all the issues discussed above. In particularly, the Australian government has identified the regional blackspots for the broadband network coverage where lengthy expensive cables are not feasible to be deployed to cover the regions. Several stake holders have been invited to present their ideas and proposals for network coverage to the regional blackspots and some of them are listed in [5]-[8].

In the literature the term optical satellite systems mainly refer to free space optics and inter satellite optical links. However, the research literature associated with this topic 'hybrid satellite-optical systems' is not at all rich, and on the other hand closely related patents exist in this field, which are given in [3], [4].

In this paper though we present some preliminary ideas considering the hybrid satellite-optical networks for satisfying the requirements for the Australian NBN to cover the regional blackspots. In particularly, we identify the existing satellite services and their related coverage areas and footprints across Australia which could potentially be used for regional broadband access, and associate them with the existing fibre optic backbone infrastructure in Australia. We present two hybrid satellite-optical ring network topologies for the NBN. We also present the optical to electronic (RF) and the electronic (RF) to optical conversions for the on ground optical-satellite uplink station and the satellite-optical downlink station transceiver architectures. It should be noted here that, because of the limited capacity of the satellite transmissions, we are not making proposals in this paper to directly compete with the optical and/or wireless systems which could provide services (if feasible) to the blackspots regions potentially with greater capacity. We mainly consider such satellite-optical systems where satellite is chosen to be the best option. There is also a major role for satellite communications in rural areas outside the major cities in Australia. In these regions, the dwellings are reasonably far apart, but there are still considerable regional population densities. Examples of these regions are the North Coastal and the South Coastal regions which are adjacent to Sydney. In these regions, fibre optical communications is not a commercially desirable option and terrestrial radio communications is not viable because of blockage from hills and because a large numbers of users are located in valleys. The total traffic from these regions is likely to exceed the traffic for the large land, but very small population density, areas in Australia. An additional major role for satellite communications is emergency and disaster communications services in which connectivity could be provided for the major cities in the event of a catastrophic outage of the fibre optical backbone. This is an extremely desirable feature in a national broadband network.

The rest of the paper is organized as follows. In Section 2 we briefly present the Australian NBN and the regional blackspots, in Section 3 we present the existing commercial satellites for coverage in Australia. The hybrid satellite-terrestrial networks based on the ring architecture are presented in Section 4, and the regional optical network with satellite access is presented in Section 5. In Section 6 we present the satellite-optical interface architecture, and finally in we provide some concluding remarks in Section Section 7.

## 2   Australia's National Broadband Network Initiative and Responses

The Australian government's initiative on the construction of a National Broadband Network (NBN) worth of 42 billion$ Australian over the next eight years has attracted many stakeholders in and around the region [1]. In particularly, the NBN had called for proposals to provide telecommunications backbone extension to the regional blackspots such as Darwin, Broken Hill, Emerald, Geraldton, Long Reach and many more areas as depicted in Figure-1. These blackspot regions are geographically situated further from the nearest metropolitan telecommunication hubs which then require cost effective extensions of the backbone to provide broadband communications. The all possible solutions to extend the backbone to the blackspot regions, which are 1) Extending the fibre-optic network, 2) Providing long range high speed wireless communications, and 3) Providing access with satellite coverage, have their own advantages and disadvantages associated with them. In this section we briefly describe the blackspots and also highlight some of the proposals made by leading stakeholders addressing solutions to the regional blackspots program.

**Fig. 1.** Australia's Regional Blackspots for the National Broadband Network

## 2.1   The Regional Blackspots

The identified regional blackspots in Australia for the NBN project are not only situated further from the metropolitan areas but also have very low population densities compared to the other cities. These two facts make a challenging task for the telecommunications service providers to provide a cost effective (lossless) services to the regions. Though the cities such as Darwin, Geraldton, Broken Hill etc. are considered as the regional blackspots for the NBN development there exist a fibre optic ring network covering some of the areas such as Darwin and Alice Springs. In some places (east coast and south-west) there are also additional inland fibre connections between major cities such as Brisbane, Sydney, Melbourne, Adelaide, Perth. There are also several satellite stations connected to the fibre network well outside of major cities rather than in major cities. The Greatest "need" for satellite coverage in Australia is mainly on the east coast in the valleys along the Gold Coast, Central Coast areas. These areas are reasonably densely populated but are not economical for fibre or even wireless coverage and are also prone to a reasonable amount of rain. The above considerations are useful in determining the configurations for the hybrid backbone network considered in our paper.

## 2.2   The Stakeholders' Proposals

In this section we summarize some of the proposals made to the regional blackspot program published by the Australian Department of Broadband, Communications and Digital Economy [1].

*Alcatel-Lucent-Australia:* The Alcatel Lucent Australia proposes to provide broadband network solutions to the blackspots by identifying two types of backhaul systems "aggregation backhaul fibre" and "access seeker backhaul fibre" [5].

They also seek wireless solutions for the less densely populated regions, hence proposing combination of fibre and wireless solutions.

*Telstra:* The Australian telecommunications giant Telstra proposes to extend its fibre backbone infrastructure further to provide broadband to the regional blackspots and points out some fundamental economic issues related to pricing [6]. Telstra also proposes low data rate wireless access for low population areas.

*Vodaphone:* Vodafone emphasizes on the fair pricing for the blackspot regions and the metropolitan regions, and favors the dark fibre backhaul access to be made available to an aggregation point (regional centres) [7] as a solution to the Australian NBN for the blackspot regions.

*Huawei:* HUAWEI proposes a Single Ethernet, Multi-Play service architecture for the regional blackspots, which is a single IP/MPLS Metro Ethernet Network powered by a single platform providing Fixed Mobile Convergence multi-play services under a single Network Management System [8] for the NBN.

## 3    Satellite Coverage for Australia

The Australian region is extensively covered by several commercial satellites delivering communications and broadcasting services. The state of the art satellite high speed communications are based on the Ka-band and the Ku-band frequency ranges providing larger bandwidths to accommodate higher data rates. The power limitation (received power) however is the major factor limiting the capacity of such links due to the enormous path loss encountered by the transmitted signals because of the larger distances between the satellites and the ground stations. The rain fading conditions will also add to the path loss degrading the performance of the satellite links further. Though the number Ku-band satellites for commercial services covering the globe is quite large, the Ka-band on the other hand which could potentially provide greater capacity is only at its preliminary stages of deployment. One of such Ka-band commercial satellites to be launched in 2010 is the Eutelsat's Ka-Sat to be delivered by EADS/Astrium [9]. On the other hand, a few test satellites and defense satellites have already been launched having the Ka-band communications payload. The Australian built and owned micro-satellite Federation Satellite-1 (FedSat) operating in the near polar low earth orbit (LEO) is an example of such a test satellite having the Ka-band payload launched in 2003 [10], another example is the Japanese WINDS satellite that reaches greater speeds in communications using the Ka-band frequencies [11].

Some of the commercial satellites operating in the Ku-band covering the Australian region capable of providing broadband links are listed in Figure-2. The Optus C1, B3, D1, D2 and D3 satellites have 24, 15, 24, 24 and 32 Ku-band transponders respectively operating in the non-regenerative bent pipe mode. The NSS-12 satellite on the other hand has 48 Ku-band transponders. The effective isotropically radiated power (EIRP) coverage map and the corresponding G/T requirements at the ground stations for the Optus-D1 satellite are depicted

| Satellite | Band | Position | Number of Transponders |
|-----------|------|----------|------------------------|
| Optus C1 (Australia) | Ku | 156°E | 24 |
| Optus B3 (Australia) | Ku | 164°E | 15 |
| Optus D1 (Australia) | Ku | 160°E | 24 |
| OptusD2 (Australia) | Ku | 152°E | 24 |
| Optus D3 (Australia) | Ku | 156°E | 32 |
| AsiaSat 3S (Hong Kong) | C Ku | 105.5°E | 28 (C band) 16 (Ku band) |
| AsiaSat 4 (Hong Kong) | C Ku | 122°E | 28 (C band) 20 (Ku band) |
| AsiaSat 5 (Hong Kong) | C Ku | 100.5° E | 26 (C band) 14 Ku band |
| Thaicom 4 (IPStar) (Thailand) | C Ku | 78.5°E | 47 (C band) 20 (Ku band) |
| NSS-12 (France) | C Ku | 57°E | 40 (C band) 48 (Ku band) (C/Ku cross-strapping) |

Fig. 2. Satellite coverage in the Australian region

in Figure-3 and Figure-4 respectively. Depending on the EIRP and the G/T values the satellite could provide (with the current standards) up to a few hundreds of Mbps of capacity. Furthermore, apart from the satellites mentioned in the table in Figure-2, there is also an experimental satellite WINDS (Japan) operating in the Ka band at a position of 143°E with link capacities of Uplink: $1.56, 24, 51, 155$ Mbps and Downlink: 155 Mbps in the regenerative mode, and $155, 622, 1244$ Mbps in the Non-regenerative Mode, giving very high throughput compared to the currently existing satellite links.

Apart from the main issue of the limitation in the throughput of the current geostationary satellites compared to the NBN needs another issue is the latency due to the distance of geostationary satellites (500 ms or more round trip delay). Considering this a possible solution would be a MEO constellation. The O3b network solution based on the MEO constellation has a higher throughput than regular Geostationary satellites and a lower latency (around 140 ms round trip delay) due to the difference in the altitude [12].

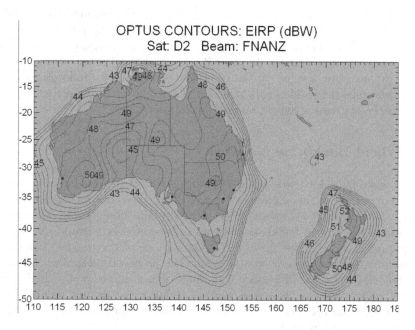

**Fig. 3.** The Optus D1 satellite coverage across Australia, transmitted EIRP dBw, reference

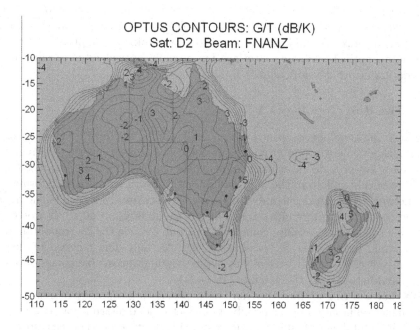

**Fig. 4.** The Optus D1 satellite coverage across Australia, G/T in dB/K

Based on the capacities of the satellites and the regional requirements (number of users in the region etc.), one or several satellites can be connected to the Australian NBN backbone in order to provide broadband access to the blackspot regions. The satellite connects to the NBN backbone and extends the coverage further by providing services to the blackspot regions. In the following sections we provide some networking topologies for the satellites to connect to the fibre optic backbone giving a hybrid satellite-optical network.

# 4   Hybrid Backbone Network

The proposed hybrid satellite-optical network architecture based on ring topologies are presented in this section. We provide two types of topologies based on 1) single satellite, and 2) two satellites, as we explain subsequently. The general idea behind the hybrid backbone network is presented in Figure-5, in the figure we provide an example for covering Darwin one of the regional blackspots in Australia and the eastern coastal areas. The proposed technology based on satellites, as mentioned in Section 1, is however considered well suited where its counterparts such as fibre and wireless technologies are not feasible to be deployed based on the terrain structure (hills and mountains) and the distance from the metropolitan cities.

As shown in the Figure-5, the satellites connect to the metropolitan fibre hub by means of one/multiple satellite link(s) which has an optical-electronic hybrid interface in the ground station to provide high speed communications. The optical-electronic interface, which is further explained in Section 6, provides the conversion from the optical signals to the electronic signals suitable for uplink satellite transmissions and vice versa in the downlink. In our proposal we also provide an optical-electronic interface for possible optical inter satellite links considering future developments.

## 4.1   The Ring Topology - 1

The first ring topology is formed with a single satellite connected to the broadband backbone network on ground as depicted in Figure-6 covering the regional blackspot. We provide an example of using the Optus-D1 satellite connected to the fibre backbone hub in the metropolitan cities Perth and Brisbane forming a ring network. The backbone hub connecting the satellites as shown in the figure can be connected to any cities that has the capabilities to do so, it would be desirable to have the satellite connected to a hub outside the metropolitan area which would have less traffic passing through the hub. The regional blackspot areas in the east coastal valleys will access the high speed backbone national broadband network via the satellite Optus-D1.

We choose a ring architecture here because the ring topology in general will have higher reliability and the possibility for better load distribution. It is important to have intelligent traffic routing or splitting to avoid bottle necks especially on the satellite links.

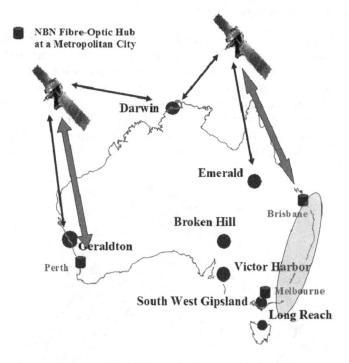

**Fig. 5.** Part of the Hybrid Satellite-Optical Network for providing broadband access to Australia's Regional Blackspots through the National Broadband Network

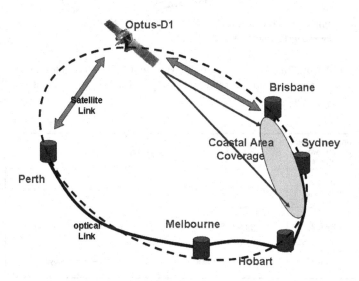

**Fig. 6.** An example of Ring topology-1 for the Australian NBN, considering AsiaSat4 and covering the blackspot region Darwin

## 4.2   The Ring Topology - 2

The second topology is formed with two satellites connected to the NBN backbone as depicted in Figure-7. This architecture forms several rings with the fibre optic backbone hubs in the metropolitan cities. We provide an example considering two satellites connecting to the fibre backbone hubs in the metropolitan or outer cities. In our proposal we also provide an inter satellite link which is considered for future systems. For the system without the inter satellite links two satellites are able to form multiple ring topologies as depicted in Figure-8. Furthermore, another ring topology is also possible in addition to the

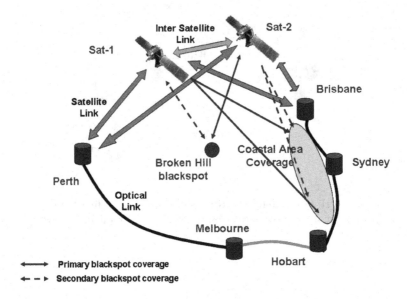

**Fig. 7.** Examples of Ring topologies for the Australian NBN, considering two satellites covering the blackspot regions Darwin and Broken Hill, where the inter satellite links are futuristic proposals

| Ring Topologies with two satellites | Topology |
|---|---|
| Ring-1 (Futuristic) | Sydney – Brisbane – Sat1 – Sat2 – Perth – Melbourne – Hobart – Sydney |
| Ring-2 | Sydney – Brisbane – Sat1 – Perth – Melbourne – Hobart – Sydney |
| Ring-3 | Sydney – Brisbane – Sat2 – Perth – Melbourne – Hobart – Sydney |

**Fig. 8.** Table showing different logical ring topologies with two satellites for the Australian NBN requirements to cover regional blackspots , of Figure-6

ones shown in Figure-8, which is given by: Brisbane-Sydney-Hobart-Melbourne-Perth-Sat1-East Coast-Sat2-Brisbane. In this topology (the latter one), the regional blackspot also becomes part of the ring connecting through the two satellites. The multiple-ring configurations, such as in Figure-7, provide more capacity and reliability at the cost of higher complexity on satellites (for inter-satellite traffic) and at ground station (for directing the traffic towards appropriate satellites according to load demands).

## 5    The Regional Optical Network

Based on the blackspot geographical size and population density, the regional network architecture could be a single metro ring connecting the satellite earth station and several other metro access nodes. This in turn could feed a passive optical network or two level architecture with one inner metro ring and one outer metro ring to provide connectivity to the whole region. The fibre-based access network that we consider here however, connected to the satellite gateway, can be considered unnecessary due to the limited satellite capacity when compared to the fibre access network. But we consider the deployment of such regional optical network assuming future expansions of satellite link capacities and/or future deployment of high speed access networks replacing the satellite links to these regions. An alternate option is to have ADSL for the access network which is quite sufficient to match the capacity of the satellite link.

In this paper we present an example with single metro ring network connecting several access points. There are several possible alternatives of passive optical networks available. The selection of suitable architecture for each of the blackspots again depends on the population, population density, and demand for the bandwidth. In this paper we will present an example with generic passive optical network and call it as FTTx (e.g., FTTH, FTTB, FTTC, FTTP, etc.), however it can be changed to EPON, GPON, WDM PON, etc.

### 5.1    Fibre to the Premises

Figure-9 shows the interface between the satellite earth station and regional optical network. The earth station antenna's are used for either for transmitting user data from the regional network such as metro ring network or FTTx to satellite or to receive the signals from satellite and send it to FTTx user. In the Figure-9 the earth station antennas are directly connected to optical ine terminal (OLT) which feeds the regional FTTx network. However, in actual deployment OLT can be placed at one of the nodes in the regional metro ring network and the earth station can be connected to the metro ring network through appropriate interfaces at some other node on the ring network. The splitter is a passive optical element which splits the optical signals and is connected to a number of optical network units (ONUs). Depending on the configuration of FTTX, ONUs can be placed at home or business or appartment to serve the end users. The architecture shown also supports existing xDSL and cable modem operators,

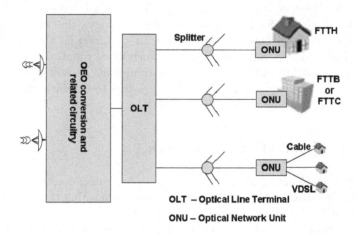

**Fig. 9.** Example of fiber to the premises regional network

which are fed by ONUs. The OEO conversion and related circuitry is required to convert RF signals that are received from earth station receiver and to route them appropriate end user(s).

# 6   The Optical Satellite Interface Architecture

The optical satellite and the satellite optical interfaces are used where ever the a conversion of signals from optical to electronic or electronic to optical respectively are required. The interfaces will lie in the optical hub on the ground for uplink and down link satellite communications. The optical to electronic conversion and the electronic to optical conversion are performed at the base band of the RF communications chain. We also propose a similar optical to electronic interface for an optical inter satellite link connecting two satellites considering future commercial systems. It is important to point out that such optical inter satellite links require on board satellite processing which is not available in many commercial satellites that are currently available.

## 6.1   Optical Part

The optical hardware that interfaces with the electronic part of the hybrid satellite-optical network is shown in Figure-10. The in/out fiber cables are connected to some optical nodes in the fiber network. The signal from the out/in fiber cables are received, amplified and demultiplexed at the fibre hub node. Then the optical signals (wavelengths) that are meant for local use are dropped using the drop module and the rest are converted to the electronic domain and routed to the satellite using the electronic circuitry and lookup tables. The look up tables can be implemented in the network layer, and the treatment of such

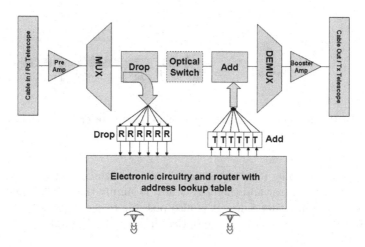

**Fig. 10.** An example of the optical-satellite hardware interface, for the optical to electronic and electronic to optical signal conversions

are beyond the scope of this paper. For the optical inter satellite link part the in/out cable interfaces are replaced with optical telescopes on board the satellite as shown in the figure. The optical signals received from the telescopes that are meant for relay to other satellite will be switched in optical domain and combined with local signals that are added in the add module. The local signals that are received from earth station are converted into electronic domain and routed to appropriate optical interfaces using lookup tables and then will be added in the add module with the pass through optical signals that are meant for relay. All combined optical signals are multiplexed and then amplified before transmitting through inter-satellite link to other satellite. The electronic circuitry contains the lookup tables and the modules that are necessary to convert the electronic signals into RF signals as described in the subsequent section.

## 6.2   Electronic Part

The electronic and the radio fr5equency (RF) hardware part to interface with the fibre optic part of the hybrid system is presented in this section. Figure-11 depicts the block diagram of such an interface unit to the optical system. In the receiver chain of the satellite RF link, the received signal is down converted to the base band with an inter mediate frequency (IF) stage and the corresponding electronic signal is passed to the electronic-optical interface for optical conversion. In the transmitter chain of the satellite RF link the optical signals are converted to electronic signals and then up converted to the corresponding frequency band (such as Ka or Ku) before transmitting it using the antenna. The base band processing unit's operation in the electronic circuitry can be specified as to what level the signals (data) are recovered before changing it to the optical signals. It is also possible to deploy a complete processing at the baseband and recovering

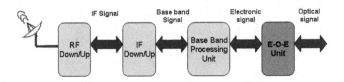

**Fig. 11.** The RF and electronic part of the hybrid satellite optical system interface, interface to teh optical system

the data before mapping it to the optical domain in which case the system acts as a repeater/regenerator and the O-E-O unit is simply the satellite and optical transceiver units on either sides. It is also possible to use buffers to store data to match the data rates between the optical link to satellite link.

## 7  Conclusion

In this paper we present the concept of hybrid satellite-optical networks for extending the coverage of the communications backbone. We present a case study on the Australian National Broadband Network requirements for providing broadband access to the regional blackspots. We present some network topologies based on the ring architecture for the hybrid satellite-optical system. We also present the interface architecture for the optical to electronic and electronic optical signal conversions that is required at the optical hubs. Furthermore, regional fibre based (FTTx) network architectures are also presented for regional network coverage on ground. It is also presented that hybrid satellite-optical network is the feasible solution for providing broadband to the regional areas in Australia such as in the valleys along the east coast.

## References

1. The Australian National Broadband Network Inititation - Department of Broadband, Communications and Digital Economy, Australia,
   http://www.dbcde.gov.au/funding_and_programs/national_broadband_network
2. Proceedings of the Future of the Internet conference : European Commission, Solvenia (March 31, 2008)
3. United States Patent: US 6,912,075 B1, by Stanislav I, et. al, The DITECTV Group Inc, Ring Architecture for an Optical Satellite Communications Network With Passive Optical Routing (June 28, 2005)
4. United States Patent: US 7,373,085 B2, by john T. Austin, The DITECTV Group Inc., Hybrid Satellite Fibre Communications Systems May 13 (2008)
5. Response to the Call for Regional Backbone Blackspots Program Submissions for the National Broadband Network in Australia, 'Backhaul Blackspots Initiative Stakeholder Consultation Paper', Alcatel-Lucent-Australia, Published by Department of Broadband, Communications and Digital Economy, Australia (May 12, 2009)

6. Response to the Call for Regional Backbone Blackspots Program Submissions for the National Broadband Network in Australia, 'Telstra Response Backhaul Blackspots Initiative Stakeholder Consultation Paper', Telstra - Australia, Published by Department of Broadband, Communications and Digital Economy, Australia (May 2009)

7. Response to the Call for Regional Backbone Blackspots Program Submissions for the National Broadband Network in Australia, 'Backhaul Blackspots Initiative: Stakeholder Consultation Paper', Vodafone - Australia, 15 May-2009, Published by Department of Broadband, Communications and Digital Economy, Australia

8. Response to the Call for Regional Backbone Blackspots Program Submissions for the National Broadband Network in Australia, 'Backhaul Architecture Discussions for Australia NBN Network', Huwei, Published by Department of Broadband, Communications and Digital Economy, Australia (May 2009)

9. Eutelasat Communications,
   http://www.eutelsat.com/satellites/upcoming-launches.html

10. CRC for Satellite Systems, Federation Satellite-1, http://www.crcss.csiro.au/

11. Japanese Aerospace and Exploration Agency, WINDS Satellite,
    http://www.jaxa.jp/pr/brochure/pdf/04/sat07.pdf

12. O3b Netrworks, http://www.o3bnetworks.com/advantage.html

# Special Session 1
# Delay Tolerant Network

# Mitigating Denial of Service Attacks in Delay-and Disruption-Tolerant Networks

Godwin Ansa, Enyenihi Johnson, Haitham Cruickshank, and Zhili Sun

Centre for Communications Systems Research, University of Surrey
Guildford, Surrey, UK
{g.ansa,e.johnson,h.cruickshank,z.sun}@surrey.ac.uk

**Abstract.** There is a growing interest in providing communications to "Challenged" environments which have been hitherto isolated and disconnected due to the lack of communications infrastructure. These are regions which lie at the edge of the current Internet. Confidentiality, integrity and availability are the three major security requirements of any secured system or network. This paper presents our work on Denial of Service mitigation in Delay-and Disruption-Tolerant Networks. We propose three examples of a light-weight bundle authenticator (DTN-cookie) based on XOR and HMAC operations to thwart DoS attacks that lead to resource exhaustion.

**Keywords:** DTN, Denial of Service, Protocol, Security.

## 1 Introduction

The success of the Internet is largely due to its ability to interconnect communication devices across the world using a homogenous set of protocols, the Transmission Control Protocol/Internet Protocol (TCP/IP) suite. The present Internet is built on the assumption of availability of a continuous bidirectional link between source and destination which supports end-to-end communication, small and relatively consistent delay in sending packets and receiving the corresponding acknowledgement packets, data rates from source to destination and vice versa are symmetric, and low error rates in terms of packet loss or data corruption [1]. However, there are networks that do not conform to the above assumptions. These networks referred to as "Challenged" networks are characterized by limited bandwidth, host and router mobility, disconnection due to interference or limited battery power [2].

These highly heterogeneous networks unlike the Internet are prone to long and variable delays, high error rates, arbitrarily long periods of link disconnection and large bi-directional data-rate asymmetries [1]. To overcome these difficulties, the DTN architecture which is based on the initial work on the Interplanetary Internet [3, 4] was conceived. DTN uses a store-and-forward message-switching technique to isolate delay and move data along the communication path. DTN is a network of regional networks [1], forming an overlay architecture which operates above the existing protocol stacks found in other network architectures [5]. Its purpose is to support interoperability among underlying challenged regional networks [2]. At the DTN

K. Sithamparanathan et al. (Eds.): PSATS 2010, LNICST 43, pp. 221–234, 2010.

nodes, a new overlay layer called the "bundle layer" sits on top of the traditional transport layers to provide end-to-end data transfers among the DTN regions. The DTN infrastructure suffers from severe resource scarcity and this has prompted some restrictions to its use through some form of authentication and access control. The DTN security architecture supports hop-by-hop authentication and integrity checks. This is to ensure bundle content correctness before forwarding and is designed to authenticate DTN nodes as legitimate senders and receivers of bundles to each other [6, 7]. The end-to-end mechanism provides authentication for the user.

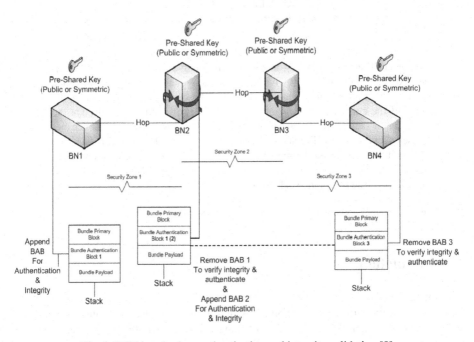

**Fig. 1.** DTN hop-by-hop authentication and integrity validation [8]

There are a number of key components in a DTN that provide critical services such as monitoring or query access points, data servers, cryptographic key servers, routers, security gateways, network uplinks and network nodes. These network components can come under serious DoS attacks when an attacker sends loads of requests which engage them in computationally intensive authentication protocol [9]. Currently, it is not possible to stop DoS attacks since most attacks are based on the use of protocols and services in an enormous scale. Solutions can only mitigate these attacks. Figure 1 shows the hop-by-hop authentication/integrity check using the Bundle Authentication Block (BAB). The BAB is used to assure the authenticity and integrity of the bundle along a single hop from forwarder to intermediate receiver. The communication path is divided into security zones as shown. Similarly, for end-to-end security services, the Payload Integrity Block (PIB) and Payload Confidentiality Blocks (PCB) are used. Further details on the DTN security architecture can be found in [10].

Our design seeks to provide a weak authentication phase using a unidirectional message exchange prior to signature verification. With this approach, communication cost is reduced significantly. Also our solution is power efficient and low in computational cost since the proposed DoS mitigation technique is lightweight and suitable for low-power devices like sensors.

## 1.2 DTN Scenario

Based on the description of a DTN, we present Figure 2 which depicts a United Nations (UN) peacekeeping scenario with three isolated regions bridged by a satellite. Region 1 and 2 are wireless sensor networks and region 3 is a satellite network and represents the UN headquarters in New York. Each region can be accessed through a security gateway (a base station in the case of regions 1 and 2, and a Network Control Centre "NCC" for region 3). The satellite network acts as a transit region (backbone in the sky) [11] for the two isolated DTN regions. In this scenario, the security gateways, sensor nodes and routers are stationary while the satellite terminals and Mobile Sink Nodes (MSNs) can be mobile. Some environmental constraints may include node failure, intentional sleep cycles, energy savings and node mobility. The patterns of connectivity can be scheduled, predicted or opportunistic.

The remainder of this paper is structured as follows. In Section 2 we highlight the threats posed by DoS attacks which prevent the DTN from fulfilling its functions. Section 3 reviews related work on DoS mitigation in terrestrial networks and the proposed techniques. Our initial design specification, the assumptions made, the

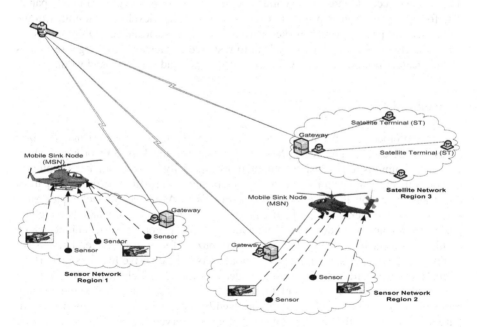

**Fig. 2.** A DTN-based wireless UN peacekeeping scenario

networking and security requirements are presented in Section 4. In section 5, we discuss time synchronization issues in DTN and analyze the proposed design. Section 6 concludes the paper and suggests the direction for future research.

## 2 Threat Analysis

Security threats can be divided into passive and active threats. A careful threat analysis of the DTN scenario depicted in Figure 2 shows that the network is susceptible to passive attacks through eavesdropping and traffic analysis. This is due to the wireless communication medium and broadcast nature of the satellite channel which allows intruders to have access to private information and the identity of the communicating entities. Also the depicted scenario is prone to active attacks such as replay attacks, masquerading, modification attacks and Denial of Service (DoS) attacks. The main focus of this paper is on DoS attacks though our design takes into consideration the active attacks mentioned above to provide a more robust solution.

Based on a classification by the Computer Emergency Response Team (CERT), there are three kinds of DoS attacks [12]:

- Destruction or alteration of configuration information
- Physical destruction or alteration of network components
- Consumption of scarce, limited, or non renewable resources

The first and second kinds of DoS attacks listed above are not dealt with in this paper. The focus of this paper is primarily on protocol or design-level vulnerabilities in the authentication process which makes it easy for attackers to launch DoS attacks on DTN security gateways which may lead to resource exhaustion. The target resources include battery power, memory, CPU time, disk space and network bandwidth.

## 3 Related Work

The very protocols we use to protect communication networks against unauthorized access can be used as a hook for DoS attacks by clever attackers. Any protocol where the server commits to expensive computations especially using public key cryptography or to memory allocation by storing protocol state information before or as part of client authentication is susceptible to network DoS. A number of techniques have been proposed to tackle this problem in terrestrial networks one of which is the client puzzle technique. In order to prevent junk mail, [13] proposed a technique which requires a sender to compute a cryptographic puzzle for each message. The cost of computing the puzzle is negligible for normal users but expensive for mass mailers.

Juels and Brainard [14] extended this idea and introduced client puzzles to tackle the problem of connection depletion attacks. The robustness of authentication protocols against DoS attacks can be improved by asking a client to commit its computational resources to the protocol run before the server allocates its memory and processing time. The solution to the puzzle requires a brute-force search for some bits of inverse of a one-way hash function. The difficulty of the puzzle is adjusted based on server load. The assurance of the server is increased when it establishes that the intention of the client is good. This is achieved gradually through a series of weak authentication prior to signature verification [15].

Another solution defined by IPSec, is the Internet Security Association and Key Management Protocol (ISAKMP) which is a framework for key exchange and security associations. It is based on an anti-clogging technique which requires a client to return a server generated cookie. This is a technique derived from the PHOTURIS protocol, and can be used to prove a client's identity and is verified by the server before any costly authentication protocol is triggered [12]. A cookie as defined by [16] *"is a unique nonce computed from the names of sending and receiving parties and local secret information available only to the sender"*. A specification of the ISAKMP anti-clogging technique which is based on the PHOTURIS protocol is given in [12] as follows:

- the cookie must depend on the addresses of the communicating parties
- the cookie is generated based on a local secret known only by its generator
- nobody must be able to forge the cookie that will be accepted by the server
- the cookie generation and verification must be efficient in CPU and memory consumption.
- the server must not keep per-client state until IP address has been verified.

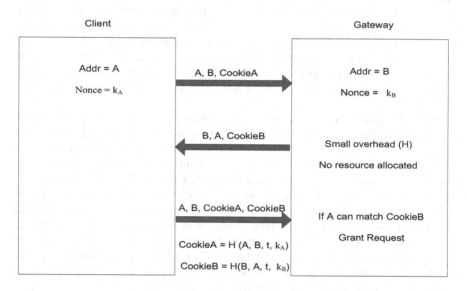

**Fig. 3.** The cookie anti-clogging technique [12]

PHOTURIS uses a keyed one-way hash function which uses both IP addresses, both UDP ports, and some locally-generated secret value (which is same for all clients but must be changed periodically). In some terrestrial systems, a threshold is placed on the rate of requests that a legitimate client can generate. In order to justify an increased rate from a single source, attackers emulate different source addresses by using false source addresses. The cookie exchange helps in the verification of a client's claim of presence at a particular IP address. See [17] for more details on the ISAKMP anti-clogging technique.

## 4  Protocol Design for DoS-Resilience in DTN

A DTN is potentially susceptible to DoS attacks due to limited connectivity, highly variable round-trip communication time, and limited computing resources at some nodes [16]. Therefore, in order to provide security additional overhead in terms of bandwidth utilization and computational costs may be introduced on the nodes. In IP Security (IPSec), bogus traffic injected into the network is carried all the way to the security destination and this consumes valuable resources [7]. As shown in Figure 1, DTN Bundle Security Protocol (BSP) includes a hop-by-hop security feature where each bundle is checked at a DTN router and any traffic that cannot be authenticated as coming from a legitimate node is discarded.

We adopt a security architecture which is domain/region-oriented. A domain/region is made up of a security gateway and nodes that are allowed to communicate with one another and our focus will be on a single domain (Region 1). In this architecture, security gateways acting as access control points use public key cryptography to authenticate clients. During a connection request, control messages are sent to the security gateway signed using the client's private key. Protocols that use strong authentication from the very beginning can be used by an attacker to cause availability problems in the network. This is due to the fact that public key algorithms use computationally expensive methods such as exponentiation and factorization to provide security. We assume that in the interaction between the attacker and a security gateway, the attacker's primary objective is to waste the gateway's resources by interacting with it.

Due to the scarcity of resources, DTN does not allow complex security mechanisms to be deployed. Therefore, the cookie and the client puzzle techniques as proposed for terrestrial networks are not suitable for implementation in DTN environments. Both methods result in longer protocol runs due to the additional messages during the initial phase of the protocol. The client puzzle technique is especially not suitable for this environment since it forces clients to work more when the security gateway load is high. A security gateway might be attending to a high volume of legitimate requests from network nodes. Devices especially sensor nodes might not have the capability to solve the puzzles. The wireless communication medium used in the sensor networks (regions 1 and 2), and the broadcast nature of the satellite channel coupled with the roundtrip delay makes the cookie anti-clogging technique as proposed for terrestrial environments unsuitable for our proposed architecture. These DoS mitigation techniques are designed to operate in low-delay, well connected networks and may not perform well in DTN environments. In order to counter the attacks listed in section 2, our design has to fulfill a number of networking and security requirements.

### 4.1  Networking Requirements

The protocol should operate when no end-to-end path exists from source to destination. Also, the protocol should be able to withstand changes in scheduling and/or in contact of nodes. It should provide support for varying data rates. The protocol must be resilient to delays and disruptions which may be in the order of minutes, hours or days. Where power-saving is a system-level requirement, the protocol should be able to run on nodes that are resource-constrained. And finally, the protocol should be able to work when faced with significant node mobility.

## 4.2  Security Requirements

We ensure availability by making sure that all security processing is performed by more capable nodes (DTN-aware nodes e.g. MSNs). We also ensure data freshness by preventing the replay of old messages through the use of timestamps, sequence numbers and nonces. All message requests must be authenticated by the security gateways in order to verify the authenticity of the entities and validity of the data source. Lastly we ensure the integrity of message requests received in order to guarantee that the contents have not been modified or deleted. The DoS mitigation technique proposed in this paper addresses these requirements.

# 5  Design Specification

In this section we describe the assumptions made during our design, and provide a detailed specification of the design including the notations used. We discuss issues relating to timestamps and time-synchronization in DTN and also provide an analysis of the design.

## 5.1  Design Assumptions

- a security gateway has bounded resources that could possibly be exhausted by a clever attacker.
- the attacker may or may not have bounded resources and may or may not have resources greater than the security gateway.
- the attacker is assumed to have the ability to replay, modify, transmit, receive, and execute the protocol.
- the attacker is within wireless communication range to the security gateway and does not need the help of other nodes to launch an attack.
- trust is established during initial registration of a node with the security gateway.
- only DTN-aware MSNs and Satellite Terminals (STs) can interact with the security gateway.
- the public/private keys are generated and pre-shared during initialization
- only nodes that are registered with the security gateway and share a secret (which is used to generate the nonce) with it can generate a valid request.
- the protocol is between two communicating parties i.e. the client (MSN/ST) and security gateway.

The client always initiates the communication between a client and a security gateway. Figure 4 shows the generic bundle (message) format exchanged between a client and a security gateway.

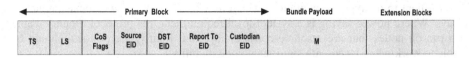

**Fig. 4.** Generic bundle format

In Figure 5, additional security extension blocks such as the Bundle Authentication Block (BAB) or the Payload Integrity Block (PIB) are added to the generic bundle as shown in Figure 4 to provide authentication or integrity checks respectively. Also a DTN-cookie is added as a last block to the bundle to provide a weak authentication phase during the verification process. This is our contribution to satisfy the requirement that control or data bundles within a domain/region do not trigger any form of DoS attack which might exhaust the resources of DTN nodes.

| Primary Block | | Source EID | DST EID | Security Block | Bundle Payload | | | |
|---|---|---|---|---|---|---|---|---|
| TS | LS | Source EID | DST EID | RSAwithSHA256 | M | h (M) | privK (h (M)) | Cookie |

**Fig. 5.** A bundle with additional security extension blocks

**Notations.** We use the following notations in the description of our design.

- TS: the timestamp which is a concatenation of a bundle creation time and a monotonically increasing sequence number which is unique for every new bundle from a source EID.
- LS: the bundle lifespan or expiration time. The LS value of a bundle equals X where X can be in days, hours or minutes.
- Source_EID: the identity of each DTN-aware node, we assume that each EID is a singleton.
- DST_EID: the identity of the destination node i.e. the entity for which the bundle is destined (security gateway).
- RSAwithSHA256: represents the ciphersuite and gives an idea to what security block is in use.
- M: the payload of the request message.
- h: is a cryptographic hash function such as MD5, SHA1 or SHA256. We will be using SHA256 as the underlying hash function to the signature algorithm.
- h (M): the hash value or message digest derived by passing the payload M through the function h.
- $pubK_{Xi}$: the public key of node $X_i$
- $privK_{Xi}$: the private key of node $X_i$

DoS attacks are not addressed fully in the current security extensions of the Bundle Protocol. At present, DTN nodes simply discard any traffic that fails the authentication and access control checks. This in itself provides minimal protection and makes it harder to launch a DoS attack. However, the potential danger is in the computation and storage overheads at DTN nodes which we seek to address. We propose three examples of a lightweight authenticator which we refer to as DTN-cookie each having varying levels of complexity. The choice of a particular type of DTN-cookie will depend on the level of DoS threat. The DTN-cookie is calculated by the bundle originator and attached as the last block of the bundle as shown in Figure 5 and must be verified by the security gateway.

(a) DTN-cookie is a nonce which represents the result when a random number generator is seeded using an Initialization Vector (IV). The IV is known only to all registered nodes in the domain/region during the initialization phase.

Nonce = RNG (IV or seed). The Initialization Vector is kept secret and changed periodically to ensure freshness.

(b) DTN-cookie is the result of an XOR operation on the timestamp and the result of the operation in (a) i.e. timestamp (TS) $\oplus$ nonce in (a).

(c) DTN-cookie is derived by passing the result of the operation in (b) through a keyed Message Authentication Code such as HMAC. The underlying hash function is SHA-1 and the secret key is shared between the client and the gateway. This is represented as follows:

DTN-cookie = HMAC ((timestamp (TS) $\oplus$ nonce) + secret key).

A secure Key Management mechanism is required for the safe generation and distribution of keys. Also, regular key refreshments are very important to thwart attacks which might attempt to use compromised keys.

## 5.2 Timestamps and Time Synchronization in DTN

Timestamps are typically used for logging events. The Bundle Protocol uses timestamps for three reasons to guarantee network efficiency and resource protection [3]:

- the useful life indicator of bundles prevents the network from storing and forwarding bundles whose useful lifespan have expired.
- the lifetime helps prevent bundles from looping continuously in the network as a result of routing loops.
- the originating timestamp helps in the unique identification of bundles and the re-assembly of bundle fragments.

The original purpose of timestamps is to help DTN intermediary or destination nodes to determine when it is appropriate to drop a bundle or determine the age of a bundle. In our design, timestamps are used to provide an accurate record of the bundle creation time and act as a freshness identifier to protect against replay attacks. Timestamps provide a more efficient way to test for freshness without introducing too much traffic into the network. This replaces the idea of the gateway broadcasting or sending a nonce as a freshness identifier at certain time intervals. Based on RFC 5050 the creation timestamp is a concatenation of the bundle creation time and a monotonically increasing sequence number. The sequence number is incremented continuously (say every second) in order to make the concatenation of source EID and creation timestamp the unique bundle identifier. With this bundles created at the same time interval by different nodes can be differentiated.

The Bundle Protocol has an in-built assumption that DTN nodes have a basic time-synchronization capability with a common, synchronized view of the Coordinated Universal Time (UTC) [3, 6]. This is based on DTN's initial design for deep space environments where the space-based agents are synchronized and highly scheduled with bandwidth and delays known in advance. This assumption becomes invalid when extended to terrestrial DTN environments due to the fact that DTN nodes are isolated or disconnected most of the time, may use discovery methods or might implement intentional sleep cycles to conserve power as in wireless sensor networks. In these different instances the clocks of such nodes can drift. It has been noted that in challenged environments like DTN, time synchronization is a problem.

The use of classical time protocols like the Network Time Protocol (NTP) is limited because it is not resilient to disruption. A very good source for UTC is the Global Positioning System (GPS) which is one non-DTN time solution. DTN nodes cannot rely on GPS due to the fact that most nodes such as sensors may lack GPS receivers and the cost implication of using GPS as a reference clock maybe too high making deployment infeasible. DTN has the in-built capability to read the local system clock values and determine the correct time. This is the reason why it possible for DTN nodes to set the creation time when bundles are created and sent into the network and checked for expiry on reception.

At present, there is on-going debate in the DTN research community on the justification for DTN reliance on time synchronization to perform store-and-forward networking as specified in RFC 5050. The use of absolute timestamps and coordinated clocks in DTN to meet the requirements stated earlier has been criticized or supported by many. There are suggestions to either strengthen or replace the lifetime mechanism with a countdown counter such as a "hops-to-live". Hops-to-live explicitly discards bundles that have traversed more than a set number of hops. This will allow bundles to expire when their lifetime is decremented to zero without any requirement for loose synchronization.

### 5.3  Analysis of Design

As a requirement, our design should be secure against masquerade by providing a mechanism to identify and discard any attack bundle on initial processing of the DTN-cookie. Also the DTN-cookie should be lightweight, efficient and simple. The DTN-cookie is the result of an XOR operation on the timestamp and a nonce generated by the client. The nonce generated by the client should match that calculated by the security gateway. The design should discourage Transport Layer Security (TLS) type of handshake but use minimized number of roundtrips i.e. only a single unidirectional message for connection establishment or access. DTN-aware nodes act as security-sources for sensor nodes that maybe IDless or have resource restrictions. We add a DTN-cookie to every bundle for quick identification of attack bundles. In our design, computational efficiency is achieved since no gateway resource is dedicated to service any attack bundle except those required to identify and discard the traffic. A client wishing to communicate with the security gateway has to generate a message request in the form of a bundle as shown in Figure 5 and send to the security gateway.

The pseudo code below shows the operation that takes place at the security gateway during the weak authentication of a bundle.

Client ⟶ Server:

request = {TS, LS, Source_EID, DST_EID, M, h (M), priv (h (M)), DTN-cookie}

Set Bundle Lifespan (Ls) = X (days, hours or minutes)

The Server performs an XOR operation:
result = timestamp $\oplus$ DTN-cookie

```
if   (result ≠ server_cookie) || (bundle_in_network > Ls) ||
        (DST_EID ≠ serverAddress)
                Discard Bundle
     else
                (retrieve public key credentials from cache)
                calculate pubK_Xi (privK_Xi (h (M)))
     if  pubK_Xi (privK_Xi (h (M))) ≠ request.h (M)
                Discard Bundle
            else
                calculate h (M)
                if   h (M) ≠ request.h (M)
                        Discard Bundle
                else
                        Accept Bundle
```

One component of the security gateway is a multiple socket server with the capability to run multiple threads simultaneously and can service more than one connection request at a time. The security gateway on receiving a bundle, evaluates it to determine if it is from a legitimate client (DTN-aware node). Every legitimate entity runs a random number algorithm. This algorithm is seeded with an Initialization Vector which the security gateway shares with all DTN-aware nodes during initialization. The security gateway also shares a secret key pair with every DTN-aware node within its domain. The value of the Initialization Vector or the secret key is only known to legitimate DTN-aware nodes. These values are prerequisites for the computation of a valid nonce or DTN-cookie. In our design specification, it is impossible to generate a valid bundle that will be accepted by the security gateway without having the capability to compute a valid nonce or DTN-cookie. Every bundle sent by an attacker is discarded during the weak authentication phase when the DTN-cookie is evaluated. Placing the DTN-cookie and signature at the end of the bundle allows memory-constrained nodes like sensors to be able to process the bundle and verify its security result.

With a single unidirectional message request, the security mechanism is able to identify attack bundles and discard them. Replay attacks aimed at modifying the timestamp field will invalidate the bundle during the weak authentication of the DTN-cookie. Also, attacks that are aimed towards substituting the payload of a legitimate message will be thwarted since any modification or tampering with the payload will be detected during the signature verification phase. If a bundle passes the weak authentication phase, a computing intensive signature verification phase will be triggered. The cost of an attack will be more on the side of the attacker since at every attempt he has to compute a nonce, generate a fake DTN-cookie, sign the bundle and send. The gateway is not affected since any client request that cannot pass the weak authentication phase is discarded and the connection closed. This is to safeguard the gateway's resources. If the signature verification phase succeeds, then the client is authenticated, request granted and resource allocated based on security gateway policy.

From our evaluation of the protocol's performance, it is clear that the protocol follows the description of Gong and Syverson's model of fail-stop protocols [18] but different because it does not use strong authentication from the very beginning. It also follows the framework proposed by Meadows [9] where the server's assurance of the client's intention is increased at every step of the protocol execution. This is achieved by introducing a weak authentication phase prior to the more expensive signature verification phase.

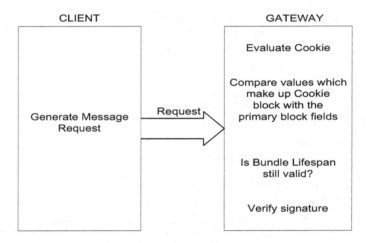

**Fig. 6.** The DTN-cookie technique

The gain in our design is that we have been able to reduce the number of message exchanges in the weak authentication phase from three (as in the PHOTURIS protocol) to one unidirectional message request thereby saving a lot of bandwidth. Also our design has achieved its objective of making the bundle authenticator (i.e. DTN-cookie) light-weight and efficient by using simple techniques like XOR and HMAC operations. Through these methods, we have been able to provide weak authentication for bundles with less overheads in the computation cost and power. In order to provide maximum protection, the HMAC variant of DTN-cookie proposed in this paper can be used. It is faster to hash the timestamp, nonce and key than hashing the entire bundle making it computationally more efficient. Also the inputs to the MAC algorithm [19] (i.e. the timestamp, nonce and key) have a very high degree of randomness as shown in their method of generation. It is hard to forge but inexpensive to verify which makes it appropriate for nodes with very low power budget. However, this comes with a slightly higher price of overheads due to the additional security processing.

# 6  Conclusion

DoS attacks are becoming a great threat to the proper functioning and survivability of networks. From section 3, it is obvious that traditional DoS mitigation methods such as the cookie anti-clogging technique and client puzzle used in terrestrial networks are not suitable for DTN environments. These methods require the exchange of several messages to achieve weak authentication or solving server generated puzzles respectively.

In our work we propose the use of a security extension block (DTN-cookie) which is added to every bundle to provide weak authentication. The weak authentication phase precedes a computationally intensive signature verification phase. The lightweight authenticator comes in three variants which is applied based on the perceived level of DoS threat. We have implemented the XOR variant of the DTN-cookie which provides moderate protection for DTN security gateways. This is to protect against resource exhaustion and ensure availability of DTN services. As future work, these mechanisms will be tested using the DTN2 Reference Implementation. We will analyze the protocol's performance against metrics such as communication cost, computation cost and power efficiency. We will broaden our scope to cover a more hierarchical hop-by-hop DoS resilient mechanism and also consider inter-domain DoS threats in DTN.

## Acknowledgements

We will like to thank the EU Information Society Technologies SATNEx II Network of Excellence VIII for supporting this research work.

## References

1. Warthman, F.: Delay Tolerant Networks (DTNs): A tutorial.v1.1 (2003)
2. Fall, K.: A Delay-Tolerant Network Architecture for Challenged Internets. In: ACM SIGCOMM Conference on Applications, Technologies, Architectures, and Protocols for Computer Communications, pp. 27–34 (2003)
3. Wood, L., Eddy, W., Holliday, P.: A Bundle of Problems. In: IEEE Aerospace Conference, Big Sky Montana (2009)
4. Farrell, S., Cahill, V., Geraghty, D., Humphreys, I., MacDonald, P.: When TCP Breaks: Delay-and Disruption-Tolerant Networking. IEEE Internet Computing 10(4), 72–78 (2006)
5. Fall, K.: A Message-Switched Architecture for Challenged Internets. Intel Research Berkeley. IRB-TR-02-010 (2002)
6. Cerf, V., et al.: Delay-Tolerant Networking Architecture. RFC 4838, Network Working Group (2007)
7. Cerf, V.G.: An Interplanetary Internet. Space Operations Communicator 5(4) (2008)
8. Bhutta, N., Ansa, G., Johnson, E., Ahmad, N., Alsiyabi, M., Cruickshank, H.: Security Analysis for Delay/Disruption Satellite and Sensor Networks. In: IWSSC 2009, Siena Italy (2009)
9. Meadows, C.: A Formal Framework and Evaluation Method for Network Denial of Service. In: Proc. IEEE Computer Security Foundations Workshop (1999)

10. Farrell, S., et al.: Delay Tolerant Networking Security Overview. DTN Research Group, Internet Draft (draft-irtf-dtnrg-sec-overview-06) (2009)
11. Franck, L.: Delay Tolerant Networking with Satellites: Overview and Research Directions. In: COST272 - 7th MCM, Telecom Paris (2004)
12. Onen, M., Molva, R.: Denial of Service Prevention in Satellite Networks. In: IEEE International Conference on Communications, vol. 7, pp. 4387–4391 (2004)
13. Dwork, C., Naor, M.: Pricing via Processing or Combating Junk Mails. Springer, Heidelberg (1998)
14. Juels, A., Brainard, J.: Client Puzzles: A Cryptographic Countermeasure Against Connection Depletion Attacks. In: Proc. Network and Distributed Systems Security Symposium, pp. 151–165 (1999)
15. Aura, T., Nikander, P., Leiwo, J.: DoS-resistant Authentication with Client Puzzles. In: Christianson, B., Crispo, B., Malcolm, J.A., Roe, M. (eds.) Security Protocols 2000. LNCS, vol. 2133, pp. 178–181. Springer, Heidelberg (2001)
16. Feng, Q., Lutz, R.: Assessing the Effect of Software Failures on Trust Assumptions. In: 19th Int'l Symposium on Software Reliability Engineering, pp. 291–292 (2008)
17. Arkinson, R.: Security Architecture for the Internet Protocol. RFC 1825 (1995)
18. Gong, L., Syverson, P.: Fail-stop Protocols: An Approach to Designing Secure Protocols. In: Proc. of IFIP DCCA-5, Illinois (1995)
19. Bellare, M., Canetti, R., Krawczyk, H.: Keying Hash Functions for Message Authentication. In: Koblitz, N. (ed.) CRYPTO 1996. LNCS, vol. 1109, pp. 1–15. Springer, Heidelberg (1996)

# Delay/Disruption Tolerant Network Architecture for Aircrafts Datalink on Scheduled Routes

Mohammed Al-Siyabi, Haitham Cruickshank, and Zhili Sun

Centre for Communication Systems Research, University of Surrey, Guildford, UK
{m.alsiyabi,h.cruickshank,z.sun}@surrey.ac.uk

**Abstract.** DTN is a relatively new research field and many applications have been identified for it. It is an overlay network working over heterogeneous networks in challenged environments where the links are less reliable and the delays are expected to be very long. Due to the difficult working conditions of DTN, all types of available links are utilized to ensure better delivery of messages including the physical transportations methods such as buses and ferries. We propose using aircrafts in scheduled routes for data transportation for DTN application. We will show an analysis of aircrafts routes and possible scenario for DTN concept realization.

**Keywords:** Delay Tolerant Network (DTN), Aircraft, Air Traffic Control (ATC).

## 1 Introduction

DTN was first introduced as a new concept for interplanetary applications and expanded from there to cover more applications such as sensor networks, ad hoc, tactical military communications, acoustic marine and environmental monitoring. DTN links availability and duration are not guaranteed and they depend on opportunistic, scheduled, and predicted contact [1]. DTN works in challenged conditions such as scarce resources, limited bandwidth and connection durations. Disruption and long delays are common features and highly expected on this network.

However, DTN concept has advantages over traditional networks by providing more protection against data loss caused by network failures and disconnectivity. This is achieved by storing the data in DTN node's persistent memory until the next contact is available. DTN uses the store and forward mechanism to rise above the disconnectivity of intermittent links by overlaying a new protocol layer called bundle layers to transfer data messages which are also called bundles. It uses persistent memory to store the messages/bundles and forward them from node to node whenever the link is available. As shown in figure 1, which represents sending a message from source to destination, in case the intermediate node is not available, the node will store the message and forward it to the next node whenever the link is available again. These characteristics confine the potential applications of DTN to the delivery of un-urgent messages because of the expected long delays.

K. Sithamparanathan et al. (Eds.): PSATS 2010, LNICST 43, pp. 235–248, 2010.

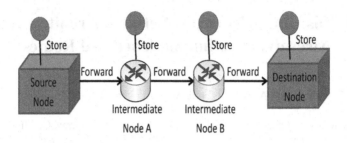

**Fig. 1.** Store and Forward DTN Architecture

Due to the challenged environment and scarce recourses in DTN, all types of available transmission means are used. Therefore, in addition to using the standard network backbone infrastructures, it has been proposed in DTN to utilize the existing transportations means such as buses, ships, ferries, bicycles, motorbikes and trains by physically transporting the saved data on a storage medium such as USP memory. There is a tendency in DTN to use physical transportation methods which is relatively a low speed movement compared with the high transmission speeds in network infrastructures. DTN is tolerant to delays and disruption; therefore, transportations are suitable to carry DTN messages at a standard transportation speed.

Using aircrafts in scheduled route as DTN bundle carrier is a novel trend for DTN applications. Throughout the DTN literature and to the best of our knowledge, there is no proposal to use commercial, private, military aircrafts for DTN applications the way we plan to introduce in this paper. There were some proposals to use motorbikes, ferries, buses, cars, bicycle and perhaps using Unmanned Aerial Vehicle (UAV) for some application [1],[2],[3],[4],[5]. Our contribution is to propose a valid application for new DTN technology by using airlines companies' aircrafts in scheduled routes to work as DTN bundles carriers during their flights along their routes.

Figure 2 shows the basic aircraft DTN architecture. The ground DTN node is located at a remote area with limited communication infrastructure under a scheduled flying route of a commercial airline company. The aircraft passes over the ground

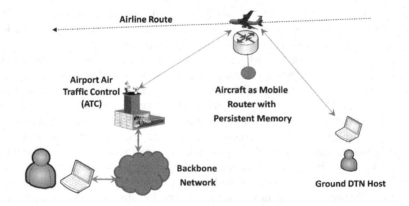

**Fig. 2.** Basic aircrafts DTN architecture

node at relatively systematic specific time intervals. The ground node has a ground to air DTN capable transceiver radio and transmits to the passing aircraft which is considered as a mobile router with persistent memory. In turn, the aircraft will store or deliver the message to the Air Traffic Control (ATC) then to its final destination through the backbone network.

This represents one way communication (up-link) from the ground node in remote areas to a user in urban areas. However, the two way communications from the user in the backbone network to the aircraft to the remote users will be more complex because it will require more coordination to enable the aircraft to decide when to download its traffic and where depending on the location of the ground remote node and the time expected for the aircraft to reach it.

## 2 Other DTN Transportation Mediums

There are many similar approaches in the literature to use transportation and scheduled transportation services to provide DTN service. However, to the best of our knowledge, this is the first time aircrafts in scheduled routes are proposed to be used for DTN services. All types of transportations are used in DTN including birds such as pigeons. In South Africa, they suffer from week broadband capacity at remote areas and an IT company wanted to prove this weakness to the media. They ran an amusing competition between ADSL speed and a humble pigeon. Winston, the pigeon, armed with a 4 GB memory stick travelled 60 miles and delivered the data while the ADSL had delivered 4 % of the data only[6].This indicates the usefulness of store and forward model for remote areas data transmission. The DTN concept works in a similar way to the pigeon transportation idea, where the data are stored in a storage medium and carried all the way to its destination. In South Africa also, they launched "Wizzy Digital Courier" [4] project in early 2003 to provide low cost internet access to schools using memory sticks carried physically to the users terminals.

In reference[2], at UMass Amherst, they deployed 40-node DTN operating on a public transit system called Diesel Net, a DTN consisting of Wi-Fi nodes attached to buses which travel on scheduled routes. Whenever they encounter other buses during their movements along their routes, they exchange data by establishing pair-wise connections between them. A similar approach can be applied to aircrafts where a number of scheduled aircrafts can exchange bundles among them along their routes. Reference [7] in Diesel Net describes how they evaluated DTN routing protocol called RAPID (Resource Allocation Protocol for Intentional DTN) using vehicular DTN test bed of 40 buses. They found out that the radio range is a parameter for optimum routing, and the same for the aircrafts radio range, which will decide the covered areas for DTN services based on the coverage range of both ground and airborne radios.

The performance of DTN depends on the number of participants, their communication capability, their storage capacity and their movements' pattern [8].This will apply to the aircrafts case where the quality will get better when there are more participating aircrafts and having high storage capacity, high data rate radio communications and their flying routes are within range of the ground terminals. The movement pattern of the aircrafts will be important to improve performance which is similar to [8] where they introduced autonomous agents or robotic agents, adopted and controlled their physical motion to the best optimum to meet the traffic demands in networks. The closest flying aircraft route to the DTN ground users is the best choice for transmitting bundles rather than one at farther distance which will degrade the radio performance.

Another approach, proposed by Li and Rus [9] algorithm, assumes peers broadcast the location of all other peers at frequent intervals using a communication channel. A similar idea can be used where one aircraft in a stable flying route is used to announce the locations and times of all other flights along their routes. This will help ground users to decide when and to whom to send. Zhao [3] proposed DTN ferries, which use ferries as DTN carriers. In his proposal, the peers schedule their movement to meet with the ferries movement in order to route their messages. This approach is more suitable to aircrafts because their flying route is fixed and therefore it is more appropriate for the ground terminals to schedule their movements and existence with the aircrafts movement.

## 3   Feasibility of Using Aircrafts for DTN Data Transport

Aircrafts transportation is the most popular, fastest, safest, widespread means of transportation on earth. Commercial air transport represents one of the major aspects of the world economy. It transports around 1.8 billion passengers annually over thousands of flights[10]. This business is growing and expected to increase the number of flights and passengers traffic to double the amount in the next 15-20 years [11].Worldwide aircrafts traffic flying routes represent a network of thousands of flights crossing the world every day. Based on Official Airline Guide (OAG) Facts, May 2009: Executive summary statistics, there are almost 81 thousand flights that take off daily worldwide and sometimes the number reaches 85 thousands in good seasons [10].

This gives indication of the potential application for this facility and might add a secondary service to airlines companies business to act as DTN bundles carriers. If aircrafts autonomously exchange and forward DTN bundles, this will be a great and big achievement for DTN technology.  Aircrafts do not have any terrain obstacles and can fly over all types of topography. There are many remote areas (such as oceans and deserts) where it is very expensive to lay the terrestrial networks and there are many flights passing over some of these places on predictable times and locations. Therefore, they can be used as mobile routers to carry DTN bundles along their routes.

Aircrafts are flying at different altitudes with horizontal and vertical separation between them. Aircrafts can't just fly without orientation. They are flying in what is called air corridor where they follow fixed routes according to set plans and directives from ATC (Air Traffic Center) which is used to direct aircrafts during their flights. ATC have communication facilities of ground to air radios to communicate with the aircrafts [12].

Figure 3 [13] represent the worldwide air traffic daily routes of thousands of flights. These aircrafts can be used to receive, store and forward DTN bundles along their flying routes from sending DTN nodes on the ground. This is the basic idea behind the novel approach of using aircrafts in commercial flying routes to act as DTC carriers.

**Fig. 3.** Worldwide aircrafts traffic routes [13]

Another detailed example is shown in Figure 4 [14] which represents an example of the flying routes over Europe. It is obvious that the widespread of this service makes it an excellent choice to be a carrier for the DTN bundles. Ground to air radios on the ground and the airborne radios can be made DTN aware to enable them to act like DTN nodes.

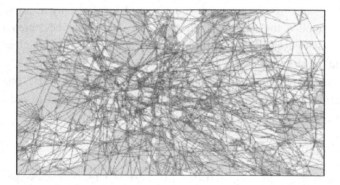

**Fig. 4.** An Example of main flying routes in Europe [14]

## 4   Aircrafts DTN Applications Concepts

DTN is an ongoing research field and aeronautical communications is also in continuous developments and is more focused on datalink applications than the traditional voice system. This research may provide the possible integration of new DTN concepts with the existing developments of aeronautical research.

### 4.1   Timing Concepts

Commercial airlines companies, cargo companies, military and governments run scheduled flights on timely fashions from airports to multi destinations. These flights are scheduled to depart daily or at any certain interval at fixed times of the day and arrive to their destination airports at the expected arrival time. Although there could be some unfortunate possible delays or flights cancellations, the aircrafts flying routes and duration time can be anticipated from ground users who can expect when they fly over their area and send their messages accordingly. Furthermore, the ground users do not need to know the destination of the passing aircraft. They can send their messages to any flying aircrafts which in turn will forward them to the nearest ATC, to the backbone network and finally to their destination.

## 4.2  Flying Aircrafts Repeaters

Flying aircrafts can be considered as repeaters/routers between terrestrial networks and satellite networks. If all flying aircrafts in the world are coordinating and coope-rating together to forward and route messages, they will certainly act as flying air repeaters in addition to their genuine function to transfer people and goods. Similar applications are used in the military such as Airborne Early Warning and Control System (AWACS) ) [15] where in addition to the detection tasks, the aircrafts might be used to extend radio coverage by acting as a repeater for ground units to transfer messages to further distances. After receiving DTN bundles, the aircrafts has two options to forward the bundles according to the applications priority and delivery options:

- At arrival: Store in persistent memory and forward only at arrival in ATC. This is applied to low priority traffic. The data might be stored in aircraft, downloaded physically into a flash memory and injected into the backbone net-work in the airport.
- During flight: Store in persistent memory and forward to ATC, other aircrafts or satellites while flying. This is applied for high priority traffic and might have higher cost to implement.

## 4.3  Fragmentation (Traffic Splitting)

Small size messages might fit into one flight while large size messages might be fragmented and sent to many aircrafts at different times. At destination, the fragments are reassembled to reestablish the messages. There might be proactive fragmentation where the messages are split in advance to be fit for the aircrafts capacity or reactive fragmentation in which case the arriving aircraft can't take the whole messages. Therefore, the ground terminal will fragment the message, send a portion of it into the approaching aircraft and schedule to send the rest of the message bundles into the next one or two coming aircrafts depending on the message size and the aircraft capacity.

## 4.4  Aircraft to Aircraft

DTN transmission can be done via more than one aircraft. In some cases, when the arriving aircraft has limited capacity which might be filled from some previous DTN nodes along the flight route, that aircraft can free its capacity by sending its load to another aircraft that is out of range of the sending ground DTN radio, while it is in the range of the aircraft. This way the aircraft capacity is enough to receive the new traffic bundles from the DTN ground terminals.

## 5    Contact Duration and Capacity Calculations

It is important to estimate the contact duration of aircrafts with respect to a fixed user on the ground in order to calculate the expected capacity of the contact. The DTN application concept is based on using a basic type of ground to air VHF transceiver which can be deployed at remote areas. VHF Datalink (VDL) mode 2 is one of the common digital links used for sending data between aircrafts and ground stations. VDL2 will be the focus of this discussion and it is assumed that there exists a mechanism to transfer DTN bundles to aircrafts. VDL2 maximum data rate *(R)* is 31.5 Kbps [16]; therefore, it is required to calculate the total contact time *(t)* which the aircrafts needs to fly over the ground node using the basic equation below

$$\text{Time} = \frac{\text{Distance}}{\text{Speed}} \tag{1}$$

Aircrafts speed varies at different altitudes and for the purpose of this paper we will assume the scenario of a cruising speed flight at altitude *(h)* of 30,000 ft = 9.144 km at a ground speed *(S)* of 900 Km/h. We need first to calculate the distance *(d)* covered by an aircraft during which it is in line of sight (LOS) with respect to the ground DTN node. As shown in figure 5A, the radio coverage range is calculated using the communication radio horizon equation which is the straight line of sight distance *(d)* in kilometers to the earth horizon

$$d = 3.569\sqrt{h(m)} \;\; km \tag{2}$$

Where *(h)* is the height above ground or sea level (in meters). As shown in figure 5B and 5C, the aircraft will become in horizon LOS with the ground node in two times:

1. From approaching the node horizon until it becomes above the node *(d1)*.
2. After leaving the node until disappearing from node horizon *(d2)*.

Therefore, the total distance *(d)* the aircraft is within the aircraft horizon is

$$d=d1+d2 \tag{3}$$

Now, for our scenario, the aircraft height *(h)* is 30,000 ft (9144 m) and hence the radio horizon distance *(d1 and d2)* is 341 km and the total distance *(d)* will be 682 Km. Accordingly, the contact time *(t)* will be 45 minutes during which the aircraft will be in LOS with the ground node. However, this whole duration can't be used for data transmissions due to radios performance. The radio range is dependent on many factors such as the transmitted power, gain and atmosphere conditions. For better accuracy, we will consider the radio range is 180 NM or 333.36 km based on VDL2 physical layer validation report [17]. Therefore, the total distance *(d)* is 666.72 km and the contact duration *(t)* will be 44.5 minutes which is almost the same as the calculated results and therefore confirms our calculations.

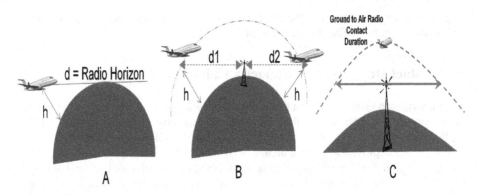

**Fig. 5.** Aircrafts contact duration calculations

For *(R)* 31.5 Kbps data rate of VDL2, the amount of data transmitted *(C)* during the contact duration will be 10 Mbytes. Therefore, for users who want to send data more than 10 Mbytes with the same aircraft speed and altitude used in our scenario, currently, this technology might not suitable due to the datalink limitations unless they fragment their load among more than one flight. However, the data rate might be improved in the future radio technology and accordingly the amount of transmitted data. Furthermore, this result is the best case scenario where the aircraft is assumed to be in direct LOS with the ground node while the real life situations will be affected by aircraft altitude, speed and angle with respect to the ground terminal plus height of the ground terminal, topography of the area, curvature of earth and radios performance.

Generally, we have derived equation (4) below to calculate the contact data capacity *(C)* (Mbytes) as a function of aircraft speed *(S)* (km/hr) and altitude *(h)* (ft) and the ground radio transceiver data rate *(R)* (kbps) for any scenario.

$$C \text{ (MB)} = 1.66 \times \frac{R \text{ (kbps)} \times \sqrt{h \text{ (ft)}}}{S \left(\frac{km}{hr}\right)} \quad \text{(MByte)} \tag{4}$$

In case HF radio transceiver is used, the HF Datalink (HFDL) provides long range communication and used by aircrafts to fly polar routes but with limited data rate *(R)* up to 19.2 Kbps [18]. Using equation (4) for the same scenario, the capacity *(C)* will be 6.15 Mbytes which is limited in today's technology but for some remote areas, would probably be of a great value.

## 6   DTN and Aeronautical Satellite

In addition to the navigation functions of satellites in aeronautical applications, they are used for voice and data communications between ground stations and aircrafts. There are non-air traffic management (ATM) uses for satellite communication which includes providing telephone services to passengers onboard the aircrafts. INMARSAT, IRIDIUM and other satellite systems are used for aircrafts satellite communication facilities [16]. Furthermore, aircrafts can provide additional services for ground

DTN nodes using their satellite facilities to provide remote ground users with data transportation services.

There are remote areas with no satellite terminal but having ground to air radios to contact aircrafts. On the other hand, there are some passing aircrafts which have access to satellite communication. In this case, the ground terminal will use their radios by connecting a laptop programmed with DTN technology. As shown in figures 6 and 7, the messages are sent from the laptop to the radio which will send it to the passing aircraft which in turn will forward it to the satellite and from there towards the final destination. In this case, the aircraft is used as a proxy hop to the satellite. This way the messages from remote areas will be sent to their destination faster and with less delay based on the best coordination between the DTN ground terminals and the passing aircraft.

**Table 1.** VHF VDL mode 2 and satellite data rates

| Technology | VHF | Satellite | | | | |
|---|---|---|---|---|---|---|
| System | VDL 2 | Inmarsat SBB | Iridium | Global Star | Thuraya | IGSAGS |
| Data rate | 31.5 Kbps | Up to 432 Kbps per channel | 2.4 kbps Full duplex channels per user | Up to 9.6 kbps per user | 9.6 kbps (per user) | 30 kbps (per user) |

Table 1 provides an overview of the VHF technology data rate and some satellite systems data links technologies[16]. First hop will be using VDL2 link from ground node to the passing aircraft at a maximum data rate of 31.5 kbps and second hop from the aircraft to the satellite at various data rate depending on the system of used satellite.

# 7 Aircrafts DTN Possible Application

There might be many applications for using aircrafts in flying routes as DTN bundles carriers because aircrafts are flying over many rural places and difficult terrain. The under-developed areas can use this service to send their messages to the backbone network. Ships in deep seas and offshore oil rigs depend on High Frequency (HF), Line Of Sight (LOS) for short distances and satellites for their communications. However, there are many flights passing over seas and oceans and big ships and oil rigs are normally fitted with ground to air radios. They can be used to send DTN bundles to the passing aircraft which might reduce cost and delay and provide alternative means of communication to them.

Military bases which are in remote areas can also use this facility along with border monitoring points which might send their monitoring reports to passing scheduled aircrafts to ensure better delivery speeds. Furthermore, environmental monitoring can take advantage of this service like the case with Zebra Net [5] where the monitoring reports can be sent to a passing aircrafts at certain set up times. Any sensor network can be adjusted to send its data to the scheduled aircrafts which might reduce the cost of setting a special purposes vehicle or flight to collect their data.

Another optimistic application might be implemented in high condensed flying areas such as Europe and USA. It might be possible to have a real time transmission during peak hours because there are many flying aircrafts which means more mobile routers and contact. As shown in figure 4 earlier, in Europe the routes are condensed and there are extra aircrafts which will secure better chances for more contacts in a real time manner of the traffic. When the ground DTN node connects to an approaching aircraft, it starts sending its bundles, which in turn forward it to other ATC backbone entities. However, as it moves away from the node, there will be more other approaching aircrafts which will mean the aircraft will hand over the receiving of bundles task to the new approaching aircraft and so on until the messages are fully transmitted. This can be applied to video streaming applications where a real time captured video can be sent via a passing aircraft to its destination. Of course in this case we assume the capacity and data rates of the transmitting radios in both ground and aircraft are enough to transmit the real time video stream.

In addition to the prime role of airlines companies to transfer goods and passengers, they might provide secondary services for DTN data transmission to ground subscribers. Every interested user might register with the airline company asking for the service and accordingly will be assigned an account with identified entitlements of the capacity, priority, traffic contract and expected Quality of Service (QoS). Therefore, the users now can transmit to any aircraft that belongs to the company fleet. Furthermore, Airlines companies can cooperate in same fashion like mobile companies to provide roaming services among their customers. If the passing aircraft doesn't belong to the registered company, the user can still send his bundles with a little agreed extra charge according to the roaming agreement between the two airlines companies. This is an optimistic application but with the rapid increase in the air transportation, we might live one day to see it happening.

## 8   Aircrafts DTN Bundles Scenarios

Bundles can be routed to destination via different possible routes. The general idea of flying DTN routing is shown in figure 6. Three example applications for this service are:

- Soldiers with handheld mobile DTN aware ground to air transceiver radio.
- Offshore oil rig in the ocean with static DTN aware ground to air base station transceiver radio.
- Remote areas with static DTN aware ground to air base station transceiver radio.

The three users are located under flying routes where tens of aircrafts pass over them every day. They want to send their messages to the backbone network i.e. Internet. They use DTN protocols applications to transfer their messages into bundles and send them to the nearest passing aircraft which can do any of the following tasks based on the traffic priorities:

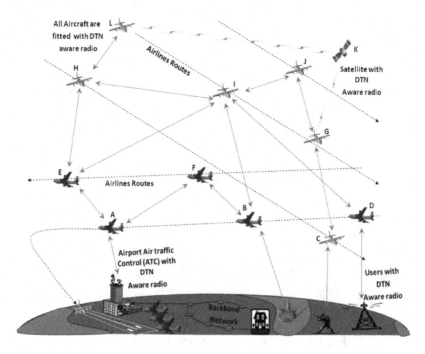

**Fig. 6.** Aircrafts DTN scenarios

- Store them all the way and download them physically using USP memory sticks in the ATC airport which will forward them to the backbone network and to their destination.
- Forward them to the ATC using the aircraft radio.
- Forward them to another aircraft in another flying route within line of sight of aircraft radio transmission. This can be repeated until the messages find their way to the ATC and then to their final destination.
- Forward them to a satellite.

There are different routes for the bundles to follow. For example, in case of the soldier to deliver or receive his messages, this can be done via routes C-G-J-I-E-A, C-G-J-I-B-F-A and so on. Another example is for the offshore oil rig where bundles can take route B-F-A, B-I-E-A, B-I-H-E-A or B-I-J-G-K-L-H-E-A. Note that the final route includes using a satellite link. It is also possible to fragment the bundles and send some via route B-F-A and some via B-I-E-A.

As shown in figure 6, aircrafts are considered as flying mobile routers with persistent memory to store the messages until finding a node accepting them or until forwarding them to a destination. In this case, the aircraft will provide custody transfer to the ground DTN node and it will be upon the aircraft to deliver the messages. The optimum route for the message delivery depends on many factors such as number of aircrafts, sender location from the air routes and speed and altitude of aircrafts.

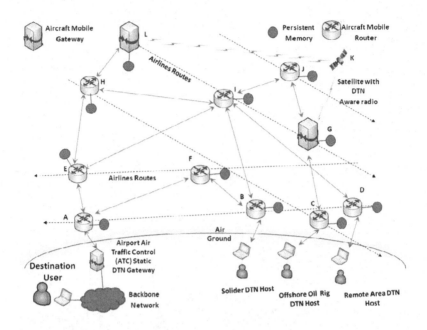

**Fig. 7.** Aircrafts as mobile routers for different scenarios

## 9 Research Opportunities

Delay Tolerant Network (DTN) itself is a new research network architecture and the DTN research group (DTNRG) in the Internet Research Task Force (IRTF) is working on its architecture and bundle protocol [19]. This novel trend for using aircrafts of airlines commercial companies in scheduled routes as DTN carriers will require a lot of research to validate its success. The research should be tied between the DTN architecture and the aeronautical communication applications of airborne radios and the ground terminal.

Routing is still under research in DTN and considered a difficult task due to the nature of lack of links connectivity. Adding the movement of aircrafts nodes to it will make it more complex. Routing might require an approach similar to the one used in MANET routing where some of the nodes are in constant movements [7].

Another research potential in this field is the DTN aircrafts addressing. Bundles source and destinations are identified by Endpoint Identifier EID and each endpoint is represented syntactically as a Uniform Resource Identifier (URI) which is used to represent the address in DTN. The aircrafts address is required to route the bundles to the correct aircraft from a group of flying aircrafts. An aircraft is identified by a system called Identifying Friendly or Foe (IFF). This system might be useful for address binding from URI address to the IFF code which belongs to a unique aircraft. More research in this is required to ensure the correct addressing of bundles to the correct aircraft in the correct route.

Radios on the ground and aircrafts need to be made DTN aware and fitted with persistent memory. Theses radios are designed mainly for voice applications between the pilot and the traffic control over VHF channels. Data link communications is already available in today's ATC tool set. Another research area is to explore the possibility of DTN application using the aircraft data link and the requirement for extra memory storage for DTN applications.

There are many research aspects in DTN security. Key management, authentication, access control, denial of service and others are among the active research in DTN bundling security architecture. Security is also implemented in aircrafts to some extent. The IFF code is used to authenticate aircrafts and likewise bundles must be authenticated before accepted in aircrafts which might be required to provide some means of bundle integrity within the custody transfer to the ground source node. The bundle protocol has identified some security blocks to enhance the security of DTN bundle transmission. These aspects might need further research to find the possible implementations within the aeronautical applications.

The notion of QoS in DTN is different from the traditional IP networks. This field has not been addressed a lot in the literature. DTN Bundle protocol has identified some bits for priority indications but the mechanism for providing quality of service for bundles flows are still not part of DTN architecture [20]. Aircrafts as DTN bundle carriers might require QoS criteria especially for its optimistic applications in condensed flying areas and peak flying times of real time transmission. Furthermore, in remote areas with limited resources and many users, contention to scarce resources might lead to traffic congestions and network degradation. These and other QoS issues are considered another research potential.

## 10  Conclusion and Future Work

DTN has good future applications and using aircrafts in scheduled routes is a promising application because flying routes are spread in vast areas and cover all types of terrain which are considered good carriers for DTN bundles. This paper presented some of the thoughts relating to this application which are considered as an introduction to a future implementation of DTN technology within aeronautical communications.

For future work, considering the three scenarios, we will expand into the contact durations estimations and capacity calculations to cover various aircrafts altitudes and speeds. Furthermore, we will look into the QoS issues within the DTN for this specific application and the impact of applying some congestion management techniques such as Admission Control to enhance the QoS of aircrafts datalink bundles delivery.

## References

[1] Farrell, S., Cahill, V.: Delay-and Disruption- Tolerant Networking. Artech House, London (2006)

[2] Zhang, X., Kurose, J., Levine, B.N., Towsley, D., Zhang, H.: Study of a Bus-based Disruption-Tolerant Network: Mobility Modeling and Impact on Routing. In: MobiCom 2007, Dept. of Computer Science, University of Massachusetts Amherst,Montréal, Québec, Canada, September 9-14 (2007)

[3] Zhao, W., Ammar, M., Zegura, E.: A Message Ferrying Approach for Data Delivery in Sparse Mobile Ad hoc Networks. In: Proc. ACM Mobihoc (May 2004)

[4] Jain, S., Fall, K., Patra, R.: Routing in a DTN. In: SIGCOMM 2004, Oregon, USA (August 2004)

[5] Farrell, S., Cahill, V.: Delay-and Disruption- Tolerant Networking, ch. 3, p. 65. Artech House, London (2006)

[6] BBC News, http://news.bbc.co.uk/1/hi/world/africa/8248056.stm [Cited: September 12, 2009]

[7] Balasubramanian, A., Levine, B.N., Venkataramani, A.: DTN routing as a resource allocation problem. In: Umass Amherst, SIGCOMM 2007, Kyoto, Japan, August 27–31 (2007)

[8] Burns, B., Brock, O., Levine, B.: MORA routing and Capacity Building in Disruption Tolerant Networks, Umass Amherst, National Science Foundation (2007)

[9] Li, Q., Rus, D.: Sending messages to mobile users in disconnected ad-hoc wireless networks. In: MobiCom 2000: Proceedings of the 6th annual international conference, Department of Computer Science, Dartmouth College, Hanover (2000)

[10] OAG Aviation 2009, Official Airline Guide June 2009: OAG FACTS June 2009: Executive Summary Report, http://www.oagaviation.com/reports.html [Cited: June 5, 2009]

[11] Pat, H.: Global Airlines competition in a transnational industry. Elsevier, London (2007)

[12] Wikipedia: The Free Encyclopedia: Air Traffic Control, http://en.wikipedia.org/wiki/Air_traffic_control [Cited: August 24, 2009]

[13] http://openflights.org/demo/openflights-routedb.png [Cited: June 10, 2009]

[14] http://infosthetics.com/archives/2009/05/visualizing_of_all_the_flights_in_24_hours.html [Cited: May 14, 2009]

[15] Brick, D., Ellersick, F.: Future Air Force Tactical Communications. Hanscom Air Force Base, MA, Communications IEEE Transactions 28(9), Part 1, 1551–1572 (1980)

[16] Gilbert, T., Dyer, G., Henriksen, S., Berger, J., Jin, J., Boci, T.: Identification of Technologies for Provision of Future Aeronautical Communications, ITT Industries, Herndon, Virginia, NASA (2006)

[17] Delhaise, P., Desperier, B., Roturier, B.: VDL Mode 2 Physical layer validation report, EUROCONTROL, DIS/COM, Mobile Communications Infrastructure, Figure 1.22, p. 37 (2007)

[18] Product Catalog Manual, The HF-9500 400-Watt airborne multimode HF system is Rockwell Collins, Airborne Communication system, Rockwell Collins Product

[19] Cerf, V., Burleigh, S., Hooke, A., Torgerson, L., Durst, R., Scott, K., Fall, K., Weiss, H.: Delay–Tolerant Networking Architecture. Internet RFC4838 (April 2007)

[20] Wood, L., Eddy, W., Holliday, P.: A Bundle of Problems. IEEEAC paper #1023 (December 23, 2008)

# Access Control Framework for Delay/Disruption Tolerant Networks

Enyenihi Johnson, Godwin Ansa, Haitham Cruickshank, and Zhili Sun

Centre for Communication Systems Research (CCSR)
University of Surrey, Guildford, United Kingdom
{e.johnson,g.ansa,h.cruickshank,z.sun}@Surrey.ac.uk

**Abstract.** The emergence of DTN as an option for sustaining communication in environments with high delay/frequent disruption have rendered existing access control mechanisms inappropriate hence the need for a new concept in DTN access control. This is primarily due to contradicting assumptions like low delay and constant connectivity on which the existing mechanisms are built. This paper discusses the security issues in DTN, investigate existing access control mechanisms and relate their design principles as well as operational mode to DTN. We proposed a lightweight hierarchical architecture based on AAA architecture concept and explored the DTN architecture to identify those features that will support the implementation of AAA architecture concept. We present the proposed architecture for an intra-domain scenario with a brief description.

**Keywords:** DTN, Security, Access Control, AAA, Authentication, Authorization, Hierarchical.

## 1 Introduction

Advancement in technology and the quest for effective communication have led to the discovery of networks that are delay/disruption tolerant where some of the assumptions on which today's Internet was built no longer hold. These networks ranging from marine networks, mobile ad-hoc networks, wireless sensor networks, military tactical networks to deep-space networks all share a common problem. This common problem is their inability to sustain communication in the face of limitations like intermittent connectivity, high/variable delay, asymmetric data rates, high error rates and heterogeneity. To address this problem, the Delay/Disruption Tolerant Networking (DTN) [1], [2] was proposed and the overlay network approach [3] was considered the most appropriate. Its emergence opens new areas of research in security which includes key management, Denial of Service (DoS) attacks, anonymity and privacy, access control amongst others. Access control is the main focus of this paper.

The need to have a common platform to carry out DTN services necessitated the introduction of a new layer called the bundle layer. The inability of the current Internet protocols to address communication problems in delay/disruption tolerant networks led to the development of DTN protocols (Bundle Protocol and Licklider Transmission Protocol) [4]. Our framework is designed to implement the Bundle Protocol [5] baring

K. Sithamparanathan et al. (Eds.): PSATS 2010, LNICST 43, pp. 249–264, 2010.

its complexity [6] because apart from being an overlay protocol, it has an in-built security mechanism to provide end-to-end data integrity and confidentiality as well as protecting the network from unwanted traffic [7]. References [1] - [9] are the existing documentations that give detailed description of DTN, its architecture and security.

The primary goal of this paper is to propose an access control framework for delay/disruption tolerant networks. To realise the goal, we evaluate security issues in DTN and identify access control related threats. We investigate existing access control mechanisms and relate their design principle as well as operational mode to DTN. We examine the DTN architecture and identify those features that support access control implementation. We propose a lightweight hierarchical architecture and justify why it suits the DTN environment.

This paper is organized as follows: In section II we review security issues in DTN, section III discusses access control and existing traditional solutions, section IV discusses the AAA architecture mentioned in [8] and the applicability of its concept in DTN access control, section V describes the DTN architecture and the existing features that supports the implementation of AAA architecture concept, section VI presents and explains the proposed access control framework, and section VII presents the conclusions.

## 2  DTN Security

The inherent constraints (like long delay, frequent disconnection and heterogeneity) in DTN and the overlay nature of the bundle protocol make security in DTN a critical issue. The inability of existing security mechanisms to address security issues in DTN environment necessitated the need for an entirely new concept in DTN security. This led to the identification of some threats during the design process of DTN security mechanisms. The identified threats according to [9] are those associated with non-DTN node, resource consumption, denial of service, confidentiality and integrity as well as traffic storm. The resource scarcity nature of the DTN demands that resource consumption related threats [9] associated with masquerading and modification attacks [10] is given serious consideration. Masquerading attack is where a malicious attacker impersonates another legitimate entity to gain access to secret information in a system or network in the case of an outsider, or to enjoy more privileges in the case of an insider. Modification attack is where an attacker attempts to modify information it is not authorized to. It exists in the form of changing existing information, removal of existing information and insertion of information.

DTN security is described extensively in [9], [11] and its goal is to ensure the protection of DTN infrastructure from these attacks through:

- Denying access to unauthenticated entities
- Preventing unauthorized entities from controlling the DTN infrastructure
- Preventing authenticated entities from carrying out unauthorized services
- Prompt detection and discarding of bundles sent by unauthorized entities
- Prompt detection and discarding of bundles with modified headers
- Prompt detection and removal of compromised entities

The above listed DTN security goals can be realised with access control [11].

# 3  Access Control

Access Control protects the network from unauthenticated entities and prevents unauthorized entities from using network resources. Reference [12] list and explain the three access control system abstractions of policy, mechanism and model. Access control can be implemented using either a centralized architecture [13] or a decentralized architecture. The decentralized architecture is either distributed [14], [15] where access control decision is fully decentralized or hierarchical [16] where access control decision is partially decentralized. A single entity manages access control in a centralized architecture while the regional security gateways are responsible for access control management in the distributed architecture. In the hierarchical architecture with combined elements of centralization and decentralization, a central entity manages access control of the network comprising the various distinct regional security gateways. The absence of an existing access control solution for delay/disruption tolerant networks to the best of our knowledge necessitated the investigation of traditional access control solutions to ascertain their suitability for the DTN environment.

Reference [12] identifies Discretional Access Control (DAC), Mandatory Access Control (MAC) and Role-Based Access Control (RBAC) as the three main traditional access control policies (solutions). Their brief descriptions are given below:

- **Discretional Access Control (DAC):** This approach is identity based and leaves a certain amount of access control to the discretion of an authorised user. The heterogeneous nature of the DTN environment makes this approach inapplicable. The absence of real assurance on the flow of information in a system and its vulnerability to Trojan horse attack will encourage modification and masquerading attacks respectively which our proposed framework is designed to address.

- **Mandatory Access Control (MAC):** This approach is rule-based and leaves access control management as well as definition of policy that cannot be modified by an authorized user to the system administrator. The use of system-wide policy and its ability to minimize abuse of applications by granting needed rights to individual participants make the approach suitable for the DTN environment. How this policy is implemented in the DTN environment will determine how limitations like complex configuration and determination of access authorization for each application are handled.

- **Role-Based Access Control (RBAC):** This approach is rule-based and access control decisions are based on roles individual users have as part of an organization. The administrative complexity of this approach increases with increase in granularity since multiple roles per user is needed for stronger security. Fewer roles per user make administration easier while weakening the security. RBAC will not be suitable for DTN environment from the stronger security perspective while it may be suitable from the easier administration perspective. Its combination with MAC is a probable solution.

The conceptualization of DTN to provide interoperability across heterogeneous networks and the need for the implementation of system-wide policy make trust a significant factor in DTN access control. Trust-based access control has been implemented using the centralized architecture with AAA (Authentication, Authorization and accounting) architecture [17] as an example. The conception of trust management for decentralized access control first mentioned in [20] led to the development of trust management systems that are either based on credential/policy or reputation [21]. The reputation-based trust management system is ideal for homogeneous networks while the credential/policy-based trust management system is ideal for heterogeneous networks. Few existing distributed trust management models used in traditional internet environments are: PolicyMaker [20], KeyNote [22], REFEREE [23] and SPKI [24].

The classical AAA architecture and the above mentioned credential/policy-based distributed trust models are not suitable for direct implementation in DTN due to: design principle, operational complexity, scalability issue and unavailability during long/variable delay and frequent disruption [25], [26]. However, the implementation flexibility offered by the AAA standard and the applicability of certain concepts with slight modification to the DTN environment underlines the suitability of AAA architecture concept to DTN.

## 4  AAA Architecture

The Authentication, Authorization and Accounting (AAA) architecture shown in fig. 1 is a framework that defines a central entity called the AAA Server to support the AAA operations. The AAA operations are Authentication, Authorization and Accounting but accounting is out of the scope of this work. The three network requirements needed for access control decision making are: the AAA server which receives and processes end users requests; AAA Client/NAS which provides end users with access to the network; and the AAA protocol which conveys AAA information between the NAS and the AAA server. Examples of AAA protocol are RADIUS (Remote Access Dial-In User Service) and DIAMETER. Additional requirements needed by the AAA server to facilitate access control decision making and resource management are:

| AAA | Authentication, Authorization and Accounting |
|-----|----------------------------------------------|
| NAS | Network Access Server |
| ASM | Application Specific Module |
| P&E R | Policy & Event Repository |
| ASD | Application Specific Database |

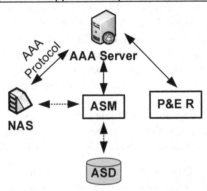

**Fig. 1.** Generic AAA Architecture

- Application Specific Module (ASM) which houses user database with application specific information.
- Policy & Event repository which stores on-going events as well as information relating to available services, resources and policy rules.

This architecture has a single point of failure, interactive, scalability problem in large networks, uses centralized Access Control List (ACL) amongst others. [17] – [19].

## 4.1  Authentication

Authentication ensures that the identity of a user requesting access to a system or services is verified before such request is granted. The three types of authentication [19] are:

- *Client Authentication* which comes in the form of either user or device authentication uses the credentials presented by the client to verify the authenticity of the client before granting access to the network.
- *Message Authentication* whose primary goal is to prevent modification attack ensures the legitimacy of the message source and data integrity while in transit.
- *Mutual Authentication* which protects a communicating party during node compromise ensures that two communicating entities at any point in time use either sequential or parallel method to authenticate each other.

Client and mutual authentication are implemented with either two-party model or three-party model [19]. Two-party model facilitates communication between two entities through a direct line without an intermediary node like a gateway or proxy. Three-party model which is our adopted model was designed to address the ineffectiveness of the two-party model in large networks. It engages the services of a third party to ensure that communicating parties only have access to resources and services they are authorized to. These models employ various authentication mechanisms that are classified using the three fundamental criteria of possession, knowledge and identity. Among the few mechanisms listed in [19], Public Key Infrastructure (PKI) scheme is considered for this work because of its numerous advantages.

## 4.2  Authorization

Authorization decides whether a certain privilege should be given to a user requesting access to the network based on submitted credentials. Entities involved in an authorization process within a single domain are User, AAA Server, and NAS. The User is an entity sending a request; AAA Server is an entity that evaluates the request and makes decision while the NAS is the entity that enforces the decision made by the AAA Server. These entities enter into relationship prior to the authorization phase which is either *contractual* (a formal contract or Service Level Agreements between user and the network) or *trust* (agreement usually initiated in the form of security association and facilitated by third party authentication server) [18], [19].

The authorization process involves the three messaging sequences of agent, pull and push [18]. The AAA Server is directly involved in entities communication in both agent and pull sequences, and not in a push sequence. Push messaging sequence as illustrated in figure 2 is discussed further because of its peculiarity to the delay/disruption tolerant environment.

Msg 1 is the request to the AAA Server for credential (ticket or certificate), Msg 2 is the response from the AAA Server including the credential and pre-information, Msg 3 is a request for a particular service or forwarding a packet and Msg 4 is a response to the request or acknowledgement of the packet which can be made optional in DTN context. NAS A functions as the User which uses a credential obtained from AAA Server to send a request while NAS B functions as the policy enforcement entity which uses a pre-information from AAA Server to authenticate a requesting party (User). Fig. 2 presents a scenario where communication between NAS A and NAS B does not involve the AAA server directly.

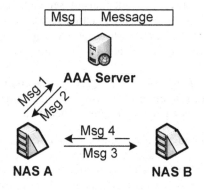

**Fig. 2.** Authorization Push Messaging Sequence

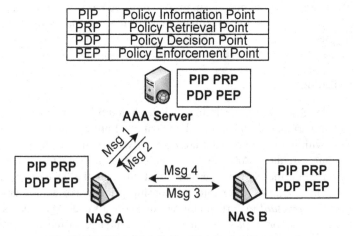

**Fig. 3.** Modified AAA Policy Distribution Framework

The push messaging sequence as employed in the generic AAA architecture cannot be directly implemented in delay/disruption tolerant networks despite reducing communication exchanges. Modifying the policy distribution framework in [18] to reflect that in fig. 3 will make the push messaging sequence suitable for environment with high delay and frequent disruption. This will make every entity custodian of the four policy elements of PIP and PRP for policy retrieval, PDP for policy evaluation and PEP for policy enforcement.

Worthy of note is the complexity and overhead that will result from this modification. The fragile nature of DTN demands a simple solution and the proposed lightweight hierarchical framework is not designed to provide complex solution. While this concept will be adopted for our proposed framework, we will avoid the use of policy elements and rather programmed the designated components to provide functionalities associated with the various policy elements.

## 5   DTN Architecture and AAA Concept Implementation

This section examines the DTN architecture [2] and its suitability to implement the AAA architecture concept. The DTN bundle node is the main component of the DTN architecture implementing the bundle layer. The bundle node comes in three different variants of host, router and gateway with persistent storage and custody transfer capability [5]. The host while acting as the source or destination sends or receives bundles but does not forward; the router forwards bundles within a single DTN region; while the gateway forwards bundles between two or more DTN regions and also provides conversions between the lower-layer protocols of the regions involved in bundle

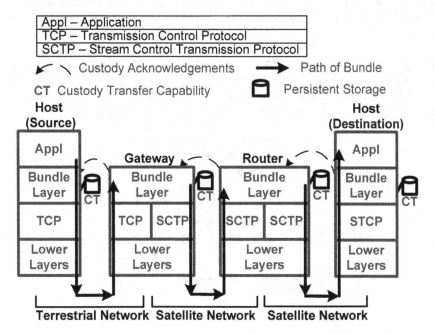

**Fig. 4.** Basic DTN Architecture

transmission. Fig. 4 shows the basic DTN architecture with the bundle node variants involved in bundle transmission between terrestrial and satellite networks.

The DTN bundle node with its components described in detail in [5] is represented in fig. 5. The three components of the DTN bundle node are:

- Bundle Protocol Agent (BPA)
- Convergence Layer Adapters (CLAs)
- Application Agent (AA) subdivided into Application Specific Element (ASE) and Administrative Element (AE).

The BPA executes the bundle protocol procedures and offer Bundle Protocol (BP) services, CLAs send and receive bundles on behalf of the BPA utilizing services of the lower layers, while the AA through ASE and AE effects purpose-specific communication through BP services utilization [5].    Comparison of the DTN bundle node structure of fig. 5 with the generic AAA architecture of fig. 1 reveals some similarity between them. The BPA, ASE and AE of the bundle node either have similar functions to the AAA Server, Application Specific Module (ASM) and Policy & Event Repository (P&E R)  of the AAA architecture respectively or have the capacity to provide similar functions.

Using BP SInt between BPA and ASE, and Prv CInt between BPA and AE makes communication between the BPA and the AA components independent. This is similar to the generic AAA architecture where communication between AAA Server and ASM is independent of that between AAA Server and P&E R. The existence of a common interface (BP Sint) between BPA and ASE as well as AE depicts the possibility of unifying the functions of ASE and AE which might be an advantage. With reference to section 4.2, BPA is designed to execute functions associated with PRP, PDP and PEP while ASE and AE are designed to execute functions associated with PIP.

| BP | Bundle Protocol | CLA | Convergence Layer Adapters |
|---|---|---|---|
| BP SInt | BP Service Interface | ASE | Application Specific Element |
| Pr CInt | Private Control Interface | AE | Administrative Element |
| BPA | Bundle Protocol Agent | AA | Application Agent |

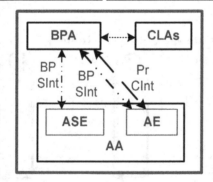

**Fig. 5.** Abstracted DTN Bundle Node Structure

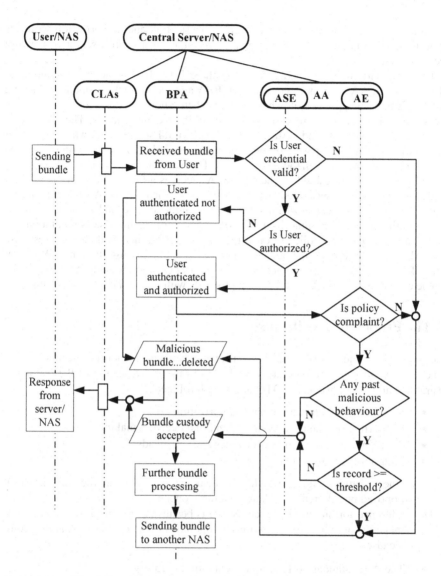

**Fig. 6.** Proposed Access Control Sequence in DTN Bundle Node

The ability of the bundle node to incorporate BPA, ASE and AE in its internal structure compared to the AAA architecture where AAA Server, ASM and P&E R are external makes it suitable for offline processing and internal decision making. The bundle node with its persistent storage can conveniently store the credential and pre-information used in access control decision making in the generic AAA architecture. Its ability to serve as policy enforcement point where it has and enforce its own policy is emphasized in [7]. The bundle node can be implemented as a server or a gateway (access server) [5], [8] and implements the Bundle Protocol (BP) [5] which is designed to fulfil the minimum requirement of the AAA protocol defined in [18].

Fig. 6 is a flowchart showing the proposed authentication and authorization sequence when the bundle node of fig. 5 is implemented either as a central server or network access server.

The flowchart in fig. 6 incorporates the three DTN bundle node components of CLA, BPA and AA with more emphasis on BPA and the AA sub-components of ASE and AE. Emphasis is placed on what happens when a node receives a bundle because access control is better enforced with the node in the receiving mode. The ASE stores the credentials like keys and certificate from the central server (CA) while AE stores the policy and history of past activities like malicious behaviour of a particular entity. The number of times the malicious activity of a particular entity must not equal or exceed is called the threshold. When the BPA receives a bundle through the CLA, it sends the requesting User's credential to ASE for verification. BPA evaluates the response from ASE to decide whether the User is authenticated and authorized. If the User is authenticated and authorized, the BPA then confirms the User's reputation and conformity with existing policy through the AE. The BPA then evaluates the response from AE to decide whether the bundle should be accepted for custody or not. Whatever action BPA enforces is communicated to the requested user through the CLA. If the bundle custody is accepted, the BPA then proceeds with further bundle processing.

## 6   The Proposed Architecture

The inability of the existing access control mechanisms to address access control issues in delay/disruption tolerant networks led to the identification of the following desirable features of a workable DTN access control mechanism:

- Separating authentication from authorization
- Supporting offline processing and internal decision making
- Reducing communication exchanges and overheads
- Simplicity and scalability

Based on these features, lightweight hierarchical access control architecture shown in fig. 7 is proposed based on the AAA architecture concept.

The preference for hierarchical architecture is because of the need for a central entity to manage the activities of the various autonomous PNs and the AAA architecture concept because:

- The AAA standard offers implementation flexibility
- The components of the generic AAA architecture provide similar functionalities to that of the DTN bundle node
- The three-party authentication model establishes trust and facilitates communication in heterogeneous environment
- Authorization push messaging sequence reduces communication exchanges and puts less load on the server
- The policy distribution framework can be modified to suit the DTN context

The architecture of fig. 7 assumes a single domain with three private networks and is designed to operate in a conflict scenario like United Nation Peace Keeping Mission. These private networks represent Peace Keeping Forces of three different nations

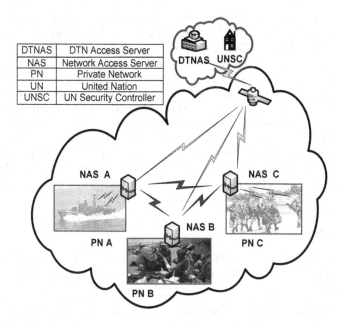

**Fig. 7.** Proposed Hierarchical Lightweight Access Control Framework

deployed to different locations within a conflict region. The private networks are sensor-based with few DTN-aware nodes. The DTN network comprises the DTNAS, NAS of the private networks and the few DTN-aware nodes within the PNs with satellite facilitating communication in the network. The security gateways (NASs) of the various PNs functions as both bundle and security sources and destinations with security zone [7] existing between them. Each NAS can add and process security blocks. The reference security blocks according to [7] are Bundle Authentication Block (BAB), Payload Integrity Block (PIP), Payload Confidentiality Block (PCB) and Extension Security Block (ESB).

## 6.1 Architecture Components and Functions

The major components of the architecture of fig. 7 are the UNSC, DTNAS and NAS. These components are described below:

- UNSC: This is the entity that registers all the private networks (countries) designated for Peace Keeping Mission and the organization commissioned to provide the DTN services. The security information obtained during this period is stored and made available to the relevant entities at different times prior to network registration/service initialization phase.

- DTNAS: This is the central server that coordinates the activities of the DTN network and registers the various Network Access Servers (NAS) into the DTN Network. During network registration and service initialization phase, the DTNAS generates and distributes Common Communication Parameter (CCP) and Certificates to all authenticated members accompanied with its public key. The CCP is used by network members for proof of authentication while the Certificate is used to verify the validity of users' request. The DTNAS can function as Key Server/Key Distribution Centre (KDC) or Certificate Authority (CA).

- NAS: These are security gateways that handle regional access control management. These servers authenticate and register entities into the respective private networks and have the capacity to generate CCP and Certificates needed within the Private Networks (PN) for communication and verification of the validity of users' request. These security gateways in addition to their regional responsibilities also store CCP and certificate from the DTNAS needed for communication and request validity verification within the DTN network. NAS together with DTNAS implements the bundle layer that houses the Bundle Protocol (BP) needed for transportation of access control information.

### 6.2 Architecture Description

The architecture is designed to implement the bundle node of fig. 5 as DTNAS, NAS or End User in the respective private networks. It is based on traditional cryptography and designed to:

- Use a Common Communication Parameter (CCP) for communication during bundle transmission
- Provide security services on a hop-by-hop and end-to-end basis
- Support policy-based access control

The complexity of the node in terms of database size and computational capability decreases from DTNAS to End User. This is demonstrated in fig. 8 together with the relationship types of the architectural components.

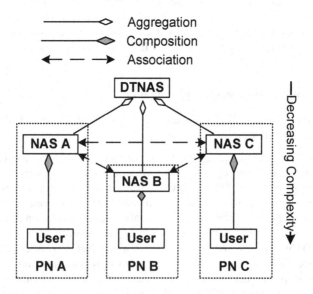

**Fig. 8.** Proposed Hierarchy and Relationship Type of Architectural Entities

The DTNAS and NAS of the various PNs are in aggregation relationship because NASs cannot operate in the DTN network without DTNAS, but can exist independently without DTNAS. NAS A, B and C are in association relationship because they hold a reference to one another through the certificate obtained from DTNAS after authentication during registration/service initialization. The End Users in the various PNs are in composition relationship with their respective NAS because the End Users cannot exist on their own since their existence in the various PNs is tied to the respective NASs. The following assumptions are considered:

- UNSC, DTNAS and NAS can generate their own key pairs
- UNSC and DTNAS cannot be compromised
- DTNAS and NAS provide UNSC with their public key and identity who in turn passes it on to designated entities together with a secret information for authentication purposes
- DTNAS has two public keys with the first one used during registration/service initialization and the second one after registration.
- Registration Request from NAS to DTNAS contains the identity of NAS and secret information obtained from UNSC while Registration Confirmation from DTNAS to NAS contains identity of DTNAS, secret information obtained from UNSC.
- All registered NAS will be in custody of certificate and CCP from DTNAS as well as the public key of DTNAS given after registration.

The Certificate and CCP are stored in the ASE of fig. 5 and the two phases considered for the description of the architecture are:

**1. Registration/Service Initialization:** During this phase, NAS sends registration request (regReq) to DTNAS which verifies the validity of request by comparing NAS identity and accompanying security information with its database content. If the credentials are genuine and other conditions met, DTNAS sends registration confirmation (regConf) to NAS accompanied by certificate and CCP. The public keys of the recipients are used by the communicating party for securing the message.

**2. Data Exchange Phase:** The security gateways (NASs) are assumed to be registered into the DTN network and in possession of the CCP, certificate from DTNAS, public key of DTNAS as well as individual key pairs. The CCP is used for BAB and other relevant keys for PIB and PCB. The use of CCP is intended to make communication within the DTN network free flowing. Any receiving node uses the CCP to access the BAB to authenticate itself and can only access the PIB and PCB if in position of the relevant keys. Since the BAB is the first security block to be accessed by the receiving node, we are of the opinion that the certificate from DTNAS should be housed in the BAB. Every receiving NAS confirms the DTNAS's identity and verify the signature in the accompanying certificate in the bundle with the public key in its custody. It also confirms the conformity of the action with the assigned role as well as the reputation of the sender. The receiving NAS accepts bundle custody if the sender is authenticated and authorized before proceeding with further bundle processing.

The sequence of action followed by DTNAS or NAS in verifying the validity of a request from another communicating party in either phase 1 or phase 2 is shown in fig. 6. The architecture is designed to be dynamic and permits execution of phase 1 after the start of phase 2. This takes place either when an existing PN leaves the DTN network or new PN joins the DTN network.

### 6.3 Future Implementation

Future work will involve modeling the proposed lightweight hierarchical architecture in C++ and the validation of the result. In the course of the implementation, the following issues amongst others will be addressed:

- How can Mandatory Access Control (MAC) be implemented in DTN to address the identified limitations?
- Will combined implementation of Role-Based Access Control (RBAC) and MAC be feasible?
- What will be the nature of the CCP and content of the certificate?
- What will qualify an existing NAS for expulsion from the DTN network and what mechanism will be appropriate?

## 7   Conclusions

This paper proposed an access control framework for DTN environment and established the applicability of AAA architecture concept. We discussed security issues in DTN relating to resource consumption, as well as existing traditional access control solutions and their limitations. We identified desirable characteristics of an operational access control mechanism in the DTN environment and explored the DTN architecture to identify those features that will support the implementation of the AAA architecture concept.

In this paper, we have presented a lightweight hierarchical architecture for an intra-domain scenario and demonstrated how the three-party authentication model as well as the authorization push messaging sequence of the AAA architecture can be modified to suit the DTN environment. We compared the DTN bundle node structure with the generic AAA architecture to highlight the similarities between them and justify the suitability of the bundle node for AAA architecture concept implementation. We have proposed an access control sequence for the bundle node as well as how the architecture entities will relate in a hierarchical arrangement. Our framework will among other benefits prevent masquerading and modification attacks, reduce communication exchanges and overheads, support offline processing and empower the entities to make access control decisions internally.

This paper focuses mainly on design and gives an overview of the solution. The implementation and validation of the design in a delay/disruptive environment will be carried out in future work.

## References

1. Farrell, S., Cahill, V.: Delay- and Disruption-Tolerant Networking. Artech House (2006) ISBN 1596930632
2. Cerf, V., Hooke, A., Torgerson, L., Durst, R., Scott, K., Fall, K., Weiss, H.: Delay-Tolerant Networking Architecture. IETF RFC 4838 (April 2007)

3. Fall, K.: A Delay-Tolerant Network Architecture for Challenged Internets. SIGCOMM, August 25-29 (2003)

4. Farrell, S., Cahill, V., Geraghty, D., Humphreys, I., McDonald, P.: When TCP Breaks: Delay- and Disruption Tolerant Networking. IEEE Internet Computing 10(4), 72–78 (2006)

5. Scott, K., Burleigh, S.: Bundle Protocol Specification. IETF RFC 5050 (November 2007)

6. Wood, L., Eddy, W., Holliday, P.: A Bundle of Problems. In: IEEE Aerospace Conference, Big Sky, Montana (2009)

7. Symington, S., Farrell, S., Weiss, H., Lovell, P.: Bundle Security Protocol Specification. Work in progress as an internet-draft, draft-irtf-dtnrg-bundle-security-07. September 9 (2009)

8. Fall, K., Farrell, S.: DTN: An Architectural Retrospective. IEEE Journal on Selected Areas in Communication (JSAC) 26(5), 828–836 (2008)

9. Farrell, S., Symington, S., Torgerson, L., Weiss, H., Lovell, P.: Delay-Tolerant Networking Security Overview. Work in progress as an internet-draft, draft-irtf-dtnrg-sec-overview-05, May 5 (2009)

10. Cruickshank, H., Pillai, P., Noisternig, M., Iyengar, S.: Security Requirement for Unidirectional Lightweight Encapsulation (ULE) Protocol. NWG RFC 5458 (March 2009)

11. Bhutta, M., Johnson, E., Ansa, G., Ahmed, N., Alsiyabi, M., Cruickshank, H.: Security Analysis for Delay/Disruption Tolerant Satellite and Sensor Networks. In: IWSSC 2009, Siena, Italy (September 2009)

12. Hu, V.C., Ferraiolo, D.F., Kuhn, D.R.: Assessment of Access Control Systems. National Institute of Standards and Technology, Interagency Report 7316 (September 2006)

13. House, T.C.: Client/Server Access: Satellite-ATM Connectivity Using Knowledge Management Approach. In: 4th International Conference on Information Technology: New Generations, Nevada, pp. 863–867 (2007)

14. Jiang, C., Li, B., Xu, H.: An Efficient Scheme for User Authentication in Wireless Sensor Networks. In: Advanced Information Networking and Applications Workshops, vol. 1, pp. 438–442 (May 2007)

15. Kim, K., Yang, J.: The Practical System Architecture for the Wireless Sensor Networks. In: International Conference on Multimedia and Ubiquitous Engineering, pp. 547–551 (April 2008)

16. Khakpour, A.R., Laurent-Maknavicius, M., Chaouchi, H.: WATCHMAN: An Overlay Distributed AAA Architecture for Mobile Ad Hoc Networks. In: The International Conference on Availability, Reliability and Security, pp. 144–152 (March 2008)

17. de Laat, C., Gross, G., Gommans, L., Vollbrecht, J., Spence, D.: Generic AAA Architecture. NWG RFC 2903 (August 2000)

18. Vollbrecht, J., Calhoun, P., Farrell, S., Gommans, G., Gross, G., de Bruijn, B., de Laat, C., Holdrege, M., Spence, D.: AAA Authorization Framework. NWG RFC 2904 (August 2000)

19. Nakhjiri, M., Nakhjiri, M.: AAA and Network Security for Mobile Access: Radius, Diameter, EAP, PKI and IP Mobility. John Wiley, Chichester (2005)

20. Blaze, M., Feigenbaum, J., Lacy, J.: Decentralized Trust Management. In: IEEE Symposium on Security and Privacy, May 6-8, pp. 164–173 (1996)

21. Bonatti, P., Duma, C., Olmedilla, D., Shahmehri, N.: An Integration of Reputation-based and Policy-based Trust Management,
http://rewerse.net/publications/download/
REWERSE-RP-2005-116.pdf

22. Blaze, M., Feigenbaum, J., Ioannidis, J., Keromytis, A.: The KeyNote Trust – Management System Version 2. NWG RFC 2704 (September 1999)

23. Chu, Y., Feigenbaum, J., LaMacchia, B., Resnick, P., Strauss, M.: REFEREE: Trust Management for Web Applications. Computer Networks and ISDN Systems 29(8-13), 953–964 (1997)
24. Ellison, C., Frantz, B., Lampson, B., Rivest, R., Thomas, B., Ylonen, T.: SPKI Certificate Theory. NWG RFC 2693 (September 1999)
25. Kagal, L., Finin, T., Joshi, A.: Trust-based Security in Pervasive Computing Environments. IEEE Computer Magazine 34(12), 154–157 (2001)
26. Blaze, M., Feigenbaum, J., Lacy, J.: The Role of Trust Management in Distributed Systems Security. In: Vitek, J. (ed.) Secure Internet Programming. LNCS, vol. 1603, pp. 185–210. Springer, Heidelberg (1999)

# ID Based Cryptography and Anonymity in Delay/Disruption Tolerant Networks

Naveed Ahmad, Haitham Cruickshank, and Zhili Sun

Center for Communication Systems Research, University of Surrey
Guildford, Surrey, UK
{n.ahmad,h.cruickshank,z.sun}@surrey.ac.uk

**Abstract.** Due to the rapid development in technology, every network, application needs full time connectivity without disruption and delays. The Delay/Disruption Tolerant Networking (DTN) concept is suitable for applications such as rural and disaster areas networks, animal and environmental monitoring plus others. However, due to the shared and unsecured nature of such challenged networks a good cryptographic framework needed in DTN. Identity Based Cryptography (IBC) compares favorably with traditional public key cryptography while generating public key on a fly as required. In this paper, we will provide anonymity solution in DTN using IBC. This has the advantage over public key cryptography with respect to end-to-end confidentiality. Also we use pseudonyms to provide anonymity and hide the identity of the end user.

**Keywords:** Delay Tolerant Network Security, Identity Based Cryptography, Anonymity, Pseudonyms, Public Key Cryptography.

## 1 Introduction

The Internet TCP/IP protocol stack networks works normally when end-to-end connectivity is available and the round trip time is relatively small. To explain the problem with TCP in certain applications we take the scenario of interplanetary communications. If a node on earth wants to send data to space (or another planet) then it must go through the process of three way handshake. In addition to that if there is no communication for few minutes between two nodes then the TCP will assume time out. If we consider the data transfer between the earth and nearest planet then it will take approximately 24 minutes to reach data and TCP will definitely fail.

A Delay/Disruption Tolerant Network (DTN) is an overlay on top of regional networks including the Internet. The DTN architecture consists of a network of independent networks each characterised by Internet-like connectivity within, but having occasional communication opportunities among them. Connectivity can be scheduled and sometimes random. These independent networks form the DTN regions and are connected through a system of DTN gateways. Each DTN region relies on its own protocol stack that best suits its communication means, infrastructure and technologies. At the DTN nodes, a new layer, called the bundle layer, is added on top of the traditional transport layers to provide end-to-end data transfers among the DTN regions. The DTN overlay architecture operates above the existing protocol stacks

K. Sithamparanathan et al. (Eds.): PSATS 2010, LNICST 43, pp. 265–275, 2010.
© Institute for Computer Sciences, Social-Informatics and Telecommunications Engineering 2010

found in other network architectures [1], [2]. DTN [3] supports heterogeneous environment and is based on idea of store and forward method. Its architecture with the help of the bundle layer supports heterogeneity of networks. In DTN, data is sent in the form of bundle through store and forward relay. Bundle protocol [4] is working as communication medium which defines rules for bundle. Figure-1 shows the layer stack of DTN where Internet is used to facilitate communication between two DTN regions. However DTN can be used for other network apart from Internet. DTN gateways are intelligent to handle different transport, network and data link layers.

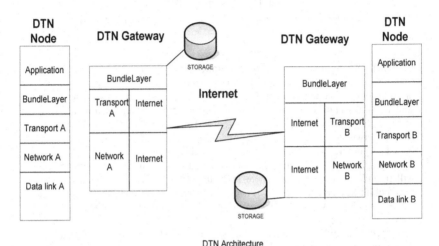

**Fig. 1.** DTN Layer Stack

In addition to space applications, DTN can be implemented in many applications [3] e.g. such as water pollution monitoring, disaster monitoring and telemedicine in rural areas. Apart from these, DTN can also support traditional applications such as Web cache, Emails and file transfer. Some applications need classification of their data as top secrete, secrete, confidential and unclassified in order to enforce security and hiding of data from intruders. However our scenario will focus on telemedicine application in rural areas. This is applicable to other rural area scenarios as well. Figure 2 depicts our scenario and will be used as a framework for our solution:

- A local doctor wants to send a patient (e.g. a village elder) medical data to a senior doctor in a main hospital in Europe for evaluation of the patient's condition. There is no communications connectivity in this rural village. So public buses can be used as part of the communications transport chain.
- The medical data is stored on the bus and then transferred to the rural area gateway (DTN gateway-1). The data will be stored until the availability of a transmission link (e.g. satellite or wireless) to the Internet.
- The bundle is passed through Internet routers to the Internet Service Provider (ISP) gateway and delivered to the hospital network gateway (DTN Gateway-2). The medical data is then transferred to the hospital local server, where the senior doctor can examine it.

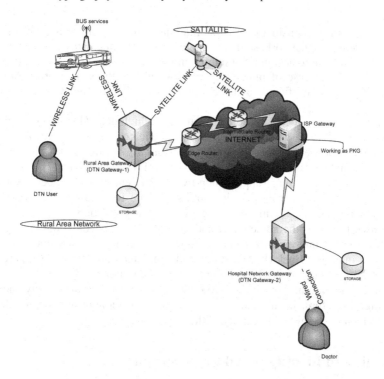

**Fig. 2.** Telemedicine scenario in rural area network

- We assumed that segmentation of the user (patient) data is performed according to the access technology (satellites, wireless and wired LAN) requirements in the DTN gateways.

This scenario shows a strong need for medical data security and patient identity privacy (anonymity). However achieving security and anonymity in such challenging network is a difficult task. Passive threats are major concern due to the broadcast nature of satellite, where an intruder can easily monitor the user sensitive data. Also there is possibility that intruder might gain access to the local buses stored information.

## 2  Security Requirements for DTN

Traditionally, security can be achieved through cryptographic functions by providing confidentiality, integrity and authentication. But due to disconnected nature of DTN, traditional cryptography is not an optimal solution. Researchers had tried to implement Identity Based Cryptography (IBC) as an alternative to traditional security techniques. Currently, the DTN related security work is focused within the DTN Research Group (DTNRG) and Internet Research Task Force (IRTF) [5], [6]. While designing security architecture, it is important to minimize the message exchanges between DTN nodes.

Another important consideration is the minimum contact with Trusted Authorities: DTN is opportunistic network, so there is no permanent connectivity among the nodes so one should take in to account that minimum interaction should be done with trusted authority, which, in case of public key cryptography is the Certification Authority (CA) which issues certificates and its equivalent the Public Key Generator (PKG) in IBC.

Current security protocols do not perform well in high delay/disruption conditions, because of underlying assumption such as end-to-end connectivity is always present; low link delays between communicating parties and low error rate on link channels. Thus, new security architecture is needed to meet DTN requirements [7], [8], [9]. The current security architecture supports hop-by-hop and end-to-end authentication and integrity validation, to ensure data is corrected before forwarding. The hop-by hop authentication/integrity is achieved using Bundle Authentication Block (BAB). The BAB is used to assure the authenticity and integrity of the bundle along a single hop from forwarder to intermediate receiver. Similarly for end-to-end security services, the Payload Integrity Block (PIB) and Payload Confidentiality Block (PCB) are used. Further details on security architecture in DTN can be found in [8].

However, the current work in DTNRG does not address user anonymity and identity hiding. Therefore, in this paper we focus on user anonymity and provide IDC based mechanisms to hide the identity of the sender and receiver.

## 3    Public and Identity Based Cryptography

Cryptography can be divided into symmetric key cryptography (same key used for encryption and decryption) and asymmetric key cryptography (different keys are used for encryption and decryption) [11]. Public key cryptography is mostly attributed to Diffie, Hellman, Rivest, Shamir and Adleman [11]. To use traditional cryptography Public Key Infrastructure (PKI) provides a framework which provides foundation for other security services. It is used in many applications such as; e-voting, e-banking and e-commerce. PKI supports security building blocks such as confidentiality, authentication, integrity and non-repudiation. The primary goal of PKI is to allow the distribution of public keys and certificates and also binding them in a secure manner [11]. In case of challenged networks (such as DTN), PKI works well in authentication and integrity aspects, but to achieve confidentiality sender requires the receiver public key to encrypt data and also checking of Certificate Revocation List (CRL) for compromised keys [12]. As such, these functions require connection availability to the CA, which is not always possible as shown in our scenario (Figure 2).

To overcome the shortcomings of public key cryptography Shamir proposed the topic of Identity Based Cryptography (IBC) in 1984 [13]. In this new cryptographic approach, user identifier information such as email address, phone number, IP address are used instead of certificates as a public key for encryption and verification of digital signature [14], [15]. In PKI, the authority which manages certificates was CA and in IBC, the Public Key Generator (PKG) is the central authority which generates private key for participants. IBC can work with exiting public key cryptographic systems e.g. RSA, DSS. The PKG is shown in Figure 2 and it is assumed to be co-located with the ISP gateway.

IBC work in the following steps:

- **System setup:** - PKG generates its own private key $S_{pkg}$ from security parameters pp (where PP is system wide parameters.).
- **Encryption:** - sender encrypts the message with the receiver public key $P_{re\text{-}ceiver}$, generated from ID of receiver.
- **Key extraction:** - PKG generates private key $S_{receiver}$ for receiver from his ID, security parameter pp and its own $S_{pkg}$ as input.
- **Decryption:** - receiver applies its private key and can decrypt message.

Shamir only implemented digital signature in his early work and later on Boneh and Franklin [16] implemented encryption as well.

The disconnected nature of DTN can cause a problem in the PKI framework, where the sender needs the receiver certificate and public key when it wants to send data. IBC can solve some of the DTN security issues. IBC has no significant advantage in authentication and integrity but it works well in confidentiality [17]. To achieve integrity and authentication in IBC Seth et al [17] suggested the avoiding of Certificate Revocation List (CRL) and proposed periodic refreshing of underlying identifier information e.g. *alice@hotmail.com 12-10-2009* is refer to Alice key whose validity is till $12^{th}$ October and the receiver can verify to look into the date. However this was challenged by S.Farrell [18] and argued that verifying Certificate from CA is similar to checking public parameter in IBC in DTN. But actually that parameter is long lived and no need to checked frequently.

## 4 Pseudonyms and Anonymity

One way of providing anonymity (identity hiding) is by using Pseudonyms. Pseudonym means falsely named (name other then the real name) and can used as an identifier of entity/node. It is created by the entity/node itself. There are four kind of pseudonym unlinkability [19]:

- **Public pseudonyms:** Linking between the subject and pseudonym are known publicly from beginning. e.g. name with phone number kept in public directory.
- **Initially non public pseudonyms:** This type limits its identity to certain parties. e.g. name with account number known by bank only.
- **Initially unlinked pseudonyms:** This provides high level of privacy and the pseudonym is known to the entity itself only.
- **Pseudonyms as public Key:** A digital pseudonym is a public key used to verify signature made by the anonymous subject of the corresponding private key [20]. This approach is also used in mobile ad hoc network (MANETS).

Encryption hides the data transmission from attackers. However sender and receiver identity, network address, packet length and packet timing (RTT) can provide useful information to adversaries to achieve traffic analysis attacks. So this gives rise to the idea of identity hiding and anonymity. The research on anonymity is dated back to the paper [20] by D Chaum's. The term anonymity according to [21] "Is state of being not identifiable within a set of subjects". Types of anonymity can be defined as:

**Sender anonymity:** - To hide the originator of the message.

**Receiver Anonymity:** - That the adversary can't determine the intended receiver if the message.

**Unlinkability:** - To hide the association of sender and receiver.

Anonymity is required in many applications e.g. e-voting, digital cash, electronic email, news reporting, telemedicine and many more. To achieve anonymity researchers define anonymous protocols that focus on initiator/sender and receiver/recipient anonymity plus their unlinkability (who is with whom). Anonymous protocol should prevent message coding attack, timing attack, message volume attack, flooding attack, intersection attack and collusion attack [20]. To achieve anonymity there should some rule what we called Anonymous Communication Protocol (ACP). Generally most of the ACP are based on idea of Mixes Network by David Chaum's and onion routing [21],[22]. Table 1 shows different ACPs in term of some performance metrics.

**Table 1.** A survey of Anonymous Communication Protocol (ACP)

| Protocol | Sender Anonymity | Receiver Anonymity | Unlink-ability | Discipline | Latency |
|---|---|---|---|---|---|
| TOR | Yes | Yes | Yes | Internet | Low |
| Tarzan | Yes | No | No | Peer-to-Peer | Low |
| Crowds | Yes | No | Yes | Web surfing | Large |
| Cypherpunk (Remailer-1) | No | Yes | Yes | Email | Large |
| Mixmaster (Remailer-2) | Yes | No | Yes | Email | Large |
| Mixminion (Remailer-3) | Yes | Yes | Yes | Email | Low |

Above all discussed protocols either use the idea of onion routing or mix networks, and provides anonymity at some level. However, the above traditional solution for anonymity doesn't work in DTN because of the disconnect nature and routing strategy of DTN. With opportunistic and variable delays source routing is not always possible [23]. In DTN, there is no complete routing topology so Onion Routing (OR) doesn't work because OR needs to know the route in advance and encrypt the message accordingly for each router. Mix networks can be applied on DTN as they hold message for random amount of time and flushes when all packets arrived. To overcome these limitations, we provide DTN anonymity architecture with pseudonym based approach.

## 5  DTN Anonymity Protocol Design

Our proposed protocol is based on IBC and Pseudonyms, where encryption, decryption, digital signature and keys are generated using IBC. The identities of users were hided through the use of pseudonyms. Each entity uses its email address as ID (for example) and generates a public key. The PKG generates private keys for each participating entity using its own secret key and security parameters pp. Considering our scenario (Figure-2), the DTN user (local doctor/patient) from rural area network wants to send medical data to a senior doctor in a major city hospital. However, we want to keep the sender and receiver identity hidden from intruders.

### 5.1  Assumptions

**1.** Sender and receiver know each other identities but unknown to other entities.
**2.** The PKG requires only once the identity of user to generate the private key. After that it stored the identity in the database and update with the date and time.
**3.** Once the entity received the key pairs, there is no need to interact with PKG anymore. and can send data to other entity.
**4.** The keys are distributed securely through traditional mechanisms such as Secure Socket Layer (SSL) to each entity. This key distribution is out of scope for this paper.
**5.** The DTN gateways are trusted. In our proposed solution, anonymity is achieved through the use of pseudonyms which allow DTN routers/gateways to know that the Pseudonym is belonging to the valid authenticated user without unveil his identity.
**6.** There is security association between each entity and their corresponding gateway. The pseudonym generated by each entity is securely send to gateway, where it stored in the persistence storage.
**7.** There is secure channel between both gateways where they exchange both the pseudonyms handed by the end entities, so that gateway-1 send the pseudonyms of the receiver node to the sender node and gateway-2 send the pseudonym of the sender node to the receiving node. In this way now both the end entities have each other pseudonym and they can generate the symmetric key and can send data securely.

We will show the message exchanges between DTN node (local doctor) and DTN gateway-1, DTN gateway-1 and DTN gateway-2, and finally will show the operation of intended receiver which senior doctor in our case.

### 1.  DTN node (local doctor/patient) and Gateway-1
The sender (DTN node) will send its data to DTN gateway-1 (via the public bus). The DTN node generates random number and then will generate its public key (e.g. its email ID). Also generates pseudonyms by hashing the ID concatenated with random number. We are assuming that the sender knows the email ID of receiver. DTN node also generates one time symmetric key by concatenating a random number with the

pseudonym of receiver. In case of simple encryption and without contacting the PKG, the bundle sender can generate the key and send bundle to receiver, which is the main advantage of IBC over PKI. The sender sends the bundle to gateway-1 as next hope address. Figure-3 shows operation of DTN node and the exchange of messages between DTN node and Gateway-1.

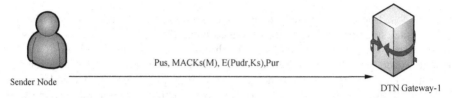

Pus, MACKs(M), E(Pudr,Ks),Pur

Sender Node

DTN Gateway-1

**Fig. 3.** Messages exchange between DTN node and gateway-1

Where the functions calculated by DTN node as:

Generation of random number r
Public key= IDdtn
Pseudonym of dtn node=Pus=H(r.IDdtn)
Symmetric key between sender node and receiver node= Ks=(r.Pus)

Here the sender node put his pseudonym as Pus, and the receiver as Pur. As he received the pseudonym of receiver from the gateway-1 via secure channel. "M" is the message (e.g. patient medical data) which we want to send securely and anonymously.

## 2. DTN gateway-1 to DTN gateway-2

Whenever DTN gateway-1 receives the bundle it will keep record of pseudonyms with their corresponding IDs. It will forward the message to DTN gateway-2. The structure of the message is shown in figure-4.

Pus, MACKs(M), E(Pudr,Ks),Pur

Gateway-1

Gateway-2

**Fig. 4.** Messages exchange between gateway-1 and gateway-2

## 3. Operation of receiving node

When bundle reach the intended receiver (hospital doctor) so it will do the same operation as of sender e.g. generating random number, public key and pseudonym. But here it will need private key to decrypt the message which was encrypted by its public key. As this network is directly connected to Internet so receiver will request for his private key to PKG the trusted authority residing at ISP server which generates private key for receiver using it security parameters pp and ID of receiver. It will securely send the generated private key through SSL. So that the receiver will first decrypt the message by its own private key and will obtain the symmetric key and will verify MAC through symmetric key. The operation which will perform by receiving node and PKG is how in figure-5 Where the functions are calculated as:

**Receiver side:-**
>               Generation of random no r
>               Public key= IDdr
>               Pseudonym of receiving node=PurH(r.IDdr)
>               Ks←Decrypt(Sdr,Ks)
>               Decrypt message with Ks for authentication.

**PKG:-**

>            pp.Spkg.IDdr= Sdr (private key)

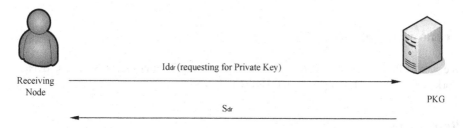

Receiving Node

Iddr (requesting for Private Key)

Sdr

PKG

**Fig. 5.** Operations of the intended receiver

The receiving node already calculated the symmetric key, pseudonym prior to the receiving of bundle, upon the receiving it just send the request for private key to the PKG, which generate key for receiving node and send via secure channel.

In this pseudonym and identity based anonymous system we clearly show the anonymity of sender and receiver. Here the adversary can correlate two pseudonyms with each other but can not identify the real identities of those pseudonyms. A user can change its pseudonym frequently. As a bundle stored at gateway-1 for the connection to be up so that adversary unable to calculate the RTT and hence can not launch traffic analysis attacks. Adversary knows only the messages exchange between gateways which will not be useful with identifying the real sender/receiver. We used traditional public cryptography for authentication and integrity and for end to end confidentiality we successful used IBC. We used date concept described earlier with private key for validity reasons. As there is only one PKG so if the key of PKG compromise then adversary can easily generates keys for participants and can encrypt or decrypt data.

## 6   Conclusions and Future Work

The DTN concept is suitable for challenged networks such as deep space mission, disaster monitoring and rural area networks. In this paper, we focused on a telemedicine application in rural areas with the objective of exchanging confidential medical data securely with a hospital in a remote city. We provide patient anonymity and identity hiding. An overview of DTN, Identity Based Cryptography and pseudonyms is presented. Also an analysis of anonymous routing protocols has shown that they are not suitable for DTN environment.

The paper presented our DTN anonymity protocol design and the message exchanges between the users and DTN gateways. The analysis showed that using pseudonym provides a convenient mechanism for user anonymity and medical data encryption. This work is at an early stage. However and in our future work, we will implement this system using Pairing Based Cryptography (PBC), where some earlier work was published by Stanford University [24]. We will implement our design in a testbed using DTN-2 reference model [25]. We also note that PKG is single point of contact in our design so our future will be extended to use hierarchical PKG and Hierarchical Identity Based Cryptography. We will also try to combine both encryption and digital signature i.e. signcryption using IBC, in order to reduce the cost of communication.

## Acknowledgement

We would like to thank the EU Information Society Technologies SATNex II Network of Excellence for supporting this research work.

## References

1. Cerf, V., et al.: Delay Tolerant Networking Architecture. IETF, Network Working Group, RFC 4838 (2007)
2. Fall, K.: A Delay Tolerant Network for Challenging Internet. In: SIGCOMM 2003 Conference on Application, Technologies, Architecture and Protocol for Computer communication, pp. 27–34 (2003)
3. Warthman, F.: A Tutorial Delay Tolerant Networks (DTNs). V 1.1, DTNRG (2003)
4. Scott, K., Burleigh, S.: Bundle Protocol Specification. IETF, Network Working Group, RFC 5050 (2007)
5. Farrell, S., Cahill, V.: Security consideration in space and delay tolerant networks. In: Second IEEE international conference, Space mission challenges for information technology, SMC-IT (2006)
6. Fall, K., Chakrabarthi, A.: Identity Based Cryptography for Delay Tolerant Networking (2003),
   http://edify.cse.lehigh.edu/EdifyTeam/edifyTeamDocs/dtn_sec.pdf
7. Symington, S.F., et al.: Bundle Security Protocol Specification. draft-irtf-dtnrg-bundle-security-08, IETF draft (2008)
8. Farrell, S., et al.: Delay-Tolerant Networking Security Overview. draft-irtf-dtnrg-sec-overview-06, IETF draft (2009)
9. Bhutta, M., Johnson, E., Ansa, G., Ahmed, N., Alsiyabi, M., Cruickshank, H.: Security Analysis for Delay/Disruption Tolerant Satellite and Sensor Networks. In: IWSSC 2009, Siena, Italy (September 2009)
10. Farrell, S., Cahill, V.: Delay and Disruption Tolerant Network (2006), ISBN. 1-59693-063-2
11. Weise, J.: Public Key Infrastructure Overview. Sun Blue Prints (2001)

12. Asokan, N., et al.: Applicability of Identity Based Cryptography in Disruption Tolerant Network. In: 1st international MobiSys workshop on mobile oppurtunistics networking, MobiOpp 2007, pp. 52–56 (2007)
13. Shamir, A.: Identity based cryptosystem and signature scheme. In: Blakely, G.R., Chaum, D. (eds.) CRYPTO 1984. LNCS, vol. 196, pp. 47–53. Springer, Heidelberg (1985)
14. Gagne, M.: Identity based encryption: A survey. RSA Labortries, Cryptobytes 6 (2003)
15. Baek, J., et al.: A survey of Identity based cryptography. In: Proc. of Australian Unix Users Group Annual Conference (2004)
16. Boneh, D., Franklin, M.K.: Identity-based encryption from the weil pairing. In: Menezes, A. (ed.) CRYPTO 2007. LNCS, vol. 4622, pp. 213–229. Springer, Heidelberg (2007)
17. Seth, A., Keshav, S.: Particle security for disconnected nodes. In: First workshop on Secure Network Protocols (NPSec), pp. 31–36 (2005)
18. Farrell, S., Symington, S., Weiss, H.: Delay Tolerant Network Security overview. Draft-irtf-dtnrg-sec-overview-08, IRTF (2008)
19. Pfitzmann, A., Hansen, M.: Anonymity, unlinkability, undetectability, unobservability, pseudonymity and identity management- A consolidated proposal for terminology (2008), http://dud.inf.tudresden.de/AnonTerminology.shtml
20. Chaum, D.: Untraceable electronic email, return address and digital pseudonym. Communication of the ACM (1981)
21. Reed, M.G., et al.: Anonymous connection and onion routing. IEEE journal on selected areas in communication, 482–494 (1998)
22. Danezis, G., Diaz, C.: A survey of anonymous communication channels. Journal of Privacy technology (2008)
23. Kate, A., et al.: Anonymity and security in delay tolerant networks. In: third international conference on security and privacy, SecureComm 2007 (2007)
24. Lynn, B.: Paring Based Cryptography (PBC) library, http://crypto.stanford.edu/pbc/
25. DTN Research group, http://www.dtnrg.org/wiki/Code

# Virtualization Technologies for DTN Testbeds

Carlo Caini[1], Rosario Firrincieli[1], Daniele Lacamera[2], and Marco Livini[1]

[1] DEIS/ARCES, University of Bologna, Bologna, Italy
[2] Sadel S.p.A., Bologna, Italy
{carlo.caini,rosario.firrincieli}@unibo.it, root@danielinux.net,
marco.livini@studio.unibo.it

**Abstract.** At present, Internet is based on the availability of a continuous path from the source to the sink node and on limited delays. These assumptions do not hold in "challenged networks", which comprise a wide variety of different environments, from sensor networks to space communications (including satellite systems). These networks are the preferred target of Delay/Disruption Tolerant Networking (DTN), an innovative networking architecture able to cope with long delays, channel disruptions and limited or intermittent connectivity. Given the increasing interest in DTN, there is urgent need for suitable tools for DTN performance evaluation. In general, there are two approaches to performance evaluation in networking: simulation and real testbeds. In this paper, after an in-depth discussion of advantages and disadvantages of both, a third way based on a virtualization is proposed and tested for DTN environments, for which it seems particularly suitable. To validate this assumption, a virtual counterpart of a real testbed is set-up using Virtual Testbed Toolkit (VTT) components. A series of tests is then performed by considering DTN transmission on a heterogeneous network including a GEO satellite link. The close match between real and virtual testbed results confirms the validity of the virtual approach for accurate performance evaluations in DTN environments.

## 1 Introduction

A key assumption of present Internet is the availability of a continuous path from the source to the sink node. This, however, is not always true in the "challenged networks", which comprise a wide variety of different environments, like sensor networks and space communications. These networks are the preferred target of Delay/Disruption Tolerant Networking (DTN) [1], [2], which provides more robust network architecture in cases of long delays, channel disruptions and limited or intermittent connectivity.

Among the many possible challenged environments, heterogeneous networks that include satellite links should be also considered. This is because of the long propagation delay (Round Trip Time – RTT – is about 600 ms in a GEO system), the possible presence of relatively high PER (Packet Error Rate) values of due to adverse propagation conditions on the satellite link and, when considering mobile satellite terminals, the presence of disruptions caused by tunnels and buildings.

K. Sithamparanathan et al. (Eds.): PSATS 2010, LNICST 43, pp. 276–287, 2010.
© Institute for Computer Sciences, Social-Informatics and Telecommunications Engineering 2010

In dealing with performance evaluation of new protocols or architectures, two approaches are possible. The first is based on simulation, the second on the use of real testbeds. Each has advantages and disadvantages, as it will be shown below. In brief, network simulators, such as ns-2 [3] and many others, by relying on a single workstation, are easy to set up and maintain, but depend on the accuracy of protocol implementations and/or modeling. Moreover, they generally require code duplication, as specific version of new protocols must be developed and maintained for the simulator environment. This can lead to measurement inconsistency, caused by bugs or other code discrepancies. Testbeds avoid this problem by making use of real protocol and architecture implementations, thus providing a test environment much closer to reality. On the negative side, testbeds imply much greater costs and higher maintenance. For PC-based testbeds, costs increase roughly linearly with the number of nodes, while in simulation the cost is independent of network layout complexity.

In this paper a third way, based on virtualization, is proposed and tested for DTN environments, to which it seems particularly suited. Virtualization expands the concept of emulation, so an entire testbed can be emulated with even one off-the-shelf fast PC. The main goal is to combine the accuracy and code commonality of real testbeds with the benefits of network simulators: lower costs, higher flexibility and reduced maintenance. With DTN architectures, an additional advantage is that the most important DTN bundle layer implementations (DTN2 and ION) are developed for Linux and there is still little support of DTN in network simulators. The paper will show that virtualization technologies are a good match for DTN environments.

## 2  Simulation vs. Real Testbeds

### 2.1  Simulation

Network simulators provide opportunities for fast and efficient experimentation. Two main categories exist: simulators that target to a very specific protocol or network type, and simulators that address a wide range of protocols. Several simulation packages, like Cnet [4], Opnet [5], Qualnet [6] and Insane [7], come into the latter category. However, at present the most commonly adopted wide scope tool is ns-2, a discrete event simulator developed and maintained for networking research by LBNL, University of California, Berkeley campus [3]. Thanks to its wide diffusion and public domain design, the network research community can easily share results and additional modules.

### 2.2  Linux Testbeds

GNU/Linux is the preferred operating system when setting up a testbed for the experimental evaluation of new protocols and architectures, for a number of reasons. Linux is free, so it can be installed with no expense other than the hardware. It is fully customizable in all its components; thanks to its GNU General Public License [9] the user is allowed to freely access and modify the source code of the Linux kernel and of all system tools. Moreover, there are a number of additional networking applications freely available on the Internet.

An essential feature of Linux is that the standard code implementing network functions is research oriented, besides also being perfectly suitable for the ordinary user. For example, Linux already offers several TCP variants in addition to the standard NewReno algorithm, such as TCP Hybla [10] without packet spacing [11] and Hoe's initial slow start threshold estimate [12]), HighSpeed TCP, TCP Westwood+, TCP CUBIC (the Linux default) and many others. Other important features, such as the SACK option and the Forward RTO (F-RTO) [13], are also available. All these TCP enhancements can be activated by means of their own individual control switches.

The GNU libraries offer a useful interface to read TCP variables during a connection through the *socket()* system call, which is the *TCP_INFO* socket option. If this option is set when creating a socket, the user application can access TCP-related values during a connection, by directly communicating with the Linux TCP layer. Another commonly used evaluation tool is the "libpcap" library and all the applications built on it, like tcpdump [14]. These latter tools make network interfaces work in "promiscuous" mode, capturing every single packet that passes through and collecting statistics on TCP flows. Despite their advantages, in particular the fact that these tools are already available, in our experience, more powerful instruments are needed for a in-depth analysis of TCP.. To this end, we added some debugging routines to the standard kernel code, using the MultiTCP [15] patch.

## 2.3   Advantages and Disadvantages of the First Two Alternatives

In this section, we compare simulation and testbeds with regard to a number of typical experimentation issues.

*Test management*
There is no doubt that it is usually much easier and faster to perform complex test campaigns by simulation than a testbed, because the latter requires a much more complex hardware and software. However, we have shown that by adopting centralized control tools, as in TATPA (Testbed on Advanced Transport Protocols and Architecture) [16], this disadvantage can be removed. It should of course be stressed that realizing such a complex management interface is in itself quite a demanding and expensive task, while for simulation it comes for free.

Another management aspect to be considered is the possibility of granting concurrent access to resources. In simulation it is usually possible to carry out several runs in parallel, and a number of users can use the simulator at the same time, although, given its relatively limited cost, it is more likely that they use of different PCs. By contrast, in the case of testbeds, where only one run can be launched at a time, the use of hardware resources must be strictly regulated, to avoid any potential conflict. But even in this case, this problem can be resolved by an appropriate interface, to manage an efficient access scheduling.

*Reproducibility*
Reproducibility is one of the main principles of the scientific method. Experimental results produced by a group of researchers are reproducible if they can be confirmed by other independent researchers in the same operational conditions. Simulators generally guarantee reproducibility if run over the same architecture and all the random sources are correctly seeded. Regarding testbeds, only partial reproducibility can be

achieved, because of the lack of synchronicity between testbed components, and unavoidable hardware and software discrepancies between different testbeds. However, the assessment of average performance parameters, such as goodput, is not impaired, provided that tests are carried out in "clean" environments, i.e. without external "interference", which is a prerequisite to assure adequate reproducibility of results. Analyses performed on "real Internet", so frequent in the literature, should eventually complement, and not substitute for, analyses in clean environments.

*Hardware Requirements*
Hardware (and related costs) is definitely a point in favor of simulation. While a simulation requires a single workstation, an emulation testbed generally requires several workstations and/or additional dedicated hardware like hubs, switches and routers. The TATPA testbed, for example, consists of up to ten PCs with one or more network cards (depending whether they act as end-points or routers) and connected by cross-cables and switches.

*Maintenance*
Maintenance includes fixing bugs, adding new features and updating software and hardware components. Ns-2 updates are frequent, and it is necessary to check how new versions impact on non standard modules, and to introduce when necessary the required modifications. Testbeds have the same problem whenever a new version of Linux kernel is released. Finally, as a testbed always consists of several units and maintenance increases with the number of components, although some savings of scale can be possible.

*Extensibility and Inter-Working*
Extensibility quantifies the ability to easily extend a system, with new features or other modifications; Inter-working is the capacity of different systems to work together, sharing information and data. Both arguments for the testbed approach, thanks to the limited number of standard network interface. As an example, to add new modules (even based on proprietary software or hardware platforms) in an Ethernet based testbed, it is enough that they adopt the same NIC (Network Interface Card) standard. With simulation, new modules can inter-work only if expressly developed for a given simulator software. This weak point of simulation can be mitigated by wide diffusion of a given the simulator (as for ns-2), which facilitates sharing of new modules.

*Layer Implementation*
Layer implementation indicates the capacity of representing the entire ISO/OSI stack as closely as possible. This important point mainly depends on the simulation and emulation tool adopted. In general there must be a trade-off between complexity and close representation. For example, a satellite connection can be simply modeled by setting a large delay and possibly a significant packet error rate (PER) [17]. More complex models can include a choice among different probability density functions for random losses (e.g. two state models for link availability), or the implementation of link functions (e.g. MAC procedures) and so on [18]. With complex models, the emulator has the additional constraint that all procedures must be performed in real time.

*Accuracy and code commonality with existing systems*

Last but not least, it should be noted that testbeds use the same protocol and architecture as real systems. There is therefore a higher level of accuracy than simulation can offer. Moreover, using the same code of existing systems speeds up the development of new versions and avoids parallel maintenance of two versions of the same code (one for simulation, one for real operating systems), which is both quite demanding and inevitably prone to error (additional bugs in code conversion). An interesting attempt to reduce this problem, limited however to TCP congestion control, is the "Linux TCP implementation for ns-2" developed by Caltech [19], which reuses Linux code for TCP congestion control algorithms on ns-2.

Finally, let us point out here that possible dual use (research and deployment) of code developed for real operating systems was certainly contemplated by the developers of the DTN2 bundle layer reference implementation for Linux. It is worth citing the DTN2 description given on the DTNRG website: "The goal of this implementation is to clearly embody the components of the DTN architecture, while also providing a robust and flexible software framework for experimentation, extension, and real-world deployment".

## 3  The Virtual Approach

Emulation is usually employed in testbeds to reproduce radio channel characteristics in real time (e.g. satellite, WLAN, cellular networks). Virtualization expands this concept to all the testbed components, so an entire testbed can be emulated with one modern PC. The main goal is to combine the advantages of real testbeds, such as extensibility, inter-working, accuracy and protocol commonality with real systems, with the benefits of network simulators, such as lower costs, higher flexibility, reduced maintenance and result reproducibility. The virtual testbed toolkit presented in this paper, based on free software, goes further and tries to preserve the real-time constraint, an essential requirement for performance evaluation of time-sensitive protocol on wireless networks.

Although the advantages of the virtualization approach are many and significant, there are also limits to its applicability. They are mainly related to the complexity of the testbed layout (number of virtual machines necessary to implement nodes) and the transmission rates supported (the higher, the more computationally demanding). These limits are closely related to the computational resources of the host machine and the efficiency of the virtualization hardware and software supports. Incidentally, to cope with demanding environments the use of multiple host machines can be considered as well, thus leading to the concept of a *distributed* virtual testbed, by contrast to an *integrated* virtual testbed, where there is just one host machine.

As regards the DTN application field, it is worth noting that in DTN environments the bandwidths are usually limited (e.g. no high-speed networks are considered), which makes it feasible to implement even relatively complex layouts, by preserving the real-time constraint. Moreover, in some cases, like security or routing experiments, real-time constraint is not essential, thus further expanding the number of nodes supported. It seems therefore that DTN environments and virtualization technologies are a perfect match. Experimental results presented below, obtained using integrated virtual testbed, confirm the validity of this assumption.

## 3.1   The Virtual Testbed Toolkit (VTT)

The idea of exploiting network virtualization to concentrate many testbed components on one PC has already appeared in the literature. To provide some examples, we cite [20], where the implementation of a virtual router based on Xen technology is presented, and [21], which describes a hybrid testbed, composed of real mesh nodes and a virtualized environment. Virtualization is further exploited in [22] and [23], where VMs are used to build testbeds dedicated to the evaluation of security issues. In [24] the aim is to create an "inbox" protocol development environment.

However, the Virtual Testbed Toolkit (VTT) used in this paper is innovative with respect to other proposals, in that it aims to preserve time accuracy, in order to offer reliable results even when dealing with time-sensitive performance tests (e.g. goodput evaluations). This is a challenge due to the limited processing resources of the real host machine. For this reason, the virtualization approach, when applied to a DTN environment, is validated by comparing virtual testbed results with those achieved by the real TATPA testbed, based on a cluster of Linux PCs.

This validation is performed by considering time-sensitive DTN performance (e.g. goodput) on a heterogeneous network scenario including satellite links. Other tests, with non time-sensitive performance, could also be carried out, but would be much less demanding.

VTT implements network nodes as independent Kernel-based Virtual Machines (KVMs), while other network devices and connections are emulated through the Virtual Distributed Ethernet (VDE) project tools [25]. A powerful graphic interface, the "Virtual NetManager", allows the user to design the desired network layout and to configure and control the network components, as shown in Fig. 1. The toolkit is

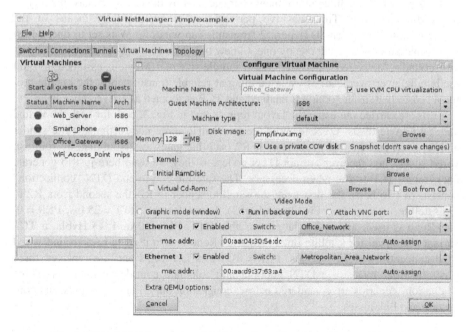

**Fig. 1.** Virtual NetManager graphical interface; virtual machine configuration

distributed under the GPL2 free license. All information about downloading and installation can be found in [26]. It should be pointed out, however, that the software is under development and some work is still necessary to improve the reliability of the most recent components.

The authors have already dealt with related issues in [27], where a virtual counterpart of the TATPA testbed, namely VITT (Virtual Integrated TCP Testbed) was proposed. However, the present work differs in many respects: first, the focus here is on DTN and not on TCP alone; second, here there is a toolkit that allows great layout configurability, and not just a fixed layout testbed; third, the Virtual NetManager interface has been introduced; fourth, VTT benefits for all the VDE enhancements introduced in the meantime.

## 4  Numerical Results

DTN bundle layer performance evaluations obtained using the VTT tools are compared here with those obtained by the TATPA testbed. The aim is to validate the reliability of virtualization when applied to DTN environments, rather than to present new performance results. In other words, the novelty of the numerical results presented here lies *in the way* they have been obtained (i.e. through VTT tools), and not in their absolute values. In fact, the environment considered is actually the same as that in [28], where TATPA results on DTN were first presented. The hardware platform used for running VTT tools is an "Intel® Core™2 Quad Q6600" with 2.4 MHz clock, support of Intel® Virtual Technology and 4 GB of RAM.

Tests refer to a satellite environment characterized by the continuous availability of the end-to-end path. Time-sensitive performance is evaluated by means of the DTNperf_2 tool [29]. The DTNperf_2 "transmission window" W is set to one, which means that bundles are sent one by one, (a new bundle is sent only at reception of previous bundle "delivered" status report). A bundle size of 1 Mbyte is assumed, to limit the bundle layer overhead; as we are aiming at reliable transmissions, the bundle protocol "custody transfer" option is enabled and TCP is adopted as convergence layer.

Tests are carried out using the layout represented in Fig. 2, both for both the virtual and TATPA testbeds. DTN features are enabled in three nodes: the satellite sender and receiver, and the intermediate node R2 (satellite gateway). Note that, by contrast, wired sender and receiver are not DTN nodes, as they are used here just to generate background TCP traffic when necessary. The satellite end-to-end DTN "connection" consists of two hops; the first from the satellite sender to R2, the second from R2 to the satellite receiver (see Fig. 2 and Fig. 3). In the former (RTT = 25 ms, PER = 0) NewReno is used, and in the latter (variable RTT, PER = 0 or 1 %) Hybla, a TCP variant optimized for satellite links [10]. NewReno is also used in background wired TCP connections (RTT = 25 ms, PER = 0). Tests last 180 s and are repeated three times in order to average DTN goodput and calculate confidence intervals. Three evaluation scenarios are considered below: congestion only, link losses only and congestion and link losses.

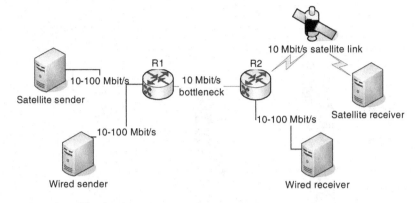

**Fig. 2.** Layout used in both virtual and TATPA testbeds

| Sat sender | Intermediate node (R2) | | Sat receiver |
|---|---|---|---|
| Application | | | Application |
| Bundle Layer | | | |
| Transport A | Transport A | Transport B | Transport B |
| IP | IP | IP | IP |
| Data Link | Data Link | Data Link | Data Link |
| Physical | Physical | Physical | Physical |

Wired Connection          Satellite Connection

**Fig. 3.** DTN protocol stack used in tests

### 4.1 Performance Comparison in the Presence of Congestion

The first evaluation scenario is a DTN transfer between satellite end nodes (with variable RTT on the satellite hop) and 5 wired TCP connections in background.

In Fig. 4, TATPA and VTT results are compared, referring to the goodput achieved by the satellite connection for three RTTs. It shows how VTT and TATPA results are very similar, for all RTTs. This confirms the accuracy of the virtual approach, with all the aforementioned advantages deriving from the use of a single PC.

As regards goodput, this is almost independent of RTT. This is due to the DTN architecture which, by splitting the satellite connection into two parts, allows a fair subdivision of the bottleneck, because the 5 TCP background connections and the satellite sender-R2 connection have the same RTT. On the satellite link, the improvements due to Hybla are limited, because there are neither congestion events nor link losses.

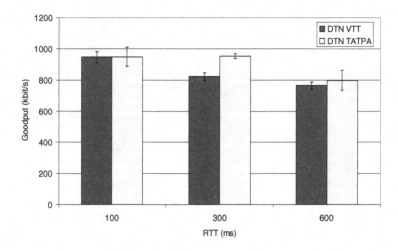

**Fig. 4.** Performance comparison between VTT and TATPA. Presence of congestion on the R1-R2 bottleneck: goodput of a satellite connection vs. its RTT; 5 background wired connection (RTT=25 ms) active.

## 4.2 Performance Comparison in the Presence of Link Losses

Unlike in the previous case, here there are no competing background connections on the first (wired) DTN hop. However, end-to-end performance is impaired by a high PER on the second DTN hop (the satellite one), which becomes the bottleneck here. Results, given in Fig. 5, show a good match between TATPA and VTT outcomes, in line with the previous case.

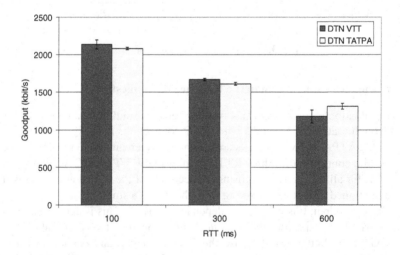

**Fig. 5.** Performance comparison between VTT and TATPA. Presence of losses (PER = 1%) on the satellite link: goodput of a satellite connection vs. its RTT; no background traffic.

Here performance very much depends on the ability of the TCP protocol used on the satellite hop to cope with random losses (i.e. losses not due to congestion). The protocol used here is Hybla, which actually provides much better resilience against random losses than other TCP variants, in particular for long RTTs. Interested readers are referred to [30] for an exhaustive comparison between Hybla and other TCP variants.

### 4.3 Performance Comparison in the Presence of Congestion and Link Losses

In the third scenario we have the simultaneous presence of both congestion on the first DTN hop and a high PER on the satellite one. Results, given in Fig. 6, refer as above to the end-to-end goodput of the DTN transfer between the two "satellite" end nodes. As in the previous scenarios, VTT and TATPA results closely match, demonstrating how, even in this complex scenario, the virtual approach can provide the same level as accuracy of a real testbed.

As regards performance, the limited impairment with RTT can be ascribed to both DTN architecture and Hybla. On the first DTN hop, where background traffic is present, the "TCP splitting" performed by the DTN architecture allows a fair sharing of bandwidth resources among all the connections on the R1-R2 bottleneck. On the second DTN hop, where a high PER affects the satellite link, Hybla resilience to random losses limits their negative impact on performance. Note that, as a result, the additional performance degradation due to PER on the satellite hop, with respect to the congestion only case (Fig. 4), is limited. Better performance could have been obtained by making use of a larger DTNperf_2 window, but this would have been outside the scope of the present tests.

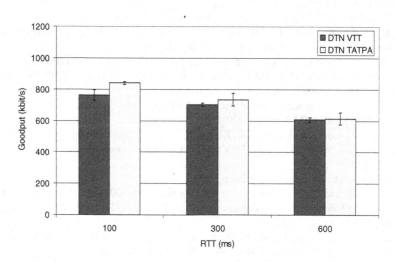

**Fig. 6.** Performance comparison between VTT and TATPA. Presence of both congestion on the R1-R2 bottleneck and losses (PER = 1%) on the satellite link: goodput of a satellite connection vs. its RTT; 5 background wired connection (RTT=25 ms) active.

# 5  Conclusions

In this paper, the use of virtualization technologies for DTN bundle protocol architecture is proposed and discussed. The aim is to set-up an entire DTN testbed in just one PC, thus combining the accuracy of real testbeds with the benefits of network simulators in terms of cost, test reproducibility, and maintenance. The results obtained by means of the Virtual Testbed Toolkit used to set up an integrated virtual counterpart of the real TATPA testbed show a good match in all benchmark tests considered. This confirms the validity of the virtualization technologies for performance evaluations in DTN environments.

# References

1. Cerf, V., Hooke, A., Torgerson, L., Durst, R., Scott, K., Fall, K., Weiss, H.: Delay-Tolerant Networking Architecture. IETF RFC 4838 (April 2007)
2. Fall, K., Farrell, S.: DTN: an architectural retrospective. IEEE Journal on Selected Areas in Commun 26(5), 828–836 (2008)
3. Network Simulator ns-2 University of California, Berkeley, http://www.isi.edu/nsnam/ns/
4. Cnet network simulator, http://www.csse.uwa.edu.au/cnet/
5. Opnet network simulator, http://www.opnet.com/
6. Qualnet network simulator, http://www.scalable-networks.com
7. Mah, B.A.: Insane Users Manual, The Tenet Group Computer Science Division. Univ. California, Berkeley (1996)
8. NCTUns, http://ns110.csie.nctu.edu.tw/
9. GNU General Public License, http://www.gnu.org/gpl
10. Caini, C., Firrincieli, R.: TCP Hybla: a TCP Enhancement for Heterogeneous Networks. Wiley Int. J. Satellite Commun. Netw. 22, 547–566 (2004)
11. Caini, C., Firrincieli, R.: Packet spreading techniques to avoid bursty traffic in long RTT TCP connections. In: Proc. IEEE Vehicular Technology Conference VTC 2004-Spring, Milano (IT), May 2004, vol. 5, pp. 2906–2910 (2004)
12. Hoe, J.C.: Improving the Start-up Behavior of a Congestion Control Scheme for TCP. In: Proc. ACM SIGCOMM 1996, pp. 270–280 (1996)
13. Sarolahti, P., Kojo, M., Raatikainen, K.: F-RTO: an enhanced recovery algorithm for TCP retransmission timeouts. ACM SIGCOMM Computer Communication Review 33(2), 51–63 (2003)
14. TCP Dump, http://www.tcpdump.org
15. Caini, C., Firrincieli, R., Lacamera, D.: A Linux Based Multi TCP Implementation for Experimental Evaluation of TCP Enhancements. In: Proc. SPECTS 2005, Philadelphia, July 2005, pp. 875–883 (2005)
16. Caini, C., Firrincieli, R., Lacamera, D., Tamagnini, S., Tiraferri, D.: The TATPA. testbed. In: Proc. of IEEE/Create-Net Tridentcom 2007, Orlando, USA (2007)
17. Parker, S., Schmechel, C.: Some Testing Tools for TCP Implementors. IETF RFC 2398 (August 1998)
18. Marchese, M.: TCP Modifications over Satellite Channels: Study and Performance Evaluation. International Journal of Satellite Communications, Special Issue on IP 19(1), 93–110 (2001)

19. Wei, D.X., Cao, P.: NS-2 TCP-Linux: an NS-2 TCP implementation with congestion control algorithms from Linux. In: Proc. of ValueTool 2006 – Workshop of NS-2, October 2006, pp. 1–9 (2006)
20. Egi, N., Greenhalgh, A., Handley, M., Hoerdt, M., Mathy, L., Schooley, T.: Evaluating Xen for Router Virtualization. In: Proc. of IEEE ICCCN 2007, Honolulu, Hawaii USA, August 2007, pp. 1256–1261 (2007)
21. Zimmermann, A., Gunes, M., Wenig, M., Meis, U., Ritzerfeld, J.: How to Study Wireless Mesh Networks: A hybrid Testbed Approach. In: Proc. of AINA 2007, Niagara Falls, Canada, May 2007, pp. 853–860 (2007)
22. Volynkin, A., Skormin, V.: Large-scale Reconfigurable Virtual Testbed for Information Security Experiments. In: Proc. of IEEE/Create-NetTridentcom 2007, Orlando, USA (2007)
23. Duchamp, D., DeAngelis, G.: A Hypervisor Based Security Testbed. In: Proc. of DETER 2007, Boston, USA (August 2007)
24. Huang, X.W., Sharma, R., Keshav, S.: The ENTRAPID Protocol Development Environment. In: Proc. of IEEE INFOCOMM 1999, pp. 1107–1115 (1999)
25. Davoli, R.: VDE: Virtual Distributed Ethernet. In: Proc. of IEEE/Create-Net Tridentcom 2005, Trento, Italy, May 2005, pp. 213–220 (2005)
26. wiki V2, http://wiki.virtualsquare.org/
27. Caini, C., Davoli, R., Firrincieli, R., Lacamera, D.: Virtual Integrated TCP Testbed (VITT). In: Proc. Create-Net Tridentcom, Innsbruck, Austria, March 2008, pp. 1–6 (2008)
28. Caini, C., Cornice, P., Firrincieli, R., Lacamera, D.: A DTN Approach to Satellite Communications. IEEE Journal on Selected Areas in Communications, special issue on Delay and Disruption Tolerant Wireless Communication 26(5), 820–827 (2008)
29. Caini, C., Cornice, P., Firrincieli, R., Livini, M.: DTNperf_2: a Performance Evaluation tool for Delay/Disruption Tolerant Networking. In: Proc. E-DTN, St. Petersburg, Russia, September 2009, pp. 1–6 (2009)
30. Caini, C., Firrincieli, R., Lacamera, D.: Comparative Performance Evaluation of TCP variants on Satellite Environments. In: Proc. IEEE ICC, Dresden, Germany, June 2009, pp. 1–5 (2009)

# Special Session 2
# Quantum Satellite Communications

# On the Polarization Analysis of Optical Beams for Use in Quantum Communications between Earth and Space

Alberto Dall'Arche[1], Andrea Tomaello[1],
Cristian Bonato[1,2], and Paolo Villoresi[1]

[1] Department of Information Engineering, University of Padova, and CNR-INFM
LUXOR Laboratory for Ultraviolet and X-ray Optical Research Via Gradenigo, 6/B,
35131 Padova, Italy
dallarch@dei.unipd.it, tomaello@dei.unipd.it, paolo.villoresi@unipd.it
[2] Huygens Laboratory, Leiden University, P.O. Box 9504, 2300 RA Leiden,
The Netherlands
bonato@molphys.leidenuniv.nl

**Abstract.** In this work we will address the transformation of the polarization state of single photons during the transmission along a Space channel and the measures to correct them in order to accomplish Quantum Communication (QC) between Space and Earth.

An open issue in space scale QC is the preservation of polarization states by the telescope and all the involved moving optical components, as well as ensuring the alignment of the polarization basis between the orbiting sender and receiver on Earth. In the following, we will treat in detail this crucial aspect, by modelling the measurement of the polarization properties of the quantum channel, expressed by its Mueller matrix, in the experimental conditions of Ref. [12] with the addition of the control of the outbound state of the photons and the measure of the polarization state of the inbound beam.

**Keywords:** Satellite quantum communication, polarization analysis, quantum key distribution.

## 1 Introduction

About a decade ago, several groups endeavored the porting of QC in general and Quantum Keys Distribution (QKD) as first example, outside the cradle of the lab, where QC was initially tested [2], [3].

The final step of this extension of the tract covered with QC is naturally Space, due to the restrictions imposed on the Earth surface by the Earth curvature as well as atmospheric turbulence. Several studies of satellite QC addressed the various aspects involved by the long leg length, the relative motion, the diffraction losses, the background radiation and the error rate ([4,5,6,7,8,9,10]).

The experimental demonstration of the feasibility of single photon exchange between Space and a ground receiver has been also demonstrated in our group recently [12].

K. Sithamparanathan et al. (Eds.): PSATS 2010, LNICST 43, pp. 291–296, 2010.

The demonstration of the control of the polarization state along the Space channel is important to pave the way to further steps in Space QC. We believe that the most suitable infrastructure to investigate this topic is the Satellite Laser Ranging System for Geodynamics.

## 2   Problems in the Transmission

Polarization analysis for an Earth-Space link as first, start with the problem of modeling a real quantum link on space. Physically, we have to deal with a free-space dynamic optical link that crosses the atmosphere. Dynamic means the fact that transmitter and receiver are in relative motion between them.

We can identify the following main issues, that have to be addressed:

- Effects due to atmospheric turbulence that causes attenuation and fluctuations in the signal received.
- Background noise: due to sunlight, moonlight and every source of photons that can be collected by the receiver.
- The relative motions beetween transmitter and receiver, that is the main source of misalignment in the polarization references of transmitter and receiver.
- Non ideal optics that can cause depolarization, attenuation and distortion.

The "Radar Link Equation" given by Degnan [11], is the common representation used to define the noise and attenuation due to atmosphere and non ideal experimental setup, and so the link budget.

Is not trivial the problem of states choosing to optimize the experimental results. Infact, the effects of noise and attenuation on measurements are related to the transmitted states.

An accurate model of the link is the winning key to desing a successfull experiment of polarization analysis.

## 3   Channel Polarization Analysis

The polarization properties of an optical system can be generally described through the use of the Mueller matrix and the Stokes formalism. The interaction between a polarized beam and a polarizing device can be described by:

$$S = \mathbf{M}S'$$ (1)

where $S'$ and $S$ are respectively the Stokes vectors of incident beam and of the emerging beam. $\mathbf{M}$ is the 4x4 Mueller matrix of the optical system. A tipical way for retrieving the Mueller matrix of an optical device is to test the device with $n$ different polarized beam (with $n \geq 4$) and measure the outcoming beam. The input state can be generated through the rotation of a quarter-wave plate at determinated angle $\theta$:

$$J = \begin{bmatrix} 1 \\ \cos^2(2\theta) \\ \cos(2\theta)\sin(2\theta) \\ \sin(2\theta) \end{bmatrix} \tag{2}$$

For $n$ different input states the equation (1) can be rewrited in matricial form:

$$\mathbf{S} = \mathbf{MA} \tag{3}$$

where $\mathbf{S}$ is the matrix of output Stokes vectors:

$$\mathbf{S} = \begin{bmatrix} S^{(0)} S^{(1)} \cdots S^{(n)} \end{bmatrix} \tag{4}$$

and $\mathbf{A}$ is the matrix of input state vectors:

$$\mathbf{A} = \begin{bmatrix} J^{(0)} J^{(1)} \cdots J^{(n)} \end{bmatrix} \tag{5}$$

Inverting equation (3) is possible to retrieve the Mueller matrix $\mathbf{M}$:

$$\mathbf{M} = \mathbf{SA}^+ \tag{6}$$

where $\mathbf{A}^+$ is the pseudo-inverse matrix of $\mathbf{A}$.

An easy way to see the effects of an optical system on a polarized beam is to plot its related Poincaré sphere. Knowing the Mueller matrix of the system we can use the relation (1) to obtain the associated Poincaré sphere. In figure (1) is

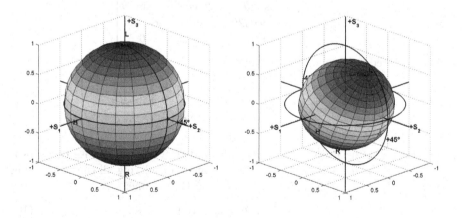

(a) Input states                    (b) Output states

**Fig. 1.** Poincaré spheres

plotted the Poincaré sphere before and after the trasformation of a collimator-radiometer system described by the Mueller matrix in the eq. (7) measured by Howell in [17]:

$$M = \begin{bmatrix} 1.0000 & 0.0338 & 0.1587 & 0.0758 \\ 0.0490 & 0.6955 & 0.0001 & -0.0653 \\ 0.1590 & -0.0001 & 0.8138 & 0.2527 \\ -0.0729 & -0.0753 & -0.2361 & 0.6346 \end{bmatrix} \tag{7}$$

As we can see the output states sphere is rotated and also smaller than the input states one. By modelling the trasformation along the space channel and measuring the Stokes parameters with a suitable polarimeter under development in our group, we will correct for the transformation induced.

## 4    Feedback Control in Quantum Communication System

An important feature of a quantum communication system is the polarization preservation. This is in general not realized in present systems, due to the non-idealities of a real channel. It's however possible to study the polarization properties of the channel by the use of Mueller matrices formalism and use it to compensate the distortion of the channel. In fact knowing the Mueller matrix of the channel it's possible to prepare an input state so that is received in the desired polarization state. Using the cascade of an half-wave plate and a quarter-wave plate is possible to choose anykind of polarization states in the Poincaré sphere. In figure (2) is represented an example of a quantum trasmission system. In Mueller formalism the matrix of the rotated quarter-wave retarder is:

$$Q(\theta) = \begin{bmatrix} 1 & 0 & 0 & 0 \\ 0 & \cos^2 2\theta & \sin 2\theta \cos 2\theta & -\sin 2\theta \\ 0 & \sin 2\theta \cos 2\theta & \sin^2 2\theta & \cos 2\theta \\ 0 & \sin 2\theta & -\cos 2\theta & 0 \end{bmatrix} \tag{8}$$

and the rotated half-wave retarder matrix is:

$$H(\theta) = \begin{bmatrix} 1 & 0 & 0 & 0 \\ 0 & \cos 4\theta & \sin 4\theta & 0 \\ 0 & \sin 4\theta & -\cos 4\theta & 0 \\ 0 & 0 & 0 & -1 \end{bmatrix} \tag{9}$$

In practice, starting from a vertically polarized state we can choose the appropriated rotation angles to send the desired state. Considering all the trasmitting system together with the channel the equation (1) become:

$$S = \mathbf{M}\mathbf{Q}(\theta_{\mathbf{Q}})\mathbf{H}(\theta_{\mathbf{H}})V \tag{10}$$

where V is the Stokes vector of the input vertical polarized state. A simple way to find the two rotation angles is to minimize the norm of the difference between the sent state and the expected received state:

$$(\theta_Q, \theta_H) = \min_{\theta_Q, \theta_H} \| S - \mathbf{M}\mathbf{Q}(\theta_{\mathbf{Q}})\mathbf{H}(\theta_{\mathbf{H}})V \|_F \tag{11}$$

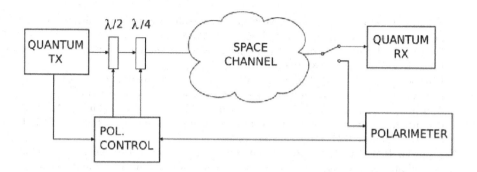

**Fig. 2.** Scheme of a quantum transmission system

In this way, knowing the Mueller matrix of the channel we can pre-compensate any retardation effect introduced by the channel. In a typical trasmitting system channel probing and information exchange share the same medium, this implies that Mueller matrix measure should not affect the single-photon exchange in the quantum channel. Two possible solution are time-multiplexing and wavelenght-multiplexing proposed by [9].

With the model here proposed and the undergoing experimental measurements, the necessary knowledge of the channel transformations will be available for the first time. With these we can predict the evolution of a time-varing channel and compensate it for changes in the polarization by means of a feedback control.

## 5   Conclusions

In conclusion, these analysis are aimed to ascertain the causes of incorrect alignment of the polarization reference of an orbiting quantum transmitter and a quantum receiver on Earth. The findings will be used to envisage the feedback system that will correct for these transformations and that will allow the demonstration of the Space QC.

The ability to analize and compensate the polarization state of photons will give us the tools and the basis for quantum communication on free-space on space scale. What we are doing, can be seen like a creation of a communication medium, in wich photons can be used to transfer informations. The problem can be compared, as were invented fiber optics. At that time the problem was the development of a media allowing the propagation of light over long distance. Now our problem is the "development" of a media in wich the photons can propagate preserving their polarization state, and the media is formed by: free-space link, polarization analyzer and compensator.

# References

1. Villoresi, P., et al.: Experimental verification of the feasibility of a quantum channel between space and earth. New J. Phys. 10, 033038 (2008)
2. Buttler, W.T., et al.: Practical free-space quantum key distribution over 1 km. Phys. Rev. Lett. 81, 3283 (1998)
3. Kurtsiefer, C., Zarda, P., Halder, M., Weinfurter, H., Gorman, P.M., Tapster, P.R., Rarity, J.: GA step towards global key distribution. Nature 419, 450 (2002)
4. Aspelmeyer, M., Jennewein, T., Pfennigbauer, M., Leeb, W.R., Zeilinger, A.: Long distance quantum communication with entangled photons using satellites. IEEE J. Sel. Top. Quantum Electron. 9, 1541 (2003)
5. Villoresi, P., et al.: Space-to-ground quantum communication using an optical ground station: a feasibility study. In: Quantum Communications and Quantum Imaging II Proc. SPIE, vol. 5551, p. 113 (2004) quantph/0408067v1
6. Peng, C.Z., et al.: Experimental free-space distribution of entangled photon pairs over 13 km: Towards satellite- based global quantum communication. Phys. Rev. Lett. 94, 150501 (2005)
7. Bonato, C., et al.: Influence of satellite motion on polarization qubits in a space-Earth quantum communication link. Opt. Express 14, 10050 (2006)
8. Bonato, C., Pernechele, C., Villoresi, P.: Influence of all-reflective optical systems in the transmission of polarization-encoded qubits. J. Opt. A: Pure Appl. Opt. 9899 (2007)
9. Bonato, C., Tomaello, A., Deppo, V.D., Naletto, G., Villoresi, P.: Feasibility of satellite quantum key distribution. New J. Phys. 11 (2009), 45017
10. Ursin, R., et al.: Space-quest: experiments with quantum entanglement in space. In: Int. Aeronautical Congress Proc. A2.1.3 (2008), arXiv:0806.0945
11. Degnan, J.J.: Millimiter accuracy satellite laser ranging: A review. Contributions of Space Geodesy to Geodynamics Technology. In: Smith, D.E., Turcotte, D.L. (eds.). AGU Geodynamics Series, vol. 25, p. 133 (1993)
12. Aiello, A., Puentes, G., Voigt, D., Woerdman, J.P.: Maximum-likelihood estimation of Mueller matrices. Optics letters 31, 6 (2006)
13. Bouwmeester, D., Ekert, A.K., Zeilinger, A.: Physics of Quantum Information. Springer, Heidelberg (2000)
14. Goldstein, D.: Polarized Light, 2nd edn. Marcel Dekker, New York (2003)
15. Ahmad, J.E., Takakura, Y.: Estimation of physically realizable Mueller matrices from experiments using global constrained optimization. Optics express (August 28, 2008)
16. Toyoshima, M., Takenaka, H., Shoji, Y., Takayama, Y., Koyama, Y., Kunimori, H.: Polarization measurements through space-to- ground atmospheric propagation paths by using a highly polarized laser source in space. Optics express (November 23, 2009)
17. Howell, B.J.: Measurement of the polarization effects of an instrument using partially polarized light. App. Opt. 18(6) (1979)

# 100 MHz Amplitude and Polarization Modulated Optical Source for Free-Space Quantum Communications at 850 nm

M. Jofre[1,*], A. Gardelein[1], G. Anzolin[1], G. Molina-Terriza[1,2], J.P. Torres[1,3], M.W. Mitchell[1], and V. Pruneri[1,2]

[1] ICFO-Institut de Ciencies Fotoniques, Mediterranean Technology Park, 08860 Castelldefels (Barcelona), Spain
marc.jofre@icfo.es
[2] ICREA-Institucio Catalana de Recerca i Estudis Avançats, 08010 Barcelona, Spain
[3] Dept. Teoria del Senyal i Comunicacions, Universitat Politecnica de Catalunya, 08034 Barcelona, Spain

**Abstract.** We report on an 100 MHz repetition rate integrated photonic transmitter at 850 nm with arbitrary amplitude and polarization modulation. The source is suitable for free-space quantum communication links, in particular for quantum key distribution applications. The whole transmitter, with the optical and electronic components integrated, has reduced size and power consumption. In addition, the optoelectronic components forming the transmitter can be space-qualified, making it suitable for satellite and future space missions.

**Keywords:** Free-space optical communications, quantum communications, quantum cryptography, faint pulse source.

## 1 Introduction

In many applications, *free-space optical* (FSO) communications is the technology of choice to transmit information, especially when fiber optical cabling is not easily achievable or its installation is too expensive [1]. FSO communication is favorable for high data-rate, long-range point-to-point links, where the terminal size, mass, and power consumption are subjected to strong limitations, such is the case of aeronautical or space platforms.

An important issue in today's information society is the security of data transmission against potential intruders, which always put at risk the confidentiality. Current methods to increase security require that two parties wishing to transmit information securely need to exchange or share one or more keys. Quantum cryptography, or more precisely *Quantum Key Distribution* (QKD), guarantees absolutely secure key distribution based on the principles of quantum physics, since it is not since it is not possible to measure or reproduce a state (eg. polarization or phase of a photon) without being detected [2].

---

* Corresponding author.

K. Sithamparanathan et al. (Eds.): PSATS 2010, LNICST 43, pp. 297–304, 2010.
© Institute for Computer Sciences, Social-Informatics and Telecommunications Engineering 2010

The first QKD scheme, due to Bennett and Brassard [3], employs single photons sent through a quantum channel, plus classical communications over a public channel to generate a secure shared key. This scheme is commonly known as the BB84 protocol. Attenuated laser pulses or *faint pulse sources* (FPS), which in average emit less than one photon per pulse, are often used as signals in practical QKD devices. The introduction of the decoy-state protocol [4] made possible a much tighter bound for the key generation rate, achieving an almost linear dependency of the latter on the channel transmittance. In this way, the technologically much simpler faint pulse systems can offer comparable QKD security with respect to single photon sources. Another key feature of QKD is that the security is linked to the one-time-pad transmission, i.e. the key has to be used once and has to be equal or similar in size to the information being transmitted. It is thus evident the importance of developing faint pulse sources and systems for QKD which can generate high key bit rates. The highest Secure Key Rate reported to date over 20 Km of optical telecom fiber is of 1.02 Mb/s [5] and 14.1 b/s over 200 Km [6], while the achieved speed over 144 Km free space link is of 12.8 Kb/s [7] and 50 Kb/s over 480 m [8].

We note that previous implementations based on multiple lasers [9,8] have attempted to achieve time-frequency indistinguishability by laser pre-selection, current and temperature adjustment, and temporal and spectral measurements. Apart from being expensive and cumbersome, this kind of tuning has limited stability due to the inevitable aging of laser diodes. It is worth noting that the temporal and spectral distributions reported to date indicate indistinguishability in the time and frequency bases, but leave open the question of distinguishability based on other pulse characteristics such as chirp.

In this paper we report the development of a novel integrated pulse source which can reach rates as high as 100 Mb/s at 850nm modulated in amplitude and polarization. For QKD applications, it has been simulated that the source could achieve a Secure Key Rate of the order of 500 Kb/s at 20 Km using decoy-state protocol. The source is capable to generate pulses at around 850 nm with at least three different intensity levels (i.e. number of photons per pulse) and four different polarization states. The proposed FPS ensures indistinguishability among the different intensity and polarization pulses and ensures phase incoherence of consecutive generated states. One of the foreseen applications is its use to overcome the distance limit of QKD in optical fibers [6,10], by creating a global security network among very distant places on earth through satellite communication [11,12,13]. In particular such a source might be used in future *European Space Agency* (ESA) missions [14].

## 2   Integrated Faint Pulse Source

The integrated source can generate pulses at 850 nm with at least three different intensity levels (i.e. number of photons per pulse) and four different polarization states. In order to use it for space applications, the proposed integrated FPS source for FSO communication consists of commercially available space-qualified

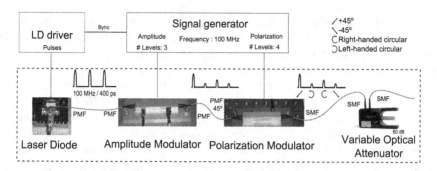

**Fig. 1.** Schematic of the QKD source. The source is composed of a laser diode, an amplitude modulator, a polarization modulator and a variable optical attenuator together with the driving electronics.

discrete components; single semiconductor laser diode emitting a continuous pulse train at 100 MHz followed by integrated (waveguide) amplitude and polarization lithium niobate (LiNbO$_3$) modulators (Figure 1). The wavelength, reduced power consumption, compactness and space qualifiable optoelectronic components constituting the source make it very suitable for space transmission, for free space quantum and classical communication links.

## 3   Side-Channel Information

In a BB84 protocol scheme implementing the decoy-state protocol different pulses should differ in polarization and amplitude while remaining indistinguishable in other characteristics, including temporal shape and frequency spectrum. If the pulses differ in spectrum, for example, an eavesdropper could use spectral measurements to infer the sent polarization without actually measuring it. Removal of this kind of *side-channel* information is thus critical to the security of the protocol. Since the information is encoded in the polarization state, the statistical similarity between pulses of different polarizations but same intensity level is more relevant than that of different intensity level but same polarization to prevent information leakage from the quantum link. Here we consider the quantum optics of side-channel information, limiting the discussion to pure states and simple measurements. A full treatment including mixed states and generalized measurements will be the subject of a future publication.

We consider a source that produces pulses with amplitudes $\mathcal{E}_l$, polarizations $\mathbf{p}_l$ and pulse shapes $\Pi_l(t)$. Without loss of generality we assume the polarizations and pulses shapes are normalized $\mathbf{p}_l^* \cdot \mathbf{p}_l = \int dt\, \Pi_l^*(t) \Pi_l(t) = 1$. In a classical description, the field envelopes are

$$\mathbf{E}_l(t) = \mathcal{E}_l \mathbf{p}_l \Pi_l(t) \tag{1}$$

The corresponding quantum state is a generalized coherent state

$$|\alpha_l\rangle \equiv D_l(\eta \mathcal{E}_l \mathbf{p}_l) |0\rangle \tag{2}$$

where $|0\rangle$ is the vacuum state and $D_l(\mathbf{x}) \equiv \exp[\mathbf{x} \cdot \mathbf{A}_l^\dagger - \mathbf{x}^* \cdot \mathbf{A}_l]$ is a displacement operator, defined in terms of the mode operator $\mathbf{A}_l \equiv \int dt\, \Pi_l^*(t)\mathbf{a}(t)$, $\mathbf{a} \equiv (a_x, a_y)$ is a vector of annihilation operators, with $[a_p(t), a_q^\dagger(t')] = \delta(t - t')\delta_{p,q}$ for $p, q \in \{x, y\}$. A scaling factor $\eta$ is included to convert from photon units to field units, chosen such that the positive-frequency part of the quantized electric field is $\hat{\mathbf{E}}(t) = \eta^{-1}\mathbf{a}(t)$. It is easy to check that $\langle \alpha_l | \mathbf{a}(t) | \alpha_l \rangle = \eta \mathcal{E}_l \mathbf{p}_l \Pi_l(t)$, so that the average quantum field $\langle \alpha_l | \hat{\mathbf{E}}(t) | \alpha_l \rangle = \mathcal{E}_l \mathbf{p}_l \Pi_l(t)$ in agreement with Equation 1.

Quantum mechanics allows measurements on the pulse-shape $\Pi$ without measurement of the polarization $\mathbf{p}$. For example, the number operator $N_l \equiv \mathbf{A}_l^\dagger \cdot \mathbf{A}_l = A_{l,x}^\dagger A_{l,x} + A_{l,y}^\dagger A_{l,y}$ counts photons in the mode $\Pi_l$ independent of $\mathbf{p}_l$. If the modes $\{\Pi_l\}$ are different, an eavesdropper could use state-discrimination techniques [15,16] to determine $l$ (and thus the secret key) *without* disturbing $\mathbf{p}$. This kind of eavesdropping would not be detected by Bob's polarization measurements. For this reason, it is critical to guarantee that this kind of *side channel* information is not present in the sent optical pulses. The similarity between the various $\Pi_l$ can be quantified by an overlap integral: $[A_{l,p}, A_{m,q}^\dagger] = \int dt\, \Pi_l^*(t)\Pi_m(t)[a_p, a_q^\dagger] \equiv S_{lm}\delta_{p,q}$, so that for example two states with equal amplitudes $|\mathcal{E}_l| = |\mathcal{E}_m|$, $\langle \alpha_m | N_l | \alpha_m \rangle / \langle \alpha_l | N_l | \alpha_l \rangle = |S_{lm}|^2$. Finally, we note that it is possible for pulses to have the same spectra and temporal shape but still be distinguishable, for example if they have different chirp. For this reason, establishing that two (or more) distinct sources produce indistinguishable pulses is not easy.

Our strategy to eliminate side-channel information in the pulse shapes is to dissociate pulse generation from the setting of polarization and amplitude levels. As described in the previous section the FPS consists of a single laser diode emitting a continuous train of optical pulses followed by an AM, a PM and a VOA. Considering that the laser operation is the same for each pulse sent, and that both the AM and PM control voltages are held constant over the duration of the pulse, we can assume that the pulse shape does not depend on the sent amplitude and polarization. The complex expression of the pulsed electromagnetic field exiting the FPS can be written as

$$\mathbf{E}(t) = \sum_i A\alpha_i e^{j\phi_i} e^{j\beta_i} \frac{\hat{\mathbf{x}} + e^{j\gamma_i}\hat{\mathbf{y}}}{\sqrt{2}} \Pi\left(t - iT\right) \tag{3}$$

where $t$ is the time, $T$ is the pulse train period and $A, \phi_i, \Pi$ are the amplitude, phase, and shape, respectively, of the optical pulse generated by the LD. $\alpha_i, \beta_i$ describe the transmission and introduced phase, respectively, of the AM. $\gamma_i$ is the phase difference between $\hat{\mathbf{x}}$ and $\hat{\mathbf{y}}$ introduced by the polarization modulator in order to generate the different polarization states.

Another security consideration is optical coherence between successive pulses, which could in principle be used for eavesdropping attacks [17]. As the LD is taken below threshold between pulses, each new pulse will start up from vacuum fluctuations, and will have a random overall phase $\phi_i$, thus eliminating coherence between succesive pulses and thus among states. Similarly, any information contained in the AM phase $\beta_i$ is washed out by the random $\phi_i$.

## 4   Experimental Results

The resulting optical pulse duration is about 400 ps. The short optical pulse duration (small duty cycle) has the advantage to increase the signal to noise ratio since the measurement window (detection time) in the receiver can be reduced. Furthermore, the optical pulse bandwidth is small enough to enter the acceptance bandwidth of the subsequent polarization modulator. The modulator "ON" window has a duration of at least 5 ns, much larger than that of the optical pulse. Therefore, only the amplitude of the optical pulse changes, while the temporal and spectral shape remain unaltered. In addition low driving voltages are needed, half-wave voltages of 640mV and 1.56V for the amplitude and polarization modulators, respectively. Making the design suitable for electronic integration with low electrical power consumption drivers. Moreover, intensity

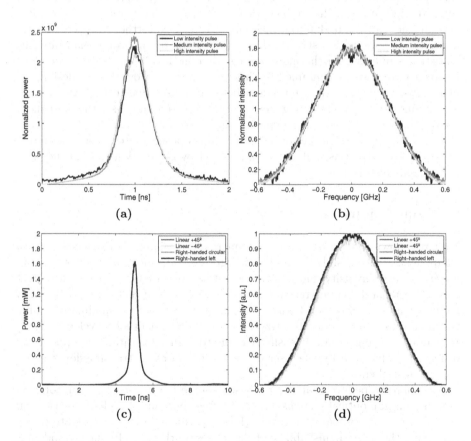

**Fig. 2.** (Top) Temporal (a) and spectral (b) profiles for pulses with three intensity levels. (Bottom) Temporal (c) and spectral (d) profiles for pulsed with four polarization states. As expected, these show a high degree of similarity, indicating minimal distortion of the pulses by the amplitude and polarization modulators.

extinction ratio and *polarization extinction ratio* (PER) higher than 25 dB have been achieved with the amplitude modulator and polarization modulator, respectively. Making the source suitable to use it to implement decoy-state QKD transmission while obtaining a low *Quantum Bit Error Rate* (QBER).

Figure 2 top subfigures (a) and (b) show pulses with the same polarization but with different intensity levels with the aim of comparing its temporal and spectral indistinguishability. A 8 GHz amplified photodiode and a 4 MHz resolution Fabry-Perot scanning interferometer where used for the temporal and spectral measurements, respectively. In order to compare pulses with different intensity levels, the different pulses are normalized to their own total intensity. Moreover, Figure 2 bottom subfigures (c) and (d) show a similar comparison, but this time pulses have the same intensity level and different polarization. As expected, there is a high degree of similarity of the pulses, independently of their polarization or intensity state, indicating minimal pulse distortion due to the AM and the PM. It has to be noticed that the small differences for the different intensity pulses are due to measurement errors. Nevertheless, as commented in section 3 polarization statistical similarity is more important than intensity statistical similarity. Furthermore, information on the absolute or relative phase between pulses is not contained in these four figures. However, by design, the phase of each pulse varies at random between pulses due to the fact that, as already mentioned, pulses are generated by taking continuously the laser diode above and below threshold, as explained in section 3.

Given the high optical performance of the proposed source, it is expected to achieve a low QBER as well as a high Secure Key Generation Rate in the order of hundreds of kHz.

## 5    Conclusions

We have shown that, starting from commercially available and space-qualifiable components, it is possible to build an integrated transmitter capable of generating the several intensity and polarization states required for decoy-state QKD. The experimental demonstration has been carried out at 850 nm with 100 MHz modulation rates. However, taking into consideration that the modulators bandwidth can go well beyond 10 GHz and operate also at other wavelengths (e.g. 1550 nm), the source can be easily scalable to higher bit rates, the upper limit being probably given by the laser diode itself, and other transmission systems (e.g. optical fibers).

Although we believe that the proposed source is of general use in polarization modulation optical systems, especially free-space links, we have focused our demonstration in preparation for a QKD experiment using decoy-state protocol, where the indistinguishability of the pulses, both in the frequency and time domain, is the key for the security of the link. Given the relatively low driving voltages of the modulators, the proposed transmitter is potentially low power consumption and also highly integrable.

# Acknowledgments

This work was carried out with the financial support of the Ministerio de Educación y Ciencia (Spain) through grants TEC2007-60185, FIS2007-60179, FIS2008-01051 and Consolider Ingenio CSD2006-00019.

# References

1. Carbonneau, T.H., Wisely, D.R.: Opportunities and challenges for optical wireless: the competitive advantage of free space telecommunications links in today's crowded marketplace. In: Wireless Technologies and Systems: Millimeter-Wave and Optical, Proc. SPIE, vol. 3232, pp. 119–128 (1998)
2. Scarani, V., Iblisdir, S., Gisin, N., Acín, A.: Quantum cloning. Rev. Mod. Phys. 77(4), 1225–1256 (2005)
3. Bennett, C.H., Brassard, G.: Quantum cryptography: Public-key distribution and coin tossing. In: Proceedings of IEEE International Conference on Computers, Systems and Signal Processing, pp. 175–179 (1984)
4. Lo, H.-K., Ma, X., Chen, K.: Decoy state quantum key distribution. Phys. Rev. Lett. 94(23), 230504 (2005)
5. Dixon, A.R., Yuan, Z.L., Dynes, J.F., Sharpe, A.W., Shields, A.J.: Gigahertz decoy quantum key distribution with 1 mbit/s secure key rate. Opt. Express 16(23), 18790–18979 (2008)
6. Chen, T.-Y., Wang, J., Liu, Y., Cai, W.-Q., Wan, X., Chen, L.-K., Wang, J.-H., Liu, S.-B., Liang, H., Yang, L., Peng, C.-Z., Chen, Z.-B., Pan, J.-W.: 200km Decoy-state quantum key distribution with photon polarization. arXiv:0908.4063v1 (2009)
7. Schmitt-Manderbach, T., Weier, H., Fürst, M., Ursin, R., Tiefenbacher, F., Scheidl, T., Perdigues, J., Sodnik, Z., Kurtsiefer, C., Rarity, A., Zeilinger, J.G., Weinfurter, H.: Experimental Demonstration of Free-Space Decoy-State Quantum Key Distribution over 144 km. Phys. Rev. Lett. 98, 010504 (2007)
8. Weier, H., Schmitt-Manderbach, T., Regner, N., Kurtsiefer, C., Weinfurte, H.: Free space quantum key distribution: Towards a real life application. Fortschr. Phys. 54(8-10), 840–845 (2006)
9. Kurtsiefer, C., Zarda, P., Halder, M., Gorman, P.M., Tapster, P.R., Rarity, J.G., Weinfurter, H.: Long Distance Free Space Quantum Cryptography. In: Proc. SPIE, vol. 4917, p. 25 (2002)
10. Takesue, H., Nam, S.W., Zhang, Q., Hadfield, R.H., Honjo, T., Tamaki, K., Yamamoto, Y.: Quantum key distribution over a 40-db channel loss using superconducting single-photon detectors. Nature Photonics 1, 343–348 (2007)
11. Hwang, W.-Y.: Quantum key distribution with high loss: Toward global secure communication. Phys. Rev. Lett. 91(5), 057901 (2003)
12. Rarity, J.G., Tapster, P.R., Gorman, P.M., Knight, P.: Ground to satellite secure key exchange using quantum cryptography. New Journal of Physics 4 (2002)
13. Bonato, C., Tomaello, A., Deppo, V.D., Naletto, G., Villoresi, P.: Feasibility of satellite quantum key distribution. New Journal of Physics 11, 045017 (2009)

14. Ursin, R., Jennewein, T., Kofler, J., Perdigues, J.M., Cacciapuoti, L., de Matos, C.J., Aspelmeyer, M., Valencia, A., Scheidl, T., Fedrizzi, A., Acin, A., Barbieri, C., Bianco, G., Brukner, C., Capmany, J., Cova, S., Giggenbach, D., Leeb, W., Hadfield, R.H., Laflamme, R., Lutkenhaus, N., Milburn, G., Peev, M., Ralph, T., Rarity, J., Renner, R., Samain, E., Solomos, N., Tittel, W., Torres, J.P., Toyoshima, M., Ortigosa-Blanch, A., Pruneri, V., Villoresi, P., Walmsley, I., Weihs, G., Weinfurter, H., Zukowski, M., Zeilinger, A.: Space-quest: Experiments with quantum entanglement in space. Europhysics News 40(3), 26–29 (2009)
15. Bergou, J.A., Herzog, U., Hillery, M.: Discrimination of quantum states. Lecture Notes in Physics, vol. 649. Springer, Berlin (2004)
16. Barnett, S.M., Croke, S.: Quantum state discrimination. Adv. Opt. Photon. 1(2), 238–278 (2009)
17. Lo, H.-K., Preskill, J.: Security of quantum key distribution using weak coherent states with nonrandom phases. Quantum Information and Computation 8(5), 431–458 (2007)

# Novel Techniques for Information Reconciliation, Quantum Channel Probing and Link Design for Quantum Key Distribution

Marina Mondin[1], Fred Daneshgaran[2], Maria Delgado[1], and Fabio Mesiti[1]

[1] Politecnico di Torino, Dip. Di Elettronica, C.so duca degli Abruzzi 24, 10129, Torino, Italy
{marina.mondin,maria.delgadoalizo,fabio.mesiti}@polito.it
[2] California State Univ., ECE Dept., 5151 State Univ. Cr., Los Angeles, CA, 90032, USA
fdanesh@calstatela.edu

**Abstract.** In this manuscript, a novel technique for forward error correction based information reconciliation is proposed, exploiting capacity achieving soft-metric based iteratively decoded block codes. The availability of soft metric and information bits reliability is also employed to efficiently perform channel probing and privacy amplification.

**Keywords:** Information reconciliation, Low Density Parity Check codes, LDPC, soft metric, log likelihood ratios, QKD, Quantum Key Distribution.

## 1 Overview

Quantum computing and information processing is at the forefront of research and development and a multitude of organizations and research centers have been pursuing this area feverishly. In this field, quantum cryptography has emerged as one of the most important practical applications of non-classical or quantum theory. One-time pad (or Vernam cipher) requires that the key used to encode the message and hence render it illegible to unintended receiver, be as long as the message itself and this is often impractical and shorter keys are often used. While the security of the traditional cryptographic techniques is based on algorithmic complexity of solving certain mathematical problems (e.g., trap door one-way functions), the security of Quantum Cryptography (QC) is founded on basic physical principles. The best known example of traditional algorithmic method is multiplication of large numbers. In fact, the difficulty of prime factorization is at the basis of the most common public key cryptosystems. The problem from a cryptographic point of view is that the existence of a fast algorithm for factorization has not been ruled out; a sudden mathematical breakthrough would make many internet communications completely insecure. Even worse, it has been proven that the possible realization of a quantum computer would allow a fast algorithm for factorization. A secure cryptosystem can be achieved if one encodes information in a quantum system. To be more precise, quantum mechanics is able to generate perfectly secure, random keys which can then be used in standard secret-key protocols.

K. Sithamparanathan et al. (Eds.): PSATS 2010, LNICST 43, pp. 305–316, 2010.

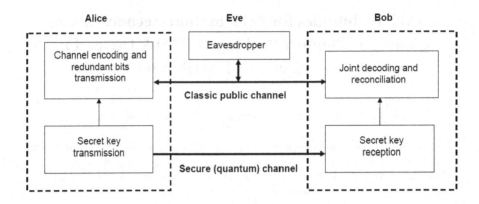

**Fig. 1.** Model of the secure and public channels involved in QKD communication

In the generic model of a secret-key cryptosystem shown in Figure 1, the sender Alice wants to transmit a plaintext message secretly to the receiver Bob. The secret key is transmitted on a secure (quantum) channel, which has typically high bit error rate (denoted QBER), so that a subsequent information reconciliation and privacy amplification operations need to be performed on a public channel. Once the secret key is known to Alice and to Bob (and only to them), Alice will encrypt the plaintext using the secret key according to the encryption rule of the system, and send the cryptogram to Bob, while Eve will not be able to recover the transmitted message. A multitude of attack strategies that could hypothetically be used by Eve have been identified and well documented in the literature. Note that the transmission rate on the QKD secret channel is generally very low (since the technology is very complex), while the actual data rate on the public channel can be very high. It is therefore important to analyze the achievable QKD rates. Furthermore, the bit error rate (BER) on the public channel is low, while the BER on the secret channel is high, and channel coding may be required to make the secret channel more reliable.

Up to now, the most famous protocol suggested for QKD is the BB84 protocol. The BB84 protocol, using the *cascade reconciliation protocol*, performs error-correction by sending very little information over the public channel and was proposed by Gilles Brassard and Louis Salvail. The cascade protocol operates in a number of rounds, and requires interaction between transmitter and receiver (Alice and Bob).

From a practical point of view, most recent attempts at long distance free space QKD have focused on using Weak laser Pulses (WLP) as opposed to true single photon sources which are still in experimental development stages. With Decoy state QKD, clever eavesdropping strategies that may be adopted by Eve can no longer be used.

The focus of this paper is on pragmatic information reconciliation using novel soft information processing techniques. The proposed techniques can be applied to QKD schemes based both on Single Photon or WLP sources, with or without decoy states. The difference among the different schemes is the use of different channel metrics. Furthermore, the information reconciliation proposed here will only use feed-forward techniques, not requiring interaction between transmitter and receiver.

## 2  Quantum Channel Communication System

In reference to the model depicted in Figure 1, the practical implementations of QKD protocols rely on solutions that are low cost, offer high levels of security, and can be rapidly deployed requiring uncomplicated setups and conventional devices. In this regard, QKD using decoy states (henceforth referred to as DQKD) is currently the most promising technique.

Among the multitude of DQKD experimental techniques proposed in the literature, the technique described in [1], allows one to achieve the desired characteristics of DQKD, with a reduced cost and leading to a robust system. This technique amounts to what communication Engineers would refer to as Pulse Position Modulation (PPM) which allows the use of extremely simple measurements (the time of arrival of a pulse).

We propose to use a Photon Counting Detector (PCD) to generate soft information at the output of the quantum channel, as opposed to hard decisions about whether a given received signal is a logic-0 or a logic-1. Note that in its original form, the proposed BB84 technique does not require the use of PCD. Consider the application of soft coding to a specific scheme, i.e., the one of [1]. In this protocol Alice transmits attenuated coherent states (i.e., modulated pulses of a CW laser) that either she prepares with a mean photon number $N$ or blocks such states and transmits vacuum pulses. The $k$-th logical bit is encoded in a two pulse temporal sequence,

$$|0_k\rangle = |\sqrt{N}\rangle_{2k-1} |0\rangle_{2k}$$

$$|1_k\rangle = |0\rangle_{2k-1} |\sqrt{N}\rangle_{2k}$$

The time of arrival allows an unambiguous discrimination of the logical qubit. In order to check the presence of an eventual eavesdropper Alice, with a small frequency $f$, transmits a decoy state,

$$|d_k\rangle = |\sqrt{N}\rangle_{2k-1} |\sqrt{N}\rangle_{2k}$$

Due to the coherence of the laser, the two component of the decoy state have a precise phase relation and thus they always exit a specific gate of an interferometer at Bob's side preceded by an unbalanced Beam Splitter (BS), with transmission $t_B$. Such correlation also exists across the boundary between two alternating bits as well. After measurements, Bob announces when the detector after interferometer clicked (set 1, bits for the check) and when the detector at the other exit of BS clicked (set 2, bits to be used for the key reconstruction). The effect of eavesdropping is a breaking of coherence and can be estimated by the measurement of the set 1. After this test, Alice and Bob run error correction and privacy amplification on set 2 thus obtaining the key.

The performance of the protocol is quantified by the achievable secret key rate

$$R_{sk} = [R + 2p_d(1-R)](1-f)(1-h(Q)-I_{Eve})$$

Where, $R = 1 - \exp(-N t t_B \eta)$ is the counting rate when the communication channel has a transmission $t$, $p_d$ is the detector dark count rate, $h(Q)$ is the binary entropy function and $\eta$ is the detector quantum efficiency. By measuring the quantum bit error rate $Q$, Alice and Bob can estimate the fraction of information $I_{Eve}$ known by Eve. Thus the protocol is based on on/off detection; either the state is observed or it is not.

Once the decoy states have been identified and erased from the useful transmitted sequence, the equivalent channel model is simply that of a binary symmetric channel with bit error probability equal to the quantum bit error rate $Q$, as shown in Figure 2-(a). However, in order to minimize the effect of dark counts, one can envisage more elaborate strategies based on "soft" encoding and decoding.

One of the main ideas of our paper is that of using a detector discriminating the number of incident photons characterized by a certain set of $n$-photon dark count probabilities $p_{d,n}$. We note that we can generate and use a form of soft information even if a PCD is not used. The key attribute in using PCD is that we can generate soft information associated with the key data transmitted on the quantum channel.

For every number of detected photons one can associate a weight by comparing $p_{d,n}$ with the probability $p_n = \dfrac{\exp(-\mu)\mu^n}{n!}$ expected for the attenuated coherent state with average photon number $\mu$.

Let $N$ be the theoretical number of photons transmitted for every information bit, $N_{max}$ the maximum number of photons that can be detected in one symbol interval, with the positive sign the transmission or reception of a logic-0 and with the negative sign the transmission or reception of a logic-1, then we can model the discrete channel generated by QKD transmission using weak laser pulses as shown in Figure 2 (b), with an input random variable $Xw$ which at the generic k-th instant may assume the values $Xw_k \in (-N,+N)$, and an output random variable $Yw$ which at the generic k-th instant may assume the values $Yw_k \in (-N_{max},...,-2,-1,0,1,2,...,+N_{max})$, where $N_{max} > N$. Note that the model below is associated with transmission of one information bit which corresponds to two time slots (hence, the positive-negative designation in the probabilistic channel model), even though the number of photons detectable in a given slot is obviously only a positive quantity.

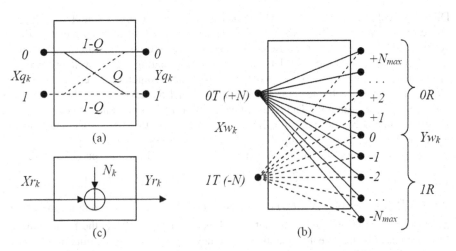

**Fig. 2.** Equivalent model for the single photon quantum channel (a), when WLP are used (b), and for the public channel (c)

The section about soft-metric based post-processing will describe how to extract useful soft metric values from the channel models of Figure 2 (a) and (b), and how to use them during the decoding and information reconciliation phases.

## 3   Classic Communication System

The public channel uses classic communication schemes, typically a radiofrequency link. Since very strong coding is allowed, the bit error rate of the classic channel is generally extremely small. Since the use of an optical link implies the presence of line of sight (LOS) between transmitter and receiver, fading can be excluded, and additive white Gaussian noise (AWGN) is generally the predominant impairment, so that the equivalent channel model shown in Figure 2 (c) can be used. In this figure, $Xr_k$ is the k-th transmitted symbol, $N_k \in \mathcal{N}(0,\sigma^2)$ is a Gaussian random variable with zero mean and variance $\sigma^2 = N_0/2 = E_b/2\eta_s$, where $\eta_s = E_b/N_0$ is the wireless link signal-to-noise ratio, and $Yr_k$ is the real sample obtained at the output of the public channel detector. If a bipolar transmission scheme is used, we can set $Xr_k \in (-\sqrt{E_b}, +\sqrt{E_b})$.

On the public link, no information bits can be transmitted, so only the redundant information of the considered feed-forward systematic block channel code with rate $R_b$ will be transmitted. If we denote by $n_q$ the number of information q-bits and by $r$ the number of redundant bits, in order to minimize the quantity of information derived by Eve from the public channel, $r$ must be minimized, and therefore the code rate,

$$R_c = \frac{n_q}{n_q + r}$$

must be maximized. For this reason, the use of long information blocks is required and Low density parity check codes (LDPC) with iterative soft decoding meet this criterion. For such codes, the information blocks of length $n = n_q + r$ in the order of tens of thousands can be used. In spite of the large block length (which guarantees high coding rate), the use of iterative soft decoding allows for acceptable decoding complexity.

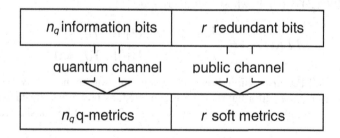

**Fig. 3.** Available bits and metrics at transmitter and receiver

Given the previous hypotheses, and denoting as $b_k$ the k-th redundant bit, we can write $Xr_k = \sqrt{E_b}(2b_k - 1)$ and $Yr_k = \sqrt{E_b}(2b_k - 1) + N_k$, where $Yr_k$ has a conditional probability density function

$$f_Y(Yr_k \mid b_k) = \frac{1}{\sqrt{2\pi\sigma^2}} \exp\left(-\frac{\left(Yr_k - \sqrt{E_b}(2b_k - 1)\right)^2}{2\sigma^2}\right)$$

The corresponding Log-Likelihood Ratio (LLR) value is,

$$LLR(Yr_k) = \log[P(Yr_k \mid b_k = 1)/P(Yr_k \mid b_k = 0)] \text{ is } LLR(Yr_k) = \frac{2Yr_k\sqrt{E_b}}{\sigma^2}.$$

This is the soft metric that will later be used by the post-processing block for the k-th redundant bit with sample value at the output of the detector equal to $Yr_k$.

### 3.1  Soft-Metric Based Post-Processing

Soft metric processing will be used for error correction, eavesdropping detection and privacy amplification, exploiting all the information available from the detectors at the output of the public and the quantum channels. This corresponds to using in the post processing algorithms not only the raw received information and redundancy bits, but all the soft information extracted from the channels, i.e., the log-likelihood ratios or LLRs [2], also denoted *soft metrics* in what follows.

### Evaluation of soft metrics for different channels

As far as the redundant bits are concerned, the real received signal samples $Yr_k \in R$ can be used to generate the soft metrics,

$$LLR(Yr_k) = 2Yr_k\sqrt{E_b}/\sigma^2.$$

As far as the information bits are concerned, when single photon transmission is used (or no soft information is extracted from a WLP based quantum channel in the absence of photon counting detector), the channel model shown in Figure 2 (a) must be considered, with transmitted bits $Xq_k \in GF(2) = \{0,1\}$ and received bits $Yq_k \in GF(2) = \{0,1\}$, whose soft metrics are [2],

$$LLR(Yq_k) = \begin{cases} \log[(1-Q)/Q] & \text{if } Yq_k = 1 \\ \log[Q/(1-Q)] & \text{if } Yq_k = 0 \end{cases}.$$

In the case of WLP transmission, however, when a photon counter is available at the receiver, additional soft information can be extracted, as previously discussed. In this case, the equivalent channel model shown in Figure 2(b) must be considered, and the soft likelihood metrics

$$LLR(Yw_k) = \log[P(Yw_k \mid b_k = 1)/P(Yw_k \mid b_k = 0)]$$
$$= \log[P(Yw_k \mid Xw_k = 1)/P(Yw_k \mid Xw_k = 0)]$$

can be expressed as

$$LLR(Yw_k = Yw(j)) =$$
$$\log[P(Yw_k = Yw(j) \mid Xw_k = 1)/P(Yw_k = Yw(j) \mid Xw_k = 1)]$$

## Joint use of metrics from different channels

In the decoding of LDPC for the information bits $Xq_k \in GF(2) = \{0,1\}$, we will use the soft metrics of the received raw bits $Yq_k \in GF(2) = \{0,1\}$

$$LLR(Yq_k) = \begin{cases} \log[(1-Q)/Q] & \text{if } Yq_k = 1 \\ \log[Q/(1-Q)] & \text{if } Yq_k = 0 \end{cases},$$

while, as far as the redundant bits $Xr_k \in GF(2) = \{0,1\}$ are concerned, we are dealing with the real received signal samples $Yr_k$ with soft metrics

$$LLR(Yr_k) = 2Yr_k \sqrt{E_b}/\sigma^2 .$$

These metrics must be jointly used and compared in the LDPC decoder. To achieve this, the metrics need to be compatible and comparable. Let us suppose that the equivalent Binary Symmetric Channel (BSC) model used in the quantum channel is obtained using 2 PAM as the modulation scheme with transmitted levels $\sqrt{Ep_b}(2b_k - 1)$, where $b_k$ are the transmitted bits, $\hat{b}_k$ are the decided raw bits, $Ep_b$ is the energy per bit and $\sigma_p^2$ is the noise variance per dimension (see Figure 4). Let us also denote the equivalent received sample as $Yp_k = \sqrt{Ep_b}(2b_k - 1) + Np_k$, so that

$$P(b_k \text{ in error}) = \frac{1}{2} erfc\left(\frac{\sqrt{Ep_b}}{\sqrt{2}\sigma_p}\right) = Q$$

where, the transmitted levels are $\pm\sqrt{Ep_b}$ and $Np_k \in \mathcal{N}(0, \sigma_p^2)$

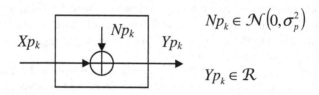

$$Np_k \in \mathcal{N}(0, \sigma_p^2)$$

$$Yp_k \in \mathcal{R}$$

**Fig. 4.** Equivalent model for the single photon quantum channel when using an equivalent 2 PAM modulation scheme

At this point we can assume that the noise is negligible, (i.e., that $Yp_k \cong \sqrt{Ep_b}(2b_k - 1) \cong \sqrt{Ep_b}(2\hat{b}_k - 1)$), allowing us to write the soft metric of the equivalent 2 PAM channel as,

$$LLR(Yp_k) = \frac{4Yp_k\sqrt{Ep_b}}{2\sigma_p^2} = \frac{4Ep_b(2\hat{b}_k - 1)}{2\sigma_p^2} =$$

$$= 4erfc^{-1}(2Q)(2\hat{b}_k - 1) = \begin{cases} +4erfc^{-1}(2Q) \text{ if } \hat{b}_k = 1 \\ -4erfc^{-1}(2Q) \text{ if } \hat{b}_k = 0 \end{cases}$$

The metric for the equivalent BSC Quantum channel shown in the last formula can be jointly used with the metric of the 2 PAM public channel for decoding.

### Iterative soft forward error correction

Once the appropriate soft (quantized on more than 1 bit) metrics have been associated with the various (information and redundant) bits, the situation is as depicted in Figure 3, and a soft metric based block decoder must be identified. Considering the basic result of Shannon's theorem that indicates that the longer the considered block length in Forward Error Correction (FEC) channel code, the larger its minimum distance and/or the higher its rate, we desire to use a very large block length $n_q + r$, which can pose huge constraints on the decoding complexity. To overcome this, Low Density Parity Check (LDPC) codes provide a viable solution.

In fact, in contrast to many classic codes, LDPC codes allow very fast iterative probabilistic decoding algorithms, in addition to being a class of linear capacity achieving codes. This makes LDPC codes attractive from both a theoretical and a practical point of view.

Finally, we can notice that the suggested decoding algorithm offers a soft-output, so that the decoded bits, obtained after a suitable and possibly variable number of iterations, are paired with their associated soft metrics as well, which can be used as an indicator on the reliability of the decoded bits.

### Convergence analysis

A typical decoded bit error performance curve of an iteratively decoded capacity achieving code transmitted over a binary symmetric channel (BSC), as a function of the transition probability P of the BSC, is illustrated in Figure 5. The performance of the code is divided into three regions: the low-performance region, the waterfall region and the (optional) error floor region.

The low-performance region is the region where transition probability P is higher than the minimum value required for the iterative decoding to converge. The value of the threshold transition probability P* depends on the size of considered code.

The performance region where a small decrease in the transition probability P results in a considerable improvement in the error probability is called the waterfall region, or sometimes the turbo cliff region when its slope is particularly steep.

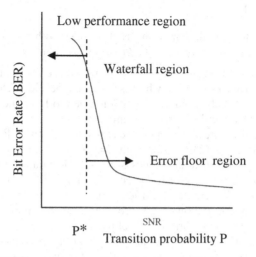

**Fig. 5.** Typical decoded BER performance curve of an iteratively decoded capacity achieving code

In the error floor region, when present, the performance does not improve significantly as the transition probability P decreases further, or however it decreases with a slope much smaller than in the waterfall region. We must note that the error floor region typically does not show a horizontal floor, but a change in slope with respect to the waterfall region.

Given these general characteristics of an LDPC code performance, and knowing that a quantum channel has a typical quantum BER $Q \approx 0.11$ or lower, and that the channel is not considered reliable because of eavesdropping if $Q > Q^* \approx 0.3$, i.e., if the QBER is larger than a given threshold $Q^*$, if an LDPC code is selected with threshold transition probability $P^* \approx Q^*$, the decoding process will not converge if the quantum channel is unreliable. The non-convergence could be detected by observing the erratic behavior of the decoded sequence reliability, allowing the use of the decoded codeword reliability monitoring as a form of quantum channel probe. Hence, we have a novel mechanism of detecting eavesdropping on the fly based on the inherent characteristics of the codes employed for information reconciliation.

**Privacy amplification**

The availability of soft output information, where the decoded bits are paired with the associated reliability, offers an instrument for performing efficient and selective privacy amplification, deleting from the decoded sequence (i.e., form the quantum key), the bits with low reliability, maintaining the most trusted information. This allows for a variable rate security key generation protocol which again to the best of our knowledge is entirely novel.

## Simulation Results

We have conducted simulations using LDPC codes with rate 0.5 and various block lengths. Weighed q-metric values $\alpha LLR(Yp_k)$ have been considered, with $0 < \alpha \leq 1$. The parameter $\alpha$ has been inserted in order to optimize the contribution of the information derived from the q-bits, which should not be too high since the q-bits are generally not very reliable, but should also not be too low, due to the fact that some information can however be extracted from them.

In Figure 6 and Figure 7 we report the simulated Bit Error Rate (BER) and Frame Error Rate (FER) of a LDPC code with $n=n_q+r=504$, $r=252$ and $R_c=0.5$ decoded with 100 iterations, for different values of the QBER parameter Q in the range 0.1 to 0.5, as a function of the weigh parameter $\alpha$. It can be observed how an optimal value of $\alpha$ in the order of 0.5 can be identified, which however depends on the QBER parameter $Q$. Optimizing $\alpha$ allows for a strong performance improvement, lowering the achievable error rates up to three orders of magnitude.

It can also be observed that the decoder performance converges to low BER and FER values only if $Q$ is smaller than roughly 0.15, allowing for reliability control, as previously described.

Finally, in Figure 8, the BER values of a $n=n_q+r=504$, $r=252$ and $R_c=0.5$ code are compared with those of a $n=n_q+r=1000$, $r=500$ and $R_c=0.5$ code, one for $Q$ in the range 0.12-0.5, showing that as expected, longer code blocks (and higher complexity) allow for better decoding performances.

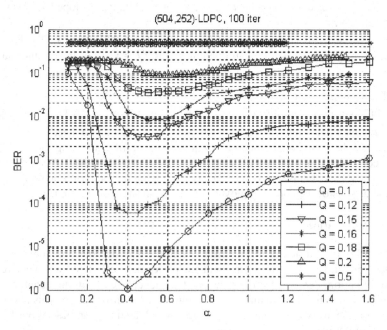

**Fig. 6.** BER performance of a LDPC code with $n=n_q+r=504$, $r=252$ and $R_c=0.5$, decoded with 100 iterations as a function of $Q$ and $\alpha$

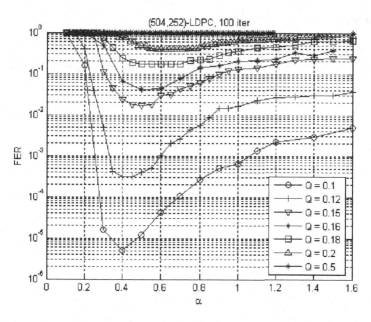

**Fig. 7.** FER performance of a LDPC code with $n=n_q+r=504$, $r=252$ and $R_c=0.5$, decoded with 100 iterations as a function of $Q$ and $\alpha$

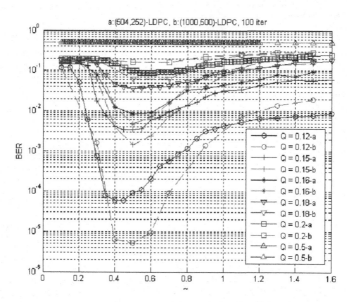

**Fig. 8.** Comparison between the BER performance of two LDPC codes with $R_c=0.5$, one with $n=n_q+r=504$, $r=252$ and one with $n=n_q+r=1000$, $r=500$ as a function of $Q$ and $\alpha$

# References

1. Stucki, D., et al.: Appl. Phys. Lett. 87, 194108 (2005)
2. Proakis, J.G., Salehi, M.: Digital Communications, 5th edn. McGraw-Hill, New York (2006)

# Using Redundancy-Free Quantum Channels for Improving the Satellite Communication

Laszlo Bacsardi, Laszlo Gyongyosi, and Sandor Imre

Department of Telecommunications, Budapest University of Technology and Economics,
H-1117 Budapest, Magyar tudosok krt. 2., Hungary
{bacsardi,gyongyosi,imre}@hit.bme.hu

**Abstract.** The quantum based systems could be the next steps in improving the satellite communication. The actual implementation of quantum cryptography systems would be invaluable, allowing for the first time the practical possibility of one-time-pad-encrypted, undecipherable communication, which will offer an essentially new degree of security in future satellite communications. They offer secure key distribution protocols, more efficient coding and communications methods than the classical solutions. However, the classical error coding methods could not be used in a quantum channel, which is required for the quantum communication. There are many quantum error coding algorithms which are based on some redundancy. However, we can construct a channel with zero redundancy error correction. In this paper we introduce three different quantum error correction approaches. The first one is based on eigenvectors and unitary transformations. In the second case we can create a redundancy-free channel using local unitary operation and unitary matrices, while the third one is based on entanglement. All of these can help to set up an efficient quantum channel for the quantum based satellite communication.

**Keywords:** quantum channel, space communication, error correction, redundancy-free.

## 1 Introduction

In last years the quantum theory based on quantum mechanical principles appeared in satellite communication offering answers for some of nowadays' technical questions. The quantum cryptography – cryptography based on quantum theory principles – gives better solutions for communication problems e.g. key distribution than the classical cryptographic methods, which have been found to have vulnerabilities in wired and wireless systems as well. The first *quantum cryptography* protocol, the BB84 [1] was introduced in 1984 and offered a solution for secure key distribution based on quantum theory principles like *no cloning*. The free-space Quantum Key Distribution (QKD) has almost a 20-year-old history. It started with the first published experiment in 1991. The 30 cm long optical path grew to 950 m under nighttime conditions in 1998 [2], and about to 10 km under daylight in 2002 [3], until the distance of 144 km was reached by an international research group in 2006 [4].

K. Sithamparanathan et al. (Eds.): PSATS 2010, LNICST 43, pp. 317–329, 2010.

The long distance quantum communication technologies in the future will far exceed the processing capabilities of current silicon-based devices. In current network technology, in order to spread *quantum cryptography*, interfaces able to manage together the quantum and classical channel must be implemented.

In our point of view, the quantum computing algorithms can be used to affirm our free-space communication in the following four ways: [5]

1. *Open-air communication*: we mean usually "horizontal" telecommunication that happens below 100-200 km height. Instead of optical cable air is used for channel.
2. *Earth-satellite communications*: it is usually between 300 and 800 km altitude. Signal encoding and decoding is used to produce quantum error correction that allows operation in noisy environment.
3. *Satellite broadcast*: the broadcast satellite is in orbit at 36,000 km and we want to send data from the satellite to the base stations located on the background. Quantum algorithms can improve the effective bandwidth, thus the brand is better utilized as in traditional cases.
4. *Inter-satellite communication*: the communication between satellites. Any kind of coding and encoding can be used, to increase stability [6].

Free space quantum communication for great distances have been developed and tested successfully. Currently, the quantum cryptographic key generation systems have been realized in metro-area networks over distances on tens kilometres, the free space based QKD solutions can achieve megabit-per-sec data rate communication. Long-distance open-air and satellite quantum communication experiments have been demonstrated the feasibility of extending quantum channel from the ground to a satellite, and in between satellites in free space. The satellite based single photon links already allow QKD on global scale.

## 2  Properties of Quantum Channel

The transmission of classical information over *satellite quantum channel* with no prior entanglement between the sender (Alice) and the recipient (Bob) is illustrated in Fig.1. The sender's classical information denoted by $A_i$ encoded into a quantum state $|\psi_A\rangle$. The encoded quantum states are sent over the satellite quantum channel, In the decoding phase, Bob measures state $|\psi_A\rangle$, the outcome of the measurement is the classical information $B_i$.

A qubit can be described by the two-dimensional Hilbert space $\mathbb{C}^2$, and the operators acting on the quantum system is generated by the Pauli matrices,

$$\sigma_x = \begin{pmatrix} 0 & 1 \\ 1 & 0 \end{pmatrix}, \ \sigma_y = \begin{pmatrix} 0 & -i \\ i & 0 \end{pmatrix}, \ \sigma_z = \begin{pmatrix} 1 & 0 \\ 0 & -1 \end{pmatrix}. \tag{1}$$

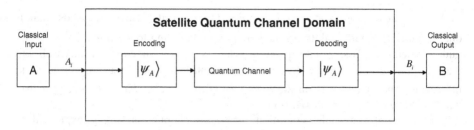

**Fig. 1.** Transmission classical information through the satellite quantum channel

In generally, for a Pauli matrix $\sigma_k$, $Tr(\sigma_k) = 0$ and $\sigma_k^2 = I$, where $k = x, y, z$. The set of states for a qubit in the computational basis $\{|0\rangle, |1\rangle\}$, is the *eigenbasis* of $\sigma_z$, thus $\sigma_z |0\rangle = |0\rangle$ and $\sigma_z |1\rangle = -|1\rangle$. A generic *pure* state can be given by

$$|\psi\rangle = \alpha|0\rangle + \beta|1\rangle, \tag{2}$$

and the *projector* of the state is $|\psi\rangle\langle\psi| = \frac{1}{2}(1 + \hat{n} \cdot \vec{\sigma})$, where $\hat{n}$ is the *Bloch vector*, and it can be given by $\hat{n} = \left(2\operatorname{Re}(\alpha\beta^*), 2\operatorname{Im}(\alpha\beta^*), |\alpha|^2 - |\beta|^2\right)$. For *pure* state the *norm* of Bloch vector is 1, and these vectors cover the Bloch sphere [1].

The *pure* quantum states of a *two-level* system can be given by unit vectors in spherical coordinates,

$$|\psi\rangle = \cos\frac{\theta}{2}|0\rangle + e^{i\varphi}\sin\frac{\theta}{2}|1\rangle \tag{3}$$

The state $|\psi\rangle$ can be given by state $|+\hat{n}\rangle$, and it is the eigenstate for the eigenvalue $+1$ of $\hat{n} \cdot \vec{\sigma}$, with $\hat{n} = \hat{n}(\theta, \varphi) = (\sin\theta\cos\varphi, \sin\theta\sin\varphi, \cos\theta)$ where $\theta \in [0, \pi]$ and $\varphi \in [0, 2\pi]$. A $\rho$ *mixed* state can be expressed by a $|\psi\rangle\langle\psi| = \frac{1}{2}(1 + \hat{n} \cdot \vec{\sigma})$ projector on a *pure* quantum state.

The quantum states sent to quantum channel can be represented by their density matrix. We denote by $\mathbf{S}(\mathbb{C}^d)$ the space of all density matrices of size $d \times d$, and we call it a *d-level* system [1, 7]. A one-qubit system is a *two-level* system [12], and its density matrix can be expressed as

$$\rho = \begin{pmatrix} \dfrac{1+z}{2} & \dfrac{x-iy}{2} \\ \dfrac{x+iy}{2} & \dfrac{1-z}{2} \end{pmatrix}, \ x^2 + y^2 + z^2 \le 1, \ x, y, z \in \mathbb{R}. \tag{4}$$

Alice's pure quantum state can be expressed by a density matrix $\rho_A$, whose rank is one, while a state with rank two is called *mixed*. According to the noise $\mathcal{N}$ of quantum channel, Alice's sent pure quantum state becomes a mixed state, thus Bob will receive a mixed state denoted by $\sigma_B$. A pure state has special meaning in quantum information theory and it is on the *boundary of the convex object*. A density matrix which is *not pure* is called *mixed state*.

For one-qubit states, the condition for $\rho$ to be pure is simply expressed as $x^2 + y^2 + z^2 = 1$, and it is on the surface of the Bloch ball [8].

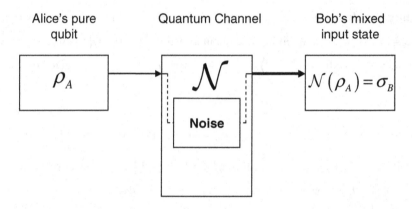

**Fig. 2.** General model of a noisy quantum channel

The map of the quantum channel is a trace-preserving and completely positive map, and it can be given by a linear transform $\mathcal{N}$ which maps quantum states to quantum states. The noise of the channel can be modeled by a linear transform

$$\mathcal{N} : M(\mathbb{C};d) \rightarrow M(\mathbb{C};d), \tag{5}$$

where $\mathcal{N}(\rho(\mathbb{C}^d)) \subset \rho(\mathbb{C}^d)$. Thus, if Alice sends quantum state $\rho(x, y, z)$ on the quantum channel, the channel maps it as follows:

$$\{(x', y', z') | \rho'(x', y', z') = \mathcal{N}(\rho(x, y, z)), (x, y, z)\}. \tag{6}$$

The image of quantum channel's linear transform $\mathcal{N}$ is an ellipsoid. To preserve the condition for density matrix $\rho$, the eavesdropper's cloning transformation $\mathcal{N}$ must be trace-preserving, i.e. $Tr\mathcal{N}(\rho) = Tr(\rho)$, and it must be completely positive, i.e. for any identity map $I$, the map $\mathcal{N} \otimes I$ maps a semi-positive Hermitian matrix into a semi-positive Hermitian matrix. Thus, in our satellite communication based, the channel is modeled by a *TPCP* map [9].

The capacity of the satellite channel $C(\mathcal{N})$ for given noise $\mathcal{N}$, can be defined as follows [9]:

$$C(\mathcal{N}) = \max_{p_1,\dots,p_n,\rho_1,\dots,\rho_n} S\left(\mathcal{N}\left(\sum_{i=1}^{n} p_i(\rho_i)\right)\right) + \sum_{i=1}^{n} p_i S(\mathcal{N}(\rho_i)), \qquad (7)$$

where $S(\rho) = -\rho \log \rho$ is the von-Neumann entropy.

For a well functioning communication we need a channel coding to handle the errors appearing in a communication channel. In quantum computing the classical error coding methods could not be used. This lead to develop quantum based error correction methods and algorithms. However, they are mostly based on quantum and not classical theorems [10]. In this paper we deal with new three redundancy-free solutions.

## 3 Achieving Redundancy-Free Channel with Eigenvectors

We would like to provide error correction with sending certain amount of qubits over a noisy quantum channel. The qubits are independent, each contains information that needs to be processed. We introduce three different redundancy-free solutions for the quantum communication. In the first one the noise of the quantum channel is modeled by a rotation angle.

The correction of the damaged quantum states is not possible in a classical representation, since the error correction of qubits is realized by unitary rotations.

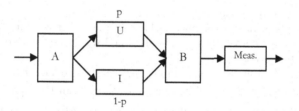

**Fig. 3.** Our channel model. $A$ transforms the initial qubits into a special form. $B$ has to produce the inverse of matrix $A$.

Our initial assumption is that the channel rotates the qubit with an $\omega$ degree, that is considered to be constant so far. We wish to create a system where error correction is possible. By this, not a complete restoration is meant. The transmission is considered successful when at the end of the channel the qubit remains in its original state's $\varepsilon$ environment.

To achieve this we mix the qubits and send them over the channel, as shown in Fig 3. What we expect is that at the measurement, the error for one qubit is distributed among the others in its environment (its neighbors). By being so, the error remains in an $\varepsilon$ environment for each qubit.

For the communication we use $n$ long qubits so that $2^n = N$, where $n$ is the length of the qubits and $N$ is the size of the space. We can construct a classical channel with zero redundancy error correction for any unitary channel, where the information itself is classical, coded into qubits. Let assume that we have a unitary channel with a $U$ unitary transformation, where the $U$ matrix is known. Because $U$ is unitary, it acts on each qubit sent over the channel and changes the qubit. After the successful transmission we have two cases for the eigenvalues

$$\text{I. } U = \begin{bmatrix} e^{j+\alpha} & 0 \\ 0 & e^{j+\alpha} \end{bmatrix} \otimes \begin{bmatrix} e^{j+\alpha} & 0 \\ 0 & e^{j+\alpha} \end{bmatrix} = \begin{bmatrix} e^{j2\alpha} & 0 \\ 0 & e^{j2\alpha} \end{bmatrix} \tag{8}$$

$$\text{II. } U = \begin{bmatrix} e^{j+\alpha} & 0 \\ 0 & e^{j+\alpha} \end{bmatrix} \otimes \begin{bmatrix} e^{j-\alpha} & 0 \\ 0 & e^{j-\alpha} \end{bmatrix} = \begin{bmatrix} 1 & 0 \\ 0 & 1 \end{bmatrix} = I \tag{9}$$

The description leads to a redundancy-free solution because the classical states are coded into the eigenvectors of the $U$ matrix. With the appropriate selection of the matrix $A$ we can restore one quantum bit sent over the channel without any other (redundant) information. The whole algorithm is described in [11] and [12].

## 4 Redundancy-Free Channel Coding

We consider the redundancy-free implementation of an unitary error correcting operator $\mathcal{R}_\theta$. The protocol achieves the redundancy-free quantum communication using *local unitary operations* and *unitary matrices*.

The whole algorithm is described in [12]. In this paper we introduce how the resources of the error correction could be used and we introduce a novel approach for multi-qubit error correcting.

The *error* of the satellite quantum channel can be modeled by a unitary rotation $\mathcal{R}_\theta^\dagger$, thus the error of the satellite quantum channel can be expressed as an angle $\theta_i \in [0, 2\pi)$. At the beginning of the communication, Alice sends her quantum state $\psi_A$ on the quantum channel, which transforms it to $|d\rangle = \mathcal{R}_\theta^\dagger(\psi_A)$ with given probability $p$. The error of the quantum channel is denoted by $\mathcal{R}_\theta^\dagger$.

In our error-correcting process if Bob tries to read the sent quantum state, he doesn't know the properties of the noise on the quantum channel. In our redundancy-free coding mechanism, Alice's initial state is $\psi_A$, the correction transformation denoted by $\mathcal{R}_\theta$. Bob uses a CNOT to correct the error of the quantum channel. In order to read the sent quantum bits correctly, Bob must rotate the $i$-th data quantum bit by the angle $\theta_i$ in the opposite direction of what the *error of the quantum channel rotated*.

Bob has a chance *not greater* than $\varepsilon = \sin^2(\theta_i)$ to correct the sent states, because he doesn't know the original rotation angle $\theta_i$ of the quantum channel's error on the $i$-th sent qubit. The rotation operation $\mathcal{R}_\theta$ of the error correcting mechanism can be given by the angle $|\theta\rangle$, where

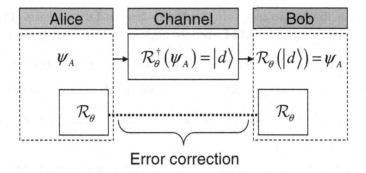

**Fig. 4.** Redundancy free error correction

$$|\theta\rangle = \frac{1}{\sqrt{2}}\left(e^{i\frac{\theta}{2}}|0\rangle + e^{-i\frac{\theta}{2}}|1\rangle\right). \tag{10}$$

The error-correcting method consists of a *control qubit, which* corresponds to the modified qubit $|d\rangle$, and a *target qubit*, which is equal to the *error-correction* angle state $|\theta\rangle$. To correct state $|d\rangle$ to $\psi_A$, Bob uses a simple CNOT transformation, thus our state is transformed to

$$|d\rangle \otimes |\theta\rangle \rightarrow \frac{1}{\sqrt{2}}\left(\mathcal{R}_\theta |d\rangle \otimes |0\rangle + \mathcal{R}_\theta^\dagger |d\rangle \otimes |1\rangle\right), \tag{11}$$

and therefore a projective measurement in the $\{|0\rangle, |1\rangle\}$ basis of the correction-state $|\theta\rangle$ will make the modified qubit $|d\rangle$ collapse either into the desired state $\mathcal{R}_\theta |d\rangle$ or into the wrong state $\mathcal{R}_\theta^\dagger |d\rangle$. Bob cannot determine the received state exactly, since he does not know angle of the error $\theta_i$. In this phase, Bob can not be sure whether the *i*-th quantum state $|d_i\rangle$ is identical to the original sent state $|\psi_i\rangle$ or not.

## 4.1  Quantum Probabilistic Channel Decoding

The noise $\mathcal{N}$ on the satellite quantum channel prepares a damaged state $|d_i\rangle = \cos\theta_i'|0\rangle + e^{i\alpha}\sin\theta_i'|1\rangle$. The damaged qubit can be identical to the original qubit $(|d_i\rangle = |\psi_i\rangle)$, with probability $\cos^2(\theta_i)$, and it differs $(|d_i\rangle \neq |\psi_i\rangle)$ with probability $\sin^2(\theta_i)$. The damaged state $|d_i\rangle$ can be projected to the original state $|\psi_i\rangle = \cos\theta_i|0\rangle + e^{i\alpha}\sin\theta_i|1\rangle$ successfully with probability

$$p_i = \cos^2\theta_i \cos^2(\theta_i - \theta_i') + \sin^2\theta_i \sin^2(\theta_i + \theta_i'). \tag{12}$$

In our system, the rotation angles are evenly distributed and the *maximum of the average probability* $\bar{p}_i$ can be reached when the angle of state $\theta_i^*$ is equal to zero. Bob gets correct angle $\theta_i$ with probability $p_i = 1 - \frac{1}{2}\sin^2 2\theta_i$, therefore Bob's total probability to receive $n$ quantum states with valid rotation angles $\theta_i$ is $P = \prod_{i=1}^{n}\left(1 - \frac{1}{2}\sin^2 2\theta_i\right)$. As we can conclude, by increasing linearly $n$, Bob's probability of error can be made arbitrarily small.

If we have sent an $N$-*length* state $\left|\theta^{(n)}\right\rangle$ on the satellite quantum channel, the $n$-qubit length unknown state $\left|\mathcal{R}_\theta^n\right\rangle$ has maximal entropy, thus

$$\int \frac{d\theta}{2\pi} \left|\mathcal{R}_\theta^n\right\rangle\left\langle\mathcal{R}_\theta^n\right| = \left(\frac{\mathbb{I}}{2}\right)^{\otimes n}, \tag{13}$$

where $\mathbb{I}$ is the identify operator. Let assume $p_\theta$ the probability of the successful transformation $\mathcal{R}_\theta\left(\mathcal{R}_\theta^\dagger|\psi_A\rangle\right) = |\psi_A\rangle$, which probability is independent of the damaged state $|d\rangle$.

## 4.2 Resources of Error Correcting

A projective measurement on the basis $\{|0\rangle, |1\rangle\}$ of the error-correcting state will make the damaged qubit collapse either into the desired state $\mathcal{R}_\theta|d\rangle$ or into the wrong state $\mathcal{R}_\theta^\dagger|d\rangle$, with each outcome having probability of 1/2. Therefore, Bob applies the gate of Fig.5. to prepare the *bad state* $\mathcal{R}_\theta^\dagger|d\rangle$ or the right state $\mathcal{R}_\theta|d\rangle$ with equal probability 1/2.

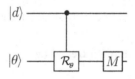

**Fig. 5.** The error correction of a damaged qubit $|d\rangle$ with single-qubit key state $|\theta\rangle$. The angle state is one qubit.

If Bob has an $l$-length qubit string $\otimes_{i=1}^{l}\left|2^{i-1}\theta\right\rangle$ to decode damaged state $|d\rangle$, Bob's failure probability will be only $\varepsilon = (1/2)^l$. The probability of wrong decoding is decreases exponentially with the size of the $|\theta\rangle$, the length of the error-correcting string denoted by $l$. Bob takes damaged qubit $|d\rangle$ as the control-bit, and takes error correcting qubit states $\otimes_{i=1}^{l}|2^{i-1}\theta\rangle$ as the target, therefore Bob evolves the transformation of $|d\rangle\otimes_{i=1}^{l}|2^{i-1}\theta\rangle$ into

$$\frac{1}{\sqrt{2^{l}}}\left(\sqrt{2^{l}-1}\,\mathcal{R}_{\theta}|d\rangle\otimes|right\rangle+\mathcal{R}_{\theta}^{(2^{l}-1)\dagger}|d\rangle\otimes|wrong\rangle\right),\tag{14}$$

where $\langle right|wrong\rangle=0$. The gate for improved decoding is shown in Fig.6.

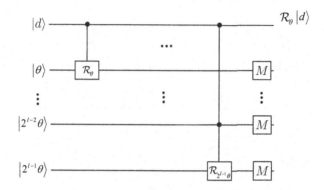

**Fig. 6.** The correction of a damaged state $|d\rangle$ with multi-qubit error-correcting state $\otimes_{i=1}^{l}|2^{i-1}\theta\rangle$. The error correcting angle is stored in an $l$-length quantum string.

Every rotation transformation $\mathcal{R}_{\theta}$ succeeds with probability $p=1-(1/2)^{l}$, with error probability $\varepsilon=(1/2)^{l}$. In Fig.7. we illustrate the simplified gate for multi-qubit error correction, the short diagonal line on the bottom line represents, that state $|\theta\rangle$ consists of several quantum bits.

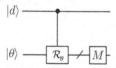

**Fig. 7.** The error correction of a damaged state $|d\rangle$ with state $|\theta\rangle$. The short diagonal line on the bottom line represents, that state $|\theta\rangle$ consists of several quantum bits.

Since Bob has a one-qubit length state for correct the damaged state, Bob fails to perform $\mathcal{R}_{\theta}\left(\mathcal{R}_{\theta}^{\dagger}|\psi_{A}\rangle\right)=|\psi_{A}\rangle$ with probability $p_{1}=1/2$. The average length of the required string is

$$\bar{l}=\sum_{l=1}^{\infty}p_{l}l=\sum_{l=1}^{\infty}\frac{l}{2^{l}}=2.\tag{15}$$

Thus, a two qubit error-correcting state for a single-qubit error correction is sufficient, on average.

## 4.3 Multi-qubit Error-Correcting

If Bob receives as $n$-bit length damaged string $|d_1\rangle\otimes...\otimes|d_n\rangle$, he can correct it with the $n$-bit length correction-key $|\theta_1\rangle\otimes|\theta_2\rangle\otimes...\otimes|\theta_n\rangle$ *in one-step*, as it is shown in Fig.8.

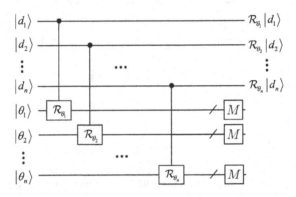

**Fig. 8.** The correction of an $n$-length multi-qubit damaged string $|d_1\rangle\otimes...\otimes|d_n\rangle$ with an $n$-length multi-qubit *string* $|\theta_1\rangle\otimes|\theta_2\rangle\otimes...\otimes|\theta_n\rangle$. The correction state is realized by an $l$-length multi-qubit string $\otimes_{i=1}^{l}|2^{i-1}\theta\rangle$.

Using our method, all the rotation transformations are realized by an $l$-length multi-qubit string, therefore every error correction transformation $\mathcal{R}_{\theta_i}$ on the corresponding damaged qubit $|d_i\rangle$ can be implemented with success probability $1-(1/2)^l$.

## 5   Achieving Redundancy-Free Channel with Entanglement

The entanglement is the ability of qubits to interact over any distance instantaneously. The EPR-states do not exactly communicate, however the results of measurements on each quantum states are correlated. The entangled pure states are those multipartite systems, that cannot be represented in the form of a simple tensor product of subsystem states $|\Psi\rangle\neq|\psi_1\rangle\otimes|\psi_2\rangle\otimes...\otimes|\psi_n\rangle$, where $|\psi_i\rangle$ are states of local subsystems. An entangled pair is a single quantum system in a superposition of equally possible states, and the entangled state contains no information about the individual particles, only that they are in opposite states. The entangled states cannot be prepared from unentangled states by any sequence of local actions of two distant partners, and the classical communication can not help to generate EPR-states. The Bell states can be defined as $\Psi^{\pm} \equiv \frac{1}{\sqrt{2}}(|00\rangle \pm |11\rangle)$ and $\Phi^{\pm} \equiv \frac{1}{\sqrt{2}}(|01\rangle \pm |10\rangle)$.

The correction of the damaged state $|d\rangle$ can be realized by a shared EPR-state between Alice and Bob. Our code uses entangled qubits to transfer classical information through the channel. During the communication process Alice encodes the classical information into entangled pairs, then keeps one qubit of the pair and sends the other one to Bob in the quantum channel. Because the information was encoded into an entangled pair, they now share classical information. After receiving the qubit, Bob performs a measurement on it. Because of the properties of entanglement, this makes the measurement on the other qubit of the pair deterministic. When Alice measures its qubit with $t_{waiting}$ time after it was sent, she gains knowledge on what Bob had measured. If the transmission was successful, which means Bob got the correct classical state after measuring, and then Alice sends the next qubit. If the measurement provided a false information, Alice waits a $t_{error}$ time before sending the next qubit, thus letting Bob know that a bit error was occurred during the communication. In that case Bob flips the measured classical bit.

This code does not need any synchronization other than a well chosen $t_{waiting}$. On any noisy channel, because Alice is monitoring the measurement results, a BER of 0% can be achieved without having to send additional qubits through the channel. This makes the efficiency of the code better than any classical and many quantum codes. The transmission on the channel is redundancy-free as well. Since only the measured states carry information, the circuit which produces the entangled pair can be simple, like a CNOT (Controlled NOT) gate. The circuit is shown in Fig.9.

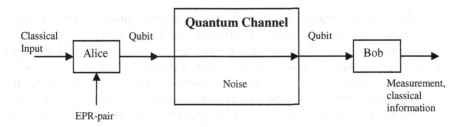

**Fig. 9.** Transmission over a quantum channel with the help of entanglement

The $t_{waiting}$ time can be conciliated during an initialization process, measuring the communication time during sending and receiving back a test message with $l$ length (and with a $t_{timestamp}$). Assuming that the channel is a bidirectional channel (the delays are same in both ways) we can calculate the $t_{waiting}$ as

$$t_{waiting} = \left(t_{sendingAlice2Bob} + t_{sendingBob2Alice}\right)/2 + \varepsilon \qquad (16)$$

where $t_{sendingAlice2Bob}$ is the period of sending the message from Alice to Bob, and $t_{sendigBob2Alice}$ is the period of sending the message from Bob to Alice, and $\varepsilon$ is an arbitrarily chosen little number.

For the successful communication the following condition should be set for $t_{error}$

$$\left(t_{waiting}/\lambda\right) < t_{error} \ll \left(t_{waiting}/2\right) \qquad (17)$$

where $\lambda$ depends on the physical properties of the channel.

However, the loss of a qubit, which happens often in the free-space communication, can cause error during the process. Thus this simple solution can be used in a free space channel only in an advanced form, where Bob knows the sending frequency of Alice, and Bob measures the time differences between two arrived qubits. If the interval between two received qubits is bigger than $t_{waiting} + t_{error} + \varepsilon$, this means that one qubit has been lost during the transmission. With elaborated $t_{waiting}$ and $t_{error}$ time we can provide a redundancy-free solution for quantum transmission, where the interval of the sending period carries the information about the possible error. With this we illustrated an EPR and time based redundancy free error correction method for free-space communication.

# 6  Conclusions

One of the primary requirements of long-distance and free-space quantum communication is the capability of the effective transmission of quantum states in non-ideal, noisy environments. The free-space and satellite quantum channel could be the way to increase significantly the distance limit of current quantum communication systems. The current earthbound free-space quantum channels have the advantage in that they can be combined with satellite quantum communication. In the future, we will be able to overcome the current distance limits in quantum communication by transmitting EPR-states from space to Earth. To exploit the advantages of free-space quantum channels, it will be necessary to use space and satellite technology. The free space optical technology has been combined successfully with entangled pairs and satellite communication.

In classical systems, error correction can be performed only by introduced redundancy within the communication. The error correction capabilities are required for any form of a large scale computation and communication. In classical systems the simplest form to give redundancy to the communication is to encode each bit more than once, however in quantum communication the error correction can be made by much more complex strategies. Currently, many quantum error correction techniques have been introduced to overcome the limitations of quantum theory principles. In these proposals, redundancy is required for successful error correction, because the quantum states are cannot be cloned perfectly, or cannot be measured nondestructively.

In our paper, we have presented a fundamentally new method to realize quantum communication with zero redundancy error correction. Our zero redundancy quantum error correction approaches are based on eigenvectors with unitary transformations, local unitary operations, and entanglement.

The presented redundancy free coding mechanisms can help to set up an efficient quantum channel for the quantum based satellite communication.

# References

[1] Imre, S., Ferenc, B.: Quantum Computing and Communications: An Engineering Approach. Wiley, Chichester (2005)

[2] Buttler, W.T., Hughes, R.J., Kwiat, P.G., Lamoreaux, S.K., Luther, G.L., Morgan, G.L., Nordholt, J.E., Peterson, C.G., Simmons, C.M.: Practical free-space quantum key distribution over 1 km (arXiv:quant-ph/9805071)

[3] Hughes, R.J., Nordholt, J.E., Derkacs, D., Peterson, C.G.: Practical free-space quantum key distribution over 10 km in daylight and at night. New Journal of Physics 4, 43.1–43.14(2002)

[4] Schmitt-Manderbach, T., Weier, H., Fürst, M., Ursin, R., Tiefenbacher, F., Scheidl, T., Perdigues, J., Sodnik, Z., Kurtsiefer, C., Rarity, J.G., Zeilinger, A., Weinfurter, H.: Experimental Demonstration of Free-Space Decoy-State Quantum Key Distribution over 144 km. Physical Review Letters, 2007 PRL 98, 10504 (2007)

[5] Bacsardi, L.: Using Quantum Computing Algorithms in Future Satellite Communication. Acta Astronautica 57(2-8), 224–229 (2005)

[6] Bacsardi, L.: Satellite communication over quantum channel. Acta Astronautica 61(1-6), 151–159 (2007)

[7] Nielsen, M.A., Chuang, I.L.: Quantum Computation and Quantum Information. Cambridge University Press, Cambridge (2000)

[8] Gyongyosi, L., Imre, S.: Fidelity Analysis of Quantum Cloning Based Attacks in Quantum Cryptography. In: Proceedings of the 10th International Conference on Telecommunications - ConTEL 2009, Zagreb, Croatia, 2009.06.08-2009.06.10. 2009, paper 53, pp. 221–228, (2009)

[9] Lamberti, P.W., Majtey, A.P., Borras, A., Casas, M., Plastino, A.: Metric character of the quantum Jensen-Shannon divergence. Physical Review A (Atomic, Molecular, and Optical Physics) 77(5), 052311 (2008)

[10] Poulin, D.: Stabilizer Formalism for Operator Quantum Error Correction, Quant-ph/0508131(2005)

[11] Bacsardi, L., Berces, M., Imre, S.: Redundancy-Free Quantum Theory Based Error Correction Method in Long Distance Aerial Communication. In: 59th IAC Congress, Glasgow, Scotland, 29 September - 3 October (2008)

[12] Bacsardi, L., Gyongyosi, L., Imre, S.: Solutions for Redundancy-Free Error Correction in Quantum Channel. In: QuantumCom 2009. LNICST, vol. 36, pp. 117–124 (2010)

# Efficient Long Range Communication by Quantum Injected Optical Parametric Amplification

Chiara Vitelli[1,2], Lorenzo Toffoli[1],
Fabio Sciarrino[1,3], and Francesco De Martini[1,4]

[1] Dipartimento di Fisica, "Sapienza" Università di Roma, piazzale Aldo Moro 5,
I-00185 Roma, Italy
chiara.vitelli@gmail.com
[2] Consorzio Nazionale Interuniversitario per le Scienze Fisiche della Materia
[3] Istituto Nazionale di Ottica Applicata, largo Fermi 6, I-50125 Firenze, Italy
[4] Accademia Nazionale dei Lincei, via della Lungara 10, I-00165 Roma, Italy

**Abstract.** Free-space optical communications over long distances are associated with severe losses while the natural limit for the energy associated to a single bit of information is just one photon. In order to enhance the transmission Efficiency we propose the use of macro qubits consisting of thousand of photons. We investigate the Fidelity of the transmission of a macro-qubit generated by quantum injected optical parametric amplification (QI-OPA) along a lossy communication channel. The realization of a QI-OPA micro-macro Teleportation protocol is considered.

**Keywords:** Quantum Communication, Quantum Teleportation, Optical Parametric Amplifier.

## 1 Transmission of Amplified Quantum States over a Lossy Channel

The transmission of quantum states between two or several space-like separated communication stations is an important task for implementing relevant quantum Information, quantum Cryptographic and Teleportation protocols. These ones generally involve the distribution between distant parties of entangled states [1] whose Fidelity is impaired by noise and by losses along the quantum channels, e.g. contributed by the dark counts of the detectors and by the absorptive losses in optical fibers. In particular, the communication resources provided by the present technology limit the distance for faithful entanglement distribution to the order of $100 km$ [2]. In order to overcome these problems it has been suggested the use of quantum repeaters, a new technology which still needs significant developments, or the adoption of free-space links [3,4]. Recently the demonstration of the successful transmission of an entangled photon pair over a $144 Km$ free-space link has been reported [5]. It has been shown that, even thought the presence of extreme attenuation due to turbulent atmospheric effects, the free-space

K. Sithamparanathan et al. (Eds.): PSATS 2010, LNICST 43, pp. 330–339, 2010.

transmission preserves the fidelity of the entangled photon pairs. However the attenuations along the communication channel due to diffraction, atmospheric absorption, turbulence and to device imperfections led to a link Efficiency for single photon communication equal to about to -30 dB.

In this work we propose a relevant improvement of that communication scenario by exploiting the transmission of a macro-qubit produced by a Quantum-Injected Optical Parametric Amplifier (QI-OPA) [6,7] over a lossy communication channel. We expect to attain a large enhancement of the communication Efficiency over the single photon transmission. Luckily enough the QI-OPA generated multiphoton state, consisting of thousands of photons depending on the non - linear (NL) *exponential amplification gain* ($g$) , has been proved to be a *unitary* and *information preserving* process that keeps all quantum properties of the injected qubit [8]. Furthermore, it has been proved to be quite resilient to decoherence and losses [9]. More specifically, when a *polarization* qubit $|\pm\rangle = 2^{-1/2}(|H\rangle \pm |V\rangle)$, being $|H\rangle$ and $|V\rangle$ the horizontal and vertical photon polarization states, are injected into the QI-OPA amplifier, the output state is expressed as:

$$|\Phi^{\pm}\rangle = \sum_{i,j=0}^{\infty} \gamma_{ij} |(2i+1)\pm, (2j)\mp\rangle \tag{1}$$

where $\gamma_{ij} \equiv \sqrt{(1+2i)!(2j)!}(i!j!)^{-1}C^{-2}(-\frac{\Gamma}{2})^j\frac{\Gamma^i}{2}$, $C \equiv \cosh g$, $\Gamma \equiv \tanh g$, being $g = \chi t$ the NL gain. There $|p+, q-\rangle$ stands for a state with $p$ photons with polarization $\vec{\pi}_+$ and $q$ photons with $\vec{\pi}_-$. The macro-states $|\Phi^+\rangle$, $|\Phi^-\rangle$ are orthonormal, i.e. $\langle{}^i\Phi|\Phi^j\rangle = \delta_{ij}$. Our goal is to investigate whether and how the distinguishability between the two states is modified after the transmission over a lossy channel.

Let us consider the macro-qubit $|\Phi^+\rangle$, obtained by the amplification of a single photon qubit state $|+\rangle$:

$$|\Phi^+\rangle = \frac{1}{C^2} \sum_{ij}^{\infty} \left(\frac{-\Gamma}{2}\right)^j \left(\frac{\Gamma}{2}\right)^i \frac{\sqrt{(2j)!(2i+1)!}}{j!i!}|(2i+1)+, 2j-\rangle_b$$

$$= \frac{1}{C^2} \sum_{ij}^{\infty} \left(\frac{-\Gamma}{2}\right)^j \left(\frac{\Gamma}{2}\right)^i \frac{(b_+^\dagger)^{2i+1}}{j!} \frac{(b_-^\dagger)^{2j}}{i!}|0\rangle \tag{2}$$

We consider the case in which the macro qubit propagates along a noisy channel, on the spatial mode b. The losses are modelled by a beam splitter $(BS)$ with transfer function

$$b_\pm = \sqrt{\tau}c_\pm + i\sqrt{1-\tau}\,d_\pm \tag{3}$$

where $\mathbf{b}$ is the propagation spatial mode of the macro-qubit and the *transmittivity* ($\tau$) represents the *efficiency* of the free-space link, see Fig.1. The macro-qubit state transmitted by $BS$ is found to be:

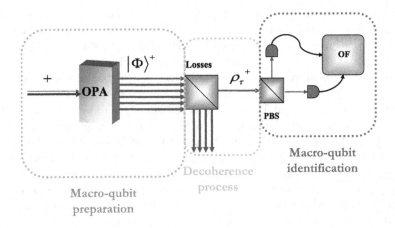

**Fig. 1.** Conceptual scheme of the proposed experiment: the macro-qubit generated by the QIOPA device undergoes a high losses transmission process, represented by the beam splitter model. The transmitted state is then analyzed and detected through a dichotomic measurement.

$$|\Phi^+\rangle^{out} = \frac{1}{C^2} \sum_{ij}^{\infty} \sum_{k}^{2i+1} \sum_{l}^{2j} \binom{2i+1}{k}\binom{2j}{l}\left(\frac{-\Gamma}{2}\right)^j\left(\frac{\Gamma}{2}\right)^i \frac{1}{j!i!}\left(\sqrt{\tau}c_+^\dagger\right)^k\left(i\sqrt{1-\tau}d_+^\dagger\right)^{2i+1-k}$$

$$\left(\sqrt{\tau}c_-^\dagger\right)^l\left(i\sqrt{1-\tau}d_-^\dagger\right)^{2j-l}|0\rangle|0\rangle = \frac{1}{C^2}\sum_{ij}^{\infty}\sum_{k}^{2i+1}\sum_{l}^{2j}\left(\frac{-\Gamma}{2}\right)^j\left(\frac{\Gamma}{2}\right)^i \frac{1}{j!}\frac{1}{i!}\frac{\sqrt{\tau}^{k+l}}{\sqrt{k!}\sqrt{l!}}$$

$$\frac{(i\sqrt{1-\tau})^{2i+1+2j-k-l}(2i+1)!(2j)!}{\sqrt{(2i+1-k)!(2j-l)!}}|k+,l-\rangle_d|(2i+1-k)+,(2j-l)-\rangle_c \qquad (4)$$

The portion of the state over the spatial mode **d** is lost over the environment while the transmitted state is represented by the density matrix:

$$\rho_\tau^+ = (Tr\rho_{out}^+) = \frac{1}{C^4}\sum_{i,j}^{\infty}\sum_{m,n}^{\infty}\sum_{w=0}^{min\{2i+1,2m+1\}}\sum_{z=0}^{min\{2j,2n\}}(-1)^{j+n}\frac{\Gamma^{j+n+i+m}}{2}\frac{(2i+1)!(2j)!}{j!i!}$$

$$\frac{(2m+1)!(2n)!}{m!n!}\frac{\tau^{i+j+m+n+1-w-z}(1-\tau)^{w+z}}{\sqrt{(2i+1-w)!(2j-z)!}\sqrt{(2m+1-w)!(2n-z)!}}\frac{1}{w!z!}$$

$$|2i+1-w,2j-z\rangle\langle 2m+1-w,2n-z| \qquad (5)$$

The measurement of the macro qubit is then realized via a dichotomic strategy involving the action of the O-Filter (OF) device, first introduced by Ref.[8]. We briefly summarize the details of the macro-qubit detection process: the multiphoton state is analyzed in polarization and detected by two photomultipliers. The two intensity signals, proportional to the orthogonally polarized photon numbers $n$ and $m$, are compared shot-by-shot by the OF electronic device whose filtering action is outlined as follows. When the number of detected photons $m_\varphi$ bearing the $\pi_\varphi$ polarization, exceeds $n_{\varphi\perp}$, bearing the $\pi_{\varphi\perp}$ polarization orthogonal to

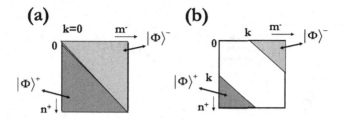

**Fig. 2.** Macro state identification: (a) If the O-Filter threshold is equal to zero, the measurement on the macro-qubit turns out to be purely dichotomic. (b) For a non-zero k value, the measurement performed on the macro state involves the presence of inconclusive results, that correspond to the non-unbalanced detected pulses.

$\pi_\varphi$, by a ceratin adjustable threshold quantity $k$, i.e. $m_\varphi - n_{\varphi\perp} > k$, the $(+1)$ outcome is assigned to the event and the detection of the macro-state $|\Phi^\varphi\rangle$ is assumed. On the contrary, when the condition $n_{\varphi\perp} - m_\varphi > k$ is met, the $(-1)$ outcome is assigned and detection of $|\Phi^{\varphi\perp}\rangle$ is assumed. Finally, an inconclusive result $(0)$ is obtained when the detected pulses are balanced: $|n_{\varphi\perp} - m_\varphi| < k$.

The OF based measurement performed on the macro state $|\Phi^+\rangle$, after transmission over the high losses channel, can be represented by the following operator:

$$R^\pm(k) = \sum_{n=k}^{\infty} \sum_{m=0}^{k} |n+, m-\rangle\langle n+, m-| \qquad (6)$$

We define the $k$−dependent Visibility $V(k)$ of the macro-state, i.e. the efficiency in discriminating the orthogonal macro-qubits, as:

$$V(k) = \frac{R_{max}(k) - R_{min}(k)}{R_{max}(k) + R_{min}(k)} \qquad (7)$$

where $R_{max} = \langle R^{+1}(k)\rangle_{\rho_T^+}$ represent the probability of identifying the macro state after the transmission as $|\Phi^+\rangle$, and $R_{min} = \langle R^{-1}(k)\rangle_{\rho_T^+}$ correspond to the probability of identifying the macro state as $|\Phi^-\rangle$. By increasing the value of $k$ a better discrimination, and hence a higher Visibility can be achieved. The Visibility is related to the Fidelity of the macro state by the relation [10]:

$$F(k) = \frac{V(k) + 1}{2} \qquad (8)$$

We are now interested in measuring the macro qubit in a dichotomic way by no O-Filtering, i.e. by choosing the threshold: $k = 0$. In these conditions let's consider the value of the obtained Fidelity $F$ as a function of the non linear gain $g$ of the amplifier. We report in fig.3 the trend of the Fidelity for different values of the transmission Efficiency of the communication channel. By plotting the value of $F(n)$ as a function of the average number of transmitted photons,

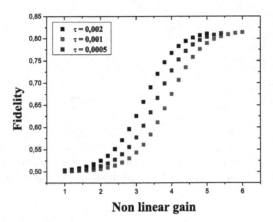

**Fig. 3.** Trend of the visibility as a function of the non linear gain of the amplifier. We observe that, by fixing the transmission efficiency, the value of the fidelity increases by increasing the gain of the amplifier. These trends are reported for different value of the transmission efficiency.

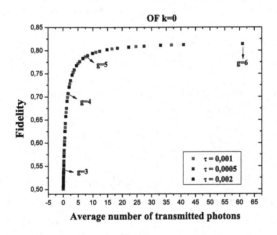

**Fig. 4.** Trend of the fidelity as a function of the average transmitted photons

we obtain the plot in fig.4, by which we deduce that the asymptotic Fidelity value that can be reached through a dichotomic measurement with: $k = 0$ is $F \sim 0.82$ corresponding to an asymptotic Visibility $V \sim 0.64$. The asymptotic value $F$ is determined by the ratio between the number of detected photons that are correctly attributed to the corresponding macrostate and the number of photons that, still belonging to the same macrostate, are interpreted incorrectly. Of course, by increasing the value of $k$ a large Efficiency and Visibility are

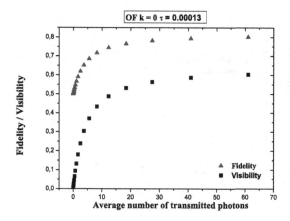

**Fig. 5.** Trend of the fidelity and visibility as a function of the transmitted photons

attained at the cost of increasing the probability of inconclusive results, i.e. of decreasing the overall measurement Efficiency ($QE$) of the apparatus.

Similar results are obtained for more realistic simulation parameters as, for instance, by considering a $-30dB$ loss of the transmission channel (as the one presented in Ref.[3]). In that case, by taking into account the reduced quantum efficiency ($QE_p \sim 0.13$) of the IR photomultipliers used to detect the macro-states we may consider the overall efficiency of the transmission process $\tau = 0.00013$. The related trends of the Fidelity and Visibility in these conditions are reported by Fig.5. Our results show that, respect to the single - photon qubit state, the transmission of the macro-qubit over a lossy channel allows to increase the Efficiency of the transmission process to its maximum value for every value of the "channel efficiency", i.e. of the model BS transmittivity $\tau$ (see Fig.6). This can be easily obtained by properly increasing the value of the exponential gain $g$ respect to the value of $\tau$. This can be easily done by increasing the power of the pump laser of the QI-OPA system.

## 2   Micro-Macro Teleportation

As already pointed out, the asymptotic values of Fidelity and Visibility shown by Figures 4 and 5 would hardly allow to perform non locality tests, as required in many QKD applications. As said, increasing values of $F(k)$ and $V(k)$, together with and a decreasing value of $QE$, can be attained by increasing the value of the threshold $k > 0$. This is shown by fig.7 in which is reported the value of the Fidelity as a function of the OF threshold k ($\tau$ and $g$ fixed).

In any case, the reported values of $F$ and $V$ obtained with $k = 0$ are sufficient to implement different quantum information protocols, such as the Teleportation. As it is well known, the latter protocol introduced by Bennett et al. in Ref.[11],

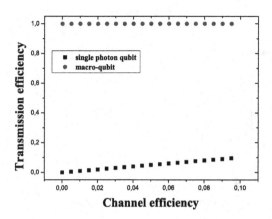

**Fig. 6.** Comparison between the transmission efficiency of the single photon qubit and of the macro-qubit state

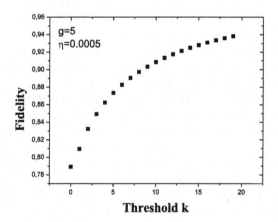

**Fig. 7.** Trend of the Fidelity as a function of the OF threshold $k$. A more sophisticated measurement allows to increase the value of the Fidelity, at the cost of decreasing the quantum efficiency of the overall process.

consists of a nonlocal transfert of the state of an unknown qubit onto another far apart particle.

With the present system we could realize the teleportation of a single-photon qubit between the Alice's site and a corresponding photonic macrostate transmitted by a long-range free space link to a Bob's site, Fig.8. More specifically, an EPR source generates a polarization entangled photon pair over the spatial modes $k_A$ and $k_B$. The single photon on mode $k_B$ is amplified by a "phase covariant cloning machine" [7,12].

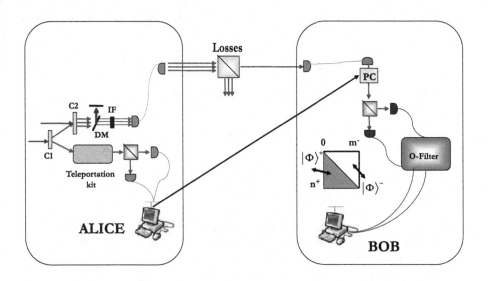

**Fig. 8.** Experimental scheme for the micro-macroscopic photonic teleportation

At the Alice's site the *Teleportation kit* realizes the conversion of polarization into momentum state, and the qubit to be teleported is encoded into the polarization degree of freedom of the single photon state. The Bell measurement at Alice's site identifies the quantum transformation that will be realized at Bob's site. At last, at Bob's site, a far apart station, the state is analyzed by an O-Filter. By a coincidence procedure between Alice and Bob the success of the Teleportation will be assessed.

Let us analyze in more details the proposed Teleportation experiment. As shown in fig.8 an entangled pair of two photons in the singlet state (9) is produced through spontaneous parametric down-conversion (SPDC) by the NL crystal 1 (C1) pumped by a pulsed UV pump beam:

$$\frac{1}{\sqrt{2}} \left( |H\rangle_A |V\rangle_B - |V\rangle_A |H\rangle_B \right) \tag{9}$$

There the labels $A, B$ refer to particles associated respectively with the spatial modes $\mathbf{k}_A$ and $\mathbf{k}_B$. The photon belonging to $\mathbf{k}_B$, together with a strong UV pump beam, is injected into an optical parametric amplifier consisting of a NL crystal 2 (C2) pumped by the beam $\mathbf{k}'_P$. The crystal is oriented for *collinear* operation over the two linear polarization modes, respectively horizontal and vertical. The interaction Hamiltonian of the parametric amplification $\widehat{H} = i\chi\hbar\widehat{a}_H^\dagger\widehat{a}_V^\dagger + h.c.$ acts on the single spatial mode $\mathbf{k}_B$ where $\widehat{a}_\pi^\dagger$ is the one photon creation operator associated to the polarization $\overrightarrow{\pi}$ [12]. The overall output state amplified by the OPA apparatus is expressed, in any polarization equatorial basis $\left\{\overrightarrow{\pi}_\phi = 2^{-1/2}\left(\overrightarrow{\pi}_H + e^{i\phi}\overrightarrow{\pi}_V\right), \overrightarrow{\pi}_{\phi\perp} = \overrightarrow{\pi}_\phi^\perp\right\}$, by the Micro-Macro entangled state:

$$|\Sigma\rangle_{A,B} = 2^{-1/2}\left(|\Phi^\phi\rangle_B |1\phi^\perp\rangle_A - |\Phi^{\phi\perp}\rangle_B |1\phi\rangle_A\right) \tag{10}$$

where the mutually orthogonal multi-particle "macro-states" are (see eq.1):

$$|\Phi^\phi\rangle_B = \sum_{i,j=0}^\infty \gamma_{ij} \frac{\sqrt{(1+2i)!(2j)!}}{i!j!} |(2i+1)\phi; (2j)\phi^\perp\rangle_B$$

$$|\Phi^{\phi\perp}\rangle_B = \sum_{i,j=0}^\infty \gamma_{ij} \frac{\sqrt{(1+2i)!(2j)!}}{i!j!} |(2j)\phi; (2i+1)\phi^\perp\rangle_B$$

When an equatorial qubit $|\varphi\rangle = |H\rangle + e^{i\varphi}|V\rangle$ is injected into the amplifier, the ensemble average photon number $N_\pm$ on mode $\mathbf{k}_B$ with polarization $\pi_\pm$ is found to depend on the phase $\varphi$ as follows:

$$N_\pm = \overline{m} + \frac{1}{2}(2\overline{m}+1)(1 \pm \cos\varphi) \tag{11}$$

where $\overline{m} = \sinh^2 g$ is the average number of photons emitted by the OPA for each polarization mode in absence of quantum injection.

To show that the Teleportation works for any basis on the "equatorial" Hilbert subspace on the qubit Bloch sphere, we choose the linearly polarized $\{\pi_+, \pi_-\}$ basis set, and the circularly polarized one $\{\pi_R, \pi_L\}$ set. In order to demonstrate that the experimental results cannot be simulated by a "classical" process, the experimental Teleportation fidelity should be found: [13,14]:

$$\mathcal{F} > \frac{3}{4} \tag{12}$$

The experimental measurement would involve the evaluation of the Visibility by taking into account the coincidences between detectors at Alice's site and the output of the OF device at Bob's site, for different choices of the preparation basis and of the analysis basis. If the Macroscopic state is projected onto the same polarization state as the teleported qubit we would obtain a maximum of coincidences $C_{max}$. On the contrary when the state is the orthogonal one, we register a minimum of coincidences $C_{min}$. Hence, in order to demonstrate the teleportation protocol we have to obtain a Visibility as large as:

$$\mathcal{V} = \frac{C_{max} - C_{min}}{C_{max} + C_{min}} > \frac{1}{2} \tag{13}$$

In conclusion, we have analyzed theoretically the transmission of Macro - qubits along lossy channel. We have found that, thanks to the robustness and to the resilience to decoherence of the Macro-state generated by a QI-OPA, a faithful information can be transmitted over a long range channel with an Efficiency nearly equal to one. By adoption of a detection O-Filter with a threshold

$k = 0$ the Fidelity of the state is less than the one achieved by a single photon transmitted state. However, the Fidelity can be largely increased by increasing the value of the OF threshold: $k > 0$.

In summary, we have proposed our Micro - Macro parametric amplification system as an appealing long - range application of the quantum Teleportation protocol. Furthermore, thanks to the high resilience to decoherence of the Macro-qubit, the present scheme can be adopted for general use in free space experiments in an uplink scenario.

# References

1. Gisin, N., Thew, R.: Quantum Communication. Nature Photonics 1, 165–167 (2007)
2. Waks, E., Zeevi, A., Yamamoto, Y.: Security of quantum key distribution with entangled photons against individual attacks. Phys. Rev. A 65, 052310 (2002)
3. Ursin, R., Tiefenbacher, F., Schmitt-Manderbach, T., Weier, H., Scheidl, T., Lindenthal, M., Baluensteiner, B., Jennewein, T., Perdigues, J., Trojek, P., Omer, B., Furst, M., Meyenburg, M., Rarity, J., Sodnik, Z., Barbieri, C., Weinfurter, H., Zeilinger, A.: Entanglement-based quantum communication over 144 km. Nature 3, 481–486 (2007)
4. Schmitt-Manderbach, T., Weier, H., Furst, M., Ursin, R., Tiefenbacher, F., Scheidl, T., Perdigues, J., Sodnik, Z., Kurtsiefer, K., Rarity, J., Zeilinger, A., Weinfurter, H.: Experimental Demonstration of Free-Space Decoy-State Quantum Key Distribution over 144 km. Phys. Rev. Lett. 98, 10504 (2007)
5. Fedrizzi, A., Ursin, R., Herbst, T., Nespoli, M., Prevedel, R., Scheidl, T., Tiefenbacher, F., Jennewein, T., Zeilinger, A.: High-fidelity transmission of entanglement over a high-loss free-space channel. Nature Physics 5, 389–392 (2009)
6. De Martini, F.: Amplification of Quantum Entanglement. Phys.Rev. Lett. 81, 2842–2845 (1998)
7. De Martini, F.: Quantum superposition of parametrically amplified multiphoton pure states. Phys. Lett. A 250, 15–19 (1998)
8. De Martini, F., Sciarrino, F., Vitelli, C.: Entanglement Test on a Microscopic-Macroscopic System. Phys. Rev.Lett. 100, 253601 (2008)
9. De Martini, F., Sciarrino, F., Spagnolo, N.: Anomalous Lack of Decoherence of the Macroscopic Quantum Superpositions Based on Phase-Covariant Quantum Cloning. Phys. Rev. Lett. 103, 100501 (2009)
10. Lombardi, E., Sciarrino, F., Popescu, S., De Martini, F.: Teleportation of a Vacuum–One-Photon Qubit. Phys. Rev. Lett. 88, 070402 (2002)
11. Bennet, C.H., Brassard, G., Crpeau, C., Jozsa, R., Peres, A., Wootters, W.K.: Teleporting an unknown quantum state via dual classical and Einstein-Podolsky-Rosen channels. Phys. Rev. Lett. 70, 1895 (1993)
12. Nagali, E., De Angelis, T., Sciarrino, F., De Martini, F.: Experimental realization of macroscopic coherence by phase-covariant cloning of a single photon. Phys. Rev. A 76, 042126 (2007)
13. Boschi, D., Branca, S., De Martini, F., Hardy, L., Popescu, S.: Experimental Realization of Teleporting an Unknown Pure Quantum State via Dual Classical and Einstein-Podolsky-Rosen Channels. Phys. Rev. Lett. 80, 1121–1125 (1998)
14. Massar, S., Popescu, S.: Optimal Extraction of Information from Finite Quantum Ensembles. Phys. Rev. Lett. 74, 1259–1263 (1995)

# Special Session 3
# Access Quality Processing and Applications of Satellite Imagery

# Semi-automatic Objects Recognition Process Based on Fuzzy Logic

Federico Prandi and Raffaella Brumana

Politecnico di Milano, Dept. B.E.S.T.
Piazza Leonardo da Vinci 32, 20133 Milano
{federico.prandi,raffaella.brumana}@polimi.it

**Abstract.** Three dimensional object extraction and recognition (OER) from geographic data has been one of most important topics in photogrammetry for a long time. Today, the capability of being able to rapidly generate high-density DSM increases the provision of geographic information. However the discrete nature of the measuring makes it more difficult to correctly recognize and extract 3D objects from these surfaces. The proposed methodology wants to semi-automate some of the operations required for clustering of geographic objects, in order to perform the recognition process. Fuzzy logic allows using, in a mathematical process the uncertain information typical of human reasoning. In this paper we present an approach for detecting objects based on fuzzy logic. In a first phase only the structural information are extracted and integrated in the fuzzy reasoning process in order to have a more generic treatment. The recognition algorithm has been tested with different data sets and different objectives.

**Keywords:** Objects Recognition, DSM, Fuzzy logic, disaster management.

## 1 Introduction

Three dimensional object extraction and recognition (OER) from geographic data has been one of most important topic in photogrammetry and remote sensing for a long time. However, most of the existing methods for automatic extraction and recognition of objects from data are based on a range of different information and make use of parametric methods. Within these systems object's vagueness behavior is basically neglected [1].

Manual intervention is still needed to reconstruct 3D models introducing a critical bottleneck to the modeling of geographic objects. Aerial photogrammetry has been, and still is, one of the preferred ways to retrieve three-dimensional information on objects, being it very well understood and since it delivers accurate results. The major drawback is that automation of the measurement process is closely related to image understanding which is a problem hard to solve.

Experience and daily practice make it possible for our brain to automatically interpret what we see. Human recognition takes advantage of a variety of acquired information rather than relying on a single descriptor of an object. Further, human perception has a tremendous potential for learning and it deals perfectly with the fuzziness of the real world. Whenever it is required to identify objects within

K. Sithamparanathan et al. (Eds.): PSATS 2010, LNICST 43, pp. 343–353, 2010.

geographic data an interpretation made by a human operator may represent an easier option. However if the process were performed by a computer, it would be very likely that none of the objects were identified.

Fuzzy logic gives the possibility to use, within a mathematical process, uncertain information which is typical of human reasoning. The purpose of this paper is to use 3D information contained in the DSM to automatically detect and recognize topographic objects in complex scenes. Furthermore, we try to use only LiDAR or Image Matching DSM. Due to this limitation our goal becomes even more challenging. As illustrated in the future work section it is possible to extend the methodology to others data sets such as multispectral or high resolution satellite images.

The proposed approach can be divided into five major steps:

- Pre-processing (data acquisition, interpolation, matching).
- DSM normalization.
- Extraction and definition of object's structural descriptor.
- Fuzzy reasoning process (membership function, IF-THEN Rules, inference process).
- Object detection.

It is clear that the problem of automatically extracting objects is still far from being solved. Now, after about two decades of research on the topic of automated recognition and reconstruction of man-made objects, there are still no fully automatic systems. The variety of methods available and the analysis of their advantages and weaknesses can provide quite a handful of hints for other scientists on how to approach the problem of 3D object extraction.

## 1.1 Related Works

As seen above, the research issues involved in the generation of 3D topographic objects for 3D GIS are very wide. They range from ICT theory of conceptual models to virtual reality and software development, passing through the development of data acquisition sensors, automation in data extraction and data analysis. Each one of these issues is related to many others: for instance in order to develop a given conceptual model it is important to be aware on how data is acquired. Similarly, when developing an algorithm for feature extraction, one has to understand which is the model to be used with those features.

In fact there is not a universal automatic or semi-automatic approach and the process of 3D reconstruction is often manual. The main task required to automatically generate a DTM from data is to divide terrain points from non-terrain points. Further it may be necessary to classify non-terrain points as belonging to buildings, vegetation or other objects (e.g. bridges), depending on the specific application.

Automatic approaches to generate DTM and building reconstruction based on radiometric images have since long been a challenging research topic. In the literature it is acknowledged that the issues related to segmentation and classification are not only an interesting research topic, but they are also very important in practice. Multiple, largely complementary, sensor data, such as color or multi-spectral aerial images and range data from laser scanners or SAR, have been used to ensure robustness and better performances in 3D ORR (Object Recognition and Reconstruction). For example, color infrared (CIR) aerial images can be combined to laser scanner data DTMs for feature extraction purposes [2].

If multispectral imagery is available, the classification approach is the most convenient way to detect building areas or urban regions [3]. Everything that exceeds a certain threshold in the nDSM (normalized Digital Surface Model) will be included, and vegetation will be then excluded by further interpreting the NDVI (Normalized Difference Vegetation Index).

In many cases however multispectral information is missing and therefore techniques to segment the DSM are adopted. Different filtering strategies have been proposed, based on deviations from a parametric surface, slope threshold, clustering, etc.

A slope-based filtering using mathematical morphology has been presented in [4] and it defines a slope threshold as the maximum allowed height difference between two points as a function of their spatial distance. Another interesting approach has been discussed in [5]: the segmentation is carried out by combining region growing with a principal component analysis (PCA). A three-stage framework has been implemented for a complete, robust and automatic classification of LiDAR data. This is composed by a region-growing technique to identify regions with a step edge along their border, a grouping of connected sets of pixels on the basis of an 8-classes partition of the height gradient orientation and a rule based scheme applied to the classification of the regions [6]. Another study [7] focuses on automatic extraction of a DTM from a high-resolution DEM produced by image correlation in urban or rural areas based on a hybrid approach. The study combines complementary aspects of both TIN-based and segmentation-based techniques.

Once the locations of features have been identified, either through automatic segmentation or manual digitization, the feature extraction process can be started. The different approaches available depend on whether image data or laser scanner data have to be processed, mainly due to the differences in the nature of the data.

The reconstruction of man-made objects is a task of major concern nowadays, and a rich variety of approaches has been proposed in recent years. A comprehensive overview is given in the proceedings of the Ascona Workshops [8].

However, despite the progress that has been made with scanning systems and digital image acquisition, achieving automatic processing of the resulting datasets is at a very early research stage. For example, nowadays laser scan data is mostly used to produce digital terrain models which can be obtained from the original (measured) point cloud through interpolation algorithms which are do not differ significantly from photogrammetric DTM modules that have been in use for the last three decades. Only in specialized applications, such as the derivation of DTM in wooded areas or the surveying of power lines, there are first approaches capable to exploit specific properties of laser scan datasets to achieve automatic extraction.

## 2 Classification Based on Fuzzy Logic

With the term recognition we refer to the process that assigns a label (e.g. "building" or "tree") to the result of a segmentation, in particular a region, based on properties (descriptors) of the region. Segmentation is the process that partitions the spatial domain of an image, or other raster datasets, like digital elevation models, into mutually exclusive parts, called regions.

Fuzzy logic can provide the link to connect computational theories with human perception. It provides a simple way to get to a specific conclusion based upon imprecise, uncertain, ambiguous, vague or missing input information. When dealing with simple 'black' and 'white' answers is no longer satisfactory, a *degree of membership* (as suggested by Prof. Zadeh in 1965) becomes the way to tackle a range of different problems. The natural description of problems, in linguistic terms, rather than in terms of relationships between precise numerical values, is the other advantage of fuzzy logic theory.

In fact fuzzy logic introduces *linguistic variables* for each descriptors characteristic of an object and *linguistic labels* to describe the fuzzy sets on the range of all possible values that those linguistic variables may be equal to.

When applied to raster images, fuzzy classification estimates the contribution of each class within each pixel. The theory assumes that a pixel is not an indecomposable unit in the image analysis. Consequently, it works on the principle of "one pixel—several classes" to provide more information about the pixel, unlike hard classification methods which perform poorly when extracting information.

The research works dealing with classification and feature extraction [9, 10] have provided several demonstrations of the capability of such fuzzy approaches.

## 3  Proposed Methodology

In the proposed fuzzy process (Fig. 1), each pixel is transformed into a matrix of degrees of membership representing the fuzzy inputs. A minimum-reasoning rule is then applied to infer the fuzzy outputs. Finally, a defuzzification step is applied to extract features [11].

The main components of the fuzzy recognition process are as follows:

- A database, which defines the membership functions of the fuzzy sets.
- A rule base, which contains fuzzy if-then rules.
- A fuzzy reasoning procedure, which performs inference operations on the rules.

The process should account for i) all available descriptors of an object (such as: 3D structure, textural information and spectral responses), ii) a fuzzy description of object properties and a fuzzy inference strategy for object recognition, iii) learning capabilities to be able to modify imprecise model descriptions and increase the potential of recognition in particular if new and unrecognized objects are encountered.

The proposed method for object extraction requires some preliminary steps that consist in: i) to locate and separate all 3D objects from the terrain and ii) to analyze and generate all the geometric properties that can describe the objects. Then, the challenge is to develop a segmentation procedure in connection with an inference process for object recognition.

A rule base should include observations of important descriptors. Moreover, it reflects the fact that people may formulate similar "fuzzy statements" to characterize how they perceive how objects appear, for instance, within aerial color images.

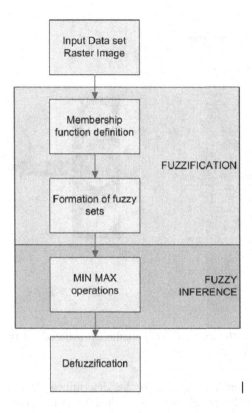

**Fig. 1.** Implementation flowchart of the steps required for fuzzy recognition process

The fuzzy inference AND or OR operators combine the membership values of the inputs in each rule for the antecedent of that rule. The MIN reasoning rule, applied on the matrix of produced fuzzy inputs, will consider, for each class, the membership degrees provided by the different fuzzy sets. Furthermore it will pick out the minimal membership degree to represent the class extent in the pixel. Then a MAX operation will be performed, as a result of each rule, to extract the element with the highest value (fuzzy output) and the corresponding class of that feature will be considered as associated fuzzy class to that pixel (fig. 2).

More specifically the steps of the fuzzy recognition process will be:

- Input raster data and structural descriptor variables are introduced.
- Membership functions are defined by using results from human heuristic knowledge.
- Definition of fuzzy logic inference rules.
- Performing raster data classification.

The OER process starts with the extraction of the Structural Descriptors (SD). Then those descriptors are analyzed to derive SD membership functions. In the next stage, the recognition operation is performed with the application of the sample if-then fuzzy rules and the MIN-MAX inference process.

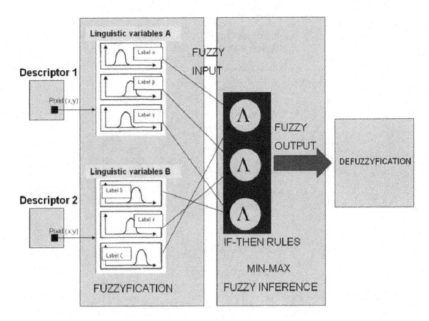

**Fig. 2.** Architecture of the explicit fuzzy method illustrated for two descriptors, two variables with three classes

The membership function parameters are determined through human heuristic knowledge. It should be noted that this method is more appropriate to situations where there is a clear linear ordering in the measurement of the fuzzy concept for instance when dealing with concepts such as tallness, heat, time, etc.

Interval estimation is a relatively simple way of acquiring the membership function and it results in membership functions that are "less fuzzy" (i.e. the spread is narrower) when compared to other methods.

The trapezoidal membership function, with maximum equal to 1 and minimum equal to 0, is used in this work. Special cases, including symmetrical trapezoids and triangles, reduce the number of parameters to three. The trapezoidal functions are modeled with four parameters ($\alpha,\beta,\gamma,\delta,$).

$$\mu_A(x,\alpha,\beta,\gamma,\delta) = \begin{cases} 0 & if\ x < \alpha \\ \dfrac{x-\alpha}{\beta-\alpha} & if\ \alpha \le x < \beta \\ 1 & if\ \beta \le x < \gamma \\ \dfrac{\delta-x}{\delta-\gamma} & if\ \gamma \le x < \delta \\ 0 & if\ x < \delta \end{cases}$$

The linguistic variables, which are variables that assume in linguistic terms values of the object's structural descriptors, have to be defined in fuzzy logic. Linguistic variables are associated to each input structural descriptor and for each linguistic variables some linguistic labels has been assigned. This assignment is mostly a mixture of expert knowledge and examination of the desired input–output data.

Through definition of linguistic variables and membership function parameters calculation the input to the fuzzy recognition process is performed. Sufficient overlap of neighboring membership functions is taken into account to provide smooth transition from one linguistic label to another.

**Table 1.** Linguistic variables and labels for the fuzzy-based object recognition process

| Structural descriptor | Linguistic labels |
|---|---|
| Height | *Very Low, Low, Medium, Tall, Very Tall* |
| Area | *Very Small, Small, Medium, Large, Very Large* |
| Gradients on segment borders | *Very Flat, Flat, Steep, Very Steep* |
| Relief | *Very Irregular, Irregular, Regular, Very Regular* |
| Height range in a point neighborhood | *Very Low, Low, Medium, Tall, Very Tall* |

As mentioned earlier, the object recognition potentials can be enhanced through the simultaneous fusion of the SD parameters extracted. For this reason our recognition strategy is based on the concept of information fusion. The descriptors are used simultaneously within the recognition engine to perform the object recognition process.

Because of the wide variety of clustering cases we have decided to use a versatile tool for the management of fuzzy clustering process. Since many spatial phenomena are inherently fuzzy or vague or possess indeterminate boundaries, fuzzy logic has been applied in many GIS scenarios, including fuzzy spatial analysis, fuzzy reasoning, and the representation of fuzzy boundaries.

In a second step the membership values which have been identified have to be combined to get to a final decision (inference process). This component of the fuzzy recognition process consists in the definition of a set of rule bases, which contain fuzzy if-then rules.

Formulation of fuzzy rules requires a profound observation of the integrative impact of the descriptors on the recognition of an object. This again depends on the experience of an operator but also on the complexity of an object. In the experiments we observed, when dealing with partition walls it is sufficient to use a relatively small number of fuzzy rules, whereas when it identifying trees the process requires a higher number of rules, probably due to their more complex shapes and variety in terms of appearance.

By taking into account the geometric properties, it is possible to overcome some problems typical of the use of image spectral characteristics. However a better result can be achieved if the descriptors are not necessarily limited to the structural descriptor values. The process of information fusion may also include other types of descriptors if they are available. If instead there are only one or two descriptors available (e.g. only spectral, or spectral and structural), the recognition process can still be executed, albeit being more prone to less reliable results. The insertion of others descriptors in the fuzzy recognition process is always possible once the membership function and the if-then fuzzy base rules are defined.

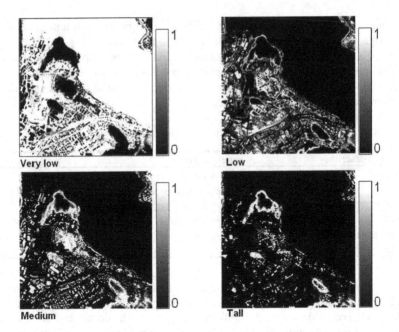

**Fig. 3.** Membership function's grids (as many as the linguistic variables associated to the descriptor) calculated for the structural descriptor "Height". The values are between zero and one.

If-then rules are statements that make fuzzy logic useful. A single fuzzy if-then rule can be formulated according to:

IF x is A; THEN y is B

Where A and B are linguistic variables defined by fuzzy sets on the range of all possible values of x and y, respectively. The antecedent may integrate several inputs using logical AND and OR. Fuzzy reasoning with fuzzy if-then rules enables linguistic statements to be treated mathematically.

Given the rules and inputs, the degree of membership to each of the fuzzy sets has to be determined. By combining the individual membership functions trough the simple rules and after the aggregation process we obtain the final result and we can then defuzzify it.

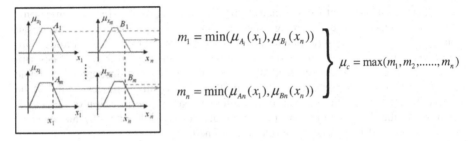

$$m_1 = \min(\mu_{A_i}(x_1), \mu_{B_i}(x_n))$$

$$m_n = \min(\mu_{A_n}(x_1), \mu_{B_n}(x_n))$$

$$\mu_c = \max(m_1, m_2, \ldots, m_n)$$

**Fig. 4.** MIN-MAX reasoning structure

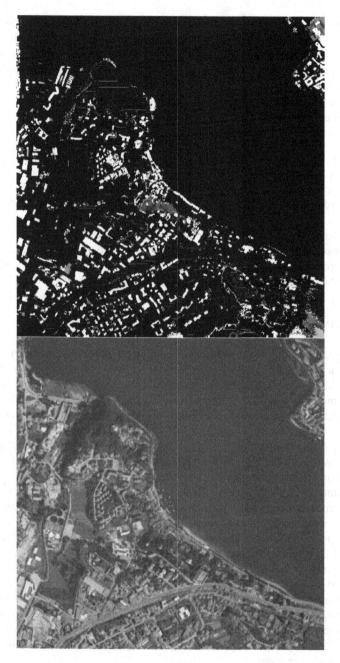

**Fig. 5.** Results of fuzzy buildings recognition (Above), the grey level are proportional to the output fuzzy value of the inference process. We can qualitatively compare the results to the aerial image (below) of the area.

Our approach for fuzzy object recognition follows the MIN-MAX concept. The membership values in the premise part are combined according to minimum values (so-called min- inference) to extract the value of each rule, where $m_i$ is the consequent for each equation rules and $\mu Ai(xi)$ the value of the membership functions for each linguistic variable of the premise part of the rule.

The final output (fig. 4) is then obtained by the MAX of the consequent equations rules and is calculated by:

$$\mu_c = \max(m_1, m_2, \ldots\ldots, m_n)$$

The qualitative results (Fig. 5) highlight a good classification of the buildings objects; in particular we have an optimal results in case of isolated buildings or urban areas. Instead more complex, with lack of recognition, is the case of building near to areas characterized by vegetation where large trees are also classified as buildings. This problem can be overcome using a spectral descriptor such as NDVI index which allows an efficient separation between objects and vegetation.

The investigations presented here have given a first demonstration of the capability of this approach. The recognition process could identify approximately 80% of the buildings objects within the area used for the test.

## 4 Conclusions and Future Works

In object recognition, human interaction remains an important part of the workflow even though the amount of work to be performed by the human operators can be reduced considerably in the global extraction process. Many automatic and semi-automatic methods proposed in the literature focus either on the reconstruction process or on feature extraction once the objects has been recognized by an operator.

The core of the system presented is an approach to recognize object's primitives through use of fuzzy logic theory. This allows analyzing the data to extract a maximal amount of information, through an explicit process that uses structural information of objects and integrates them within a fuzzy reasoning process.

In our approach detection, classification and modeling of objects is based exclusively on structural description, without additional information like GIS data.

Further, in this way we have been able to assess i) the versatility of the fuzzy recognition process in different challenging clustering situations, ii) the efficacy to recognize 3-D structural information iii) the capability to solve difficult problems by using the property to benefit from uncertain or vague concepts, typical of human thinking and language.

Despite this further investigation and developments might be carried out. With regard to data used as input, different object descriptors, such as textural or multispectral properties, could be considered in the recognition process. Moreover the generation of structural descriptors has to be improved by considering the sensitivity of the algorithms to coarse input.

Another important improvement is to provide learning capability through neural-networks. The learning capability of neural networks can be introduced in the fuzzy recognition process by taking adaptable parameter sets into account thus moving towards a neuro-fuzzy approach.

Finally data acquired from different sensors, such as high density airborne laser scanning, high resolution satellite images, or from other technologies such as Unmanned Aerial Vehicles (UAV), could be used to improve the recognition process and their effectiveness can be assessed.

# References

1. Samadzadegan, F., Azizi, A., Hahn, M.T., Lucas, C.: Automatic 3D object recognition and reconstruction based on neuro-fuzzy modelling. ISPRS Journal of Photogrammetry & Remote Sensing 59, 255–277 (2005)
2. Hahn, M., Stätter, C.: A scene labeling strategy for terrain feature extraction using multisource data. IAPRS 32 Part 3/1, 435–443 (1998)
3. Knudsen, T., Olsen, B.: Automated Change Detection for Updates of Digital Map Databases. Photogrammetric Engineering & Remote Sensing 69(11), 1289–1296 (2003)
4. Vosselmann, G.: Slope based filtering of laser altimetry data. In: IAPRS, Amsterdam, The Netherlands, vol. 33(B3), pp. 935–942 (2000)
5. Roggero, M.: Object segmentation with region growing and principal component analysis. IAPRS 34(3A), 289–294 (2002)
6. Forlani, G., Nardinocchi, C., Scaioni, M., Zingaretti, P.: Complete classification of raw LIDAR data and 3D reconstruction of buildings. Pattern Analysis Application 8, 357–374 (2006)
7. Baillard, C.: A Hybrid Method for Deriving DTMs from Urban DEMs IAPRS, XXXVII Part B3b Commission III p.109 (2008)
8. Workshops on Automatic Extraction of Man-Made Objects from Aerial and Space Images, Ascona/Switzerland in 1995, 1997 and 2001
9. Mohammadzadeh, A., Tavakoli, A., Zoej, M.J.V.: Automatic Linear Feature Extraction of Iranian Roads from High Resolution Multi-spectral Satellite Imagery. IAPRS XXXV part B3, 764 (2004)
10. Wuest, B., Zhang, Y.: Region Based Segmentation Of Quickbird Imagery Through Fuzzy Integration. IAPRS WG VII/4 XXXVII Part B7, 491 (2008)
11. Melgani, F., Al Hashemy, B.A.R., Taha, S.M.R.: An Explicit Fuzzy Supervised Classification Method for Multispectral Remote Sensing Images. IEEE Transactions On Geoscience And Remote Sensing 38(1) (2000)

# GeoEye-1: Analysis of Radiometric and Geometric Capability

Mattia Crespi[1], Gabriele Colosimo[1], Laura De Vendictis[2],
Francesca Fratarcangeli[1], and Francesca Pieralice[1]

[1] Geodesy and Geomatic Area, University of Rome La Sapienza,
Via Eudossiana 18, 00184 Rome, Italy
{mattia.crespi,gabriele.colosimo,francesca.fratarcangeli,
francesca.pieralice}@uniroma1.it
http://w3.uniroma1.it/geodgeom/
[2] e-Geos S.p.A. - via Cannizzaro 71, 00156 Rome, Italy
guest517.devendictis@e-geos.it

**Abstract.** The Geoeye-1 satellite, launched in September 2008, is able to acquire imagery in panchromatic mode, with a spatial resolution of 0.41 m at nadir, offering the most powerful way to obtain detailed imagery actually commercially available.

The aim of the work is to evaluate the quality of the GeoEye-1 products through radiometric and geometric analysis; the area test is the city of Rome.

Radiometric quality of the image has been evaluated estimating the level of noise and the characteristic of the Modulation Transfer Function - MTF, that gives an index about the image sharpness.

The second part of the research is focused on the evaluation of the geometric capability of Geoeye-1 satellite. The image has been oriented using two different methods: the rigorous model and the Rational Polynomial Function (RPFs) model with the Rational Polynomial Coefficients (RPCs). The results were analysed in order to compare the orientation quality obtained from different model and different software, in terms of accuracy achievable from the image.

**Keywords:** HRSI, image orientation, radiometric quality.

## 1 Introduction

The Geoeye-1 satellite, launched in September 2008, is able to acquire imagery in panchromatic mode, with a spatial resolution of 0.41 m at nadir, and in multispectral mode, with a spatial resolution of 2.0 m at nadir, offering the most powerful way to obtain detailed imagery actually commercially available.

The aim of the work is to evaluate the quality of the GeoEye-1 products through radiometric and geometric analysis; the area test is the city of Rome.

The panchromatic analysed image was acquired on 21 September 2009, it has 0.5 m pixel size and belongs to the Geo product class. The Geo products are radiometrically corrected map oriented image, suitable for a wide range of uses.

K. Sithamparanathan et al. (Eds.): PSATS 2010, LNICST 43, pp. 354–369, 2010.
© Institute for Computer Sciences, Social-Informatics and Telecommunications Engineering 2010

In addition to being suitable for visualization and monitoring applications, the Geo is shipped with the sensor camera model in Rational Polynomial Coefficients (RPCs) format. Geo images are projected onto an "inflated" ellipsoid, derived from the WGS84, choosing a certain ellipsoidal height. This kind of pre-processed images are usually mentioned as level 1B imagery.

Radiometric quality of the image has been evaluated estimating the level of noise and the characteristic of the Modulation Transfer Function - MTF, that gives an index about the image sharpness.

As regards the image noise, following the methods proposed from Baltsavias [1], the level of noise has been analysed by the standard deviation of the Digital Number of pixel selected in non-homogenous areas, so that a possible dependence between noise and radiometric intensity is evaluated.

The sharpness of the images has been analysed through the study of the Modulation Transfer Function; this function, in the spatial frequency domain for a chosen direction, represents the spatial resolution of the image. In order to estimate the MTF, an "edge method", proposed by Choi [2] and revised by De Vendictis [5], has been applied, using natural targets detected on the image.

The second part of the research is focused on the evaluation of the geometric capability of Geoeye-1 satellite. Tests of image orientation, using commercial and scientific software, have been performed. The image has been oriented using two different methods: the rigorous model and the Rational Polynomial Function (RPFs) model with the Rational Polynomial Coefficients (RPCs).

The results were analysed in order to compare the orientation quality obtained from different models in terms of accuracy achievable from the image. Two different software have been used: the commercial software PCI Geomatica 10.2 in which is included the rigorous model developed by Toutin, and the scientific software SISAR developed by the Geodesy and Geomatic Area of the University of Rome "La Sapienza".

The rigorous model implemented in SISAR is based on well know collinearity equations, with the reconstruction of the orbital segment during the image acquisition, the satellite position and attitude parameters.

Besides in the SISAR software it is possible to use RPCs and refine the image orientation on the basis of a set of GCPs. A possible refinement of the model, allowing for bias compensation, is accomplished in a quite common way with the introduction of a simple first order polynomial in the RPF, whose parameters are estimated.

## 2   Radiometric Quality Analysis

Within the chain from image sensing to the final value-added product, the imagery quality plays obviously a crucial role. Nowadays, most of the linear array sensors have the ability to provide more than 8-bit/pixel digital images; anyway we have still to consider some radiometric problems as the variations in the sensor view angle, the sun angle and shadowing, the image noise that can influence the image matching algorithms and the image unsharpness, due to CCD line jitter, kappa jitter and motion blur, and deficiencies of the lens system [11].

Image quality may be represented by several parameters as the radiometric resolution and its accuracy, represented by the noise level and the geometrical resolution and sharpness, described by the Modulation Transfer Function (MTF).

## 2.1   Noise Analysis

Here the noise level is evaluated through the standard deviation of the Digital Number (DN) in non-homogeneous areas according to the method proposed in Baltsavias et al. [1] and Zhang [11], that allow an analysis of the noise variation as a function of intensity. Usually the image noise is estimated using the standard deviation of the DN in homogeneous areas where one type surface's pixels should have the same DN; in any case homogeneous areas are not really representative of a standard acquisition and, moreover, the use of inhomogeneous areas allows an analysis of the noise variation as a function of intensity.

Nevertheless, if inhomogeneous areas are considered, it has to be taken in account on the entire image that the DN differences can be due both to the different texture and to the noise; then the objective is to separate the noise from the effect of texture variations.

In order to achieve this aim a small squared window $n \times n$ pixels (for e.g., $3 \times 3$ pixels) wide is moved within the area by a 3 pixel step and the DN mean ($M_w$) and the standard deviation ($\sigma_w$) is calculated for each window. The total DN range is divided in classes and the standard deviations are assigned to a class according to the mean DN of each window. At this stage, each class contains all the standard deviations attaining to those windows whose mean DN is within the DN limits of the class. It is reasonable that the lowest standard deviation are mainly due to the noise, whereas the other and for sure the highest are due to texture variations. Therefore in each class, the standard deviations are sorted, and the noise is estimated as the mean of the 5% smallest standard deviations. A check of the effectivenes of this hypothesis over a suitable simulated image is illustrated in [3].

## 2.2   Post-Flight Modulation Transfer Function (MTF) Analysis

The MTF of an imaging system describes the transfer of an input in spatial frequency domain. It is well known that MTF is a useful tool to describe the sharpness of an imaging system. Most of the time, the MTF characteristics are measured before the launch; however, they may change due to the vibration during the launch or some change in material properties in time. For that reason, for on-orbit MTF determination it is necessary to have an up-to-date performance assessment of spaceborne sensors.

Here it was evaluated according to the "Edge Method" proposed by Choi [2] and revisited by De Vendictis [5].

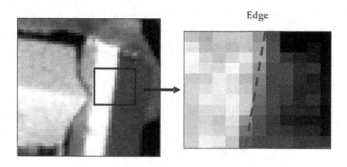

**Fig. 1.** Edge example

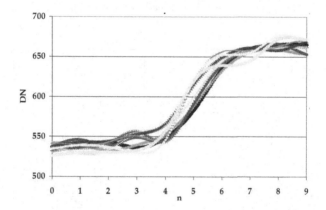

**Fig. 2.** Splines interpolating perpendicular lines

The initial task of the Edge Method is the identification of target edges useful for the analysis. Edges should show a blurred line edge between two almost uniform regions (at least in the neighborhood of the edge) of different intensities. Possible natural edges can be the separation line between the two layers of a roof, two fields with different cultivations, a roof edge and the ground, a road border and so on (Fig. 1).

After the selection of some suitable edges, at first the algorithm estimates the edge locations at sub-pixel accuracy; under the assumption that the chosen edges lie on a straight line, the alignment of all edge locations is LS estimated. The edge profiles, which are centered at each edge pixel and have the direction perpendicular to the edge, are interpolated with cubic spline functions (Fig. 2).

These cubic spline functions, differently from Choi, are averaged and interpolated with an analytical function in order to obtain an empirical Edge Spread Function (ESF) (Fig. 3).

The ESF is then differentiated to obtain the Line Spread Function (LSF). Finally the LSF is Fourier-transformed and normalized to obtain the corresponding

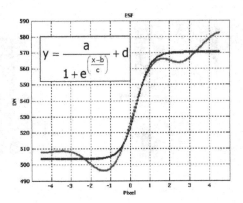

**Fig. 3.** Empirical Edge Spread Function in blue color

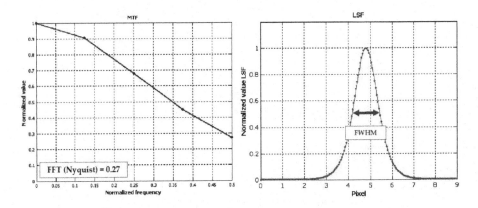

**Fig. 4.** MTF at Nyquist frequency and Full Width at Half Maximum

MTF. Finally, after the Fourier transformation, the computed MTF is scaled in the frequency axis in order to represent the calculated MTF in terms of the Nyquist frequency of the image. In addition, the Full Width at Half Maximum (FWHM) value is also computed from the estimated LSF (Fig. 4).

The details of both procedures are described exhaustively in [3].

## 3    Results of Radiometric Quality Analysis

Geoeye-1 imagery are collected in 11-bits format (2048 grey levels) but, even if the peak is less pronounced, the 99% of the DN vary between 110 and 780. For this reason, in order to perform the signal-to-noise ratio analysis, the imagery DN interval between 110 and 782, with the exclusion of the histogram tails (0-110 DN and 782-2047 DN), has been divided in different classes, 32 grey levels wide.

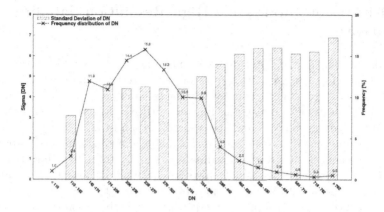

**Fig. 5.** Geoeye-1 noise level estimation

The analysis results are reported in Fig. 5 showing that the noise is intensity dependent, in fact it is increasing with increasing grey values.

The MTF was estimated detecting, on the whole image, 30 well distributed linear structures, oriented both along- and across-track. The MTF values at Nyquist frequency and the FWHM values were estimated for all the selected edges; the results were combined into average values for the along- and across-track direction (Tab. 1).

**Table 1.** MTF and FWHM estimation

| Off Nadir | Sun elevation | Resampling | Edges along-track | | Edges cross-track | |
|:---:|:---:|:---:|:---:|:---:|:---:|:---:|
| | | | MTF at Nyquist | FWHM (pixel) | MTF at Nyquist | FWHM (pixel) |
| 12° | 50° | CC | 0.42 | 1.05 | 0.34 | 1.18 |

The results achieved show that the MTF values and the FWHM values seem to be similar for along and cross track direction, considering their standard deviation at the level of 0.15.

They seem to be slightly better than those displayed in [8], that states as reference for Geoeye-1 a MTF value at the Nyquist frequency of approximately 0.24 along-track and 0.26 across-track; due to the high MTF standard deviation this issue has to be investigated repeating the analysis on other images. Anyway it has to be noticed that tests discussed by Kohm were carried out on images acquired just 6 months after the launch, which could suffer for an initial non optimal radiometric calibration.

# 4   Orientation Models for High Resolution Satellite Imagery

Image distortions, due to acquisition system and geometry, could be removed by an orientation process, estimating a set of parameters for an orientation model. Remote sensing community usually adopts two different types of orientation models for High Resolution Satellite Imagery (HRSI): the physical sensor models (also called rigorous models) and the generalized sensor models.

The rigorous models are based on a standard photogrammetric approach where the image and the ground coordinates are linked through collinearity equations. The involved parameters have physical meaning. Besides, they require the knowledge of the specific satellite and orbit characteristics.

On the contrary, the generalized models are usually based on the RPFs which link image and terrain coordinates by the RPCs and do not need the knowledge of sensor and acquisition features. The RPCs can be calculated by the final users via a LS estimation directly from GCPs, or are generated by the sensor managing companies by using their own physical sensor models and disseminated to the users through the image metadata. Nevertheless, the first strategy (also called terrain-dependent) is not recommended if a reliable and accurate orientation is required. In the second strategy, they can be generated according to a terrain-independent scenario based on a known physical sensor model.

This section will discuss many features of the orientation models. Specifically, in Sect. 4.1 discussions will be focused on the rigorous model for the orientation of the image projected to a specific object surface (usually an "inflated" ellipsoid derived from the WGS84) (level 1B). The RPCs model is discussed in Sect. 4.2 and Sect. 4.3.

## 4.1   The Rigorous Model for Level 1B Imagery

This specific rigorous model has been developed for the management of level 1B imagery [4]. In this case it has to be noted that the images are projected onto a specific object (usually an "inflated" ellipsoid, derived from the WGS84 choosing a certain ellipsoidal height). The collinearity equations link points on the ground and points projected on the mentioned "inflated" ellipsoid (Fig. 6).

Each point on the ground surface corresponds to a point on "inflated" ellipsoid, identified from line of sight (LOS), i.e. the line directed from the perspective centre to the point on the ground. The collinearity condition is satisfied when $\hat{u}_{SI}$ (the unit vector directed from perspective centre to image point) coincides with $\hat{u}_{ST}$ (the unit vector directed from perspective centre to ground point), i.e., ground point and image point are lined up on LOS. The collinearity equations may be conveniently expressed in the ECEF system in vector form:

$$\hat{u}_{SI} = \mathbf{R} \cdot \hat{u}_{ST} \qquad (1)$$

where $\mathbf{R}$ is a rotation matrix. In fact, relative "small" translation of ground with respect to ellipsoid can be expressed with an infinitesimal rotation around the

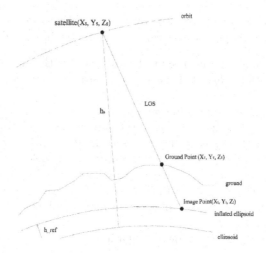

**Fig. 6.** Model geometry of level 1B image

perspective center, because the height of satellite platform ($h_S$) is much higher than the difference of elevation between ground surface and the "inflated" ellipsoid ($\Delta h$). Under this infinitesimal rotation hypothesis ($cos\phi, \theta, \psi \cong 1\ sin\phi \cong \phi, sin\theta \cong \theta, sin\psi \cong \psi$) the rotation matrix **R** is reduced to the sum of the unit matrix and an antisymmetric matrix:

$$R = I + \delta R = \begin{bmatrix} 0 & \varphi & \theta \\ -\varphi & 0 & \psi \\ -\theta & -\psi & 0 \end{bmatrix} \Rightarrow R = \begin{bmatrix} 1 & \varphi & \theta \\ -\varphi & 1 & \psi \\ -\theta & -\psi & 1 \end{bmatrix} \tag{2}$$

where the attitude angles are supposed to be modelled by a time-dependent function up to the second order (3).

$$\begin{cases} \varphi = a_0 + a_1\tau + a_2\tau^2 \\ \vartheta = b_0 + b_1\tau + b_2\tau^2 \\ \psi = c_0 + c_1\tau + c_2\tau^2 \end{cases} \tag{3}$$

$\tau$ is the time, in seconds, such as $\tau = J_s \cdot \Delta t$ where $\Delta t$ is the time needed to scan a row on the ground and $J_s$ is the row of the pixel.

The (1) can also be expressed in the following way:

$$\begin{bmatrix} X_I - X_S \\ Y_I - Y_S \\ Z_I - Z_S \end{bmatrix} = \rho R \begin{bmatrix} X_T - X_S \\ Y_T - Y_S \\ Z_T - Z_S \end{bmatrix} \tag{4}$$

where

- $\varrho$ is the scale factor, (ratio of perspective centre-image point distance $d_{SI}$ and perspective centre-ground point distance $d_{ST}$: $\rho = d_{SI}/d_{ST}$)
- $X_T, Y_T, Z_T$ are the ground coordinates in the ECEF system

- $X_I, Y_I, Z_I$ are the image coordinates in the ECEF system
- $X_S, Y_S, Z_S$ are the perspective centre coordinates in the ECEF system

The model parameters that need to be estimated with the LS adjustment are the nine coefficients $(a_i, b_i, c_i)$. Their initial approximate values are simply fixed to zero.

As regards the satellite position, in general detailed information are not supplied for the level 1B images; therefore the satellite coordinates can be roughly computed only on the basis of the angles (azimuth and elevation) that define satellite position with respect to image center. Nevertheless, this way is often rather inaccurate, so that it is necessary to follow an other strategy.

In particular in this work Direct Linear Transformation (DLT) is used, establishing a rough relation between image coordinates and ground coordinates in a Cartesian Local system.

The DLT is based on the following equations:

$$
\begin{aligned}
I &= \frac{L_1 \cdot E + L_2 \cdot N + L_3 \cdot U + L_4}{L_9 \cdot E + L_{10} \cdot N + L_{11} \cdot U + 1} \\
J &= \frac{L_5 \cdot E + L_6 \cdot N + L_7 \cdot U + L_8}{L_9 \cdot E + L_{10} \cdot N + L_{11} \cdot U + 1}
\end{aligned}
\tag{5}
$$

where $(I, J)$ are the image coordinates, $(E, N, U)$ are the ground coordinates respect to the Cartesian Local system centered in the center of the image and the $L_i$ are the DLT parameters.

Starting from some GCPs coordinates, the DLT parameters are estimated; satellite position in the Cartesian Local system, related to the image center, is computed using the DLT parameters for a fixed height of the satellite.

Local coordinates are transformed into ECEF coordinates, and from the unique satellite position it is possible to reconstruct the orbit segment. Due to the short lenght of the orbital arc related to the image acquisition, it is possible to approximate it with an arc of circumference. Details on this computation, which is conveniently done in the orbital system, are illustrated in [4].

## 4.2 RPC Usage and Orientation Refinement in RPF

As mentioned before, some companies (for example DigitalGlobe for QuickBird and WorldView and Space Imaging for Ikonos and GeoEye-1, India Space Research Organization for Cartosat-1) usually supply the RPCs, as part of the image metadata to enable image orientation via RPFs.

The RPFs relate object point coordinates (latitude $\varphi$, longitude $\lambda$ and height $h$) to pixel coordinates $(I, J)$, as a physical sensor models, but in the form of ratios of polynomial expressions:

$$
I = \frac{P_1(\varphi, \lambda, h)}{P_2(\varphi, \lambda, h)} \qquad J = \frac{P_3(\varphi, \lambda, h)}{P_4(\varphi, \lambda, h)}
\tag{6}
$$

where $\varphi, \lambda$ are the geographic coordinates, $h$ is the height above the WGS84 ellipsoid and $(I, J)$ are the image coordinates. The order of these four polynomials is usually limited to 3 so that each polynomial takes the generic form:

$$P_n = \sum_{i=0}^{m_1} \sum_{j=0}^{m_2} \sum_{k=0}^{m_3} t_{ijk} \varphi^i \lambda^j h^k \qquad (7)$$

with $0 \leq m_1 \leq 3;\ 0 \leq m_2 \leq 3;\ 0 \leq m_3 \leq 3$ and $m_1 + m_2 + m_3 \leq 3$, where $t_{ijk}$ are the RPCs [9].

The ground and image coordinates $(\varphi, \lambda, h;\ I, J)$ in the equation (6) are normalized to (-1, +1) range using normalization parameters supplied in the metadata file, in order to improve the numerical precision during the computation.

Since the residual bias may be present into the RPCs, the orientation can be refined on the basis of the known GPs, acting as GCPs. A possible refinement of the model (6) (written in normalized coordinates), allowing for bias compensation, is accomplished in a quite common way with the introduction of a simple first order polynomial in the RPFs (8) whose parameters are estimated, provided a suitable number of GCPs is known [7].

$$
\begin{aligned}
I_n &= A_o + I_n \cdot A_1 + J_n \cdot A_2 + \frac{P_1(\varphi_n, \lambda_n, h_n)}{P_2(\varphi_n, \lambda_n, h_n)} = \\
&= A_o + I_n \cdot A_1 + J_n \cdot A_2 + \frac{a_0 + a_1\lambda_n + a_2\varphi_n + a_3 h_n + a_4\lambda_n\varphi_n + \ldots + a_{17}\lambda_n^3 + a_{18}\varphi_n^3 + a_{19}h_n^3}{1 + b_1\lambda_n + b_2\varphi_n + b_3 h_n + b_4\lambda_n\varphi_n + \ldots + b_{17}\lambda_n^3 + b_{18}\varphi_n^3 + b_{19}h_n^3} \\
J_n &= B_o + J_n \cdot B_1 + I_n \cdot B_2 + \frac{P_3(\varphi_n, \lambda_n, h_n)}{P_4(\varphi_n, \lambda_n, h_n)} = \\
&= B_o + J_n \cdot B_1 + I_n \cdot B_2 + \frac{c_0 + c_1\lambda_n + c_2\varphi_n + c_3 h_n + c_4\lambda_n\varphi_n + \ldots + c_{17}\lambda_n^3 + c_{18}\varphi_n^3 + c_{19}h_n^3}{1 + d_1\lambda_n + d_2\varphi_n + d_3 h_n + d_4\lambda_n\varphi_n + \ldots + d_{17}\lambda_n^3 + d_{18}\varphi_n^3 + d_{19}h_n^3}
\end{aligned}
$$
$$(8)$$

where $(I_n, J_n)$ are the normalized images coordinates, and $P_i$ are third order polynomial functions of object space normalized coordinates $(\varphi_n, \lambda_n, h_n)$; $A_i$ and $B_i$ terms describe image shift and drift effects in particular:

- $A_0, A_1, A_2, B_0, B_1, B_2$ describe a complete affine transformation
- $A_0, A_1, B_0, B_1$ model the shift and drift
- $A_0, B_0$, describe a simple coordinate shift

### 4.3   RPC Generation by SISAR Rigorous Model

In this Section will be discuss the strategy for the RPCs generation using the already established physical sensor model.

A 2D image grid covering the full extent of the image is established and its corresponding 3D object grid with several layers (e.g., four or more layers for the third-order case) slicing the entire elevation range is generated. The horizontal coordinates $(X, Y)$ of a point of the 3D object grid are calculated from a point $(I, J)$ of the image grid using the physical sensor model with an a priori selected elevation $Z$. Then, the RPC are LS estimated with the object grid points and the image grid points. This terrain-independent computational scenario can make the RPFs model a good replacement to the physical sensor models, and has been widely used to determine the RPCs.

It has to be underlined that in the usually adopted terrain-independent approach, the LS solution is often carried out through a regularization, since unknown RPCs may be highly correlated so that the design matrix is almost rank deficient. In order to overcome the regularization requirements, an innovative algorithm for the RPCs extraction, with a terrain independent approach, has been proposed in [4] and is shortly summarized hereafter.

In details, at first an image discretization is made, dividing the full extent image space in a 2D grid. Then, the points of the 2D image grid are used to generate the 3D ground grid: the image is oriented and by the knowledge of the rigorous orientation sensor model, the collinearity equations were derived and used to create the 3D grid, starting from each point of the 2D grid image. In this respect, it has to be noted that the 2D grid is actually a regular grid, whereas the 3D one is not strictly regular, due to the image attitude. Moreover, the 3D grid points were generated intersecting the straight lines modelled by the collinearity equations with surfaces (approximately ellipsoids) concentric to the WGS84 ellipsoid, placed at regular elevation steps. So, the dimension of the 3D grid is both based on the full extent of the image and the elevation range of the terrain (Fig.7).

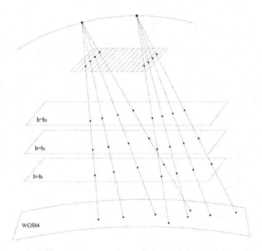

**Fig. 7.** Grid for RPC generation in the terrian-independet approach

The RPCs least squares estimation is based on the linearization of the generic RPFs equations, which can be written as:

$$I_n + b_1\lambda_n I_n + b_2\varphi_n I_n + ... + b_{19}h_n^3 I_n - a_0 - a_1\lambda_n - a_2\varphi_n... - a_{19}h_n^3 = 0$$
$$J_n + d_1\lambda_n J_n + d_2\varphi_n J_n + ... + d_{19}h_n^3 J_n - c_0 - c_1\lambda_n - c_2\varphi_n... - c_{19}h_n^3 = 0 \quad (9)$$

where $a_i, b_i, c_i, d_i$ are the RPCs (78 coefficients for third order polynomials), $(I_n, J_n)$ and $(\varphi_n, \lambda_n, h_n)$ are the normalized coordinates, with scale and offset factors computed according to:

$$\begin{cases} w_{offset} = \min(w_k) \\ w_{scale} = \max(w_k) - \min(w_k) \\ I_{offset} = J_{offset} = 1 \\ I_{scale} = n^\circ column - 1 \\ J_{scale} = n^\circ row - 1 \end{cases} where \ w = \varphi, \lambda, h \quad (10)$$

where $k$ is the number of available GCPs and n° column/row are the overall columns/rows of the image; the normalization range is (0, 1).

The new proposed estimation approach is based on the Singular Value Decomposition (SVD) and QR decomposition which are employed to evaluate the actual rank of the design matrix and to select the actual estimable coefficients; again, the SVD based subset selection procedure is due to Golub, Klema and Stewart [6]. This method permits to select only the really estimable and significant parameters, avoiding an over-parametrization; so, the number of estimated coefficients is usually less than the vendors one (about 1/2 ,1/3 coefficients).

# 5   Results of Geometric Analysis of GeoEye-1 Image

This Section is focused on the evaluation of the geometric capability of Geoeye-1 satellite. The data analysed is a GeoEye-1 image, that has been oriented using two different methods: the rigorous model and the RPFs model with the RPCs.
Orientation has been performed with two different software:

- the commercial software PCI Geomatica 10.2, in which is embedded the OrthoEngine module, equipped with the rigorous model developed by Toutin [10]
- the scientific software SISAR developed by the Geodesy and Geomatic Area of "La Sapienza" University of Rome, in which the rigorous model and a routine for RPC generation are included

The results were analysed in order to compare the orientation quality obtained from different models and different software in terms of accuracy achievable from the image.

In the Tab. 2 the features of the GeoEye-1 image are listed. The panchromatic analysed image was acquired on 21 September 2009, it has 0.5 m pixel size and belongs to the Geo product class.

The GPs were surveyed with static or fast static procedures by a Trimble 5700 GPS receiver and their coordinates are estimated by Trimble Geomatic Office software with respect to available GPS permanent stations (M0SE at Rome Faculty of Engineering). The mean horizontal and vertical accuracies of the coordinates are between 10 and 20 cm.

The entire scene is split into two tiles, and each of them is provided with a specific vendors RPC file. In the case of orientation with rigorous model it possible to stitch two tiles and to handle the entire scene. On the other hand, in the case of RPCs model the two tiles have to be oriented separately, because they have two different RPCs files.

Thanks to the SISAR routine for the RPCs generation, a unique RPCs file can be obtained, suitable to orientate the entire scene with RPCs model; moreover the SISAR RPCs can be easily loaded into any commercial software.

## 5.1   Rigorous Model Results

The image has been oriented with rigorous models implemented in SISAR and in OrthoEngine. The orientation tests have been performed varying the number

**Table 2.** Features of GeoEye-1 image

| Area | GSD [m] | Off-nadir [°] | Scene coverage [Km x Km] | GPs |
|------|---------|---------------|--------------------------|-----|
| Rome | 0.50 | 12 | 16 × 15 | 37 |

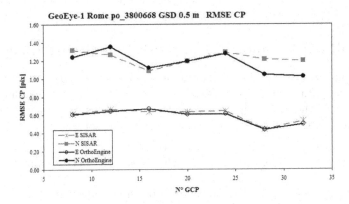

**Fig. 8.** Rigorous model - Image accuracy vs. GCP number for GeoEye-1 image of Rome

of GCPs and the image accuracy, represented by the RMSE computed over Check Points (CPs) residuals (CPs RMSE), was been analyzed. The RMSEs were computed both for the North and East residual components separately.

RMSE trend is similar for both software and accuracy value is around the GSD value; in particular CPs RMSE is approximately 0.30 m in East component and 0.60 m North component.

## 5.2    RPCs Vendors Results

As mentioned, the Rome GeoEye-1 scene is composed by two tiles, that are provided with two different RPCs files; therefore the two tiles have been oriented separately, which could be a remarkable drawback for several applications. In Tab. 3 the results, obtained using the vendors RPCs, are listed respectively for the first and the second tile of the Rome scene. Accuracy in terms of CPs RMSE has been evaluated for the RCPs orientation performed without adjustment, estimating both shift and affine trasformation using 5 GCPs.

Note that the results are quite different for the two tiles; moreover, the accuracy for the East component is always in the order of one pixel, whereas for the North component the shift and affine transformation improve the results significantly; it has to be underlined that the shift transformation performs slighly better and seems to be enough to model the correction, as already proven with other level 1B imagery (for example Ikonos ones).

**Table 3.** Results of GeoEye-1 image orientation with vendors RPCs

| | | RMSE CP [pix] | | | | |
|---|---|---|---|---|---|---|
| | | OrthoEngine | | | | |
| | | First Tile | | | Second Tile | |
| | n° GCP | EAST | NORTH | n° GCP | EAST | NORTH |
| Without correction | - | 0.91 | 8.41 | - | 1.06 | 8.29 |
| Shift transformation | 5 | 0.68 | 1.02 | 5 | 1.07 | 2.08 |
| Affine transformation | 5 | 0.87 | 1.07 | 5 | 1.13 | 2.13 |
| | | SISAR | | | | |
| | | First Tile | | | Second Tile | |
| | n° GCP | EAST | NORTH | n° GCP | EAST | NORTH |
| Without correction | - | 1.24 | 7.66 | - | 0.74 | 2.79 |
| Shift transformation | 5 | 0.66 | 0.90 | 5 | 1.03 | 1.78 |
| Affine transformation | 5 | 0.93 | 0.87 | 5 | 1.10 | 1.54 |

## 5.3   SISAR RPCs Results

In Fig. 9 and in Fig. 10 results of SISAR RPCs application are shown. The RPCs file has been obtained by a routine implemented in the software SISAR, that computes the coefficients on the basis of the rigorous model. A unique file, with 20 significant coefficients only, has been generated in order to orientate the entire scene.

SISAR RPCs are tested in the scientific SISAR software and in the commercial software OrthoEngine. It has to be noticed that the results are totally comparable with the rigorous ones, and the CPs RMSE trend is quite similar for the two software. Moreover, the results obtained using a shift and an affine transformation are respectively presented; again, the affine model does not improve significantly the accuracy achivable with the RPCs.

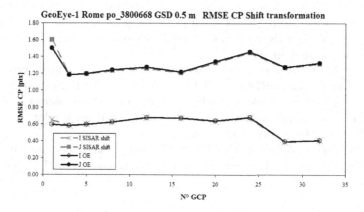

**Fig. 9.** SISAR RPCs, shift transformation - Image accuracy vs. GCP number for GeoEye-1 image of Rome

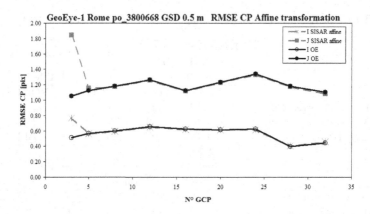

**Fig. 10.** SISAR RPCs, affine transformation - Image accuracy vs. GCP number for GeoEye-1 image of Rome

# 6    Conclusions

The GeoEye-1 satellite is able to acquire panchromatic and multispectral images at very high resolution. The paper presents an analysis about the radiometric and geometric features of a very recent image acquired on September 2009 over Rome (Italy).

As regard to the radiometric analysis, the results show that the noise is intensity dependent, in fact it is increasing with increasing grey values.

The MTF values at Nyquist frequency and the FWHM values were estimated for all the selected edges; the results were combined into average values for the along- and across-track direction. The results achieved show that the MTF values and the FWHM values seem to be similar for along and cross track direction, considering their standard deviation at the level of 0.15.

As regard to the geometric capability, the accuracy of the orientation performed with two software (PCI OrthoEngine and SISAR) is on the order of the pixel size, both using rigorous model and RPCs model, almost twice better in East than in North component.

In particular, the autonomously generated SISAR RPCs, which overcome the problem of the vendors RPCs related to two separated tiles, can be used also by commercial software (like OrthoEngine); commercial software results using SISAR RPC are comparable with the results obtained using vendors RPC in the same software and globally even better.

Moreover it possible to note that the simple shift adjustment eliminates almost the totality of RPC geolocation errors, as already encountered with level 1B imagery.

# References

1. Baltsavias, E.P., Paieraki, M., Zhang, L.: Radiometric and Geometric Evaluation of IKONOS Geo Images and Their Use for 3D Building Modeling. In: Joint ISPRS Workshop on High Resolution Mapping from Space (2001)
2. Choi, T.: IKONOS Satellite on Orbit Modulation Transfer Function (MTF) Measurement using Edge and Pulse Method. Master Thesis, South Dakota State University (2002)
3. Crespi, M., De Vendictis, L.: A Procedure for High Resolution Satellite Imagery Quality Assessment. Sensors 9(5), 3289–3313 (2009)
4. Crespi, M., Fratarcangeli, F., Giannone, F., Pieralice, F.: Chapter 4 - Overview on models for high resolution satellites imagery orientation. In: Li, D., Shan, J., Gong, J. (eds.) Geospatial Technology for Earth Observation data. Springer, Heidelberg (2009)
5. De Vendictis, L.: Quality assessment and enhancement of High Resolution Satellite Imagery for DSM extraction. PhD Thesis, Area di Geodesia e Geomatica Dipartimento di Idraulica Trasporti e Strade, Sapienza Universit di Roma (2007)
6. Golub, G.H., Van Loan, C.F.: Matrix Computation. The Johns Hopkins University Press, Baltimore and London (1993)
7. Hanley, H.B., Fraser, C.S.: Sensor orientation for high-resolution satellite imagery: further insights into bias-compensated RPC,
   http://www.isprs.org/istanbul2004/comm1/papers/5.pdf
8. Kohm, K., Mulawa, D.: On-Orbit Geolocation Accuracy andImage Quality Performance of the GeoEye-1High Resolution Imaging Satellite. In: GeoEye JACIE Conference Fairfax, Virginia (2009)
9. Tao, C.V., Hu, Y.: 3D reconstruction methods based on the rational function model. Photogrammetric Engineering & Remote Sensing 68(7), 705–714 (2002)
10. Toutin, T.: Geometric processing of remote sensing images: models, algorithms and methods (review paper). International Journal of Remote Sensing 10, 1893–1924 (2004)
11. Zhang, L.: Automatic Digital Surface Model (DSM) Generation from Linear Array Images. PhD Dissertation, Institute of Geodesy and Photogrammetry, ETH Zurich (2005), ISBN 3-906467-55-4

# Local Detection of Three-Dimensional Systematic Errors in Satellite DSMs: Case Studies of SRTM and ASTER in Lombardy

Maria Antonia Brovelli, Xuefei Liu, and Fernando Sansò

DIIAR, Politecnico di Milano, Polo Regionale di Como
Via Valleggio 11, 22100 Como, Italy
{maria.brovelli,fernando.sanso}@polimi.it,
xuefei.liu@mail.polimi.it

**Abstract.** In this paper we present a method for detecting three-dimensional systematic errors of Digital Surface Models (DSMs) derived from satellite data. The detection process is realized via a three-dimensional comparison with reference altimetric models of better accuracy, by a matching process based on a 3D geospatial transformation without scale factor correction. The matching process of the two altimetric models is based on the estimation of the six parameters of a geospatial transformation between two 3D surfaces, minimizing the Euclidean distances between the surfaces by least squares method; this procedure does not require the *a priori* availability of homologous points. The method is applied on comparison of GPS surveys over Lombardy Region of Northern Italy, with SRTM (3 arc sec) and ASTER (1 arc sec) DSMs in the same region; tests of statistical significance are performed confirming, in the latter case, the existing 3D systematic error.

**Keywords:** DSM, GPS, systematic errors, 3D transformation.

## 1 Introduction

The Digital Surface Model (DSM) is a topographic representation of the earth's surface that includes buildings, vegetation, roads, as well as natural terrain features. DSMs provide us with a geometrically correct reference frame over which other data layers can be draped. They can also be used as a comparatively inexpensive means to ensure that cartographic products such as topographic line maps, or even road maps, have a much higher degree of accuracy than would otherwise be possible.

Digital surface models may be prepared in a number of ways: field surveys based on Global Positioning System (GPS) represent an optimal choice to produce high accuracy DSMs, yet they are used in few cases because of the high cost; instead, remote sensing surveying techniques are frequently used. One powerful technique for generating digital surface models is interferometric synthetic aperture radar (InSAR): two passes of a radar satellite or a single pass if the satellite is equipped with two antennas, like the Shuttle Radar Topography Mission (SRTM) instrumentation. The phase difference information between the SAR images is used to measure precisely

K. Sithamparanathan et al. (Eds.): PSATS 2010, LNICST 43, pp. 370–380, 2010.
© Institute for Computer Sciences, Social-Informatics and Telecommunications Engineering 2010

changes in the range, on the sub-wavelength scale, for corresponding points in an image pair. Analysis of the differential phase, and therefore change in distance, between the corresponding pixel centers and the observing antenna can provide information on terrain elevation. The vertical accuracy of the SRTM-3 generated DSM, with grid spacing of 3 arc-seconds, about 90 m, is stated as 16 m with 90% confidence level [1]. Alternatively, stereoscopic pairs can be employed using the digital image correlation method, where two optical images acquired with different angles taken from the same pass of an airplane or an Earth Observation Satellite, such as the visible and near-infrared (VNIR) band of the Advanced Spaceborne Thermal Emission and Reflection Radiometer (ASTER), an advanced multispectral imager, launched on board NASA's Terra spacecraft in December, 1999. The viewing geometry of ASTER is suitable for a global DSM generation with horizontal spatial resolution of 15 m and a near-pixel-size vertical accuracy. Pre-production estimated accuracies for the global product were 20 m at 95% confidence for vertical data and 30 m at 95% confidence for horizontal data, with a horizontal posting of 30 m [2].

The exterior quality (i.e. accuracy) of a DSM can be examined through a comparison with reference elevation data which did not participate in the generation of the DSM. The reference model can be either another DSM or irregularly distributed 3D points, in addition, these data are supposed to possess much better accuracy than the input data( at least one order of magnitude better than the DSM to be examined). In this way, systematic errors of the DSM may be revealed. Researches with a similar approach have been conducted in recent years, for instance, Koch et al. have published their results in SRTM quality assessment using algorithm based on the spatial similarity transformation [3].

In this paper we focus on the satellite DSM exterior quality evaluation and height accuracy calibration, via comparisons between DSM and GPS surveying data, SRTM- and ASTER-derived DSMs for the Lombardy region, in northern Italy were compared with GPS measurements, systematic errors were detected in these satellite DSMs.

## 2 Methodology: Least Squares Matching

An accuracy evaluation for a DSM can be performed by comparing it to reference elevation data, which can be either another DSM or irregularly distributed 3D points. The reference elevation data should be characterized by an accuracy of at least one order of magnitude better than the DSM to be examined. Moreover, in order to be compared, the models need to be transformed into a unique datum. For example, local products, usually given in a national datum, should be converted to a global one by a grid-based datum adjustment before they are compared to international models.

If there is only a simple translation between the two models, the classic two-and-a-half-dimensional (2.5D) calibration, which considers merely the average altimetric distance between the models, should be enough. Unfortunately this is not always the case (Figure 1): on the contrary, georeferentiation difference is often tridimensional, i.e. both rotation and translation exist between the two models: systematic errors in elevation data can be recognized to consist of mainly two components, the horizontal, often referred as positional accuracy, and the vertical component or accuracy of the attribute. However, positional and attribute accuracy generally cannot be separated;

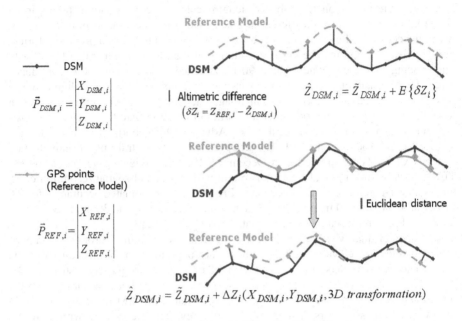

**Fig. 1.** From the traditional 2.5 D to the 3D calibration

the error may be due to an incorrect elevation value at the correct location, or a correct elevation for an incorrect location, or certain combination of the two.

Consequently a complete three-dimensional transformation between the two models is indispensable. Since both the DSM and the reference model describe the same terrain in the common geodetic datum, the difference between the two models is rather small, thus we can reasonably assume that between the two models there is no scale variation and the rotation is infinitesimal. Therefore DSM calibration methodology is based on the estimation of a spatial Helmert transformation without scale correction, minimizing the Euclidean distances between the surfaces by least squares method.

$$min \sum_i \left| \vec{P}_{DSM,i} - (I + R)\vec{p}_{REF,i} - \vec{t} \right|^2 \tag{1}$$

in which:

$$\vec{P}_{DSM,i} = \begin{bmatrix} X_{DSM,i} \\ Y_{DSM,i} \\ Z_{DSM,i} \end{bmatrix}, \quad \vec{p}_{REF,i} = \begin{bmatrix} X_{REF,i} \\ Y_{REF,i} \\ Z_{REF,i} \end{bmatrix},$$

$$R = \begin{bmatrix} 0 & R_z & -R_y \\ -R_z & 0 & R_x \\ R_y & -R_x & 0 \end{bmatrix}, \quad \vec{t} = \begin{bmatrix} T_x \\ T_y \\ T_z \end{bmatrix}$$

$X_{REF,i}, Y_{REF,i}, Z_{REF,i}$ are the Cartesian coordinates of reference data with greater accuracy, while $X_{DSM,i}, Y_{DSM,i}, Z_{DSM,i}$ are those of the DSM under examination;

$T_x, T_y, T_z$ and $R_x, R_y, R_z$ are the three parameters of translation and the three parameters of an infinitesimal rotation of the transformation, respectively.

Elevation values inside every DSM grid cell can be determined via a bilinear interpolation, calculated at the position corresponding to reference model's planimetrical coordinates. Consequently the DSM vector can be expressed as a function of horizontal coordinates of the reference model:

$$\begin{cases} X_{DSM,i} = X_{REF,i} \\ Y_{DSM,i} = Y_{REF,i} \\ Z_{DSM,i} = \tilde{Z}_{DSM,i} = Z_{bilinear}(X_{REF,i}, Y_{REF,i}) \end{cases} \tag{2}$$

in which:

$\tilde{Z}_{DSM,i}$ is the interpolated elevation at the position $(X_{REF,i}, Y_{REF,i})$,

$Z_{bilinear}(\bullet)$ is a bilinear interpolation function, which is then applied at every reference point position $(X_{REF,i}, Y_{REF,i})$.

Since the homologous points for the calibration process are calculated based on the DSM grid data and at every reference point position $(X_{REF,i}, Y_{REF,i})$, the whole procedure does not require *a priori* availability of homologous points.

The transformation therefore can be written as follows:

$$\begin{bmatrix} X_{GPS,i} \\ Y_{GPS,i} \\ Z_{bilinear}(X_{REF,i}, Y_{REF,i}) \end{bmatrix} = \begin{bmatrix} T_x \\ T_y \\ T_z \end{bmatrix} + \begin{bmatrix} 1 & R_z & -R_y \\ -R_z & 1 & R_x \\ R_y & -R_x & 1 \end{bmatrix} \begin{bmatrix} X_{REF,i} \\ Y_{REF,i} \\ Z_{REF,i} \end{bmatrix} \tag{3}$$

The six parameters ($T_x, T_y, T_z$ and $R_x, R_y, R_z$) of the 3D transformation are estimated by least squares method, adopting equation (3) for all the reference points; potentially existing systematic errors are revealed by examining these parameters. The residuals of the transformation can be considered as either local systematic errors or random ones.

## 3   Data Overview

The study area of this work lies in Lombardy Region, in the north of Italy, between 44° to 47° North latitude and 8° to 11° East longitude. Lombardy is located in Alpine and Pre-Alpine area, characterized by both smooth plain (Padana Plain) and hard reliefs (Rhaetian Alps and Bergamo Alps). All elevation data used in this work cover all the three distinct natural zones (mountains, hills and plains) in Lombardy region, data coverage is shown in Figure 2.

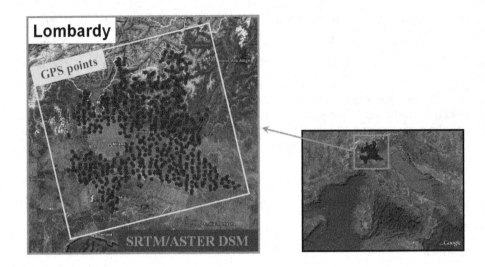

**Fig. 2.** Data coverage in the study zone

Two kinds of satellite DSMs have been used in this work: the global DSM derived from SRTM (version 4 from the CGIAR-CSI GeoPortal) and the ASTER-derived DSM. The global SRTM DSM has a grid spacing of 3 arc second (approx. 90 m) and the global vertical accuracy is assessed as 16 m with 90% confidence level; while pre-production estimated accuracies for the ASTER global product are 20 m at 95% confidence for vertical data and 30 m at 95% confidence for horizontal data, with a posting interval of 1 arc second (approx. 30 m). Both SRTM and ASTER data are georeferenced in geographic lat/long coordinates in WGS84 horizontal datum, with orthometric heights referenced to the EGM96 geoid [4][5].

On the other side, reference model for the calibration has constituted of 3D sparse points obtained by direct GPS measurements, with vertical and horizontal accuracy of a few centimeters; these points are characterized by stablility and accessiblity with materializations average distance among them of 20 km. GPS data were produced by Lombardy Region - General Department of Land and Urban Planning, Organizational Unit Infrastructure for Spatial Information (Regione Lombardia - Direzione Generale Territorio e Urbanistica - Unità Organizzativa Infrastruttura per l'Informazione Territoriale), GPS data are supplied in geographic lat/long coordinates in WGS84 horizontal datum, with height referenced to WGS84 ellipsoid.

## 4   Experiment

### 4.1   Data Preprocessing

The first part of data elaboration consists in searching the homologous points. As mentioned in previous section, homologous points for the calibration have been calculated automatically based on the DSM grid data and at every reference point position, using a MATLAB®-based module [6].

In this way we obtain the homologous points in the form:

$$\begin{cases} (\varphi_{GPS,i}, \lambda_{GPS,i}, h_{GPS,i}), \text{ referenced to the WGS84 Ellipsoid;} \\ (\varphi_{DSM,i}, \lambda_{DSM,i}, H_{DSM,i}), \text{ referenced to the WGS84 / EGM96 Geoid.} \end{cases}$$

The undulation of the geoid $N$ in the study area has been calculated using EGM96, the NASA and NIMA global geopotential model [7], since:

$$h_i = H_i + N_i \tag{4}$$

in which: $h_i$ is the ellipsoidal height of a point, while $H_i$ is the orthometric elevation of the point; $N_i$ expresses the corresponding undulation of the geoid.

So we obtain:

$$\begin{cases} (\varphi_{GPS,i}, \lambda_{GPS,i}, h_{GPS,i}) \\ (\varphi_{DSM,i}, \lambda_{DSM,i}, h_{DSM,i}) \end{cases}, \text{ both referenced to the WGS84 Ellipsoid.}$$

Subsequently all data in geographic coordinates have been converted into geocentric Cartesian coordinates:

$$\begin{cases} X_i = (N_i + h_i) \cos \varphi_i \cos \lambda_i \\ Y_i = (N_i + h_i) \cos \varphi_i \sin \lambda_i \\ Z_i = (N_i (1 - e^2) + h_i) \sin \varphi_i \end{cases} \tag{5}$$

in which: $N_i = \dfrac{a}{\sqrt{1 - e^2 \sin^2 \varphi_i}}$ , $e^2 = 1 - \dfrac{b^2}{a^2}$

For the WGS84 Earth Ellipsoid:

Semi-major axis a= 6 378 137.0000 m

Semi-minor axis b≈ 6 356 752.3142 m

Then the data have been converted into a local Cartesian coordinate system via the following 3D rototranslation:

$$\begin{bmatrix} x_i \\ y_i \\ z_i \end{bmatrix} = \begin{bmatrix} -\sin \lambda_0 & \cos \lambda_0 & 0 \\ -\sin \varphi_0 \cos \lambda_0 & -\sin \varphi_0 \sin \lambda_0 & \cos \varphi_0 \\ \cos \varphi_0 \cos \lambda_0 & \cos \varphi_0 \sin \lambda_0 & \sin \varphi_0 \end{bmatrix} \cdot \begin{bmatrix} X_i - X_0 \\ Y_i - Y_0 \\ Z_i - Z_0 \end{bmatrix} \tag{6}$$

in which: $(X_0, Y_0, Z_0)$ represents the barycenter of the homologous points expressed in geocentric Cartesian coordinate system, while $(\varphi_0, \lambda_0)$ are the corresponding geographic coordinates.

As a result, both GPS measurements and the DSM data in homologous points are expressed in local Cartesian coordinate system:

$$\begin{cases} (x_{GPS,i}, y_{GPS,i}, z_{GPS,i}) \\ (x_{DSM,i}, y_{DSM,i}, z_{DSM,i}) \end{cases}, \text{ referenced to the local Cartesian coordinate system.}$$

The proposed 3D transformation is based on the hypothesis that the possible horizontal errors in DSM would not exceed its grid cell size (this allows us to interpolate the DSM elevation values considering only the four vertices of each pixel in which the GPS measurement falls). This hypothesis has been verified by comparison tests between the satellite DSMs and an available high resolution local LIDAR (Laser Imaging Detection and Ranging) DSM, which covers a significant subpart of Lombardy; the accuracy of the LIDAR DSM has been calibrated by GPS Real-Time Kinematic measurements in previous work [8]. Satellite DSMs are compared with the local LIDAR DSM at pixel level at an offset position and its adjacent parts (in a few pixels scale); by examining the linear correlation coefficients of the two DSMs and by testing for the significance of correlation coefficient we confirmed that the maximum correlation of both SRTM and ASTER DSM with respected to LIDAR DSM was obtained without shift more than one pixel (In a few cases the actual sample maximum can be displaced by a pixel, yet its value is not significantly different from the one that we find within the pixel).

At this point we can perform the 3D transformation between the GPS data and the DSMs, in local Cartesian coordinate system; the systematic errors between the two models will be detected, by examining the transformation results.

## 4.2  Comparison of SRTM DSM with GPS Data

The first three-dimensional calibration test is conducted on four SRTM DSM tiles which cover the entire Lombardy region, using the GPS data in the same zone as reference model. The calibration is computed by the least squares estimation on the calculated homolougous points in the previous step.

Table 1 reports the statistics before the transformation estimation: a 2.5D bias of 0.36 m with a standard deviation of 10.33 m has been detected between the SRTM and GPS data.

**Table 1.** 2.5D statistics of comparison SRTM DSM - GPS measurements

| Number of points | 608 |
|---|---|
| 2.5D bias (m) | -0.36 |
| $\sigma$ (m) | 10.33 |
| min (m) | -68.53 |
| max (m) | 44.57 |

Table 2 shows the estimated parameters and residuals of the transformation. The application of the 3D transformation improves the differences standard deviations (from the original 10.33 m to 5.95 m after the transformation). Statistical significance of these residual parameters has been verified by a standard F-test; it turned out that the parameters are slightly significant (empirical Fisher Test: 2.29, theoretical (95%): 2.10), which confirms a systematic difference, however small it is, exists between the SRTM data and the GPS measurements.

**Table 2.** Parameters and residuals of the 3D transformation SRTM - GPS

| *Transformation parameters* | |
|---|---|
| Tx (m) | -0.00541 |
| Ty (m) | -0.00043 |
| Tz (m) | -0.33305 |
| Rx (rad) | -2.4102E-006 |
| Ry (rad) | -1.6044E-005 |
| Rz (rad) | -5.7450E-008 |
| *Transformation residuals* | |
| 2.5D bias (m) | 0 |
| σ (m) | 5.95 |
| min (m) | -67.18 |
| max (m) | 44.20 |

Transformation results show that the vertical translation may be mainly responsible to the global systematic errors, compared to the planimetric shifts. To better investigate the significance of planimetric shifts and rotations, an identical calculation has been applied on the same sets, with the 2.5D bias removed *a priori*.

Table 3 reports the 2.5D bias-free statistics, the transformation parameters and the residuals statistics for the comparison between SRTM and GPS data. All the parameters remain equal to their counterparts of the complete transformation, except for the vertical shift, whose reduction corresponds exactly to the 2.5D bias. The empirical Fisher Test value decreases from 2.29 to 1.92, making the parameters of the transformation no longer significant. This confirms that vertical shift plays a principal role in the systematic errors detected in SRTM DSM compared to GPS data.

**Table 3.** Parameters and residuals of the 3D transformation (2.5 bias-free) SRTM - GPS

| *2.5 bias-free transformation parameters* | |
|---|---|
| Tx (m) | -0.00541 |
| Ty (m) | -0.00043 |
| Tz (m) | 0.02961 |
| Rx (rad) | -2.4102E-006 |
| Ry (rad) | -1.6044E-005 |
| Rz (rad) | -5.7450E-008 |
| *2.5 bias-free transformation residuals* | |
| 2.5D bias (m) | 0 |
| σ (m) | 5.95 |
| min (m) | -67.18 |
| max (m) | 44.20 |

### 4.3   Comparison of ASTER DSM with GPS Data

The three-dimensional calibration test is then conducted on eleven ASTER DSM tiles all over the entire Lombardy region, using again the GPS data in the same zone as reference model.

Table 4 reports the statistics before the 3D transformation application: a 2.5D bias of 5.77 m with a standard deviation of 9.25 m has been detected between the ASTER and GPS data.

**Table 4.** 2.5D statistics of comparison ASTER DSM - GPS measurements

| Number of points | 608 |
|---|---|
| 2.5D bias (m) | 5.77 |
| σ (m) | 9.25 |
| min (m) | -53.21 |
| max (m) | 53.09 |

Table 5 shows the estimated parameters and residuals of the transformation. Similar as in the case of SRTM vs. GPS comparison, 3D transformation application improves the differences standard deviations (from the original 9.25 m to 5.18 m after the transformation). F-test confirms the presence of a considerably significant systematic error of the ASTER-derived DSM with respect to the GPS measurements (transformation parameters lead to an empirical Fisher value of 144.64, while the theoretical (95%) value is 2.10).

**Table 5.** Parameters and residuals of the 3D transformation ASTER - GPS

| *Transformation parameters* | |
|---|---|
| Tx (m) | -0.00848 |
| Ty (m) | 0.00858 |
| Tz (m) | 5.63768 |
| Rx (rad) | -3.9744E-005 |
| Ry (rad) | -2.1638E-005 |
| Rz (rad) | -7.8187E-008 |
| *Transformation residuals* | |
| 2.5D bias (m) | 0 |
| σ (m) | 5.18 |
| min (m) | -57.46 |
| max (m) | 44.74 |

Again, a 2.5 bias-free transformation is applied on the same ASTER and GPS data set, in order verify the vertical translation's role in the global systematic errors detected in ASTER data.

Table 6 reports the 2.5D bias-free statistics, the transformation parameters and the residuals statistics for the comparison between ASTER and GPS data. All the parameters remain equal to their counterparts of the complete transformation, except for the vertical shift, whose reduction corresponds exactly to the 2.5D bias between the two altimetric models. The empirical Fisher Test value has decreased dramatically from 144.64 to 19.23, yet the test result remains positive: transformation parameters are still statistically significant. This result shows that even though the 2.5D bias is largely responsible in the systematic errors in ASTER DSM compared to GPS data, a full three-dimensional transformation is indispensable in order to remove all the systematic errors detected in ASTER DSM.

**Table 6.** Parameters and residuals of the 3D transformation (2.5 bias-free) ASTER - GPS

| *2.5 bias-free transformation parameters* | |
|---|---|
| Tx (m) | -0.00848 |
| Ty (m) | 0.00858 |
| Tz (m) | -0.12798 |
| Rx (rad) | -3.9744E-005 |
| Ry (rad) | -2.1638E-005 |
| Rz (rad) | -7.8187E-008 |
| *2.5 bias-free transformation residuals* | |
| 2.5D bias (m) | 0 |
| σ (m) | 5.18 |
| min (m) | -57.46 |
| max (m) | 44.74 |

## 5   Conclusions

This paper shows results of evaluation of the proper georeferencing of a DSM derived from satellite data, by determining its accuracy compared to local GPS measurements of a high accuracy; the algorithm used is based on a spatial similarity transformation without scale variation on the two altimetric data sets which have to be in the same datum. This algorithm does not require any *a priori* availability of homologous points. Experiments have been conducted on SRTM-derived and ASTER-derived DSM data in Lombardy Region, Northern Italy, both in 2.5D and in complete 3D comparison.

Systematic errors have been detected both in SRTM DSM and in ASTER DSM, compared to GPS data; in both cases vertical shifts play a principal role in the DSM systematic errors. However, three dimensional systematic errors in SRTM DSM are not significant, while in ASTER DSM case, a significant rototranslational systematic error has been confirmed. We can conclude that before the further application of the global ASTER DSM, a complete three-dimensional calibration is necessary.

# References

1. Jarvis, A., Rubiano, J., Nelson, A., Farrow, A., Mulligan, M.: Practical use of SRTM data in the tropics: comparisons with digital elevation models generated from cartographic data. In: Working document no. 198, Centro Internacional de Agricultura Tropical, CIAT (2004)
2. ASTER GDEM Validation Team (METI/ERSDAC-NASA/LPDAAC-USGS/EROS): ASTER Global DEM Validation Summary Report (2009)
3. Koch, A., Heipke, C., Lohmann, P.: Quality Assessment of SRTM DTM: methodology and practical results. In: Symposium on Geospatial Theory, Processing and Applications, Ottawa (2002)
4. CGIAR Consortium for Spatial Information (CGIAR-CSI),
   `http://srtm.csi.cgiar.org`
5. ASTER Global Digital Elevation Model (ASTER GDEM)-Earth Remote Sensing Data Analysis Center (ERSDAC), `http://www.ersdac.or.jp`
6. Brovelli, M.A., Caldera, S., Liu, X.: 3D comparison of DTMs without the use of homologous points. In: The 6th International Symposium on Digital Earth, Processing, Beijing (2009)
7. Lemoine, F.G., Kenyon, S.C., Factor, J.K., Trimmer, R.G., Pavlis, N.K., Chinn, D.S., Cox, C.M., Klosko, S.M., Luthcke, S.B., Torrence, M.H., Wang, Y.M., Williamson, R.G., Pavlis, E.C., Rapp, R.H., Olson, T.R.: The development of the joint NASA GSFC and NIMA geopotential model EGM96. NASA/TP-1998-206861. In: Goddard Space Flight Center, Greenbelt, Maryland (1998)
8. Brovelli, M.A., Caldera, S., Liu, X., Sansò, F.: Valutazione dell'accuratezza tridimensionale di un modello digitale del terreno. In: Convegno nazionale SIFET Dalle misure al modello digitale, Mantova, pp. 31–36 (2009)

# Interactive Access and Processing of Multispectral Imagery: The User in the Loop

Bruno Simões[1], Stefano Piffer[1], Angelo Carriero[2], Giuseppe Conti[1,*],
and Raffaele De Amicis[1]

[1] Fondazione Graphitech,
Via Alla Cascata 56C, Trento, Italy
Tel.: +39 0461 283397, Fax: +39 0461 283398
{bruno.simoes,stefano.piffer,giuseppe.conti,
raffaele.de.amicis}@graphitech.it
[2] Provincia Autonoma di Trento – Servizio Foreste e Fauna
Via G.B. Trener, 3, Trento, Italy
angelo.carriero@provincia.tn.it

**Abstract.** Accessing and processing of multispectral imagery in an interactive way is essential to a number of operational scenarios. This paper illustrates their use in the context of forest management and planning, by presenting the results of a system that allows operators to access large repositories of geographical data, including multi-spectral imaging, and to process them in a very user friendly way. The project has seen the involvement of personnel from a local planning authority and it has provided the chance to confront with a number of issues related to today's large availability of airborne and satellite data. This is challenging current technologies, creating a potential information overload. The paper will illustrate how the use of interactive 3D technologies to access and process multi-spectral data within a comprehensive framework capable to manage a large variety of different geographical information, can be beneficial to reduce access time to information and to improve the entire decision-making process.

**Keywords:** environmental planning, satellite imaging, web-based access, 3D GeoVisual analytics.

## 1 Introduction

Geographic Information (GI) repositories are constantly growing in size and complexity [1]. Data within these repositories is usually generated by Geographical Information Systems (GIS), Computer-Aided Design software (CAD), image processing systems and by a large number of specifically designed software providing real-time information coming from different sensors (e.g. pollution, traffic etc.).

The field of GI is being also characterized by the success enjoyed by consumer-oriented 3D geobrowsers such as Google™ Earth and Microsoft® Bing™ Maps 3D. These have fundamentally contributed to extend the scope of the GI domain, far

---

* Corresponding author.

K. Sithamparanathan et al. (Eds.): PSATS 2010, LNICST 43, pp. 381–395, 2010.
© Institute for Computer Sciences, Social-Informatics and Telecommunications Engineering 2010

beyond the exclusive domain of a small elite of experts, with the introduction of 3D interactive visualization systems. In fact although 3D geobrowsers have been designed for consumer use, indeed their widespread success has determined their perhaps inadequate use in professional contexts. Nonetheless this trend, in turn, has contributed to the development of 3D visualization capabilities in other software tools specifically engineered for professional and expert use.

Both professional Geographic Information Systems (GIS) as well as general-purpose geobrowsers are heavily dependent on accurate and up-to-date high-resolution airborne and satellite imagery. Geobrowsers heavily rely on Digital Elevation Models (DEM) acquired by satellites since they require accessing DEM at large if not near-global scale. Within these systems satellite data plays undoubtedly a key role both in that it essential to represent the Earth surface as well as to ensure access to complex information, for instance through multi-spectral data over vast coverage.

However the constantly increasing availability of high resolution airborne and satellite data, is causing a critical "information overload". A remarkable example of this is the recent data centre built by Microsoft for its 3D solution Virtual Earth which has been designed to accommodate up to 15 Petabytes (15*1015 bytes) of satellite imaging or the Earthscope project that expects to generate daily outputs of over 10 terabytes. In order to support the operators' decision making process within several scenarios, including land use and planning, environmental monitoring and management to name but a few, it is necessary to develop efficient software technologies capable to provide intelligent access and filtering of available information through automatic or semi-automatic extraction of thematic information.

Such an information overload is yielding two potential criticalities. The first is related to the difficulty to access, manage and distribute through the network data in an efficient manner. Equally importantly, this growth in data available is challenging interoperability, an essential requirement within the domain of Geographical Information. In fact, today's enterprise-wide, network-based, GIS infrastructures heavily relay on standards and protocols which appear increasingly unfit to cope with such a fast expanding data growth.

Additionally, along with this information explosion, operators are facing an increasing difficulty to assess the accuracy of a particular dataset and its suitability for a given task. In fact a number of domain-specific scenarios require frequent update of large operational geographical datasets, often relying on complex enterprise-wide GIS systems, referred to as Spatial Data Infrastructures (SDI), where the traditional process of review and update of Geographical Information (GI), typically based on field survey, can be extremely time consuming and costly, if not impracticable. It has became necessary to develop methods for supporting, through automatic or semi-automatic processes the management of huge, complex and high dimensional datasets.

This paper presents the results of a project dealing with the aforementioned issues, where operators from the Forest Department of the Autonomous Province of Trento in Italy, needed to be able to assess, very efficiently and in a very user-friendly way, three dimensional distribution of the different vegetation species over relatively large forested areas. To do so operators needed a be able to access interactively different bands of multispectral imagery and to render them interactively over a 3D representation of a digital terrain  (both as DSM – Digital Surface Model and DTM – Digital Terrain Model) created from satellite or airborne high resolution LIDAR data.

This first assessment was essential to quickly identify specific portions of forest where further onsite in-depth survey needed to be scheduled. The availability of an interactive tool capable of ensuring interactive access and processing to the variety of information available ranging from LIDAR, to multispectral imaging, to standard GIS information, has significantly improved their operational efficiency. Due to the nature of the application, it was required that operators could access a very user-friendly fast responding interface, whose use would require short training time.

## 2  Outlook

In the case of the project described within this paper, the Forest and Fauna Unit of the Province of Trento, Italy, together with the local university had started a project to assess the use of remote sensing data in the context of forest management. A first feasibility study had highlighted the potential, in terms of assessment of dendrologic features, of using LIDAR and hyper spectral data.

The process includes the identification of a number of macro-tasks such as analysis of the main requirements and pre-processing of data, classification and identification of different species, assessment of forest density, assessment of forest structure, assessment of biomass height within the forest, assessment of scalability of the project to the entire Provincial territory.

For this reason a first set of LIDAR and hyper spectral data were acquired within three sample areas representatives of the most important forest pattern in the area ranging from coppice to alpine spruce forests. These sample areas were chose in Val di Sella (Sella valley) in the area of Padergnone and within the Paneveggio Forest for a total surface of about 1500 hectares.

As far as the LIDAR data were concerned, a point cloud was retrieved as a tuple {x, y, z, I} (I being the intensity of laser) and with a density not lower than 5 points per square meter. As far as hyper spectral data were concerned these included 64 bands within the 400 and 100 nm range. All the information have undergone a geo-referencing and radiometric correction process, both on single passes and on the entire mosaic, at the spatial resolution of 1 meter.

Concurrently, within the same areas, onsite surveys were conducted with the aim of assessing precision of remote sensing procedures according to the different forest layouts. The onsite surveys were planned to collect two specific datasets, respectively to create an assessment model and for its validation.

More precisely 165 sample areas were identified, all localized within the different forest types, ranging from beechwood, norway spruce to holm oak forests. Through the use of LIDAR and hyper spectral data it was possible to assess, with high precision, the following parameters: plant height, forest species, horizontal and vertical structure, density and biomass.

From this experience it become clear that forest classification, also within most complex forest configurations such as mixed forest, yielded good results. For this reason it was chosen to develop a technology that could be used by forest expert during the editing of forest plans. For this reason it was decided to create a 3D tool that could enable interactive manipulation of:

- LIDAR data, with the possibility to create real-time cross section to detect forest structures (e.g. single plane, multiple plane, irregular etc.).
- Hyper spectral data with the possibility to visualize, in false color (RGB), three different bands among the 64 available, in order to highlight the different species on the basis of the hyper spectral characteristic triad of the species of interest.

## 3   State of the Art

In the past, the domain of 3D scientific visualization has explored several techniques to ensure access to complex data patterns in an interactive way through the use of 3D visualization that could support the understanding of an evolving phenomenon.

3D visualization can be extremely effective to ensure reasoning over such a vast range of n-dimensional information. With the correct design in terms of interface layout and information items, large amount of data can be quickly and easily comprehended by a human observer through the use of 3D graphics [2]. In fact it is well acknowledged that visualization provides an additional cognitive support that improves context awareness   [3]. When information is presented visually, efficient innate human capabilities can be used to perceive and process data. Information visualization techniques amplify cognition by increasing human mental resources, reducing search times, improving recognition of patterns, increasing inference making, and increasing monitoring scope [3] [4] all essential elements of environmental management process [5] [6] [7] [8].

However visualization alone often does not suffice to support analysis, to provide model and hypothesis-making. In recent years scientists have developed a discipline that combines the benefits of data mining and information visualization within a geospatial context, which is referred to as GeoVisual Analytics (GVA) [9]. GVA is capable to provide integrated visualization, filtering and reasoning solutions to better support operators looking for design decision support [4]. Through GVA tools, users can typical acquire visual cues that can help them formulate a set of viable models.

An ideal environment for GVA in fact should provide seamless integration of computational and visual techniques. For instance, the visual overview may be based on some preliminary data transformations appropriate to the data and task. Interactive focusing, selecting, and filtering could be used to isolate data associated with a hypothesis, which could then be passed to an analysis engine with informed parameter settings. Results could be superimposed on the original information to show the differences between the raw data and the computed model, with errors highlighted in a visual manner. This process could be iterated if the resulting model did not match the data with sufficient accuracy, or the analyst could refocus on a different subspace of information [10]. For this reason GVA is essential in contexts such as understanding of complex spatial relationships among information spaces and different datasets, for instance to define the most appropriate evacuation routes or to plot an emergency plan [11] [12] [13].

In the specific context of forest cover management and analysis, several authors [14] agree on the fact that concurrent access to satellite and GIS data is essential to create maps and to assess indicators such as cover changes, forest recolonization dynamics, forest structures evolution to name but a few.

Furthermore providing web-based access to forest-related data is an essential priority as acknowledged by experts operating in the field of forest management. Works such as [15] and [16] clearly indicate how the possibility to concurrently access different information including satellite imaging, cartography and alphanumerical data through web-based repositories is key to their operational activities.

Last but not least within the wider European context, the European Commission has clearly acknowledge the importance of providing standardized access geospatial information related to the environment. In fact The EC is promoting the creation of a Infrastructure for Spatial Information in Europe (INSPIRE) (http://inspire.jrc.it/home.html) to improve utilization of geographic information of environmental interest on a European level. The INSPIRE directive [17] together with GMES (Global Monitoring for Environment and Security) [18] programme based on data received from Earth Observation satellites whose results will converge into GEOSS - Global Earth Observation System of Systems [19] by Group on Earth Observations (GEO), SEIS - Shared Environmental Information System [21] [22] all clearly testify the great attention paid by the international community to this issue.

## 4 The System Developed

The application developed has been engineered to provide strong support to operators looking for decision support in the context of forest planning, monitoring and management. Typically operators have to refer to an extremely wide range of heterogeneous multi-source, multi-dimensional, time-varying information sources, including GIS maps, morphology of the terrain and forest canopy through LIDAR data (Digital Terrain Model - DTM or Digital Surface Model – DSM). The very nature of the processes, which are intrinsically cooperative -as diverse operators may be involved- underlines the importance of developing user-friendly universal interfaces. Navigation and data access must be complemented with functions that enable operators to analyze interrelations between spatial information, data patterns and environmental effects through interactive processing of a range of satellite and airborne data.

Within this scenario the complexity of most standard Geographical Information Systems (GIS) and 3D GIS [22] [23] [24] in fact is far too complex for decision makers. For this reason a Geo-Visual Analytical approach was preferred. The goal was to deliver a web-based 3D solution capable to provide interoperable access to geographical information and satellite imaging that was able to provide strong links between data transformation and visualization to better support analysis. The tool should also provide the capability to define customized processing functionalities, for instance to cross-relate data from multi-spectral datasets, in a very user friendly manner. For this reason it was imperative to provide alternative visual and user friendly solutions to traditional programming of simulation procedures, which notably require extensive training and time.

The system developed has been engineered as an articulated enterprise level Service-Oriented Architecture designed to provide all the functionalities required to access, manage and process large sets of multi-dimensional GIS and satellite data through OGC – OpenGIS Consortium compliant web services. The entire infrastructure has been designed to benefit from the web services abstract model to provide access to complex operational workflows and simulations which are essential to complex daily analysis, yet retaining high usability and fast response.

At client level, operators can benefit of a very user-friendly 3D interface, which allows them for instance to navigate within the 3D territory, to visualize and compose images from different bands of multispectral datasets and perform complex processing functionalities in a very visual way.

### 4.1 Client Side

The client application developed is capable to render a 3D scene of a large scale environment containing a multitude of different data sets ranging from satellite imaging, to multi-spectral data, to vector-based geographical information. Altimetry information on the terrain are streamed, via web service, from a server to the client as raw height maps at variable level of resolutions, built from SRTM30Plus (Shuttle Radar Topography Mission) dataset generated during the Space Shuttle Endeavour mission in 2000. This publicly available dataset ensures near global scale coverage at convenient resolutions ranging from 30 to 90 meters. The use of relatively low precision data allows fast rendering with standard computing hardware, while retaining the overall morphology of the terrain. Moreover this allows saving bandwidth to the benefit of high resolution airborne of satellite imaging.

As illustrated in Figure 1, operators can conveniently access cartographies, sensor data, multi-band datasets and overly them within the same scene to perform analyses and studies. Most relevantly, as it will be illustrated in a later section, the client can also be used to easily configure simulations over a variety of data. This is done in a visual way following a visual programming approach where operators can drag and drop processing unit, represented as icons, and connect them to create a meaningful processing sequence. The computations requested for the processing are then performed at server level, in a completely transparent manner and results of simulation are sent back to the client in an interoperable format. This ensures high scalability and allows the creation of very lightweight client applications.

Additional information on interoperable access to processing functionalities is beyond the scope of this paper. Full details on the technology developed can be read from previous works of the authors [25] [26] [1].

The application has been developed on Java extending the World Wind APIs [27] with regard to 3D geo-visualization and it makes use of Java Web Start [28] technology to assist the deployment of client applications.

Following the architecture described in Figure 2, the client application has been engineered with the goal of delivering a web-based 3D access to data exposed on the network via a number of OpenGIS Consortium (OGC) standards. This in fact was considered essential to ensure access to the variety of geographical information and satellite imagery available within enterprise-level infrastructures. Specifically interoperability is enforced through support of a number of OGC standards including Web Map Service (WMS) for raster cartography and airborne or satellite imaging [29],

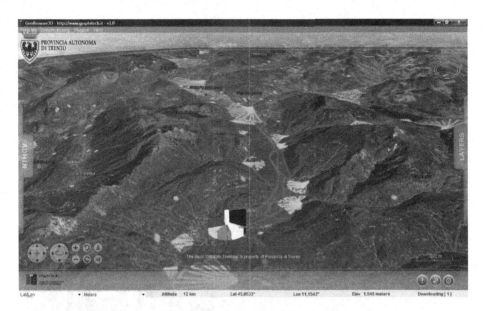

**Fig. 1.** The image of the system where the user concurrently accesses satellite imaging, real-time sensor information, GIS vector layer within a single environment

Web Feature Service (WFS) [30] for vector based information, Web Coverage Service (WCS) [31] for time-varying data related to coverages of portions of territory and Web Processing Service (WPS) [32] essential to expose processing functionalities via the web through a standard interoperable format. All these services are exposed by a federation of server geographically distributed.

As illustrated in Figure 2 this architecture enables the client software to make use of data and services coming from multiple sources in multiple formats and process them, if necessary, by using distributed processing [1] providing strong support to operators looking for decision support through an ideal environment for analysis that integrates computational and visual techniques.

Furthermore processing of complex and large dataset, typical of Earth Observation data, takes place between components at server level where computing performance is highest and bandwidth can be very high. We shall see how this feature, in the scenario analyzed, has brought to considerable advantages in terms of computing and networking resources optimization.

As a matter of fact this approach requires dealing with scalability at the server side as these becomes responsible for the processing of work load from all the client applications [1]. Furthermore this architecture can easily be extended to benefit from the potential of cloud computing for any processing activity. Following this approach, the operator can pay for temporarily computing resources, if they are only necessary for some peek period. These resources are then transparently accessed from clients applications, optimizing investments and resource allocation.

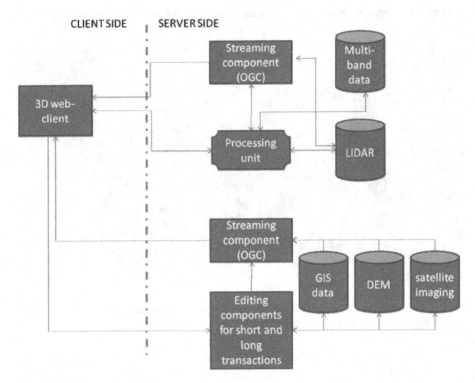

**Fig. 2.** The overview of the architecture

## 4.2  Processing of Multi-spectral Data

As mentioned in the previous section the approach followed allows to distribute the processing capabilities over a federation of servers each exposing its processing capabilities through a standardized communication interface. With such a distributed infrastructure it becomes possible to develop lightweight client applications which are only required to interact with processing parameters and to show the final results, once these are received from the network. The client is also responsible for ensuring orchestration of services when services (processes) chains are composed.

An example will help us illustrate the benefits of this approach when the user has to perform some processing over a very high-resolution dataset. The datasets used for the test were 32 multi-band imagery each containing 63 or 126 bands (from approximately 400 to 1000 Mhz) each represented by raw 256 color grayscale image. If the user wants to see the content of each band of the multispectral dataset this is sent from the server to the clients, as compressed image (PNG) through the WMS protocol, where each band is visualized as a gray image. The operator can use several tools available at the client side to visualize and process this data. Additionally operators needed, within the same environment, to visualise and overlay the multi-band imagery to LIDAR datasets (both DTM and DSM) with a resolution of 1x1 meter. The areas covered by the different datasets, i.e. muti-spectral imaging and LIDAR, did not coincide although they overlapped for most of the areas covered.

**Fig. 3.** The area identifying high-resolution multi-spectral data is available

The client software shows automatically all the areas containing multispectral or LIDAR data available from the servers, which are identified by a blue bounding box as shown in Figure 3. These bounding boxes are retrieved automatically from the server at run-time, enabling in this way the operator to be aware of any high-resolution data available on one or more servers prior to visualising. Due this approach the client initially only needs to render bounding boxes and it requests the full dataset only when required.

Once the operator decides to see the multi-spectral data he/she can seamlessly integrate his other airborne or satellite imagery, combine them with several maps, all retrieved through standard Web Map Services (WMS) within the same virtual environment. When a multi-spectral dataset is received for the first time, it is cached locally, at the client side, and re-used, if static, on following requests, thus further improving performances and reducing bandwidth usage. The transparency of each of these datasets, dealt with by the client as a different information layer, can also be adjusted in real time for better analysis and visualization. Furthermore the different datasets can be superimposed at wish by selecting the proper stacking order. This for instance was considered an essential requirement for the operators to be able to provide better support to decisions.

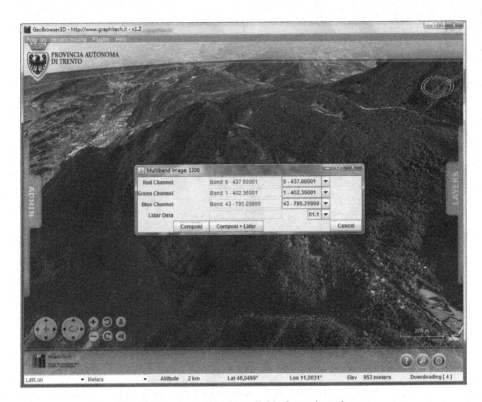

**Fig. 4.** Selection of bands available for a given dataset

One important aspect during operational activities is the concurrent visualization of different bands, to be used for interpretation. Photo-interpretation of different combinations of bands allows the operators to determine regions of interest and important features in the forest identifying areas which require further analysis or on site survey.

To visualize multispectral images, a Red-Green-Blue (RGB) composite image is usually generated from the data through a number of statistical methods. As a data compression algorithm, this approach provides a n:1 image compression ratio, while preserving edge feature information. For remote sensing community, this application provides a visualization tool for realizing the full edge information content in hyperspectral images, such as those obtained through satellite imaging. Such high-dimensional photometric data is not easily tractable by traditional geobrowsers [33].

When the user wants to compose a RGB image from three bands of a given multispectral dataset then he/she only needs to click on the corresponding bounding box. As shown in Figure 4, a new windows will appear where he/she can select the desired bands to compose the image. When the operator confirms the operation, the request is sent to the server for processing and the resulting composed RGB image is returned through the WMS service and located at the proper location within the virtual scene as shown in Figure 5. The process is very fast, since only the final composed image is sent over the network and since the merging process is performed by a dedicated server. A further advantage is that if a new, more efficient version of the service is

**Fig. 5.** The final composed RGB image with the selected bands

available, all the user can immediately benefit from it in a completely automatic and transparent manner.

As mentioned previously, in order to maximise rendering performance at the client level and to reduce network traffic, information on the altimetry of the terrain is sent to the client by default at low resolution based on the SRTM30Plus (Shuttle Radar Topology Mission) dataset. However this type of information, although suitable for general-purpose large-scale navigation falls short when detailed analysis of a specific area are needed. In this case, when the standard Digital Elevation Model (DEM) resolution provided by the client application does not suffice, the operator can also use a high resolution sub-metric LIDAR dataset. This high-resolution datasets can be acquired through airborne LIDAR (Laser Imaging Detection and Ranging) technology, can easily scale up in order of Gigabytes just for some thousands of km2.

Sending this information by default would be unsustainable for the client (it would require extremely performing graphical hardware) and for the network, instead keeping this information at server side thus optimizing the overall system's performances.

When the operator needs to perform a more detailed analysis he can opt to combine the LIDAR dataset with the multispectral information available in order to have more accurate results. If the operator confirms this option, the LIDAR data (DSM or DTM) is then used to create a very high-resolution scene covering a limited area, as selected by the user, comprising the processed multi-band data superimposed to the high resolution

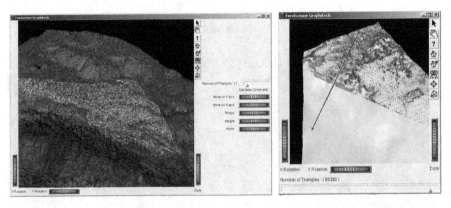

**Fig. 6.** The high resolution scene built combining LIDAR data with multi-spectral information

terrain. This information is prepared by the server, compressed and sent to the client that renders it on a new window together with a set of tools necessary to perform real-time cross sections and other analysis necessary to the operator as visible in Fig. 6.

### 4.3   Additional Processing Capabilities

Additionally to the processing illustrated in the previous section the operator can potentially perform any other processing task from his/her client if this is made available on the network through the interoperable WPS standard. The client in fact can be used by the operator to combine different elementary processing functionalities to create complex simulations in a very user friendly way. The operator, through their 3D client, can access the different processing functionalities made available through the network by a federation of processing services.

As illustrated in Figure 7, at the client side each processing unit is represented by a black box that receives data and provides an output as a result of its computing. These components are accessible  within a menu of the graphical user interface. Each black box provides access, in an interoperable way, to processing functionalities through web services as presented in previous works of the authors [34] using the Web Processing Service(WPS) protocol.

Such black boxes can dragged and dropped within the 3D scene and the operator can create complex graphs representing articulated simulation routines by composing graphs whose nodes represent an elementary processing unit.

For instance, in order to perform further and more complex multispectral data processing, the operator could use the WPS interface to retrieve specific multispectral bands, pass them as input to another web process, in order to perform some image analysis and then retrieve the final result for presentation at client level. It should be noted that the operator can create an arbitrarily complex process chain without the need to download them to the client software since the code is being run at the server level.

Through this approach client applications not only avoid heavy computational workloads, but the entire system save network bandwidth, since all necessary data for processing is transferred directly between servers where connection can be assumed to be much higher.

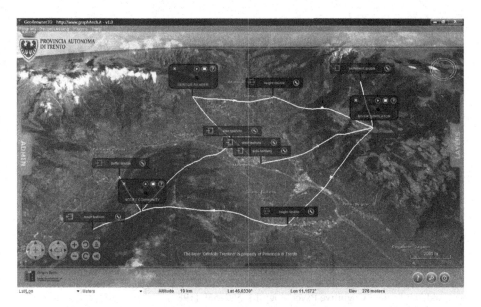

**Fig. 7.** An image showing a chain of process being created within the 3D scene

## 5 Conclusions

This paper presents the result of a system developed around the specific requirement of a user who needs to access large airborne and satellite data within an environment capable to render them together with other GIS data of relevance. Additionally the paper presents how the system developed has answer to the need of providing analysis feature, by allowing operators to perform specific processing tasks required for their operational activities.

The entire system has been engineered to benefit from a distributed Service Oriented Architecture where functionalities, including streaming of data, editing of dataset as well as processing features, are all available through interoperable open standards from the OGC – OpenGIS Consortium. This approach brings a considerable advantage in that it allows using services from a number of other applications complying with those standards. Additionally, as discussed throughout the paper, this has allowed a number of optimisations especially during the access and processing of large dataset since transactions requiring very high bandwidth can be reduced considerably.

**Acknowledgments.** Part of the achievements discussed in this paper as well as the data shown in the images were financed by the project - "Sviluppo di una Infrastruttura Dati Territoriali secondo una Architettura Orientata ai Servizi" commissioned by the Servizio Semplificazione e Sistemi Informativi, Department of Innovation, Research and ICT of the Autonomous Province of Trento, Italy.

# References

1. Simoes, B., Conti, G., Piffer, S., De Amicis, R.: Enterprise-level architecture for interactive web-based 3D visualization of geo-referenced repositories. In: Web3D 2009: Proceedings of the 14th International Conference on 3D Web Technology, Darmstadt, Germany, pp. 147–154. ACM, New York (2006)
2. Wright, W.: Business visualization applications. Computer Graphics and Applications (1997)
3. Card, S., Mackinlay, J., Shneiderman, B.: Readings in Information Visualization. Morgan Kaufmann, San Francisco (1999)
4. De Amicis, R., Conti, G., Simoes, B., Lattuca, R., Tosi, N., Piffer, S., Pellitteri, G.: Geovisual analytics for urban design in the context of future internet. International Journal on Interactive Design and Manufacturing, IJIDeM (2009)
5. Reddy, M., Leclerc, Y., Iverson, L., Bletter, N.: TerraVisionII: Visualizing massive terrain databases in VRML. IEEE Computer Graphics and Applications 19(2), 30–38 (1999)
6. Vinson, N.: Design Guidelines for Landmarks to Support Navigation in Virtual Environments. In: Proceeding of CHI 1999, pp. 278–285. ACM Press, New York (1999)
7. Thorndyke, P., Hayes-Roth, B.: Differences in Spatial Knowledge Acquired from Maps and Navigation. Cognitive Psychology 14, 560–589 (1982)
8. Darken, R., Sibert, J.: Navigating in Large Virtual Worlds. The International Journal of Human-Computer Interaction, 49–72 (1996)
9. De Amicis, R., Stojanovic, R., Conti, G.: GeoVisual Analytics: Geographical Information Processing and Visual Analytics for Environmental Security. Springer, Heidelberg (2009)
10. Thomas, J.J., Cook, K.A.: Illuminating the Path: The Research and Development Agenda for Visual Analytics, National Visualization and Analytics Center (2005)
11. Gore A.: The digital Earth: Understanding our planet in 21st century,
    http://www.isde5.org/al_gore_speech.htm
12. Grasso, V., Singh, A.: Global Environmental Alert Service (GEAS). In: Advances in Space Research, vol. 41, 11, pp. 1836–1852. Elsevier Ltd., Amsterdam (2008)
13. Grasso, V., Cervone, G., Singh, A., Kafatos, M.: Global environmental alert service. In: Proceedings of American Geophysical Union, Fall Meeting (2006)
14. Urbinati C., Benetti R., Viola F., Ferrari C.: (in Italian): Dinamismi della copertura forestale in Val di Tovel dal 1860 ad oggi. In: Studi Trentini di Scienze Naturali, Acta Biol., 81 (2), pp. 39-52, Museo Tridentino di Scienze Naturali, Trento (2006), ISSN 0392-0542
15. Päivinen, R., Köhl, M.: EFI Technical Report 17: European Forest Information and Comunication System. European Forest Institute, Joensuu Finland (2005)
16. Fior, C., Notarangelo, G.: (in Italian): Proposte per facilitare accesso e scambio via internet delle informazioni dei piani di assestamento forestale. In: FOREST@, The Italian Society of Silviculture and Forest Ecology (2007)
17. INSPIRE, Directive 2007/2/EC of the European Parliament and of the Council of 14 March 2007 establishing an Infrastructure for Spatial Information in the European Community
18. GMES - Global Monitoring for Environment and Security, http://www.gmes.info/
19. GEOSS - Global Earth Observation System of Systems,
    http://www.earthobservations.org/geoss.shtml
20. SEIS - Shared Environmental Information System,
    http://ec.europa.eu/environment/seis/index.htm
21. European Commission: Communication from the Commission to the Council - Towards a Shared Environmental Information System (SEIS), COM (2008) 46 final (2008)

22. Zlatanova, S., Rahman, A., Pilouk, M.: Trends in 3D GIS development. Journal of Geospatial Engineering 4, 1–10 (2002)
23. Brooks, S., Whalley, J.: Multilayer hybrid visualizations to support 3D GIS. Elsevier, Amsterdam (2008)
24. Köller, D., Lindstrom, P., Ribarsky, W., Hodges, L.F., Faust, N., Turner, G.: Virtual GIS: A real-time 3D geographic information system. In: Proceedings of the IEEE conference on visualization 1995, pp. 94–100 (1995)
25. Conti, G., De Amicis, R.: Service-Based Infrastructures For The New Generation Of Interactive Territorial Management Systems. In: Proceedings of the Symposium on Engineering and Management of IT-Based Organizational Systems, Germany (2008)
26. Conti, G., Andreolli, M., Piffer, S., De Amicis, R.: A 3D web based geographical information system for regional planning. In: proceedings of Webist 2008, Funchal, Madeira, Portugal (2008)
27. NASA WorldWind, http://worldwind.arc.nasa.gov
28. Sun Microsystems, Java Web Start, http://java.sun.com/javase/technologies/desktop/javawebstart/index.jsp
29. OGC, Web Map Service, http://www.opengeospatial.org/standards/wms
30. OGC, Web Feature Service, http://www.opengeospatial.org/standards/wfs
31. OGC, Web Coverage Service, http://www.opengeospatial.org/standards/wcs
32. OGC, Web Processing Service, http://www.opengeospatial.org/standards/wps
33. Socolinsky, D.A., Lawrence, B.W.: A New Visualization Paradigm for Multispectral Imagery And Data Fusion. In: IEEE Computer Society Conference on Computer Vision and Pattern Recognition. IEEE Computer Society, Los Alamitos (1999)
34. Conti, G., De Amicis, R., Simoes, B., Piffer, S.: Interactive Processing Service Orchestration of Environmental Information within a 3D web client. In: Proceedings of Geographic information technologies and spatial data infrastructure 11 (GSDI), Rotterdam, The Netherlands (2008)

# Time Series Analysis of the Digital Elevation Model of Kuwait Derived from Synthetic Aperture Radar Interferometry

K.S. Rao and Hala K. Al Jassar

Physics Department, Kuwait University, P.O. Box 5969, Safat 13060, Kuwait
{ksrao,hala}@kuc01.kuniv.edu.kw

**Abstract.** The digital elevation model derived from SAR Interferometry is prone to atmospheric, penetration into soil medium, system noise and decorrelation errors. Eight ASAR images are selected for this study which have unique data set forming 7 InSAR pairs with single master image. It is expected that all the DEMs should have the same elevation values spatially with in the noise limits. However, they differ very much with one another beyond the noise levels indicating the effects of atmosphere and other disturbances. The 7 DEMs are compared with the DEM of SRTM for the estimation of errors. The spatial and temporal distribution of errors in DEM are analyzed by considering several case studies.

**Keywords:** Digital Elevation Model, SAR Interferometry, phases, penetration depth.

## 1 Introduction

Synthetic Aperture Radar Interferometry (InSAR) is a powerful technique for deriving Digital Elevation Models (DEMs) with high spatial (a few tens of meters) and vertical (a few meters) resolutions [1,2] . The operational satellite systems such as Environmental satellite (ENVISAT), European Remote Sensing Satellite (ERS), Radar Satellite (RADARSAT), Japanese Earth Resources Satellite (JERS) etc., provide SAR data suitable for repeat pass InSAR. The repeat pass InSAR has limitations in deriving accurate DEM due to tropospheric phase delay as has been reported by several authors in the past [3, 4]. In view of several applications of DEM, both civilian and defense, there is an interest to develop models to minimize the tropospheric errors in repeat pass InSAR.

Kuwait, being a desert, has additional problems. The desert sand, being completely dry, allows microwaves to penetrate into the soil medium. The penetration depth depends on soil moisture. The annual variation of soil moisture over Kuwait desert will be from 3% to 10% by volume. Therefore, the measured phases in different SAR scenes used in repeat pass InSAR will be diffused leading to more errors in the derived DEM. Kuwait desert has some specific features such as scattered settlements, grazing of sheep, wind blow. These features will disturb the top soil layers leading the decorrelation of phases of the two SAR images used in repeat pass InSAR.

K. Sithamparanathan et al. (Eds.): PSATS 2010, LNICST 43, pp. 396–406, 2010.

The climate of Kuwait desert is arid with very hot dry summers and mild rainy winters [5]. There are generally four seasons in Kuwait: winter, spring, summer and autumn, within are several seasons. Sub-seasons are periods of distinct weather, such as frequent dust storms. Winter is the wettest and coldest season and begins in December and ends in mid-February. Spring begins in by mid-February and generally last through May. The temperatures vary between $-4.0°$ C to $+50°$ C. The mean annual rainfall is 115 mm with variability from year to year (28-260 mm) and from place to place. There are no rains during the period May – October.

## 2  ASAR Data and DEM of SRTM

On March 1, 2002 ENVISAT satellite was launched by an Ariane 5 launcher. Among several payloads, ASAR is one of the main instruments on board ENVISAT satellite. ASAR images the land at C-band (5.3 GHz or 5.63cm) with choice of 5 polarizations and 3 modes (http://envisat.esa.int /instruments/asar/). Through a project (C1F-3807) sponsored by European Space Agency (ESA), we have been receiving ASAR data in Single Look Complex (SLC). We started receiving the data since the year 2005 and by now we have 29 scenes. The data is acquired in the descending mode for the track /swath no (464/I1) at VV polarization.

The basis for selecting ASAR data for generating DEM is the $B^\perp$. The relation between $B^\perp$ and its sensitivity to topography is given in [6] and the simplified form is as follows:

$$h = \frac{\lambda r \sin\theta}{4\pi B_\perp}\varphi$$

where h is the topographic elevation, $\lambda$ is the wavelength, r is the range from satellite to the ground pixel, $\theta$ is incident angle, and $\varphi$ is the interferometric phase. The height per fringe ($h_a$) is given by

$$h_a = \frac{\lambda r \sin\theta}{2B_\perp}$$

Therefore, higher $B_\perp$ means more sensitive to elevation. At the same time, very large $B_\perp$ leads to de-correlation of interferometric phases. Therefore, $B_\perp$ in the range 200 m – 400 m is selected for this study. Following the above condition, 7 pairs are possible with one master image of December 2007. Though we generated all the DEMs, in this study we are discussing only these 7 DEMs. Since the master image is common for all these DEMs, they are automatically registered and so direct comparison is possible without separately registering them with one another.

### 2.1  DEM of SRTM with 90 m Spatial Resolution

Ninety meter spatial resolution DEM generated from SRTM is freely available in the internet. DEM of 90 m spatial resolution is downloaded from the site http://srtm.sci.cgiar.org/ and used in this study as a reference. DEM of SRTM will be registered and re-sampled to ASAR resolution so that it can serve as a standard reference for error analysis of DEM of repeat pass InSAR. Though the topography of

Kuwait desert is flat and gently sloping down towards west, Burgan oil field has a ridge of 120 m height extending North – South direction.

The DEM of SRTM is one of the best data sets available freely to the scientific community. This has been extensively validated and used for many scientific publications [7]. To assess the elevation accuracy of DEM of SRTM over Kuwait Desert terrain, it is compared with spot values (benchmarks) given in topographic map of Kuwait. RMSE for DEM of 90 m is 3.3 m and RMSE for DEM of 50 m is 1.7 m. Since there is a large gap in time between SRTM and survey of Kuwait topographic map, it is quiet possible that some locations might have been disturbed.

## 3   Generating DEM Using Repeat Pass InSAR Technique

The flowchart for generating DEM is shown in Figure 1. GAMMA interferometric modules are used for generating DEM of Kuwait. A brief description of various steps shown in flowchart are explained here. A rough estimate of offset between the two ASAR images (master and slave images) is done at Multi Look Intensity (MLI) image by averaging 2 range x 10 azimuth pixels and it is fine tuned at Single Look Complex (SLC) using intensity cross-correlation approach with search window 64 x 128 pixels. The slave (second) image is registered (by identifying 48 x 48 registration locations equally distributed through out the image) with master (first) image.

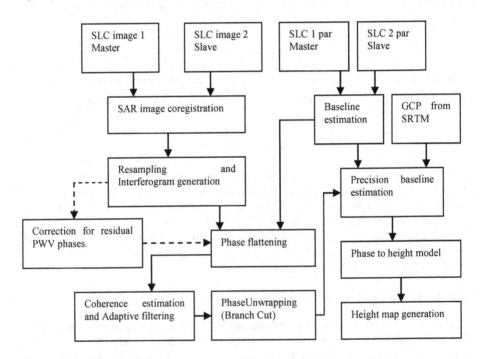

**Fig. 1.** Flow chart for generating DEM through InSAR including PWV corrections

Initial baseline is estimated using state vectors and then refined using 99 Ground Control Points (GCPs) obtained from DEM of SRTM. The spatial distributions of GCPs are shown in Figure 10. It can be seen from Figure 10 that the GCPs form two groups; one corresponding to Burgan oil field and another Manaqish (Umm Qudayr) oil fields. Though the study area is only Burgan, the GCPs are selected over other oil fields for better accuracy. Outside the oil fields (in the open areas), the interferometry was not possible due to decorrelation of the phases.

Phase unwrapping is performed after removing the flat terrain fringes (estimated based on $B_\perp$), applying adaptive filtering and estimating coherence. Branch Cut (BC) approach followed by bridges is used for phase unwrapping. Finally the interferometric phases are converted into elevations using phase – height model. The baseline components and their variation with azimuth are estimated using least square approach.

# 4  Results and Discussions

There are several reasons for the errors in repeat pass InSAR such as (1) different models used in processing ASAR data, (2) instrument noise, (3) error in baseline estimation, (4) atmospheric water vapor and clouds, (5) desert dry soil penetration of the microwaves, etc.

## 4.1  Temporal and Spatial Comparison of Errors in Different DEMs of Burgan Oil Filed

While processing the data sets, several problems were encountered.  Since Kuwait is a desert area, the sand moves frequently destroying the phase coherence even with the day difference of 35 days. From the phase coherence point of view, Kuwait can be classified as three main classes namely built-up city areas, open areas and protected areas. All the installations and Oil fields are protected with a metallic wire fence. The open areas are the places where scattered settlements are seen and grazing takes place. City areas having buildings show high phase coherence; fenced areas with least disturbance have good phase coherence where as open areas have low phase coherence.  Figure 2 shows the visible image of Kuwait and the protected areas.

Therefore, interference fringes are formed only on the protected areas such as oil fields and built-up city areas. Several processing parameters in GAMMA modules are adjusted to get the best results. Also the threshold limit for signal to noise is adjusted for best registration of the two images selected to eliminate weak registration points where the signal strength is very low. 99 GCSs  are selected covering uniformly both the main oil fields of Kuwait to help in precession estimation of baseline components and their variation with azimuth. The elevations of these GCPs are extracted from the 90 m spatial resolution DEM of SRTM after resampling and registering with ASAR image.

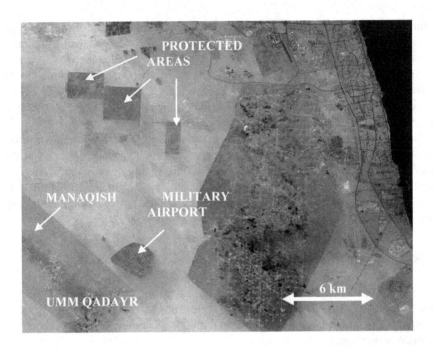

**Fig. 2.** TM Landsat-7 image of Kuwait oil fields. Band 2 (R), Band 3 (G), Band 4 (B)

To highlight the errors in the DEM generated through repeat pass InSAR, 90 m DEM of SRTM is transformed into ASAR geometry and registered with InSAR DEM and then subtracted. Since DEM of SRTM is free from atmospheric and other (penetration of waves into desert sand etc.,) errors as both the images are acquired simultaneously, it is taken as a reference in this study. Figures 3a-g show errors (subtraction of DEM of repeat pass InSAR from DEM of SRTM) in seven DEMs of Burgan. Table 1 gives RMS and STD errors considering the entire oil field and at two distinct locations indicated in Figure 3a. It can be seen from Table 1 that STD and RMS values are more or less same. This is because the mean error is close to zero. The STD is to know the variance in the errors where as RMS is a measure of the deviation of InSAR DEM from the DEM of SRTM. The mean error is close to zero indicates that there is no bias between DEMs of SRTM and InSAR. The STD values vary from 2.2 to 9.4 m. The spatial and temporal distributions of errors are evident from Figures 3a-g. They are arranged in the increasing order of day-diff. The colour coading is done in the interval of 3 m as shown in Figure 3. The gray colour all around Burgan oil field in Figure 3 refers to low phase coherence and so they are made as Zeros just to exclude for the analysis.

- Figure 3a shows the spatial distribution of errors for the interferogram of 35 day difference having a phase coherence of 0.93. It can be seen from Figure 3a that errors over Burgan oil field are mostly within ±3 m. However, on the southern side, it shows a high gradient with an error poorer than -10 m. Similarly, on the left – middle portion, brown colour indicates the range of 3 to 6 m. The average error is only -0.38 with STD of 3.8 m.

**Table 1.** Errors in elevation values (in m) for two locations P1 and P2. Also for the entire study area Burqan. The common master image is of Dec. 2007. The RMS and STD are same (upto one digit after the decimal point) for most of the cases where the mean error is close to zero.

| DEM pair | Day-diff | P-1 | P-2 | RMS |
|---|---|---|---|---|
| October 07 | 35 | -1.32 | 0.28 | 3.8 |
| August 07 | 105 | 0.17 | -0.01 | 2.5 |
| July 07 | 140 | -0.09 | -0.43 | 2.2 |
| June 07 | 175 | -2.16 | 3.14 | 3.8 |
| January 07 | 315 | -3.56 | 0.57 | 5.3 |
| September 06 | 455 | -0.08 | -3.48 | 5.4 |
| June 06 | 525 | 5.63 | -6.45 | 9.8 |

- There is a good consistency in the values of Figures 3b and 3c where the RMS error is only 2.5 m and 2.2 m respectively. Also the errors are in the range of ±3 m (blue and green colours and a few locations brown colour. 105 and 140 days are the day-diff in these two cases. The coherence (0.9 and 0.89) is also very high.
- Figure 3d corresponding to 175 day difference shows values in the range -3 m to 10 m at some locations, though the overall range is ±3 m. There is no definite trend in the results. The average value is 0.36 m with RMS of 3.8m
- Figure 3e corresponds to 315 day difference shows values varying in the range ±10 m. The trend resembles to some extent with Figure 3a in the southern portion of Burgan. Though the average error is only 0.31m, the STD is 5.33 m. The average coherence in this case is 0.72.
- Figure 3f refers to day-diff of 455 days which has least errors in the middle portion of oil field. On the southern side, the values are positive and turned to negative around Northern side. In this case, the average coherence is 0.75. The mean value is 2.16 m with STD of 4.9 m.
- Figure 3g corresponds to 525 day difference is the worst of all the others. Though the average error is 2.55m, the STD is as high as 9.4 m with a coherence of 0.69.

In general, there is no either spatial or temporal consistency in the errors (Figure 3). However, the errors within ± 3 m should not be taken into account as the reference DEM of SRTM itself has an error of this order. In this respect, the central portion of Burgan oil field has errors within the limits in most of the cases.

Figures 3b and 3c are very good. Figures 3a, 3e and 3g show vertical fringe like patterns with large errors on the Southern portion of the oil fields. To some extent, the range of errors increases with day-diff after a particular period which in turn has effect on coherence, there is no consistency in the spatial distribution. Since water vapour and soil moisture patterns are very dynamic in spatial variations, the observed trends can be understood in these terms. The RMS error does not seem to be a good indicator of overall errors. Even though the spatial distribution of errors in some pockets of the study area are as high as 10m, the RMS value is still very low as the percentage of these pixels does not influence the RMS considerably.

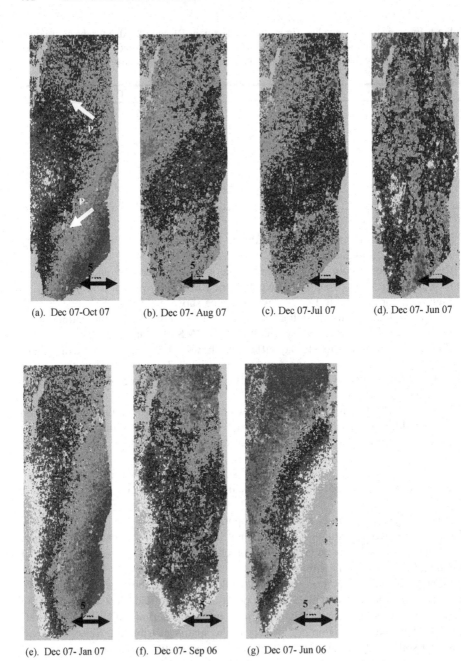

(a).  Dec 07-Oct 07      (b). Dec 07- Aug 07      (c). Dec 07-Jul 07      (d). Dec 07- Jun 07

(e).  Dec 07- Jan 07      (f).  Dec 07- Sep 06      (g) Dec 07- Jun 06

**Fig. 3.** Errors in the DEM of Burqan (SRTM- InSAR)

## 4.2  Study on the Quantitative Consistency of the Elevations

Since the errors in the derived DEMs are varying spatially and temporarily, it is worthwhile to go for a quantitative analysis of these errors. Therefore, two specific locations are selected as shown in Figure 3a : One location P1 at the southern portion of the oil field and the other P2 at the Northern portion of the study area. Figure 4 shows the errors as a function of day difference for points P1 and P2. It can be seen from Figure 4 that there is not much consistency in the results as a function of time. The errors are in the range ±6 m.

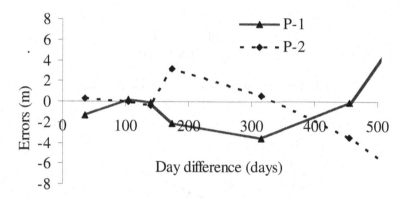

**Fig. 4.** Elevation as a function of Day-diff for two selected points in Burqan oil field

## 4.3  Relation between Day-Diff, Coherence and RMS Errors

To investigate into the other possible reasons of the errors in the DEMs, average co-herence is plotted as a function of day-diff as shown in Figure 5a. The coherence steadily decreases with increase in day-diff. Second degree polynomial shows better fitting with the data. The equation of fitting is given in the figure itself. Since the study area is protected, desert and no human activities, the coherence is not supposed to decrease with day-diff. The observed decrease can be due to the change in vegeta-tion cover which is protected from the cattle grazing. As the day-diff increases, some changes are natural to take place on the ground in terms of vegetation cover.

Figure 5b shows the RMS error as a function of day-diff. Except a few cases, the RMS error steadily increases with day-diff. Since coherence has an effect on the reli-ability of the phases, the decrease of coherence leads to increase in RMS error. The observed linear relation may not hold for higher day-diff. Similarly Figure 5c shows the relation between RMS error and the average coherence which is self explanatory.

## 4.4  Effect of Variation of Soil Moisture on the Accuracy of DEM

The presence of precipitable water vapour in the atmosphere delays the microwave signals. The differential delays causes errors in the elevation data. Atmospheric cor-rections are implemented for the DEMs using the models reported by [4]. MERIS PWV is used for the corrections. It has been noticed that the corrections did not im-prove the results as the variation of PWV over desert is seen to be not significant.

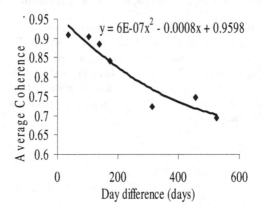

**Fig. 5a.** Relation between Day difference and Coherence

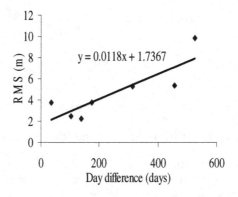

**Fig. 5b.** RMS error as a function of Day difference

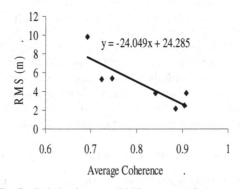

**Fig. 5c.** Relation between RMS error and Coherence

The processing steps are checked again and again to make sure that there are no errors in generating repeat pass DEM. The speckle and instrument noises are minimized by averaging the pixles to a resolution of 60 x 60 m and by filtering using adopt filter.

The presence of precipitable water vapour in the atmosphere delays the microwave signals. The differential delays causes errors in the elevation data. Atmospheric corrections are implemented for the DEMs using the models reported by [4]. MERIS PWV is used for the corrections. It has been noticed that the corrections did not improve the results as the variation of PWV over desert is seen to be not significant.

The other possible sources of errors can be the penetration of microwaves into the soil medium. It is reported [8] that there is considerable spatial variation in rainfall rate. This is also confirmed by studying the spatial variation of soil moisture by [9] . Since there is no improvement after tropospheric corrections, the possible error sources can be the diffusion of phases due to differential penetration of microwaves in to soil medium. The patterns observed in Figures 3a, 3e and 3g may be due to penetration of the waves into moist soils. A detailed investigation needs to be carried out in this direction.

Finally the decorrelation of the phases with increase in day difference can be partly responsible for errors.

## 5  Conclusions

After a detailed investigation into the errors in DEM of repeat pass InSAR in terms of spatial and temporal variations, patterns etc., the following conclusions are gained:

- Spatial distribution of Water vapour is fairly constant over Burgan oil field, though there is a temporal variation.
- RMS error is  not a true representation of the actual errors.  The large errors in some pockets of the study area may not be reflected in the RMS errors due to their less population.  In the present context, we are interested in such pockets.
- Three factors are investigated as responsible for errors in the DEMs namely PWV, Soil moisture and temporal decorrelation.
- PWV corrections to InSAR has no significant effect on the accuracy of DEM.
- Temporal decorrelation has some influence on the accuracy of the derived DEM. Up to day difference of 455 days,  the errors are acceptable.  Beyond this period, the errors in DEM steeply increase.
- Spatial and temporal variability of soil moisture has influence on the accuracy of DEM.  This needs to be further investigated.  This can be checked by installing some Corner Reflectors over the Burgan oil field.  For the study and calibration of land subsidence over Burgan oil field, there is a planning of installing 25 corner reflectors all over the Burgan oil field.

**Acknowledgments.** The authors are thankful to European Space Agency (ESA) for sponsoring the project . (C1F:3807) and providing (ASAR and MERIS) data sets free of charge.  Also thanks to Research Administration, Kuwait University for sponsoring this project (SP: 02/08).

# References

1. Zebker, H.A., Goldstein, R.M.: Topographic mapping from interferometric synthetic aperture radar observations. Journal of Geophysical Research 91(B5), 4993–4999 (1986)
2. Hanssen, R.F.: Radar interferometry: data interpretation and error analysis, vol. xviii, 308 p. Kluwer Academic, Dordrecht (2001)
3. Hanssen, R.F.: Atmospheric heterogeneities in ERS tendem SAR interferometry, 136 p. Delft University press, Delft (1998)
4. Li, Z.: Correction of atmospheric water vapour effects on repeat-pass SAR interferometry using GPS, MODIS and MERIS data. Ph. D. thesis, Department of geomatic Engineering, University college London (2005)
5. Al Jassar, H.K., Rao, K.S., Sabbah, I.: A model for the retrieval and monitoring of soil moisture over desert area of Kuwait. International journal of remote sensing 27(1-2), 329–348 (2006)
6. Rao, K.S., Kumar, V.P.B., Al Jassar, H.K.: An iterative technique to estimate baseline parameters in SAR Interferometry, Kuwait. Journal of Science and Engineering 34(2a), 91–109 (2007)
7. Rao, K.S., Phalke, S.M., Sakalley, J., Al Jassar, H.K.: Assessment of Geo-coding and Height Accuracy of the DEM derived from preliminary data sets of X-ba-nd SRTM. Journal of the Indian Society of Remote Sensing 34(IV), 369–375 (2006)
8. Marc, P.M., Elfatih, A.B.E.: The Hydroclimatology of Kuwait: Explaining Variability of Rainfall at Seasonal and Interannual Timescales (2008), doi:10.1175/2008JHM952.1, http://ams.allenpress.com/perlserv/?request=get-abstract&doi=10.1175%2F2008JHM952.1&ct=1
9. Al Jassar, H.K., Rao, K.S.: Validation of soil moisture retrieval models of Aqua satellite (AMSR-E) over Kuwait desert area. International Journal of Remote Sensing (will appear in the issue of 2010)

# Special Session 4
# Satellite Based Emergency Services

# Cooperative Strategies of Integrated Satellite/Terrestrial Systems for Emergencies

Simone Morosi, Sara Jayousi, and Enrico Del Re

Department of Electronics and Telecommunications
University of Florence - CNIT
Via S. Marta 3, 50139, Florence, Italy
Tel.: +39 055 4796485; Fax: +39 055 472858
{simone.morosi,enrico.delre}@unifi.it, sara.jayousi@cnit.it

**Abstract.** In this paper some simple cooperative relaying strategies which rely on the exploitation of the Delay Diversity technique and the Maximal Ratio Combining (MRC) receive diversity algorithm are proposed for a DVB-SH compliant hybrid satellite/terrestrial network. These strategies are investigated in a public emergency scenario where the adoption of an integrated heterogeneous network combined with the cooperative diversity techniques guarantees the connection between the incident area and the external areas: particularly, the drawbacks of the Non-Line-Of-Sight (NLOS) propagation are mitigated. The NAV/COM capabilities of the cooperative DD algorithm in a DVB-SH Single Frequency Network (SFN) are discussed, highlighting the suitability of these schemes in emergency situation management. A comparison analysis of the proposed schemes is performed, describing the assumptions required and the simulation results with respect to the satellite-only and the terrestrial-only cases.

**Keywords:** NAV/COM System, Cooperative, Satellite/Terrestrial network, Emergency Communication, Delay diversity, Maximal Ratio Combining.

## 1 Introduction

In the last few years the increasing number of natural or antrophic disasters pushes the scientific communities to further investigate the research topic of communications and networking technologies for public safety and security. In the provision of emergency telecommunication facilities, particular attention has been given to the integration of satellite and terrestrial segments with the goal to exploit the complementary capabilities of both systems and overcome the drawbacks of each scheme [24] [2] [22].

The integration of satellite and terrestrial segments is required for both communication and navigation systems:

- *Communication system*: The satellite can complement the terrestrial networks while the gap fillers allow the communication with an end-user whose satellite link is characterized by bad channel condition.

K. Sithamparanathan et al. (Eds.): PSATS 2010, LNICST 43, pp. 409–424, 2010.
© Institute for Computer Sciences, Social-Informatics and Telecommunications Engineering 2010

- *Navigation system*: a GPS NLOS visibility receiver can achieve navigation capabilities through the exploitation of satellite and terrestrial cooperation.

Together with the integration of satellite and terrestrial components, also the integration of navigation and communication systems can be seen as one of the main needs for the emergency network [13]. The NAV/COM capabilities allow the exploitation of both navigation information for communication purpose [19] (optimization of communication techniques, interference reduction and location-based information services delivery) and communication supports for navigation purpose [16] (cooperative localization techniques, high precision achievement).

Therefore an efficient emergency rescue management is based on the fast implementation of an integrated satellite-terrestrial NAV/COM network, which enables the Emergency Control Centre (ECC) to properly coordinates the rescue teams interventions.

In this paper we study hybrid satellite/terrestrial cooperative relaying strategies which can be adopted in public emergency situations with the aim of guaranteeing communication between the emergency area and the external areas.

Simple and suitable solutions to overcome the performance loss of the NLOS environment are analysed. In particular we propose the combination of the hybrid satellite/terrestrial network OFDM-based proposed by the DVB-SH standard (SH-A Architecture) with the Cooperative *Delay Diversity* (DD) relaying technique [18] [8] [17] [7] [5]. Moreover, we analyse the adoption of the MRC receive diversity scheme together with the Cooperative Delay diversity technique with the aim of guaranteeing a more robust communication link. Finally to highlight the importance of a NAV/COM satellite/terrestrial network for emergency management we briefly address the double-use capabilities of the proposed system for communication and navigation purposes.

## 2   System Model: Hybrid Satellite/Terrestrial Cooperative Relaying Network

The basic building blocks of a satellite/terrestrial cooperative relaying system are the following: the Satellite Component (SC), the Complementary Ground Component (CGC) and the receiver (D), acting as the source, the relay and the destination respectively.

Analysing a single frequency network (SFN) we combine the hybrid cooperative relaying scheme with the Delay Diversity technique in order to cope with the NLOS propagation condition through the exploitation of the channel propagation properties.

The system model, which has been considered in this paper, is depicted in Fig.1. In particular two different types of cooperative-relay nodes are considered:

- CGC-Gap Fillers (CGC-GFs) which process the received signal according to the *Amplify and Forward* (AAF) algorithm.
- CGC-Transmitters (CGC-TXs) which complement the satellite reception in those areas where the satellite coverage is not guaranteed.

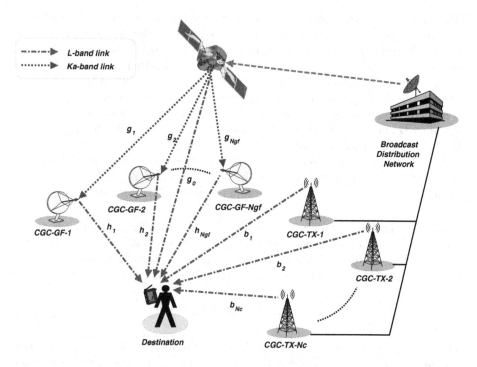

**Fig. 1.** Hybrid satellite/terrestrial *N-Relay Cooperative Delay Diversity* system with different types of CGCs: GFs (Gap Fillers) and TXs (Transmitters)

Both cooperative nodes can be seen as *relays* between the satellite or the broadcast distribution network and the destination node.

## 2.1   Hybrid Cooperative Delay Diversity Algorithm

In a satellite/terrestrial cooperative relaying network, where $N_{gf}$ relays act as gap fillers and $N_C$ relays are directly connected to the broadcast distribution network, $(N_{gf}+N_c+1)$ different faded and delayed copies of the same information data arrive at the destination node. The delay diversity gain is achieved through the increase of the delay spread of the channel, and, therefore, the raise of the frequency selectivity [25].

   In order to describe the delays of the DD technique, we analyse separately the two different types of CGCs involved in the cooperative network. In particular we assume as a reference the propagation delay ($\delta_0$) of the signal through the direct path (from SC to D).

**CGC-Gap Filler Delays.** Denoting as $\delta_i$ the propagation delay of the signal of the indirect path from SC to D through CGC-CF-i (with $i = 1, .., N_{gf}$), since $d_{(SC,CGC^{(GF)}-i)} \simeq d_{(SC,D)}$, the *delays* ($\delta_{CGC^{(GF)}-i}$) of the DD scheme are:

$$\delta_{CGC^{(GF)}-i} = \delta_i - \delta_0 \simeq \frac{d_{(CGC^{(GF)}-i,D)}}{c} \quad , \quad c = \text{speed of light.} \quad (1)$$

Therefore, the DD technique can be seen as a natural cooperative-relaying transmission: in fact, no additional operation is required at the destination node. In order to keep the complexity low, each gap filler can work according to the *Amplify and Forward* algorithm, amplifying and retransmitting the received signal.

Nonetheless, some simple operations have to be considered; in fact to make a gap-filler simultaneously receive and retransmit the signal a frequency conversion is needed. According to the DVB-SH standard the satellite transmits the same signal to D and CGC on different frequencies: in fact, the link SC-D is in Ka-Band, while the link SC-CGC is in L-Band. Therefore the gap filler amplifies and retransmits the received Ka-Band signal after converting into L-Band. In this way different delayed L-band copies of the signal arrive at D, allowing the implementation of the DD technique in a hybrid satellite/terrestrial network.

**CGC-Transmitters Delays.** Assuming a synchronization condition between both types of CGCs (SFN network) the delays of the CGCs which are directly connected to the distribution network are the effective propagation delays between the CGC-TX-z (with $z = 1, ... N_c$) and the destination:

$$\delta_{CGC^{(TX)}-z} = \frac{d_{(CGC^{(TX)}-z,D)}}{c} \qquad (2)$$

Therefore, both the delays of the signals coming from the CGC-GFs and the ones coming from the CGC-TXs depend on their position and their mutual distance.

Otherwise, assuming at D a synchronization condition between the signal coming from the SC and the one coming from the CGCs directly connected to the distribution network, the cooperative nodes have to delay artificially the transmitted signal with the aim to create a time diversity at the receiver end. In particular the delays can be taken equal to the effective propagation time intervals between the CGC-TXs and the destination.

## 2.2   Validation of the Proposed System

With the aim to validate the efficiency of the scheme described in the previous subsection and highlight the importance of the cooperation between the satellite and the terrestrial segments, we analyse a particular case of the proposed system: the N-Way Relay cooperative DD scheme, which is characterised by the absence of the direct link SC-D ($g_0 = 0$, see Fig.1). Particularly, D selects and processes only the signals coming from the CGCs involved in the transmission scheme. As the simulation results confirm (see Section 1.7), neglecting the signal coming directly from the satellite does not imply any advantages, even if the channel between SC and D is modelled as an alternation of LOS/NLOS cases. On the contrary, we can observe a performance degradation, which also depends on the environment considered. The absence of a path implies a reduction of the frequency selectivity of the equivalent channel transfer function and therefore the diversity introduced by the DD technique is less with respect to the one introduced in the original system.

Besides, it is important to highlight that the implementation of the proposed cooperative DD schemes does not require any change in the standard. In fact:

- the CGCs considered in the paper are the ones which are defined in the standard specs;
- the frequency conversion at the gap filler is standard-compliant;
- the SFN synchronization performed in DVB-SH network allows the presence of a delayed replica of the original signal, which fulfil the DD constrain.

## 2.3   Receive Diversity in a Hybrid Cooperative DD System

In order to increase the diversity order we can assume the presence of two antennas at the receiver-end. In particular we consider the N-relay scheme depicted in Fig.1, replacing D with a double antenna equipped destination node.

A Maximal Ratio Combiner (MRC) is adopted with the aim to not increase the complexity of the destination node by the implementation of additional operations. Due to the frequency used and the height of the receiver, it is realistic to consider that the several copies of the transmitted signal, which arrive at D, are affected by independent channel coefficients.

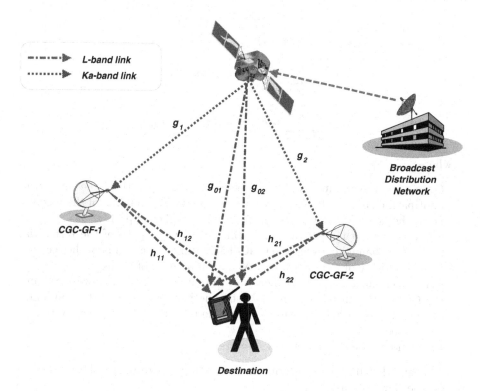

**Fig. 2.** Hybrid satellite/terrestrial *2-Relay Cooperative Delay Diversity* with MRC at the double antenna equipped receiver-end

Without losing in generality, we consider the two gap fillers case which is depicted in Fig.2: in this case independent faded copies of the transmitted signal are received either from the SC or from the gap fillers; this is true for both the elements of the receiver antenna. In particular the copies coming from each gap filler are characterized by a specific delay, which can be derived from the expression 1.

## 3     Analysis of the Equivalent Channel Impulse Response

In order to highlight the relationship between the Cooperative Delay Diversity technique and the channel properties, we describe the effect of the application of this scheme on the channel impulse response.

In particular we analyse a hybrid satellite/terrestrial cooperative relaying network, where $N_{gf}$ relays act as gap fillers and $N_C$ relays are directly connected to the broadcast distribution network, while the receiver is equipped with two receive antennas. Denoting with $s(n)$ the complex-valued transmitted signals in the time domain, after the removal of a cyclic prefix and neglecting the AWGN noise, the received signal at the $r$-antenna $(r = 1, 2)$ of the Destination node can be written as:

$$y_r(n) = \alpha g_{0r} s(n)$$
$$+ \sum_{i=1}^{N_{gf}} \sum_{p=0}^{N_{max}} \beta_i g_i h_{ir}(n, p) s(n - \delta_i - \tau_p)$$
$$+ \sum_{z=1}^{N_C} \sum_{q=0}^{N_{max}} \gamma_z b_{zr}(n, q) s(n - \delta_z - \tau_q) \tag{3}$$

where

- $h_{ir}(n, p)$ is the channel complex coefficient of the p-path of the terrestrial multipath channel between the CGC-GF-$i$ and the $r$-antenna of the receiver D, $\tau_p$ the delay of the $p$-path and $N_{max}$ the number of paths;
- $b_{zr}(n, q)$ is the channel complex coefficient of the q-path of the terrestrial multipath channel between the CGC-TX-$z$ and the $r$-antenna of the receiver D, $\tau_q$ the delay of the $q$-path and $N_{max}$ the number of paths;
- $g_i$ is the channel complex coefficient of the satellite channel between SC and the CGC-GF-$i$; in particular $g_{0r}$ is the one between SC and the $r$-antenna of the receiver D and it assumes the value 0 if the N-Way Relay system is considered;
- $\alpha$, $\beta_i$ and $\gamma_z$ are the power scale factors.

Analysing the DD effects in terms of channel impulse response, the expression (3) can be rewritten as:

$$y_r(n) = s(n) * h_{equ}^{(r)}(n) \tag{4}$$

where $h_{equ}^{(r)}(n)$ is the equivalent channel impulse response which is perceived by the $r$-antenna at the receiver:

$$
\begin{aligned}
h_{equ}^{(r)}(n) &= \alpha g_{0r}\delta(n) \\
&+ \sum_{i=1}^{N_{gf}} \sum_{p=0}^{N_{max}} \beta_i g_i h_{ir}(n,p)\delta(n - \delta_i - \tau_p) \\
&+ \sum_{z=1}^{N_C} \sum_{q=0}^{N_{max}} \gamma_z b_{zr}(n,q)\delta(n - \delta_z - \tau_q)
\end{aligned}
\tag{5}
$$

According to this analysis, switching from the non-cooperative to a cooperative mode, the Destination node experiences an increase of the frequency selectivity of the propagation channel; in fact the receiver cannot discriminate whether the propagation path comes from the effect of the cooperative relaying DD technique or the channel itself. Therefore, as highlighted in (5) , from the $r$-antenna point of view, transmitting delayed copies of the same signal through a propagation channel makes the MISO channel (Multiple-Input Single-Output) transform into a SISO (Single-Input Single-Output) channel with increased frequency selectivity [11]. We can conclude that in the cooperative scheme proposed the spatial diversity is transformed into frequency diversity, which makes the error distribution change: this feature can be exploited by the use of FEC codes with a remarkable improvement of the performance.

In the previous expressions, the satellite channel between SC and the gap fillers and D is assumed to be in LOS or NLOS condition, while the one between the CGCs (both types) and D is supposed to be a NLOS multipath channel (with Rayleigh Distribution). It is important to notice that the equivalent channel perceived by D is an hybrid channel, which consists in terrestrial and satellite components and is characterized by a mixed LOS/NLOS propagation conditions. In general the adoption of the DD technique combined with the presence of a LOS component carries to a loss in performance: particularly, the increase of frequency selectivity involves the presence of deep fades which are the responsible of the performance degradation [12]. However, we analyse hybrid cooperative schemes, which have to be evaluated with the satellite channel model. Therefore the alternation of LOS/NLOS state (environmental dependent) of the satellite channel makes the DD technique more suitable with respect to the terrestrial case with a LOS component.

Despite the low complexity of the proposed system, the increase of frequency selectivity of the channel propagation perceived by the receiver involves an accurate channel estimation. In fact, the reduction of the coherence bandwidth as far as the delays increase make a conventional SISO channel estimator unable to correctly estimate the channel. [6] addresses the problem of the channel estimator in a DD OFDM system, while a trade off study of the maximum tolerable delay with respect to the channel estimation impacts has been conducted in [23]. Even though all these topics are beyond the aim of this paper, they are under investigation and will be considered in the future works.

## 4    Some Consideration on NAV/COM Integration through Hybrid Cooperative Relaying DD System

The integration of NAV/COM capabilities is strictly required in an emergency context. The hybrid cooperative delay diversity system proposed can easily make the receiver in GPS NLOS visibility acquire self-positioning information. The receiver can estimate its location through the combination of the cooperative relaying scheme in a Single Frequency Network (SFN) and the implementation of the Time Differences of Arrivals (TDoA) algorithm. In particular we address to the case, where almost three (2D-positioning) or four (3D-positioning) CGCs are in GPS LOS visibility or alternatively their positions are known. The synchronization of the CGCs, which is the fundamental requirement for navigation applications based on TDoA, is achieved in a DVB-SH SFN of emitters. In this context the receiver through an accurate channel estimation can obtained the required TDoA measurements, which enable the positioning [20].

Therefore the implementation of the cooperative system proposed allow the receiver to:

- improve the performance of the communication system, which can be evaluate in terms of coverage extension, power consumption reduction or robustness of the radio link;
- estimate its position even in case of GPS NLOS visibility.

## 5    Emergency Scenario

Among the different phases of a public emergency situation management (preparedness, response, recovery and mitigation), we consider the first response phase of a disaster (fire, earthquake, flood, explosion), where several rescuers organised in teams act with the aim of saving lives and preserving the environment during emergencies.

The implementation of the hybrid cooperative system proposed in the emergency scenario (Fig.3) allows the connection of the rescuers operating in the emergency area with the outside world even when the satellite-team link is characterised by bad channel condition.

In this context the relays can be represented by:

- CGC-gap fillers which enable the rescue teams to communicate with the Emergency Control Centre in absence of the terrestrial infrastructure network, which is often only partially available or completely destroyed due to the disaster effects. In particular the gap fillers can be represented by a temporary, mobile stations placed at the perimeter of the disaster site.
- CGC-TX, assuming a partially available terrestrial infrastructure; in particular we supposed the presence of a still available CGC, which is directly connected to the broadcast distribution network.

Besides the destination node equipped by a two element antenna, which implements the MRC receive diversity scheme, can be represented by an anchor

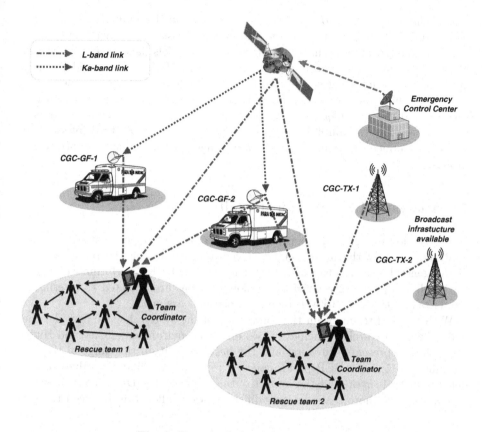

**Fig. 3.** Hypothetical emergency scenario

node able to coordinate the rescuers of its team according to the information received from the emergency control centre. With these assumptions the presence of two antennas at the receiver end does not represent a limitation in terms of equipment cost and size. In fact, thanks to the performance achieved with this diversity scheme, just one anchor node is required for a team of rescuers.

## 6   Simulation Parameters and Assumptions

According to the DVB-SH (SH-A Architecture) specifications [3] [21] [4] , an OFDM system is implemented both for satellite component and for the CGCs and a cyclic prefix is introduced to avoid ISI at the receiver. In particular the most important DVB-SH compliant parameters which are adopted in the simulations are: signal bandwidth 5 MHz, mode 1K, OFDM Sampling Frequency 40/7 MHz, OFDM Symbol Duration $179.2\mu s$, OFDM Guard Interval $44.8\mu s$, QPSK modulation, Turbo Code (code rate 1/4).

Besides at the receiver after the removal of the cyclic prefix, the Zero Forcing equalization is performed, assuming the knowledge of channel state information.

The channel propagation models which are used in the simulations are: Lutz model and TU6 model for the satellite and the terrestrial channel, respectively [4]. Even though more accurate satellite channel models have been proposed in [9], with the aim to not loose in generality, we consider the Lutz model, which is one of the models suggested in the DVB-SH implementation guidelines.

In the simulations we also assume that: the satellite channels between the satellite and the gap fillers are always in LOS, the gap fillers can be seen as a transparent relay (no amplification is performed) and the DVB-SH interleavers are not introduced to make clear the advantages of the cooperative strategies proposed.

## 7   Analysis of Simulation Results

In this section we verify the performance of the hybrid cooperative DD system, analysing some of the most significant comparisons among the possible cases of the general scheme proposed. In particular in all BER-performance graphs the satellite and the terrestrial stand-alone systems are depicted as a terms of reference and the same total transmitted power is assumed.

With the aim to maintain the complexity of the system low we consider the one-relay and two-relay schemes in two different environments: City and Highway, which represents the worst and the best case within the range of the environments [15]. The BER-performance is reported for different values of the delay in order to represent the impact of this value on the DD scheme; besides, to implement a more realistic case, different power allocation between the CS

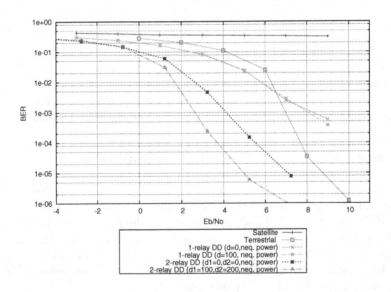

**Fig. 4.** Performance comparison of DVB-SH system among: satellite-only, terrestrial-only, 1-Relay Cooperative DD and 2-Relay Cooperative DD in City environment

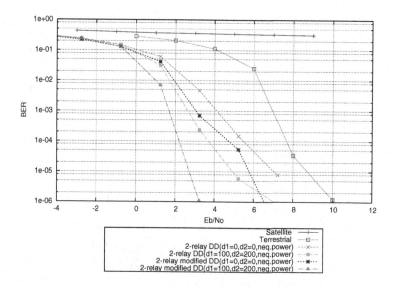

**Fig. 5.** Performance comparison of DVB-SH system among: satellite-only, terrestrial-only, N-Relay Cooperative DD and N-Relay Modified Cooperative DD, with $N = 2$ in City environment

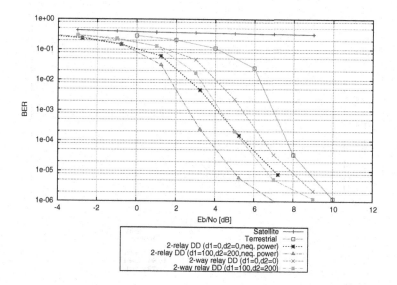

**Fig. 6.** Performance comparison of DVB-SH system among: satellite-only, terrestrial-only, N-Relay Cooperative DD and N-Way Relay Cooperative DD, with $N = 2$ in City environment

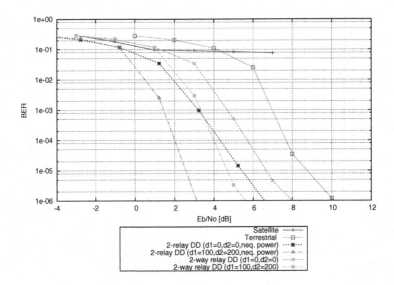

**Fig. 7.** Performance comparison of DVB-SH system among: satellite-only, terrestrial-only, N-Relay Cooperative DD and N-Way Relay Cooperative DD, with $N = 2$ in Highway environment

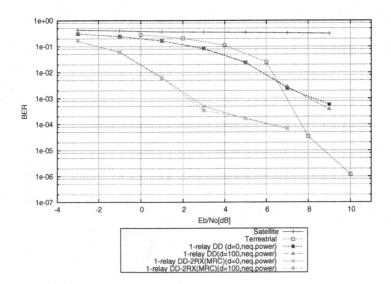

**Fig. 8.** Performance comparison of DVB-SH system among: satellite-only, terrestrial-only, N-Relay Cooperative DD and N-Relay Cooperative DD combined with MRC, with $N = 1$ in City environment

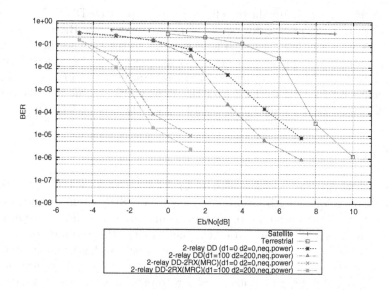

**Fig. 9.** Performance comparison of DVB-SH system among: satellite-only, terrestrial-only, N-Relay Cooperative DD and N-Relay Cooperative DD combined with MRC, with $N = 2$ in City environment

and the CGC is assumed (not equal power): particularly, the copies of the signals coming from the CGCs (all types) are characterised by a higher level of power with respect to the signal directly transmitted from the satellite.

In order to highlight the BER-performance of the *N-Relay Cooperative DD system* with only CGC-GFs, the $N = 1$ and $N = 2$ cases are depicted in Fig.4, where the two cooperative relaying schemes are compared in the City environment. In particular the 2-relay system gains 4-5dB ($\delta$-depending) for BER=$10^{-3}$ over the 1-relay system. Therefore the presence of more than one relay, increasing the frequency selectivity of the channel transfer function, permits to achieve a performance improvement in term of bit error rate.

In Fig.5 two versions of the *N-Relay Cooperative DD system* with $N = 2$ are compared: the 2-relay-case characterized by the presence of two CGC-GFs and the 2-relay modified-case, in which the two relays are represented by one CGC-GF and one CGC-TX. In particular the 2-Relay modified system gains 1-2dB ($\delta$-depending) for BER=$10^{-4}$ over the 2-Relay system. These results are justified by the fact that the CGC-TX transmits an exact copy of the original signal.

In Fig.6 and in Fig.7 the *N-Relay Cooperative DD system* and the *N-Way Relay Cooperative DD system* (with the $N = 2$) are compared in City and Highway setting respectively. In particular the N-Relay system gains 1-1.8dB and 1.5-2dB ($\delta$-depending) for BER=$10^{-4}$ over the N-Way Relay system in City and Highway environment respectively, validating the effectiveness of the first scheme.

Finally, in order to highlight the effect of the cooperative DD technique combined with the MRC receive diversity scheme, we analyse the BER performance of the 1-relay (Fig.8) and 2-relay (Fig.9) systems in the City setting, assuming a double-antenna equipped receiver. The combination of the cooperative DD technique with the MRC receive diversity algorithm makes the 1-relay DD-2RX system gains 6dB for BER=$10^{-3}$ over the 1-relay DD scheme and the 2-relay DD-2RX system gains 5-6dB for BER=$10^{-4}$ over the 2-relay DD scheme.

## 8    Conclusions

Simple and feasible cooperative relaying strategies based on the *Delay Diversity* (DD) technique have been proposed for a DVB-SH compliant hybrid satellite/terrestrial network in order to reduce the impairments caused by the NLOS condition in the satellite propagation channel. Besides the combination between the cooperative DD system and the MRC diversity scheme has been investigated.

The proposed cooperative schemes are characterized by a significant gain with respect to the satellite system and therefore represent a promising solution to guarantee communication in public emergency situations, particularly, in the first response phase of a disaster, without any additional complexity requirement.

Simulation results show that combining the cooperative DD technique with the MRC receive diversity scheme permits to achieve interesting BER-performance overcoming the performance of a terrestrial system through the exploitation of the channel propagation features and the spatial diversity gain.

Moreover the double-use (communication and navigation purpose) of the cooperative DD algorithm in a SFN DVB-SH system has been discussed, highlighting the NAV/COM capabilities and therefore the suitability of these schemes in emergency situation management.

**Acknowledgments.** This work has been supported by Italian Research Program (PRIN 2007) Satellite-Assisted Locallzation and communication system for Emergency services (SALICE) [1]. Partners of the project are: University of Florence (coord.), Polytechnic of Turin, University of Rome Tor Vergata, University of Reggio Calabria, University of Trento.

## References

1. Salice web site, `http://lenst.det.unifi.it/salice`
2. ETSI Recomandation TS 102 181 V.1.1, Requirements for communication between authorities/organizations during emergencies, emtel (2005)
3. ETSI TS 102 585 V1.1.1 (2007). System specifications for satellite services to handheld devices (sh) below 3 ghz european (2007)
4. ETSI TS 102 584 V1.1.1 (2008-12). Dvb-sh implementation guidelines (2008)
5. Antó, A.: Cyclic delay diversity in cooperative communications and single hop systems. M. eng. thesis 2007, KTH School of Information and Communications Technology (2007)

6. Auer, G.: Channel estimation for ofdm with cyclic delay diversity. In: 15th IEEE International Symposium on Personal, Indoor and Mobile Radio Communications, PIMRC 2004, September 2004. vol. 3, pp. 1792–1796 (2004)
7. Slimane, S.B., Li, X., Zhou, B., Syed, N., Dheim, M.A.: Delay optimization in cooperative relaying with cyclic delay diversity. In: IEEE International Conference on Communication (ICC 2008), May 2008, pp. 3553–3557 (2008)
8. Ben Slimane, S., Osseiran, A.: Relay communication with delay diversity for future communication systems. In: VTC 2006, pp. 1–5 (2006)
9. Burzigotti, P., Prieto-Cerdeira, R., Bolea-Alamanac, A., Perez-Fontan, F., Sanched-Lago, I.: Dvb-sh analysis using a multi-state land mobile satellite channel model. In: 4th Advanced Satellite Mobile Systems, ASMS 2008, pp. 149–155 (2008)
10. Choi, S., Park, J.-H., Park, D.-J.: Randomized cyclic delay code for cooperative communication systems. IEEE Communications Letters 12, 271–273 (2008)
11. Dammann, A., Plass, S.: Cyclic delay diversity: Effective channel properties and applications. In: Proc. of the WWRF17-WG4-06, pp. 1–7 (2006)
12. Dammann, A., Raulefs, R., Plass, S.: Soft cyclic delay diversity and its performance for dvb-t in ricean channels. In: Global Communications Conference 2007, November 2007, pp. 4210–4214 (2007)
13. Dominici, F., Marucco, G., Mulassano, P., Defina, A., Charqane, K.: Navigation in case of emergency (nice): An integrated nav/com technology for emergency management. In: 5th IEEE Consumer Communications and Networking Conference, CCNC 2008., January 2008, pp. 608–612 (2008)
14. Lodhi, A., Said, F., Dohler, M., Aghvami, H.: Performance comparison of space-time block coded and cyclic delay diversity mc-cdma systems. IEEE Wireless Communications 12, 38–45 (2004)
15. Lutz, E., Cygan, D., Dippold, M., DolainSky, F., Papke, W.: The land mobile satellite communication channel-recording, statistics and channel model. IEEE Transactions on Vehicular Technology 40, 375–386 (1991)
16. Mensing, C., Dammann, A.: Positioning with ofdm based communications systems and gnss in critical scenarios. In: 5th Workshop on Positioning, Navigation and Communication, WPNC 2008., March 2008, pp. 1–7 (2008)
17. Osseiran, A., Logothetis, A., Ben Slimane, S., Larsson, P.: Relay cyclic delay diversity: Modeling and system performance. In: IEEE International Conf. on Signal Processing Communication (November 2007)
18. Plass, S., Dammann, A.: Cellular cyclic delay diversity for next generation mobile systems. In: VTC 2006, pp. 1–5 (2006)
19. Raulefs, R., Plass, S.: Combining wireless communications and navigation - the where project. In: IEEE 68th Vehicular Technology Conference, VTC 2008, September 2008, pp. 1–5 (Fall 2008)
20. Thevenon, P., Julien, O., Macabiau, C., Serant, D., Ries, L., Corazza, S., Bousquet, M.: Positioning principles with a mobile tv system using dvb-sh signals and a single frequency network. In: 16th International Conference on Digital Signal Processing, pp. 1–8 (July 2009)
21. ETSI EN 302 583 V1.1.1(2008). Framing structure, channel coding and modulation for satellite services to handheld devices (sh) below 3 ghz (2008)
22. Vanelli-Coralli, A., Corazza, G.E., Karagiannidis, G.K., Mathiopoulos, P.T., Mathiopoulos, D.S., Mosquera, C., Papaharalabos, S., Scalise, S.: Satellite communications: Research trends and open issues. In: IWSSC 2007, pp. 71–75 (2007)

23. Wei, C., Hu, T., You, X.: Cyclic delay diversity performance in ofdma based system. In: 14th European Wireless Conference, EW 2008, June 2008, pp. 1–5 (2008)
24. SES-SatEC working group. Overview of present satellite emergency communication resources. Technical Report ETSI TR 102 641 V1.1.1 (2008)
25. Zhang, Y., Cosmas, J., Bard, M., Song, Y.-H.: Diversity gain for dvb-h by using transmitter/receiver cyclic delay diversity. IEEE Transactions on Broadcasting 52, 464–474 (2006)

# Software Defined Radio Assisted Localization for Emergency Scenarios

Enrico Del Re[1], Luca Simone Ronga[1], Luca Vettori[1], Simone Morosi[1],
Letizia Lo Presti[2], Emanuela Falletti[3], and Marco Pini[3]

[1] Dipartimento di Elettronica e Telecomunicazioni, Università di Firenze, Italy
[2] Dipartimento di Elettronica, Politecnico di Torino, Italy
[3] NavSAS Group, Istituto Superiore Mario Boella (ISMB) Torino, Italy

**Abstract.** In the following lines we introduce a Software Defined Radio prototype terminal for Emergency Situations. More specifically this integrated terminal will have NAV/COM functions and so it will be composed by two modules: the Localization and Communication Components, running on the same machine and connected each other via TCP/IP protocol. The Localization component will have to find out the terminal position itself and the Communication component will have to communicate it to other terminals. Both components of this prototype, thus, will be interfaced by their own front-ends, so providing the navigation and communication services.

**Keywords:** emergency situations, assisted localization, NAV-COM devices, software defined radio terminal.

## 1 Introduction

The activities of the scientific research communities have been recently motivated towards the topics of the communications and networking technologies for public safety and security. This trend has been enforced by the terrorist menace and the attention which has been given to catastrophic events.

As a result, a big research activity has been accomplished at international level in order to define modern, interoperable communications and networking standards for emergency response and public safety. Communication and navigation services in an emergency scenario are characterized by extremely different requirements from the classical ones. Access to permanent bidirectional links between a control center and teams of interveners (e.g., first aid groups) is crucial in handling emergencies and must be available for the entire duration of the intervention. Besides, knowing on time and accurately the position of the rescue entities (persons and means) is a fundamental enhancement in the coordination and planning of emergency and disaster relief operations, both in terms of efficacy and safety of the interventions. Indeed, the ETSI Recommendation TS 102 181 [1] recognizes the importance of providing "real-time information regarding the position of personnel or vehicles to a command point". Therefore the integration of communication services and positioning/navigation capabilities in

K. Sithamparanathan et al. (Eds.): PSATS 2010, LNICST 43, pp. 425–435, 2010.

a unique, portable, robust and user-friendly terminal (professional NAV/COM device) results a key feature in this kind of applications.

Navigation capabilities, for example using GNSS (Global Navigation Satellite Systems) services, are necessary to provide the 3D terminal position (with better accuracy possible). Then, localization information should be automatically transmitted to the suitable entities as soon as it is available, without human intervention. Unfortunately, GNSS signal reception is dramatically impaired by Line-Of-Sight (LOS) obstructions and multipath, especially in urban environments, as well as by strong attenuations due to walls and slabs in indoor conditions. Several strategies to improve positioning performance in critical conditions have been studied [3,4,5,6]; among them, the concept of "cooperative localization" seems to be particularly suitable for the scenario addressed in this work, in order to improve overall system reliability by the exploitation of all the available technology at the maximum extent, as expected for a system that can save human lives. The basis for the cooperative localization investigate here is an Assisted GNSS (AGNSS)-like approach, which exploits the COM network architecture with specifically added feature to improve localization performance.

The main objective of this paper is the definition of a prototypical architecture for a reconfigurable and flexible user terminal open to host the requirements of a professional NAV/COM device for emergency interventions. The Software Defined Radio (SDR) technology is the technique chosen to reach this requirements because of its intrinsic flexibility and reconfigurability [2]. As it is well known SDR is a technique for moving digital signal processing as close as possible to the antenna. This kind of solutions also claims for a higher flexibility at the physical layer and a smarter intelligence at the other lower layers: as a result, the enabling SDR technologies are often considered together with a new radio paradigm that implements self-reconfigurability, the so-called Cognitive Radio (CR).

This paper is organized as follows. In Section 2 the Integrated NAV/COM Terminal and considered scenario are presented. In Sections 3 and 4 the Location and Communication components are better described. In Section 5 we present the concluding remarks.

## 2    Integrated Terminal Architecture

As stated in the introduction, the indoor/outdoor location and tracking capability with better possible accuracy has been recognized as the single most important technological development enhancing emergency response operations. A single GPS receiver has good performance of providing optimal capability outdoor. Nonetheless, a challenging situation is when a terminal attempts the localization both in indoor and in the outdoor with hostile environment (e.g., because of foliage or heavy scattering from dense and metallic structure).

In the considered scenario (depicted in Fig. 1), one or more terminals (associated to a first aid group, for instance) are spread on the territory of the intervention. A certain fraction of the terminals are in LOS visibility with four

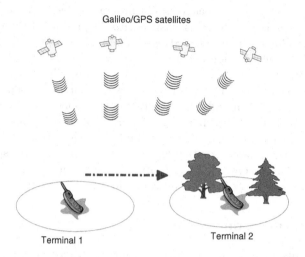

**Fig. 1.** Considered scenario: the Terminal 1 is in LOS visibility, whereas Terminal 2 is in Non-LOS condition

or more GPS satellites, as Terminal 1 in the figure. On the contrary, the other terminals (Terminal 2 in the figure) are in a Non-LOS condition so that their GPS receiver is severely impaired, but not completely blocked. In this case, an AGNSS-like solution seems profitable, since terminals with reliable GPS position (that could be seen as "anchor nodes") may send their navigation parameters to the impaired ones, such as the ID of satellites with the best $C/N_o$, Doppler frequencies and orbital parameters. Although these local information needs to be refined in the impaired receiver, it could significantly improve performance of the impaired nodes in at least two ways:

1. strongly reducing the acquisition time and false-alarm probability for the medium-impaired terminals, as well as easing the tracking mode;
2. enabling the acquisition and tracking of the necessary satellite signals for strongly-impaired terminals, whose autonomous acquisition process would be too much prone to errors to be reliable.

Notably in such situations the presence of multiple sets of assistance information, received from multiple anchor terminals, should be exploited in the most fruitful way as a form of information diversity, able to potentially increase the reliability and accuracy of the AGNSS procedure.

Consequently, the integration of communication systems to localization/ navigation services in the rescuer's terminal can be extremely effective in a scenario like that has just been envisaged. More specifically a reconfigurable NAV/COM radio terminal may be the key element in the design of an effective and robust emergency network.

With the goal of developing a prototype of such a professional NAV/COM terminal we consider a software-defined radio approach, that is the terminal becomes a software program loaded into a programmable device equipped with proper RF front-ends. Only what is feasible with the present CPU technology will be considered. This reconfigurable SDR terminal will have to take into account heterogeneous communication networks based on terrestrial radio interface and so TETRA, Wi-Fi/WiMAX and UMTS/LTE systems will be considered.

The prototype architecture of our integrated terminal is based on two main modules: the Localization and Communication Component. They are expected to become nothing but two separated software programs running on the same PC, properly interfaced with each other and with their respective navigation and communications radio front-ends, for instance resident on specific USB-connected boards. Thereby, the PC prototype becomes, in fact, a real NAV/COM terminal with cooperative localization capabilities.

## 3 Localization Component

The SDR localization component is based on the N-Gene platform, an 8-bits fully software GNSS receiver, able to receive the Global Positioning System (GPS) Coarse Acquisition (C/A) code on L1, with the ability to process more than 12 channels in real time, and track live GIOVE-A and GIOVE-B[1] signals transmitted on the E1 band. The receiver has been completely developed at the NavSAS lab in Politecnico di Torino/ISMB during the last two years, with the aim of equipping the lab with a powerful, quickly usable and extremely versatile tool to receive and analyze GNSS signals; the fully-software reprogrammability, together with the real-time processing capability, allow lab researchers to quickly test new receiving algorithms and architectures directly to real or simulated signals, as well as performing completely controlled data collections and signal analysis campaigns. In fact, the receiver can be used with any RF front-end that exports data through an USB interface. The 8-bits quantization allows for implementing all of those signal processing blocks requiring a fine resolution, as for example notch filters for interference mitigation, pulse blanking techniques and multipath mitigation techniques based on the estimation of the parameters of the input signal. The reconfigurability of its software modules makes N-Gene the optimal tool to realize the Integrated Terminal architecture with NAV/COM capabilities introduced in the previous section.

The high level of flexibility is the prominent feature that has made SDR architectures an indispensable tool to evaluate competing designs and has opened the possibility of multi-profile core platforms at commercially affordable costs, which can switch to different application profiles and different performances by means of a few simple software instructions. As a step forward, future GNSS SDR receivers could adaptively reconfigure their own architecture to the most appropriate one for the immediate environment they have to cope with, in order to maximize their efficiency. In a research lab, a real-time fully software architecture represents the ultimate simulation/testing environment, since it provides a

---

[1] GIOVE-A and GIOVE-B are the two first satellites of the European GNSS system, Galileo).

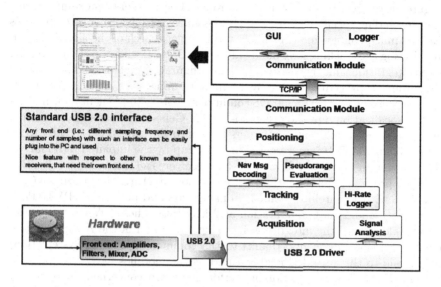

**Fig. 2.** N-Gene block diagram

single architecture able to process simulated signals generated in controlled environment and live signals. It allows in this way to test and validate novel receiving architectures and signal monitoring procedures without replacing hardware components: all the necessary updates become a software matter. These are the fundamental reasons that has led to the proliferation of SDR solutions in the field of GNSS receivers since the last decade [7].

Figure 2 shows a high level block diagram of the N-Gene software architecture. The left part of the diagram represents the front end, which is the only piece of dedicated hardware required. The USB 2.0 connection makes the receiver particularly versatile to be connected to virtually any RF front-end with USB interface. At the moment the platform has been successfully tested with different commercial and prototype front-ends, featuring 3-to-6 MHz IF bandwidth @L1/L2 and 1-to-8 quantization bits using a sampling frequency in the range 13-to-20 MHz. The right part of Figure 2 represents the N-Gene software routines. The USB driver controls the data flow from the ADC, while the acquisition and tracking blocks are the core of the baseband signal processing. The former seeks for the satellites in view, while the latter synchronizes the incoming codes and carriers with local replicas. As soon as the receiver tracks at least four satellites, it is able to compute the user position and velocity, through the estimation of the distance between the user and the set of satellites (i.e.: pseudorange estimation).

The receiver is controlled by the Graphical User Interface (GUI) through a TCP/IP protocol. This design allows for controlling the receiver from a remote PC, in case this is needed, and in this project represents the enabling feature for the implementation of a cooperative localization architecture among two or more terminals. Indeed, thanks to the software flexibility, the user is allowed to configure the receiver by specifying a wide range of parameters, for example by assigning/excluding specific signals (i.e.: GPS, Galileo or EGNOS) or satellite codes to each channel, configuring thresholds and Doppler search of the signal acquisition, selecting the tracking loop bandwidths, the Delay Lock Loop (DLL) spacing and the integration time. Evidently, similar configuration rights could be assigned to an automatic procedure driven by a remote terminal that provides assistance to the receiver in case of critical LOS conditions, so as to implement a form of cooperative localization. On the other side, the N-Gene-based assistance terminal is able to output its relevant parameters thanks to the same TCP/IP link to an additional "virtual GUI," represented in this setup by the impaired terminal.

The current operative platform of the SW receiver is a Gentoo Linux. Running on a 3 GHz processor (Intel Pentium 4 standard architecture) the maximum CPU load is 50% with 12 satellite channels in navigation and performing PVT (Position, Velocity and Time) computation at 2 kHz rate. These SW characteristics are favorable toward the integration in a single terminal of the Navigation and Communication Components, thanks to the common Operative System (OS) platform and to the fair CPU load featured by the modules.

As far as the N-gene positioning performance are concerned, in open sky the receiver achieves a position accuracy lower than 10 meters rms, using code-based measurements and without applying carrier smoothing techniques. In case of "cold start," the Time-To-First-Fix (TTFF) is lower than 45 s. These performance figures show that the receiver is surely competitive with respect to any other commercial/mass-market solution in terms of positioning performance, while it gains in versatility of use.

For example, it can be used to accurately monitor the signal $C/N_o$ ratio in passing from a LOS (open sky) condition to a partially blocked condition (partial non-LOS), for instance under foliage or in a area populated by high buildings, thanks to its accurate procedure to estimate the $C/N_o$ [8]. As soon as the measure falls below a certain threshold for satellites above the elevation mask, a procedure can be started to decide if assistance is needed and, in the case, to broadcast an assistance request through the Communication Module. A companion receiver, whose Communication Module has sensed the assistance request and whose signal quality control parameters have declared good signal quality, will activate a procedure to communicate back the subset of assistance parameters.

The assistance procedure can be borrowed and re-adapted from the AGNSS standards (N-Gene can already host specific software routines to recovery AGNSS data using an OMA-SUPL protocol [10]). AGNSS is a network-assisted augmentation method that integrates GNSS with information provided by the cellular network (namely, GSM/GPRS and UMTS) to the aim of reducing TTFF and increasing the receiver sensitivity. GNSS receiver sensitivity might be enhanced by reducing the acquisition search space in both Doppler shift and phase domains, thanks to a rough information about the most probable Doppler shift and code phase computed and transmitted by the cellular network. Without resorting to the complete GSM/GPRS/UMTS assistance protocols [9,10], which necessitate in any case of the availability of connection to public services,

**Table 1.** Possible assistance parameters in AGNSS

| Assistance data |
| --- |
| Visible satellites |
| Position of the visible satellites (azimuth, elevation) |
| Predicted codes phase (and confidence interval) |
| Code phase confidence intervals ("search window") |
| Predicted Doppler shifts and Doppler rates |
| Satellite ephemeris |
| Satellite almanac |
| Satellite clock corrections |
| Navigation time (GNSS time) |
| Navigation data bits |
| user terminal location (either coarse or precise estimation) |

possibly damaged or overloaded in emergency situations, it is possible to derive ad ad-hoc assistance procedure for the integrated terminal, lighter and possibly more flexible than the standard AGNSS. The list of the common assistance data that may by included in an assistance message is shown in Table 1.

The N-Gene software architecture features a TCP/IP socket and allows for recovering all the parameters involved in the assistance procedure from a remote server. This characteristic is used to connect the receiver to the communication component described below and implement an efficient hybrid NAV/COM system suitable in emergency situations.

## 4    Communication Component

GNU Radio [11] is an open source software toolkit for building and deploying Software Defined Radios. It is a platform for signal processing on commodity hardware. In fact, when combined with a minimal hardware, GNU Radio allows the construction of radios that the transmitted (and received) waveforms are defined by software.

More in specific GNU Radio is a hybrid system C++/Python that works on several operating systems among which Linux that we will use. The radiocommunication chain can be represented by a graph where the vertexes are the signal processing blocks and the edges represent the data flow between them. The signal processing blocks are implemented in C++ and the graphs are constructed and run in Python. Therefore, Python is used to "glue" the signal processing blocks constituting the communication chain. One interesting feature of GNU Radio is that the parameters, and even the inner structure, of the graph can be changed "on the fly". Thus, our terminal can change its inner structure to adapt to the existing communication systems.

The hardware platform usually combined to GNU Radio is the Ettus Universal Software Radio Peripheral (USRP)[12], a general purpose motherboard that gives access to the radio frequency spectrum and can be connected with any computer (that support GNU Radio) with a USB 2.0 port. The USRP is designed to allow general purpose computers to function as high bandwidth software radios. In essence, it serves as a digital baseband and IF section of a radio communication system.

It has 4 high-speed analog to digital converters (ADCs), each at 12 bits per sample, 64MSamples/sec. There are also 4 high-speed digital to analog converters (DACs), each at 14 bits per sample, 128MSamples/sec. These 4 input and 4 output channels are connected to an Altera Cyclone EP1C12 FPGA. The FPGA, in turn, connects to a USB2 interface chip, the Cypress FX2, and on to the computer. Usually the USRP motherboard supports four daughterboards, two for receiving side and two for transmitting side.

RF front-ends are implemented on these daughterboards. There are some type of them depending by the frequency, ranging from baseband up to 2.9 GHz. We use the daughterboards that operate in the 2.4 GHz band. The basic design philosophy behind the USRP has been to do all of the waveform-specific processing, like modulation and demodulation, on the host CPU. All of the high-speed general purpose operations like digital up and down conversion, decimation and interpolation are done on the FPGA. Finally, to complete the communication chain we use Radio Shack 15-215 Antenna.

For what concerns the physical layer for our terminal, we will consider the OFDM modulation because it is efficiently used in latest broadband wireless communications system, like IEEE 802.11 (Wi-Fi), 802.16 (WiMAX), HYPERLAN and 3GPP Long Term Evolution (LTE). Now we introduce a brief overview of OFDM modulation. The sequential data stream (that could be a PSK or QAM symbol) is converted to a parallel stream and the vectors of which are interpreted as signal in the frequency domain. By applying an inverse fast Fourier transform (IFFT), these data are transformed into the time domain and transmitted on a set of orthogonal carriers with separation $\Delta f^2$. To avoid intersymbol interference (ISI) the last $L$ samples of the body of the OFDM symbol ($N$ samples long) are copied on the head of the symbol, called *cyclic prefix*, to form the complete OFDM symbol. At the receiver we have the inverse blocks of the transmitter and the data are retrieved by means of a fast Fourier transform (FFT).

GNU Radio provides the signal processing blocks implementing the OFDM transmitter/receiver flow graph (depicted in Fig.3). In particular the transmitting chain has a block used to insert "pre-modulated" preamble symbols before each payload. Instead on the receiving side we have a block for the symbol synchronization (realized with Maximum Likelihood method or Pseudo-Noise Sequence correlation) and another block that build an OFDM correlator and equalizer using the known preamble symbols.

More specifically for our simulation we consider a simple OFDM symbol structure for data transmission. We use 200 sub-carriers on 512 elements for the FFT operation with 128 samples for the value of cyclic prefix. Consequently, utilizing the USRPs we obtain a subcarrier spacing equal to 625 Hz (that essentially

---

[2] To preserve orthogonality between subcarries $\Delta f = \frac{1}{T_u}$ where $T_u$ is the useful OFDM symbol period.

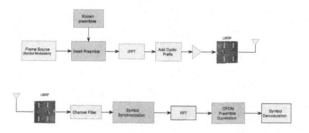

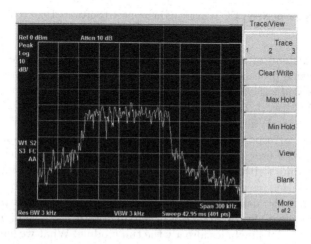

**Fig. 3.** Transmitting and Receiving chain of OFDM communication system on GNU Radio platform

**Fig. 4.** Bandwidth of ODFM signal created by USRP

depends on the ADC's number of samples and interpolation rate) for a maximum bandwitdh of 125 kHz and a theoretical bitrate of 100 kbps (utilizing a BPSK modulation for every sub-carrier). These values are confirmed by the Fig. 4 that represent the output screen of a spectrum analyzer placed close to the transmitting USRP. Finally, we could consider the implementation of simple coding channel (e.g. block or convolutional coding) in order to increase the performance in term of error rate.

For what concern the interface between NAV and COM modules a reasonable choice seems to be the use of TCP sockets realized by, for instance, Python routines, as we can see from the Fig. 5.

Another interesting feature of GNU Radio is the opportunity to have particular drivers, called universal TUN/TAP drivers [13] for "tunneling" the packets from the USRP to the Linux kernel (via USB 2.0). These TUN/TAP drivers provide the reception and transmission of packet for user space processes. In fact it can be seen as a simple Point-to-Point or Ethernet device, which, instead of receiving packets from physical media, receives the packets from user space

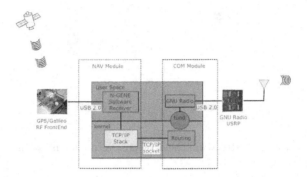

**Fig. 5.** Integration of NAV/COM Systems in proposed Software Defined Radio Terminal

process and instead of sending packets via physical media writes the packets to the user space process. In order to use the driver, the program has to open /dev/net/tun and issue a corresponding ioctl() to register a network device with the kernel. A network device will appear as tunXX or tapXX, depending on the driver chosen. When the program closes the file descriptor, the network device and all corresponding routes will disappear. Depending on the type of device chosen, the userspace program has to read/write IP packets (with tun) or Ethernet frames (with tap). Another interesting application using TUN/TAP is pipsecd, an userspace IPSec implementation that can use complete kernel routing. GNU Radio using these TUN/TAP drivers can create a program that provides a framework for building our own MAC protocols. The Linux 2.6 kernel (used in Ubuntu 8.10) includes already the tun module. What we have to do is to run two copies of this program on two different machines. So in this situation we can allow two machines to talk each other with the TCP/IP protocols. Thanks to this IP tunnel we can copy with a problem born considering the scenario in Fig.1. In fact, in order to reduce time acquisition by the impaired terminals (like Terminal 2 in figure 1) we have to maintain a time-synchronization between Terminal 1 (in full LOS visibility) and Terminal 2. So, we will try to realize this time-synchronization with the Network Time Protocol (NTP), a client-server TCP/IP protocol used to synchronize the internal clock of computers inside a network. It can be used on Linux platform, by easily configuring the daemon NTPd. Even the Precision Time Protocol, PTP (a protocol similar to NTP but that achieves more accuracy) and the Linux daemon PTPd will be investigate to achieve more accuracy compared to NTP.

## 5   Concluding Remarks

SDR represents in this work the enabling technology to realize the prototype of an integrated NAV/COM terminal intended to be used by first responders intervening in public emergency situations. The challenging feature is the provision of positioning capabilities in satellite-blocked (or partially blocked) environments, as are likely e.g. in urban or forest interventions. Such critical signal scenarios can be coped with a cooperative localization approach, which involves the exchange of navigation data between two NAV/COM terminals. Two SDR modules are then realized for each user terminal: a Localization SW module connected via TCP/IP to a Communication SW module. Thanks to the fully SW implementation, the presence of hardware components is reduced to the minimum extent, and the whole prototype can be hosted in a general purpose PC, this allowing to easily perform field test campaigns at really affordable costs.

## Acknowledgment

This work has been supported by the Italian Ministry of the Education, University and Research (MIUR), under the PRIN 2007 program "SALICE" (http://lenst.det.unifi.it/salice/).

## References

1. ETSI Recommendation TS 102 181 V.1.1.1 (2005-12), Emergency Communications (EMTEL); Requirements for communication between authorities/organizations during emergencies
2. Del Re, E. (ed.): Software Radio Technologies and Services. Springer, London (2001)
3. van Diggelen, F.: Indoor GPS theory & implementation. In: IEEE/ION Position Location and Navigation Symposium, PLANS 2002, pp. 240–247 (April 2002)
4. Sahmoudi, M., Amin, M.G.: A Maximum-Likelihood synchronization scheme for GPS positioning in multipath, interference, and weak signal environments. In: IEEE Vehicular Tech. Conf., VTC 2006 (September 2006)
5. Razavi, A., Gebre-Egziabher, D., Akos, D.M.: Carrier loop architectures for tracking weak GPS signals. IEEE Trans. on Aerospace and Electronic Systems 44(2), 697–710 (2008)
6. Dovis, F., Lesca, R., Margaria, D., Boiero, G., Ghinamo, G.: An assisted high-sensitivity acquisition technique for GPS indoor positioning. In: IEEE/ION Position, Location and Navigation Symposium, PLANS 2008, pp. 1350–1361 (May 2008)
7. Won, J.H., Pany, T., Hein, G.W.: GNSS Software Defined Radio. Inside GNSS Magazine, 48–56 (July/August 2006)
8. Falletti, E., Pini, M., Lo Presti, L., Margaria, D.: Assessment on low complexity $C/N_0$ estimators based on a M-PSK signal model for GNSS Receivers. In: IEEE/ION Position Location and Navigation Symposium (PLANS) (May 2008)
9. 3GPP Specications. Requirements for support of assisted global positioning system. 3GPP TS 25.171, v.7.1.0 (June 2006)
10. Open Mobile Alliance (OMA). Secure User Plane for Location (SUPL), OMA-TS-UPL, v.1.0 (June 2007)
11. GNU Radio Website (2009), http://www.gnuradio.org
12. Ettus Research LLC Website (2009), http://www.ettus.com
13. VTun, http://vtun.sourceforge.net

# Hybrid System HAP-WiFi for Incident Area Network[*]

G. Araniti[1], M. De Sanctis[2], S.C. Spinella[1], M. Monti[2], E. Cianca[2],
A. Molinaro[1], A. Iera[1], and M. Ruggieri[2]

[1] Department D.I.M.E.T, University Mediterranea of Reggio Calabria,
Via Graziella Loc. Feo di Vito, 89100 Reggio Calabria, Italy
{araniti,silverio.spinella,antonella.molinaro,
antonio.iera}@unirc.it
[2] Department of Electronics Engineering, University of Rome "Tor Vergata",
Via del Politecnico 1, 00133 Roma, Italy
{mauro.de.sanctis,marco.monti,ernestina.cianca,
ruggieri}@uniroma2.it

**Abstract.** Recent large scale disasters have highlighted the importance of a robust and efficient public safety communication network able to coordinate emergency operations even when existing infrastructures are damaged. The Incident Area Network (IAN) is a self-forming temporary network infrastructures brought to the scene of an incident to support personal and local communications among different public safety end-users. In this work we are interested in investigating how the High Altitude Platform (HAP) can effectively support Multimedia Broadcast/Multicast Service (MBMS) in a scenario wherein the preexistent terrestrial network is not available. To this aim, we propose an efficient policy of Radio Resource Management (RRM) based on cooperation framework between HAP and Mobile Ad-Hoc NETwork (MANET). The proposed solution has been successfully tested through a comprehensive simulation campaign.

**Keywords:** Incident Area Networks, Cooperative Multicast, MBMS, HAP, MANET, WiFi.

## 1 Introduction

Broadband communications are particularly significant features in those areas involved in catastrophic incidents, where effective and efficient communication means, infrastructures and procedures are required to react to the accident. In this context the communication infrastructure at the incident area is often completely destroyed or only partially available. As a consequence, to ensure radio communications for an efficient organization of the relief operations, a possible solution is the deployment of ad-hoc wireless networks as an Incident Area Network (IAN). It is a self-forming temporary network infrastructure brought to the scene of an incident to support personal and local

---

[*] This work has been supported by Italian Research Program (PRIN 2007) Satellite-Assisted LocalIzation and Communication system for Emergency services (SALICE)", http://lenst.det.unifi.it/salice

K. Sithamparanathan et al. (Eds.): PSATS 2010, LNICST 43, pp. 436–450, 2010.

communications among different public safety end-users (fire brigade, police, medics, etc) and their connection with a gateway [1], [2]. In particular, considering the users involved in post-disaster operations (for instance, Emergency Vehicles - EVs, First Rescues - FRs, etc.), the IAN can replace the damaged network infrastructure. This can guarantee the continuity of standard communications (for example voice traffic with the Coordination Centre) and allows the exchange of information data related to the particular situation (hereinafter Rescue Communications), such as data on location of FRs and EVs, alert information, electronic maps, video of the monitored area to support aid forces during their motion within the disaster zone. In such a situation, broadcast and multicast communications could allow an efficient utilization of limited IAN radio resources. For example, several FR teams are likely to operate simultaneously within the critical area; each team may need to establish multicast communications for specific information delivery or co-ordination among operators. Multicast service delivery can be easily guaranteed to users by utilizing point-to-multipoint MBMS (Multimedia Broadcast/Multicast Services) architecture [3], specifically designed within the third-generation (3G) cellular systems. Notwithstanding, a terrestrial MBMS segment cannot be adequate to match the exacting requirements arising in disadvantaged operational scenarios like the above-mentioned ones. High Altitude Platforms (HAPs) are very attractive in the view of assisting incident area networks in offering broadcast and multicast services [4]. This paper aims at defining the system architecture of the IAN, as proposed by the SALICE project [5], and the cooperation framework between HAP and Mobile Ad-hoc NETworks (MANET), specifically designed to increase the effectiveness of HAP in supporting multicast transmissions in a IAN. In particular, objective of this work is evaluate the advantages introduced by a possible HAP-WiFi cooperative architecture and to define a feasible Radio Resource Management policy to manage multicast traffic delivery in presence of *multiple* MBMS sessions.

The remain part of this paper is organized as follows. Section 2 describes the systems architecture of the IAN. Section 3 illustrates the transport channels features used for MBMS services from HAPs systems and, furthermore, it introduces the cooperative HAP/MANET policy proposed for the IAN. While the results of a exhaustive simulation campaign, aiming at defining the RRM policy, are the focus of Section 4. The performance degradation of the throughput of WiFi links caused by interference is discussed in Section 5. Finally, conclusive remarks are given in Section 6.

## 2   System Architecture

This section aims at identifying the end-to-end architecture and topology of the IAN, including space and ground network systems. As mentioned above, the end-to-end architecture proposed could be split into two different sub-networks, based on their coverage features: *Short-Range Network*, used to carry out communications within the Incident Area Network, and *Long-Range Network*, utilized for the communications toward external zones. Long-Range Network could consist of both a space and a terrestrial segment, while the Short-Range Network takes into account only the last one. Space segment comprises satellite (GEO and LEO) and UAV systems, while the terrestrial segment consists of several mobile/wireless communication systems, such as WWAN (UMTS, TETRA), WMAN (WiMAX standard), WLAN (WiFi standard),

WPAN (IEEE 802.15.3 & IEEE802.15.4 standards). These kinds of terrestrial networks are very different in terms of offered data rate, delay, security issues and communication range. This strong heterogeneity poses several problems about the definition of an efficient integration scheme which allows a smart and quick communication between the various system actors. The IAN should be conceived as the result of integration between *(i)* existing and active systems not impaired by the disaster (i.e.: satellite systems, HAP platforms and also active cellular networks) to support long distance communications, and *(ii)* terrestrial networks quickly deployed in the emergency scenario that allow users either to communicate within the same area and to access the subsystems for connections with external zones by means of an IAN Gateway. In fact, the IAN will include several Master Mobile Nodes (MMN) with gateway functionalities, equipped with different interfaces: UMTS, Satellite Networks, HAP Networks, etc. According to our proposal, a IAN should be used for both voice/video/data transmissions and wireless sensor communications in the local and/or personal area [6]. In particular, in this research work we aim at investigating how efficient HAPs can be in supporting Multimedia Broadcast/Multicast Service (MBMS) in a IAN scenario in which this multicast services cannot be provided by the terrestrial coverage. Therefore, the approach to the definition of a IAN for emergency service management is the following (see Fig. 1).

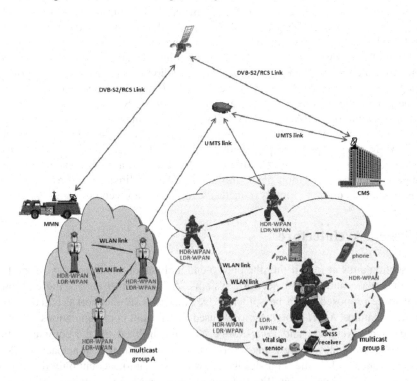

**Fig. 1.** System Architecture

The user (relief team member) is provided with a Relief Member Unit (RMU) which is a network node with multi-standard capabilities and bridge functionalities. The wireless standard used by the RMU are IEEE802.15.4, IEEE802.11 and possibly UMTS to allow communication with HAP system. All devices also equipped with HAP/UMTS interface could assume the role of *Anchor Node* during a multicast cooperative transmission. IEEE802.11 standard is used for communication between users in ad-hoc mode. UMTS link is used by the *Anchor Node* for relaying communications outside the IAN. Furthermore, the user is surrounded by two Wireless Personal Area Networks (WPANs) that can exchange information through the RMU:

- A LDR-WPAN composed by a set of sensors for location and context detection (e.g. vital sign sensor, temperature sensor, GNSS receiver, indoor positioning devices) with an energy-efficient Low Data Rate (LDR) WPAN air interface. The PHY transmission bit rate of the LDR interface ranges from few bps to 250 kbps [7].
- A HDR-WPAN based on IEEE802.15.3/Wimedia composed by a set of devices with a High Data Rate (HDR) WPAN air interface (e.g. Personal Digital Assistants, Phones, etc.). The PHY transmission bit rate of the HDR interface ranges from 10 Mbps to 50 Mbps [8].

This IAN should allow processing and fusion of location/context data collected by sensors of the LDR-WPAN in the RMU, and data delivery between network nodes in the HDR-WPAN and the access network. Since the above mentioned wireless systems for HDR-WPAN and LDR-WPAN exploit unlicensed frequency bands and they can be partially or totally overlapping in frequency, in this approach coexistence issues have to be carefully addressed and a solution beyond cooperation has to be identified, based on the concept of simultaneous use of different devices.

## 3  Cooperative Multicast

In order to optimize the coordination among different rescue  teams, an efficient utilization of the limited radio resources have to be guaranteed. The employment of Multimedia Broadcast/Multicast Services provided by HAP in an incident area can enhance the overall system performance, since multicast emergency transmissions can be delivered to groups of receivers at the same time; thus avoiding data duplications both in the core network and over the air interface [9]. MBMS is the multicast technology developed by the 3rd Generation Partnership Project (3GPP). It is a downlink point-to-multipoint protocol thought for the delivery of a multicast and broadcast stream from a single source.

### 3.1  Transport Channels Supported by MBMS/HAP

The MBMS data can be delivered to users by utilizing any of three different transport channels: Dedicated Channel (DCH), Forward Access Channel (FACH), and High Speed Downlink Shared Channel (HS-DSCH). The selection of the appropriate radio bearer for a MBMS service should be done with respect to the other exiting MBMS sessions in the local emergency area and with respect to available power by HAP.

In this work we assumed to utilize only FACH and DCH channels, where the first one is utilized to deliver alerting information for all the population and rescue teams involved in the disaster area; while the second one is employed to deliver particular-ized multicast services to a given rescue team for their coordination (through Anchor Nodes, as it will be described in following). We decided not to use the shared chan-nel, because in an emergency situation a dedicated channel (DCH) could be more reliable with respect to HS-DSCH that shares the resource with all the others users located in the same area.

Hence in this section, we briefly recall the modality to assign the transmission power to such two channels. The transmission power assigned to the DCHs can vary depending on: *(i)* the multicast users number; *(ii)* the users position with respect to the centre of the area covered by the HAP; *(iii)* the bit rate of the application.

In Eq. (1) it is shown how to define the transmission power assigned to a DCH serving the *i*-th user in a given cell (named *own cell* in the following) [10]:

$$P_{DCH,i} = (C/I)_i \frac{\sum_{j=1}^{N_{other\_cell}} P_j^{other} G_j^{other}(\theta_i, d_i) + p \sum_{k=1}^{N_{user}} P_k^{own} G_k^{own}(\theta_i, d_i) + P^{com} G_i^{own}(\theta_i, d_i) + N_d}{G_i^{own}(\theta_i, d_i)} \quad (1)$$

where the terms reported at the numerator represent: *(i)* the interference due to the transmitted power ($P_j^{other}$) from the *j*-th adjacent cell (the total number of interfering cells is $N_{other\_cell}$); *(ii)* the interference due to the transmission power ($P_k^{own}$) from the *k*-th user belonging to the *multicast group* that receive data within the *own cell* (the total number of own cell users is $N_{user}$); *(iii)* the interference due to the power used for transmission over the downlink common control channels ($P^{com}$); *(iv)* the Additive Gaussian White Noise (AGWN) ($N_0$). Furthermore, $p$ is the orthogonality factor which can be zero in case of perfect orthogonality, $G_i^{own}(\theta_i, d_i)$ is the link gain related to the *i*-th user with respect to its *own cell*, $G_j^{other}(\theta_i, d_i)$ is the link gain with respect to the *neighboring cells* while $G_k^{own}(\theta_i, d_i)$ is the one in the *own cell*; both are still related to the *i*-th user.

In general, $G(\theta, d)$ and $C/I$ (the Carrier-to-Interference ratio) are defined respec-tively by (2) and (3).

$$G(\theta, d)_{dB} = g(\theta)_{dB} - L_p(d)_{dB} \quad (2)$$

$$(C/I)_{dB} = (E_b/N_0)_{dB} - (P_g)_{dB} \quad (3)$$

$\theta$ is the angle representing the boresight direction, $g(\theta)$ is the Antenna Gain calcu-lated in the boresight direction, $L_p(d)$ is the attenuation value caused by the Path Loss for the user at a distance equal to $d$ from the centre of the HAP coverage area. $E_b/N_0$ is the Energy per Bit-to-Noise Power Spectral Density while $P_g$ is the Processing Gain.

The FACH is a Point to Multipoint (PtM) channel with a power level high enough to guarantee an acceptable service in the whole coverage area [11]; it transmits at a fixed power level since fast power control is not supported in this channel. Both bit rate of the MBMS services and the cell coverage area affect the power allocated to FACHs.

High data rate MBMS services might not be deliverable by FACH, since excessive downlink transmission power would be required. High bit rates can only be offered to users located very close to the centre of the area covered by the HAP.

## 3.2  Hybrid Radio Resource Management Policy for IAN

Multicast transmissions have increased power requirements and consume a large portion of the available power resources of the HAP. As a consequence, the number of parallel multicast sessions that a HAP could support is limited. A promising means to overcome MBMS intrinsic limitations consists in integrating MANET technologies into HAP network. This solution foresees that RMUs cooperate in the multi-hop access to the HAP infrastructure by exploiting their short-range Wi-Fi interface. In so doing, a SALICE terminal will play the role of *Anchor Node* receiving the multicast traffic from the UMTS interface through a DCH; subsequently, it conveys the received packets, across the Wi-Fi interface, to its neighbour terminals within the MANET. This means that the users cooperate with each other to achieve the common goal of enjoying a multicast service at a given quality of service and, at the same time, cooperation between the MANET and the HAP network is established to increase the overall capacity and coverage of the IAN. The choice of the terminal to use as an *Anchor Node* is taken according to policies that may account for different parameter values.

Figure 1 shows an incident area, where a HAP serves two rescue teams (police and fire brigade) interested in downloading and streaming multicast services (i.e.: plans, video, electronic pictures and maps of the emergency site). It is worth noting that the number of users utilizing the same *Anchor Node* depends on the their mutual reachability that in turn is related to the *Wi-Fi radius coverage* ($WF_{Radius}$) and the *maximum number of allowed hops* ($H_{Max}$). For each rescue team the election of either one or more *Anchor Nodes* is foreseen.

To the purpose of reducing the adverse impact of multicast transmissions on the whole IAN traffic, an efficient Radio Resource Management (RRM) policy based on a HAP/MANET cooperative architecture is needed.

The RRM utilized for such a scenario has a threefold objective to: *(i)* define the access modality to the HAP/MBMS infrastructure from mobile terminals either directly (by means of FACH or DCH channels) or indirectly (multi-hop through the ad-hoc networks terminating to an *Anchor Node*); *(ii)* monitor continuously the conditions of network and terminals to the purpose of implementing the right policy for the election and the management of the *Anchor Nodes* at HAP level, on the basis of the signalling information sent by the cooperative terminals; *(iii)* monitor periodically rescue team priorities in order to deliver multicast information to the team with major need.

When a user terminal, for instance, a fireman's terminal, requests the access to a given multicast service, it checks in advance whether a FACH is already active for the same service. Should this be the case, then it joins the multicast group by accessing the local HAP FACH channel according to the MBMS rules. Otherwise, during a *listening* phase it searches for a reachable MANET handling a group/subgroup of users receiving the same multicast service. Following the identification of a target MANET, a *join* procedure is triggered by means of a *connect query* and the terminal keeps waiting for a reply from the Anchor Node. This latter, first checks if the acceptance of the new user in the MANET causes the trespassing of the threshold ($Thr_{QoS}$) on either the maximum number of users it is allowed to serve or the maximum  number of hops. In this case the new user will become a member of the multicast group/subgroup; while, in case of negative reply, the user requests a DCH channel to the HAP network.

Logically, in the latter case, the new user becomes a potential new Anchor Node of a MANET that will support any future request of the same multicast service. In case a novel terminal enters/leaves a MANET, the relevant Anchor Node updates its *local database* and signals the event to the HAP, which updates its *global database*. In so doing, any time an Anchor Node leaves the system (*Old Anchor Node*), the HAP network should be able to re-elect a novel Anchor Node (*New Anchor Node*) among the multi-interface terminals previously connected to the Old Anchor Node. Moreover, if the remote CMS (Control Master Station) identified a priority assistance team with higher need for better bit rate to coordinate the emergency operations, this can request from a HAP more radio resources using a multiple DCH channels and deallocating, if it is necessary, radio resources from other teams or from FACH.

The cited procedure exploits metrics such as: *Signal to Noise Ratio* (in the following A); *Minimum distance from the Old Anchor Node* (in the following B); *Mobility level* (in the following C); *Battery level* (in the following D). Similarly to the Cluster Head (CH) election procedure in [12] with reference to a sensor network, we apply an *Analytic Hierarchy Process* (AHP) [13] to decide the relative weights of an evaluative criteria set according to the aforementioned metrics. The AHP is a theory of measurement through pair wise comparisons and relies on the judgements of experts to derive priority scales. The node with the highest weight will be chosen by the RNC to be the new AN. In our case, the following decreasing priority order is established: D, B, A, and C.

The proposed RRM policy foresees a power computation phase where, by processing the data received from the Broadcast Multicast Service Centre (BM-SC) and Radio Network Control (RNC), the required power is computed to be allocated for any MBMS session. In the Radio Bearer ($R_b$) selection, the $P_{DCH}$ (power required for DCHs) and the $P_{FACH}$ (power required for FACH) are computed and the services priority are defined. We define $P_{total}$ as the sum of the power assigned to all the active MBMS sessions in each cell. This power will be compared to the maximum available power assigned by the network provider to MBMS sessions ($P_{MBMS}$).

Furthermore, we introduced two new procedures: (*i*) AN Selection and (*ii*) AN Election/Re-election. The former allows to evaluate if a new user can become a member of the multicast group/subgroup managed by an AN. The latter decides if a MBMS user can become a new AN to support users requiring the same multicast service. The user, obviously, starts an AN Selection procedure if a common transport channel is already active and cannot be activated for its multicast service. We define a new metric named *per-node throughput* that will be used by RNC during this procedure. This parameter is defined as the ratio of bit rate received by a multicast group member over the expected bit rate. As shown in the following, it depends either on the maximum number of users in the MANET and on the maximum number of allowed hops. Thus, it is compared with the $Thr_{QoS}$:

- a *per-node throughput* $\geq Thr_{QoS}$ means that the new user will join the AN;
- a *per-node throughput* $< Thr_{QoS}$ means that the new user likely will utilize a DCH channel.

For the *AN Election/Re-election procedure*, instead, the UE parameters evaluated at RNC level are the metrics in input to the aforementioned AHP, in order to choose the best AN.

If $P_{total} < P_{MBMS}$, then the suitable transport channel is assigned to the MBMS session. Differently, when $P_{total} \geq P_{MBMS}$, a session reconfiguration procedure should occur due to the fact that there are not enough radio resources available in the Node B to serve all the MBMS sessions. Possible reconfiguration events could be considered: *(i)* the reduction of the transmission rate of a MBMS session; *(ii)* the pause of alerting information for a short period of time; *(iii)* the cancellation of the service with low priority, *(iv)* the reduction of $Thr_{QoS}$. In so doing, as we will show in the following, a higher number of users will join the AN.

# 4   Simulation Results

A thorough simulation campaign has been conducted to demonstrate that the integration between HAP and MANET networks can improve the performance of system in an IAN scenario, in terms of capacity and coverage area, while providing access to multicast streaming services. In particular, the impact of the proposed architecture on *standard* MBMS is evaluated in an emergency situation, by highlighting introduced advantages and observed limitations.

Our RRM algorithm has been implemented in NS2 (Network Simulator 2) simulation environment [14]. Results described in this section are obtained with a 95% confidence interval. The main assumptions during the performed test campaigns are shown in Table I. A Poisson distributed call inter-arrival time is assumed and the values of the *multicast offered traffic (Erlang/cell)* depend on the specific simulation objective and vary during the tests. As reported in Table I, we conducted our simulation considering both fixed and mobile users. In particular we consider a user speed varying in the range [0:3] km/h, according to UMTS technical specifications. User mobility doesn't increase the power computation for HAP system. Nevertheless, high mobility could reduce the MANET performances in term of throughput, connectivity and as a consequence the capacity of the overall system could decrease.

We assumed (refer to Table I) several multicast groups receiving different MBMS streaming services at the same time from the same HAP. Indeed, in presence of a single multicast service per HAP, the complexity deriving from the integration between HAP and MANET is not justified.

As mentioned in previous sections, FACH will be activated to provide alerting information, while DCHs will be employed to particularized multicast services to a given rescue team through Anchor Nodes. Table II reports power values required by the FACH channel for different service bit rates and coverage areas [15]. In our simulation campaign we assumed to provide alerting services with 64 kbps in the overall incident area ($P_{FACH} = 12.6$ W).

However, in case of need, the alerting services will be stopped and this power will be assigned to rescue teams.

Figure 2 shows the capacity gain, defined as the ratio of the capacity of the integrated HAP/MANET with multi-hop cooperative access ($C_{HAP/MANET}$) over the capacity of the standalone HAP system ($C_{HAP}$):

**Table 1.** Simulation Assumptions

| | Features | Values |
|---|---|---|
| **HAP Features** | HAP High | 22 km |
| | Cell Radius | 2,6 km |
| | Cell Layout | Hexagonal grid |
| | Number of Neighboring Cell | 6 |
| | Maximum HAP Tx Power | 40 W |
| | Other BS Tx Power | 10 W |
| | Common Channel Power | 2 W |
| | Path Loss | Free Space affected by Rooftop Scattering and Mult. Screen Diffraction |
| | Multipath Channel | Vehicular A (3km/h) |
| | BLER Target | 10% |
| | Gmax | 32,2 dBi |
| | Thermal Noise | -100 dBm |
| | Orthogonality Factor | 0,5 |
| | User Speed | [0:3] km/h |
| **MANET Features** | Coverage radius | [10:100] m |
| | Multicast Routing Protocol | ODMRP |
| | Propagation Model | 2-Ray Ground Reflection |
| | Data Rate | 11 Mbps |
| | Number of hops | 1,2,3,4 |
| **Multicast Traffic** | Multicast Services (over dedicated/shared/common channels) | 64 kbps |
| | Frame Size | 400 bytes |
| | Frame Speed | 20 frame/s |
| | Video Duration | 300 s |
| | Number of Active Multicast Groups | More than 4 |
| | User Geographical Distribution | Uniform |
| | Offered Traffic | 400 Erlang/cell |

**Table 2.** FACH power in function of cell coverage and service bit rate [15]

| Cell Coverage / Service Bit Rate | 50% | 95% |
|---|---|---|
| 64 Kbps | 5.6 W | **12.6 W** |
| 128 Kbps | 15.2 W | 31.6 W |

$$Capacity\_Gain = \frac{C_{HAP/MANET}}{C_{HAP}} \qquad (4)$$

This metric allows to perceive the increase in the capacity consequent to the introduction of a multi-hop cooperative access into the integrated HAP/Wi-Fi system. Capacity gain values increase with $WF_{Radius}$ and with $H_{Max}$. This increasing does not require any HAP infrastructure augmentation, because the additional Wi-Fi access capability is directly provided by the RMUs. It is worth noting that choosing a given Wi-Fi coverage radius correspond to define a given level of transmission power of the

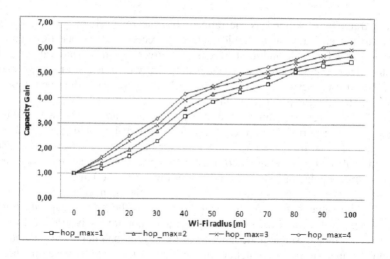

**Fig. 2.** Capacity Gain

802.11 terminal interface. Obviously, a higher transmission power entails both a greater Wi-Fi coverage radius and a greater number of users served by a single Anchor Node. Similar behavior is obtained increasing $H_{Max}$.

The price to pay is in terms of throughput reduction for multicast users, as a consequence of the increase in the maximum number of multicast multi-interface terminals that access the system through a given Anchor Node. Indeed, Figure 3 shows the per-node throughput values for a given multicast MANET receiver when varying the Wi-Fi radius and the maximum number of allowed hops.

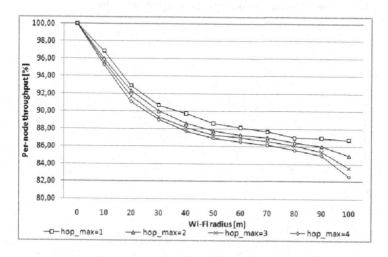

**Fig. 3.** Per-node throughput when varying $WF_{Radius}$ and $H_{Max}$

This parameter is defined as the ratio of bit rate received by a multicast group member to the bit rate which should have been received. Per-node throughput has been calculated for each multicast MANET receiver and the mean value has been evaluated. The per-node throughput values decrease with $WF_{Radius}$ and $H_{Max}$, because the number of users served by a single Anchor Node increases and, as consequence, a higher packets collision is experienced.

Other two interesting parameters to take into account are the delay and jitter that are respectively reported in Figures 4 and 5. Although both indexes increase with $WF_{Radius}$ and $H_{Max}$, still the assumed values are such as not to adversely affect also the perceived quality of a potential video streaming application. In fact, the video streaming can tolerate a delay of 5 seconds and a jitter lower than 100 ms.

By summarizing, it can be stated that increasing the number of nodes allowed to connect to the same *Anchor Node* means to increase the system capacity (and the Grade of Service level); at the same time, this does not adversely affect the QoS degree perceived by any single node in terms of mean jitter and delay but it could imply a potential reduction in the throughput of the multicast service. A wise dimensioning study is thus required to enable the RNC to best choose the values of $WF_{Radius}$ and $H_{Max}$ (i.e. the ones which, at the same time, allow a system capacity and the multicast user throughput within their relevant acceptability ranges) for any given loading condition. The simplest RNC policy could consist in monitoring the offered load, choosing the best combination of Wi-Fi transmission power and number of allowed hops, and in communicating them to the multicast terminals. The introduction of these new features in the RNC imply some simple modifications also in the routing protocol. In particular, new Signaling and Control Packets has to be introduced with the aim to vary the maximum number of allowed hops and to manage efficiently the multicast MANET receivers connected to the Anchor Node. This dynamic parameter tuning always could maximizes the system capacity, while still maintaining system blocking probability and multicast user throughput at acceptable levels.

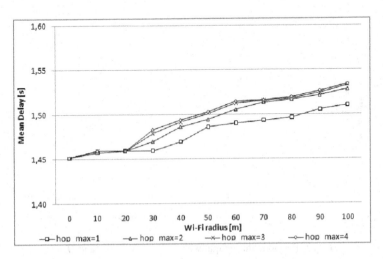

**Fig. 4.** Mean Delay when varying $WF_{Radius}$ and $H_{Max}$

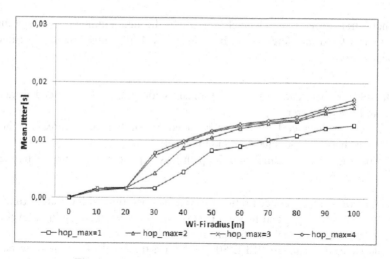

**Fig. 5.** Mean Jitter when varying $WF_{Radius}$ and $H_{Max}$

# 5   Interference Issues

The architecture proposed in the SALICE project for the IAN foresees the utilization of at least two different license-exempt wireless communications standards in ISM band at 2.4 GHz, namely: IEEE 802.11/WiFi and IEEE 802.15.4/ZigBee. These standards are implemented in the RMU multi-standard node, hence resulting in co-located systems interference when two or more standards are used simultaneously. However, even if there were no interference between the air interfaces included in the RMU, the high concentration of relief team members in a small area generates interference issues between the air interfaces of RMUs of different members.

The performance of WiFi links as simulated in the previous Section and ZigBee links are highly affected by interference. In fact, the frequency band used by such wireless networks can be totally or partially overlapped, hence resulting in co-channel or adjacent-channel interference which reduce the performance. Co-channel interference occurs when the interfering signal has the same carrier frequency of the useful information signal. Co-channel interference can be reduced by using e.g. power control, directional antenna beam pointing control, interference cancellation schemes.

Adjacent Channel Interference can be categorized into in-band interference and out-of-band interference. In-band interference occurs when the centre of the interfering signal bandwidth falls within the bandwidth of the desired signal.

Out-of-band interference occurs when the centre of the interfering signal bandwidth falls outside the bandwidth of the desired signal. This kind of interference can be experienced when transmitters and receivers operate close together in terms of the two main variables that determine their degree of isolation from each other: distance and frequency separation. Out-of band interference may be caused over short to medium distances when there is insufficient isolation. This interference is not directly caused by co-channel emissions, but by having the energy of emissions at other frequencies transferred to co-channel frequencies through a number of special mechanisms. Out of band interference can be reduced with filtering. The level of interference depends on:

- the physical layer technologies;
- the relative difference between the transmission power of the intended transmitter and the interferer;
- the relative distance between the intended transmitter and the receiver and the distance between the interferer and the receiver;
- the propagation modalities and the path loss exponent; the range of frequencies that are overlapped.

In a IAN there is a high concentration of systems operating with different (uncoordinated) wireless standards, and hence, the situation of experiencing a high level of co-channel or adjacent-channel interference is very likely.

As shown in the standard IEEE 802.15.4 [16], the level of interference between WiFi and ZigBee nodes and vice versa depends on the distance between the interferer and the intended receiver and the channel frequency of the two networks. According to the level of frequency separation, the interference between WiFi and ZigBee can be in-band or out-of-band. It is shown that below the distance of 1 m, the *PER* is about 1 for any value of the channel separation, and hence almost every packet is corrupted.

The performance degradation of a WiFi or ZigBee link can be expressed in terms of goodput degradation. We propose to use the following formula for the computation of the goodput:

$$goodput = T \cdot \varepsilon \cdot (1 - PER) \tag{5}$$

Where $T$ is the throughput of the link computed without interference as shown in the previous Section, $\varepsilon$ is the duty cycle of the transmission and *PER* is the packet error rate. The duty cycle is also the channel utilization ratio which is equal to 1 if no coexistence mechanism based on time division alternation are used.

Assuming a distance from 10 to 20 cm between the WiFi and the ZigBee air interfaces co-located in the RMU, then the goodput of each link is zero. When the level of interference is high, i.e. the *PER* is about 1 and the goodput is zero, a coexistence mechanism is required. There are two categories of coexistence mechanisms [17]:

1) collaborative coexistence mechanisms, where the two interfering networks exchange information;
2) non-collaborative coexistence mechanisms, where the exchange of information is not allowed.

Collaborative coexistence mechanisms are more efficient but they are not always applicable. The possibility of exchanging information is quite easy when the two interfering air interfaces are co-located in the same multi-mode terminal, which is an assumption valid for the RMU. The advantages and drawbacks of well known interference management mechanisms that can be used for our purposes are reported in Table 3.

**Table 3.** Summary of interference management methods

| Method | Description of the Method | Advantages | Drawbacks |
|---|---|---|---|
| Transmission power control | Dynamically increases and decreases the level of transmit power according to performance and interference metrics. The performance of the method depends on the channel gain and the number of devices. | Simple and well experimented implementation | Manage the interference to reduce the effects as much as possible without any minimum guaranteed quality |
| Dynamic frequency selection | The center carrier frequency is selected on the basis of channel occupation | Does not decrease the link capacity. Simple implementation. | The channel is not always selectable. Requires channel estimation on different bands. |
| Beamforming | Beam shape of the antenna is adapted with the aim to have a null towards the direction of the interferer. | Does not decrease the link capacity | Complex implementation. |

# 6  Conclusion

This paper illustrated the analysis of a Radio Resource Management to be implemented in a multi-hop scenario in which MANETs cooperate with a HAP system to reach the common goal of enhancing the access to MBMS services. Through an exhaustive simulation campaign we demonstrated that it is possible to increase the number of multicast sessions, in a IAN scenario characterized by an intrinsic radio resource limitation. Obtained results may represent a valid support to the effective system design activity. This preliminary work provides just one of the potentials output on the cooperative behavior of HAP and MANET systems in a configuration specifically thought to provide multicast users with a multi-hop access in a IAN infrastructure. Furthermore the evaluation of the effects of interference in terms of goodput degradation is provided. Future studies will be finalized to provide a trade-off between the maximum capacity and the guarantee QoS allowed to MANET nodes different user mobility and system load conditions.

# References

1. de Graaf, M., et al.: Easy Wireless: Broadband Ad-Hoc Networking For Emergency Services. In: The Sixth Annual Mediterranean Ad Hoc Networking WorkShop, Corfu, Greece, June 12-15 (2007)
2. Hoeksema, F., Heskamp, M., Schiphorst, R., Slump, K.: A node architecture for disaster relief networking. In: First IEEE International Symposium on New Frontiers in Dynamic Spectrum Access Networks (DySPAN 2005) (2005)
3. 3GPP TS 25.346 V7.0.0 (2006-03): Introduction of the Multimedia Broadcast/Multicast Service (MBMS) in the Radio Access Network (RAN), Stage 2 (Release7)

4. Araniti, G., Iera, A., Molinaro, A.: The Role of HAPs in Supporting Multimedia Broadcast and Multicast Services in Terrestrial-Satellite Integrated Systems. Wireless personal communications, Special Issue on High Altitude Platforms: Research and Application Activities 32(3-4), 195–213 (2005), ISSN: 0929-6212

5. http://lenst.det.unifi.it/salice

6. Huang, Y., He, W., Nahrstedt, K., Whay, C.: Requirements and System Architecture Design Consideration for First Responder Systems. In: IEEE Conference on Technologies for Homeland Security (2007)

7. IEEE Std. 802.15.4-2003, Standard for Telecommunications and Information Exchange Between Systems—Local Area Metropolitan Area Networks—Specific Requirements — Wireless Medium Access Control (MAC) and Physical Layer (PHY) Specifications for Low Rate Wireless Personal Area Networks (WPAN)

8. IEEE Std. 802.15.3-2003, Standard for Telecommunications and Information Exchange Between Systems—Local Area Metropolitan Area Networks—Specific Requirements — Wireless Medium Access Control (MAC) and Physical Layer (PHY) Specifications for High Rate Wireless Personal Area Networks (WPAN)

9. Wittman, R., Zitterbart, M.: Multicast Communications – Protocols and Applications. Morgan Kaufmann, San Francisco (2000)

10. Taha-Ahmed, M., Calvo-Ramòn, L., de Haro-Ariet, L.: On the High Altitude Platfom (HAP) W-CDMA system capacity. Radio engineering 13(2) (2004)

11. IST-2003-507607 (B-BONE). Deliverable D2.5. Final results with combined enhancements of the air interface

12. Yin, Y., Shi, J., Li, Y., Zhang, P.: Cluster head selection using analytical hierarchy process for wireless sensor networks. In: IEEE 17th PIMRC, Helsinki, Finland, pp. 1–5 (2006)

13. Saaty, T.L.: Fundamentals of Decision Making and Priority Theory with the Analytic Hierarchy Process. RWS Pubs. (2000)

14. The Network Simulator–ns-2, http://www.isi.edu/nsnam/ns/

15. Raschellà, A., Araniti, G., Iera, A., Molinaro, A.: Radio resource management policy for multicast transmissions in high altitude platforms. In: ICSSC (2009)

16. IEEE Std. 802.15.4, Standard for Telecommunications and Information Exchange Between SystemsLocal Area Metropolitan Area NetworksSpecific Requirements Wireless Medium Access Control (MAC) and Physical Layer (PHY) Specifications for Low Rate Wireless Personal Area Networks (WPAN), September 8 (2006)

17. De Sanctis, M., Monti, M., Ruggieri, M., Prasad, R.: A Collaborative Coexistence Mechanism for IEEE 802.15.3 and 802.15.4 WPANs. In: The 20th IEEE International Symposium On Personal, Indoor and Mobile Radio Communications (PIMRC 2009), Tokyo, Japan, September 13-16 (2009)

# Author Index

Printed in the United States
By Bookmasters